Philipp von Stosch: Collecting, Drawing, Studying and Publishing Engraved Gems

Monumenta Graeca et Romana

Editor-in-Chief

Troels Myrup Kristensen (*Aarhus University, Denmark*)

Editor-in-Chief Emeritus

John M. Fossey FRSC (*Musée des beaux-arts de Montréal, Canada*) †

Associate Editor

Beaudoin Caron (*Université de Montréal*)

Assistant Editors

Laure Sarah Ethier & Marilie Jacob (*Université de Montréal*)

Editorial Board

Anna Collar (*University of Southampton, UK*)
Søren Handberg (*University of Oslo, Norway*)
Kathleen M. Lynch (*University of Cincinnati, USA*)

Editorial Advisory Board

Andreas Konecny (*Universität Graz, Austria*)
Duane Roller (*Ohio State University, USA*)
Massimo Osanna (*Ministry of Culture, Italy*)
Peter Stewart (*University of Oxford, UK*)
Lea Stirling (*University of Manitoba, Canada*)

VOLUME 29

The titles published in this series are listed at *brill.com/mgr*

Philipp von Stosch: Collecting, Drawing, Studying and Publishing Engraved Gems

By

Paweł Gołyźniak
Ulf R. Hansson
Hadrien J. Rambach

BRILL

LEIDEN | BOSTON

This is an open access title distributed under the terms of the CC BY-NC-ND 4.0 license, which permits any non-commercial use, distribution, and reproduction in any medium, provided no alterations are made and the original author(s) and source are credited. Further information and the complete license text can be found at https://creativecommons.org/licenses/by-nc-nd/4.0/

The terms of the CC license apply only to the original material. The use of material from other sources (indicated by a reference) such as diagrams, illustrations, photos and text samples may require further permission from the respective copyright holder.

The research for this work was financially supported by the National Science Centre, Poland (statutory research project no. 2019/33/B/HS3/00959 (Opus)). Publication co-financed by the Faculty of History of the Jagiellonian University.

Cover illustration: Vienna, Albertina, inv. no.: 1266, Pier Leone Ghezzi, *Baron Stosch disputing over gems and coins with antiquarians in his house, Pier Leone Ghezzi in the background*, pen and brown ink, 270 × 353 mm, © The ALBERTINA Museum, Vienna.

The Library of Congress Cataloging-in-Publication Data is available online at https://catalog.loc.gov

Typeface for the Latin, Greek, and Cyrillic scripts: "Brill". See and download: brill.com/brill-typeface.

ISSN 0169-8850
ISBN 978-90-04-71253-9 (hardback)
ISBN 978-90-04-71255-3 (e-book)
DOI 10.1163/9789004712553

Copyright 2025 by Paweł Gołyźniak, Ulf R. Hansson and Hadrien J. Rambach. Published by Koninklijke Brill BV, Plantijnstraat 2, 2321 JC Leiden, The Netherlands.
Koninklijke Brill BV incorporates the imprints Brill, Brill Nijhoff, Brill Schöningh, Brill Fink, Brill mentis, Brill Wageningen Academic, Vandenhoeck & Ruprecht, Böhlau and V&R unipress.
Koninklijke Brill BV reserves the right to protect this publication against unauthorized use. Requests for re-use and/ or translations must be addressed to Koninklijke Brill BV via brill.com or copyright.com.
For more information: info@brill.com.

This book is printed on acid-free paper and produced in a sustainable manner.

Contents

Foreword   VII
Acknowledgments   X
List of Figures and Photo Credits   XII

PART 1
Philipp von Stosch in the Circle of Eighteenth-Century Collectors and Enthusiasts of Gems

1   Philipp von Stosch: A Lifetime of Collecting   3
    Ulf R. Hansson

2   Collecting Engraved Gems in the Circle of Stosch   20
    Ulf R. Hansson

PART 2
The Art of Gem Drawings – Philipp von Stosch and the Circle of His Draughtsmen

3   Drawings of Engraved Gems from the Late Mediaeval until the Nineteenth Century   37
    Hadrien J. Rambach

4   Stosch and the Circle of His Draughtsmen of Gems   66
    Paweł Gołyźniak and Hadrien J. Rambach

PART 3
Philipp von Stosch and His Paper Museum of Gems

5   Stosch's Corpus of Gem Drawings in the Archives   97
    Paweł Gołyźniak

6   *Pierres gravees par Stosche* in the Princes Czartoryski Museum in Krakow   103
    Paweł Gołyźniak

7   *Pierres gravées du roi avec figures* in the Kunstbibliothek in Berlin   123
    Paweł Gołyźniak

8   Stosch's *Paper Museum of Gems* Rediscovered   131
    Paweł Gołyźniak

PART 4
Philipp von Stosch and His Studies of Engraved Gems

9   Stosch's *Magnum Opus – Gemmae antiquae caelatae* 1724 in the Context of His Life, Collecting and Studying Engraved Gems   213
    Hadrien J. Rambach

10 Gemmae antiquae caelatae II   236
    Paweł Gołyźniak

11 Stosch and His Contribution to the Development of Gem Studies and Antiquarianism   280
    Paweł Gołyźniak and Hadrien J. Rambach

Bibliography   313
Index   338

Foreword

Philipp von Stosch was one of the most controversial figures in the history of collecting and antiquarianism. Active in Rome and Florence in the first half of the eighteenth century but travelling extensively in his youth around northern Europe, he built an impressive network of useful contacts and positioned himself well into the learned, social and political circles. He is known today primarily as a collector of engraved gems who was expelled from Rome for spying on the exiled Stuart court on behalf of the British government. In January 1731 a dramatic night-time assault forced him to flee to Florence, where he found shelter under the friendly auspices of Gian Gastone de'Medici. He transferred his *Museo Stoschiano* there, comprising numerous antiquities, old master paintings, drawings, prints and maps, engraved gems, coins and medals, arms and armour, naturalia, erotica and above all an enormous, priceless library. Stosch was certainly a highly respected figure, an 'oracle' to the fellow antiquarians with whom he eagerly shared his knowledge and kept the doors of his house-museum open for study and consultation until his death in 1757. His opinion was seldom disregarded and thus Johann Joachim Winckelmann made it his priority to establish contact with Stosch upon his arrival in Italy. Ultimately, he became his spiritual heir, cataloguing his enormous collection of engraved gems that was regarded as superior even to that of the King of France and was ultimately purchased in 1764 by Frederick the Great of Prussia. Stosch recommended Winckelmann to his close friend Cardinal Alessandro Albani, who made the young, promising scholar his librarian, which proved decisive for his later career.

Stosch enjoyed a wonderful career as an antiquary selling valuable items to wealthy and important, mainly British, collectors. He advised on works of art to Emperor Charles VI and became the royal antiquary at the court of Dresden. His impressive network of personal contacts included popes, kings, statesmen, cardinals and notable members of the *Republic of Letters*. However, intersecting with so many important people and amassing so vast and valuable collections exposed him to criticism and jealousy as well. Stosch's reputation deteriorated greatly but not only by his work as a political agent, which continued in Florence. His personality was eccentric, so to speak. He was an outspoken radical libertine, freethinker and freemason, and one rather open about his own sexuality. He was one of the key founders of the first masonic lodge in Florence in 1733. His library was full of controversial books listed in the pope's *Index Librorum Prohibitorum*, and the Inquisition attempted to have him expelled from Italy through the Lorena administration while in Florence. In addition, he is said to have lived with an owl and a boar as his pets and he used to wear a monocle, for which he was often ridiculed as a 'cyclops'. Rumours, anecdotes and far-fetched stories circulated already during his lifetime, building up the negative picture of his figure. They were repeated over centuries, perpetuating an image of a morally corrupt and greedy collector concerned only with personal gain, often acting in ambiguous ways, and accused of theft and forgery of engraved gems on a regular basis.

This book is designed to show and discuss another facet of Stosch that would argue with the dense mythology clouding the true nature of his accomplishments as an antiquarian, collector, patron and scholar. This is possible due to discovery and study of a substantial part of Stosch's, previously considered lost, enormous collection of drawings of engraved gems. Most of Stosch's archives and correspondence is now lost and separate from the collection of engraved gems; the rest of his *museo* was dispersed shortly after his death. Nearly 3200 rediscovered unique specimens in total illuminate us on a substantial production of documentary archaeological drawings made by several artists, including Pier Leone Ghezzi, Girolamo Odam, Bernard Picart, Anton Maria Zanetti, Markus Tuscher, Theodorus Netscher, Georg Martin Preißler, Johann Justin Preißler, Georg Abraham Nagel and Johann Adam Schweickart, tirelessly working in a studio organised by Stosch on the faithful documentation of vast numbers of engraved gems. These drawings were made for a variety of purposes – documentary, study, correspondence, advertising and publishing alike. They provide an opportunity to present Stosch not only as one of the most important representatives of eighteenth-century collecting, but they expose his crucial role in the creation and transfer of knowledge that contributed immensely to the transformation of eighteenth-century antiquarianism towards a more scholarly archaeological science.

The study consists of several chapters which not only discuss the rediscovered materials but also contextualise them within the framework of antiquarian culture developing in Italy in the first half of the eighteenth century. The first two are concerned with Stosch, his life and career and they present him as a part of a broad circle of antiquarians to whom collecting and studying of engraved gems became the most vital part of investigation of Antiquity at the time. The following two chapters discuss the importance of illustrating of engraved gems from the late mediaeval times up to the nineteenth century, with a particular focus put on the artists working for Stosch in his house, creating visual documentation of intaglios and cameos for his various projects. It is not a coincidence that Stosch was literally obsessed with faithful visual reproduction of engraved gems, gaining a reputation of being the best in training young artists in this difficult activity – combining art, science and craftsmanship together. It was the time when illustrations became central for collection and processing of data about antiquities and further dissemination of knowledge produced as a result of their careful analysis in general. Stosch and his house-studio were a part of a greater phenomenon and, as one now discovers, making an important impact on the development of antiquarianism towards the late 1750s. Having the context drawn on the figure of Stosch, gem collecting and illustrating, the core of the study concerns the discovered drawings of engraved gems produced under Stosch's close supervision. This starts from the analysis of relevant archival materials that suggest the existence of a substantial *Paper Museum of Gems* once owned by Stosch. The comparison to the famous, although for a long time also neglected, *Museo Cartaceo* of Cassiano dal Pozzo here is not merely a coincidence. There is a link between Stosch and Pozzo since the first was clearly fascinated by the accomplishments of the latter having direct contact with Pozzo's *Paper Museum* while it was owned by Stosch's close friend Cardinal Albani. A critical analysis of two major collections – *Pierres gravees par Stosche* in the Princes Czartoryski Museum in Krakow and *Pierres gravées du roi avec figures* in the Kunstbibliothek in Berlin – proves that a significant part of Stosch's *Paper Museum of Gems* survived. Stosch indeed built a considerable pictorial database of engraved gems that served as a reference source for his various studies, day-to-day investigations, consultations, advertising and public discussion of particular gems, visual documentation of his own collection and notably his publishing projects, those both finished and unfinished. The most important one was his book *Gemmae antiquae caelatae* – a study of gems signed by ancient masters – published in 1724 in Amsterdam by Bernard Picart. It is still regarded as a milestone in the study of ancient glyptics for its subject matter but its contribution to the overall development of accurate and faithful visual reproduction of antiquities must also be stressed. Stosch planned and worked on a sequel to this important volume which never appeared. Some of the discovered drawings combined with information extracted from his surviving correspondence and other archives allow this project to be reconstructed to a significant degree.

All of this proves Stosch's substantial contribution to the transformation of gem studies and the antiquarianism movement overall into archaeological science in a scholarly sense. Stosch re-emerges as one of the most instrumental figures stimulating these developments. His wide-ranging activities as a whole, his collection of original gems, pastes, casts, drawings and prints, his library, his book and other scientific projects were intimately connected to his patronage over artists documenting original gems as drawings. His almost obsessive accumulation of everything related to the glyptic art was driven by his desire to investigate it from various angles, including techniques of engraving, chronology and iconography. All his activities paved the way for Comte de Caylus, Mariette and notably Winckelmann to take the studies of Antiquity to a new level in the 1750s and 1760s. Winckelmann particularly benefited from Stosch by cataloguing his collection of engraved gems under the title *Description des Pierres gravées du feu Baron de Stosch* and most notably accessing his vast archives and collections in Florence prior to their dispersal. This was a critical step in his career and also for writing the first synthesis of ancient art – *Geschichte der Kunst des Alterthums* published in 1764. In this context, Stosch, much like Cassiano dal Pozzo, whom he admired, by collecting substantial visual evidence of antiquities (i.e. engraved gems), is a true pioneer delivering essential tools for the holistic study of gems and Antiquity.

As it happens, this study is being published exactly three hundred years after the appearance of Stosch's book *Gemmae antiquae caelatae*. This occasion, combined with the rediscovery of a number of original drawings that were made notably by Girolamo Odam, Pier Leone Ghezzi and Bernard Picart during the production process of this volume, justifies looking at the gems selected by Stosch for publication once more and making a reassessment. Therefore, the book is accompanied with the Appendix 1, in which Stosch's original French text is set together with a study of those glyptic masterpieces from a contemporary perspective, taking into account the contributions of scholars who commented on them over the past three hundred years. This, on the one hand, gives us a sense of development and progress in archaeological science regarding intaglios and cameos over centuries of research. On the other hand, it facilitates appreciation of Stosch's connoisseurship and scholarship. Moreover, the production process of his book was complex and included some controversies and even arguments over the faithfulness of visual reproductions provided by Odam and Picart. As a result, the text is supplemented with all original drawings as well as photographs of original gems or at least their impressions and casts that could be identified. This allows a judgement to be made on the accuracy and faithfulness of the work of all those engaged in the process of the book's production. Furthermore, it highlights the particular importance of illustrations in the studies of Antiquity in the Age of Enlightenment.

Finally, the book is supplemented with a catalogue of all original drawings and prints that have been rediscovered as originating from Stosch's *Paper Museum of Gems* – Appendix 2. This catalogue is divided into three main collections – *Pierres gravees par Stosche* in the Princes Czartoryski Museum in Krakow, *Pierres gravées du roi avec figures* in the Kunstbibliothek in Berlin and all original drawings (as well as their counterproofs) made by Bernard Picart for Stosch's book that were found or identified over the years of research. All the drawings from Krakow are illustrated, while only a selection of the drawings from Berlin could be illustrated here due to their considerable fragility which, so far, prevented digitization without considerable and costly conservation efforts. All the ca. 3200 items are works of art in their own right, but most importantly they document engraved gems from Stosch's collection as well as all other contemporary cabinets imaginable. Many of the documented gems are likely to be lost now and the drawings constitute their only visual recording, significantly enriching the general corpus of all known intaglios and cameos with unknown types, variants and forms.

Publication of all these materials would fulfil Stosch's vision, albeit centuries later. All hope of recovering his lost pictorial legacy seemed in vain, yet now, it can be brought back to life to the benefit of archaeologists, historians, art historians, curators, collectors and all enthusiasts of ancient engraved gems, eighteenth-century drawings, as well as studies and history of collecting and scholarship alike.

Paweł Gołyźniak
Krakow 2024

 All supplementary material, e.g. the revised edition of Stosch's book of 1724 (Appendix 1) and catalogues of all discovered gem drawings made for Stosch's *Paper Museum of Gems* and other projects (Appendix 2), have been made available online at figshare.com. They may be accessed via this QR code and the following link: https://doi.org/10.6084/m9.figshare.27992171.

Acknowledgments

This book may never have seen the light of day if it had not been for the many people who advised and assisted us so generously while doing the research on this project. First and foremost, it is our great pleasure to acknowledge here the support of Andrzej Betlej (the former Director of the National Museum in Krakow, now the Director of the Royal Wawel Castle in Krakow) and Andrzej Szczerski (the current Director of the National Museum in Krakow) for the permission to conduct the research and publish the drawings discovered in the Princes Czartoryski Museum in Krakow. We are also very grateful to Ewa Nogieć-Czepiel (emerita), Bożena Chmiel and Barbara König (The Princes Czartoryski Museum in Krakow) for their kind assistance and all remarks during the studies of the collection. Likewise, we owe gratitude to Moritz Wullen (the Director of the Kunstbibliothek in Berlin) and Joachim Brand (the Deputy Director of the Kunstbibliothek in Berlin) for kind permission to study and publish our research on the part of Stosch's gem drawings corpus discovered in Berlin as well as to Elke Blauert (emerita) and Jana Hettmann (The Kunstbibliothek in Berlin) for kind assistance in the research done in Berlin. Regarding location and access to Bernard Picart's drawings the following individuals are greatly acknowledged: Hein Maassen and Jeroen Vandommele (The Royal Library of the Netherlands in The Hague), Brooks Rich and Dorothy J. del Bueno (The Department of Prints, Drawings, and Photographs at the Philadelphia Museum of Art), Alexander Stavrou (The Department of the History of Art, University of Oxford), Jonathan H. Kagan, Tom Lecky and private collectors.

Secondly, our special thanks go to those who helped and supported our work with their expertise, commentaries and experience (in alphabetical order): Angelamaria Aceto, Sébastien Aubry, Mathilde Avisseau-Brouste, Grażyna Bartnik-Szymańska, Max Bernheimer, David Biedermann, Edward Bigden, Karl-Magnus Brose, Isabella Chapman, Véronique Dasen, Elena Dmitrieva, Melissa A. Eppihimer, Richard Falkiner, Sash Giles, Ittai Gradel, Maria Barbara Guerrieri Borsoi, Malcolm Hay, Thomas Heneage, Herbert Horovitz, Sandra Hindman, David Jaffé, Monique Kornell, Jöern Lang, Kenneth Lapatin, Tomasz Łojewski, Marianne Maaskant-Kleibrink, Zofia Maniakowska-Jazownik, Ewa Manikowska, Attilio Mastrocinque, Max Michelson, Arianna D'Ottone-Rambach, Janusz Pezda, Agata Pietrzak, Lucia Pirzio Biroli Stefanelli, the late Gertrud Platz-Horster, Daniel Thomas Potts, Crispian Riley-Smith, Greg Rubinstein, Frank Rumscheid, Diana Scarisbrick, Agnieszka Smołucha-Sładkowska, Jeffrey Spier, Joachim Śliwa, Gabriella Tassinari, Claudia Wagner and Erika Zwierlein-Diehl.

Apart from those, we are very grateful to dozens of museums, libraries, galleries, scholars and curators who so willingly helped us with queries during our visits, to get information about and photographs of original gems published within this project and discussed some issues, in particular: Ajaccio, Palais Fesch; Alnwick Castle, The Beverley Collection (Lisa Little); Baltimore, The Walters Art Museum (Laura Seitter); Berlin, Ägyptisches Museum und Papyrussammlung, Staatliche Museen zu Berlin (Rebekka Pabst); Berlin, Antikensammlung, Staatliche Museen zu Berlin (Agnes Schwarzmaier); Berlin, Museum für Islamische Kunst, Staatliche Museen zu Berlin; Berlin, Vorderasiatisches Museum, Staatliche Museen zu Berlin (Nadja Cholidis, Giulia Russo, Alrun Gutow); Boston, Museum of Fine Arts (Carolyn Cruthirds); bpk Bildagentur (Cornelia Reichert and Sabine Schumann); Braunschweig, Herzog-Anton-Ulrich Museum; Cambridge, The Fitzwilliam Museum (Emma Darbyshire); Cambridge (MA), Harvard Art Museums (Jeff Steward); Chatsworth, the Devonshire Collection (Amber Rebeka); Copenhagen, The Berthel Thorvaldsen Museum; Cortona, Museo dell'Accademia Etrusca (Paolo Bruschetti); Dresden, Staatliche Kunstsammlungen Dresden, Skulpturensammlung (Saskia Wetzig); Florence, Biblioteca Marucelliana (Paolo Turcis); Florence, Gallerie degli Uffizi (Eike Schmidt); Florence, Museo Archeologico Nazionale (Mario Iozzo); Glasgow, The National Galleries Scotland (Beth Dunant); Leiden, Rijksmuseum van Oudheden; Leipzig, GRASSI Museum; Lisbon, The Calouste Gulbenkian Museum (Marta Areia); London, The British Museum (Natasha Lawson, Thorsten Opper and Elizabeth Bray); London, the Victoria & Albert Museum (Freya Levett); London, Christie's/Bridgeman Images; London, Sotheby's (Christopher Mason), Montepellier, Musée Fabre (Florence Hudowicz); Naples, Museo Archeologico Nazionale (Floriana Miele); New York, The Metropolitan Museum of Art; New York, The Morgan Library Museum (Kaitlyn Krieg); Oxford, The Ashmolean Museum; Oxford, The Beazley Archive, University of Oxford (Peter Stewart); Paris, Artcurial (Elisabeth Bastier); Paris, Bibliothèque nationale de France (Alla Giraud); Paris, Galerie Kugel; Philadelphia, Museum of Art (Heather Hughes and Jonathan Hoppe); Princeton (NJ), Princeton University Art Museum (Kelly Flaherty); Rome, Musei Capitolini (Claudio Parisi Presicce and Angela Carbonaro); Rome, Museo Nazionale Romano (Valeria Intini); The Vatican City,

Biblioteca Apostolica Vaticana, Gabinetto di Manoscritti (Federica Orlando); The Vatican City, Biblioteca Apostolica Vaticana, Gabinetto delle Medaglie (Eleonora Giampiccolo); Venice, Museo Archeologico Nazionale (Daniele Ferrara); Vienna, Kunsthistorisches Museum (Ilse Jung); Würzburg, Martin-von-Wagner Museum (Jochen Griesbach).

The English was revised by Leah Morawiec (Szałsza). However, some last-minute changes were made to the text, for which we take full responsibility. Natalia Sawicka is acknowledged for the layout of Appendix 1 and 2. Last but not least, the editorial contribution of the Brill team should be singled out as well. The authors are very grateful especially to Giulia Moriconi, Vincent Oeters, Troels Myrup Kristensen and Fem Eggers for their guidance and help during the publishing process and the wonderful form that the book received.

Figures and Photo Credits

1.1 (Plate 1)	Berlin, Skulpturensammlung und Museum für Byzantinische Kunst, Marble bust of Philipp von Stosch, inv. no.: M204, 85 cm, Edmé Bouchardon, 1727	16
1.2 (Plate 1)	The Hague, Historical Museum, inv. no.: 1948x0009-SCH, Portrait of François Fagel by Philip van Dijk, 1735, oil on canvas, 103,5 × 56 cm	16
1.3 (Plate 1)	Leiden, Rijksmuseum van Oudheden, inv. no.: GS-10347, 16 × 12 mm, glass paste made after an intaglio by Lorenz Natter (ΝΑΤΤΕΡ ΕΠΟΙΕΙ), portrait of cardinal Alessandro Albani (1692–1779), 18th century	16
1.4 (Plate 1)	Ajaccio, Palais Fesch, inv. no.: MFA 852.1.660, Pier Leone Ghezzi self-portrait, oil on canvas, 62 × 46 cm	16
1.5 (Plate 2)	Markus Tuscher, portrait medallion of Stosch, 1738, private collection	17
1.6 (Plate 2)	Florence, Palazzo Pitti, Museo degli Argenti, inv. no.: Gemme 1921, n. 328, white sapphire, 21 × 18 mm, Portrait of Stosch by Carlo Costanzi	17
1.7 (Plate 2)	Pier Leone Ghezzi, Philipp von Stosch in his house with a servant holding up a flask, pen and brown ink, 306 × 214 mm, Jonathan H. Kagan collection, New York	17
1.8 (Plate 2)	New York, Metropolitan Museum of Art, acc. no.: 48.141, Anton Rafael Mengs, Portrait of J.J. Winckelmann, ca. 1777, oil on canvas, 63,5 × 49,2 cm	17
1.9 (Plate 3)	Exemplary selection of Stosch's gems and glass pastes:	18
1.9a	Berlin, Antikensammlung, inv. no.: FG 359, carnelian scaraboid, third quarter of the 4th century BC	18
1.9b	Berlin, Antikensammlung, inv. no.: FG 364, sardonyx scaraboid, second quarter of the 4th century BC	18
1.9c	Berlin, Antikensammlung, inv. no.: FG 1934, sard intaglio, 12 × 10 mm, second half of the 1st century BC	18
1.9d	Berlin, Antikensammlung, inv. no.: FG 2168, carnelian intaglio, 1st century BC	18
1.9e	Berlin, Antikensammlung, inv. no.: FG 3137, glass gem, 1st century BC	18
1.9f	Berlin, Antikensammlung, inv. no.: FG 4361, glass gem, 1st century BC	18
1.9g	Berlin, Antikensammlung, inv. no.: FG 7120, carnelian intaglio, 13 × 11 mm, second half of the 1st century BC	18
1.9h	Berlin, Antikensammlung, inv. no.: FG 6907, carnelian intaglio, 10 × 11 mm, 1st century AD	18
1.9i	Berlin, Antikensammlung, inv. no.: FG 2640, carnelian intaglio, late 1st century BC–early 1st century AD	18
1.9j	Berlin, Antikensammlung, inv. no.: FG 6730, carnelian intaglio, 17 × 16 mm, early 1st century AD	18
1.9k	Berlin, Antikensammlung, inv. no.: FG 7484, carnelian intaglio, 2nd century AD	18
1.9l	Berlin, Antikensammlung, inv. no.: FG 6714, chalcedony intaglio, 1st–2nd century AD	18
1.9m	Berlin, Antikensammlung, inv. no.: FG 7097, carnelian intaglio, 2nd century AD	18
1.9n	Berlin, Antikensammlung, inv. no.: FG 7774, carnelian intaglio, 16 × 12 mm, 2nd century AD	18
1.9o	Berlin, Antikensammlung, inv. no.: FG 8340, nicolo intaglio, 2nd–3rd century AD	18
1.10 (Plate 4)	Exemplary selection of Stosch's gems and glass pastes:	19
1.10a	Berlin, Ägyptisches Museum, inv. no.: 9752, steatite scarab, New Kingdom Period, ca. 1550–1070 BC (Egyptian)	19

FIGURES AND PHOTO CREDITS XIII

1.10b	Berlin, Ägyptisches Museum, inv. no.: 9786, sardonyx cameo, 28 × 21 mm, 1st century BC (late Hellenistic) 19
1.10c	Berlin, Ägyptisches Museum, inv. no.: 9788, turquoise intaglio, 13 × 12 mm, 2nd–3rd century AD (magical gem) 19
1.10d	Berlin, Ägyptisches Museum, inv. no.: 9782, chalcedony intaglio, 13 × 12 mm, 2nd century AD century (magical gem) 19
1.10e	Berlin, Ägyptisches Museum, inv. no.: 9796, red jasper magical gem, 19 × 15 mm, 2nd–3rd century AD 19
1.10f	Berlin, Museum für Islamische Kunst, inv. no.: VA 2724, carnelian intaglio, 14 × 21 mm, 1st–2nd century AD 19
1.10g	Berlin, Museum für Islamische Kunst, inv. no.: VA 1438, agate stamp seal, 5th century AD (Sassanian) 19
1.10h	Berlin, Ägyptisches Museum, inv. no.: 9798, carnelian intaglio, 14 × 12 mm, early 18th century 19
1.10i	Berlin, Ägyptisches Museum, inv. no.: 9794, glass paste 19
1.10j	Berlin, Ägyptisches Museum, inv. no.: 9818, glass paste 19
1.10k	Berlin, Ägyptisches Museum, inv. no.: 9863, glass paste 19
2.1 (Plate 5)	Baudelot de Dairval, Ch.C. 1717. *Lettre sur le prétendu Solon des pierres gravées. Explication d'une medaille d'or de la famille Cornuficia*. Paris: chez Jean-Baptiste Lamesle. Cover 32
2.2 (Plate 5)	Baudelot de Dairval, Ch.C. 1717. *Lettre sur le prétendu Solon des pierres gravées. Explication d'une medaille d'or de la famille Cornuficia*. Paris: chez Jean-Baptiste Lamesle. Plate with illustrations 32
2.3 (Plate 5)	Chatsworth, the Devonshire collection, inv. no.: IRN 6637 Old Master Drawing 641, Pier Leone Ghezzi, pen and ink on pale buff paper, 365 × 255 mm, *Due Famosi antiquari – Baron Philip von Stosch showing an antique gem to Sabbitini* 32
2.4 (Plate 6)	Biblioteca Apostolica Vaticana, inv. no.: Cod. Ott. lat. 3116, fol. 191bis, Pier Leone Ghezzi, *Congresso de' migliori antiquarj di Roma* (dated 10 October 1728), pen and brown ink 33
2.5 (Plate 6)	Vienna, Albertina, inv. no.: 1265, Pier Leone Ghezzi, *Congresso de' migliori antiquarj di Roma* (dated 1725), pen and brown ink, 270 × 395 mm 33
2.6 (Plate 7)	Valesio, F., Gori, A.F. and Venuti, R. 1750. *Museum Cortonense*. Rome: Giovanni Generosis. Cover 34
2.7 (Plate 7)	Borioni, A. and Venuti, R. 1736. *Collectanea antiquitatum Romanarum: quas centum tabulis aeneis incisas et a Rodulphino Venuti Academico Etrusco Cortonensi notis illustratas exhibet Antonius Borioni*. Rome: Ex Typographia Rochi Bernabò. Cover 34
2.8 (Plate 7)	Gori, A.F. 1731–1732. *Museum Florentinum: exhibens insigniora vetustatis monumenta quae Florentiae sunt*, vols 1–2. Florence: Ex typographia Michaelis Nestenus et Francisci Moücke. Cover 34
2.9 (Plate 7)	Gori, A.F. and Zanetti, A.G.F. 1750. Venice: ex typographio Joan. Baptiste Albritii Hier. f. sumtibus auctoris. Cover 34
3.1 (Plate 8)	Trompe l'oeil with engraved gems, private collection 53
3.2 (Plate 8)	Trompe l'oeil with engraved gems, private collection 53
3.3 (Plate 9)	Paris, Musée du Louvre, inv. no.: 10383r, Pietro Buonaccorsi (1501–1547), sanguine, 120 × 77 mm 54
3.4 (Plate 9)	Malibu, the J. Paul Getty Museum, acc. no.: 86.GG.469, Nicolas Poussin (1594–1665), ca. 1635, Pen and brown ink and brush and brown wash over traces of black chalk, 157 × 135 mm 54
3.5 (Plate 9)	Oxford, Ashmolean Museum, inv. no.: WA1989.74, Peter Paul Rubens, 1626, 100.7 × 78 cm, *The Great Cameo of France* 54

3.6 (Plate 9)	Paris, Bibliothèque nationale de France, inv. no.: Camée.264, sardonyx cameo, 310 × 265 mm, first quarter of the 1st century AD 54
3.7 (Plate 10)	Paris, Musée du Louvre, inv. no.: INV 23849r, Edmé Bouchardon, ca. 1737, 123 × 173 mm, *Seal of Michelangelo* 55
3.8 (Plate 10)	Florence, Biblioteca Marucelliana, Ms. A.XLVIII, c. 13r, between 1688–1731, *Gemmae antiche da esso [Senatore Bonaroti] delineate* 55
3.9 (Plate 10)	Johann Heinrich Lips (1758–1817), *Minerva salutifera*, 162 × 125 mm, private collection 56
3.10 (Plate 10)	New York, The Metropolitan Museum of Art, acc. no.: 2014.461, Anton Raphael Mengs (1728–1779), *Oedipus at Colonnos before the temple of the Eumenides*, ca. 1760–1761 56
3.11 (Plate 11)	Augustin Pajou (1730–1809), 'un triton d'après une médaille', 175 × 138 mm, private collection 57
3.12 (Plate 11)	Edinburgh, The National Galleries of Scotland, inv. RSA 1349 (David Laing bequest), Jan Wandelaar (1690–1759), *Portrait of the Roman Dictator Sylla*, black chalk on paper, 310 × 250 mm 57
3.13 (Plate 11)	Montpellier, Musée Fabre, inv. no.: 837.1.443, François-Xavier Fabre (1766–1837) 57
3.14 (Plate 11)	Montpellier, Musée Fabre, inv. no.: 837.1.460, François-Xavier Fabre (1766–1837) 57
3.15 (Plate 12)	Joseph-Marie Vien (1716–1809)? 235 × 180 mm, private collection 58
3.16 (Plate 13)	Joseph-Marie Vien (1716–1809)? 235 × 180 mm, private collection 59
3.17 (Plate 14)	Jacques-Louis David (1748–1825), private collection 60
3.18 (Plate 14)	Harvard Art Museums/Fogg Museum, inv. no.: 1943.1815.19.8.A, Jacques-Louis David (1748–1825), *Copy of a Roman Cippus* (The Roman Album) 60
3.19 (Plate 14)	Paris, Musée du Louvre, inv. no.: 26139.bis recto – *Femme jouant de la lyre d'après un camée antique*, black chalk on paper, 211 × 144 mm 60
3.20 (Plate 15)	Genevosio drawings, sheet 1, 400 × 265 mm, private collection 61
3.21 (Plate 16)	Genevosio drawings, sheet 2, 400 × 265 mm, private collection 62
3.22 (Plate 17)	Genevosio drawings, sheet 3, 400 × 265 mm, private collection 63
3.23 (Plate 18)	Genevosio drawings, sheet 4, 400 × 265 mm, private collection 64
3.24 (Plate 19)	Genevosio drawings, sheet 5, 400 × 265 mm, private collection 65
4.1 (Plate 20)	Vienna, Albertina, inv. no.: 1266, Pier Leone Ghezzi, *Baron Stosch disputing over gems and coins with antiquarians in his house, Pier Leone Ghezzi in the background*, pen and brown ink, 270 × 353mm 89
4.2 (Plate 20)	The British Museum, inv. no.: 1859,0806.93, Pier Leone Ghezzi, *Baron Stosch disputing over gems and coins with antiquarians in his house*, pen and brown ink, 369 × 487mm 89
4.3 (Plate 21)	Portrait of Pier Leone Ghezzi, 415 × 256 mm, red chalk, Edmé Bouchardon (1698–1762), 1728, The Yale University Art Gallery, acc. no.: 1958.44 90
4.4 (Plate 21)	Portrait of Girolamo Odam, 192 × 142 mm, brown ink, Pier Leone Ghezzi (1674–1755), 30 August 1730, The British Museum, inv. no.: 1871,0812.1047 90
4.5 (Plate 21)	Portrait of Theodorus Netscher, ca. 170 × 190 mm, etching, Jacobus Houbraken (1698–1780, engraver) after Aert Schouman (1710–1792, drawing), 1750 90
4.6 (Plate 21)	Portrait of Anton Maria Zanetti, 171 × 191 mm, etching, Giovanni Antonio Faldoni (ca. 1690–ca. 1770, engraver) after Rosalba Carriera (1673–1757, drawing), ca. 1725, The Metropolitan Museum of Art, New York, acc. no.: 32.12.2(2) 90
4.7 (Plate 22)	Portrait of Bernard Picart, 291 × 238 mm, etching, Nicolaas Verkolje (1673–1746, engraver) after a painting by Jean-Marc Nattier (1685–1766), 1715, Collectie Stadsarchief Amsterdam: tekeningen en prenten, inv. no.: 010097014572 91

4.8 (Plate 22)	Portrait of Johann Justin Preißler, 263 × 180 mm, coloured etching, Pier Antonio Pazzi (1706–1766), 1762, Wolfenbüttel, Herzog August Bibliothek, inv. no.: A 16916 91
4.9 (Plate 22)	Head of Agrippina (signed *JJ Preisler d.*), 125 × 158 mm, pen and black ink with grey wash over red chalk, Johann Justin Preißler, ca. 1730–1736, private collection 91
4.10 (Plate 22)	Head of Agrippina (signed *JJ Preisler d.*) detail, 125 × 158 mm, pen and black ink with grey wash over red chalk, Johann Justin Preißler, ca. 1730–1736, private collection 91
4.11 (Plate 23)	Mars ("War") standing to the front-right with shield and spear, 120 × 100 mm, red chalk, unidentified artist, first half of the 18th century, private collection 92
4.12 (Plate 23)	Justitia ("Justice") standing to the front-left with scepter and balance, 120 × 100 mm, red chalk, unidentified artist, first half of the 18th century, private collection 92
4.13 (Plate 23)	Mask frontally, 120 × 100 mm, red chalk, unidentified artist, first half of the 18th century, private collection 92
4.14 (Plate 23)	Head of Silenus frontally, 120 × 100 mm, red chalk, unidentified artist, first half of the 18th century, private collection 92
4.15 (Plate 23)	Combination: head of an elephant emerging from a nautilus shell, 120 × 100 mm, red chalk, unidentified artist, first half of the 18th century, private collection 92
4.16 (Plate 23)	Combination: Hippalectyron made of a protome of a horse conjoined with Silenus' and ram's heads standing on roster's legs, 120 × 100 mm, red chalk, unidentified artist, first half of the 18th century, private collection 92
4.17 (Plate 24)	Portrait of Georg Martin Preißler, 352 × 260 mm, etching, Valentin Daniel Preißler (1717–1765, engraver) after Philipp Wilhelm Oeding (1697–1781, drawing), 1756 93
4.18 (Plate 24)	Markus Tuscher self-portrait, 266 × 216 mm, black chalk, ca. 1743–1751, The Royal Collection of Graphic Art in Copenhagen, inv. no.: KKSgb6375 93
4.19 (Plate 24)	Portrait of Georg Abraham Nagel, ca. 170 × 190 mm, etching, Pier Antonio Pazzi (1706–1766, drawing and engraving), 1750 93
4.20 (Plate 25)	Harpocrates standing to the front, 150 × 127 mm, pen, black ink with grey wash, Georg Abraham Nagel, 1754, private collection 94
4.21 (Plate 25)	Athena/Minerva standing next to a column, 150 × 127 mm, pen, black ink with grey wash, Georg Abraham Nagel, 1754, private collection 94
4.22 (Plate 25)	A hunter walking with a staff with birds on his shoulder, 150 × 127 mm, pen, black ink with grey wash, Georg Abraham Nagel, 1754, private collection 94
4.23 (Plate 25)	A woman (Amymone?) dressed in a chiton and himation standing with a vessel next to a fountain, 150 × 127 mm, pen, black ink with grey wash, Georg Abraham Nagel, 1754, private collection 94
6.1 (Plate 26)	The collection of 28 volumes of gem drawings in the Princes Czartoryski Museum in Krakow 118
6.2 (Plate 26)	Portrait of Izabela Czartoryska, 63,5 × 52 cm, oil on canvas, Alexander Roslin (1718–1793), 1774, The Princes Czartoryski Museum in Krakow, inv. no.: MNK XII-A-616 118
6.3 (Plate 26)	Portrait of Adam Jerzy Czartoryski, 35 × 31 cm, oil on canvas, unknown painter, ca. 1840–1850, The Princes Czartoryski Museum in Krakow, inv. no.: MNK XII-A-613 118
6.4 (Plate 26)	François-Xavier Fabre self-portrait, 72,5 × 59 cm, oil on canvas, 1835, Musée Fabre de Montpellier Méditerranée Métropole inv. no.: 837.1.30 118

6.5 (Plate 27)	A copy of Stosch 1724 *Gemmae antiquae caelatae* (The Czartoryski Library, inv. no. 1237 IV), recto of the front cover endpaper with a paper note	119
6.6 (Plate 27)	Spine of volume 1 with *Pierres gravees par Stosche* embossed in gold	119
6.7 (Plate 27)	Watermark: legend *Koten Schlos* and Strasbourg's lily (*Fleur-de-Lis*) at the top and a coat of arms with a bend	119
6.8 (Plate 27)	Watermark: legend L.T.F.v.T N	119
6.9 (Plate 27)	Watermark: Strasbourg's lily in a coat of arms with a crown in the upper part and the initials WR in the bottom. On the side there is a countermark IV (Jean Viledary) and C & I Honig below.	119
6.10 (Plate 27)	Watermark: appendage of the coat of arms in the form of Honigh family's beehive mark accompanied with the name of the factory J Honig & Zoonen	119
6.11 (Plate 28)	Krakow No. 171, attributed to Girolamo Odam, ca. 1715–1726/31, 115 × 154 mm, drawing transferred onto new paper	120
6.12 (Plate 28)	Berlin, Antikensammlung, inv. no.: FG 8422, red jasper intaglio, 2nd century AD	120
6.13 (Plate 28)	Krakow No. 171, fragment of surviving original sheet, 225 × 220 mm	120
6.14 (Plate 29)	Krakow Rr. 1497, attributed to Girolamo Odam, ca. 1715–1726/31, 155 × 120 mm, drawing transferred onto new paper	121
6.15 (Plate 29)	Berlin, Antikensammlung, inv. no.: FG 8044, sard intaglio, 1st–2nd century AD	121
6.16 (Plate 29)	Krakow No. 171, fragment of surviving original sheet, 225 × 220 mm	121
6.17 (Plate 30)	Krakow No. 73, attributed to Georg Abraham Nagel, ca. late 1730s–early 1740s, 120 × 132 mm, drawing with Izabela Czartoryska's commentary	122
6.18 (Plate 30)	Berlin, Antikensammlung, inv. no.: FG 7882, carnelian intaglio, 12 × 13 mm, 1st century AD	122
6.19 (Plate 30)	Berlin, Antikensammlung, inv. no.: FG 1100b, amethyst intaglio, 15 × 11 mm, 2nd–1st century BC (Hellenistic)	122
6.20 (Plate 30)	Krakow No. 174, attributed to Girolamo Odam, ca. 1715–1726/31, 115 × 154 mm, drawing with commentary and real-size gem drawing by Izabela Czartoryska	122
6.21 (Plate 30)	Krakow No. 661, attributed to Girolamo Odam, ca. 1715–1726/31, 170 × 137 mm, drawing with Izabela Czartoryska's commentary extended later	122
6.22 (Plate 30)	Krakow Rr. 308, attributed to Girolamo Odam, ca. 1715–1726/31, 153 × 128 mm, with a commentary by Izabela Czartoryska's assistant	122
7.1 (Plate 31)	Cover of *Pierres gravées du roi avec figures* vol. I	127
7.2 (Plate 31)	Title page of *Pierres gravées du roi avec figures* vol. I	127
7.3 (Plate 31)	Stamp of Koenigliche Museen	127
7.4 (Plate 31)	Stamp – Ex Biblioth Regia Berlinensi	127
7.5 (Plate 31)	Old and new inventory numbers	127
7.6 (Plate 32)	Berlin vol. V, pl. 112, with text by Stosch in pencil	128
7.7 (Plate 32)	Berlin, Antikensammlung, inv. no.: FG 349, carnelian intaglio, 13 × 11 mm, first half of the 1st century BC	128
7.8 (Plate 32)	Berlin, Antikensammlung, inv. no.: FG 7397, carnelian intaglio, first half of the 1st century AD	128
7.9 (Plate 32)	Berlin vol. IV, pl. 25, with text by Stosch in pencil	128
7.10 (Plate 33)	Berlin vol. I, pl. 40, with provenance information in the bottom	129
7.11 (Plate 33)	Berlin, Ägyptisches Museum, inv. no.: 9764, nicolo intaglio, 12 × 10 mm, mid-2nd century AD	129
7.12 (Plate 33)	Berlin vol. II, pl. 10, with fragment of provenance information in the bottom	129

FIGURES AND PHOTO CREDITS

7.13 (Plate 33)	Berlin vol. II, pl. 69 recto, with impression of Krakow No. 327 on the recto side	129
7.14 (Plate 33)	Krakow No. 327, attributed to Girolamo Odam, ca. 1715–1718, 137 × 169 mm, documentary drawing which 'offprint' is on the recto of Berlin vol. II, pl. 69	129
7.15 (Plate 34)	Berlin vol. VI, pl. 64 recto, with double impression of Berlin vol. 6, pl. 65 on the recto side	130
7.16 (Plate 34)	Berlin vol. I, pl. 22 recto, with impression of Berlin vol. I, pl. 23 once it was on original sheet	130
7.17 (Plate 34)	Berlin vol. I, pl. 23 verso	130
8.1 (Plate 35)	Krakow No. 1029, attributed to Girolamo Odam, ca. 1715–1718, 268 × 187 mm, preliminary drawing for Stosch's book *Gemmae antiquae caelatae*	171
8.2 (Plate 35)	London, the British Museum, inv. no.: 1867,0507.318, blue beryl (aquamarine) intaglio, 24 × 20 mm, third quarter of the 1st century BC	171
8.3 (Plate 35)	London, the British Museum, inv. no.: 1913,0307.326, agate cameo, 23 × 21 mm, 16th century	171
8.4 (Plate 35)	Krakow No. 1220, attributed to Girolamo Odam, ca. 1715–1718, 261 × 182 mm, preliminary drawing for Stosch's book *Gemmae antiquae caelatae*	171
8.5 (Plate 36)	Oxford, Ashmolean Museum, acc. no.: WA2014.49, 517 × 369 mm, pen and brown ink and grey wash on laid paper, Girolamo Odam, 1722	172
8.6 (Plate 36)	Philadelphia, Philadelphia Museum of Art, acc. no.: 1978-70-373, 409 × 277 mm, pen and brown ink (possibly iron gall) on laid paper mounted on paper, Girolamo Odam, ca. 1715	172
8.7 (Plate 36)	Krakow No. 1254, attributed to Girolamo Odam, ca. 1715–1718, 263 × 181 mm, preliminary drawing for Stosch's book *Gemmae antiquae caelatae*	172
8.8 (Plate 36)	London, the British Museum, inv. no.: 1867,0507.389, chalcedony intaglio, 28 × 24 mm, ca. 50 BC	172
8.9 (Plate 37)	Krakow No. 1384, attributed to Pier Leone Ghezzi, ca. 1715–1718, 115 × 105 mm, preliminary drawing for Stosch's book *Gemmae antiquae caelatae*	173
8.10 (Plate 37)	Chatsworth, the Devonshire collection, inv. no.: IRN 5013, carnelian intaglio, 13 × 11 mm, late 1st century BC–early 1st century AD	173
8.11 (Plate 37)	Private Collection, sardonyx cameo, 20 × 17mm, 16th century, by Alessandro Cesati (1510–1564)	173
8.12 (Plate 37)	Krakow No. 2141, attributed to Pier Leone Ghezzi, ca. 1715–1718, 121 × 107 mm, preliminary drawing for Stosch's book *Gemmae antiquae caelatae*	173
8.13 (Plate 38)	Krakow No. 391, counter-proof of Bernard Picart's drawing for Stosch's book *Gemmae antiquae caelatae*, ca. 1719–1733, 127 × 87 mm	174
8.14 (Plate 38)	Würzburg, Martin-von-Wagner Museum, inv. no.: G296-300, glass paste	174
8.15 (Plate 38)	Berlin, Antikensammlung, inv. no.: FG 2305, rock crystal intaglio, 37 × 29 mm, ca. 20–10 BC	174
8.16 (Plate 38)	Krakow No. 392, attributed to Bernard Picart, ca. 1719–1723, 268 × 185 mm, drawing for Stosch's book *Gemmae antiquae caelatae*	174
8.17 (Plate 39)	Krakow No. 175, attributed to Girolamo Odam, ca. 1715–1726/31, 182 × 151 mm	175
8.18 (Plate 39)	Florence, Museo Archeologico Nazionale, inv. no.: 14712, green chalcedony intaglio, early 1st century AD	175
8.19 (Plate 39)	Krakow No. 1019, attributed to Girolamo Odam, ca. 1715–1726/31, 139 × 171 mm	175
8.20 (Plate 39)	Krakow No. 1857, attributed to Girolamo Odam, ca. 1715–1726/31, 187 × 153 mm	175

8.21 (Plate 40)   Krakow No. 283, attributed to Girolamo Odam, ca. 1715–1726/31, 150 × 182 mm, lost gem once in the Michel Ange de La Chausse (1660–1724) collection   176

8.22 (Plate 40)   Krakow No. 2221, attributed to Girolamo Odam, ca. 1715–1726/31, 148 × 181 mm, lost gem once in the Francesco de'Ficoroni (1664–1747) collection   176

8.23 (Plate 40)   Krakow No. 306, attributed to Girolamo Odam, ca. 1715–1726/31, 187 × 153 mm, lost gem once in the Girolamo Odam and Francesco Vettori (1692–1770) collections   176

8.24 (Plate 40)   Krakow No. 1687, attributed to Girolamo Odam, ca. 1715–1726/31, 188 × 157 mm, lost gem once in the Prior Anton Maria Vaini's (1660–1737) collection   176

8.25 (Plate 41)   Krakow No. 74, attributed to Girolamo Odam, ca. 1715–1726/31, 240 × 250 mm, drawing of the so-called *Seal of Michelangelo*   177

8.26 (Plate 41)   Paris, Bibliothèque nationale de France, inv. no.: 58.2337, carnelian intaglio, 11 × 15 mm, early 16th century (by Pier Maria Serbaldi da Pescia (ca. 1455–after 1522))   177

8.27 (Plate 42)   Krakow No. 1726, attributed to Girolamo Odam, ca. 1715–1726/31, 145 × 178 mm, gem from Philipp von Stosch collection   178

8.28 (Plate 42)   Berlin, Antikensammlung, inv. no.: FG 2342, chalcedony intaglio, 17 × 21 mm, second quarter of the 3rd century AD   178

8.29 (Plate 42)   Berlin, Antikensammlung, inv. no.: FG 5172, glass gem, 11 × 10 mm, 44–40 BC   178

8.30 (Plate 42)   Krakow No. 1355, attributed to Girolamo Odam, ca. 1715–1726/31, 156 × 122 mm, gem from Philipp von Stosch collection   178

8.31 (Plate 43)   Krakow No. 250, attributed to Girolamo Odam, ca. 1715–1726/31, 184 × 151 mm, gem from Girolamo Odam collection   179

8.32 (Plate 43)   Krakow No. 569, attributed to Girolamo Odam, ca. 1715–1726/31, 150 × 182 mm, gem from Girolamo Odam collection   179

8.33 (Plate 43)   Krakow No. 2168, attributed to Girolamo Odam, ca. 1715–1726/31, 120 × 160 mm, gem from Girolamo Odam collection   179

8.34 (Plate 43)   Biblioteca Apostolica Vaticana, inv. no.: Cod. Ott. lat. 3108, fol. 141, 120 × 160 mm, pen and ink with grey wash, graphite, attributed to Pier Leone Ghezzi, ca. 1724–1740   179

8.35 (Plate 44)   Krakow No. 1964, attributed to Johann Justin Preißler, 1726–1738, 153 × 128 mm, drawing of a lost intaglio, with hatched background   180

8.36 (Plate 44)   Krakow No. 1804, attributed to Johann Justin Preißler, 1726–1738, 156 × 133 mm, drawing of a lost cameo, with hatched background   180

8.37 (Plate 44)   Krakow No. 1792, attributed to Johann Justin Preißler, 1726–1738, 156 × 133 mm, drawing of a hematite scarab, with background in wash   180

8.38 (Plate 44)   London, the British Museum, inv. no.: 1772.3-15.433/E48508, hematite scarab, 27 × 45 mm, Neo-Assyrian (7th century BC)   180

8.39 (Plate 45)   Krakow No. 996, attributed to Johann Justin Preißler, 1726–1738, 127 × 150 mm, drawing with inscriptions in the caption field   181

8.40 (Plate 45)   Dresden, Staatliche Kunstsammlungen Dresden, Skulpturensammlung, inv. no.: Hase2 105/111, amethyst intaglio, 13 × 16 mm, early 1st century AD   181

8.41 (Plate 45)   Krakow No. 409, attributed to Johann Justin Preißler, 1726–1738, 153 × 129 mm, drawing with inscriptions in the caption field   181

8.42 (Plate 45)   Etching by J.S. Klauber (1790), based on Johann Justin Preißler's drawing, after Schlichtegroll 1792b, pl. XI   181

8.43 (Plate 46)   Private collection, 125 × 139 mm, pen and ink with grey wash over red chalk, signed *J.J. Preisler. d.*, ca. 1730–1736   182

8.44 (Plate 46)   Krakow No. 1293, attributed to Johann Justin Preißler, 1726–1738, 127 × 151 mm   182

FIGURES AND PHOTO CREDITS

8.45 (Plate 46)	Private collection, 121 × 132 mm, pen and ink with grey wash over red chalk, signed *J.J. Preisler. d.*, ca. 1730–1736 182
8.46 (Plate 46)	Berlin vol. II, pl. 175, attributed to Johann Justin Preißler, 1726–1738, 130 × 150 mm 182
8.47 (Plate 47)	Krakow No. 1493, attributed to Markus Tuscher, ca. 1728–1741, 120 × 105 mm 183
8.48 (Plate 47)	Krakow No. 1644, attributed to Markus Tuscher, ca. 1728–1741, 128 × 152 mm, drawing of Stosch's gem, with hatched background 183
8.49 (Plate 47)	Berlin, Antikensammlung, inv. no.: FG 5413, glass gem, 1st century BC/AD 183
8.50 (Plate 47)	Krakow No. 1341, attributed to Markus Tuscher, ca. 1728–1741, 152 × 129 mm, drawing of a lost gem, with hatched background 183
8.51 (Plate 48)	Berlin vol. I, pl. 35, attributed to Markus Tuscher, ca. 1728–1741, 155 × 135 mm, drawing of Stosch's gem, with background in wash 184
8.52 (Plate 48)	Berlin, Antikensammlung, inv. no.: FG 6748, glass gem, 14 × 11 mm, last third of the 1st century BC 184
8.53 (Plate 48)	Equestrian monument to King Frederick V in Amalienborg Square, drawing in pen and ink with wash, 355 × 472 mm, Markus Tuscher, 1750, The Royal Collection of Graphic Art in Copenhagen, inv. no.: KKSgb6957 184
8.54 (Plate 49)	Krakow No. 245, attributed to Georg Abraham Nagel, ca. late 1730s–early 1740s, 135 × 108 mm, drawing of a gem with hatched background 185
8.55 (Plate 49)	Baltimore, Walters Art Museum, inv. no.: 42.1283, carnelian intaglio, 11 × 9 mm, 1st century AD 185
8.56 (Plate 49)	Alnwick Castle, the Beverley collection, inv. no.: 10662, carnelian intaglio, 15 × 12 mm, late 1st century BC 185
8.57 (Plate 49)	Krakow No. 268, attributed to Georg Abraham Nagel, ca. late 1730s–early 1740s, 152 × 129 mm, drawing of a gem with hatched background 185
8.58 (Plate 50)	Krakow No. 1699, attributed to Georg Abraham Nagel, ca. late 1730s–early 1740s, 161 × 205 mm, drawing of a gem with background in wash 186
8.59 (Plate 50)	Boston, Museum of Fine Arts, acc. no.: 99.109, turquoise cameo, 31 × 38 mm, early 1st century AD 186
8.60 (Plate 50)	Krakow No. 277, attributed to Georg Abraham Nagel, ca. late 1730s–early 1740s, 161 × 205 mm, drawing of a lost cameo 186
8.61 (Plate 51)	Krakow No. 1289, attributed to Georg Abraham Nagel, ca. late 1730s–early 1740s, 131 × 153 mm, lost gem once in the Pietro Andrea Andreini (1642–1729) collection 187
8.62 (Plate 51)	Krakow No. 224, attributed to Georg Abraham Nagel, ca. late 1730s–early 1740s, 157 × 128 mm, lost gem once in Gabriel Medina (?–?) collection 187
8.63 (Plate 51)	Krakow No. 963, attributed to Georg Abraham Nagel, ca. late 1730s–early 1740s, 153 × 130 mm, instead of a real-size gem on the left side lines inscribed *Camei Altitudo/Camei Latitudo* 187
8.64 (Plate 51)	Private collection, sardonyx cameo, 37 × 28 mm, 2nd–1st century BC 187
8.65 (Plate 52)	Krakow No. 403, attributed to Georg Abraham Nagel, ca. late 1730s–early 1740s, 155 × 130 mm, instead of a real-size gem on the left side lines inscribed *Gemae Altitudo/Gemae Latitudo* and *N* in the bottom-right corner – initial of Nagel's name 188
8.66 (Plate 52)	Florence, Museo Archeologico Nazionale, inv. no.: 14714, sardonyx intaglio, 35 × 27 mm, late 1st century BC–early 1st century AD (Augustan) 188
8.67 (Plate 52)	Krakow No. 27, attributed to Georg Abraham Nagel, ca. late 1730s–early 1740s, 155 × 130 mm, lost cameo, *N* in the bottom-right corner – initial of Nagel's name 188

8.68 (Plate 52)	Krakow No. 1578, attributed to Georg Abraham Nagel, ca. late 1730s–early 1740s, 155 × 130 mm, lost intaglio, *N* in the bottom-right corner – initial of Nagel's name	188
8.69 (Plate 53)	Private collection, 150 × 127 mm, pen and ink with grey wash, attributed to Georg Abraham Nagel, ca. 1754, a gem from the Carlo della Torre di Rezzonico (1693–1769) collection	189
8.70 (Plate 53)	Private collection, 150 × 127 mm, pen and ink with grey wash, attributed to Georg Abraham Nagel, ca. 1754, a gem from the Carlo della Torre di Rezzonico (1693–1769) collection	189
8.71 (Plate 53)	Krakow No. 1378, attributed to Georg Abraham Nagel, ca. late 1730s–early 1740s, 149 × 128 mm, the so-called Phocion cameo, background in wash	189
8.72 (Plate 53)	Krakow No. 1769, attributed to Georg Abraham Nagel, ca. late 1730s–early 1740s, 153 × 129 mm, lost intaglio with lining	189
8.73 (Plate 54)	Krakow No. 1183, engraving, Johann Adam Schweickart, ca. 1756, 121 × 95 mm, the *Tydeus Scarab*	190
8.74 (Plate 54)	Berlin, Antikensammlung, inv. no.: FG 195, carnelian scarab, 14 × 11 mm, first quarter of the 5th century BC (Etruscan)	190
8.75 (Plate 54)	Krakow No. 1182, attributed to Georg Abraham Nagel, ca. late 1730s–early 1740s, 156 × 130 mm, drawing of the *Tydeus Scarab*	190
8.76 (Plate 55)	Krakow No. 395, attributed to Pier Leone Ghezzi, ca. 1715–1731, 94 × 85 mm, lost carnelian intaglio once in Girolamo Odam collection, 'caricatural style'	191
8.77 (Plate 55)	Krakow No. 1253, attributed to Pier Leone Ghezzi, ca. 1715–1731, 125 × 112 mm, lost cameo, 'caricatural style'	191
8.78 (Plate 55)	Krakow No. 1588, attributed to Pier Leone Ghezzi, ca. 1715–1731, 350 × 228 mm	191
8.79 (Plate 55)	Private collection, 32 × 25 mm, tiger's eye cameo, ca. 1600 AD	191
8.80 (Plate 56)	Krakow No. 974, unknown artist, ca. 1720s–1750s, 173 × 156 mm, with fragments of original sheet and framing	192
8.81 (Plate 56)	Florence, Museo Archeologico Nazionale, inv. no.: 14774, carnelian intaglio, 32 × 23 mm, 16th–17th century	192
8.82 (Plate 56)	Krakow No. 23, unknown artist, ca. 1720s–1750s, 168 × 149 mm, with original real-size gem drawing	192
8.83 (Plate 56)	Krakow No. 1004, unknown artist, ca. 1720s–1750s, 152 × 125 mm, transferred on new paper and real-size drawing by Izabela Czartoryska	192
8.84 (Plate 57)	Krakow No. 1256, unknown artist, ca. 1720–1726, 125 × 110 mm, red chalk sketch of Stosch 1724 pl. XXX with Gori's reading of the signature	193
8.85 (Plate 57)	Krakow No. 1360, unknown artist, ca. 1720–1726, 177 × 134 mm, pen and brown ink sketch of Stosch 1724 pl. XXVI with Gori's notes	193
8.86 (Plate 57)	Krakow No. 1124, unknown artist, ca. 1720–1726, 127 × 107 mm, red chalk sketch of Stosch 1724 pl. XXXI	193
8.87 (Plate 57)	Krakow No. 1354, unknown artist, ca. 1720–1726, 127 × 107 mm, red chalk sketch of Stosch 1724 pl. II with Gori's correction of the signature	193
8.88 (Plate 58)	Berlin, Skulpturensammlung und Museum für Byzantinische Kunst, Marble bust of Philipp von Stosch, inv. no.: M204, 85 cm, Edmé Bouchardon, 1727	194
8.89 (Plate 58)	Krakow No. 1665, Johann Justin Preißler, ca. 1727–1738, 284 × 187 mm, red chalk drawing after marble bust by Edmé Bouchardon	194
8.90 (Plate 58)	Krakow No. 1665, Georg Martin Preißler, ca. 1727–1738, 330 × 190 mm, engraving made after the drawing by Johann Justin Preißler published in the luxury edition of Winckelmann 1760 catalogue	194

8.91 (Plate 59)	Krakow No. 2058, attributed to Girolamo Odam, ca. 1715–1726/31, 155 × 128 mm 195	
8.92 (Plate 59)	Krakow No. 1806, attributed to Johann Adam Schweickart? ca. 1742–1757, 158 × 106 mm 195	
8.93 (Plate 59)	Krakow No. 1061, unknown artist, ca. 1724–1757, 206 × 145 mm 195	
8.94 (Plate 59)	Krakow No. 1753, unknown artist, ca. 1724–1757, 102 × 73 mm 195	
8.95 (Plate 60)	Krakow No. 1980, attributed to Georg Abraham Nagel, ca. late 1730s–early 1740s, 158 × 133 mm, lost cameo, *N* in the bottom-right corner – initial of Nagel's name, gem drawing within a frame stuck down on laid paper 196	
8.96 (Plate 60)	Krakow No. 1291, attributed to Girolamo Odam, ca. 1715–1726/31, 183 × 150 mm, gem drawing within a frame drawn by hand, with provenance information and gemstone type given by Odam 196	
8.97 (Plate 60)	Krakow No. 468, attributed to Johann Justin Preißler, 1726–1738, 155 × 128 mm, drawing subject matter description and object type indicated 196	
8.98 (Plate 60)	Krakow No. 148, attributed to Johann Justin Preißler, 1726–1738, 152 × 128 mm, drawing subject matter description and object/gemstone type indicated 196	
8.99 (Plate 61)	Berlin vol. III, pl. 70, attributed to Markus Tuscher, ca. 1728–1741, 150 × 130 mm, drawing of Stosch's gem, with subject matter description corrected by Stosch 197	
8.100 (Plate 61)	Berlin, Antikensammlung, inv. no.: FG 917, carnelian intaglio, late 2nd–early 1st century BC 197	
8.101 (Plate 61)	Berlin, Antikensammlung, inv. no.: FG 3085, carnelian intaglio, 50 BC–AD 50 197	
8.102 (Plate 61)	Berlin vol. IV, pl. 71, attributed to Georg Abraham Nagel, ca. late 1730s–early 1740s, 150 × 130 mm, drawing of Stosch's gem, with gemstone type information added or confirmed by Stosch in pencil 197	
8.103 (Plate 62)	Krakow No. 413, attributed to Girolamo Odam, ca. 1715–1726/31, 122 × 160 mm 198	
8.104 (Plate 62)	Krakow No. 412, attributed to Johann Justin Preißler, 1726–1738, 152 × 128 mm 198	
8.105 (Plate 62)	Krakow No. 1207, attributed to Girolamo Odam, ca. 1715–1726/31, 152 × 125 mm 198	
8.106 (Plate 62)	Krakow No. 1208, attributed to Georg Abraham Nagel, ca. late 1730s–early 1740s, 152 × 129 mm 198	
8.107 (Plate 63)	Krakow No. 488, attributed to Girolamo Odam, ca. 1715–1726/31, 171 × 137 mm 199	
8.108 (Plate 63)	Krakow No. 487, attributed to Markus Tuscher, ca. 1728–1741, 155 × 139 mm 199	
8.109 (Plate 63)	Berlin vol. III, pl. 7, attributed to Johann Justin Preißler, 1726–1738, 150 × 130 mm 199	
8.110 (Plate 63)	Berlin, Antikensammlung, inv. no.: FG 8888, carnelian intaglio, 16th–17th century 199	
8.111 (Plate 64)	Krakow No. 213, attributed to Georg Abraham Nagel, ca. late 1730s–early 1740s, 142 × 111 mm, one of Stosch's gems 200	
8.112 (Plate 64)	Berlin, Ägyptisches Museum, inv. no.: 9808, limestone magical gem, 18 × 15 mm, 2nd–3rd century AD 200	
8.113 (Plate 64)	Berlin, Ägyptisches Museum, inv. no.: 9793, onyx cameo and intaglio, 25 × 12 mm, 1st century BC (Side A)/2nd–3rd century AD (Side B)? 200	
8.114 (Plate 64)	Krakow No. 1803, attributed to Girolamo Odam, ca. 1715–1726/31, 117 × 158 mm, one of Stosch's gems 200	
8.115 (Plate 65)	Krakow No. 1885, attributed to Georg Abraham Nagel, ca. late 1730s–early 1740s, 136 × 159 mm, a gem from an identified collection 201	

8.116 (Plate 65)	Cortona, Accademia Etrusca, inv. no.: 15742, carnelian intaglio, 11 × 13 mm, second half of the 1st century BC	201
8.117 (Plate 65)	London, Victoria & Albert Museum, inv. no.: 629-1871, engraved gold ring, 23 × 25 mm, 7th century AD	201
8.118 (Plate 65)	Krakow No. 1759, attributed to Georg Abraham Nagel, ca. late 1730s–early 1740s, 124 × 105 mm, a gem from an identified collection	201
8.119 (Plate 66)	Krakow No. 442, attributed to Girolamo Odam, ca. 1715–1726/31, 154 × 117 mm, once in the Marcoantonio Sabbatini (1637–1724) and later in Stosch collection	202
8.120 (Plate 66)	Berlin, Antikensammlung, inv. no.: FG 2816, glass gem, 24 × 18 mm, late 1st century BC (Augustan)	202
8.121 (Plate 66)	Berlin, Antikensammlung, inv. no.: FG 2503, green chalcedony intaglio, 1st century AD	202
8.122 (Plate 66)	Krakow No. 1518, attributed to Girolamo Odam, ca. 1715–1726/31, 124 × 157 mm, once in the Francesco de'Ficoroni (1664–1747) and later in Stosch collection	202
8.123 (Plate 67)	Krakow No. 441, attributed to Girolamo Odam, ca. 1715–1726/31, 170 × 138 mm, unidentified gem	203
8.124 (Plate 67)	Krakow No. 1361, attributed to Georg Abraham Nagel, ca. late 1730s–early 1740s, 153 × 130 mm, unidentified gem	203
8.125 (Plate 67)	Krakow No. 1813, attributed to Girolamo Odam, ca. 1715–1726/31, 189 × 156 mm, unidentified gem	203
8.126 (Plate 67)	Krakow No. 1783, attributed to Girolamo Odam, ca. 1715–1726/31, 138 × 169 mm, unidentified gem	203
8.127 (Plate 68)	Krakow No. 1221, engraving, Vincenzo Franceschini (1680–ca. 1750), pre-1718, after a drawing of the gem by Pier Leone Ghezzi (1674–1755) and frame design by Girolamo Odam (ca. 1681–1741), 358 × 239 mm, the *Meleager Gem*	204
8.128 (Plate 68)	Berlin, Antikensammlung: sard intaglio, inv. no.: FG 9296, 18 × 12 mm, early 18th century	204
8.129 (Plate 68)	Berlin, Antikensammlung: carnelian scarab, inv. no.: FG 194, 13 × 16 mm, 500–480 BC (Etruscan)	204
8.130 (Plate 68)	Krakow No. 1180, engraving, Johann Adam Schweickart, ca. 1756, 231 × 146 mm, the *Stosch Gem*	204
8.131 (Plate 69)	Krakow No. 416, attributed to Georg Abraham Nagel, ca. late 1730s–early 1740s, 153 × 130 mm, a drawing with an explanatory commentary	205
8.132 (Plate 69)	Naples, Museo Archeologico Nazionale, inv. no.: 25837/5, sardonyx cameo, 51 × 42 mm, late 1st century BC	205
8.133 (Plate 69)	Krakow No. 579, attributed to Georg Abraham Nagel, ca. late 1730s–early 1740s, 153 × 129 mm, a drawing of a lost gem with an explanatory commentary	205
8.134 (Plate 69)	Krakow No. 169, attributed to Georg Abraham Nagel, ca. late 1730s–early 1740s, 156 × 129 mm, a drawing of a lost gem with an explanatory commentary and reference to the coins of Macrinus	205
8.135 (Plate 70)	Krakow No. 39, attributed to Johann Justin Preißler, 1726–1738, 163 × 133 mm, a drawing with reference to Winckelmann 1760 catalogue by Joannon de Saint Laurent in the bottom-right corner and another one added between 1783 and 1800 in the caption field	206
8.136 (Plate 70)	Berlin, Antikensammlung, FG 2393, green chalcedony intaglio, 16 × 11 mm, 1st century AD	206
8.137 (Plate 71)	Krakow No. 1467, attributed to Girolamo Odam, ca. 1715–1726/31, 181 × 149 mm, a drawing with reference to Winckelmann 1760 catalogue by Joannon de Saint Laurent in the bottom and another one added between 1783 and 1800 in the caption field	207

FIGURES AND PHOTO CREDITS XXIII

8.138 (Plate 71)	Berlin, Antikensammlung, inv. no.: FG 8139, carnelian intaglio, 12 × 10 mm, 1st century AD 207
8.139 (Plate 72)	Krakow No. 1467, attributed to Girolamo Odam, ca. 1715–1726/31, 116 × 157 mm, a drawing with reference to Winckelmann 1760 catalogue by Joannon de Saint Laurent in the bottom of the gem 208
8.140 (Plate 72)	Berlin, Antikensammlung: inv. no.: FG 2744, glass gem, 1st century BC/AD 208
8.141 (Plate 72)	Berlin, Antikensammlung, inv. no.: FG 8192, nicolo intaglio, 11 × 8 mm, 2nd century AD 208
8.142 (Plate 72)	Krakow No. 628, attributed to Girolamo Odam, ca. 1715–1726/31, 153 × 115 mm, a drawing with reference to Winckelmann 1760 catalogue by Joannon de Saint Laurent (*1833*) in the bottom of the gem improved between 1783 and 1800 with additional *No:* and *p. 302* 208
8.143 (Plate 73)	Berlin vol. I, pl. 32, attributed to Johann Justin Preißler, 1726–1738, 155 × 125 mm, a drawing with reference to Winckelmann 1760 catalogue by Joannon de Saint Laurent in the bottom 209
8.144 (Plate 73)	Berlin, Ägyptisches Museum, inv.no.: 9823, red jasper intaglio, 10 × 8 mm, 2nd century AD 209
8.145 (Plate 73)	Berlin vol. I, pl. 20, attributed to Johann Justin Preißler, 1726–1738, 150 × 130 mm, a drawing with reference to Winckelmann 1760 catalogue by Joannon de Saint Laurent in the bottom and in the upper-right corner 209
8.146 (Plate 73)	Berlin, Antikensammlung, inv. no.: FG 100, agate scarab, 18 × 15 mm (with mount), 6th century BC (Cypriot, with Egyptian, Greek and Phoenician influence) 209
8.147 (Plate 73)	Berlin vol. VI, pl. 10, attributed to Markus Tuscher, ca. 1728–1741, 120 × 100 mm, a drawing with reference to Winckelmann 1760 catalogue by Joannon de Saint Laurent in the bottom of the gem corrected several times 209
8.148 (Plate 73)	Berlin vol. IV, pl. 24, engraving attributed to Johann Adam Schweickart, ca. 1742–1757, 130 × 115 mm, a fragment of an illustration from the luxurious edition of Winckelmann 1760 catalogue with reference to relevant entry by Joannon de Saint Laurent in the bottom 209
8.149 (Plate 74)	Krakow No. 346, attributed to Girolamo Odam, ca. 1715–1726/31, 136 × 170 mm, a drawing with reference to Winckelmann 1760 catalogue in the caption field and rewritten gemstone type added between 1783–1800 210
8.150 (Plate 74)	Krakow No. 1382, Niccolò Mogalli (1723–1767), ca. 1755–1767 or engraving after his preliminary drawing made by 1784? 226 × 148 mm, with a reference to Winckelmann 1760 catalogue below the caption field 210
8.151 (Plate 74)	Krakow No. 1442, attributed to Girolamo Odam, ca. 1715–1726/31, 171 × 138 mm, a drawing with reference to Winckelmann 1760 catalogue by Joannon de Saint Laurent (*496*) in the bottom of the gem improved between 1783 and 1800 with additional *No:* and *p. 111* and another reference added by the same hand in the caption field and gemstone type as well 210
8.152 (Plate 74)	Berlin, Antikensammlung, inv. no.: FG 6697, chalcedony intaglio, late 1st century BC–early 1st century AD 210
9.1 (Plate 75)	Latin title-page of Philipp von Stosch (1691–1757), *Gemmæ antiquæ cælatæ scalptorum nominibus insignitæ/Pierres antiques gravées, sur lesquelles les graveurs ont mis leurs noms*, Amsterdam 1724 231
9.2 (Plate 75)	French title-page of Philipp von Stosch (1691–1757), *Gemmæ antiquæ cælatæ scalptorum nominibus insignitæ/Pierres antiques gravées, sur lesquelles les graveurs ont mis leurs noms*, Amsterdam 1724 231
9.3 (Plate 75)	After Caylus 1752–1767, vol. II, p. 143, pl. 48.3 231
9.4 (Plate 75)	Krakow No. 1066, attributed to Georg Abraham Nagel, ca. late 1730s–early 1740s, 160 × 135 mm 231

9.5 (Plate 76)	François-Joseph Marteau (d. 1757), *Portrait of Philipp von Stosch (1691–1757)*, 1727, bronze medal (reverse with Diogenes), 40,72 mm diameter – Staatliche Kunstsammlungen Dresden Münzkabinett, inv. no.: 1991/A5545 232
9.6 (Plate 76)	Johann Karl von Hedlinger (1691–1771), *Portrait of Philipp von Stosch (1691–1757)*, 1728, bronze medal (reverse with inscription: VIRI · GENEROSISSIMI · AC · DE · REB · ANTIQUS · OPTIME · MERITI · EFFIGIEM · AMICO · ADFECTU · AETERNITATI · DICARUNT · N · KEDER · NOBIL · SVEC · ET · I · C · HEDLINGER · EQUES · MDCCXXVIII), 41,5 mm diameter – Staatliche Kunstsammlungen Dresden Münzkabinett, inv. no.: 1991/A5546 232
9.7 (Plate 76)	Berlin, Ägyptisches Museum, inv. no.: 9795, Stosch's glass paste 232
9.8 (Plate 76)	Berlin, Ägyptisches Museum, inv. no.: 9844, Stosch's glass paste 232
9.9 (Plate 77)	Philadelphia, Philadelphia Museum of Art, acc. no.: 1978-70-373, 409 × 277 mm, pen and brown ink (possibly iron gall) on laid paper mounted on paper, Girolamo Odam, ca. 1715 233
9.10 (Plate 77)	Krakow No. 1254, attributed to Girolamo Odam, ca. 1715–1718, 263 × 181 mm, preliminary drawing for Stosch's book *Gemmae antiquae caelatae* 233
9.11 (Plate 77)	*Bernard Picart (1673–1733), Medusa, engraving from Philipp von Stosch, Pierres antiques gravées, Amsterdam 1724, pl. LXIII* 233
9.12 (Plate 77)	London, the British Museum, inv. no.: 1867,0507.389, chalcedony intaglio, 28 × 24 mm, ca. 50 BC 233
9.13 (Plate 78)	Private collection, Bernard Picart, red chalk, 200 × 145 mm, drawing of an unsigned gem 234
9.14 (Plate 78)	The Hague, Koninklijke Bibliotheek, inv. no. Thoms' portfolio 72A20, serie 3, pl. 18, Bernard Picart, red chalk, 150 × 120 mm, preparatory drawing for Stosch 1724, pl. VII 234
9.15 (Plate 78)	The Hague, Koninklijke Bibliotheek, inv. no. Thoms' portfolio 72A20, serie 3, pl. 10, Bernard Picart, red chalk, 150 × 120 mm, preparatory drawing for Stosch 1724, pl. LV 234
9.16 (Plate 78)	The Hague, Koninklijke Bibliotheek, inv. no. Thoms' portfolio 72A20, serie 3, pl. 12, Bernard Picart, red chalk, 150 × 120 mm, drawing of an unsigned gem 234
9.17 (Plate 79)	Berlin vol. VI, pl. 55, attributed to Girolamo Odam, ca. 1715–1718, 120 × 100 mm 235
9.18 (Plate 79)	The Hague, Koninklijke Bibliotheek, inv. no. Thoms' portfolio 72A20, serie 3, pl. 6, Bernard Picart, red chalk, 150 × 120 mm, counterproof of a drawing of an unpublished gem related to Stosch 1724, pl. LXII 235
9.19 (Plate 79)	Rome, Musei Capitolini, inv. no.: Med 6730, carnelian, 21 × 25 mm, early 18th century, Rome, Musei Capitolini, Medagliere Capitolino 235
10.1 (Plate 80)	Leipzig, the GRASSI Museum, inv. no.: 1952.055/501, garnet (almandine) intaglio, 22 × 16 mm, first third of the 1st century BC 263
10.2 (Plate 80)	Krakow No. 1749, attributed to Markus Tuscher, ca. 1728–1741, 182 × 167 mm 263
10.3 (Plate 80)	Berlin, Antikensammlung, inv. no.: FG 11063, agate cameo, 18 × 15 mm, ca. 10 AD 263
10.4 (Plate 80)	Biblioteca Apostolica Vaticana, inv. no.: Cod. Ott. lat. 3106, fol. 38, 160 × 120 mm, pen and ink with grey wash, graphite, attributed to Pier Leone Ghezzi, ca. 1724–1740 263
10.5 (Plate 81)	Berlin, Antikensammlung, inv. no.: FG 6984, carnelian intaglio, l20 × 16 mm, ca. 40 BC 264
10.6 (Plate 81)	Berlin vol. VI, pl. 48, attributed to Johann Justin Preißler, 1726–1738, 120 × 100 mm 264

10.7 (Plate 81)	Head of Sextus Pompey by Agathangelos (signed *JJ Preisler d.*), 126 × 163 mm, pen and black ink with grey wash over red chalk, Johann Justin Preißler, ca. 1730–1736, private collection	264
10.8 (Plate 81)	Illustration of a carnelian intaglio with Hellenistic ruler as Zeus with an inscription ΝΕΙϹΟΥ, after a drawing by Johann Justin Preißler, ca. 1728, after Schlichtegroll 1792b, pl. XX	264
10.9 (Plate 82)	Krakow No. 1024, unknown artist, ca. 1715–1730, 108 × 186 mm	265
10.10 (Plate 82)	Intaglio with head of satyr to the left signed ΛΟΥΚΤΕΙ, after Gronovius 1695, vol. II, p. 44, no. 506	265
10.11 (Plate 82)	Krakow No. 668, attributed to Johann Justin Preißler, 1726–1738, 121 × 105 mm	265
10.12 (Plate 82)	Würzburg, Martin-von-Wagner Museum, inv. no.: G53-233, 14 × 11 mm, 18th century	265
10.13 (Plate 83)	Krakow No. 1745, attributed to Johann Justin Preißler, 1726–1738, 228 × 147 mm	266
10.14 (Plate 83)	London, the British Museum, inv. no.: 1890,0601.126, red jasper intaglio, 14 × 12 mm, early 2nd century AD	266
10.15 (Plate 83)	Krakow No. 1670, attributed to Georg Abraham Nagel, ca. late 1730s–early 1740s, 142 × 111 mm	266
10.16 (Plate 83)	Malibu, the J. Paul Getty Museum, acc. no.: 2019.13.17, black chalcedony intaglio, 35 × 29 mm, ca. 131–138 AD	266
10.17 (Plate 84)	Krakow No. 71, attributed to Johann Adam Schweickart, ca. 1742–1757, 255 × 175 mm	267
10.18 (Plate 84)	Current whereabouts unknown, aquamarine intaglio, Giant, inscription ΔΙΟϹ, once in the Zanetti collection, after Worsley 1824, p. 143	267
10.19 (Plate 84)	Leiden, Rijksmuseum van Oudheden, inv. no.: GS-11394, garnet (almandine) intaglio, 15 × 14 mm, first third of the 18th century	267
10.20 (Plate 84)	Krakow No. 251, attributed to Georg Abraham Nagel, ca. late 1730s–early 1740s, 152 × 128 mm	267
10.21 (Plate 85)	Leiden, Rijksmuseum van Oudheden, inv. no.: GS-00276, banded agate intaglio, 17 × 10 mm, second half of the 1st century, with inscription ΑΞΕΟΥ added in the first third of the 18th century	268
10.22 (Plate 85)	Krakow No. 1262, attributed to Georg Abraham Nagel, ca. late 1730s–early 1740s, 153 × 131 mm	268
10.23 (Plate 85)	Leiden, Rijksmuseum van Oudheden, inv. no.: GS-00258, glass gem, 12 × 9 mm, second half of the 1st century BC	268
10.24 (Plate 85)	Krakow No. 1540, attributed to Johann Justin Preißler, ca. 1726–1738, 103 × 126 mm	268
10.25 (Plate 86)	Leiden, Rijksmuseum van Oudheden, inv. no.: GS-10225, glass cameo, 15 × 21 mm, early 1st century AD	269
10.26 (Plate 86)	Krakow No. 324, attributed to Georg Abraham Nagel, ca. late 1730s–early 1740s, 153 × 132 mm	269
10.27 (Plate 86)	Leiden, Rijksmuseum van Oudheden, inv. no.: GS-10089, sardonyx cameo, 42 × 31 mm, early 17th century	269
10.28 (Plate 86)	Krakow No. 1357, attributed to Georg Abraham Nagel, ca. late 1730s–early 1740s, 157 × 130 mm	269
10.29 (Plate 87)	London, the British Museum, inv. no.: 1913,0307.189, burnt carnelian intaglio, 23 × 17 mm, second half of the 1st century BC	270
10.30 (Plate 87)	Illustration of Aulos and Quintus gems owned by Vettori engraved by Paolo Pilaia after a drawing and design of Girolamo Odam, after Vettori 1739, p. XXVII	270

10.31 (Plate 87) Biblioteca Apostolica Vaticana, inv. no.: Cod. Ott. lat. 3108, fol. 124, 260 × 175 mm, pen and ink with grey wash, graphite, attributed to Pier Leone Ghezzi, ca. 1724–1740   270

10.32 (Plate 87) Berlin vol. II, pl. 89, attributed to Georg Abraham Nagel, ca. late 1730s–early 1740s, 150 × 130 mm   270

10.33 (Plate 88) Electrotype cast of a sardonyx cameo with a female goddess crowning a warrior and Victory behind him on biga to the right, signed ΑΛΦΗΟΣ (Alpheios), 19th century   271

10.34 (Plate 88) Krakow No. 455, attributed to Georg Abraham Nagel, ca. late 1730s–early 1740s, 114 × 152 mm   271

10.35 (Plate 88) Krakow No. 116, attributed to Georg Abraham Nagel, ca. late 1730s–early 1740s, 126 × 153 mm   271

10.36 (Plate 88) Krakow No. 117, attributed to Johann Adam Schweickart, ca. 1742–1757, 255 × 177 mm   271

10.37 (Plate 88) Naples, Museo Archeologico Nazionale, inv. no.: 25848/16, onyx cameo, 35 × 29 mm, ca. 150 BC   271

10.38 (Plate 89) Krakow No. 2047, attributed to Georg Abraham Nagel, ca. late 1730s–early 1740s, 158 × 133 mm   272

10.39 (Plate 89) Sulphur cast of a sardonyx cameo featuring chained Cupid leaning on his pickaxe to the right with a genuine signature of Aulos (ΑΥΛΟΣ), late 18th century   272

10.40 (Plate 89) Krakow No. 1991, attributed to Georg Abraham Nagel, ca. late 1730s–early 1740s, 153 × 130 mm   272

10.41 (Plate 89) London, the British Museum, inv. no.: 1913,0307.178, amethyst intaglio, 16 × 16 mm, second half of the 1st century BC   272

10.42 (Plate 90) Krakow No. 1055, attributed to Georg Abraham Nagel, ca. late 1730s–early 1740s, 152 × 132 mm   273

10.43 (Plate 90) Private collection, carnelian intaglio, 17 × 14 mm, 1st century BC   273

10.44 (Plate 90) Krakow No. 972, attributed to Georg Abraham Nagel, ca. late 1730s–early 1740s, 127 × 154 mm   273

10.45 (Plate 91) Krakow No. 1002, attributed to Georg Abraham Nagel, ca. late 1730s–early 1740s, 127 × 154 mm   274

10.46 (Plate 91) London, the British Museum, inv. no.: 1890,0601.77, carnelian intaglio, 10 × 14 mm, early 1st century AD   274

10.47 (Plate 91) Biblioteca Apostolica Vaticana, inv. no.: Cod. Ott. lat. 3107, fol. 184, 115 × 150 mm, pen and ink with grey wash, graphite, attributed to Pier Leone Ghezzi, ca. 1724–1740   274

10.48 (Plate 92) Berlin vol. III, pl. 35, attributed to Georg Abraham Nagel, ca. late 1730s–early 1740s, 120 × 100 mm   275

10.49 (Plate 92) London, the British Museum, inv. no.: 1890,0601.50, carnelian intaglio, 12 × 9 mm, ca. 20 BC   275

10.50 (Plate 92) Berlin vol. III, pl. 32, attributed to Georg Abraham Nagel, ca. late 1730s–early 1740s, 100 × 120 mm   275

10.51 (Plate 92) Naples, Museo Archeologico Nazionale, inv. no.: 25844/248, onyx cameo, 24 × 17 mm, mid-1st century BC   275

10.52 (Plate 93) Berlin, Antikensammlung, inv. no.: FG 6269, glass gem, 25 × 20 mm, ca. 30 BC   276

10.53 (Plate 93) Krakow No. 874, attributed to Johann Adam Schweickart, 1745, 261 × 180 mm   276

10.54 (Plate 93) Krakow No. 936, attributed to Johann Adam Schweickart, ca. 1742–1757, 253 × 176 mm   276

10.55 (Plate 93)	London, the British Museum, inv. no.: 1913,0307.150, carnelian intaglio, 11 × 11 mm, early 18th century 276	
10.56 (Plate 94)	Baltimore, the Walters Art Museum, inv. no.: 42.109, garnet (almandine) intaglio, 18 × 15 mm, second half of the 1st century BC 277	
10.57 (Plate 94)	Krakow No. 1516, attributed to Johann Adam Schweickart (1722–1787), ca. 1742–1757, 258 × 178 mm 277	
10.58 (Plate 94)	Krakow No. 286, attributed to Johann Adam Schweickart (1722–1787), ca. 1742–1757, 255 × 175 mm 277	
10.59 (Plate 94)	Boston, Museum of Fine Arts, acc. no.: 27.734, garnet (almandine) intaglio, 21 × 15 mm, ca. 100 BC 277	
10.60 (Plate 95)	Krakow No. 1458, attributed to Georg Abraham Nagel, ca. late 1730s–early 1740s, 123 × 102 mm 278	
10.61 (Plate 95)	Krakow No. 1444, attributed to Johann Adam Schweickart (1722–1787), ca. 1742–1757, 257 × 176 mm 278	
10.62 (Plate 95)	Berlin, Antikensammlung, inv. no.: FG 7051, carnelian intaglio, 1st century AD 278	
10.63 (Plate 95)	Krakow No. 1593, attributed to Johann Adam Schweickart (1722–1787), ca. 1742–1757, 255 × 176 mm 278	
10.64 (Plate 96)	Krakow No. 1800, attributed to Anne Claude de Tubières-Grimoard de Pestels de Lévis Comte de Caylus, ca. 1730–1752, 86 × 143 mm 279	
10.65 (Plate 96)	Paris, Bibliothèque nationale de France, inv. no.: camée.182, agate cameo, 27 × 31 mm, 3rd–2nd century BC 279	
10.66 (Plate 96)	Illustration of agate cameo, 3rd–2nd century BC, Griffin fighting with a serpent entwined around its leg signed ΜΙΔΙΟΥ, after Caylus 1752–1767, vol. I, 144, pl. LIII.4 279	
11.1 (Plate 97)	Krakow No. 1799, attributed to Markus Tuscher, ca. 1728–1741, 245 × 192 mm, drawing of an Egyptian scarab 306	
11.2 (Plate 97)	London, the British Museum, inv. no.: EA7911/BS.7911 (Birch Slip Number)/H431 (Miscellaneous number), green porphyry heart scarab, 52 × 34 × 26 mm, ca. 664–332 BC – Late Period (Egyptian) 306	
11.3 (Plate 97)	Krakow No. 1801, attributed to Girolamo Odam, ca. 1715–1726/31, 168 × 135 mm, drawing of a lost cameo said to be Egyptian 306	
11.4 (Plate 97)	Krakow No. 1797, attributed to Johann Justin Preißler, ca. 1727–1738, 153 × 130 mm, drawing of a lost Egyptian scarab 306	
11.5 (Plate 97)	Krakow No. 1785, attributed to Georg Abraham Nagel, ca. late 1730s–early 1740s, 160 × 136 mm, lost cameo taken as Egyptian 306	
11.6 (Plate 97)	Krakow No. 1802, attributed to Johann Justin Preißler, ca. 1727–1738, 127 × 150 mm, drawing of a Sassanian seal taken as an Egyptian gem 306	
11.7 (Plate 98)	Krakow No. 1793, attributed to Girolamo Odam, ca. 1715–1726/31, 179 × 143 mm, drawing of a Neo-Babylonian seal taken as Persian 307	
11.8 (Plate 98)	Berlin, Vorderasiatisches Museum, inv. no.: VA 769, chalcedony stamp seal, 27 × 15 mm, 8th century BC (Neo-Babylonian) 307	
11.9 (Plate 98)	London, the British Museum, inv. no.: 1772,0315,GR.418/89303, hematite cylinder seal, 22 × 14 mm, ca. 1900–1800 BC (Old Babylonian period) 307	
11.10 (Plate 98)	Krakow No. 1794, attributed to Johann Justin Preißler, ca. 1727–1738, 128 × 152 mm, drawing of an Old Babylonian cylinder seal taken as Persian 307	
11.11 (Plate 99)	Krakow No. 570, attributed to Girolamo Odam, ca. 1715–1726/31, 121 × 155 mm, drawing of an Etruscan gem 308	
11.12 (Plate 99)	Berlin, Antikensammlung, inv. no.: FG 243, carnelian scarab, 3rd century BC (Etruscan *a globolo*) 308	

11.13 (Plate 99)	Berlin, Antikensammlung, inv. no.: FG 369, carnelian scarab with the beetle cut off, 5th–4th century BC (Etruscan) 308
11.14 (Plate 99)	Krakow No. 1365, attributed to Girolamo Odam, ca. 1715–1726/31, 171 × 137 mm, drawing of an Etruscan gem 308
11.15 (Plate 100)	Krakow No. 387, attributed to Girolamo Odam, ca. 1715–1726/31, 163 × 125 mm, drawing of a Greek gem 309
11.16 (Plate 100)	Berlin, Antikensammlung, inv. no.: FG 321, glass scaraboid, 4th century BC (Classical Greek) 309
11.17 (Plate 100)	Krakow No. 1189, attributed to Girolamo Odam, ca. 1715–1726/31, 118 × 150 mm, drawing of a Greek gem 309
11.18 (Plate 100)	Krakow No. 1195, attributed to Girolamo Odam, ca. 1715–1726/31, 153 × 125 mm, drawing of a Greek gem 309
11.19 (Plate 101)	Krakow No. 1329, attributed to Girolamo Odam, ca. 1715–1726/31, 138 × 170 mm, drawing of a Roman gem 310
11.20 (Plate 101)	Florence, Museo Archeologico Nazionale, inv. no.: 15012, carnelian intaglio, 19 × 25 mm, second half of the 1st century BC 310
11.21 (Plate 101)	Florence, Museo Archeologico Nazionale, inv. no.: cat. Migliarini n. 2388, nicolo intaglio, 2nd century AD 310
11.22 (Plate 101)	Krakow No. 1575, attributed to Girolamo Odam, ca. 1715–1726/31, 138 × 170 mm, drawing of a Roman gem 310
11.23 (Plate 102)	Krakow No. 2077, attributed to Girolamo Odam, ca. 1715–1726/31, 156 × 124 mm, drawing of a Roman gem 311
11.24 (Plate 102)	Florence, Museo Archeologico Nazionale, inv. no.: 14730, sardonyx intaglio, 1st century BC 311
11.25 (Plate 102)	Krakow No. 1327, attributed to Johann Justin Preißler, ca. 1727–1738, 151 × 129 mm, drawing of a Roman gem 311
11.26 (Plate 102)	Krakow No. 1033, attributed to Georg Abraham Nagel, ca. late 1730s–early 1740s, 152 × 130 mm, drawing of a Hellenistic gem 311

Photo Credits

After https://commons.wikimedia.org/wiki/File:GeorgMartinPreislerValentinDanielPreisler1756.jpg – Fig. 4.17.

After Caylus 1752–1767, vol. I, 144, pl. LIII.4 – Fig. 10.66

After Caylus 1752–1767, vol. II, p. 143, pl. 48.3 – Fig. 9.3

After Gronovius 1695, vol. II, p. 44, no. 506 – Fig. 10.10

After Johan van Gool 1750. *De nieuwe schouburg der Nederlantsche kunstschilders en schilderessen*, p. 112a, pl. C – Fig. 4.5

After Marrini, O., Moücke, F. and Pazzi, A. 1765–1766. *Serie di ritratti di celebri pittori dipinti di propria mano: in seguito a quella già pubblicata nel Museo Fiorentino, esistente appresso l'abate Antonio Pazzi*, vol. II, p. 379 – Fig. 4.19

After Schlichtegroll 1792b, pl. X – Fig. 8.42

After Schlichtegroll 1792b, pl. XX – Fig. 10.8

After Stosch 1724, pl. LXIII – Fig. 9.11

After Vettori 1739, p. XXVII – Fig. 10.30

After Worsley 1824, p. 143 – Fig. 10.18

©Artcurial – Fig. 9.13

©Ashmolean Museum, University of Oxford – Figs 3.5, 8.5

©Beazley Archive, University of Oxford – Figs 10.33, 10.39

©Biblioteca Apostolica Vaticana – Figs 2.4, 8.34, 10.4, 10.31, 10.47

FIGURES AND PHOTO CREDITS

©Biblioteca Marucelliana, photo by Donato Pineider – Fig. 3.8
©Bibliothèque nationale de France – Figs 3.6, 8.26, 10.65
©Christie's Images – Fig. 8.64
©Collection Haags Historisch Museum, The Hague, the Netherlands – Fig. 1.2
©Collection of the Duke of Northumberland, photography by Claudia Wagner – Figs 8.56
©Cortona, Accademia Etrusca, photo by Gerardo Ruggiero – Figs 8.116
©Courtesy of Les Enluminures – Fig. 8.79
©Courtesy of Victoria and Albert Museum, London – Fig. 8.117
©GRASSI Museum in Leipzig, photo Marion Wenzel – Fig. 10.1
©Herzog August Bibliothek Wolfenbüttel in 3.0 CC BY-SA – Fig. 4.8
©Jonathan H. Kagan collection, New York – Fig. 1.7
©Koninklijke Bibliotheek The Hague – Figs 9.14–16, 9.18
©Kunstbibliothek in Berlin, photo by Dietmar Katz – Figs 7.1–6, 7.9–10, 7.12–13, 7.15–17, 8.46, 8.51, 8.99, 8.102, 8.109, 8.143, 8.145, 8.147–148, 9.17, 10.6, 10.32, 10.48, 10.50
©Max Michelson – Fig. 10.43
©Medagliere Capitolino Roma, Sovrintendenza Capitolina ai Beni Culturali – Fig. 9.19
©Musée du Louvre, dist. RMN-Grand Palais – Fig. 3.3
©Musée du Louvre, dist. RMN-Grand Palais – Photo S. Nagy – Fig. 3.7
©Musée du Louvre, dist. RMN-Grand Palais – Photo L. Chastel – Fig. 3.19
©Musée Fabre de Montpellier Méditerranée Métropole – photographie Frédéric Jaulmes – Figs 3.13–14, 6.4
©Palazzo Pitti, Museo degli Argenti con concezione di Ministerio dei beni e delle attivita culturali e del turismo Gallerie degli Uffizi – Fig. 1.6
©Paweł Gołyźniak – Figs 9.1–2
©Paweł Gołyźniak with kind permission to use granted from The National Museum in Krakow – Figs 6.1, 6.5–11, 6.13–14, 6.16–17, 6.20–22, 7.14, 8.1, 8.4, 8.7, 8.9, 8.12–13, 8.16–17, 8.19–25, 8.27, 8.30–33, 8.35–37, 8.39, 8.41, 8.44, 8.47–48, 8.50, 8.54, 8.57–58, 8.60–63, 8.65, 8.67–68, 8.71–73, 8.75–78, 8.80, 8.82–87, 8.89–98, 8.103–108, 8.111, 8.114–115, 8.118–119, 8.122–127, 8.130–131, 8.133–135, 8.137, 8.139, 8.142, 8.149–151, 9.4, 9.10, 10.2, 10.9, 10.11, 10.13, 10.15, 10.17, 10.26, 10.28, 10.34–36, 10.38, 10.40, 10.42, 10.44–45, 10.53–54, 10.57–58, 10.60–61, 10.63–64, 11.1, 11.3–7, 11.10–11, 11.14–15, 11.17–19, 11.22–23, 11.25–26
©Philadelphia Museum of Art: Bequest of Anthony Morris Clark, 1978, 1978–70–373 – Figs 8.6, 9.9
©Photo in Public Domain – Figs 1.3, 2.1–2, 2.6–9, 3.4, 4.7, 4.18, 8.53, 10.16, 10.25, 10.27
©Photograph 2024 Museum of Fine Arts, Boston – Figs 8.59, 10.59
©President and Fellows of Harvard College, 1943.1815.19.8.A – Fig. 3.18
©Private collection – Figs 1.5, 3.1–2, 3.9, 3.11, 3.15–17, 3.20–24, 4.9–16, 4.20–23, 8.11, 8.43, 8.45, 8.69–70, 10.7
©RMN-Grand Palais/cliché Gérard Blot. Avec l'aimable autorisation du Palais Fesch-musée des Beaux-Arts d'Ajaccio – Fig. 1.4
©Skulpturensammlung, Staatliche Kunstsammlungen Dresden – Fig. 8.40
©Staatliche Kunstsammlungen Dresden Münzkabinett, photo by Kathleen Dittrich – Figs 9.5–6
©Staatliche Museen zu Berlin, Antikensammlung, photo Franziska Vu – Figs 1.9.1–6, 9–12, 14–15, 6.12, 6.15, 6.18–19, 7.7–8, 8.49, 8.52, 8.100–101, 8.110, 8.120–121, 8.128, 8.136, 8.138, 8.140–141, 8.152, 10.5, 10.52, 10.62, 11.12–13, 11.16
©Staatliche Museen zu Berlin, Antikensammlung, photo Johannes Laurentius – Figs 1.9.7–8, 8.129, 8.146
©Staatliche Museen zu Berlin, Antikensammlung, photo Johannes Kramer – Figs 1.9.13, 8.15
©Staatliche Museen zu Berlin, Antikensammlung, photo Ingrid Jeske – Fig. 8.74
©Staatliche Museen zu Berlin, Antikensammlung, CC BY-NC-SA 4.0 – Figs 8.28–29, 10.3
©Staatliche Museen zu Berlin, Ägyptisches Museum und Papyrussammlung, photo: Sandra Steiß – Figs 1.10.1–5, 8–11, 7.11, 8.112–113, 8.144, 9.7–8

©Staatliche Museen zu Berlin, Museum für Islamische Kunst, CC BY-NC-SA 4.0. – Figs 1.10.6–7
©Staatliche Museen zu Berlin, Skulpturensammlung und Museum für Byzantinische Kunst / Jörg P. Anders, CC BY-NC-SA 4.0. – Figs 1.1, 8.88
©Staatliche Museen zu Berlin, Vorderasiatisches Museum, photo Olaf M. Teßmer – Fig. 11.8
©Su concessione del Ministero della Cultura – Museo Archeologico Nazionale di Napoli – foto di Giorgio Albano – Figs 8.132, 10.37, 10.51
©Su concessione del Museo Archeologico Nazionale di Firenze (Direzione regionale Musei della Toscana) – Figs 8.18, 8.66, 8.81, 11.20–21, 11.24
©The Devonshire Collections, Chatsworth. Reproduced by permission of Chatsworth Settlement Trustees – Figs 2.3, 8.10
©The Metropolitan Museum of Art, photo in public domain – Figs. 1.8, 3.10, 4.6
©The National Galleries of Scotland – Fig. 3.12
©The National Museum in Krakow, photo in Public Domain – Figs 6.2–3
©The Walters Art Museum, Baltimore – Figs 8.55, 10.56
©Trustees of the British Museum – Figs 4.2, 4.4, 8.2–3, 8.8, 8.38, 9.12, 10.14, 10.29, 10.41, 10.46, 10.49, 10.55, 11.2, 11.9
©Yale University Art Gallery – Figs 4.3
©Vienna, Albertina, photo in Public Domain – Figs 2.5, 4.1
©Würzburg, Martin-von-Wagner Museum, photo by C. Kiefer – Figs 8.14, 10.12

PART 1

*Philipp von Stosch in the Circle of Eighteenth-Century
Collectors and Enthusiasts of Gems*

∵

CHAPTER 1

Philipp von Stosch: A Lifetime of Collecting

Ulf R. Hansson

1   Introduction

Philipp von Stosch's prominence in the history of gem scholarship and collecting has long been acknowledged, and his book on gems signed by their engravers, the *Gemmae antiquae caelatae* (1724), is recognised not only as a milestone in the history of learning but as a scholarly work in the modern sense. Although in some respects rather conventional and even disappointing, its consistent focus on engraved gems as the original output of individual artists, no doubt inspired by Baudelot de Dairval's interest in the work of the Greek engraver Solon,[1] was seen as novel at the time and proved decisive for the field.[2] The selection of gems, by Stosch himself,[3] and the meticulous illustrations of them by the group of draughtsmen whom Stosch had carefully chosen for this task, turned out to be the principal and lasting merits of this book. A sequel was planned and advertised but never realised, although Stosch continued to work on the project for decades, procuring casts, impressions, drawings and written documentation for his personal archive.[4] The reception history of this remarkable publication is as interesting as the shifting posthumous reputation of its author. But it is only with the renewed interest in recent years in Stosch's persona and legacy that the true extent and significance of his contribution and wider influence, in no way limited to his book, are beginning to be unveiled, if not yet fully understood. The rediscovery of a major part of the thousands of drawings of gems that Stosch commissioned over the years for his various projects adds significantly to our knowledge and understanding of this half-forgotten figure, whom his contemporaries considered to be a prominent member of the transnational *Republic of Letters*, indeed something of an oracle for collectors.

Stosch was a man of many parts, his interest in ancient intaglios and cameos should be viewed in the light of his overall engagement with the overlapping worlds of collecting and learning. A collector and connoisseur, patron and art agent, political agent and informant, freemason and radical libertine, Stosch laid the foundations to his later successes during his early travels in northern Europe and Italy in the 1710s, when he was still in his 20s. It was during this decisive period that he became seriously interested in antiquarian matters and started building his legendary collections and library. It was also during these years that he forged many useful friendships and alliances in learned, political and radical circles. A combination of personal interest, social skills and opportunity allowed him to acquire and cultivate a personal web of contacts which over the years came to include popes, cardinals, royalty, statesmen and numerous prominent members of the *Republic of Letters*. Letters of recommendation from these opened the doors to courts around Europe and to art collections, in which Stosch acquired unparalleled first-hand knowledge of especially gems and coins, and an expert eye in distinguishing ancient originals from clever modern copies and classicising works. This latter ability no doubt became increasingly useful as the century wore on and the demands of an insatiable art market turned the copying and forgery of ancient originals into a lucrative business. With his interest in artists and signatures, Stosch directly contributed to these developments and his book provided the market with many new names of ancient gem engravers and illustrations of their work. Moreover, there were rumours that he even participated in the production or sale of fake ancient gems.[5] Stosch also became instrumental in the resurgence of gem-engraving as a popular neoclassical art form by sponsoring artists such as Flavio Sirleti, Carlo Costanzi, Francesco Ghinghi, Lorenzo Masini, Lorenz Natter and Markus Tuscher, and boosting popular interest in intaglios and

---

1   Baudelot de Dairval 1717. Cf. also De'Rossi and Maffei 1707–1709, vol. IV, pp. 36–39 (esp. p. 38) and pl. 28.
2   In addition to providing a careful illustration of each work, Stosch's insistence on the original, a specific original, resulted in information categories such as inscription (name of engraver), present whereabout (collector), material and measurements.
3   With one exception, a gem from the Duke of Devonshire's collection, added by the publisher/illustrator, Bernard Picart. Stosch 1724, p. 69, pl. XLVIII.
4   E.g. Heringa 1976; Zazoff 1983, pp. 24–50; Whiteley 1999; Hansson 2013. Cf. Chapter 10 here in particular.

5   E.g. the Vaini sale in Florence 1734, referred to by Capponi (Vatican, Biblioteca Apostolica Vaticana (henceforth BAV) ms Capp. IV, 585). Cf. Guerrieri 2010, pp. 40–41; Tassinari 2010, pp. 31–33.

cameos.[6] His systematic collection of casts and impressions of gems in all the major collections of the period, which he kept for reference purposes, sparked the cultural phenomenon of the cast cabinets or *dactyliothecae*. The first important workshop for serially produced *zolfi* (sulphur gem impressions) was set up in Rome in 1739 by Christian Dehn, who had learnt the craft by assisting Stosch in the 1720s and 30s. Parts of Stosch's impressive cast collection, said to have originally numbered 28 000 items, later mostly ended up with James Tassie, one of the more well-known cast producers of the late eighteenth century.[7]

Stosch's collecting was not only governed by aesthetic principles or the search for unique pieces; he wanted a collection that was as complete and representative of ancient gem-engraving as possible.[8] We should understand his engagement in the field as totalising. Stosch strived towards a holistic understanding of every single aspect of the craft, from the materials, shapes, engraving techniques and repertoires of ancient engravers to the study, collection, reproduction and illustration of their work and onwards to the renewal of the craft in his own times. Even Winckelmann's famous publication of Stosch's gems, which for a long time remained a model for how collections should be structured and published, was based on the manuscript catalogue and structural principles of Stosch himself and his brother Heinrich.[9] Thus, Stosch's considerable influence within this field, at the centre of antiquarian and popular interest, was both direct and indirect.

Over the decades that he was active in Rome and Florence, Stosch's reputation became increasingly tarnished by his work as a political agent and art dealer. He was targeted by the Inquisition for his library and involvement in the circulation of problematic books, and his standing in antiquarian circles was constantly undermined by his enemies and competitors on the art market. Even so, throughout his life he seems to have remained highly respected for his learning and expertise and was frequently consulted. After his voluntary exile from Rome in 1731, the Museo Stoschiano in Florence continued its function as a key site for antiquarian culture and the radical Enlightenment, in addition to being a popular sight for foreign visitors. It did so right up until Stosch's death in 1757. It is not difficult to imagine why Winckelmann on his arrival in Italy wanted to establish contact with his both illustrious and notorious compatriot, whose learning and networks were probably as attractive as his vast collections.[10]

2 Formative Years and Early Travels (1691–1715)

Philipp Stosch was born on 22 March 1691 in Küstrin, Neumark Brandenburg (Fig. 1.1).[11] His father, Philipp Siegismund, was a medical doctor and mayor of Küstrin, and his mother Louise Vechnerinn. Together they had five children, three sons and two daughters.[12] The family was middle-class Silesian but boasted an aristocratic past.[13] The young Philipp attended the local Lutheran school and at the age of 15 he was sent to Frankfurt an der Oder to study theology under Samuel Strimesius, with the intention of becoming a priest. According to his *Geschichte*,[14] his interest in collecting can be traced back to this early period when he, encouraged by his father and under the influence of the Berlin antiquary Johann Carl Schott, began collecting coins on a modest scale. After only two years at Frankfurt, he left the university and embarked on a period of travelling, visiting a series of German cities and towns and arriving in the autumn of 1709 at Leiden, where he matriculated at the university to resume his studies in theology and classical philology.[15] However, he soon

---

6 See also Tassinari 2010 and refs. It was, for example, Stosch who suggested the use of the diamond point to Sirleti, and encouraged Natter to study and copy ancient originals. Natter 1754, p. XXXII: 'Nor did I copy any antiques till after my arrival at Florence, where Baron Stosch, being struck with my taste and application to engraving, did every thing to make me apply wholly to it'. In the case of Tuscher see *idem*, p. XXX: 'Mr Mariette is also mistaken with regard to Mr Mark Tuscher of Nuremberg, who never engraved on precious stones. He was a painter, who had a weakness to want to pass too for an engraver'.

7 Raspe and Tassie 1791, p. LXIV. Catherine II of Russia bought a double set, in sulphur and glass paste, of Tassie's whole stock. For Stosch as patron of gem engravers, see also Kagan 1985.

8 'Stosch war ein Typus italienischen Antiquarentums, "Er hat das schöne in der Kunst nie kennen lernen"'. Justi 1923, vol. II, p. 269, citing Winckelmann (letter to H.D. Berendis, 5 Feb. 1758).

9 Winckelmann 1760. See also Justi 1923, vol. II, pp. 293–294 and 297; Rügler in Winckelmann 2013, p. XVII.

10 '(…) *Mich verlangt, sein Angesicht zu sehen, wie ich irgend etwas in der Welt wünsche*' ['I long to see his face, more than anything in the world'] Letter from Winckelmann to W. Muzell, Aug. 1757, Winckelmann, 1952–57, vol. 1, pp. 298–299 no. 185.

11 Modern Kostrzyn, Nowa Marchia. Unless otherwise stated, the biographical information is from Stosch's *Geschichte*, published in J.C. Strodtmann's *Das neue gelehrte Europa*, in all probability authored by Stosch himself, therefore, referred henceforth and in bibliography as Stosch 1754, 1757 and 1758.

12 Ludwig, a physician and botanist, Heinrich Siegismund, also a medical doctor, Luise Hedwig (married Mutzel), and Elisabeth (Pfeil).

13 At some point in their history, the family had to renounce their title due to financial difficulties. It was restored to Philipp Stosch in 1717 by Emperor Charles VI. Stosch 1754, pp. 31–32.

14 *Supra* n. 11.

15 Stosch followed the lectures of philologists Ludolf Küster and Tiberius Hemsterhuis, and the radical theologian Jean le Clerc.

abandoned these again and transferred to The Hague. It was there that Stosch's extraordinary trajectory through social space truly began and the foundations of his future successes were laid.

In The Hague Stosch moved in with his cousin, Wolfgang Baron von Schmettau, who was Brandenburg Envoy to the Dutch States General and very well situated to introduce his young relative in local political, diplomatic and intellectual circles. In these milieux, we find the influential François Fagel, registrar of the States General, who became Stosch's mentor and sponsor (Fig. 1.2).[16] Over the next few years, Fagel, who was a collector of some note,[17] sent his protégé on minor diplomatic missions abroad and at the same time employed him as his agent in the procurement of artworks, medals and books for his own collections. It was, moreover, Fagel who encouraged Stosch's more serious collecting ambitions and suggested he position himself in antiquarian circles with a learned treatise of some sort.[18] Fundamental to Stosch's cultural formation and early experience in *antiquaria* and diplomacy, this generous patronage and close friendship continued until Fagel's death in 1746.

Two early longer sojourns in English and France proved especially decisive. In the spring of 1712, at the height of the Mohock riots, Stosch was sent to London in the company of the Dutch envoy on a vague diplomatic mission which lasted a whole year. On the ship crossing the channel, he was introduced to Prince Eugene of Savoy, a freemason with strong cultural interests, who knew John Toland and his circle and whose library was especially strong in radical texts.[19] Contact with these radical circles, in Holland and then in London,[20] proved significant for Stosch's philosophical and religious orientation. In London, Stosch was introduced to notable collectors such as Sir Hans Sloane and Sir Andrew Fountaine, and had the opportunity to study several important coin and gem collections, including those of Arundel and Devonshire.[21] He would remain in contact with several of these English collectors throughout his life. Stosch, who sent weekly reports to François Fagel, mostly on coins and medals and their collectors, moreover visited Cambridge, residing for several months in Trinity College as the guest of its master, Richard Bentley, who seems to have been instrumental in expanding Stosch's network within the *Republic of Letters*.

The second decisive sojourn was in Paris, where we find Stosch moving in the circles of Madame Palatine and her son Philippe II, Duke of Orléans. Arriving in May 1713 and taking lodgings in rue de Tournon,[22] Stosch forged several important friendships with key figures of learning in the Orléans circle, notably Bernard de Montfaucon, Pierre Crozat and Jean-Paul Bignon.[23] It was under the influence of this cluster of scholars and collectors that his interest in ancient engraved gems manifested itself and he decided that the learned treatise he intended to write must be on some aspect of this fast emerging field of study.[24] This refocus did in no way mean that Stosch lost interest in coins and medals, he rather expanded his antiquarian interest into this exciting new field which he found had considerable potential. The Duke of Orléans, who was an avid gem collector, had employed Wilhelm Homberg as his private physician, and it was from Homberg that Stosch learnt the useful craft of reproducing intaglios in coloured glass paste.[25] Stosch's interest in gems inscribed with names of ancient master-engravers was no doubt inspired by the lively discussions in these circles. A few years later, Charles-César Baudelot de Dairval, whom Stosch had befriended and later cited in his book, published his famous study where he argued that the name 'Solon', inscribed on the famous Strozzi, Orsini and other gems referred to the engraver of these stones, not to the Greek lawgiver.[26]

Furnished with letters of recommendation from Madame Palatine, Montfaucon and Bignon, Stosch left Paris after a few months and travelled south through France and northern Italy in the company of von Schmettau, en

---

16 To the young Stosch, Fagel became a '*friend and father*', whose generosity '*knew no bounds*'. Justi 1872, p. 296. Fagel was Greffier of the States General 1690–1744, see: Heringa 1976, 1981 and 1972.

17 Heringa 1981. See also *infra*.

18 Fagel no doubt assumed that the publication would be on coins and medals. Stosch 1724, p. III; Stosch 1754, p. 26.

19 Much has been written about the circle of John Toland, recently e.g. Israel 2001; Champion 2006; Lucci 2017; Davis 2018. On Prince Eugene's library, e.g. Feola 2014. Eugene's visit to London was related to the war of the Spanish succession.

20 Stosch might actually have met all three, Toland, Collins and Prince Eugene, in Holland in 1709–1710. In London he was introduced to the theologian William Whiston, recently expelled from Cambridge for his religious views.

21 On Stosch's network of English collectors, see *infra*; Burnett 2020, vol. III, p. 1567 and *passim*.

22 Letter from Stosch to Fagel, dated 16 February 1714 (NA, inv. 1726 fol. 11).

23 The *Geschichte* also mentions Anselmo Banduri, François de Camps, François Sévin, the classical scholars Anne and André Dacier, Jacques Boileau, and the numismatist Étienne Chamillard.

24 In a letter to Fagel dated 13 April 1714, he confessed that ancient engraved gems had now become '*ma passion ou si Vous voulez ma folie dominante*' (NA, inv. 1726 fol. 22). Stosch was already familiar with glyptics, having previously examined the Arundel and other collections in England.

25 Homberg had experimented extensively with glass paste and also published his results. Homberg 1712; Stosch 1724, p. XIX; Stosch 1754, p. 11.

26 Baudelot de Dairval 1717. He was not the first, though. Cf. De'Rossi and Maffei 1707–1709, vol. IV, pp. 36–39 (esp. p. 38) and pl. 28.

route to Rome on yet another unknown mission. Making numerous stops along the way,[27] visiting collectors and scholars such as Ludovico Antonio Muratori, Scipione Maffei, Apostolo Zeno and Luigi Fernando Marsigli, they reached Rome in February 1715. Stosch continued on his own to Naples, where he was introduced in intellectual circles with the help of the antiquaries Matteo Egizio and Francesco Saverio Valletta. *'Of all the products of Italian minds'*, he later wrote to Egizio, *'none coincide as well with my own mind than those of you erudite Neapolitans, in history and philosophy as well as in literature'*.[28] Together with Egizio, he also visited Portici and climbed down the excavation trenches to inspect the earliest finds from the buried city of Herculaneum that were beginning to surface on the property of the Duke of Elbeuf.[29]

3   Stosch's First Sojourn in Rome (1715–1717)

After a visually and intellectually full fortnight in Naples, Stosch returned to Rome, where he hired the ablest of *ciceroni*, Francesco de'Ficoroni. A letter of introduction from Montfaucon opened the doors to the papal court of Clement XI Albani and to the local antiquarian community, where he befriended local and visiting notables. Among these, we find the papal antiquaries Francesco Bianchini and Marcantonio Sabbatini and the collectors Leone Strozzi and Pietro Andreini, who owned several gems inscribed with the name of their engraver. Especially significant was perhaps his friendship with the pope's nephew Alessandro Albani, with whom he explored ruins in the Roman Campagna and interacted with the antiquarian community (Fig. 1.3).[30] He described what he did and saw in his weekly reports to his generous sponsor Fagel in The Hague. Surviving documentation indicates that Stosch participated actively in the local antiquarian culture, contributing in no small part to the circulation of both artworks and information, updating himself on new discoveries in the field and on items in collections that changed hands. In this way Stosch quickly acquired first-hand knowledge not only about the Roman monuments and art collections, but about collectors and the art market, becoming both *dotto* (learned) and *pratico* (experienced),[31] which made him attractive as a *cicerone* in Rome for German-speaking visitors. Among these, we find Prince Frederick William of Brandenburg-Schwedt and Johann Mattias, Reichsgraf von der Schulenburg, the latter an ardent collector.

Working hard on his book project on signed gems, Stosch had also started his own modest collection of originals and pastes, which he complemented with gem impressions, casts and drawings, thus building a reference library. He was always on the lookout for suitable draughtsmen who could provide him with the accurate drawings that he required, and he found in particular two skilled draughtsmen associated with the studio of Carlo Maratta, Girolamo Odam and Pier Leone Ghezzi, whom he felt were able to provide what he needed in terms of precision (Fig. 1.4). They both worked from originals in Roman collections, but mostly from impressions and casts that Stosch had procured from various fellow collectors. Odam alone is said to have made 2700 drawings for Stosch, but Stosch's collaboration with Ghezzi turned out to be more long-term.[32]

The papal circles in which Stosch moved during these years included the influential cardinals Lorenzo Corsini, the future pope Clement XII, and the learned Cardinal Giuseppe Renato Imperiali, at the time Prefect of the Congregation of Buon Governo. Stosch would perhaps have liked to stay in Rome longer. But with the unexpected death of his brother Ludwig in Paris in February 1717, he announced his departure after having been summoned home by his father.[33] Whether or not he really intended to return either to Küstrin or Paris remains unknown, but in fact he never did. At his farewell audience, Clement XI presented him with a papal pension as well as with several valuable books and letters of recommendation to the papal nuncios in Vienna and Dresden.

---

27   The places and people visited are mentioned in Stosch 1754, pp. 12–22.
28   *'Di tutte le produttioni di Cervelli italiani nissune convengono pio col mio genio, che fanno quelle de Vostri Eruditi Napolitani sia in Istoria sia Philosophia sia Literatura'*. Letter from Stosch to M. Egizio, dated 20 March 1723 (Engelmann 1908, p. 338).
29   This was decades before the official excavations were begun. Stosch 1754, pp. 22–23.
30   '(...) *this friendship grew stronger every day, and they were almost never apart*' (Stosch 1754, p. 25). Field projects at Albani's properties at Castel Gandolfo and Anzio are mentioned, in addition to Nemi, Grottaferrata, Tusculum, Tivoli and Praeneste (Stosch 1754, p. 25). For Albani's early archaeological interest and explorations, see: Cacciotti 2001.
31   Cf. Griggs 2008, pp. 285–286 on Ficoroni.
32   Zazoff 1983, p. 23 and refs.
33   '(...) *daß aber der Tod seines Bruders, welcher den 14 Februar zu Paris verstorben, eben zu einer Zeit, da der König ihn zu einer ansehnlichen Bedienung bey seiner höchsten Person bestimmt hatte, nöthigte, dem Befehle seines Vaters zu gehörsamen, und sich nach seinem Vaterlande zurück zu begeben, um seiner Familiensachen wahrzunehmen'* ['... but that the death of his brother, who died in Paris on February 14, at a time when the king had appointed him to a considerable service to his highest person, compelled him to obey his father's request and to return to his Fatherland to take care of his family affairs'] (Stosch 1754, p. 27).

4 Vienna, Dresden and the Dutch Republic (1717–1722)

Departing from Rome in May 1717, Stosch made a number of significant stops along his rather unhurried way back north. In Livorno, he was introduced to Gian Gastone de' Medici, and in Florence a few days later to Cosimo III, who allowed him to make impressions in sulphur or wax of the intaglios and cameos in the grand ducal collection.[34] Stosch was also welcomed by notables in the local scholarly community such as Anton Maria Salvini, Anton Francesco Gori, Filippo Buonarroti, Anton Francesco Marmi, Scipione Maffei and Francesco Cerretani – the latter in whose collection Stosch found another signed ancient gem for his book project.[35]

Onwards to Vienna where he was introduced to Emperor Charles VI and renewed contact with Prince Eugene.[36] This sojourn proved equally rewarding. Stosch showed some of Odam's and Ghezzi's gem drawings to the emperor, asking for his patronage for the book project, which was granted.[37] He also showed these drawings and some engraving proofs to Pierre-Jean Mariette.[38] Towards the end of his stay in Vienna, the emperor restored Stosch's lapsed title of Freiherr (Baron) for unspecified services relating to the imperial art collections.[39]

In Vienna, Stosch also met the Saxon envoys Count Joseph Wackerbarth-Salmour and Count Jacob Heinrich von Flemming, who offered him an attractive position as royal antiquary to August II; again, this offer seemed combined with some sort of political assignment. Making short halts in Prague and Dresden, Stosch was sent back to the Dutch Republic, now as the envoy of Saxony-Poland.[40]

In The Hague, Stosch reconnected with his generous sponsor and mentor Fagel,[41] and renewed contact with radical and masonic circles.[42] An avid bibliophile, he collected what he could get his hands on and afford, *'per uso mio e ornamento della mia libraria'*.[43] By 1721, he had already built a discerning library that contained *'presque tous les auteurs qui serve à l'intélligence de toute sorte d'Antiquités et Curiosités modernes comme ausi pour*

---

34 Alessandro Albani had written to Cosimo III, advertising Stosch's arrival in Florence: *'Sento che sia venuto lettera alla corte del Sr Alessandro [Albani] onde sia venuto ordine di fargli vedere medagli e cammei'* ['I hear that a letter has arrived to the court from Sr Alessandro [Albani] with the request to show him [Stosch] medals and cameos'], Letter from Filippo Buonarroti to Leone Strozzi, dated Florence 12 May 1717 (ASF, Carte strozziane ser. III, 63, cart. Filippo Buonarroti-Leone Strozzi, fol. 31 r.). Stosch was assisted by the keeper of the collections, Sebastiano Bianchi.

35 *'Ier sera il S.r Filippo Stoch [sic] Prussiano [sic] che ha fatto la gita a Livorno avendo presa la traversa mi presentò la sua del 19 Aple ed i suoi saluti e già mi ha cominciato a far vedere de suoi intagli ed ho veduto il Meleagro e la Baccante che ha legati in anelli e potei vedere dalla veglia che fece da me che è molto esperto di materia d'antichità. Io lo servirò in quello mi comanderà e la ringrazia specialmente d'avermelo fatto conoscere. (...) Iarsera l'altra ebbi per l'ultima volta il Sr Prussiano (...) e credo che il Prussiano parta domattina e mi ha donato le cere di molti suoi intagli ed ha preso alcune cere de miei intagli e specialmente dei vetri e veramente è intelligissimo del buono ed è erudite e ha cognizione ancora del mondo e delle corti e veramente è stata una buona conversazione e si desiderò che Mosignore Strozzi fossi a vederci'* ['Last night the Prussian Sr Filippo Stoch who had made the trip to Livorno making a detour presented himself to me on 19 April and immediately started to show me his intaglios. I have seen the Meleager and the Baccante which he has had mounted on rings and I could see already that night at my place that he is an expert in the field of antiquities. I will try my best to assist him in what he needs and thank you especially for having presented him to me. (...) The night before last I had here for the last time the Prussian gentleman (...) and I believe the Prussian will depart tomorrow morning. He has given me wax impressions of many of his intaglios and he has made wax impressions of some of my intaglios and especially glass pastes. He is really very intelligent of the good sort and he is learned and has knowledge of the world and of the courts. It was really a very good conversation and I wish that Monsignor Strozzi had been here to see us'] – letter from Filippo Buonarroti to Leone Strozzi, dated Florence 12 May 1717 (ASF Carte strozziane, ser. III, 63, cart. Filippo Buonarroti-Leone Strozzi, fols 31–32 r). Cf. also a letter from Alessandro Gregorio Capponi to Francesco Marmi, dated Rome 1717 (BNCF, fondo magliabechiano, cl. VIII, MS. 1062, fol. 7 r. cit. in Gialluca 2014, p. 304 n. 118).

36 Stosch was presented to the Emperor either by Prince Eugene or the papal nuncio Giorgio Spinola. As a strategic courtesy, Stosch offered to sell the famous Tabula Peutingeriana to Eugene, which he had recently discovered in one of the many collections he had visited, together with a cache of valuable letters written by the thirteenth-century jurist Pietro della Vigna.

37 Stosch 1754, p. 30.

38 These prints were apparently done in Italy, cf. Chapter 8 here. Mariette, who at the time was working for Prince Eugene, mentions specifically the Medusa Strozzi and the famous Meleager (1750, vol. I, p. 332).

39 Stosch 1754, p. 32. Stosch was later also offered the post of Imperial Librarian, which he turned down (letter from Stosch to Karl Gustav Heraeus, dated Rome 19 December 1722 – Schneider 1907).

40 Stosch received 600 Reichstaler annually for his services. He was Saxon envoy to The Hague 1719–1721, but kept the title of royal antiquary longer, whether officially or not remains unknown.

41 '(...) *welcher ihm mit der That an Vaterstelle war, mit vieler Zärtlichkeit empfangen*' ['(...) who being almost like a father to him, received him with much tenderness'] (Stosch 1754, p. 34).

42 Stosch was for a while vaguely associated with the so-called *Chevaliers de Jubilation* (Knights of Jubilation) in The Hague. On this loose grouping, e.g. Jacob 1970 and 1981, and the response by Fielding and Berkvens-Stevelinck 1983.

43 Letter from Stosch to M. Egizio, dated 26 September 1722 (Engelmann 1908, p. 335).

connoissance des livres et manuscrits'.⁴⁴ In addition, he had substantial holdings in theology, philosophy, diplomacy, medicine and the new natural sciences. His library was especially rich in radical and clandestine publications, in the circulation of which he participated actively, connecting his networks in England, Holland and Italy.⁴⁵ These circles in the Dutch Republic included printers, booksellers and bibliophiles, at the heart of which we find the 'radical Huguenot coterie': Prosper Marchand, Charles Levier, Bernard Picart, Jean Aymon and possibly also Jean Rousset de Missy.⁴⁶ Stosch's involvement in these circles enabled him to retrieve a valuable book stolen by Aymon from the French royal library, for which he was generously rewarded by Philippe II d'Orléans, as well as locating a copy of a rare book that Frederick William I of Prussia had been searching for in vain.⁴⁷ These and other favours to regents and members of the highest social echelons indicate that Stosch had direct access to and was able to move freely in these milieux, forging relations based on *do ut des* principles.

In The Hague, Stosch also cemented his friendship with the collector Pierre Crozat, whom he accompanied on a tour of the Netherlands, advising on art acquisitions. Stosch's own collecting, moreover, took a new turn during this decisive period in Holland. Again, Fagel seems to have been instrumental in Stosch's decision to expand his already considerable collection of maps and drawings of cities and monuments that he had acquired on his travels, with the aim of creating a gigantic topographical atlas of *'the whole world'*.⁴⁸ This project, inspired by Cassiano dal Pozzo's *Paper Museum*, which Stosch had admired in the Albani library in Rome, and the 50-volume atlas of Laurens van der Hem based on Joan Blaeu's *Atlas Maior*, soon developed into his second most important undertaking: a more or less systematic collection of old, new and especially commissioned maps, prints and drawings of cities, fortifications, buildings and monuments. Two years later this collection already filled fifty folio volumes.⁴⁹

Towards the end of Stosch's second Dutch period, John Carteret, whom he had previously met in London, passed through The Hague on his way back to London from St Petersburg to take up his position as Secretary of State for the Southern Department.⁵⁰ Carteret realised that Stosch's numerous contacts at the papal court in Rome, combined with his budding international reputation as an antiquary and art agent, would make him an ideal informant on the exiled court of the Stuart Pretender, James Francis Edward Stuart, in Rome. Stosch saw the opportunity to return to the city that had made such an impression on him and thus let himself be recruited.⁵¹ But before leaving the Netherlands, he delivered the drawings and gem impressions for his book project to Bernard Picart, whom he commissioned to engrave the plates and also print his book, which was now more or less completed.⁵²

5   Stosch Settles Permanently in Rome (1722–1731)

Thus, on the secret payroll of the British and in the convenient cloak of art agent of August the Strong and François Fagel, who continued their patronage,⁵³ Stosch was able to return and settle permanently in Rome in January 1722. These incomes were welcome, as the death of Clement XI the previous year had deprived Stosch of his papal pension. As the British had no official representation in the city because of the pope's official recognition of the Stuart Pretender, Stosch's protection was instead negotiated with the imperial legate, Cardinal Cienfuego, who initially seems to have been unaware of Stosch's real mission.⁵⁴ The deal was to send weekly intelligence reports to London,

---

44   Letter from Stosch to Count Flemming, dated 18 March 1721 (Justi 1871, pp. 6–7, no. 11).
45   On Stosch library, see: Hansson 2025c.
46   Israel 2001, p. 696.
47   Stosch 1757, p. 36. On Aymon's book theft, see: Omont 1891.
48   Stosch 1754, pp. 34–35; Winckelmann 1760, pp. 578–596; Eggers 1926; Kinauer 1950.
49   Letter from Stosch to Count Flemming, dated 13 May 1721 (Justi 1871, p. 10). For this specific project see also Stosch 1754, pp. 34–35; 1757, pp. 285–287; Winckelmann 1760, pp. 578–596; Eggers 1926; Kinauer 1950.
50   John Carteret's father, George 1st Baron Carteret (1667–1695), had been a coin collector, although most of his collections had been sold by his widow (to John Kemp) at the time of Stosch's visit. Burnett 2020, vol. I, pp. 376–377, vol. II, pp. 783, 960, 1051 and 1124–57, vol. III, p. 1238. Still, this might have been the original reason for their meeting.
51   On Stosch's work as a British informant, see esp. Keyßler 1751, Brief XLVIII, pp. 467–472; Stosch 1757, pp. 288–299; Lewis 1961, and Corp 2011.
52   '(...) so übergab er alle Zeichnungen dieses Werkes dem berühmten Kupferstecher, Bern. Picard, und gab ihm auch die Abdrücke der Steine selbst, um sie aufs neue mit dene Zeihnungen zusammen zu halten' ['So he handed all drawings for this work to the celebrated engraver Bern. Picart, and he also gave him the impressions of the actual gems, in order to keep them together again with the drawings'] (Stosch 1754, p. 38). '*Imagines a Picarto elaborate sunt fatis splendidae atque magnificae, vera gemmae mensura ubique addita, tanta vero cura caelatae, ut quo diutius eas inspicias, eo plus nitoris, elegantiae, artis detegas*' (*Acta eruditorum* 1725, pp. 337–340 (p. 340)). On the illustrations to Stosch 1724, see esp. Heringa 1976; Whiteley 1999, and chapter 9 in this volume.
53   Justi 1871, pp. 12–15; Lewis 1961, p. 57.
54   Letter from R. de Rialp to Cardinal Cienfuego, dated 13 October 1722 (Noack 1928–1929, p. 41). De Rialp does not mention Stosch's

and he could otherwise devote himself to the scholarly and collecting activities that interested him.

Stosch was already well-known at the papal court and had soon repositioned himself at the very centre of the antiquarian community.[55] *'I live here in great peace'*, he wrote to the imperial librarian Carl Gustav Heraeus in Vienna, *'working quietly for my master who pays me generously and punctually, and enlarging my library and my collection of engraved gems every day; herein lies my only happiness'*.[56] He was then residing in the Strada Rasella,[57] near the Albani palace on the Quirinal Hill. His work as an undercover political agent did, however, not remain secret for very long. Although it tarnished his antiquarian reputation and sometimes proved socially awkward, it provided him with an unofficial political status that seems to have been not altogether negative.[58] There is no doubt, however, that his relations with the British put Stosch in an advantageous position on the art market as it gave him direct access to British collectors. Most of those who visited Rome, if not all, would have come into contact with Stosch, whose only real competitor in these early decades of the century was the indefatigable Ficoroni.[59] Stosch's close relations with Cardinal Alessandro Albani, which were now further cemented, proved equally significant in this respect. Their lifelong close association was mutually profitable and survived Stosch's later exile from Rome.

Stosch's long advertised book was finally published in 1724 by Picart in Amsterdam, and early copies of it reached Rome towards the end of that year. Its wide acclaim across Europe firmly established Stosch, who was already an authority on coins and medals,[60] as the foremost expert in this field of study that was by then a core antiquarian practice in Rome with a fast growing market.[61] The book had a long introduction by Stosch himself and catalogue entries ghostwritten by the abbate Francesco Valesio.[62] Stosch later announced a forthcoming second volume.[63] Although the project was never realised, he continued to collect material for it throughout his life, soliciting help from fellow collectors, scholars and artists.[64] He commissioned drawings not only for this planned 'supplement', as he called it, but on a much vaster scale, as is apparent from the present publication.[65]

Stosch participated actively in the Roman antiquarian community and, increasingly, the art market. His second

---

intelligence work for the British, only that he is an antiquarian that the emperor wishes Cienfuego to oblige.

55 For Stosch's Rome period 1722–1731, see e.g. Hansson 2022.
56 *'Je vis icy d'un grand calme, faisant tranquillement les affaires de mon maître qui me paye largement et punctuelle et en augmentant ma bibliothèque et recuei de pierres gravees tous le jours, en quoy consiste mon unique bonheur'* – letter from Stosch to C.G. Heraeus, dated 12 December 1722 (Schneider 1907, p. 347).
57 Noack 1928–1929, p. 41.
58 His correspondence from these years reveals that he was often troubled by his difficulties in Rome and wished to return to Holland or England.
59 The historian Hanns Gross (1990, p. 319) is exaggerating in his claim that: *'Stosch was perhaps the most notorious example of a foreigner who profited from Europe's greed for the treasures of ancient Rome by dubious means. But his misfortune, if we may call it such, was that he lived in the first half of the eighteenth century'*. But it is certainly true that Stosch was an important figure, in some sense perhaps even instrumental, in this trade decades before it was transformed into a major international market.
60 *'Er hat von seinen Wissenschaften in griechisch und lateinischen Altertümern schöne Proben abgelegt, und sind dadurch in Rom einen solchen Ruhm erworben, daß sein Ausspruch über die dahin gehörige Dinge, und wenn eine Münze oder ein altes Sigillum beurtheilet warden soll, nicht leicht vorbeygegangen wird'* ['He has given us wonderful evidence of his knowledge of Greek and Latin antiquities, and has because of this won such fame in Rome, that his expert opinion in such matters, and if a coin or old seal is being examined, is not easily ignored'] (Keyßler 1751, p. 471).
61 *'Dieses prächtige und überaus gelehrte Werk, welches das einzige in seiner Art ist, machet allein der Namen unseres Freyherrn in der gelehrten Welt unsterblich. Die meisten gelehrten Monatschriften von einigem Werte haben es an dem Lobe desselben nicht ermangeln lassen'* ['This magnificent and learned work, which is the only one of its kind, contributed on its own to make our Baron's name immortal in the world of learning. Most monthly journals of any note have not lacked in praise of it'] (Stosch 1754, p. 41). Zazoff (1983, p. 18) detects a difference in attitude towards Stosch when comparing Ghezzi's 1725 and 1728 drawings.
62 Possibly preferring not to be named in the book, Valesio's participation is nevertheless confirmed by Ghezzi (Cod. Ott. lat. 3112, fol. 115) and much later by Giovanni Lami (1742, pp. 197–9 and 1757, p. 722), and indirectly by Stosch himself, who refer to him without mentioning his name in the foreword to the book (p. v: *'Ainsi, c'est un bonheur dont je ne puis assez me féliciter, que tant d'habiles gens aient concouru, sans aucun motif de jalousie, à la perfection de cet Ouvrage'* ['Thus, it is a pleasure of which I cannot congratulate myself enough, that so many talented people have contributed, without any reason for jealousy, to the perfection of this work']). Stosch later commissioned a portrait medallion of Valesio from the artist Markus Tuscher carrying the ambiguous inscription *'bene qui latuit bene vixit'* ['he who has lived in hiding has lived well'], a paraphrase of Ovid's *bene vixit, bene qui latuit* (*Tristia* 3.4). The whole inscription reads: BENE. QUI. LATUIT. BENE. VIXIT. PH. B. DE. STOSCH. AM. OPT. G.A.M.F.C. ROMAE. MDCCX – X. – Rizzini 1889, p. 187 no. 1212; Nagler 1871, p. 691, no. 2193; Pennestrì 2021, p. 210, no. 209, pl. XLV; Hansson 2025b. According to Zazoff (1983, p. 24), Valesio had asked specifically not to be mentioned in the text. Interestingly, correspondingly, Valesio never mentions Stosch in his diary (1978).
63 E.g. Vettori 1739, p. 7; Letter from Stosch to Venuti, dated 24 February 1739 (Engelmann 1908, pp. 330–331). Also Mariette 1750, vol. I, p. 334; Stosch 1754, p. 50.
64 Letter from Stosch to Venuti, dated 16 August 1746 (Engelmann 1909, pp. 333–335 no. 3).
65 See Chapter 10 in this volume.

important project during his Roman years was of course the already mentioned *Topographical Atlas*, for which he had begun collecting material in 1719. In Rome, numerous older architectural drawings by Giovanni Battista da Sangallo, Francesco Borromini and others were added to its 'Roman section', which came to fill sixty-three volumes that also included new drawings of buildings and careful archaeological visual documentation commissioned from trusted artists.[66] Stosch had even acquired a reputation for training local draughtsmen in this difficult art.[67] Among these, Ghezzi, '*très-excellente peintre*',[68] who moved freely in Roman antiquarian circles and reported on everything he saw and heard, became something of Stosch's house artist and principal source of information.[69] Underneath one of his caricatures of the baron, Ghezzi scribbled that Stosch was '*my great friend, a man learned in everything, and very knowledgeable of antiquities, and I've learned a great deal from him*'.[70] On another drawing he wrote '*peccato che sia eretico*'.[71] Being a 'heretic' Protestant seems not to have been much of an obstacle to Stosch's operations in Rome however. Rumours of radical libertinism and involvement in the circulation of forbidden or problematic books on the other hand proved damaging.[72]

In a short period of time, Stosch had managed to establish himself, like no other foreigner at the time, at the very centre of the local antiquarian community in Rome, turning his home into a key site for the transfer of antiquarian knowledge and culture. In these cramped and not very tidy lodgings, Stosch's collections grew and he started building a new library, as most of the old books that he had acquired in northern Europe were still with Charles Levier and Fagel in The Hague.[73] This library, with its large holdings of controversial topics in theology, philosophy and the new natural sciences, attracted much interest and soon also the unwanted attention of the Inquisition. In 1723, Stosch moved to larger premises in the Strada dei Pontefici, and in 1725, after the arrival of his brother Heinrich, he moved to the Vicolo del Merangolo just behind the Palazzo Borghese.[74] Stosch's manservant Christian Dehn and the Nürnberg artist Johann Justin Preißler also resided at this latter address, and in 1728 Markus Tuscher, another Nürnberg artist, joined them.[75] The travel writer Johann Georg Keyßler has provided us with a colourful description, albeit brief, of this curious and not very tidy *casa-museo*, complete with a domesticated boar and two owls (Figs 1.5–1.7).[76] Ghezzi's two well-known drawings of an imagined coin auction[77] taking place on these premises, the so-called *Congresso de' migliori antiquarj di Roma* (Figs 2.4–2.5), show the baron as the only foreigner in the group, seated and receiving some of the city's notable antiquaries such as Ficoroni, Fontanini, Sabbatini and Bianchini.[78] Stosch's connections, moreover, included collectors like Cardinal Melchior de Polignac, the marchese Alessandro Gregorio Capponi, the keeper of the Museo Kircheriano, Contuccio Contucci, Francesco Vettori, Cardinal Filippo Antonio Gualterio and many others not included in Ghezzi's drawings. Of these, Capponi in particular, but also Vettori, were enthusiastic fellow students and collectors of gems.[79] No noteworthy antiquities or artworks seem to have been dug

---

66   Kinauer 1950. The *Atlas* is now divided between the Albertina and the Austrian National Library, the exception being Sangallo's drawings in the *Codex Stosch* or *Codex Rootstein Hopkins*, which is now in the RIBA Library in London (Campbell and Nesselrath 2006). The Roman material was collected in vols CC–CCLXII (Winckelmann 1760, pp. 590–593). According to the heir Muzell-Stosch, this part of the *Atlas* had cost Stosch more than 8000 scudi (letter from Muzell-Stosch to Albani, dated 15 November 1–57 – Noack 1928–1929, p. 68).

67   Letter from Walton [Stosch] to Lord Carteret, dated 28 February 1722 (Kew, National Archives (hereafter NA Kew) SP 85/14 fols 9–12).

68   Stosch 1724, p. v.

69   But those who drew gems for him were especially valued (Zazoff 1983, p. 57 and ref.).

70   'e molto mio amico, Uomo Letterato in tutto, et eruditissimo nelle antichità, et io vi o' imparato assai' (BAV, Cod. Ott. lat. 3112, fol. 115).

71   BAV, Cod. Ott. lat. 3112, fol. 131r.

72   An outspoken freethinker, well-read in theology and the philosophy of religions, Stosch took an interest in radical deism and other currents popular at the time. Preserved correspondence indicate that he was indeed involved in the importation and circulation of clandestine literature in Italy, functioning as an important link between intellectual clusters in Naples and the Papal States and printers and booksellers in the north (Totaro 1990; 1993; Hansson 2025c).

73   Hansson 2025c, p. 442 and refs.

74   The *Status Animarum* of 1725 places Stosch in the Strada dei Pontefici towards Via Paolina [modern via del Babuino], parish of San Lorenzo, where he resided together with his manservant Cristiano Collaur [possibly Christian Dehn] and cook Giuseppe Susterli (Pampalone 2005, pp. 103 and 127 n. 387–388). This was probably shortly before the arrival of Heinrich Sigismund Stosch. See also Noack 1928–1929, p. 41.

75   Israel 2002, pp. 83–84.

76   Keyßler 1751, Brief XLVIII, pp. 471–472. Stosch used an engraved gem with an owl to seal letters, e.g. the letter from Stosch to Gori dated 22 September 1744 (Justi 1871, p. 20 no. IX).

77   Zazoff 1983, pp. 11–12. There are both coins and gems in the two drawings, and many of the portrayed antiquaries took an interest in both.

78   Vienna, Albertina, inv. 1263 (dated 1725); BAV, Cod. Ott. lat. 3116, fol. 191 (dated 10 October 1728). For a list and discussion of connoisseurs included in these drawings, see Chapter 2 in this volume.

79   Vettori 1739; Ubaldelli 2002.

up, changed hands or surfaced on the market in the city during the 1720s without Stosch's knowledge, and often involvement.[80] This decisive decade saw much antiquarian and proto-archaeological field activity taking place in and around the city; on the Palatine Hill, along Via Appia and Via Latina, on Albani's property at Anzio, at Tivoli and in various locations in the Roman Campagna.[81]

Stosch participated enthusiastically or kept himself updated on all this for a decade, more or less. But his presence in the Papal State had become increasingly precarious, and with the election in July 1730 of Clement XII Corsini, who was no longer a friend, his situation deteriorated rapidly. Late at night on 21 January 1731, Stosch's carriage was halted by a gang of masked men who threatened the baron at gunpoint and told him to leave the city within the next few days or he would be dead.[82] Stosch complained to his protector at the time, Cardinal de Polignac, and the authorities opened an inquiry that led to nothing, so he hurriedly advertised for his creditors, packed his bags and went into exile to the Grand Duchy of Tuscany, never to return.[83] Ghezzi noted in his diary entry for 15 February that Stosch had left Rome for Livorno that morning together with his brother and his manservant Cristian Dehn, adding that his departure had pleased all of Rome.[84] Stosch decided to take refuge in Florence, which he reached via Livorno. The artist Tuscher also accompanied the Baron, while Preißler seems to have remained in Rome for a while.[85] Dehn returned to Rome after a few years.

6 Florence (1731–1757)

Stosch received a warm welcome in Florence from the anticlerical Gian Gastone, with whom he had already established good relations and whom he presented with the suitable gift of a pocket thermometer. He quickly established himself in antiquarian circles, where he was already well-known and had been well received on his earlier visits in 1717 and 1722.[86] He moved into commodious lodgings in via de' Malcontenti close to the basilica of Santa Croce, and in the 1740s he transferred to even more spacious rooms in the Borgo degli Albizi, where he stayed until his death.[87] Like in Rome, the *Museo Stoschiano* became an important meeting-place for a motley assembly of local *letterati*, freemasons, English expatriates and a stream of foreign visitors.[88] Stosch's presence in the city coincided with the decades of Etruscomania created in the wake of Filippo Buonarroti's and Thomas Coke's posthumous publication of Thomas Dempster's *De Etruria Regali* (1723–1724) followed by a series of publications

---

80 Cf. Ubaldelli 1998, pp. 40–41: '*Stosch, pendant toute la durée de son séjour à Rome (1722–1731), est le personnage central autour duquel gravite toute ce milieu d'amateurs d'antiquités*'.
81 E.g. Kammerer Grothaus 1979; Oeschlin 1979; Miranda 2000; Cacciotti 2001.
82 Stosch 1754, pp. 44–45. Stosch had attended a late *conversazione* at Cardinal Cornelio Bentivoglio's palace in the Piazza di Spagna. There exist several other versions of this dramatic incident, which sent shockwaves through Rome and the courts of Europe: letter from Stosch to the French envoy de Polignac (Noack 1928–1929, p. 42) and to the British government (Walton 25 November 1731 – NA Kew, SP 98/32 fols 146–149; Lewis 1961, 87–90); also by Pier Leone Ghezzi (Dorati da Empoli, 2001, pp. 62–63) and by Graf Wackerbarth-Salmour (Justi 1871, pp. 14–15). Cf. also Ingamells 1997, p. 151 s.v. Buckingham, Katherine, Duchess of, and ref. The specific motives behind Stosch's forced exile remain unknown, but his work as an informant is a likely explanation, in combination with allegations of atheism and libertinism.
83 Noack (1928–1929, p. 87) cites a letter from a German visitor to Rome, who mentions that Stosch was visiting the city in 1756 and staying in via Giulia, and that on this occasion he met with Winckelmann and A.R. Mengs. This probably refers to Stosch's nephew Heinrich Wilhelm von Muzell, who visited the city on his way to Florence.
84 '*Questa mattina alle ore 11 giornata di giovedì, è partito di Roma il baron Stosch con il suo fratello, e Cristiano [Dehn] suo cameriere per Livorno che di questa partenza ne ha goduto tutta Roma e non vi è stata persona che gli sia dispiaciuto*' (Memorie del Cavalier Leone Ghezzi scritte da sé medesimo da gennaio 1731 a luglio 1734 – Rome, Biblioteca Casanatense, MS 3765, fol. 3v. (Dorati da Empoli 2008, pp. 59–128)).
85 Tuscher is not mentioned in the *Status Animarum* of 1725 or in Ghezzi's diary entry, but he was staying with Stosch at the time of his departure from Rome, as is clear from Stosch's commissions, e.g. of the portrait medallion of Valesio. Preißler remained in Rome – letter from Stosch to Preißler, Florence 29 May 1731 (Leitschuh 1886, pp. 23–24). After Stosch's departure, he drew some gems for Capponi (Ubaldelli 2001, p. 136 and ref.).
86 For various reasons, Stosch's Florentine period is better known than his perhaps more decisive decade in Rome, e.g. Borroni Salvadori 1978a; Hansson 2014, 2021a and 2024c.
87 Stosch and his brother resided in separate lodgings at no. 46 Via dei Malcontenti, opposite the bell tower of S. Croce, where they still resided in April 1740 (Morelli Timpanaro 2003, p. 735), before moving to the piano nobile in the Palazzo Ramirez de Montalvo (Ginori Lisci 1985, vol. I, pp. 487–490 (p. 489)).
88 '(…) *non sa che cosa sia Antichità, e quanto ampla in tutte le sue più rare parti, chi non vede l'invidiabil Museo del Sig. Barone De Stosch* (…) *perché è ora uno de' bei pregi di Firenze e si può dire il compendio de' più scelti musei*' ['He who has not seen the enviable Museum of Baron von Stosch cannot grasp Antiquity in its fullness, and how rich in all its rare parts (…) because it is today one of the marvels of Florence and, you might say, a compendium of the most select museums'] (Gori 1742, CCXXXV–CCXXXVI). Among the foreign visitors who commented on their visit were Charles de Brosses (1885, pp. 259–260), Horace Walpole (1937–1983, passim) and Jean-Jacques Barthélemy (1802, pp. 25–26, lettre IV).

on Etruscan antiquities by Anton Francesco Gori and others.[89] This naturally affected Stosch's scholarly interests and collecting, and he made some notable acquisitions, in particular Etruscan bronzes and scarab gems, among which the famous Gemma Ansidei and the Tydeus.[90] It was a period of relative cultural regeneration in the Grand Duchy, which saw the establishment of academies and learned societies such as the *Accademia Etrusca* (1727) at Cortona and the *Società Colombaria* in Florence (1732/1735) and Livorno (1751). Stosch participated enthusiastically in their activities, corresponding and sending a steady flow of artworks from his collections to be inspected and discussed at their sessions.[91] This was an effective way of boosting his growing collections and of introducing items on the market.[92] Stosch, moreover, founded and sponsored a learned journal, *Giornale de' Letterati di Firenze*, launched in 1742 in opposition to Giovanni Lami's *Novelle Letterarie di Firenze*, which had published critical articles on Stosch and his library assistant, Lorenzo Mehus.[93]

Closely associated with the learned circles in Florence was the masonic lodge, which Stosch was instrumental in setting up in 1733 together with a group of Englishmen and some locals.[94] This lodge, which was an offshoot of the Grand Lodge of England and the earliest one in Italy, rapidly became a preferred site for the local scholarly community, with a membership that overlapped intensively with the various Tuscan learned societies. It soon attracted the attention and considerable displeasure of the Inquisition, which tried its best to have the lodge closed down. It eventually succeeded following the so-called 'Crudeli affair', in which the lodge's secretary Tommaso Crudeli became the scapegoat in the general conflict between the Catholic Church and English Freemasonry. Inquisition documents and correspondence confirm that a main target concerning the Florentine lodge was in fact Stosch, whom the Inquisition wanted expelled from Italy.[95] His home in via de' Malcontenti, and especially his library and its frequenters are repeatedly referred to in the interrogation protocols. Stosch was very active in the circulation of books within Italy and between Italy and northern Europe, using his network of northern European booksellers and printers to acquire publications that were difficult to obtain in Italy and vice versa, dealing frequently with local Florentine booksellers and their clients who often found themselves in trouble with the Inquisition.[96] His already considerable library was greatly expanded in 1739 when Stosch sent for the 208 large crates full of the books that he had left behind for safe-keeping in The Hague.[97]

Stosch continued to collect intelligence on the exiled Stuart court on behalf of the British and sent weekly reports to London, which relied heavily on information from a number of sources in Rome, notably Alessandro Albani, with whom he remained in close contact.[98] Over the years, the two had created a powerbase on the art market where English collectors were concerned, and they occasionally exploited British diplomatic channels to

---

89 Such as the *Museum Florentinum* (1723–1737), *Museum Etruscum* (1737) and *Museum Cortonense* (1750).

90 E.g. Zazoff 1974; Micheli 1984; Hansson 2014, pp. 22–24.

91 He seems not to have been an elected member of any of these associations, but their archive material are full of evidence of his numerous transactions with them.

92 According to the summary lists in his *Geschichte* (Stosch 1757, pp. 258–287), Stosch was a serious collector of a wide spectrum of materials: I Antiquities, II Medals, III Coins, IV Engraved Gems, V Old Master Paintings, VI Etchings and Woodcuts, VII Manuscripts, VIII Books, IX Naturalia, X Arms and Armour, XI Topographical Atlas.

93 Stosch helped financially to launch this journal, published between 1742 and 1753 and modelled on Apostolo Zeno's *Giornale de' Letterati d'Italia*. He was no doubt also directly involved editorially (Borroni Salvadori 1978a, pp. 596–601 and passim). Lorenzo Mehus worked for Stosch from the early 1730s onwards. It was his edition of Cyriacus of Ancona's *Itinerarium* (BAV Cod. Ott. lat. 2967), a manuscript in Stosch's possession at the time, that sparked this conflict (*Dizionario biografico degli italiani*, s.v. Mehus, Lorenzo (M.C. Flori); Borroni Salvadori 1978a, pp. 596–602 and refs).

94 Among them the physician and anglophile Antonio Cocchi, Robert Montagu, the young Charles Sackville, Earl of Middlesex, one Capt. Spencer, one Mr Shirley, and one Mr Clarke. The bibliography on the Florentine lodge is extensive, but see e.g. Baldi 1960; Sbigoli 1967; Casini 1972. Also Corsi and Crudeli 2003.

95 E.g. Casini 1972; Gianfermo 1986; Morelli Timpanaro 2003; Corsi and Crudeli 2003; Hansson 2025c.

96 Notably Prosper Marchand and Charles Levier at The Hague, Pieter Boudewijnsz van der Aa in Leiden, and Gaspar Fritsch in Leipzig (Heringa 1981, p. 57; Totaro 1990, p. 115 and 1993). On the Florentine booksellers Bernardo Paperini, Giuseppe Rigacci and Antonio Ristori, e.g. Borroni Salvadori 1978a, p. 581; Chapron 2009, pp. 49–51 and *passim*. Cf. also letter from Stosch to F. Venuti, Florence 24 February 1739 (Engelmann 1908, pp. 328–329).

97 Stosch 1754, p. 48; Engelmann 1908, pp. 328–329. It was both impractical and expensive to travel with books, and also risky in view of the many controversial publications that Stosch possessed, which is why he left them with Charles Levier and François Fagel at The Hague: '*Parceque je me trouve entièrement déstitué des moyens de le faire autrement. Car les seuls droits de sortie de la douane de mes livres me coûteroient plus de 800ƒt*' ['Because I completely lack the funds for doing otherwise. Because the custom charges for my books would cost me more than 800 Florins'] (letter from Stosch to Count Flemming, The Hague 17 May 1721 (Justi 1871, p. 12)). On Stosch's library, see esp. Hansson 2025c.

98 Although much of their correspondence seems lost (Noack 1928–1929, pp. 43–45).

traffic antiquities out of Italy via the port of Livorno with the help of the British minister plenipotentiary Sir Horace Mann. Albani and Stosch regularly introduced and recommended useful acquaintances to one another, the most well-known example being Winckelmann, whom Albani met through Stosch. In Florence, Stosch apparently called himself a Royal British Minister and Royal Polish Counsellor,[99] and he enjoyed the protection of three consecutive British envoys, Francis Colman, Charles Fane, and notably Horace Mann (in Florence from 1737), the latter who no doubt was a much closer friend and ally than his ironic correspondence with Horace Walpole suggests. Mann directed a steady stream of English visitors to the *Museo Stoschiano* and came to its owner's rescue on several critical occasions, far more than his duty required – not least on the occasions when Stosch was threatened to be expelled from the Grand Duchy.[100] After the death of Gian Gastone in 1737, Stosch continued to enjoy the protection of the Prince of Craon, who became viceroy under the Lorrain Regency.

Although he rarely left his house in his later years, Stosch continued to be involved in the increasingly international trade in art and antiquities, buying, selling and exchanging, corresponding with fellow collectors and freely offering expert opinions in exchange for information.[101] In 1755, the French numismatist Jean-Jacques Barthélemy visited the *Museo Stoschiano* and reported back to le Comte de Caylus in Paris, on whose behalf he had brought Stosch some gem impressions, that Stosch had '*plundered all of Italy and still kept the country in chains through his many contacts*' – a clear reference to the remarkably efficient overlapping networks that Stosch over the years had managed to create or enter and strategically position himself within, participating in the circulation of both information and objects.[102] He added, with disapproval, that he '*had been shown everything, but given nothing*'.[103]

Certainly a *faux pas* in the *Republic of Letters*, but in fact Stosch was also known for strategic gift giving, at times quite extravagant.[104] He also continued to be generous in admitting scholars, collectors, artists and tourists to the *Museo Stoschiano*, giving them full access to his vast collections and freely offering expert advice on artworks and collecting.

As mentioned, Stosch continued to work on a sequel to his book, but the project was never realised. As is clear from this volume, his collecting of originals as well as visual documentation continued unabated – drawings, prints, imprints and casts of gems in other collections that interested him. Together with his brother Heinrich (Enrico), he was also working on a manuscript catalogue of his own gem collection, which at the time of his death counted 3065 originals, 379 pastes and some 28 000 sulphur impressions '*of all the stones in the world*' that Stosch had collected for reference purposes.[105] The collection was constantly changing, however, as originals, pastes and impressions were traded, bought or sold, individually or in groups. A group of Egyptian scarab gems, for example, was sold to Giovanni Carafa, Duca di Noja, shortly before or after Stosch's death.[106] During the final years of his life, Stosch was on the lookout for potential buyers for his vast collections, something that was indirectly advertised in his *Geschichte* of 1757.[107] His brother Heinrich had died in 1747 and as Stosch, like his brother, had never married and had no children, he had no natural heir to whom he could pass on his considerable legacy.[108] Instead he sent for his nephew, Heinrich Wilhelm Muzell (hereafter Muzell-Stosch), an officer in the French army, who at

---

99 Stosch 1754, p. 1. Although there is no documentation to support his claim of being a Polish diplomat this late, decades after the death of Flemming and August II.

100 Mann later also helped Stosch's heir circumvent the statutory estate tax and tried to find suitable buyers in England for parts of the estate. Walpole 1937–1983, vol. I, p. 308.

101 Cf. Gross 1990, p. 319: '*Stosch was perhaps the most notorious example of a foreigner who profited from Europe's greed for the treasures of ancient Rome by dubious means. But his misfortune, if we may call it such, was that he lived in the first half of the eighteenth century*'. See also Hansson 2021a.

102 On Stosch's networks, e.g. Lang 2007.

103 '*Il a dépouillé toute Italie e la tient encore asservie par ses correspondans (…) il ma tout montré e ne ma rien cédé, je me suis abbaissé jusqu'aux prières*' (Barthélemy 1801, pp. 24–26).

104 His *Geschichte* mentions gifts of valuable books, gems, and a pocket thermometer. Stosch also offered to sell objects from his own collections at low prices, although invariably for strategic reasons it seems. An example is the *Gladiator with a Vase* gem that Horace Walpole wanted to buy for an exorbitant price, but which Stosch offered for considerably less to William Ponsonby – in return for securing Stosch's pension from the British. Walpole 1937–1983, vol. XXI, p. 151. This gem is no. XXVI in Natter's (1761) catalogue of the Bessborough collection.

105 Winckelmann 1760; Winckelmann 1952–1957, vol. I, pp. 442–444 no. 261. Barthélemy (1802, pp. 24–26), who visited in 1755, mentions 25 000 *soufres*.

106 Hansson 2014, p. 26 n. 86 and refs. On Carafa's gem collecting, Di Franco and La Paglia 2019, pp. 62–69; Gołyzniak 2023a.

107 Stosch 1757, pp. 258–287 summary catalogue in 11 sections.

108 Often described as an uncloseted homosexual, Stosch occasionally also boasted affairs with women. It is certainly true that he preferred to move in male homosocial milieux dominated by so-called 'non-marrying men' and 'warm brothers', although these relations were not necessarily of a sexual nature (Lang 2022; Hansson 2025a).

the time was living in Paris.¹⁰⁹ Muzell arrived in Florence in 1756, was promptly adopted and designated sole heir of the considerable property. The locals nicknamed him *Stoschino*, little Stosch.

7 Stosch's Death and the Dispersal of the Museo Stoschiano

Stosch died after a short illness on 6 November 1757 at the age of sixty-six. He left behind an estate valued at 100 000 ducati, which was a low estimate created for tax purposes – taxes that his heir Muzell-Stosch nevertheless tried his best to avoid with the help of Albani and Horace Mann.¹¹⁰ Mann was, together with Stosch's friend the abbate Ottaviano Bonaccorsi, also executor of Stosch's will.¹¹¹ Except for a few minor antiquities which went to the two will executors and an ancient stone relief depicting Daedalus and Icarus that went to Albani,¹¹² Muzell-Stosch was the sole beneficiary of the vast estate. As he planned to embark on costly travels in the Ottoman empire, Muzell-Stosch was in need of cash, and therefore wanted to sell everything as quickly as possible.

The collections were first offered to the Holy Emperor Francis I, who declined because of the exorbitant sum requested, and they had to be broken up and various prospective buyers approached with the offer of buying either the gem collection, the *Atlas* or the library, notably the valuable manuscripts.¹¹³ The prospective buyers included the emperor (again), the pope, the King of Spain, the Prince of Wales and lesser collectors such as John Constable of Burton Constable, but to little avail.¹¹⁴ Muzell-Stosch renewed his uncle's previous offer to Winckelmann to publish the gem collection, which was expected to fetch a considerable sum (Fig. 1.8).¹¹⁵ Muzell-Stosch wanted a simple sales catalogue to attract buyers, but Winckelmann, who found the gem collection superior even to that of the King of France,¹¹⁶ insisted on a comprehensive catalogue raisonné, an ambitious project that in the end took Winckelmann considerable time to complete.¹¹⁷ The collection of originals and pastes were finally purchased in 1764 by Frederick II of Prussia for his *Antiken-Tempel* at Sanssouci, while the majority of the sulphurs was sold at auction in Berlin in 1783 and ended up in London with James Tassie, who reproduced them in various materials and selections to great success (Figs 1.9–1.10).¹¹⁸ Other parts of the collections are said to have been offered for sale in Hamburg in 1758 or 1759, while the 334 large folio volumes containing the 31 500 maps, prints and drawings of the *Topographical Atlas* were auctioned in London in 1764 and acquired by the Habsburgs, with the exception of the da Sangallo drawings.¹¹⁹ There were also important auctions in London in 1760 (old masters prints, drawings and paintings) and 1764 (bronzes), and in 1783 the remaining estate of Muzell-Stosch, including numerous gem drawings, were sold at auction in Berlin.¹²⁰ But most of

---

109 Wilhelm Muzell was the son of Stosch's sister, Louise Hedwig, and Friedrich Muzell.
110 Noack 1928–1929, pp. 67–68.
111 Stosch's will was made in 1754 and deposited with Mann. It is published in Morelli Timpanaro 1996, pp. 425–428. On Albani's attempts to help Muzell avoid tax, Noack 1928–1929, pp. 67–68.
112 Letter from Muzell to Albani, Florence 4 November 1757 (Noack 1928–1929, p. 67).
113 A number of summary lists and manuscript catalogues survive in various archives, one is published by Noack (1928–1929, pp. 68–70). On the sale of the estate and its different turns, e.g. Noack 1928–1929, pp. 67–71; Borroni Salvadori 1978a, pp. 612–614 and refs. It is also frequently mentioned in the Walpole-Mann correspondence.
114 There exists an undated letter to W. Constable (aft. 1750) with an offer to sell him the gem collection. Beverley, E. Riding Record Office, DDCC/145/34. I am grateful to David Connell for this information. Stosch came into contact with Constable probably through the jeweller William Dugood, whom Stosch had rescued after he had been arrested for religious '*discours galliards*' in Rome in 1722. They met again in Florence in 1731 (Ingamells 1997, p. 317 s.v. Dugood, William).
115 As Stosch and Winckelmann never met in person, the offer was initially made in the correspondence between Stosch and Winckelmann following Winckelmann's gift of a copy of his first book together with a flattering letter brought to Stosch in Florence by the artist A.F. Harper (letter from Winckelmann to Stosch, Rome early June 1756 – Winckelmann 1952–1957, vol. I, p. 227 no. 146).
116 Winckelmann 1952–1957, vol. I, pp. 444–445. no. 262.
117 On Winckelmann's work on the gem collection, see e.g. Zazoff and Zazoff 1983, pp. 71–134; Décultot 2012; Rügler in Winckelmann 2013, pp. XI–XXVI; Hansson 2014.
118 Auction Muzell-Stosch 1783, pp. 76–77. Only 17 407 sulphurs survived the shipment to Hamburg (letter from Winckelmann to A. Baldani, Florence 26–30 September 1758 – Winckelmann 1952–1957, vol. I, p. 418–19, no. 240). On Tassie's acquisition, Raspe and Tassie 1791, p. LXIV. For a complete discussion on the fate of Stosch's sulphurs, cf. Chapter 5, n. 19 in this volume.
119 It is now divided between the Albertina and the Austrian National Library, Vienna. A printed catalogue, not Winckelmann's abridged version (1760), is mentioned in one of Mann's letters (Walpole 1937–1983, vol. XXI, p. 192). The *Codex Stosch/Rootstein Hopkins* was not included in the purchase, but resurfaced at auction in 2005 (Lyon & Turnbull, Edinburgh, Sale 125 Lot 1). It is now in the RIBA Library, London.
120 Langford & Son, London, 6 February 1760 (old master prints and drawings), 12 March 1760 (old master paintings), 21–23 March 1764 (bronzes), 24 March 1764 (remaining bronzes) – Auction Stosch I–IV; Böhme, Berlin, 22 April 1783 (gem drawings) – Auction Muzell-Stosch 1783, pp. 63–64, lots 886–907.

Stosch's enormous collection of such gem drawings were lost from view only to resurface in recent years. The precious collection of ancient and modern coins and medals was probably broken up and auctioned off locally. Among Stosch's more prized collections, valued at 10 000 scudi, it is remarkable that almost no traces of it survive.[121] Two separate catalogues of the library contents were issued, no doubt compiled by Stosch's assistant Lorenzo Mehus.[122] The first one had no indication of prices, as the books were expected to go to a single buyer. But as no such buyer was forthcoming, a second version was printed giving prices for each book. Numerous volumes ended up in the Biblioteca Marucelliana. Its librarian, Angelo Maria Bandini, also acquired many of the unlisted controversial books.[123] Bandini also inventoried the 571 manuscripts on behalf of the Biblioteca Apostolica Vaticana and its librarian, Cardinal Silvio Passionei, who acquired the entire collection for the sum of 700 crowns, which was considerably below its market value.[124] Much later it was discovered that many of the items that the Vatican had bought had actually been stolen from the same library at some point, although the theft had gone unnoticed. Stosch had no doubt acquired the manuscripts in good faith, as he never made any secret of the fact that they were in his possession.[125] Also excluded from the sales catalogue was the sizable collection of erotica, some of which was acquired by Frederick II.[126] The rest of the vast collections was mostly sold piecemeal to various local collectors and visitors.[127] The extraordinary Museo Stoschiano was thus dispersed, leaving large parts of it difficult or impossible to reconstruct.

---

121 Stosch 1757, pp. 260–268, nos II–III; Noack 1928–1929, p. 69. Some medals were acquired by the Prince of Wales. Also, some of Stosch's medals were drawn by Tuscher and published posthumously Johann Karl Wilhelm Möhsen in 1773 (cf. Chapter 4 here).
122 Stosch 1757 and 1759.
123 Borroni Salvadori 1978a, p. 614; Totaro 1990, p. 111.
124 BAV, MS Codex Vat. Lat. 7806a fols 81–85 (Borroni Salvadori 1978a, p. 613; Walpole 1937–1983, vol. XXI, p. 284).
125 Manteyer 1897–1899. Engelmann (1909) convincingly argued that Stosch himself was unlikely to have been involved in the actual theft, but cf. MacKay Quynn 1941, esp. 342–344.
126 Walpole 1937–1983, vol. XXI, p. 202.
127 James Adam, for example, bought some *'fragments of bas-reliefs and little statues very cheaply'* from the estate (Fleming 1962, p. 278).

FIGURE 1.1

FIGURE 1.2

FIGURE 1.3

FIGURE 1.4

PLATE 2

FIGURE 1.5

FIGURE 1.6

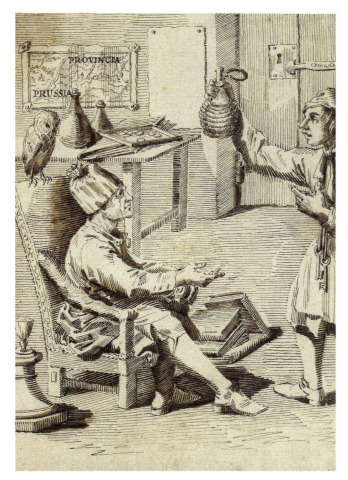

FIGURE 1.7

FIGURE 1.8

FIGURE 1.9A

FIGURE 1.9B

FIGURE 1.9C

FIGURE 1.9D

FIGURE 1.9E

FIGURE 1.9F

FIGURE 1.9G

FIGURE 1.9H

FIGURE 1.9I

FIGURE 1.9J

FIGURE 1.9K

FIGURE 1.9L

FIGURE 1.9M

FIGURE 1.9N

FIGURE 1.9O

PLATE 4

FIGURE 1.10A FIGURE 1.10B FIGURE 1.10C

FIGURE 1.10D FIGURE 1.10E

FIGURE 1.10F FIGURE 1.10G

FIGURE 1.10H FIGURE 1.10I FIGURE 1.10J FIGURE 1.10K

CHAPTER 2

Collecting Engraved Gems in the Circle of Stosch

Ulf R. Hansson

1   Introduction

For half a century, from 1708 when he left his native Küstrin until his death in Florence 1757, Stosch had been busy building and cultivating remarkable personal networks of contacts which bridged and overlapped with his various interest and which he expertly combined to his great advantage. Through these highly effective channels, Stosch participated actively in the circulation of artefacts and information and kept himself updated on all that was happening in the world of collecting and learning. Where gems were concerned, we can safely assume that he had met, corresponded or otherwise interacted with or possessed information about more or less every collector, scholar, gem engraver, draughtsman and dealer worth knowing at the time. Even though most of his vast correspondence is now lost, a good indication of the extent of these powerful networks is provided by his collection of tens of thousands of impressions, casts and drawings of gems in major and minor collections to which he in one way or another had managed to gain access over the years.

Stosch had discovered the attraction of the engraved gems of the ancient Greeks and Romans already in the early 1710s in London and especially Paris, where '*la curiosité des pierres Antiques est a present icy a la mode*'.[1] But it was of course in Rome that Stosch found the ideal setting and conditions for cultivating his interest. The city boasted a number of prominent collections, the study of gems was well-established as a core antiquarian practice, and the art of gem-engraving was practised by skilled engravers, such as Flavio Sirleti, Antonio Pichler and Carlo Costanzi. As has been noted,[2] the period which coincided with Stosch's sojourns in the city saw a considerable surge in interest in this craft, developments to which he in no small way contributed, indeed was even instrumental in. The 1720s proved especially decisive when the interests and priorities of the circles in which Stosch then operated had a substantial impact, not only locally but in a long-term European perspective. This was the formative period in which the collecting and dealing in gems became more widespread across Europe, fueled by illustrated publications such as Stosch's own book and the commercial production of gem casts and *dactyliothecae*. Roman collections were sold and dispersed, and new ones formed. Looking back at these developments, which represent a rather interesting cultural phenomenon highly characteristic of the period and of its popular reception of ancient art and mythology, Stosch's name is omnipresent in the contemporary sources, and in almost every aspect of these developments, his contribution and influence can be detected.

Many of the collections that were well known in Stosch's times are now dispersed and thousands of gems lost. Important sources in their reconstruction are the numerous cast collections of the period such as Lippert, Dehn-Dolce, Paoletti, Tassie-Raspe and Cades.[3]

2   The Formative Period

According to his *Geschichte*, composed and tidied up in the mid 1750s, Stosch's interest in collecting had already begun in his early teens when, encouraged by his father, he began collecting coins on a modest scale.[4] His interest in coins and medals were further strengthened through contact with a series of scholars and collectors during his early travels in northern Europe, the earliest of whom was the Berlin numismatist Johann Carl Schott, whom Stosch met in 1709. A student of the numismatists Andreas Morell and Ezechiel Spanheim, Schott was the nephew and assistant of the famous Lorenz Beger,[5] whom he had succeeded as keeper of the coin cabinet of Frederick I of Prussia.[6] It was in Schott's study and in the Berlin *Antikenkabinett*, which

---

1   Letters from Stosch to Fagel, Paris 9 October 1713 and 17 April 1714 (The Hague, Nationaal Archief (hereafter NA), inv. 1726 fols 22 and 36).
2   Ubaldelli 1998, p. 40.
3   On dactyliothecae, see e.g. Kockel and Graepler (eds) 2006; Knüppel 2009; Pirzio Biroli Stefanelli 2007 and 2012. Many cast collections are published online, e.g. those in the Beazley Archive in Oxford. For Tassie, see catalogue published by Raspe in 1791 (Raspe and Tassie 1791). Versions exist in London, Edinburgh and St Petersburg.
4   Unless otherwise stated, biographical information is from Stosch 1754; 1757 and 1758.
5   Beger was the author of the famous *Thesaurus Brandenburgicus Selectus*, 1696–1701.
6   Zazoff 1983, p. 35.

was the first coin and gem collection of any note that he saw, that Stosch decided to abandon altogether the idea of becoming a clergyman and instead become a scholar.[7]

This interest in coins was further cemented a year later, when Stosch was first introduced to François Fagel, who became his mentor and sponsor, and whose sizeable collection he was commissioned to expand during his diplomatic missions.[8] Working for Fagel and using his diplomatic and collector channels gave Stosch a gratifying status as art agent and offered him ample opportunity to befriend collectors and build his own networks. His early letters to Fagel are full of information about collectors, collections and sales, and it is evident that he worked for both his patron and himself. In The Hague, Stosch also met Jacob de Wilde, a notable collector who had recently published his own collection of gems, which after his death was acquired by William IV of Orange.[9] The interest in coins and medals would later go hand in hand with that in gems, and Stosch was to acquire extensive first-hand knowledge of both materials in the numerous collections he visited over the next decade, before settling permanently in Rome in 1722. It is significant that he was considered the leading authority in both these related fields in a city like Rome, which already boasted numerous experts.[10]

3   England

During his sojourn in England 1712–1713, Stosch gained access to several important art collections, chiefly to look at coins on behalf of Fagel.[11] One of the more important encounters in London seems to have been with Sir Andrew Fountaine, a keen numismatist with whom he forged a long-lasting *'genuine bond of friendship'*.[12] The two met again in Rome in 1715. Fountaine, a notable collector himself, was also the art agent of Thomas Herbert, 8th Earl of Pembroke, and it was probably through him that Stosch gained access to Pembroke's collections, maybe also those of Daniel Finch, 7th Earl of Winchilsea and 2nd Earl of Nottingham. Most likely through Fountaine, he also got the opportunity to examine the cameos and intaglios in the Arundel collection, then in the possession of Sir John Germain and containing two signed gems that Stosch later chose to include in his book, one depicting Diomedes and Odysseus inscribed with the name Felix, and the famous Tryphon gem depicting the marriage of Cupid and Psyche.[13] Most or all of the 200 or so gems had been acquired by Thomas Howard, Lord Arundel, in 1638 from the collection of the Gonzagas, Dukes of Mantua.[14] Examining this collection might well have sparked Stosch's interest in glyptics. The Arundel gems were incorporated into the Marlborough collection in the early 1760s together with the Bessborough gems, making this the largest and most important in Britain.[15] The previous year, the Duke had acquired many of Anton Maria Zanetti's gems in Venice.[16] Stosch further met William Cavendish, 2nd Duke of Devonshire, another notable gem collector with whom he later corresponded and possibly interacted through his son, Lord Cavendish, who was in Rome in 1723 and again in 1730–1732.[17] Devonshire later acquired from Stosch the well-known intaglio of a Cow signed by

---

7   'Und dadurch verlor sich allmählich der Vorlaß, ein Geistlicher zu warden, ganz und gar' (Stosch 1754, p. 7). Schott has a modest reputation today for having practised an early form of 'archaeological art history'. For Schott see esp. Heres 1987.

8   Stosch's and Fagel's regular correspondence lasted until Fagel's death in 1746. Many of the letters are now in the NA Hague, Collectie Fagel. On Fagel's collecting activities and patronage, see: Heringa 1976; 1981 and 1982.

9   De Wilde 1703, illustrated by his daughter, Maria (M. Cornelia Maria de Wilde), who later married the philologist and collector Tiberius Hemsterhuis. Stosch (1754, p. 8) records the meeting but does not mention de Wilde's gem collection or his catalogue.

10   J.G. Keyßler, who visited Rome and the *Museo Stoschiano* in 1730 commented that: '*as to his skills in the Greek and Latin antiquities, he is in such reputation at* Rome *that in all things of that kind, as when an explanation of an ancient medal or intaglio is to be determined, his judgment is generally appealed to*' (Keysler 1760, vol. II, p. 154, Letter XLVIII). In the German original: '*nicht leicht vorgegangen*' ['not easily disregarded'] (Keyßler 1751 [1740], p. 471, Brief XLVIII).

11   Stosch 1754, p. 10–11; Burnett 2020, vol. II, pp. 997–1081. For the English collectors and Stosch's dealings with them, see: Burnett 2020, vol. III, p. 1567 and *passim*.

12   Stosch 1754, p. 10.

13   Stosch 1724, pp. 49–50, pl. XXXV (Diomedes and Odysseus, signed by Felix – in fact a copy from Andreini's collection, cf. discussion in Appendix 1, pl. XXXV here) and pp. 94–95, pl. LXX (Cupid and Psyche, signed by Tryphon). Germain, said to be the illegitimate son of William III, '*displayed them* [the gems] *to royalty and aristocracy*' (Boardman *et al.* 2009, p. 7). Fountaine compiled an unpublished catalogue of the collection, which later passed to George Spencer, 4th Duke of Marlborough.

14   The collection contained 130 cameos and 133 intaglios, most of them probably from the Gonzaga collection, purchased through the Venice dealer Daniel Nys (Scarisbrick 1996; Boardman *et al.* 2009, ch. 1). On the Gonzaga collection, e.g. Venturelli 2005.

15   Boardman *et al.* 2009.

16   An exception was the famous Leopard, which Horace Walpole wanted to buy (letter from H. Walpole to H. Mann, London 4 January 1762 – Walpole 1937–84, vol. XXI, pp. 561–563 (p. 562)). These gems were acquired by John Spencer, 1st Earl Spencer in 1764 (Scarisbrick 1979, p. 425).

17   Ingamells 1997, p. 190 s.v. Cavendish, Charles Lord.

Apollonides, and also had one of the Preißler brothers and other draughtsmen draw his best gems for a catalogue that never appeared, although some of the drawings were later printed and circulated.[18]

In London, Stosch also met Sir Hans Sloane (a 'great friend'), whose gem collection at the time already numbered several hundred items.[19] The gems are not specifically mentioned in Stosch's *Geschichte*, but it can be assumed that he saw at least some of them when admiring Sloane's coin collection and remarkable cabinet. Sloane acquired many gems from the Rome dealer Bernardo Sterbini, originally from the sale of Cardinal Filippo Antonio Gualtieri.[20] Having grown to some 700 gems by 1725, the collection was acquired by the British Museum after Sloane's death in 1753.[21]

Henry Howard, Viscount Morpeth, after 1738 4th Earl of Carlisle, is not mentioned in the account of Stosch's sojourn in England, but the two certainly met later in Rome in 1715 and Stosch included two of Morpeth's gems in his book.[22] They met again in Florence in 1739 and seem to have kept in touch via correspondence. Henry Howard took a keen interest in gems, especially signed ones, and built an excellent and important collection, keeping in direct contact with several dealers and collectors whom he had met in Italy, notably Ficoroni, Zanetti and Stosch.[23] He acquired numerous gems from Ficoroni and from Cardinal Pietro Ottoboni, some of which were gifts.[24] Some 170 gems from his cabinet were acquired by the British Museum in 1890.[25]

Stosch had, in fact, plenty of opportunity to interact with English collectors, directly and through correspondence, in London in 1712–1713, but especially later in Rome and Florence.[26] Among the British collectors who visited these two cities during his long residency in Italy, apart from those already mentioned, we find the Cambridge librarian and collector Conyers Middleton, who was in Rome from November 1723 to April the following year, and who most certainly met Stosch although no documentation survives.[27] According to preserved correspondence, Middleton acquired a small collection of gems, 'with some erudition in them' mainly from the dealer and papal antiquary Francesco Palazzi, but he also knew Francesco de' Ficoroni and Bernardo Sterbini, who were all part of Stosch's circle.[28] Middleton published some 14 of his own gems and eventually sold them to Horace Walpole.[29] Middleton's approach to glyptic material was a widespread one at the time. In a letter to Walpole he explained that his interest in gems was not artistic, but the same as that of the ancients, who '*collected them* [not] *out of any regard to their beauty or sculpture, but as containing what the Italians call some erudition in them, and illustrating some rite or custom of old Rome, alluded to by the ancient writers*'.[30]

William Ponsonby, Viscount Duncannon and from 1739 2nd Earl of Bessborough, visited Florence and met Stosch in 1737 and again in 1738.[31] Ponsonby acquired numerous gems in Italy and even more at home in England, notably from Philip Dormer Stanhope, 4th Duke of Chesterfield (1754) and from the estate of Gabriel Medina, which was sold at auction in London in 1761.[32] His collection, which contained around 200 gems, was published by Lorenz Natter in 1761 and sold the following year to George Spencer, 4th Duke of Marlborough, as mentioned.[33] In 1750, Bessborough was allowed to purchase Stosch's famous garnet with an athlete, signed by Gnaios, in return for securing Stosch's continued payment from the British government.[34] This was the famous *Gladiator with the*

---

18 Devonshire 1730; Kagan 1997, p. 111.
19 Sloane collected mainly between the 1680s and 1720s.
20 F. Valesio, diary entry 21 June 1731 (Valesio 1977–1979, vol. V, p. 371).
21 Rudoe 1996, p. 198; Kagan 2010, pp. 103–104.
22 Stosch 1724, pp. 6–7, pl. VI and pp. 20–21, pl. XVI.
23 In Italy in 1714–1715 and 1738–1739 (Ingamells 1997, p. 181 s.v. Carlisle, Henry Howard 4th Earl). For his collecting, see: Scarisbrick 1987; Kagan 1997, pp. 107–109. Rudoe (1996, p. 200) claims that Carlisle started collecting gems in 1739, the same year that he met Stosch in Florence, which is surely wrong since two of his gems are in Stosch's book, *supra*, n. 22. For Carlisle and Zanetti, see: Kowalczyk 2022.
24 BAV, Cod. Ott. lat. 3107, fol. 184.
25 Dalton 1915 and Walters 1921, *passim*.
26 His weekly reports to the British government, now at NA Kew (SP Walton) gives detailed information about the Britons who Stosch met over the years 1722–57. Stosch's name also appears in numerous entries in Ingamells 1997.
27 Ingamells 1997, p. 658 s.v. Middleton, Conyers; Spier 1999; Spier and Kagan 2000; Kagan 2010, p. 102.
28 The correspondence between Middleton and Palazzi contains numerous references to gems (Spier 1999; Spier and Kagan 2000).
29 Middleton 1745, pp. 225–250 and pl. 21. Both Middleton and Walpole wrote descriptions of their collections, meant to be published together, but nothing came of this project. Instead, Middleton published his gems separately in 1745 (e.g. Spier 1999).
30 Letter dated 15 April 1743 (Walpole 1937–1983, vol. XV, pp. 15–16).
31 Ingamells 1997, p. 781 s.v. Ponsonby, Hon. William.
32 Langford and Son, London 10–12 Feb. 1761, 70 lots (Medina Sale 1761).
33 Natter 1761. Cf. also Kagan and Neverov 1984; Boardman, Kagan and Wagner 2017.
34 Bessborough was also allowed to buy the famous Venus sculpture fragment, a 2nd century CE Roman copy of a Greek original vaguely recalling the Venus Capitolina, said to have been found near the Pantheon in Rome. Later in the Henry Blundell collection, now in the National Museums Liverpool, inv. 59.148.63 (Michaelis 1882, p. 356 no. 63).

Vase that Horace Walpole had seen on a visit to the *Museo Stoschiano* and later tried to acquire to no avail with the help of Sir Horace Mann.[35] Walpole also admired Stosch's Meleager. A favourite subject in the correspondence between the two Horaces, Walpole presumably met Stosch several times during his visit to Florence in the winter of 1739–1740.[36]

4 France

It was in Paris in 1714, in the circle of Philippe d'Orléans, that the engraved gems of the Ancients had become Stosch's *'folie dominante'*.[37] Philippe II was a notable gem collector,[38] in whose circles the collection, reproduction and study of gems had become a widespread practice. These circles included collectors and scholars such as Anselmo Banduri, Jean-Paul Bignon, Bernard de Montfaucon, Wilhelm Homberg, Pierre Crozat and Charles-César Baudelot de Dairval. Of these, Montfaucon, who provided introductions for Stosch, and Baudelot de Dairval, whom he referred to as his friend, were the great gem scholars. Crozat was the leading collector and connoisseur, while Homberg had advanced knowledge about how to reproduce gems in glass.

A widely known connoisseur, the wealthy financier Pierre Crozat was perhaps the most important French collector that Stosch encountered and stayed in contact with. He later accompanied him and his brother Antoine on acquisition trips in the Netherlands to buy old master paintings. Shortly after Crozat's death in 1740, his entire collection of close to 1400 intaglios and cameos was acquired by the Duke of Orléans. According to Mariette, it was the most beautiful collection of engraved gems ever in private hands.[39] Orléans, of course, already possessed a sizeable collection which Stosch had the opportunity to study in 1714, being in the good graces of the duke and his mother, Madame Palatine.[40] In 1741, Mariette published an unillustrated summary catalogue of Crozat's gems already in Orléans' cabinet, and it was his intention to also publish a fully illustrated catalogue of all the gems in the royal cabinet, which, apart from the two mentioned collections, was one of very few prominent ones in the city at the time.[41] It was Stosch's visit to this latter collection at Versailles that gave rise to the tall tale recounted by de Brosses of him swallowing the famous Michelangelo Seal.[42] Winckelmann later claimed that Stosch's own collection was superior even to the French royal collection, which he knew through Mariette's work.[43] Mariette and Stosch had met, although not in Paris but a few years later in Vienna, when Mariette was working for Prince Eugene of Savoy. On that occasion, the two discussed Stosch's already well underway book project, and examined some of the drawings for it that Stosch had commissioned in Rome in the years 1715–1717, including some prints that were never published.[44] This was before his book project was publicly advertised, which Mariette says happened in 1721.[45]

Baudelot de Dairval's much talked about study of the name 'Solon' on engraved gems was surely decisive in Stosch's choice of focus (Figs 2.1–2.2). He later cited Baudelot's work and referred to him as a great savant and friend.[46] Montfaucon was no doubt also a key figure, not only because of his ambitious and lavishly illustrated study of the art of the Ancients that he was working on, but also for providing Stosch with letters of recommendation to useful contacts in Rome. Homberg, whom Stosch refers to in the introduction to *Gemmae antiquae caelatae* without actually mentioning his name, had experimented extensively with glass paste and published a study on how to reproduce engraved gems in coloured glass, an art that Stosch himself continued to practice and refine.[47]

---

35 *'I find I cannot live without Stosch's intaglia of the Gladiator with the vase'*, Walpole confessed in a letter to Horace Mann, who tried his best to secure it for his friend for 100 pounds, but in vain: *'Stosch has grievously offended me'*, Walpole later exclaimed, *'I still think it one of the finest things I ever saw and am mortified at not having it'* (Walpole 1937–1983, vol. XVII, pp. 232–233 and vol. XX, p. 157). This episode is indicative of the considerable attraction that intaglios and cameos had in these circles. This gem is Natter 1761, no. XXVI. On Ponsonby and his gems, e.g. Kagan 2010, p. 109; Boardman, Kagan and Wagner 2017.
36 Ingamells 1997, p. 974–6. Stosch is frequently mentioned in Walpole's correspondence (Walpole 1937–1983).
37 Letter from Stosch to Fagel, Paris 13 April 1714 (NA The Hague, coll. Fagel, inv. 1726 fol. 22).
38 Mariette 1750, vol. II; Le Blond and de la Chau 1780–1784.
39 *'Peut à peu, il avoit formé la plus belle collection de pierres gravées qui fût jamais entre les mains d'aucune particulier'* (Mariette 1853–1854, vol. II, p. 44).

40 Stosch 1754, pp. 10–11.
41 Mariette 1741 and 1750, vol. II, *Les pierres gravées du cabinet du roy*.
42 De Brosses 1858, vol. I, p. 290.
43 Winckelmann 1952–1957, vol. I, pp. 444–445, no. 262.
44 Stosch 1754, p. 30; Mariette 1750, vol. I, p. 332: *'Ce que M. de Stosch avoit commencé de faire graver en Italie, & qui n'a point été rendu public valoit, selon moi, beaucoup mieux. Je n'en ai vu que deux planches, dont il me donna des épreuves en 1718.'*
45 Ibid.
46 Stosch 1724, p. 37.
47 Homberg 1712; Stosch 1724, p. XIX; Stosch 1754, p. 11.

5 Italy – Rome

In Rome, Stosch found himself in a city with several notable papal and princely gem cabinets, where vast quantities of gems in original and reproduction were on offer, and their study widely practised by authorities such as Marcantonio Sabbatini, Michel-Ange de la Chausse, Leone Strozzi and Francesco de' Ficoroni. Stosch, who positioned himself at the very centre of the circulation of gems, impressions, casts and drawings, was instrumental in revitalising the field by introducing a whole new scale and systematicity to the study, collection, mechanical reproduction and visual documentation of gems (Fig. 2.3). In the case of both the modest scholarly cabinets of antiquarians as well as papal and palatial collections in Rome, the collection of gems was often part of a more general interest in the 'the Ancients' and in diverse categories of surviving material and visual culture such as sculpture, inscriptions, coins and medals, and increasingly also curious objects from the daily life of the ancient Romans, unearthed from tombs in the *vigne* along the Via Appia and elsewhere. Inventories, catalogues, correspondence, etc., provide important documentation of gem collecting at the time, although our picture is still fragmentary. Stosch's *Geschichte* and partially preserved correspondence and other sources offer general insights and at times very specific glimpses of how the field was perceived by Stosch himself.[48] Another important source is the artist Pier Leone Ghezzi, who moved freely in collector circles and was very knowledgeable about glyptic material as such and its study and collecting. Encouraged by patrons such as Leone Strozzi and Stosch, whose 'eyes and ears' he was, Ghezzi studied and drew gems in various collections, collected originals and casts, and even practised engraving.[49] Some of his drawings, and especially two well-known ones of the *Congresso de' migliori antiquarj di Roma*, a gathering of local antiquaries at Stosch's house, offer interesting insights about the local art market, dealers and collectors (Figs 2.4–2.5).[50] Especially interesting among the figures depicted besides Stosch and his draughtsmen Ghezzi and Odam[51] are Marcantonio Sabbatini, Francesco Valesio, Francesco de' Ficoroni, Leone Strozzi, Francesco Palazzi and Antonio Borioni, whom archival sources indicate were very active where gem collecting was concerned. A third important source for the Roman context is provided by the acquisitions journal and correspondence of the marchese Alessandro Gregorio Capponi, a collector who emerged as a notable figure in these circles precisely in the 1720s when Stosch resided in Rome.[52] This decade and the following years saw a considerable surge in interest and activity.[53] The collection and study of gems became more widespread practices, collections changed hands or were dispersed, for example those of Mario Piccolomini and Cardinal Gualterio in 1728,[54] Vleughels in 1737, and Barberini and Ottoboni in 1740,[55] and new ones were formed, such as those of Stosch and Capponi. As gems were beginning to disappear in a steady flow abroad, the papal authorities tried to control these developments in the edict of 1733, which specifically mentions cameos and intaglios as a category along with other antiquities, the handling of which were important to regulate in the face of an increasingly greedy market, which led to the sale and dispersion of valuable collections.[56] Even forgeries

---

48 Stosch's correspondence is preserved in various archives in Italy, England and Holland, notably in NA The Hague, coll. Fagel. Some relevant correspondence is published and commented on in: Justi 1871; Schneider 1907; Engelmann 1908 and 1909a–b; Heringa 1976; Hansson 2022.
49 See chapter 4 in this volume.
50 Vienna, Albertina inv. 1263 (dated 1725); BAV, Cod. Ott. lat. 3116, fol. 191 (dated 1728). For the two drawings, see: Kanzler 1900. The Albertina version depicts Marcantonio Sabbatini, Stosch, Francesco Valesio, Pietro Andreoli, Giusto Fontanini, Ficoroni, Paolo Vitri, Francesco Palazzi, Girolamo Odam, Francesco Bianchini, Francesco Grazini, Luigi Fernando Marsili, Leone Strozzi, and Ghezzi himself. The later Vatican version depicts Stosch, Ghezzi, Sabbatini, Valesio, Fontanini, Marsili, Bianchini, Vitri, Strozzi, Palazzi, Antonio Borioni, Giuseppe Campioli, Paolo Forier, Ficoroni, Grazini, and Andreoli, but omits Odam.
51 On Odam, see: Gołyźniak 2023b.
52 'Memorie di acquisti fatti dal marchese Alessandro Gregorio Capponi di medaglie ed altro' – BAV, MS Capponi 293 (transcribed excerpts are published in Ubaldelli 2001, pp. 381–487). For Capponi and gems see esp.: Gasparri 1977; Ubaldelli 1998 and 2001; and more generally Donato 1993a–b and 2017.
53 Ubaldelli 1998, p. 40.
54 Not much is known about Gualterio's gem collection, apart from the fact that he possessed numerous gems. On his collecting in general, see: Fileri 2001 a–b and 2002. There exist 40 plates illustrating objects from Mario Piccolomini's collection including many gems – 'Raccolta di 40 tavole riproducenti varie opere d'arte del museo del signor Mario Piccolomini di Roma' (BAV Capponi III/129) and an inventory in BAV, MS Capponi 276/1, cc 127r–129r, ref. in Ubaldelli 2001, p. 57 n. 235. Some Piccolomini gems are published in De' Rossi and Maffei 1707–1709; Borioni and Venuti 1736; Scarfò 1739b; La Chausse 1746.
55 Ubaldelli 2001, p. 95 and nn. 377 and 379. On the sale of the Barberini and Ottoboni collections, see: letter from H. Walpole to R. West, dated 7 May 1740 (Walpole 1937–1983, vol. XIV, pp. 211–214).
56 '(...) e perché rispetto alli Cammei, Intagli, Medaglie di tutte sorti, o simili Bronzi figurati, che sono fra le cose più pregievoli dell'antichità o che rendono così cospicui li Musei di Roma, si è da alcuni introdotto un segreto mercimonio, mediante il quale o vengono le cose suddette impunemente vendute ed esitate fuori di Roma e dello Stato Ecclesiastico, o con discredito del pubblico commercio alterate o falsificate, e poi dai Mezzani, e Sensali vendute a

were mentioned in the edict, which indicates that this clandestine production had become problematic, perhaps already a minor industry.

There was already considerable interest in engraved gems within the local antiquarian community at the time of Stosch's first sojourn in the city from 1715 to 1717. A number of larger and lesser collections[57] had been formed in the course of the sixteenth and especially seventeenth centuries, such as the gem cabinet of the antiquary Fulvio Orsini (Ursinus), which Cardinal Odoardo Farnese inherited at the turn of the century 1600 and incorporated into the great Farnese collection.[58] Removed from Rome already in the mid seventeenth century, the Farnese gems were on display until the 1730s in the Galleria Ducale at Parma, where Stosch was allowed to examine and reproduce them.[59] The collection was later moved to Naples. The Barberini,[60] Colonna,[61] Chigi, Massimo[62] and Boncompagni-Ludovisi families had also built considerable collections that were often poorly documented and not always easy to access, something that Winckelmann later experienced.[63] Christina of Sweden had built a modest gem collection, which was later purchased along with her other collections by Prince Livio Odescalchi, from whom Cardinal Pietro Ottoboni acquired many gems.[64] There were also several minor collections, such as those of Rondanini[65] and Spada,[66] which became very numerous in the eighteenth century, for example Capponi, Borioni, Vettori, Ficoroni and several others.

The papal collections in the Museo Sacro and Profano contained numerous gems from various sources, but many of the more notable acquisitions date from after Stosch's departure from the city. In 1741, for instance, the museum acquired a collection previously owned by Cardinal Gaspare di Carpegna, who had died in 1714. Among the 185 intaglios and 52 cameos was the famous Augustus bust in chalcedony as well as the large Bacchus and Ariadne cameo, which Filippo Buonarroti included in his catalogue of Carpegna's coins and medals.[67] In 1751, the Vatican museum also acquired 75 original gems, including many early Christian ones, and a collection of red wax impressions from the *Museum Victorianum*, some of which had previously been published by their owner, the prolific numismatist and antiquary, Francesco Vettori, who later acquired some other Christian gems from Stosch's estate.[68] The considerable collections of originals and sulphurs of Ficoroni and Ghezzi also ended up here. A number of the museum's originals were removed to Paris following the Treaty of Tolentino in 1797, never to be returned. An exception was the small collection of *gemmae litteratae* of Cardinal Francesco Saverio de Zelada. All or large parts of the gem cabinet in the Museo Kircheriano were transferred by the same Cardinal Zelada to the papal museums following the suppression of the Jesuit order in 1773.[69] The keeper of the Kircheriano, Contuccio Contucci,

---

Forastieri per prezzi esorbitanti.' Proibizione dell'estrazzione delle statue di marmo, o metallo, pitture, antichità e simile, 10 Sept. 1733 (Mariotti 1892, pp. 218–220).

57 E.g. Anon. 1664; Righetti 1955 and 1954–1956; Sölch 2007, p. 249.

58 Anon. (1664, p. 36) mentions Fulvio Orsini's '*studiolo d'intagli & di gemme antiche*', in particular a *Leda and Swan* cameo, and an intaglio depicting the emperor Trajan on horseback pursuing a barbarian (Gasparri (ed.) 1994). The jeweller William Dugood, whom Stosch knew and held in high esteem, was for a period employed by the Farnese household and allowed to make several thousand casts of the gems, of which many originals survive in the Museo Archeologico Nazionale in Naples (Connell 2009). For the Farnese collection, e.g. Gasparri (ed.) 1994, for the eighteenth century, see esp. pp. 101–106 (L. Pirzio Biroli Stefanelli).

59 Stosch 1754, p. 18. The Jesuit padre Paolo Pedrusi, who showed Stosch the collection, intended to include a catalogue of the gems in the last two volumes of his multi-volume catalogue of the coins and medals in the collection, published between 1694 and 1724. A large number of drawings were executed for the project, which was never published (Giove and Villone in Gasparri (ed.) 1994, p. 31).

60 Ficoroni 1744, vol. II, p. 54: '*L'altro tesoro consiste nei camei, e gemme incise, del quale in Roma non vi è il secondo*'.

61 Ficoroni 1744, vol. II, p. 55: '*Si vede uno studiolo ricco di gemme, d'argenti, ametisti lavorati, ed antichi Camei*'.

62 Anon. 1664, pp. 33–34, mentions esp. a famous portrait cameo of Cicero. Mariette (1750, vol. I, p. 333) writes that de Thoms had acquired gems from Cardinal Massimi, including the Augustus by Dioskourides (Stosch 1724, pp. 32–34, pl. XXV).

63 Zazoff and Zazoff 1983, pp. 33 and 76. Exception was the Boncompagni-Ludovisi gem collection, which Winckelmann finally managed to access in 1763 after several attempts: '*io sono il solo in Roma che gli abbia veduto, e mi fu permesso di levarne qualche impronta*' (letter from Winckelmann to Muzell-Stosch, Rome 17 December 1763 – Muzell-Stosch 1781, vol. II, pp. 10–12, no. 100).

64 The Odescalchi collection was later published by Pietro Sante Bartoli (1751–1752).

65 Anon. 1664, p. 48: '*la Dattiliotheca delle gemme intagliati, e de' preziosi Camei*'.

66 Virgilio Spada is mentioned by Gasparri (1977, p. 26) as a minor collector of gems. The collections were left to the Vallicelliana Library. The only trace I have been able to find is 51 *zolfi* (Finocchiaro 1999, p. 216, nos 1277–1278).

67 Buonarroti 1698, pp. 45 and 427. Righetti 1954–1955, pp. 287–288; Giroire in Cornini and Lega (eds) 2013, pp. 85–96.

68 Vettori 1732, *passim* and 1739; Di Fiore 2010; Cornini and Lega (eds) 2013, p. 41 n. 23 and refs. On Vettori's acquisition from Stosch's estate, Justi 1871, p. 24.

69 Stefanelli 1996, p. 193; Gasparri 1977, p. 30; Pirzio Biroli Stefanelli 1996, p. 193.

had secured many important donations, including gems from Capponi,[70] Strozzi and Ficoroni.[71]

In addition to the papal and princely collections mentioned above, an important gem cabinet often mentioned in contemporary sources is that of the Boncompagni-Ludovisi family, usually under the name of the Prince or Princess of Piombino collection, which is reputed to have consisted of more than five hundred intaglios and cameos, including well-known works previously owned by the sixteenth-century gem-interested antiquary Lelio Pasqualini, whose heirs had sold them to Cardinal Francesco Boncompagni in the early 1610s.[72] Inherited by Gaetano Boncompagni-Ludovisi, Prince of Piombino in 1721, the collection remained in the Piombino family until it was sold and dispersed in the late nineteenth century. Parts of it can, however, be reconstructed through various archival sources, including cast collections.[73] Paolo Alessandro Maffei intended to write a catalogue of the whole collection, but his project was never realised.[74] The collection contained the well-known Demosthenes amethyst carrying the name of Dioskourides, now in the J. Paul Getty Museum, as well as two signed items published by Stosch: an intaglio depicting Neptune inscribed with the name of Quintillus, and the *Maecenas* or *Cicero* gem signed by Solon.[75] About sixty of the mounted gems later resurfaced in the Via Alessandrina treasure that was discovered in 1933.[76]

The marchese Alessandro Gregorio Capponi, whose gem collecting to a large extent coincided with the decisive decade when Stosch resided in Rome, acquired numerous gems on the market, including a few which carried artists' signatures.[77] He managed to build a significant collection. Like Stosch, Capponi relied on associates such as the draughtsmen Ghezzi, Odam and Gaetano Piccini,[78] as well as scholars such as the abbate Francesco Valesio, the collector and dealer Antonio Borioni and Monsignor Giusto Fontanini, all of whom over the years acquired considerable knowledge of the field and its market. Although Capponi and Stosch knew each other and moved in the same circles already during Stosch's first and especially his second sojourn,[79] the baron is conspicuously absent from Capponi's mentioned acquisitions diary, which covers the period 1717–1746. After Stosch left Rome for Florence, Capponi continued to remain informed about his activities through their mutual associate, the Florentine librarian and collector Anton Francesco Marmi.[80] After his death, Capponi left his gems to the Jesuit Museo Kircheriano in the Collegio Romano.

The papal antiquary Marcantonio Sabbatini occupies a central position in Ghezzi's two depictions of *i migliori antiquarj*, as indeed he did in these circles.[81] The eccentric Bolognese Sabbatini had been the art advisor of Charles VI, papal antiquary to Clement IX and mentor of the pope's nephew, Alessandro Albani, in whose honour he founded the *Accademia Alessandrina*.[82] He was a prominent numismatist and gem connoisseur, whose own collection had at one time included the famous Althorp Leopard, which Stosch reputedly selected as Albani's gift to Prince Eugene, and the Medusa signed by the gem engraver Solon. Some of Sabbatini's gems were published

---

70 Capponi's gems entered the collections in 1745 (Gasparri 1977, p. 29 and ref.).
71 Bruni 1998.
72 Stefanelli 1996, p. 194; La Monica 2002.
73 These include an inventory list from the mid-seventeenth century (Pirzio Biroli Stefanelli 1993, pp. 194–197; La Monica 2002). Casts can be found in e.g. the Capitoline Museums, Rome, the British Museum, London (T. Cades, *Catalogo del Museo del Principe di Piombino. Collezione di 68 impronti cavati da gemme antiche appartenenti a S.E. il Sig.r Principe di Piombino*, 68 casts), and the Beazley Archive, Oxford. Many gems were later acquired by the dealer Francesco Martinetti and the collector Michel Tyszkiewicz, e.g. Pirzio Biroli Stefanelli in Mura Sommella (ed.) 1990, pp. 33–37.
74 Mariette 1750, vol. I, p. 279: '*Le chevalier Maffei, sollicité par tout ce qu'il y avoit de grand dans Rome, promettois de donner encore deux volumes, dans lesquels il auroit faire connoître toutes les pierres gravées de la Princesse de Piombino, mais cet engagement qu'il avoit pris avec le Public n'as pas eu lieu, et c'est grand dommage*'. For the inventory list, see: La Monica 2002.
75 Demosthenes amethyst – Malibu, J. Paul Getty Mus, inv. no.: 2019.13.15 (Boardman and Wagner 2018, no. 107). For an aquamarine with Neptune signed by Quinilius and a copy of *Maecenas* or *Cicero* signed by Solon, cf. Appendix 1, pls LVII and LXII here respectively.
76 See Pirzio Biroli Stefanelli in Mura Sommella (ed.) 1990, pp. 33–37 and cat.

77 Capponi collected gems during the period 1717–1746. His signed gems were: Ubaldelli 2001, nos 149 (Aulos), 169 (Myron), 208 (Neikepohoros), 233 (Gnaios), and a gem signed by Natter, which Capponi took for ancient (no. 198).
78 E.g. Capponi, diario 23 January 1729: '*Essendosi trattato e convenuto col signor Gaetano Piccini (col mezzo del signor cavalier Ghezzi) per farle disegnare et insieme intagliare in rame a bulino tutte le mie pietre e gioie intagliate e cammei*' (Ubaldelli 2001, p. 403).
79 See letters from Capponi to Anton Francesco Marmi, Rome February 1717 (BNCF, fondo magliabechiano, VIII, MS. 1062, fol. 7 r. and Galvano Landi to Capponi, dated 25 September 1721 – cited in Noack 1928–1929, p. 41).
80 After Stosch went into exile in Florence, Capponi nevertheless repeatedly asked for news about him from A.F. Marmi (Ubaldelli 2001, p. 28 and refs).
81 As is the case with several of the figures in these assemblages, Ghezzi used earlier drawing versions.
82 On Sabbatini, see: Guerrieri Borsoi 2022.

by La Chausse and Maffei.[83] The Medusa gem was later acquired by Monsignor Leone Strozzi, also present in both of Ghezzi's drawings, and the Leopard was purchased by Anton Maria Zanetti di Girolamo.[84] Monsignor Strozzi, who is often called *Il Fiorentino* but was in fact born in Rome, was one of the more prominent gem collectors of the period and owned several signed gems and works believed to be by Greek engravers.[85] Famous gems in his collection also included a Germanicus head, a satyr head, an Aesculapius, a Heracles, and of course the Julia Domna portrait.[86] Many of them were stolen years after the collector's death in 1722.[87] Some ended up as mentioned in the Museo Kircheriano.[88] The learned Strozzi, who also built a large lithotheca of *marmi colorati*, had the intention of writing a book on hard stones and/or gems, an ambitious project which Paolo Alessandro Maffei commented on, but it remained unfinished.[89] It was, moreover, Strozzi who inspired the young Ghezzi to start collecting gem impressions.[90]

One of the earliest contacts of Stosch's in Rome was Ficoroni, the prince of antiquarians, whom the baron had employed as his *cicerone*.[91] Few people had a better grasp of the local antiquarian community and antiquities market at the time than Ficoroni, through whose hands numerous gems passed. While he sold many of them, quite a few stayed in his own collection, which later entered the Museo Kircheriano and the papal collections.[92] Ficoroni was one of the foremost and more knowledgeable dealers where gems were concerned, with considerable first-hand knowledge. He was often in trouble with the papal authorities over his dealing activities, but trusted by international clients such as the Earl of Carlisle.

Pier Leone Ghezzi, who built a collection of several thousand sulphurs and pastes,[93] was primarily a draughtsman and one may presume that the two practices were intimately connected and began when he started drawing gems on a massive scale, for himself and on commission from connoisseurs such as Stosch – '(...) *eruditissimo nelle antichità, et io vi o' imparato assai*'[94] – and later Marchese Capponi. Drawings of gems played an extremely important role in antiquarian circles in Rome, and artists like Ghezzi,[95] commissioned to draw gems, acquired considerable ability, although of course drawings could never be as exact as the imprints and casts which these artists often used when the originals were unavailable. Having carefully studied numerous gems for his drawings, Ghezzi had acquired an intimate knowledge of the subject matter and techniques of ancient engravers.

---

83 When Sabbatini was tutor to the young Alessandro Albani, he sold this gem to his student, but later bought it back (Smith 1888, p. 148, no. 1256). Gems from Sabbatini's collection are illustrated in: La Chausse 1707, pls 23 (Brutus), 30 (S. Severus), 41 (Venus and Triton); De'Rossi and Maffei 1707–1709, vol. I, pls 6, 12 and 34, vol. II, pls 19, 34, 59 and 79, vol. III, pls 64, 68 and 76, vol. IV, pls 28 and 71.

84 Many of Strozzi's gems, including the Medusa, later ended up in the Duc de Blacas' collection and are now in the British Museum.

85 Stosch (1724) published eight signed items from the Strozzi collection: pls VII (Allion), XVIII (Aulos); XX (Axeochos), XXIII (Gnaios), XXVI (Dioscurides), XXXII (Epitynchanos), LVIII (Skylax) and LXIII (Solon) and used Strozzi's impressions for publishing another four: pls XXXVII (Hellen), XLIII (Myrton), LII (Philemon) and LXI (Solon). Ficoroni 1744, vol. II, pp. 49–50: '*ammirabile sono la colleczione delle antiche gemme incise, essendo celebre la testa di Medusa ed altre insigni, come pure molti frammenti lavorati da Greci incisori*'. On Strozzi see e.g. Guerrieri Borsoi 2004, pp. 26–36; Campanelli 2021, pp. 29–52.

86 '*Cum proximis diebus in instructissima sua Sphragidotheca, sive potius omnium elegantiarum thesauro, quam suavissime versaremur, inter innumerabilia antiquae scalpturae miracula incidimus in caput Juliae Piae sive Domnae*', ['In the last few days spent in his well-furnished Sphragidotheca, or rather of all the refinements in the treasure which we were most pleasantly engaged with, among the innumerable miracles of ancient carving, we came upon the head of Julia Pia or Domna'] cit. in Campanelli 2021, p. 33. On Strozzi's gems, also De'Rossi and Maffei 1707–1709, vol. II, pp. 117–134.

87 More precisely in 1746. BAV, Cod. Ott. lat. 3112, fol. 66r.: '*Monsignor Leone Strozzi de' Principi di Forano, che raccolse il celebre Museo che in buona è stato rubato l'anno passato 1746*'.

88 Many of the gems ended up in the Duc de Blacas' collection and then in the British Museum.

89 '*Huc addimus ex Musaeo Strozzio aliud aureum exquisitae notae, quod servatur penes dignissimum Romanae Curiae Praelatum Leonem Strozzium, cujus insigne opus de re Lapidaria utinam publico Reipublicae literariae beneficio tandem prodeat in lucem, sicut et reliqua quae vetustatis eruditae amantissimus assiduo studio paravit multiplicique doctrina decorare sategit*', ['To this we may add from the Strozzi Museum another exquisite jewel, which is kept by the most worthy of the Roman court, the prelate Count Leone Strozzi, whose remarkable work on the matter of lapidary may at last come to light for the benefit of the Republic of Letters, just as the rest which this learned lover of Antiquity has prepared with constant diligence and multiplicity of learning'] – Maffei's commentary to Sectani 1700, vol. II, p. 299. On Strozzi's project, see: Guerrieri Borsoi 2004, p. 28. A manuscript survives – ASF fondo Strozzi V serie MS 1254.

90 '*Sino da giovanetto assieme con Mons. Leone Strozzi*' (Ghezzi 1734).

91 That Ficoroni considered Stosch to be an 'arch-imposter' reported in MacKay Quynn (1941, p. 336) is erroneous and actually refers to Ficoroni's opinion of Maffei (Justi 1872, 337).

92 On Ficoroni in general, see: Ridley 2017.

93 His sulphurs now in the Vatican number 3710 (Gołyźniak, forthcoming – Ghezzi, against the number of 6669 reported by Gasparri (1977, pp. 26–27)).

94 '(...) *very knowledgeable of antiquities, and I've learned a great deal from him*' (Vatican, BAV, Cod. Ott. lat. 3112, fol. 115).

95 On Odam and Ghezzi as collectors, see: Chapter 4 in this volume and Gołyźniak 2023b.

The leading collector cardinal Pietro Ottoboni,[96] who acquired some of Christina of Sweden's collections from the estate of Livio Odescalchi,[97] built a notable collection of gems. He possessed four signed originals which Stosch included in his book, and numerous other intaglios and cameos.[98] Ottoboni presented some of his cameos to Henry Howard as a gift.[99]

Some of the figures depicted in Ghezzi's *Congresso de' migliori antiquarj* should be briefly mentioned. The scholar and diarist Francesco Valesio was a close collaborator and correspondent of Stosch responsible for writing the learned entries to Stosch's book.[100] He is not known as a collector, but moved in these circles and had acquired considerable knowledge of the field, which he combined with his classical erudition. For this, he was greatly appreciated within the antiquarian community. Valesio, who remained in contact with Stosch even after the latter's departure from Rome, continued to work for Stosch by providing him with descriptions and comments on specific gems. An early academician of the Accademia Etrusca at Cortona, Valesio furnished the Academy with descriptions of gems in the possession of its members, many of which were later included in the *Museum Cortonense* volume (Fig. 2.6).[101] Like Stosch, Valesio was known for his well-furnished library, which constituted a favourite meeting place for local connoisseurs.

The apothecary and dealer Antonio Borioni, '*un des meilleurs antiquaires*', who had a shop in Via Paolina (now Via del Babuino) and in Via dei Greci, was another significant figure in this context, very active in the art and antiquities market and himself an avid collector, some of whose treasures were published by Ridolfino Venuti in a lavishly illustrated volume (Fig. 2.7).[102] His gems, many of which were published by himself and Venuti,[103] were later acquired by the wealthy Leiden collector Count Frederick de Thoms, who purchased numerous gems on a visit to Italy in the 1730s.[104] Francesco Palazzi, Alessandro Albani's chamberlain and papal commissary of antiquities from 1733 to 1744, was also an avid collector and dealer, some of whose gems were published by Borioni and Venuti.[105] Palazzi, who learnt the trade from Sabbatini and Ficoroni and seems to have been an expert on coins and medals, and apparently was also involved in their forgery,[106] sold a few gems to Conyers Middleton.[107] The abbate Bernardo Sterbini was a dealer, who sold many gems to Sir Hans Sloane on a visit to London in the early 1730s,[108] and had among his clients in Rome Sir Charles Frederick and Conyers Middleton.[109] Sterbini had organised the sale of Cardinal Gualterio's collection in 1728.[110] Capponi recounts that numerous modern gems from the collection of the Prior Anton Maria Vaini, were sold as ancient in 1734.[111] The diarist Francesco Valesio writes in the diary entry for 21 May 1731 that many of these gems had been sold in London by Sterbini.[112]

The diplomat and collector Michel-Ange de la Chausse, who was active in Rome from 1683 until his death in 1724,

---

96 On Ottoboni as collector, Mastiti 1997; Olszewski 2002.
97 Montanari 1997. The gems in the Odescalchi collection were published by Bartoli and Galeotti 1751–1752.
98 Stosch 1724, pls XIII (Aspasios), LXV (Sosokles), LXVI (Sostratos) and LXVII (Sotratos).
99 BAV, Cod. Ott. lat. 3107, fol. 184.
100 Lami 1757, p. 722. But see Heringa 1976.
101 Gori, Valesio and Venuti 1750. For the manuscript see: Bruschetti 1984. Cortona, Biblioteca Comunale e dell'Accademia Etrusca, ms. 448. The manuscript consists of 33 prints, 21 drawings and 36 pages of written descriptions.
102 BAV Cod. Ott. lat. 3116, fol. 29 v: '*Antonio Borioni Spetiale alli Greci il quale fa l'Intendente di cose antiche quanto farebbe meglio a fare i servitiali alle budella, e non alla Borsa, e per sopra nome si chiama lo spetialetto*'. Cf. also de Brosses (1861[1768], vol. II, p. 268): '*Un des meilleurs antiquaires est Borioni lo Speziale, qui a rassemblé un recueil fort curieux en lampes sépulchrales de bronze et de terre cuite, en vases e meubles antiques, en pierres et petits bronzes égyptiens, en pierres gravées, camés, intagli etc. Il fait graver tout en un volume de cent ou cent cinquante estampes, dont le chevalier Venuti que j'ai vu à Naples s'est, à ce que l'on m'a dit, chargé de donner les explications*'.
103 Borioni and Venuti 1736, pls 29 (Serapis), 31 (Apollo), 37 (Venus Paphiae), 39 (Amor with trophy), 40 (Three cupids in a shell boat), 41 (Cupid driving a swan biga), 42 (Cupid driving a butterfly biga), 43 (Psyche in a boat drawn by dolphins), 46 (Iole), 49 (Nereid), 50 (Head of Medusa), 51 (Faun), 52 (Hermaphrodite), 53 (Satyr and goat), 54 (Meleager), 60 (Apollonius Tyanaeus), 62 (Antonia Augusta), 63 (Caligula), 65 (Trajan), 67 (Commodus), 69 (Augustae Rogus), 73 (war ship), 76 (Comedian), 79 (Man's Three Ages) and 81 (Egyptian Amulet).
104 Thoms was in Rome in 1737 and in Naples in 1738–1739 (Noack 1928–1929, p. 44; D. Levi in Barocchi and Gallo (eds) 1985, p. 176 and ref.). He also acquired some gems from Girolamo Odam (Maaskant-Kleibrink 1978, pp. 25 and 32–33 and refs; Gołyźniak 2023b).
105 Gems: Borioni and Venuti 1736, pls 31 (Apollo and Marsyas), 56 (Hector), 58 (Mars and Rhea Silvia), 59 (Euripides) and 74 (Mons Argaeus). For Palazzi, see: Ridley 1992, pp. 137–138; Spier and Kagan 2000; Griggs 2008, pp. 301–302.
106 Spier and Kagan 2000, appendix B: contemporary unauthored manuscript biography of Palazzi.
107 Spier and Kagan 2000, pp. 42–43.
108 *A Catalogue of Signor Sterbini's Curious Collection Lately Brought from Rome … Mr Cock's Room in the Great Piazza, Covent Garden 13–15 March 1733*.
109 Valesio 1977–1979, vol. V, p. 371; Spier 1999; Spier and Kagan 2000; Griggs 2008; Burnett 2020, vol. II, pp. 979–980.
110 Fileri 2001, p. 370.
111 BAV, ms Capp. IV, 585.
112 Valesio 1977–1979, vol. V, p. 29. For Vaini see: Dorati da Empoli 2008, p. 65 n. 42; Guerrieri 2010, pp. 40–41.

published two widely known books on gems and owned a collection of some two hundred gems, which included some dubious items.[113] Most of these were bequeathed to Pierre Crozat and later entered the Orléans collection together with the Crozat gems,[114] while some were acquired by Stosch and by Richard Mead.[115]

6 Italy – Florence, Venice and Naples

In Florence, during his first brief visit in 1717, Stosch had the opportunity to meet several scholars and collectors interested in engraved gems. The Grand Ducal collections of course contained numerous intaglios and cameos, which Stosch was shown by the keeper Sebastiano Bianchi. Naturally, the Medici glyptic collection was later featured prominently in Gori's *Museum Florentinum* and other widely popular publications (Fig. 2.8).[116] In the city, Stosch came into contact with the prominent antiquaries Filippo Buonarroti, Anton Maria Salvini, and the latter's student Anton Francesco Gori, who no doubt introduced him to other Tuscan collectors. Chiefly among these we find the abbate Pietro Andrea Andreini, who is not mentioned in the *Geschichte*, but to whom an interesting letter from Stosch dated 16 September 1720 survives in The Hague.[117] Andreini was a respected antiquary and collector of art and antiquities, perhaps the most important gem collector in Florence at the time, who is even credited with introducing gem collecting as a core antiquarian practice in the Grand Duchy.[118] Together with Salvini, Buonarroti, Maffei and Gori, he was positioned at the very centre of the Florentine antiquarian community. It was Andreini, Buonarroti and the custode of the grand ducal art collections who in 1710 were commissioned to bring order to the vast Medici gem collection.[119] Once antiquary to Cardinal Leopoldo de' Medici, Andreini had advised the cardinal on gem acquisitions and enriched the Grand Ducal collections with numerous intaglios and cameos, including the Camilli collection,[120] and in 1731, two years after his death, Grand Duke Gian Gastone purchased some 319 of Andreini's gems from his heirs. Andreini had previously sojourned in Naples and Rome where he moved in the circles of Christina of Sweden and Livio Odescalchi, whom he advised on gems, and befriended Jean Mabillon, Giovanni Pietro Bellori, Leonardo Agostini, Sabbatini and Strozzi. By the time Stosch knew him, he had retired to the Villa I Busini outside Florence to devote himself to study and collecting. Andreini enjoyed a wide reputation for his ability to detect even the cleverest gem forgeries and also for distinguishing highly skilled works from mediocre ones.[121] In his letter, Stosch informs Andreini that a gem inscribed with the name of Polykleitos that had been stolen from the collector was now in the hands of Count Carlo Silvestro of Rovigo.[122] According to Justi, the abbate Andreini specifically collected gems inscribed with engravers' names and owned no less than eleven such items, of which five were included in Stosch's book.[123] A number of them are included in the first two volumes of Gori's *Museum Florentinum*, but only four of the signed gems entered the Medici collections; the others were stolen.[124] Buonarroti collected gems, as did Gori of course, and both were key figures in the Florentine context. Another collector who deserves to be mentioned is Giovanni Battista Cerretani, some of whose gems were published in the *Museum Florentinum*.[125] He is named in Stosch's *Geschichte*, but little is known about him. Another prominent Florentine collector was the Marchese Vincenzo Riccardi, who knew Stosch through Méhus and who acquired many of Stosch's books for his library. Riccardi possessed a large collection of gems, some of which were included in the *Museum Florentinum*.[126]

The Accademia Etrusca at Cortona constitutes an interesting example and provides important evidence of the

---

113 La Chausse 1700.
114 Mariette 1741; Kagan and Neverov 2000, pp. 64–69.
115 Zwierlein-Diehl 2023, p. 448. Mead built a considerable gem collection, comparable to that of Sir Hans Sloane. It was sold by Langford and Son in London in 1755 (Boardman, Kagan and Wagner 2017, p. 226).
116 Gori 1731–1732, vol. I.
117 Justi 1871, p. 4 no. I.
118 On Andreini, see: Ranieri 1729; Gaetani 1766, vol. II, p. 279; Borroni Salvadori 1978a, *passim*; Battista 1993; Paoli 2015.
119 Battista 1993, p. 56 and ref.
120 Thirty-one gems from the collection of Salvador Camilli. Battista 1993, p. 54.
121 D. Levi in Barocchi and Gallo (eds) 1985, p. 176 and ref.
122 Letter from Stosch to Andreini, The Hague 16 September 1720 (Justi 1871, p. 4, no. III).
123 Justi 1871, p. 5. Stosch included five of Andreini's gems: pls V (Agathopos), XLV (Onesas), XLVI (Onesas), LIV (Polykleitos) and LXVIII (Teukros). In addition, he owned gems inscribed with the names Gnaios, Solon, Antiochos, Kleon, and Chronios. For Andreini's inscribed gems, see: Gori 1727, pp. 154–155 and in general Gori 1731–1732, vols I–II, *passim* and esp. Battista 1993; D. Levi in Barocchi and Gallo (eds) 1985, p. 176.
124 Gori 1727, p. 175; Gori 1731–1732, vol. I, p. XIV; Zwierlein-Diehl 2005, p. 325.
125 Gori 1731–1732, vol. I, pl. 86.9, II, pls 58.3–4 and 68.3.
126 Gori 1731–1732, vol. I, pls 39.2 and 6; 46.1–5 and 9–12; 48.6–7 and 49.2–4.

role that ancient intaglios and cameos played for its members in the decades following its foundation in 1727.[127] Several local members were collectors, among whom can be noted its founder Onofrio Baldelli, who donated his collection of gems at the time of the foundation, and Gori, who was a collector of a vast array of materials, including engraved gems.[128] Other members included Galeotto Ridolfino Corazzi, who had a sizeable collection,[129] the brothers Marcello, Ridolfino and Filippo Venuti, and Count Vincenzo Ansidei.[130] Many members of the Roman community such as Capponi, Ghezzi, Vettori and others were also regular or corresponding members.[131] Shortly before his death in 1742, Francesco Valesio had completed a catalogue of the gems in Baldelli's collection, some of which were also published in 1750 together with other curious antiquities in the collections of some of the academy's members in the volume *Museum Cortonense*.[132]

At Livorno, the Jewish merchant Gabriel di David Medina built a widely known collection of considerable size containing some 125 intaglios and 100 cameos that were summarily published in 1742.[133] Some of the inscribed names of engravers on gems in the collection were reputedly added by the engraver Flavio Sirleti, who had worked for Medina, as later recounted by Bracci.[134] In 1756, Barthélemy visited Medina to examine the coins and gems in the cabinet – and perhaps also purchase some items, as Medina asked for his help in selling the collection.[135] Nothing came of that sale, and after Medina's death a few years later, in 1761, his heirs sold the collection at auction in London.[136] Bessborough and Thomas Hollis were among the buyers.

The Venetian Count Anton Maria Zanetti di Girolamo was another gem collector that Stosch corresponded with.[137] Although not mentioned in Stosch's *Geschichte*, the two might have met on Stosch's two visits to Venice in 1714 and 1717.[138] A skilled draughtsman, Zanetti contributed two drawings to Stosch's book project, a sardonyx cameo with an image of Herakles playing a lyre inscribed with the name of Skylax in the Tiepolo collection in Venice,[139] and a carnelian intaglio representing a seahorse and inscribed with the name of Pharnakes, then in the Farnese collection at Parma.[140] Zanetti also offered to draw the gems of fellow collectors such as the Earl of Carlisle, with whom he stayed in contact,[141] and notably provided the illustrations to the catalogue of his own collection of 46 cameos and 24 intaglios. Zanetti's collection was built during his travels in Europe in 1721 and added to later through contacts with notable collectors such as the Duke of Devonshire, Pierre Crozat, Joseph Wenzel I, Prince of Liechtenstein and Maria Anna Victoria of Savoy, heiress to Prince Eugene. Further gems were acquired in Italy and Venice. Zanetti's *dactyliotheca* included then well-known items such as the head of Antinous in black jasper with the damaged inscription ANT,[142] the aforementioned

---

127   E.g. Gori 1737; Gori, Valesio and Venuti 1750; D. Levi in Barocchi and Gallo (eds) 1985, pp. 176–189; Bruschetti 1987.
128   Gambaro 2008, pp. 145–152, nos G1–90 and plates.
129   For the Corazzi collection, see: Galestin 1990.
130   On Buonarroti, see e.g. Gallo 1986; Gialluca in Bruschetti *et al.* 2014, pp. 291–305.
131   Ubaldelli 2011, *passim*. On Gori see: Kagan 2006; Gambaro 2008; Carpita 2012.
132   Gori, Valesio and Venuti 1750.
133   125 intagli and 100 cameos (Medina 1742).
134   Bracci 1784–1786, vol. I, p. 147, n. 7: '*Alcune gemme del celebre Museo Medina in Livorno rese famoso per i nomi degli Artefici, sono antiche e di lavoro eccellente, benchè i nomi degli Artefici siano stati incisi da Flavio Sirleti, alcune altre poi e il lavoro, e i nomi sono del sopramentovato artefice, come l'Agrippina col nome d'ASPASIO sotto la figura di Cerere*'.
135   Letter from J.J. Barthélemy to Le Comte de Caylus, Florence 28 September 1756: '*J'ai été à Pise et à Livourne. On m'avoit parlé de plusieurs cabinets de médailles qui étoient dans cette dernière ville; j'y ai vu effectivement d'assez bonnes choses. J'ai vu aussi les pierres gravées du juif Médina qui m'a promis une bonne recompense si je pouvois lui en procurer la vente. Vous savez bien que c'est me prendre par mon foible: je me suis bien promis de ne faire aucune démarche pour lui. Il a quelques camées très-beaux, la suite est nombreuse; vous en aurez peut-être vu le catalogue: je vous l'enverrai, si vous voulez, à condition que vous n'achèterez pas le cabinet*' ['I've been to Pisa and Livorno. I had been told about several medal cabinets in the last mentioned town. I also saw the engraved gems of the Jewish merchant Medina, who promised to recompense me well if I could help him with the sale. You know well that this is tempting my weakness. I have promised myself not to give in to him. He has some very fine cameos, the collection is numerous; you may have seen the catalogue. I will send it to you, if you want, on condition that you will not buy the cabinet'] (Barthélemy 1802, pp. 169–170).
136   Langford and Son, London, 10–12 February 1761 (Medina Sale 1761). Cf. letter from A.M. Zanetti to the Earl of Carlisle, Venice 25 October 1740(!): '*De celles de Medina ses heretiers n'ont pas encore fait la vente; ils veulent trop d'argent: il y a des belles choses; mais assez d'ordinaires*' (Scarisbrick 1987, p. 97 no. 2).
137   Although very little documentation survives. On Zanetti's gem collecting, see: Gori and Zanetti 1750; Scarisbrick 1987; Bandinelli 1996; Bortoluzzi 2014, pp. 63–82; Favaretto 2018. On his contacts with Stosch, Hansson 2021b.
138   The *Geschichte* (Stosch 1754, p. 20) mentions the poet Giovanni Battista Recanati, the poet Apostolo Zeno, the antiquaries Lorenzo Patarol and Scipio Maffei (1714), and Domenico Pasqualigo (1717), the latter a collector of coins and medals.
139   Stosch 1724, p. 83, pl. LIX.
140   Stosch 1724, pp. 71–72, pl. L.
141   Letter from Zanetti to Carlisle, Venice 25 October 1740 (Scarisbrick 1987, p. 97). The project was never realised.
142   Gori and Zanetti 1750, pp. 43–44, pl. XX. Today in the J. Paul Getty Museum, inv. no.: 2019.13.17.

so-called spotted Leopard cameo,[143] an intaglio with Herakles and Iole inscribed with the name of Teukros,[144] and two intaglios inscribed ΔΙΟϹ, interpreted as an abbreviation of the name Dioskourides: a hermaphrodite in amethyst and a giant in aquamarine.[145] Zanetti seems to have begun preparatory work for the catalogue, at least its illustrations, already by 1728, but it was not completed until much later. In a letter dated 1728, Zanetti informed the fellow antiquary Niccolò Gaburri of his intentions to write and illustrate a learned study on ancient gems and cameos.[146] He commissioned Gori to write the learned commentaries in Latin, which in the publication appear with translations in Italian.[147] The work was published in 1750 (Fig. 2.9).[148]

Another collector who was important at the time in Venice was the merchant and banker Joseph Smith, known simply as 'Consul Smith', who had settled in the city in 1700 and served as British consul from 1744 to 1760. Smith collected paintings, drawings and books on an ambitious scale, but also had a sizeable gem collection. One hundred intaglios and cameos were studied and published by the prolific Gori and printed posthumously by Giovanni Battista Pasquali after many of them, along with paintings, drawings and books, had been purchased in 1762 by George III for £20 000.[149]

A notable collector in Naples, Giovanni Carafa, 7th Duke of Noja, built a considerable collection of glyptics, of which some cylinder seals and Egyptian scarabs had been acquired from Stosch's collection.[150] Although the younger Carafa knew Stosch through correspondence, these items entered his collection shortly before or after Stosch's death through his heir Muzell, and thus were not part of the estate when Winckelmann arrived in Florence to work on Stosch's gems.

These are only some of the more significant or otherwise interesting of the numerous contemporary gem collectors who formed part of Stosch's circle or his wider networks. As substantial parts of his extensive correspondence are now lost, any direct interaction within these collector circles or circulation of specific items and information are today difficult and mostly impossible to reconstruct. One can only guess at the true extent and significance of these channels, which we nevertheless have good reason to assume were highly efficient. Unfortunately, published data is still lacking for many of the individual actors in the local Roman context, even instrumental ones such as Bernardo Sterbini, Francesco Palazzi, Antonio Borioni, Paolo Vitri, Paolo Forier and Giuseppe Campioli, who were obviously very active on the market. The same is true for the city of Florence and elsewhere. What remains clear from surviving evidence, however, is the position that the *Museo Stoschiano* occupied in Rome and Florence in the first half of the eighteenth century as a key site for antiquarian culture and intersection point of extensive networks of connoisseurs and collectors across Europe. This guaranteed a continuous flow of information, of original gems and of casts, impressions, drawings and prints – even from quarters where Stosch was perhaps gradually more tolerated than liked. These networks and information channels constituted Stosch's real powerbase, which he continuously and expertly cultivated, expanded and combined to great success, right up until the last years of his life.

---

143 Scarisbrick 1979.
144 Gori and Zanetti 1750, pp. 108–109, pl. LIII.
145 Gori and Zanetti 1750, p. 115, pl. LVII and pp. 66–68, pl. XXXIII.
146 Letter from Zanetti to Niccolò Gabburri, Venice 24 July 1728: '(…) onde io bramerei ancora, quantunque ne ho diverse, fare uno studio distino di pietre antiche e cammei' (Bottari 1757, vol. II, pp. 147–150, no. LXXIV).
147 On Zanetti and Gori, see esp.: Bortoluzzi 2014, pp. 63–74.
148 Gori and Passeri 1750.
149 Gori 1767. The catalogue numbers 100 gems, among which a copy of the Strozzi Medusa (no. XXI).
150 On Carafa's gem collection, see: Di Franco and La Paglia 2019, esp. pp. 62–68; Gołyzniak 2023a.

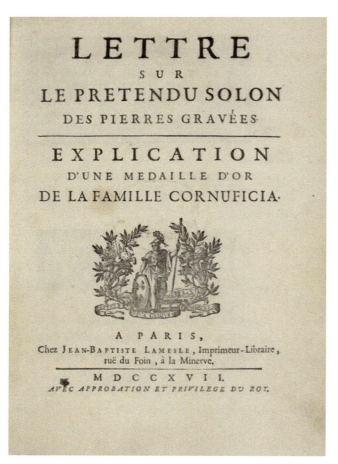

FIGURE 2.1

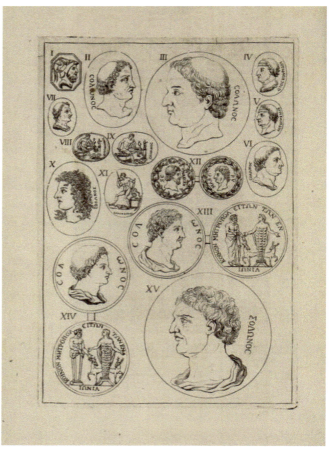

FIGURE 2.2

FIGURE 2.3

FIGURE 2.4

FIGURE 2.5

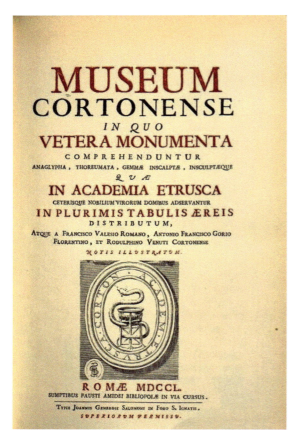

FIGURE 2.6

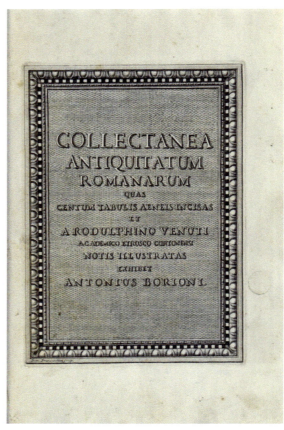

FIGURE 2.7

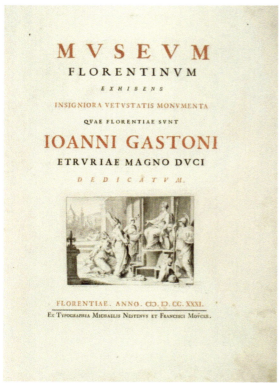

FIGURE 2.8

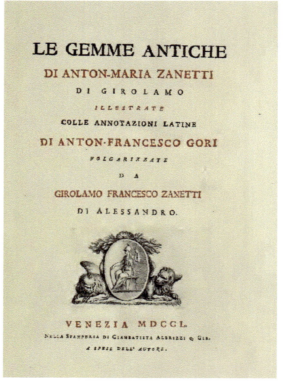

FIGURE 2.9

PART 2

The Art of Gem Drawings – Philipp von Stosch and the Circle of His Draughtsmen

∴

CHAPTER 3

Drawings of Engraved Gems from the Late Mediaeval until the Nineteenth Century

Hadrien J. Rambach

1   The *Genre* of Gem Drawings

The identification of the artists who produced the nearly 2300 drawings and prints of gems, contained in 28 volumes preserved at the Prints and Drawings cabinet of the National Museum (Princes Czartoryski Museum) in Krakow,[1] as well as the 830 additional drawings in the Kunstbibliothek Berlin, is no simple task. Indeed, questions such as: who drew them, for whom, and when[2] are made challenging by the number of artists who attempted that *genre*, from mediaeval times onwards. Therefore, our study in this volume of the drawings in Krakow, Berlin and some others should include a general reflection on drawings 'after the antique',[3] and attempt a corpus of artists known to have drawn gems. Ultimately, they must all be considered to be possible authors of the Krakow and Berlin drawings.

Edmé Bouchardon's drawing of the *Seal of Michelangelo* gem was exhibited at the Salon in 1737: the genre of *disegni di gemme* was obviously admired, even if aimed utilitarianiously at being engraved (by Pierre Soubeyran) to illustrate a book, rather than being art-for-art's sake. To reliably reproduce a gem, whilst simultaneously creating an attractive work of art, is a challenge; so much so that a drawing connoisseur such as Stosch would use gem drawing as a test of skills for the artists that he was considering to use (also for his *Atlas*).[4] Bernard Picart, for Stosch's book, '*was said to have used a microscope to examine the particular manner of each master*',[5] and he both drew most of the gems and engraved their printing plates.

Whoever wanted to publish a book on gems had a double-worry: obtaining good drawings and having those well-reproduced: this later '*quest marked the production of the* Recueil Crozat, *for which new printmaking techniques were devised to more closely replicate the qualities of wash drawings, and for which Crozat went to so far as to have presses installed in his* hôtel *so that he could supervise the printing of the plates*'.[6] But the question of the exactitude of the drawings could be debated. For example, Mariette assured his readers in 1750 that '*one can count on their* [i.e. Bouchardon's drawings] *exactitude … eyes enlightened by the constant study of nature and the antique have guaranteed it*',[7] adding that the artist '*permitted himself neither licence nor innovation*'.[8] Anyhow, the sculptor Falconet disagreed, '*arguing* [in 1770] *that Bouchardon had, in fact, imposed Mariette's ideal of antique style onto his drawings after the gems* [and that] *Bouchardon could transform even the ugliest Chinese* magot *into the most beautiful Greek figure*'.[9]

Due to the great development of copper-plate engravings (and illustrated books) in the early eighteenth-century, a number of collectors commissioned drawings of their gems. In England for example, '*à l'exception de Milord Duc de Devonshire*,[10] *personne, que je sçache, n'a encore songé en Angleterre à publier ses Pierres gravées. Encore est-il arrivé que la mort de cet Amateur, si digne de posséder de belles choses, ayant interrompu son projet, il n'a rien paru des Planches qu'il avoit fait préparer. J'en ai vû seulement des épreuves de quatorze; mais on m'assûre qu'il y en a environ*

---

1 Gołyźniak 2021.
2 And: what are/where were/where are the gems depicted on them?
3 Not in the sense of being drawn in a Classical style (*all'antica*), but meaning that they document actual ancient artefacts, such as the drawings (now at Eton College – Windsor) which were acquired by Richard Topham (1671–1730), whose '*collection as a whole constitutes a magnificent (albeit incomplete) survey of those classical sculptures, both the famous and less well known pieces, contained in Roman collections of the period c. 1725–30*' (Macandrew 1978; see also Connor Bulman 2008 and Fabréga-Dubert 2020). On illustrated catalogues of antiquities collection, see: Gallo 1997.
4 This is confirmed by a letter from Walton [Stosch] to Lord Carteret, sent on 28 February 1722 (NA Kew, SP 85/14 fols 9–12), mentioned in Hansson 2021b, p. 62, n. 17 and Chapters 4 and 5 in this volume.

5 '*C'est avec un soin & une application toute particulière, que B. Picart a exécuté ce bel Ouvrage: car non seulement il l'a gravé lui-même, mais il en a de plus fait les Desseins à l'aide du Microscope, & y a observé, autant qu'il a été possible, la manière particuliére de chaque Maitre*' (Vincent and Picart 1734, p. 8, quoted in Smentek 2014, p. 205).
6 Smentek 2014, p. 204, refers to Haskell 1988, p. 24.
7 Mariette 1750, vol. I, p. 60, translated in Smentek 2014, p. 204.
8 Mariette 1750, vol. II, p. XI, translated in Smentek 2014, p. 204.
9 Falconet 1781, pp. 256–259, cited in Smentek 2014, p. 204.
10 William, 2nd Duke of Devonshire (1673–1729).

© HADRIEN J. RAMBACH, 2025 | DOI:10.1163/9789004712553_004
This is an open access chapter distributed under the terms of the CC BY-NC-ND 4.0 license.

quatre-vingt en état de voir le jour. Ce que j'en puis dire, c'est que pour l'exécution de la Gravûre & le goût du Dessein, elles répondent très-mal à l'excellence des Morceaux curieux qu'elles veulent représenter. Et l'on peut m'en croire, puisque le Dessinateur[11] & le Graveur[12] étant François, je devrois être disposé à en dire du bien'.[13] In Holland too, *'un autre Ouvrage se préparoit depuis quelques années en Hollande, & qui, suivant toutes les apparences, n'aura pas un sort meilleur que celui du Duc de Devonshire. La mort de l'Auteur mettra encore un obstacle à sa publication, & c'est une perte. On y auroît vû avec plaisir des Antiques de toute espèce que M. de Thoms*[14] *avoit rassemblées dans le cours de ses voyages. Il promettoit de n'y faire entrer que des morceaux rares, ou qui n'avoient point encore paru. A en juger par ce que j'en ai vû, les Planches auroient été gravées avec beaucoup de propreté, peut-être sans assez de goût; car ce Curieux employoit pour son Dessinateur un homme d'un génie trop froid & trop languissant.*[15] *Il m'a fait présent, lorsqu'il étoit à Paris, des épreuves d'une vingtaine de ces Planches, & j'en ai compté six qui dans la grandeur d'un in-folio, & dans la même disposition que celles du Cabinet de Florence,*[16] *contiennent une cinquantaine de Pierres gravées, dessinées au simple trait'.*[17]

A distinction should be made between drawings after antiques or after prints which were made as an exercise, and drawings made to document (and often illustrate books) original artefacts or casts.[18] In fact, there were various types of gem drawings. Some, such as those discussed in this essay, were high-quality works of art, executed by recognised artists, aimed at illustrating luxury publications (usually one gem per plate). Others were documentary drawings – often life-size (indicated by the inscription *gemmae magnitudo*) or not much larger, which were which were used for documenting entire collections. A third type that can visually resemble either of the two previous ones is the drawing meant to accompany correspondence: an example is a letter from Markus Tuscher to Anton Francesco Gori[19] from 1735 with which was enclosed *'il Disegno e tre improntì della Pietra'*.[20]

It is noteworthy that 'drawings' of gems might not actually have been drawn after gems. Our study of the 1724 book by Stosch already mentions that several preliminary drawings were made after casts of the original engraved stones. But, in case of drawings made as training exercises or as studies of details for a forthcoming work,[21] they might also be drawn after a secondary source such as prints or drawings. This is the case for a *Bacchanale* drawing by Théodore Géricault (1791–1824), which was executed ca. 1815 after a book-illustration rather than after the actual gem (which was in Florence whilst the artist was still in Paris). It was also the case when Nicolas Poussin (1594–1665), who drew details of Grimani gems – not executed after the actual cameos in Venice but after the 1550s engravings by Enea Vico and Battista Franco.

---

11 Augustin Gosmond de Vernon (1697–176?).
12 Claude Dubosc (fl. 1711–1740).
13 Mariette 1750, vol. I, pp. 337–338.
14 Frederick de Thoms (1669–1746).
15 Pier Leone Ghezzi (1674–1755)?
16 Gori 1731–1732.
17 Mariette 1750, vol. I, p. 338.
18 I must note the exceptional series of auction-catalogues on which Gabriel de Saint-Aubin (1724–1780) sketched drawings of some of the works for sale (e.g. the *Catalogue d'une précieuse collection de tableaux, médailles, pierres gravées montées en bagues, bijoux, dessins encadrés & en feuilles, estampes encadrées, en feuilles & en recueils, livres, & autres objets de curiosité, la plus grande partie venant de l'étranger; dont la vente se fera la mercredi 5 mai 1779 & jours suivans, de relevée, rue Saint Honoré, à l'Hôtel d'Aligre*; Bibliothèque nationale de France, Estampes, RESERVE 8-YD-136, catalogue of the collection of marquis Charles-François de Calvière (1693–1777)).

19 It seems to be Gori himself, who copied Stosch 1724 in 30 sanguine drawings in Florence, Biblioteca Marucelliana (Micheli 1986, p. 38) and another 30 in Krakow, the Princes Czartoryski Museum (cf. Chapter 8 here). These drawings originally accompanied *'a very diligent and accurate summary of Stosch's volume'* dated 15 May 1726 (Tassinari 2010b, p. 100). The group from Florence also contains two other drawings by another hand, in brown ink, which equally copy gems published by Stosch. In Krakow, there is one more drawing of this type. On Gori, see: Gambaro 2008.
20 Letter sent from Livorno on 9 September 1735, Ms. B.VIII.5, c. 359, Biblioteca Marucelliana in Florence; noted in Borroni Salvadori 1978b, pp. 104–105, nn. 102 and 105. Rather than a drawing, another option was to send an impression of a gem, either in wax or simply in paper (a rubbing). An attractive example of the latter is found on a letter sent by Stosch to Fagel on 2 February 1726 with the paper imprint of a gem portrait of the Pretender (illustrated in Heringa 1981, p. 62). Stosch's preference for sending drawings of them is noteworthy: they were less fragile than casts, but more costly, and somehow less reliable, as noted by Peiresc in a letter from 14 February 1629 sent to Jean L'Empereur: *'Que s'il se trouve là quelque orfèvre ou autre ouvrier qui en sût faire une empreinte, mouleur de plomb en sable ou en plâtre, mon obligation en serait bien plus grande, car j'y pourrais voir la vraie figure du caractère plus fidèlement que si on les dessine à la plume attendu qu'il est malaisé de les portraire assez fidèlement, pour empêcher les équivoques de l'un a l'autre'* (cited in Meyer 2022, p. 26). But, *'le dessin présente aux yeux des numismates érudits au moins deux avantages. Ils sont, d'abord, une étape important dans l'autopsie: dessiner une monnaie oblige à la regarder de près. Ils sont surtout l'intermédiaire obligée entre le cabinet et la planche gravée'* (Meyer 2022, p. 37).
21 This is the case with Pajou's drawing of *Love riding a lion*, copying a cameo in Florence (Stosch 1724, pl. LIII), which is undoubtedly preparatory to his 1778 terracotta of the same subject (Draper and Scherf 1997, pp. 42–43, since then sold at Artcurial, 27 March 2019, lot 132).

2 The Middle Ages and the Renaissance

Illustrating engraved gems in the mediaeval times and the Renaissance is a subject that requires a separate study, but it should be noted here that intaglios and cameos can be often found on the borders of illuminated manuscripts. For example, the gem of Apollo, Olympos and Marsyas (so-called *Seal of Nero*)[22] is depicted in several volumes such as: Iacopo do Poggio Bracciolini's *Commento sopra il Trionfo della Fama*,[23] 1475–1478, with illuminations by Gherardo del Fora;[24] Didymus the Blind's *De Spiritu Sancto*,[25] 1488–1489, with illuminations by Monte di Giovanni di Miniato (1448–1532), for Matthias Corvinus, King of Hungary (1443–1490); Filostrato's *Eroiche*,[26] with illuminations by Boccardino il Vecchio; St. Gregorio Magno's *Dialoghi de vita e miraculis patrum italicorum*,[27] 1489, with illuminations attributed to Gherardo or Monte del Fora or Attavante; Petrarch' *Sonnectorum et Cantilenar. Liber*,[28] commissioned by Filippo Strozzi (1428–1491), with illuminations by Gherardo di Giovanni del Fora (1445–1497); Petrarch's *Trionfi*,[29] 1490s, with illuminations by Gherardo or Monte del Fora and Philostratus's *Heroides, Icones, Vitæ Sophistarum*[30] (translated by Antonio Bonfini), 1487–1490, with illuminations by Boccardino il Vecchio for Matthias Corvinus, King of Hungary (1443–1490). The same gem can be found in the illuminations added to present-copies of some *incunabulae*: on a copy[31] of Homer's *Opera*, Florence 1488, illuminated in 1489 by Gherardo di Giovanni for Piero de' Medici; on a copy[32] of Pliny's *Historia naturalis*, (translated by Cristoforo Landino), Venice 1476, illuminated in 1479–1482 by Gherardo di Giovanni for Filippo Strozzi; and on a copy[33] of Giovanni Simonetta's *Res a Francisco Sforza gestæ*, Milan 1486, illuminated by an anonymous Milanese miniaturist and presented to Maximilian I (probably in 1494).

In 1972, Nicole Dacos wrote a seminal ground-breaking essay for the exhibition catalogue on the art collections of Lorenzo de' Medici entitled: *Saggio di inventario delle opere ispirate da gemme Medici nel Rinascimento* ('A Study of the Inventory of Works Inspired by Medici Gems in the Renaissance'),[34] and indeed a number of works of art (including sculptural and architectural) have included details or entire engraved gems in their iconography. A remarkable example is the so-called *Felix Gem*,[35] which inspired Andrea Mantegna (1431–1506) for two paintings: one of his *Triumph of Caesar* and his *Battle of the Sea Gods*.[36] Similarly, Bertoldo di Giovanni (aft. 1420–1491) was inspired by a Roman cameo of *Herakles and Diomedes* (from the Medici collection)[37] for his bronze group of *Bellerophon taming Pegasus*.[38]

The Mantegna paintings have already been mentioned and so will be (cf. below) Rubens' painting of the *Great Cameo of France* in grisaille (Figs 3.5–3.6). Another pair of paintings, in *trompe-l'oeil*, should be highlighted because they include numerous copies of gems (Figs 3.1–3.2).[39] But the greatest number of artistic renderings of engraved gems are on paper rather than on canvas. The early works

---

22   On which see Rambach 2011. The cameo to which this article is devoted has entered the collection of the Cabinet des Médailles et Antiques de la Bibliothèque nationale de Lu i-même: inv. no.: 2020.29.
23   Florence, Biblioteca Medicea Laurenziana, *Ms. Ashburnham* – *65.1* – D'Ancona 1914, vol. II, no. 928; de la Mare 1985, vol. I, p. 458; Lenzuni 1992, nos 2–49; Garzelli 1996, vol. I, p. 168; Fusco and Corti 2006, p. 104.
24   The manuscript bears the Strozzi coat of arms, but it is dedicated to Lorenzo de'Medici and was in his 1492 inventory (*Libro* 152: '*Trionfo di Fama, schritto di mano di Jacopo di messer Poggio, overo la mandò a Lorenzo de' Medici*').
25   New York, Morgan Library, inv. no.: *MS.496, fo –. 2r* – Csapodi and Csapodi-Gárdonyi 1969, pp. 61, 84, 192, 194 and 320, pls 51–52; Garzelli 1985, vol. I, pp. 310–311; Alexander 1994, no. 13; Wyss 1996, pp. 49 and 51–52.
26   Vienna, Österreichische Nationalbibliothek, inv. no.: *Cod.hist.pr* – *f.66* – Fusco and Corti 2006, p. 246, n. 45.
27   Modena, Biblioteca Estense, inv. no.: *Cod.Lat – 449A* – Fusco and Corti 2006, p. 106.
28   Florence, Biblioteca Nazionale Centrale, inv. no.: *BR 227 fol 9r* – Wyss 1996, pp. 48–49. Fusco and Corti 2006, p. 246, n. 45.
29   Baltimore, Walters Art Gallery, inv. no.: *Ms.10.755, fol – 47r* – Miner 1968–1969, p. 113, fig. 50; Garzelli 1996, vol. I, p. 169; Wyss 1996, pp. 46–48, app. 19; Fusco and Corti 2006, p. 106.
30   Budapest, Széchény Library, inv. no.: *Cod.lat.417, fo –. IV* – D'Ancona 1914, pp. 803–804, no. 1592; Wyss 1996, pp. 52–53; Fusco and Corti 2006, p. 246, n. 45.
31   Naples, Biblioteca Nazionale Vittorio Emanuele III, inv. no.: *S.Q.XXXIII.K22, fol. – 244r* – Wyss 1996, pp. 46–48; Fusco and Corti 2006, p. 246, n. 45.
32   Oxford, Bodleian Library, inv. no.: *Arch.Gb.6* (*former Douce – 310*) – Pächt and Alexander 1966–1973, vol. II, p. 109, pr. 48; Garzelli 1996, vol. I, p. 168; Wyss 1996, pp. 49–50; Fusco and Corti 2006, p. 106.
33   Florence, Biblioteca Riccardiana, inv. no.: *E.R.428, fo –. IV* – Longhi 1958, p. 146, no. 460, pl. 180; Wyss 1996, pp. 54–55.
34   Dacos *et al.* 1973, pp. 131–162.
35   Boardman *et al.* 2009, no. 165. From the collections of Nicolo Niccoli; Cardinal Ludovico Trevisan; Pope Paul II (Cardinal Pietro Barbo); Cardinal Francesco Gonzaga; bequeathed to his brother Marquis Federico I of Mantua (father-in-law of Isabella d'Este); Arundel; Marlborough; Sir Arthur Evans; Captain E.G. Spencer-Churchill, now in the Ashmolean Museum in Oxford, inv. no.: *AN1966.1808* – for a full discussion, cf. Appendix 1, pl. XXXV here.
36   Vickers 1983.
37   Spier 2014.
38   Ehrlich 2018.
39   Offered for sale by Galerie Kugel at The European Fine Art Fair, Maastricht, March 2020.

related to that *genre* are difficult to identify. For example, a sketch of four ancient coins is ascribed to Pisanello (1380/1395–1450/1455), and it would then be unlikely that the artist never copied gems too.[40] Michelangelo (1475–1564) should be also mentioned. Though he did not directly copy specific intaglios or cameos *per se*, his drawings certainly reproduce several details of engraved gems.[41] The difficulty is that he could have copied a detail (such as a single figure), which may not be identifiable as a gem unless surrounded by an oval border. However, there are some rather explicit and exceptional cases like the drawing of the Farnese cup by Muhammad b. Mahmudshah al-Khayyam executed ca. 1430.[42]

The appreciation for engraved gems by the Renaissance artists and their studies of intaglios and cameos that included drawing them laid the foundations for some ambitious projects later on. The best example of this is the museum on paper of Cassiano dal Pozzo (1588–1657) that included gem drawings, some in pen and wash,[43] some in brown ink.[44] This name is not mentioned here by chance, as there is a link with Stosch, to whom this volume is dedicated. Indeed, '*the collection of drawings and antique remains assembled by Cassiano dal Pozzo in the seventeenth century ... was acquired by Clement XI, who in 1714 passed it on to Alessandro Albani. Stosch must therefore have had plenty of opportunity to consult it during both his sojourns in Rome, and it cannot be mere coincidence that his own patronage of artists in connection with his Atlas and the publication of his* Gemmae *is so very much in the same vein*'.[45]

3 Sixteenth and Seventeenth Centuries

Over the next centuries, there were numerous artists who occasionally drew some engraved gems. In the sixteenth century,[46] one should note, for example, Hans von Aachen (1552–1615), whose two gem drawings are now in the Österreichisches Staatsarchiv in Vienna.[47] If it were not for those drawings, one would not know the appearance of the cameos owned by Count François Perrenot de Granvelle de Cantecroix (1559–1607) and searching for them would be hopeless. Piero Bonaccorsi (1501–1547) should also be mentioned, as two of his gem drawings can be found in the Musée du Louvre in Paris (Fig. 3.3).[48] Moreover, the famous *Tazza Farnese* inspired Annibale Carracci (1560–1609) for a drawing.[49]

In the seventeenth century, Antoine Bouzonnet-Stella (1637–1682), the nephew and student of Jacques Stella, drew engraved gems for Cardinal Antonio Barberini (to whom he had been introduced by Giovanni Pietro Bellori) during his stay in Rome in 1658–1664. Giovanni Angelo Canini a.k.a. Giannangiolo (1609–1666) drew ancient gems and coins.[50] A notable example is Nicolas Poussin (1594–1665), who drew details of the Grimani gems – not executed after the actual cameos in Venice but after the engravings by Battista Franco.[51] Moreover, the 1627 volume, which depicts gems belonging to Pietro Stefanoni (1589–1627), was apparently illustrated by engravings after drawings by Poussin.[52] An attractive *Votary of Bacchus*, ca. 1635, in pen and ink and wash, attributed to the hand of Poussin, is most likely based on a broken Roman gem (Fig. 3.4).[53]

But, above all, Peter Paul Rubens (1577–1640) was seriously interested in engraved gems as a collector, artist and

---

40 Paris, Musée du Louvre, inv. no.: 2315r.
41 See e.g. Dunkelman 2010, p. 368. About his relationship to gems, see also Rambach 2011.
42 D'Ottone-Rambach, Rambach and Zwierlein-Diehl 2020, pp. 157–158.
43 E.g. London, the British Museum, inv. no.: 2005,0928.70 – *Leaning Cupid*, 110 × 87 mm; inv. no.: 2005,0928.69 – *Seated Eros playing the kithara*, 95 × 91 mm; inv. no.: 2005,0928.68 – *Eros trying to catch a bird in a tree* after a gem in the Albani collection, 118 × 91 mm.
44 E.g. eight drawings of 85 × 65 mm in the British Museum (inv. no.: 2005,0927.87). See: Vaiani 2016.
45 Lewis 1967, p. 326.
46 On the question of '*drawing after the antique in the early Renaissance workshop*', see: Aymonino and Varick-Lauder 2015.
47 Vienna, Österreichisches Staatsarchiv, *Triumph of Bacchus* and *Head of a young woman*, 1597–1600 – Ježková 2015.
48 Paris, Musée du Louvre, inv. no.: 10383r, *Amour et Psyché* (after a cameo in the Museo Archaeologico in Florence), sanguine, 120 × 77 mm.
49 DeGrazia Bohlin 1979, pp. 456–465.
50 '*Les talens de Jean Ange Canini ne se bornoient pas à la connoissance de l'Antiquité, il étoit habile Peintre: de plus il excelloit à dessiner les Pierres gravées & les Médailles, qu'il touchoit avec un esprit & une légèreté de main admirable*' (Canini 1731, p. VIII).
51 Bonfait and Brugerolles 2019, pp. 42–44 – notably amongst a sheet with several drawings in ink and black chalk, 315 × 218 mm (Paris, Musée du Louvre, inv. no.: 32511v), and a sheet with ink and wash, 102 × 125 mm (Paris, Ecole des Beaux-Arts, inv. no.: PM 3005).
52 Friedlaender and Blunt 1974, pp. 45–46 and 53–54; Bull 1997, pp. 119–121; Micheli 2000, pp. 560–561.
53 Blunt 1974, pp. 243–244, no. 3: '*It is extremely close to Poussin in style, but whether it is actually from his own hand must remain a matter of personal judgment*'; Blunt 1979, pp. 139–140, pl. 17a – then in the Anthony Frederick Blunt collection, sold by Ars Libri to the J. Paul Getty Museum, (inv. 86.GG.469). There is another version of this drawing, 155 × 135 mm, also in pen and ink and wash in which Bacchus is holding a torch rather than a vase (Blunt 1979, pp. 139–140, pl. 17b – then in the inventory of G.T. Siden/Seiden, now in the Fondation Jan Krugier).

even scholar.⁵⁴ He planned to publish a volume of drawings after ancient cameos and coins which, however, never came to light.⁵⁵ His exceptional painting of the *Great Cameo of France* in *grisaille* on large canvas is well known (Figs 3.5–3.6).⁵⁶ Rubens also drew a number of gems in various media, life-size and enlarged, sometimes only their details.⁵⁷ In addition, some more seventeenth-century artists are said to have drawn gems gems in various techniques like Joachim von Sandrart (1606–1688),⁵⁸ and Jacob van Werden (fl. 1643–1669).⁵⁹

4 Eighteenth Century

In the eighteenth century, the considerable rise in popularity of engraved gems among collectors of antiquities and their growing importance for the development of antiquarianism resulted in parallel growth of the production of gem drawings. They were made for a variety of purposes – documentary, artistic, correspondence and publishing alike.⁶⁰ Philipp von Stosch was decidedly the

---

54 A 224pp. volume, bound in 1648 for the brothers Pierre (1582–1651) and Jacques Dupuy (1591–1656), now in the Bibliothèque nationale de France (inv. no.: Dupuy 667), contains 17 red-wax impressions of phallic intaglios sent on 28 July 1623 by the painter Rubens to Nicolas-Claude Fabri de Peiresc (1580–1637). The same volume also contains various drawings of gems ('*Camée ou pierre gravée antique, représentant un homme tourné à droite, barbu et coiffé d'une sorte de bonnet phrygien, avec la signature fausse: dessin peint en camaïeu; Pierre gravée antique, représentant Germanicus tourné à droite, casqué: dessin à la plume; Pierres gravées antiques, représentant Agrippine et son fils: dessins à la plume*') by an unidentified artist.

55 '*In 1626, Rubens sold a large portion of his collection of paintings, sculptures, coins, and gems to George Villiers, 1st Duke of Buckingham. ... The sale of the cameos may well have had a deleterious effect on the Gem Book, for soon afterwards the project languished, and by 1627 Rubens seemed to have lost interest*' (Spier 2021, 62). The existence of this book project was well known, and on 21 June 1624 Girolamo Aleandro (1574–1629) wrote to Peiresc from Rome '*E venuto quà nuova della morte del pittore Rubenio, la quale fara facilmente svanire la raccolta, ch'egli andava facendo de' dissegni de' camei e medaglie antiche*' (letter at the Bibliothèque nationale de France in Paris), i.e. that the death of Rubens might (!) abort his project to publish a volume of drawings after ancient cameos and coins. Actually, a book published by Gerard Van der Gucht (1696–1776) in 1740 is entitled *Antique Greek and Roman Coins, Gems, &c. Engraved from Original Drawings of RUBENS by G: Vandergucht*, and contains thirty plates. The attribution to Rubens of these drawings, '*poor as they are*', has been discussed in van der Meulen (1994, pp. 214–216).

56 Oxford, Ashmolean Museum, inv. no.: WA1989.74, 1626, 100.7 × 78 cm. '*In addition to the grisaille painting made for Peiresc, now in the Ashmolean Museum, Oxford, a drawing of the Grand Camée by Rubens is in Antwerp* [Plantin-Moretus Museum, inv. no.: PK OT 00109, brown ink and wash drawing, 327 × 270 mm, publ. Cojannot-LeBlanc and Prioux 2018, p. 107], *and an anonymous engraving is known as well. Rubens's preparatory drawing of the Gemma Augustea survives in the St. Annen-Museum, Lübeck* [inv. no.: AB245, brown ink and wash drawing, 225 × 250 mm, publ. Cojannot-LeBlanc and Prioux 2018, p. 113], *along with an anonymous engraving made in 1623, which is noted in Peiresc's correspondence. Another engraving, by Nicolaas Ryckemans, also exists, but differs significantly from the drawing*' (Spier 2021, p. 62).

57 De Grummond 1977. Some examples of Rubens' gem drawings are: London, the British Museum, inv. 1919,1111.22, *The Triumph of Licinius* (?), brown ink, 189 × 249 mm (enlarged wih indication of the size), publ. Cojannot-LeBlanc and Prioux 2018, p. 118 (original gem: Paris, Cabinet des Médailles, inv. no.: camées 308, 59 × 73 mm); Winterthur, Oskar Reinhart Museum, Briner & Kern foundation, inv. 1, *Head of Alexander the Great*, brown ink with white and brown wash, 60 × 50 mm, publ.

Cojannot-LeBlanc and Prioux 2018, p. 120 (original gem: Paris, Cabinet des Médailles, inv. no.: camées 222, 32 × 30 mm); Berlin, Kupferstichkabinett, inv. no.: 3384, *Claudius and Messalina – as Triptolemos and Demeter*, brown ink, 148 × 223 mm (lifesize), publ. Cojannot-LeBlanc and Prioux 2018, p. 130 (original gem: Paris, Cabinet des Médailles, inv. no.: camées 276, 122 mm diameter); London, the British Museum, inv. Oo,9.20.e, *Bacchus singing*, brown ink, 54 × 37 mm, publ. Cojannot-LeBlanc and Prioux 2018: p. 132, n. 404 (original gem: Paris, Cabinet des Médailles, inv. no.: camées 94, 40 × 28 mm).

Like he did with marble sculptures, Rubens often only drew details (a single figure for example) of specific gems (e.g. *Bacchus singing*), which not only renders difficult the identification of the actual stone, but even renders likely that one does not realise that the drawing is a copy of a gem.

58 Dresden, Kupferstich-Kabinett, inv. no.: C 7203: *Krönungsszene mit Lorbeerkranz über zwei Adlern (Gemme)*, sanguine over pencil, 154 × 186 mm.

59 Some intaglios and cameos, such as a drunken Silenos, can be found on a group of 36 drawings of gems '*Ex Dactyliotheca Chiffletiorum*', i.e. from the collection of Jean-Jacques Chifflet (1588–1673) (Bibliothèque municipale de Besançon, inv. no.: Pâris.A.5–14), but also amongst some 172 gem impressions on paper (!), pasted on 12 sheets in a volume that bears the manuscript ex-libris of Jean Chifflet (Bibliothèque municipale de Besançon, inv. no.: 219533). It seems that these drawings were then used to illustrate Macarius l'Hureux 1657, which was edited by Chifflet's son. Some 127 drawings by van Werden for that book are also conserved in The Hague at the Plantin Moretus Museum, acquired in 1876 by Edward Moretus.

60 Charles-Nicolas Cochin (1715–1790) drew '*l'Etude des Médailles & des camées utiles aux Arts*' in sanguine of 6 pouces by 8 pouces 6 lignes (collection of Laurent-François Prault, sold at auction on 27 November 1780, lot 59, for 160/163 livres to either Jean-Baptiste Feuillet or de La Mure). The dimensions are different, but this is likely the same drawing as '*l'Etude des Médailles & des camées*' in sanguine of 4 pouces by 6 pouces (collection of de La Mure, sold at auction on 19 April 1791, lot 51). And the estate sale of Augustin de Saint-Aubin (1736–1807), Paris 4–9 April 1809, comprised (p. 5, lot 20): '*Cochin, fils. (Charles-Nicolas) Les Dessins pour le Frontispice et pour la vignette du premier volume des Pierres gravées du cabinet d'Orléans, faits à la sanguine, etc. douze dessins*'. But I am not aware of any gem drawings by him.

most prolific commissioner of those, and his example was apparently followed by others of which a good example is a wealthy English country gentleman, antiquary and collector Charles Townley (1737–1805), who also gathered several artists around himself to document his collection of engraved gems and other antiquities.[61]

The list of artists living in the eighteenth century who drew engraved gems on a single or multiple commissions is long and arranged here alphabetically. To start, let us evoke a letter from Thomas Jenkins sent on 17 June 1780 to Charles Townley in which he indicated that: '*Anders is now making a drawing of Mengs Cameo, which the Empress of Russia has purchased for 3000 Crowns*'.[62] The mentioned 'Anders' is Friedrich Anders (fl. until 1816), whose drawing was ultimately sent to Townley attached to another letter and is now preserved in London in the British Museum.[63] Francesco Bartolozzi (1727–1815) executed graphite drawings to illustrate his 1780–1791 *Marlborough Gems* book.[64] Sometimes only fragmentary information of the (apparently considerable) production of gem drawings is available, like in the case of Anton Daniele Bertoli (1677–1743),[65] Félix Boissielier (1776–1811)[66] or Jean-Jacques de Boissieu (1736–1810).[67]

However, there are much better documented examples as well, like that of Edmé Bouchardon (1698–1762).[68] His drawing of the *Seal of Michelangelo* gem, acquired by the French King at the Mariette sale and now in the Musée du Louvre in Paris,[69] has already been mentioned (Fig. 3.7) and it is also noteworthy due to its remarkable mount, for a wax impression of the original gem is pasted on it.[70] Bouchardon collaborated with Caylus and most importantly Mariette for whom he would draw gems and some of his original works may survive.[71] While the

---

According to Mariette (1750, vol. I, p. 338), Pierre Crozat (1661–1740) had apparently considered publishing a catalogue of his gems: '*J'ai toûjours oüi dire à M. Crozat, qu'il vouloir faire graver toutes ses Antiques*'. Might he have commissioned already some drawings before abandoning the project? In the 1741 *Description sommaire des desseins des grands maistres du cabinet de feu M. Crozat*, of which he had 19 000, there are no drawings of gems, though it lists numerous 'études' and 'desseins d'après l'antique'.

One can also mention a superb eighteenth-century anonymous drawing depicting a seemingly undocumented amethyst intaglio of the three-quarter facing bust of Herakles, signed 'Dioscurides' in Greek, the drawing being inscribed: '*Ercole Romano quasi di faccia in Ametisto di poco scagliata, opera di Artefice Eccelent(e) e di perfetta maniera, grande quanto una noce. Dalla Vigna di casa Altieri [sull'Esquilino a Roma]*'. Its current location is unknown.

61   The British Museum preserves hundreds of gem drawings made for Townley apparently attributed to such artists as: Christian Borckhardt (1762–1826), William Chambers (fl. 1794–1795), Franz Gabriel Fiessinger (1723–1807), G. Kirtland (fl. 1795), William Skelton (1763–1848), James Stephanoff (ca. 1786–1874), which remain to be studied.

62   TY 7/394. In another letter from Thomas Jenkins to Townley, dated 1 July 1780, one learns that: '*After what I mentioned to you in my last about the sale of the Mengs' cameo, your curiosity will naturally be excited to see the drawing of it, which is enclosed (…)*' – TY 7/ 395 – https://www.britishmuseum.org/collection/object/G_2010-5006-74 [retrieved on 4 August 2023].

63   London, the British Museum, inv. no.: 2010,5006.74, 187 × 170 mm, inscribed in pencil: '*Sardonyx cameo formerly the property of Menx [sic] the painter purchased by Mr Jenkins for £400 and sold by him to the Empress of Russia for £500*'. The cameo of *Perseus and Andromeda* the drawing reproduces is now in St. Petersburg, the Hermitage Museum, (inv. no.: ГР-12685).

64   E.g. the *Bust of Julia Domna* (copy of Boardman et al. 2009, no. 462) illustrated vol. I, pl. XXIV, is in the British Museum (inv. no.: 1856,0510.1175); and the *Head of Ptolemy* (copy of Boardman et al. 2009, no. 270) illustrated vol. II, pl. I, is in the British Museum (inv. no.: 1868,0822.7588) too. The different provenance of these two drawings indicates that the group was dispersed early on. Tassinari was possibly mistaken to write that this '*lussuosa opera*' was '*illustrate da incisioni di Francesco Bartolozzo su disegni di Giovanni Battista Cipriani*' (Tassinari 2018, p. 30, n. 22).

65   On 7 July 1727, '*il Ghezzi corregge il disegno del Bertoli del cameo con Iside*' (Ubaldelli 2001, p. 85).

66   76 drawings executed between 1795 and 1805 after La Gravelle 1732–1737 (Ottinger 1997).

67   AuctionArt and Mirabaud Mercier, Paris, 17 December 2019, lot 73 was a large in-12 drawing-book of over 200 drawings on 75 sheets, bound by Lavaux. Amongst the titled drawings were '*Pierres gravées d'Orléans*' and '*Pât. antique*'.

68   Pforr and Roserot 2016; Kopp 2017, pp. 54–59.

69   Paris, Musée du Louvre, inv. no.: 23849, the *Seal of Michelangelo*, ca. 1737, red chalk, 123 × 173 mm (lot 1125 in the Mariette sale).

70   Dmitrieva 2018, fig. 18.

71   The plates 4–10 of Caylus and Bouchardon 1737 reproduce engraved gems. Bouchardon made a series of drawings for Mariette's *Traité des pierres gravées* (1750). As noted in Kafker and Pinault-Sørensen 1995, p. 227, 'Soubeyran, Pierre (Genève, 1709–Genève, 1775). … collabore à la gravure des Pierres gravées antiques du Cabinet du Roi *d'après Bouchardon faisant partie du* Traité des Pierres gravées *de Mariette*'. Indeed, Mariette's auction also contained, by Bouchardon, '*Cent quatre-vingt-quatorze petits Sujets & Têtes, dessinés à la sanguine, d'après les pierres gravées antiques du Cabinet du Roi, & qui sont connus par les Estampes qui sont insérées dans le Traité des pierres gravées de M. Mariette, en 2 vol. in-folio: tous ces dessins sont dans deux boîtes de maroquin jaune, de forme in-4°*' (lot 1147 sold 2812 livres to A.-J. Paillet but '*rendu à Mr Clerisseau pour 3000*', their fate is unknown). Also lost are Bouchardon's '*soixante-cinq petits Dessins à la sanguine, en contr'épreuves, faits pour les Pierres gravées du Cabinet du Roi*' sold in June 1786 by the estate of Claude-Henri Watelet and bought for 599 livres 19 sold by Perrin (lot 155). A group of four simple works, all in red chalk, was sold by Piasa without provenance (Paris, 26 March 2003, lot 41): *Apollo and Marsyas* (100 × 90 mm) = Mariette 1750, vol. II, pl. XIII; *Apollo and Love* (100 × 85 mm) = Mariette 1750, vol. II, pl. XIV; *Mars and Venus* (100 × 90 mm) = Mariette 1750, vol. II,

artistic virtuosity of Bouchardon was exceptional, others would draw rather simple sketches in a large number to document collections of hundreds of gems. A good example of that is Filippo Buonarroti (1661–1733) and his manuscript notebook, including numerous drawings of gems from his own and other Florentine collections (notably those of Fabretti and Andreini) (Fig. 3.8).[72] The drawings of Giovanni Domenico Campiglia (1691–1768),[73] as well as Asmus Jakob Carstens (1754–1798),[74] were probably made in a similar vein.

Around 1730, the Jesuit Pietro Piovene wrote a short list of the 1823 gems in the Farnese collection (then in Parma), and mentioned the ongoing cataloguing to be printed with drawings by Giovanni Caselli (1698–1752), who (future head of the painting workshop of the Capodimonte Porcelain Manufactory) 'drew each gem enlarged so that it can be seen and enjoyed fully; its true dimensions are nearby'.[75] Anne Claude de Tubières-Grimoard de Pestels de Lévis de Caylus (1692–1765) apparently drew gems on his own.[76] Regarding William Chambers/Chalmers

---

pl. XIX; and *Victorious athlete* (100 × 88 mm) = Mariette 1750, vol. II, pl. CXXII: might the belong to Mariette's or to Watelet's group?

The attribution to Bouchardon of drawings found on the market would need to be confirmed. E.g. the Lex Aitken and Alfredo Bouret Gonzalez collection, sold by Christie's in London on 4 June 2014 (lot 117 – unsold), contained '*Four studies* [on three separate sheets] *of classical cameos, two with indications of their original size, one inscribed* "de la propre grandeur de la piere [sic]", *red chalk, one with black chalk, 11.2 × 18 cm and smaller (sheet sizes)*' which the auction-house attributed to Bouchardon (the three lots illustrated in the catalogue depicted busts). And Karl & Faber (Munich) offered on 3 December 2010 (lot 123) a drawing of *Bacchus and followers* on blue paper (ca. 350 × 450 mm), an unusual item that does not relate to any plate in *Mariette 1750*.

72 *Gemmae antiche da esso [Senatore Bonaroti] delineate*, Florence, Biblioteca Marucelliana, Ms. A.48, between 1688–1731 (some of the drawings of Strozzi gems are reproduced in Guerrieri Borso 2004, p. 36, fig. 21). On this hand-drawn volume, '*in cui sono raccolti numerosi disegni di gemme di collezioni romane e fiorentine (tra queste le collezioni Fabbretti e Andreini) con l'indicazione, per ogni gemma, del possessore e del tipo di pietra usata*' (Mastrocinque 1993, pp. 18–19), see Quartino 1978. On Buonarroti himself, see: Gallo 1986.

73 Gem drawings preserved in Florence, Gallerie degli Uffizi, Gabinetto dei Disegni e delle Stampe, inv. 5151–5568 (Gennaioli 2007, p. 77, figs 26–27). These are probably the '*disegni di gemme*' which were inventoried in 1784 in the Florentine museum ('*Classe III: disegni, stampe e libri. Articolo I: disegni. 288. Un volume grande in cartapecora segnato di n. I, di c. 124, che contiene i rami del Museo Fiorentino e in esso vi sono compresi soltanto i fregi in numero di quarantadue; le lettere iniziali in numero di venticinque e le gemme in tavole cento. 289. Uno detto simile segnato di n. II, di c. 100, che contiene disegni di gemme in tavole cento*', according to the *Inventario della R. Galleria. Indice dei disegni*, 1784, by Giuseppe Pelli Bencivenni: Florence, Archivio Gabinetto Disegni e Stampe degli Uffizi, ms. 102, transcribed online by the Fondazione Memofonte). Valentina Campiglia mentions that '*Il primo volume [di disegni] contiene … cento tavole raffiguranti gemme*' (Rubechini 2016, p. 110), that '*I disegni contenuti in questo volume in realtà corrispondono a quelli riprodotti nel secondo del* Museum Florentinum, *edito nel 1732, nella parte dedicata alle gemme*' (Rubechini 2016, p. 111), and that '*Nel secondo volume trovano posto le cento tavole relative ai disegni di gemme (in realtà raffigurati nel primo tomo dell'opera a stampa, come già detto, e uscito nel 1731, con la dedica a Gian Gastone dei Medici)*' (Rubechini 2016, p. 117). She also noted that '*L'attribuzione a Campiglia di tutte le tavole, comprese quelle in cui cammei sono realizzati con una semplice linea di contorno, è a mio avviso dubbia e non si può affermare che l'artista abbia adottato questo stile in virtù del soggetto da raffigurare, poiché per alcune gemme si riscontra al contrario un'attenzione al chiaroscuro tipica dell'artista lucchese*' (Rubechini 2016, p. 118). Campiglia was described in 1736 as '*a Florentine gentleman and artist in drawing and painting employed by the present Pope to make out the grand collection of antique statues and bustos, for which he had a large salary*' (Donato 2004, p. 159, n. 64; citing Cunyngham 1853, p. 237).

74 Paweł Gołyźniak kindly informed me of the presence of 5 drawings after gems by Carstens at the Kupferstichkabinett in Berlin. But for *Aurora und Cephalus*, all depict sea-related scenes: *Nereus und Doris mit zwei Kindern*, two versions of *Amphitrite mit Seerossen*, and *Scylla*.

75 '*Databile intorno al 1730 e quindi all'incirca contemporaneo alle prime due lettere del Ghinghi, è il catalogo sommario delle gemme Farnese, allora alla corte di Parma, compilato dal gesuita Pietro Piovene (Strazzullo 1979, pp. 76–78; Giove-Villone 2006, p. 31). In questo inventario, le 1823 gemme sono divise in soggetti religiosi, storici, teste illustri e di imperatori, divinità, animali, iscrizioni, simboli, ecc … Vi sono attestate pressoché tutte le pietre; i lapislazzuli sono 28; le « altre cose moderne » 21. Mandando questo catalogo al re, Piovene specifica che costituisce una sezione del Real Museo e che si è cominciato e in buona parte compiuto un magnifico inventario che verrà stampato. In questa opera il rinomato pittore e miniatore piacentino Giovanni Caselli (1698–1752), attivo per i Farnese, in seguito capo del laboratorio di pittura della Manifattura di Porcellana di Capodimonte, ha disegnato ogni gemma ingrandita così che si può vedere e godere pienamente; vicino vi sono le sue vere dimensioni. Accanto al disegno vi è un testo esplicativo, in latino e in italiano, sulla qualità della gemma, il suo significato e i nomi degli Autori più celebri che hanno trattato di quell'esemplare. Purtroppo non si è rinvenuta traccia di questo libro (Pannuti 1994, p. 8; Giove-Villone 2006, p. 31. Sul Caselli si vedano Arisi 1978; Capobianco 1997)*' – Tassinari 2010b, p. 105.

76 A drawing from an otherwise-unknown *recueil* is ascribed to Caylus in Malgouyres 2022, pp. 101–102: '*Le comte de Caylus a dessiné avec soin quelques planches du recueil de Gori, dessins reliés en un précieux petit album*', but without justification. '*Comme le remarquait Gisela Richter, d'un catalogue à l'autre, les mêmes pierres gravées passent d'antiques à modernes puis redeviennent antiques*' (Malgouyres 2022, p. 104), but in this book the gems are not dated at all. Whilst proofreading errors are easily forgiven, such as the description of a portrait of Caracalla as garnet p. 74 but as ruby p. 262, it is regrettable that a book devoted to such a rich collection contains an unsatisfactory bibliography (e.g. Lapatin 2011 is missing regarding information on the grotesques, Rambach 2011 about the *Seal of Nero*, Nardelli 1999 about the Jupiter *Aegiochus*, etc.). Also missing are proper

(fl. 1794–1795), it is known how much he was paid for his gem drawings,[77] while Giovanni Battista Cipriani (1727–1785) is believed to have drawn some gems from the Marlborough collection in pen and ink ca. 1762–1785.[78]

Salvatore Ettore was hired by Alessandro Gregorio Capponi (1683–1746) to draw some of his gems.[79] There is also evidence that Jean-Honoré Fragonard (1732–1806),[80] and Vincenzo Franceschini (1680–?) drew gems as well,[81] while Pier Leone Ghezzi (1674–1755) did so on a regular basis while executing the commissions of others, including Philipp von Stosch, as well as to satisfy his personal interest in glyptic art.[82] Jan Goeree (1670–1731) contributed to a number of numismatic books,[83] but he also drew gems.[84] Augustin Gosmond de Vernon (1697–176?) had been commissioned by the 2nd Duke of Devonshire in 1724 in preparation of an illustrated catalogue of his gems and he is said to have produced 99 gem drawings for its sake.[85]

Most collectors of gems relied upon regular artists as far as illustrations of their intaglios and cameos was concerned. However, Frans Hemsterhuis (1721–1790) apparently attempted to draw them on his own as well.[86] Nowadays, Hemsterhuis is mostly remembered as a philosopher and for his links to Diderot, but he took sculpture lessons from the German gem engraver Lorenz Natter (1705–1763), which testifies to his in-depth interest in glyptics. There is also evidence that he held Stosch's contribution to gem studies in high esteem.[87] Indeed, Stosch and

---

acknowledgments, such as mentioning that Spier's email quoted p. 128 endnote 14 was sent to me, as well as some provenances: for example, the cameo no. 71 was sold on 26–27 January 1920 as part of the collection of William Talbot Ready.

77 Chambers was paid £2.2.0 in February 1795 for 'drawings' from the collection of Charles Townley (1737–1805), and again £1.1.0 in August 1795 for 'drawing gems' (Sloan 2000, no. 167). Several of them survive, such as the ink and wash drawing of a paste intaglio (British Museum, inv. no.: 2010,5006.1426 – Walters 1926, no. 3312) and the drawing of an intaglio in graphite (British Museum, inv. no.: 2010,5006.1432 – Walters 1926, no. 1623).

78 E.g. the *Hercules Bibax* (copy of Boardman et al. 2009, no. 667), 193 × 132 mm, in the British Museum (inv. no.: 1868,0822.6503).

79 Ubaldelli 2001, pp. 133–134. Capponi, on whom see: Prosperi Valenti Rodinò 2004 and Donato 2017, would send gem impressions to his hired artists for them to copy his cameos and intaglios. Like many of his contemporaries, Capponi was a real devotee to scholarship rather than just a collector, and a noteworthy element is that he spent 13.52 scudi to publish in 1727, in 200 printed copies, using the engravers Girolamo Frezza and Vincenzo Franceschini, a gem which he had bought for 12 scudi in 1724 (Donato 2004, p. 159, n. 60). For him, like Stosch, ownership was not sufficient; he had to understand and to share.

80 E.g. *Leda and the swan*, black chalk on paper, 235 × 185 mm (Harvard Art Museums/Fogg Museum, inv. no.: 1979.70.6).

81 Franceschini, on whom see Chapter 8 in this volume, was the engraver of Stosch's *Meleager* gem (after the drawing by Ghezzi within a frame by Odam). Might he have drawn gems too?

82 See Chapter 4 in this volume and Gołyźniak (Ghezzi – forthcoming).

83 Such as Bogaert 1697, Foy-Vaillant 1701, Foy-Vaillant 1703, La Chausse 1706 and van Loon 1723–1731.

84 For the first volume of van der Aa 1729, pls 9a–d. The original drawing for the plate 9c (one which is illustrated a relief already illustrated in Spon 1685, p. 104) has survived: pen, ink and wash drawing over indications in red chalk, 307 × 181 mm (offered at Karl & Faber's auction 243 on 27 April 2012, lot 133, est. €3500–4500; offered at Winterberg Kunst's auction 86 on 20 April 2013, lot 162, est. €4500; Colnaghi and Laue 2013, no. 47, £7500).

85 Gosmond 1730. According to Kagan (2010, p. 111), Gosmond *'produced 99 drawings before he left England and these, along with several more made by a member of the Preißler family of Nuremberg artists* [supposedly Johann Justin Preißler (1698–1771)], *were printed by the illustrator Claude Dubosc (fl. 1711–1740)'*. I am not aware whether these drawings survive.

86 Whilst the title page of Hemsterhuis 1762 is illustrated with a vignette depicting an amethyst intaglio of Nereid riding a hippocamp across the sea to the left, two dolphins beneath her legs (signed by Dalion – a gem now in Leiden, Rijksmuseum van Oudheden, inv. no.: GS-01167), signed '*J.V. Schley delin. et sculpsit*' (i.e. drawn and engraved by Jakob van der Schley 1715–1779), the title page of Hemsterhuis 1769 is illustrated with a vignette depicting – carved on some ruins in nature – an intaglio of a bearded, half-cladded hammerman, seated under a tree, working on a metal crater with his tools, signed '*F.H. inv. J.V.S. sculp.*' (i.e. drawn by Hemsterhuis and engraved by Schley).

87 Following what is on offer at auctions and in the antiquarian trade makes it possible not only to discover unpublished drawings, but also manuscripts. For example, the lot 170 sold by Leclere enchères, in Marseille on 28 February 2017, was an in-quarto manuscript of 19 pp., entitled '*Catalogue d'une collection de pierres gravées antiques rassemblées par feu Mr Hemsterhuys lui-mêmei même ainsi que son père parmi les antiquaires les plus célèbres de nos jours. Connu encore par différents ouvrages qui réunissent aux charmes de la diction, une grande profondeur et beaucoup d'érudition et lui ont mérité le nom de laton moderne; tels sont L'homme et – ses Rapports – Aristée ou la Divinité. Simon ou des facu – tés de l'ame – Alexis ou l'age d'or*'. This list contains 69 entries, the first 41 being copied from those written by the collector himself, the Dutch philosopher François Hemsterhuis (1721–1790), on whom see: Brummel 1925, Hammacher 1971, Moenkemeyer 1975, Viellard-Baron 1975, Pelickmans 1987, and Fresco, Geeraedts and Hammacher 1995. About his collection of engraved gems in particular, see: Zadoks-Josephus 1952; Maaskant-Kleibrink 1978, pp. 34–39; Zwierlein-Diehl 2007, pp. 264 and 275–276. A serious connoisseur, attested to have corresponded with engravers, such as Lorenz Natter (King 1860, p. XXVIII), and to have visited various cabinets, including Bentinck's in 1767 (Camper 1794, p. 10), and he is the author of a brochure entitled *Lettre sur une pierre antique du cabinet de Monsieur Théod. De Smeth*.

This interesting figure is related to our subject, as he was the preceptor of the young Frans Fagel (1740–1773), which provides a link to François Fagel (1659–1746), the Dutch statesman and secretary to the States General who became Grand Pensionary of Holland in 1727, who was a friend and sponsor of Stosch, and

his book on gems signed by ancient master engravers were influential throughout the eighteenth century, which is clear from the drawing of the red jasper featuring Athena Parthenos and signed by Aspasios, executed by Johann Heinrich Lips (1758–1817) (Fig. 3.9).[88]

A 1778 painting of *Perseus and Andromeda* by Anton Raphael Mengs (1728–1779)[89] is said to have been inspired by an antique cameo belonging to Mengs' wife.[90] Mengs must have studied gems closely and used them as inspiration, which is confirmed by some of his surviving drawings (Fig. 3.10).[91] Willem van Mieris (1662–1747) was prolific in drawing gems, as he drew 183 of those supposedly belonging to Johan Hendrik Graf van Wassenaer-Opdam (1683–1745).[92] Georg Abraham Nagel (1712–1779) drew hundreds of gems for Stosch and some for other collectors.[93] Johann August Nahl the Younger (1752–1825) contributed with his gem drawings to the publication of some Stosch's gems by Johann Friedrich Schlichtegroll.[94] The famed gem engraver Johann Lorenz Natter (1705–1763) also did a number of drawings after famous intaglios and cameos to illustrate a never-published volume entitled *Museum Britannicum*.[95] Except for one drawing made for Stosch's book, Theodorus Netscher (1661–1728) is otherwise unknown for drawing gems on a greater scale.[96] Pietro Antonio Novelli (1729–1804) was involved in the illustration of Anton Francesco Gori's *Dactyliotheca Smithiana*.[97]

Pietro Nucherini was another artist working for the collector of engraved gems Alessandro Gregorio Capponi.[98] Girolamo Odam (ca. 1681–1741) was an accomplished illustrator of gems working notably for Stosch and several other collectors in Rome, but he was also a collector and dealer of intaglios and cameos.[99] Augustin Pajou (1730–1809) drew some artefacts 'from life' during his 'Italian years', but he mostly copied illustrations (including those of gems) published in old books for training (Fig. 3.11).[100] Thanks to

---

whose nearly 1200 letters to the latter survive. In 1710, Stosch had been recommended to Fagel by his uncle, the Prussian minister Wolfgang von Schmettau (1648–1711), see: Heringa 1981. For Hemsterhuis' appreciation of Stosch, see Chapter 5 in this volume.

88 Private collection, *Minerva salutifera*, 162 × 125 mm, sold by Dietrich Schneider-Hann, Seefeld, auction on 26 June 2019, lot 543. This drawing might have inspired Lips for a military vignette of 1802 (Kruse 1989, pp. 305–306, fig. 241). The title of the drawing, written in exergue, suggests that it was a copy of Stosch 1724, pl. XIII, rather than drawn from the original gem in Rome.

In the same 2019 auction, the lot 425 was a *Bildnis Sokrates in der Art einer Kamee* (in fact Michelangelo?) by Vincenzo 'Girolamo' Gozzini (ca. 1788–aft. 1840), sanguine, sheet 98 × 80 mm, drawing 51 × 45 mm (previously sold by the same auctioneer in Munich on 11 May 1992, lot 159, 'Aus einem gräflichen Album').

89 St. Petersburg, the State Hermitage Museum, inv. no.: ГЭ-1328.
90 Also in St. Petersburg, the State Hermitage Museum, inv. no.: ГР-12685. See: Dmitrieva (Russian buyers – forthcoming), who notes that Charles Townley annotated a drawing by Friedrich Anders (London, the British Museum, inv. no.: 2010,5006.74): 'Sardonyx cameo formerly the property of Menx the painter, purchased by Mr. Jenkins for £400 and sold by him to the Empress of Russia for £500' (cf. above), and that Catherine II herself, on 23 September 1780, wrote that this cameo 'réellement est d'une grande perfection'.
91 Two drawings of '*Oedipus at Colonnos before the temple of the Eumenides*' (also called *Oedipus before the Temple of the Furies between his Daughters Antigone and Ismene*) survived: in Florence (Uffizi) and in New York (MET), see: Giuliano 1973 and Pirzio Biroli Stefanelli 2012, p. 31, no. V-108. The latter drawing was annotated by Sir Thomas Robinson (1738–1786) '… *this drawing was done by Mengs at Rome as an Imitation of the Antique in order to be engraved. Pichler accordingly copied it for me in 1763 … Montagu has it's* (sic!) *Companion, Priam at Achilles's feet, drawn by Mengs & engraved by Pichler*' (sold to the MET at Sotheby's on 5 July 2013, lot 340, from the collection of Holland). Interestingly, this drawing had been attributed to Pichler when sold to Ralph Holland (1917–2012) at Christie's in 1969, though no drawing by him is known and though the annotation is rather explicit, but it was included in Roettgen 1999, vol. I, pp. 44–45, no. Z65.

92 See Platz-Horster 2012, p. 14, n. 31 and Chapter 4 in this volume. Examples of these drawings are illustrated in Platz-Horster 2017, p. 59, fig. 8b and Wagner 2017, p. 118, fig. 7.
93 See Chapter 4 in this volume.
94 '*Il y avoit à peu près une douzaine des plus belles pierres [de la collection Stosch] que l'éditeur [Johann Friedrich Frauenholz (1758–1822) de Nuremberg] avoit déjà fait graver, d'après les superbes dessins du célèbre artiste Nahl, dans le même modèle que celles du premier volume*' (Millin 1805, 437). These were engraved by Johann Gotthard Müller (1747–1830) and illustrate Schlichtegroll 1797 and Schlichtegroll 1805.
95 With '*213 plates [presenting] 512 gems from 23 British Cabinets*' – see Boardman, Kagan and Wagner 2017.
96 See Chapter 4 in this volume.
97 Gori 1767 is illustrated with '100 *plates engraved by Brustolon, mostly in a severely neoclassical style … The only concession to the more painterly, Baroque style is an endplate of Perseus and the Head of Medusa, engraved by Brustolon from a drawing by Pietro Antonio Novelli, an artist almost as closely associated with Pasquali as Piazzetta was with Albrizzi*' (Haskell 1980, p. 337).
98 Hired by Capponi in 1728/29 (Ubaldelli 2001, p. 138).
99 See Chapter 4 in this volume and Gołyźniak 2023b.
100 '*C'est la glyptique qui a provoqué chez lui le plus grand nombre d'images. Les gemmes se sont accumulées sur plusieurs pages huilées de recueils. Grâce aux possibilités offertes par les publications de Gori* [Gori 1731–1732] *et de La Chausse* [La Chausse 1706], *Pajou pouvait suivre de près les manières des Anciens de fixer les traits de leurs mythes favoris. … Calquant directement d'après les planches, … il accumule les références, régulièrement, suivant le processus académique de la copie minutieuse. Mais ceci n'est qu'un aspect de ses recherches dans le domaine de la glyptique, où il se montre souvent très clairvoyant dans ses choix. … On peut*

constater qu'il dessina parfois directement d'après l'original: sa copie libre du fabuleux camée du Centaure … est accompagnée d'une annotation prouvant qu'il le dessina à Capodimonte. De même, sans doute, son étude d'après la Lutte de Neptune et de Minerve, *autre pièce laurentienne*' (Draper and Scherf 1997, p. 24). On Pajou's drawings, see also Draper and Scherf 1998 and Roland Michel 1999.

Most of these studies were preserved in three albums of drawings which were on offer at Pajou's estate sale (12–13 January 1829, lot 110), two of which are now in Paris at the ÉNSBA. Numerous annotations '(*d'après une*) *médaille antique*' are erroneous, which confirms that most of these drawings were executed after prints, rather than originals.

The ÉNSBA therefore preserves a number of such drawings (numbers from Draper and Scherf 1997): no. 1-19 (chalk, 230 × 142 mm) depicts a Roman cameo of Athena and Poseidon in the Museo Archeologico Nazionale in Naples (Rambach 2011, p. 274); no. 1-45 (chalk, pen and ink, 150 × 85 mm) depicts a Roman cameo of a centaur in the Museo Archeologico Nazionale in Naples (Pannuti 1994, pp. 199–200, no. 167, Giuliano 2009, pp. 111–112, no. 35); no. 1-18 (chalk, 200 × 147 mm) depicts a cameo of Ganymede feeding Jupiter's eagle from the engraving in Bartoli 1697, pl. 110 ('*nobilissimo cameo fatto in materia di musaico trovato nelle catacombe di S. Bastiano*'); no. 11-118 (chalk on tracing-paper, 216 × 305 mm) depicts a cameo of Hercules from the engraving in La Chausse 1706, pl. XLVII, as well as a cameo of Victory's chariot from La Chausse 1706, pl. XLIII, a cameo of Romulus, Remus, the she-wolf and Faustulus (La Chausse 1706, pl. XLVIII), a cameo of Bacchus's chariot drawn by two centaurs (La Chausse 1706, pl. XLII), an intaglio with the attributes of Minerva (La Chausse 1706, pl. XLIV), and a paste intaglio of Venus and Cupid with Eneas' arms (La Chausse 1706, pl. XL); no. 1-66 (chalk, pen and ink, 149 × 92 mm) depicts an intaglio of Neptune riding a dolphin, and a cameo of Amphitrite in the Museo Archeologico Nazionale in Florence (perhaps Tondo and Vanni 1996, pp. 36 and 113, no. 28); no. 1-27 (chalk, 150 × 85 mm) depicts an unidentified intaglio of the head of Hercules, and an unidentified intaglio of the heads of Hercules and Omphale; no. 1-16 (chalk, pen and ink, 182 × 152 mm) depicts an intaglio by Antonio Pichler of a female head, a paste intaglio of a standing Muse by Onesas in the Museo Archeologico Nazionale in Florence (Stosch 1724, pl. XLV), and a Victory driving a quadriga as on the reverse of a denarius by L. Plautius Plancus; no. 1-28 (chalk, pen and ink, 200 × 135 mm) depicts a red jasper intaglio of Minerva by Aspasios in the Museo Nazionale in Rome (Stosch 1724, pl. XIII); no. 11-80 (chalk and ink, 218 × 153 mm) depicts an unidentified intaglio of Ajax in the Museo Archeologico Nazionale in Florence; no. 11-32 (chalk, pen and ink, 180 × 122 mm) depicts a carnelian intaglio of a vase from Stosch's collection (Winckelmann 1760, class V, no. 108, p. 487; Berlin, Antikensammlung, inv. no.: FG 7113), which also drawn by Ghezzi (Vatican Cod. Ott. lat. 3100, fol. 83) and by Odam (Krakow No. 1454); no. 1-60 (chalk, pen and ink, 210 × 158 mm) depicts an intaglio portrait of King Massinissa in the Museo Archeologico Nazionale in Florence (Tondo and Vanni 1996, pp. 174 and 207, no. 99); no. 1-55 (chalk, pen and ink, 150 × 93 mm) depicts an unidentified engraved gem of a nude male riding a seahorse, and a left-facing eagle head (copied from a coin of the fifth-century BC from either Sinope or Olympia); no. 1-57 (chalk, pen and ink, 197 × 140 mm) depicts an unidentified intaglio of a nude warrior with his dog, an unidentified intaglio of a nude

Pietro Giovanni Palmieri's drawings, two engraved gems are ascribed to the collection of Carlo Antonio Pullini.[101] Gaetano Piccini (fl. 1710–1730) was one more artist in the service of Alessandro Gregorio Capponi from 1728/1729.[102] He was introduced to Capponi by Ghezzi, and he was also employed by both Stosch and Ficoroni.[103] Giovanni Battista Piranesi (1720–1778) illustrated four gems from Anton Maria Zanetti's collection but he probably never saw them and copied their images from an earlier publication of Gori.[104]

man sculpting a vase, and a sphinx attacking a nude man next to a vase; no. 1-65 (chalk, pen and ink, 210 × 138 mm) depicts an unidentified intaglio of a Bacchant seated on a chimera which she feeds, and an unidentified intaglio of Hercules killing the bull; no. 1-8 (chalk, pen and ink, 130 × 82 mm) depicts an unidentified intaglio depicting Nemesis (type Furtwängler 1900, vol. I, pl. XL-9); no. 1-17 (chalk, pen and ink, 183 × 130 mm) depicts an unidentified intaglio of '*La mere de Rémus et de Romulus d'apres un pier antique a Rome*'. Additionally, seventy gems are copied on tracing-paper (Draper and Scherf 1997, pp. 24 and 70, no. 20, copied from Gori 1731–1732, vol. I, pls 25, 27–28, 33, 39, 44, 46, 58, 60, 62–64 and 72; Draper and Scherf 1997, p. 70, no. 11-3, copied from Gori 1731–1732, vol. I, pls 34–38 and 65–67).

It is supposedly from the third Roman album that a group of 26 studies in ink, wash and pen, from the collection of a 'collectionneuse bruxelloise' (sold Artcurial, Paris, 25 March 2020, lots 81–83), come. Amongst them, there were '*une naïade d'après un camée*' (146 × 177 mm), '*un triton d'après une médaille*' (175 × 138 mm), and '*trois études d'après des intailles*'. Only two of these gem-drawings were illustrated in the auction catalogue, and I am grateful to Paweł Gołyźniak for noticing that the drawing of *Athena* is a simplified version of a carnelian intaglio in Florence, Museo Archeologico Nazionale (Gori 1731–1732, vol. II, pl. 55.1; Zwierlein-Diehl 1986, pp. 148–149, no. 301; Gołyźniak 2020, no. 10.211), of which there is also a drawing by Nagel (Krakow No. 386).

Numerous engraved gems depict dolphins with human figures, winged or not (such as that illustrated on a drawing in the Pozzo collection, see: Borbein, Kunze and Rügler 2019, p. 255). The drawing of a *dolphin-rider* is annotated to be '*d'après une médaille*' (i.e. 'after a medal') but illustrates in fact a 3rd-century BC aquamarine scarab, 13 × 11 mm, from the collection of Paul von Praun (1548–1616) in Nürnberg, reproduced in impression by Lippert in the 1770s (Raspe and Tassie 1791, pl. 31, no. 2686; Zwierlein-Diehl 1986, p. 89, no. 120; Zwierlein-Diehl 2013, pp. 249–250, no. 11.V.3.3). The type also evokes the cameo of '*Triton sur un dauphin: achat-onyx, 1 ½ p. 1 3/8 p.*' in the van Wassenaer-Opdam collection (lot 193 of the 1769 sale). Maritime scenes are also found on other gem-like drawings, such as an ink and wash drawing, 140 × 240 mm, depicting women and nereids '*d'après Perino del Vaga*' (former collection of Mr. S, sold by Millon, Paris, 12 March 2020, lot 15).

101   Property of the family, ill. in Palma Venetucci 1994, p. 21.
102   Ubaldelli 2001, p. 138.
103   Ubaldelli 2001, p. 133, n. 496.
104   Piranesi 1765, pl. V, the drawing of which has survived ('*Bought of Piranesi in Rome, March 1770 by Joseph Rose*'; later sold Christie's, London, 4 July 1989, lot 105, then in the collection of Ian

Johann Justin Preißler (1698–1771) was certainly one of the most talented artists who reproduced gems faithfully on his drawings, notably for Stosch, but also antiquarians Borioni and Venuti.[105] Some gem drawings of Gabriel de Saint-Aubin (1724–1780) circulated on the art market,[106] and Augustin de Saint-Aubin (1736–1807) was involved in the publication of the gem collection of the Duke of Orléans.[107] Johann Adam Schweickart (1722–1787) worked primarily as an engraver in the studio organised by Philipp von Stosch,[108] while Johann Henrich Wilhelm Tischbein's (1751–1829) *Odysseus and the Cyclops* and *Homer inspired by the Muses* are in fact engravings of two gems formerly in the Sir William Hamilton's collection.[109] Carl Markus Tuscher (1701–1751) was another artist working for Stosch,[110] but the study of drawings may sometimes lead to unexpected discoveries about glyptics, as it is in the case of Jan Wandelaar's (1690–1759) *Portrait of the Roman Dictator Sylla* inscribed '*Wandelaar. D'après une pierre gravée par Natter, de Sylla*', thus providing information about an otherwise undocumented gem carved by Lorenz Natter (Fig. 3.12).[111]

Jean-Baptiste Wicar (1762–1834) produced hundreds of gem drawings,[112] whereas Anton Maria Zanetti *the Elder* was a passionate collector and dealer of engraved gems and drawings (1680–1767).[113] Zanetti *il Vecchio* had met Stosch in Venice in 1717, who later commissioned him to draw two gems from North Italian collections; those drawings were then engraved for publication by Picart.[114] On 25 October 1740, from Venice, Zanetti offered to draw the gems in the Carlisle collection, according to a letter which he sent to Henry Howard, 4th Earl of Carlisle, probably in order to enter his good graces.[115] In 1750, Zanetti published a catalogue of his collection of intaglios and cameos, for which Gori provided the commentaries, but Zanetti himself drew all 80 plates.[116] Anton

---

Woodner in New York; Scarisbrick 1990). The potential source of Piranesi's inspiration was Gori and Zanetti 1750, pl. XXXIII, pl. XXXVII, pl. LXV and pl. LXVII.

105   See Chapter 4 in this volume.
106   The collection of Hippolyte Destailleur (1822–1893), sold at auction in Paris by Mᵉ Maurice Delestre, 26–27 May 1893, contained a drawing described as: '*L'Amour enchaîné par l'Amitié. Pierre gravée de Guay dessinée à la plume. Au bas de la main de l'artiste: Inventé par Mme de Pompadour et dessiné par Boucher. Gravé sur une sardoine par M. Guay et sur cuivre par M. Fessard, 1755*' (lot 66a), and two drawings described as: '*Hercule appuyé sur sa massue; 2 dessins de camées à la plume et au crayon*' (lots 75–76).
107   In the words of the Goncourt brothers: '*La Description des Pierres gravées du duc d'Orléans compte, à elle seule, plus de deux cents planches d'Augustin de Saint-Aubin. Les dessins de ces pierres gravées se trouvent actuellement à la bibliothèque Mazarine à laquelle ils ont été offerts par* MM. *Lachaud et Leblond*'. A watercolour vignette by Saint-Aubin, 142 × 133 mm, reproduced in Le Blond and La Chau 1780–1784, vol. I, p. 216, formerly in the collection of Alfred-Emmanuel-Louis Beurdeley (1847–1919), by whom sold to the State Hermitage Museum in St. Petersburg, was sold by C.G. Boerner in Leipzig on 4 May 1932, lot 119. Saint-Aubin owned a few intaglios and cameos (his estate sale, Paris 4–9 April 1809, lots 320–323), and coins (lots 324–330) as well, but no related drawings were included in his sale, despite the indication in the catalogue preface (p. VI) that the Orléans gems were not the only ones which he had engraved: '*Ce Maître a exécuté beaucoup de Vignettes et de Planches, d'après des Pierres gravées et des Médailles, dans lesquelles règnent la finesse, l'esprit et la pureté qui caractérisent ses ouvrages. Au nombre des Planches, d'après des Pierres gravées, on distingue celles du Cabinet d'Orléans; l'exécution de cette Suite lui fut confiée par* MM. *De la Chau et le Blond, il en fit les Dessins, d'après les Pierres gravées, et composa pour cet ouvrage, divers Culs-de-lampes et d'autres ornemens, productions marquées au coin du génie, et qui prouvent son érudition*'.
108   See Chapter 4 in this volume.
109   Jenkins and Sloan 1996, p. 104.
110   See Chapter 4 in this volume.
111   Edinburgh, The National Galleries of Scotland, inv. RSA 1349 (David Laing bequest), Jan Wandelaar (1690–1759), *Portrait of the Roman Dictator Sylla*, black chalk on paper, 310 × 250 mm.
112   These were the preliminary drawings for Wicar 1789–1807, on which see Savattieri 2007. They were sold at auction on 20 March 1800 by Louis François Jacques Boileau (commissaire-priseur) and François Léandre Regnault Delalande (expert), lots 1–66, the seller being apparently Etienne Lacombe (his publisher) or Philippe-Laurent de Joubert de Sommières et de Montredon (Lacombe's financial backer). Their buyer(s) has/have not been recorded.
113   See Lorenzetti 1917, Borroni 1956, Scarisbrick 1987, Scarisbrick 1990, Maggioni 1991, Bandinelli 1996, Sacconi 1996, Bettagno 2001, Bandinelli 2002, Toutain 2007, Magrini 2009, Piva 2012, Crosera 2013, Bortoluzzi 2014, Craievich 2018, Lucchese 2020, Favaretto 2021, Tassinari 2022. Many of the drawings he assembled are now at the Museo Correr in Venice, as noted by Hansson (2021b, p. 64, n. 33).
114   Stosch 1724, pls L and LIX, see Chapter 4 in this volume.
115   '*je me charge de en faire les desseins de tout les pieces, que vous m'envoyerez, et dessiner dans le totel goust de l'antique, sans aucun imaginable fraix; mais simplement pour vous temoigner la grande estime, et la veneration, que je vous ay concue*' (Scarisbrick 1987, p. 97).
116   Since before 1744 (he had started '*di disegnare, et fare intagliare la mia Raccolta di gemme*'; letter quoted in Bortoluzzi 2014, pp. 52 and 65 with conflicting dates), in preparation for his own gem catalogue (Gori and Zanetti 1750), which was published with Latin commentaries by Anton Francesco Gori, translated into Italian by Zanetti's own cousin. Zanetti drew himself each of the 80 plates, though it was erroneously indicated that '*Each of its 80 plates was engraved by the owner himself, from drawings by yet another of his relations, and his namesake, Antonio Maria Zanetti the Younger*' (Kagan 2006, p. 87), Zanetti himself wrote that '*io stesso di mia propria mano ho disegnato le* Gemme *tutte, con quanta diligenza per me si potè maggiore*' (introduction of Gori and Zanetti 1750), as confirmed by one of his contemporaries: '*il est actuellement occupé à les faire graver, sur les Desseins*

Maria Zanetti *the Younger* (1706–1778), was a son of the cousin of Anton Maria Zanetti *the Elder*. He was called Anton Maria Zanetti *il Giovane* and he was commissioned to draw the gems from the collection of Joseph Smith (ca. 1674–1770) in preparation of their publication by Anton Francesco Gori in 1767.[117]

5 Nineteenth Century

In the nineteenth century the number of artists drawing engraved gems dropped considerably, which was due to a significantly lower interest in glyptic art overall towards the end of the century. There are a number of anonymous drawings from this period, but some artists stand out too.[118] For example, Tommaso Benedetti (1797–1863) drew and engraved the gems from the collection of Joseph Barth (1745–1828) (described by Steinbüchel), now in the British Museum. Théodore Chassériau (1819–1856) drew a series of engraved gems and ancient coins,[119] and Jacques Louis David (1748–1825) certainly took inspiration from intaglios and cameos while composing some of his works, but he also executed about 1000 of drawings of various kinds of antiquities, including engraved gems.[120] His second pupil, François-Xavier Fabre (1766–1837), drew a good number of engraved gems; he was as much interested in Antiquity as his master (Figs 3.13–3.14).[121]

Franz Gareis (1775–1803) apparently produced a group of gem drawings in the final years of his life,[122] and so did Théodore Géricault (1791–1824).[123] Jean Auguste Dominique Ingres (1780–1867) drew a detail of an ancient cameo,[124] while Johann Georg Mansfeld (1772–1817) was commissioned by Jean-Baptiste Mallia (1756/1757–1812) to draw and engrave gems from his collection.[125] Gustave Moreau (1826–1898) is attested to have drawn several engraved gems,[126] and so is Jean-Baptiste Muret (1795–1866).[127] Michel Nitot *dit* Dufresne (1759–1828) was an unusual figure, who signed as 'Charles Dufresnes'.[128] He

---

       qu'il en a fait' (Mariette 1750, vol. I, p. 297). Those 80 drawings in pen and ink were auctioned in New York on 29 October 2013 by Christie's (collection of Arthur and Charlotte Vershbow, lot 763, acquired in 1980 from Colnaghi, previously with the dealer Hans M. Calmann 1899–1982). Christie's mentioned that they had also previously belonged to the collector Erasmus Phillips, but the dates of life of Sir Erasmus Phillips (1699–1743) do not seem compatible. Recently, the drawings were sold again in Paris at Giquello (The Sale of Alain Moatti Library, 22 March 2024, lot 61) with the same provenance information.

117 Vivian 1971, p. 89.

118 E.g. Edinburgh, The National Galleries of Scotland, inv. no.: RSA 1147 (David Laing bequest) – an anonymous nineteenth-century drawing depicting *Hebe feeding Jupiter's eagle* was made after an engraved gem.

119 Paris, Musée du Louvre, inv. no.: RF 26284r – *Intaille et monnaie*, brown ink, 158 × 110 mm.

120 On David and his interest in Antiquity, see also: Haskell 1993, pp. 394–400. See also Chapter 6 in this volume.

121 As noted in Chapter 6 in this volume, the Musée Fabre in Montepellier holds a series of drawings after engraved gems by Fabre, e.g. inv. nos 837.1.414, 837.1.431, 837.1.438, 837.1.443, 837.1.442, 837.1.450, 837.1.579, 837.1.581, 837.1.582, 837.1.584, 837.1.585, 837.1.587.

122 A group of 19 drawings in wash, ascribed on the basis of one of them being signed 'F. Gareis Paris' (and therefore supposedly dating from 1801–1803), '*Figürliche Studien, Gemmen, Sternkreiszeichen*' – Galerie Bassenge, auction 116, Berlin, 27 November 202, lot 6769, est. EUR 2000 and sold EUR 4674 incl. premium. I am grateful to the auction house for providing me with pictures of each individual sheet, but I am not convinced that the entire group was by the same hand. Gareis was a student of Giovanni Battista Casanova (whose gem collection is now at the State Hermitage Museum in St. Petersburg – Neverov 1976, p. 8).

123 Bonfait and Brugerolles 2019, pp. 104–106. His drawing of *Bacchanale/cortège de Silène*, ca. 1816–1817, 185 × 257 mm, pen, ink, wash and watercolour (Ecole nationale supérieure des Beaux-Arts, don His de la Salle 1867: EBA 953), which illustrates a jasper intaglio in Florence (Gori 1731–1732, vol. I, pl. 91.1; Raspe and Tassie 1791, p. 277, no. 4399; Krakow No. 989), is in fact copied from its 1789 engraving by Wicar.

124 Musée de Montauban, inv. no.: MI.867.289/20 F15 SV/893 – *Détail d'un camée*, black chalk on paper, 131 × 107 mm.

125 On this collector, and Köhler's manuscript *Catalogue of the Engraved Gems of J.B. Mallia* [Katalog reznym kamnyam Zh.B. Mallia] of 1813 (archive of the State Hermitage Museum, St. Petersburg – Fund I, *opis*' 6 'C', *delo* 18a), see Dmitrieva 2022b.

126 Paris, Musée Gustave Moreau, inv. no.: des. 6138 – *Camée avec Arion*, inv. no.: des. 8766 – *Scène antique d'après un camée*, inv. no.: des. 8788 – *Homme nu dans un camée antique* and inv. no.: des. 9275 – *Camée ovale*.

127 On '*Muret, dessinateur du Cabinet des Médailles*' – see Colonna and Haumesser 2019; Wall 2019 and https://digitalmuret.inha.fr/s/digital-muret/page/glyptique [retrieved on 5 August 2023].

128 '*Le point essentiel était d'obtenir des dessins finis, corrects, et surtout empreints de ce style pur, gracieux et soutenu qui distingue les belles médailles grecques. M. Nitot-Dufresne, dessinateur habile et versé dans l'étude des monuments antiques, ne m'a laissé rien à désirer de ce qui pouvait, sous le rapport des formes et du caractère, contribuer à la perfection de la gravure. Ses dessins de médailles, au jugement des connaisseurs, sont les plus précieux que l'on ait encore faits dans ce genre*' (Landon and du Mersan 1818, vol. I, p. XII). Nitot *a.k.a.* Dufresne engraved at least 8 plates of « *Pierres gravées, médailles, etc., à l'eau forte* » (Duchesne 1826, p. 164, no. 564, 2 francs), and – as noted in Ratouis de Limay 1949 – the Bibliothèque du Musée des Arts Décoratifs in Paris preserves notes and sketches by him (who was the author of the illustrations of the *Numismatique du jeune Anacharsis ou médailles des beaux temps de la Grèce/Essai sur la science des médailles* by Landon and du Mersan in 1823). Many of his works went on the

became an opera singer during the French Revolution.¹²⁹ An acquaintance of Fragonard, his manuscript notes and drawings are precious art historical documents,¹³⁰ and his illustrations of Homer after John Plaxman are esteemed, as well as his many engravings after Old Masters. Dominique Vivant Denon (1747–1825) owned 8 *eaux-fortes* of engraved gems and medals by him,¹³¹ which remain unidentified to this day.

Bartolomeo Pinelli (1781–1835) made some drawings of the famous Poniatowski gems,¹³² and Karl Friedrich Schinkel's (1781–1841) gem drawings can be now found in the Kupferstichkabinett in Berlin.¹³³ Even if one knows the artist, identifying the gem can remain a challenge, as in the case of an oval drawing depicting *A cherub (Love) giving his right hand to Venus who holds an arrow in hers*, signed by Léon Barraband and dated 1864, in blue paint and pencil.¹³⁴

6 The Issue (Problem) of Attribution

The long list of artists, collectors and scholars producing gem drawings over centuries makes one aware of the great scale of this phenomenon. At the same time, one realises how difficult it is to attribute drawings featuring various engraved gems to specific artists due to their usual documentary character. Most gem drawings have not yet been or cannot be attributed.¹³⁵ An example is an attractive sheet with pencil and ink drawings of eight gems,

---

market a few years ago: a lot of 20 drawings after the antique (Reims, Mᵉ Dapsens, 16 December 2007, lot 218); an album (340 × 265 mm) of 168 signed drawings after the antique (Paris, Piasa, 10 April 2008, lot 112); and an album of ca. 1270 studies of animals and after Old Masters (Paris, Mᵉ Millon and Mᵉ Cornette de Saint Cyr, 20 June 2009, lot 160). These are probably the source of the three oval drawings, 185 × 130 mm (*Venus and love*), 125 × 125 mm (*hero*) and 150 × 95 mm (*figure writing*), which were offered by Mᵉ Pillon on 7 April 2013 (Versailles, lot 28), again on 29 September 2013 (lot 28), on 8 December 2013 (lot 52), on 6 April 2014 (lot 26), and finally sold on 12 October 2014 (lot 6). In the same style, a group of five drawings after coins and gems, in pen, ink and wash, was acquired from Jean-Luc Cougnard in June 2008 by a private collector: one of them, ca. 147 × 137 mm, the copy of a Sicilian silver tetradrachm struck in Akragas (Agrigento) around 415 BC, was then acquired in August 2009 by Jonathan Kagan; three of the others have oval shapes that suggest copies of engraved gems (ca. 136 × 121 mm, ca. 126 mm wide and ca. 145 mm wide) – though the first one is in fact after a Paeonian silver tetradrachm struck in Audoleon around 315–286 BC (offered Mᵉ Millon – Mᵉ Cornette de Saint Cyr, Paris, 8 December 2009, lot 756); and the last one is rectangular, 128 mm wide. They came from the Parisian trade, and their earlier provenance was not revealed. Of very different style, and unsigned, an ink drawing (140 × 104 mm) of two naked ladies standing by a fountain annotated '*Camée*', which bears a scale, was offered for sale by Marta Bryl/Keramion Archeologie in March 2018 as the work of Nitot-Dufresne.

129 On him, see Renouvier and de Montaiglon 1863, pp. 152–153; Ratouis de Limay 1949. We are not aware of any link with the jewellers Marie-Etienne Nitot (1750–1809) and his son François-Régnault (1779–1853), who created the cameo-diadem of Empress Josephine in 1811.

130 Preserved at the Bibliothèque du Musée des Arts Décoratifs in Paris.

131 Catalogue of his estate, Paris 1826, p. 164, lot 564.

132 The only illustration of '*a group of seven mythological scenes, including, Perseus and Medusa, Hercules and the Cretan bull, and Hercules killing the giants Alcyoneus and Porphyrion*' (sold Sotheby's, London, 5 July 2013, lot 383), from the collection of Ralph Holland (1917–2012), was directly copied Giovanni Calandrelli's (1784–1853) *Perseus cutting off the head of Medusa*, which he carved for Prince Stanislas Poniatowski (1754–1833) in sardonyx with a pseudo-signature of Dioskourides (reference Christie's 1839 no. 1324, Tyrell collection no. 483; original drawing – Berlin, Antikensammlung inv. no.: Z.II.23). I am grateful to Greg Rubinstein (Sotheby's) for confirming by email '*that the attribution is partially based on the signed associated sheet [illustrating the Golden Ass of Apuleius, signed and dated Pinelli fece 1813 Roma], and also on general stylistic criteria*', and to Claudia Wagner (University of Oxford) that Pinelli's drawing seems to copy Calandrelli's actual gem rather than its preliminary drawing.

133 Paweł Gołyźniak kindly informed me of the presence of several drawings after gems, ca. 1825/30, at the Kupferstichkabinett in Berlin.

134 Sold by Corinne Noublanche (ArtGallery – Galerie2014) on eBay on 20 May 2019.

135 It is even the case of relatively recent drawings, such as the nineteenth-century '*carnet de 24 dessins d'intailles égyptiennes et grecques*' in the library of the Institut national d'histoire de l'art in Paris (inv. no.: MS 637).

A particular difficulty, when studying these drawings, is not just that it is difficult to recognise an artist's hand when he is constrained to faithfully depict an existing item, but also that cataloguers (especially commercial ones) do not hesitate to compensate their incompetence with self-assurance, therefore making ascriptions or commentaries meaningless. As an example, the Christie's catalogue of 12 December 2003 (lot 544), in which there were three drawings of gems by Picart from the Spencer-Churchill album (two of which – only? – depicting signed gems), indicates that these drawings had been '*engraved by the artist for P.J. Mariette's* Traité des Pierres gravées du Cabinet du Roi, *Paris, 1750*' which is obviously incorrect, and suggests a confusion between Picart and Bouchardon.

I must also mention here the intriguing description, in the ACR Auctions catalogue of their auction 13 (Rome, 30 October 2014, lot 45), of a copy of the gem Stosch 1724, pl. XVIII (Aulos's 20 × 9 mm carnelian intaglio from the Strozzi collection which is now in the British Museum), which was said to be a '*Head of Asklepios, 19th century, rock crystal, 26 × 24 × 7 mm, An high quality engraved rock crystal intaglio with a bust of Asklepios. Ion front of the head the name of the engraver. Traces of gold in the hair and beard. Stosch, Philipp Von (1691–1757) collection, Christie's sale*' (sic).

numbered and titled '*tabvla IV–tabvla VIII*', which have a common theme of winged cherubs.¹³⁶ Additionally, one must be cautious when ascribing unsigned drawings. As an example, Gabriella Tassinari has not been able to determine with certainty whether a group of 23 gem drawings of Udine were by Leopoldo Zuccolo (1760/1761–1833) or by his brother Santo Zuccolo.¹³⁷

Another example is a group of nineteen drawings¹³⁸ in black chalk, attributed to Joseph-Marie Vien (1716–1809), and hypothesised to have been drawn for Jeanne-Antoinette Poisson, duchesse de Pompadour (1721–1764) (Figs 3.15–3.16)?¹³⁹ Indeed, Pompadour did commission ca. 1753 a group of 63 drawings¹⁴⁰ from Edmé Bouchardon (1698–1762), François Boucher (1703–1770), Charles-Nicolas Cochin (1715–1790) and Joseph-Marie Vien,¹⁴¹ to commemorate the important events of her lover's reign – King Louis XV (1710–1715–1774).¹⁴² Might those drawings be Vien's works? Possibly, though there is no actual argument for it. What is certain instead, is that they are not the drawings commissioned by Pompadour, as they are not allegories but depict instead actual engraved gems along with their sizes. Should one rather consider that these might be preparatory drawings for the plates of Mariette 1750? The differences in style and proportions suggest not, as well as the presence of some gems that do not belong to Mariette 1750. Moreover, the differences between one of the drawings and the gem of *Apollo and a Muse* in Paris, is intriguing and remains unexplained. In any case, there seem to be no grounds to ascribe these to a specific artist.

Even in the case of drawings for which one knows the commissioner, such as the group of 216 drawings of objects in the collection of Francesco de'Ficoroni (1664–1747),¹⁴³ several unidentified artists were employed.¹⁴⁴ Researching the question of gem drawings is exceedingly difficult, full of obstacles which cannot always be overcome. As an example, Horace Walpole (1717–1797) owned '*one hundred and fifty beautiful Drawings, in folio, from coins, medals, bronzes, &c.*'¹⁴⁵ which, so imprecisely described, can obviously not be identified anymore. It may seem surprising that gifted artists would be willing to execute copy-drawings in such quantities, but that is in fact a reflection of the times. As an example, Pierre '*Rosenberg is completely convincing when he tries to list the merits and methods of a given painter, e.g. when he suggests the reasons for which David made more than a thousand drawings of antiquities in Italy*'.¹⁴⁶

This reference to Jacques-Louis David¹⁴⁷ is not simply in order to mention one of the most celebrated neoclassical artists, but because there is an ink drawing on tracing paper of a gem which belongs to a group¹⁴⁸ ascribed to

---

136 Grafische Sammlung Stern, 275 × 212 mm.
137 Tassinari 2007a; Tassinari 2007b.
138 Offered by Doutrebente Enchères, Paris, 12 December 2014, lot 16. Offered by EVE Enchères, Paris, 19 May 2015, lot 125. Offered by an unidentified auctioneer, 12 October 2015, lot 212. Offered by Fraysse Enchères, Paris, 31 May 2016, lot 242. Sold by EVE Enchères, Paris, 28 April 2017, lot 88, described as '[*Pompadour (Mme de)*] – *Vien (Joseph-Marie) Ensemble de cinq feuilles d'études de dix-neuf camées, avec sous chaque projet la forme ovale ou ronde de l'entaille. Graphite. Collé sur feuille (piqûres et rousseurs) Chaque feuille de support: H. 23.5 – L. 18 cm*' (expertise by Patrice Dubois).
139 Regarding Pompadour and her passion for glyptics, see: Avisseau-Broustet 2002.
140 In the following few years, Jacques Gay (1711–1797) carved those drawings into hardstones, and Pompadour herself etched those into the *Suite d'estampes gravées par madame la marquise de Pompadour d'après les pierres gravées de Guay, graveur du Roi* (s.l. s.d.) – Chabouillet 1858, p. 344.
141 Vien's (lost) drawings depicted: *La Chambre de Justice en 1716* (Gaehtgens and Lugand 1998, no. 446b), *Le Triomphe de Fontenoy en 1745* (Gaehtgens and Lugand 1998, p. 270, no. 430; illustrated on the title page of Mariette 1750), *La Victoire de Lawfeld en 1747* (Gaehtgens and Lugand 1998, no. 434a), *Les Préliminaires de la Paix de 1748* (Gaehtgens and Lugand 1998, no. 431), *L'action de grâces pour le rétablissement de la santé du Dauphin en 1752* (Gaehtgens and Lugand 1998, no. 432), *Le Génie de la Poésie* (Gaehtgens and Lugand 1998, no. 435), *Minerve* (Gaehtgens and Lugand 1998, no. 434), *L'enlèvement de Déjanire* (Gaehtgens and Lugand 1998, no. 436), *Une tête de femme à l'Antique* (Gaehtgens and Lugand 1998, no. 445), *Une tête de satyre* (Gaehtgens and Lugand 1998, no. 446), seven *Têtes d'hommes* (Gaehtgens and Lugand 1998, nos 438–444), *Le Portrait d'un prélat* (Gaehtgens and Lugand 1998, no. 437), *Une tête d'évêque* (Gaehtgens and Lugand 1998, no. 446a), *L'adoration des Anges* (Gaehtgens and Lugand 1998, no. 446d), and a series of *Vases dans le goût de l'Antique* (Gaehtgens and Lugand 1998, no. 446d).
142 Gaehtgens and Lugand 1998, p. 270, nos 430–446.

143 On Ficoroni, see: Lavia 2004; Griggs 2008; Griggs 2009; Ridley 2017.
144 Mounted in one album (The J. Paul Getty Trust, accession no. 2014.M.3). From the collection of the Honorable Edward Bouveries and descendants, and thereafter in the collection of Charlotte and Arthur Vershbow (sold Christie's, London, Important old master drawings auction, 10 April 1985, lot 68A).
145 1842 auction catalogue, p. 56, lot 12, sold £2/8/0.
146 '*Quando Rosenberg si prova ad elencare I meriti e I metodi di un dato pittore è del tutto convincente: quando ad esempio suggerisce i motivi per i quali **David** esegui più di mille disegni in Italia ordinandoli scrupolosamente come un dizionario dell'antichità*' (Gonzalez-Palacios 2014, p. 249).
147 Coggins 1968, no. 8; Mongan 1975 figs 204–209; Prat 2011, p. 17; Rosenberg and Prat 2002, nos 452–482; Sérullaz 1991; Simonet-Lenglart 1979; Wolohojian 2003, p. 29, cat. no. 16; Stein 2022.
148 Sold by Mᵉ Loudmer, Paris, Hôtel Drouot, 17 December 1973, in a lot; acquired by Mr S.; sold by Mᵉ Millon, Paris, Hôtel Drouot, 12 mars 2020, lot 134: '*Ecole de Jacques Louis David (Paris 1748 – Bruxelles 1825). Quatre vignettes sur le même montage études*

the circle of David. The gem depicted is a typical combination (*gryllos*¹⁴⁹): the protome of a boar to the left, conjoined with a female mask facing right (Fig. 3.17).¹⁵⁰ The ascription of this drawing comes from the presence amongst this group of the drawing of a *Roman cippus*,¹⁵¹ inscribed DIS MANIB | OCTAVIAE | DE CASARI | UXORI [to the eternal shades | Octavia | Caesar's | wife], which is almost identical to David's *Copy of a Roman Cippus* from 'the Roman Album' which is now in Harvard (Fig. 3.18).¹⁵²

A similar *cippus*, but with a different inscription is said to have existed,¹⁵³ and a different *cippus* (surmounted by a crater with cover) with the same description was also drawn by David.¹⁵⁴ This *cippus* (not directly relevant to the question of gems) is now lost, but what matters is that the album in Harvard is one of the '*twelve that preserved David's drawings from his student period at the French Academy in Rome, illustrate classical sculpture from the Capitoline Museums, Villa Negroni, Villa Medici, and Giustiniani collection*',¹⁵⁵ and that David – when invited to dinner at *Villa Madama*, is known to have sketched a funerary *cippus*. Considering that the gem drawing is also likely copied from David (unless by himself?),¹⁵⁶ it also suggests that it is a drawing made directly after an actual artefact which was visible in Rome around 1776–1780. Last but not least, some of David's drawings of gems are now in Paris in the Musée du Louvre (Fig. 3.19).¹⁵⁷

Finally, one last group of drawings. Vittorio Luigi Modesto Ignazio Bonaventura Genevosio (1719–1795) was an important collector of engraved gems.¹⁵⁸ Thanks to an 8 × 8 mm ink-stamp,¹⁵⁹ we know that he was also

---

d'après l'Antique? Plume et encore noire sur papier calque. 65 × 50 cm. Doublées, annotées et numérotées.

The post-mortem auction of 1826 contained '*douze grands livres de croquis composés d'études d'après l'antique*', which remained in the family and were sold – separately this time – on 11 March 1835. Michel, Sérullaz and Sandt (1981–1982) noted that the album #1 is at the Harvard Arts Museum/Fogg Art Museum, the album #3 is in the Stockholm Nationalmuseum, that the albums #7 and #9 are in the Louvre, and that the other albums were undoubtedly split and were the source of the various drawings after the antique that regularly appear on the market.

An album of 587 drawings, authenticated in June 1949 by André Schoeller to be genuine works by David (but the authenticity of these drawings on tracing-paper has been doubted in Michel, Sérullaz and Sandt 1981–1982, p. 69, note 46), was dispersed: 289 of them were included in the copies of the book Adhémar 1953. The fate of the other drawings is unknown. Jean Adhémar mentioned in his preface the number of *cippi* amongst them, though his book illustrates very few: these four drawings mentioned here below are not amongst those illustrated, but fit their styles and subject. According to Adhémar, '*un texte de 1826, postérieur à la vente, affirme que "la famille de David conserve encore plusieurs cahiers de croquis et de dessins très importants". Puis ils ont disparu; ils ont reparu assez récemment, et ils ont fait aussitôt sensation. M. Claude Roger-Marx les a vus alors dans une exposition à la Galerie Schneider*' (but these were likely the same 12 albums which the family had bought back at the sale).

149 The gryllos, γρῦλλος or *gryllus*, '*image of human madness*' according to the philosopher Michel Foucault (Foucault 1971, p. 20), is a fanciful combination of human, animal and vegetable elements. Most of the depictions of grylloi were double-sided creatures, part man, part animal (or bird). According to Pliny and Quintilian, the Alexandrian painter Antiphilus in the 4th century BC had painted such pictures. Plutarch indicated that they were worn '*for their supposed efficacy in averting the evil eye*' (Plutarch, *Questiones convivialis*, V, 6, 681 sqq.). For a scholarly study of the type on engraved gems, see: Lapatin 2011.

150 The sheet is numbered '*463*'. The gem depicted on the drawing might be a green chalcedony or praser intaglio once in the Riccardi collection, published by Gori (1731–1732, vol. I, pl. LI.7).

151 Pen and ink on tracing paper, annotated '*villa negroni*' and the sheet is numbered '*7*'.

152 Harvard Art Museums/Fogg Museum, inv. no.: 1943.1815.19.8.A, black crayon on cream laid paper, mounted on cream laid paper. 180 × 150 mm, inscribed by David in black crayon, lower left: '*a la villa negroni*', paraphs of Eugène and Jules David (L. 839; L. 1437) in brown ink at lower centre and right. Provenance (the album): David sale, A.N. Pérignon, Paris, April 17, 1826, and following days, part of no. 66 (withdrawn); second David sale,

Hôtel des Ventes, Paris, March 11, 1835, part of no. 16; acquired by '*baron J. (Jules?) David*'; Henri, vicomte de Béranger; acquired from him through Martin Birnbaum by Grenville L. Winthrop, January 1936 (FFr 30 000); his bequest to the Fogg Art Museum, 1943. Published: Mongan 1996, pp. 42–43.

153 Montfaucon 1719–1724, vol. V, pl. XXVIII.

154 Florisoone 1948, p. 108–109, n. 89. This funerary urn is a detail of a larger scene, *Caracalla killing his brother in front of their mother*, ca. 1782 (ink and wash, 242 × 305 mm). It belonged to the Wildenstein gallery at the time of the exhibition.

155 Lyons 2003, p. 502.

156 A possible copyist is David's student, Elie Honoré Montagny (1782–1864).

157 Paris, Musée du Louvre, inv. no.: 26139.bis recto – *Femme jouant de la lyre d'après un camée antique*, black chalk on paper, 211 × 144 mm and inv. no.: 26149.bis recto – *Guerrier tenant une lance* (after a cameo of Mars), black chalk on paper, 107 × 150 mm.

158 And I hope to publish an article on his belongings in the future.

159 Lugt 1921, no. 545. Two variants of the stamp exist, the crown being with five or six pearls, and Lugt wondered if the collector may have been a count (the stamp depicts a 5-pearl crown) but noticed that counts in Piedmont wore a 9-pearl crown. In 1956, he rightly hypothesised that he may in fact have been a commander rather than a count. It is only in 1994 that Aidan Weston-Lewis published that this collector should be identified with Genevosio. Lugt online (2011): '*L'identification de la marque, qui a longtemps posé un problème, avait pourtant été donnée dès 1803, comme en témoigne une note de Morel d'Arleux, conservateur du Cabinet des dessins, dans son inventaire manuscrit des dessins du Louvre où, à côté de la description d'un dessin pour une façade de maison (Perino del Vaga, MA 573; inv. 602), son croquis de la marque est accompagné de la mention « com. genevoso de turin »; la même identification est à nouveau donnée à la fin de*

the (proud) owner of a group of 22 drawings of gems,[160] mounted together on 5 sheets (seemingly for Genevosio himself) (Figs 3.20–3.24).[161] As usual when facing unpublished drawings, some basic questions arise: who drew them (this group is coherent and all can be ascribed to a single hand), when, for whom, and what do they depict? None of the gems depicted match the descriptions of Genevosio's gems, which is coherent with the fact that the draughtsman was active in the sixteenth century (according to the auction house's expert), so it would be interesting to know where and when Genevosio acquired these drawings.[162] The gems depicted are rather remarkable, which simplifies their identification – cameos from the collection of Cardinal Domenico Grimani (1461–1523).[163]

And those are well-known for art historians because of the three plates by Enea Vico (1523–1567) after drawings by Battista Franco (bef. 1510–1561).[164] It would be simple to relegate those drawings into oblivion by describing them as later – anonymous – copies of the original drawings. But it has been already noticed that Franco himself, or his circle, were probably copying his drawings: '[Battista] *Franco may have drawn both series in Rome – the gems and the animals – and then, having moved to the court of Urbino, could have taken his Roman drawings with him. It is quite likely that copies of his drawings circulated, perhaps made by Franco himself, perhaps by other copyists or draftsmen, and that these copies were acquired by Lafréry*'.[165] So are we even sure that the Genevosio drawings would be the copies rather than the originals? Some of them depict gems that are not found on those etchings[166] – does this suggest that these drawings are the original ones, some of which only were then engraved?[167] This volume is not the place to answer such questions, but it illustrates well the importance of building a corpus of all known drawings of engraved gems, in the hope to identify their respective authors, but also in order to gain information on the past owners of gems and their collecting history.

---

    la notice (Musée du Louvre, Département des Arts graphiques, Minutes, t. 1, fol. 89–90, n° 31)'.

160 Audap & Mirabaud (auctioneers), de Bayser (experts), auction, Paris – Hôtel Drouot, 27 March 2015, lot no. 1, described as '*Ecole italienne du XVI*ᵉ *siècle. Copies d'après des antiques et des intailles. Ensemble de vingt-deux dessins à l'encre brune répartis sur cinq planches. Cachet de collection en bas à droite du Comte de Gelosi. Planche: Haut.: 39,5 cm; Larg.: 26 cm.*'.

161 According to Lugt online (2011), '*Les dessins (de la collection de Genevosio) sont montés sur papier (ou carton), entouré de plusieurs filets d'encadrement à la plume et encre noire, une bande de papier doré et une ou plusieurs bandes coloriées de lavis vert clair, séparées par les filets blancs du papier*', but this does not actually seem to be the case of all Genevosio drawings. For example, the mount of the drawing attributed to Antonio Vassilacchi (1556–1629) of *Two allegorical figures flanking the lion of St Mark on a pedestal* (London, the British Museum, inv. no.: 1946,0713.584) does not bear gilt paper, nor green wash, but instead three lines brown-ink of varying thickness like those gem drawings (which are mounted on 5 sheets, seemingly according to visual effect).

162 Genevosio is attested to have acquired drawings in the 1741 auction of Pierre Crozat, and in the 1775–1776 auctions of Pierre-Jean Mariette, both of whom were famed gem collectors, likely candidates to have owned such drawings. Mariette owned Bouchardon's '*Le Cachet de M. Ange: Sujet très-connu & fait à la sanguine, d'un précieux fini*' (lot 1125 sold to Jean-Denis Lempereur for 780 livres), and Bouchardon's '*194 Dessins très-finis, d'après les pierres gravées du Cabinet du Roi*' (lot 1147 sold to Alexandre-Joseph Paillet for 2812 livres), but I could not identify those 22 drawings in his estate sale, nor in Crozat's. Clearly, identifying individual unsigned drawings in antiquarian catalogues is always challenging: the lot 236, for example, containing '*Quarante feuilles de différentes Etudes de compositions, Tombeaux, Figures & Têtes, faites à la plume & au bistre*' by Michelangelo, without any additional information on the subjects, material or sizes.

163 On whom see: Ferrara and Bergamo-Rossi 2019 (*non vidi*).

164 Franco etched 42 subjects (Bartsch 1818, p. 146, nos 81–93) and Vico etched 33 of these, in reverse (Bartsch 1813, p. 318, nos 101–133).

165 '*Pertanto si individuano due serie grafiche, incentrate sul medesimo soggetto archeologico, realizzate in due contesti editoriali e con due cronologie diverse. … Il [Battista] Franco potrebbe aver disegnato a Roma le due serie – le gemme e gli animali – e poi, passato alla corte urbinate, avrebbe portato con sé i suoi disegni romani. E legittimo supporre che circolassero alcune copie dei suoi disegni, forse di mano dello stesso Franco, forse di altri copisti o disegnatori, e che poi tali copie sarebbero entrate in possesso di Lafréry e utilizzate per le Speculum. Questo caso delle raffigurazioni di animali fornisce quindi un modello di produzione, un canovaccio, che potrebbe essere stato seguito in più casi*' (La Monica 2014, p. 808).

166 Two at least of the drawings cannot be found on the plates.

167 In which case, at least 17 drawings from this group would be lost, as only 20 of the 22 rediscovered drawings are among the 37 gems engraved and published by Franco.

    And actually, who chose which of the Grimani gems were to be drawn by Franco? What was his criteria, and/or aim? For example, the gems drawn do not include any portrait, even though the Grimani collection did include some (e.g. the Livia bust = Neverov 2002, no. 25), not even heads of Medusa or Herakles. The plates do not include either any animal on its own, any inscription, or any fragment.

PLATE 8

FIGURE 3.1

FIGURE 3.2

FIGURE 3.3

FIGURE 3.4

FIGURE 3.5

FIGURE 3.6

FIGURE 3.7

FIGURE 3.8

FIGURE 3.9

FIGURE 3.10

PLATE 11

FIGURE 3.11

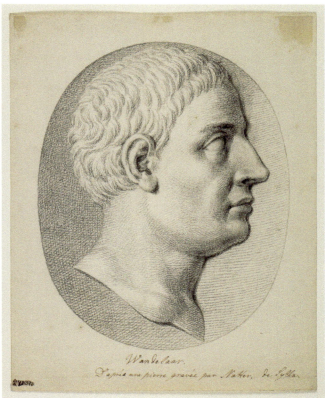

FIGURE 3.12

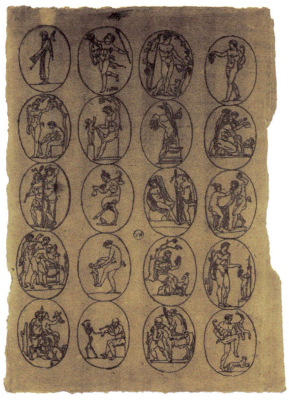

FIGURE 3.13

FIGURE 3.14

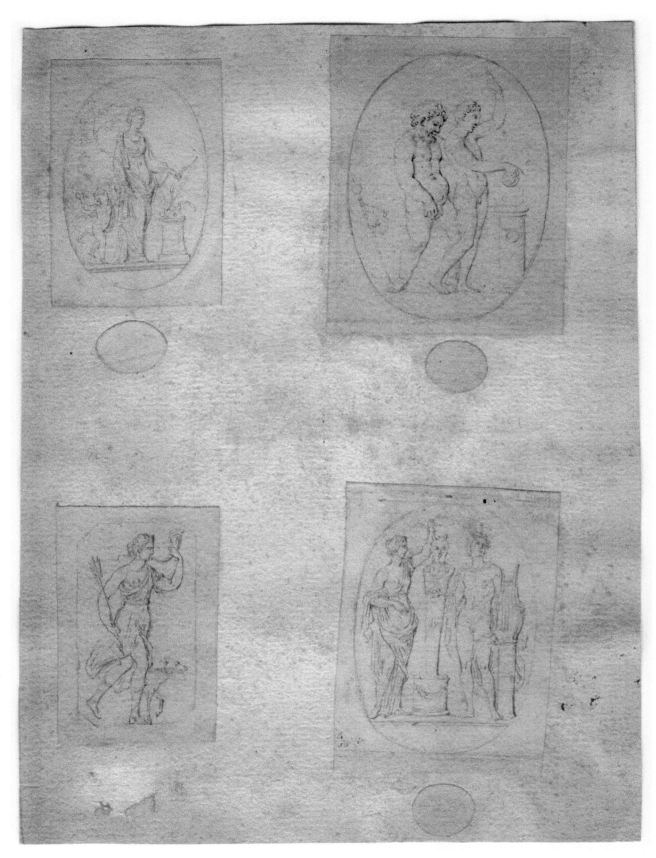

FIGURE 3.15

PLATE 13

FIGURE 3.16

FIGURE 3.17

FIGURE 3.18

FIGURE 3.19

PLATE 15 61

FIGURE 3.20

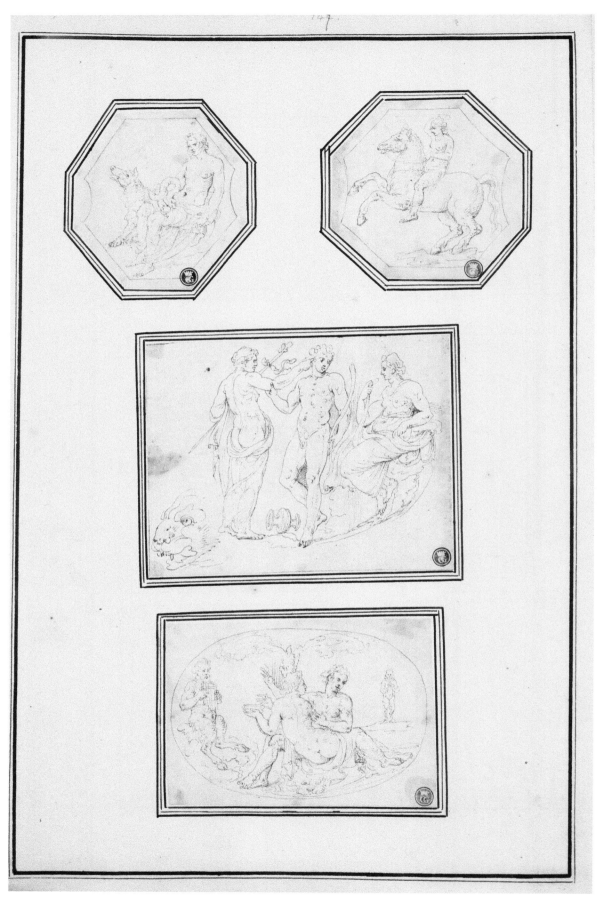

FIGURE 3.21

PLATE 17

FIGURE 3.22

FIGURE 3.23

PLATE 19

FIGURE 3.24

CHAPTER 4

Stosch and the Circle of His Draughtsmen of Gems

Paweł Gołyźniak and Hadrien J. Rambach

1   The Circle of Stosch's Draughtsmen of Gems

In the course of the eighteenth century, drawing engraved gems became one of the most popular forms of their documentation, reproduction and illustration, apart from making casts and impressions in sulphur, plaster and other materials (cf. Chapter 3).¹ Philipp von Stosch was one of the pioneers and leaders in that matter because during his lifetime he established a number of useful contacts with various artists who documented gems for him and they collaborated on his scholarly projects preparing illustrations. In a letter from 1722 to Lord Carteret, Stosch wrote that he had earned a good reputation in Rome by having trained young artists in the difficult art of making accurate visual documentation of ancient engraved gems and other antiquities.² He is said to have judged his draughtsmen mainly according to the extent to which they succeeded in reproducing gems.³ It was suggested that Stosch had all his gems drawn by artists like Johann Justin Preißler, Markus Tuscher, Georg Abraham Nagel and Johann Adam Schweickart who all lived in his house in Rome and later in Florence over different periods of time.⁴ His list is incomplete though. For example, it is known that Stosch conducted his own excavations in 1727 in Villa Casali on the Caelian Hill, but he also would send Pier Leone Ghezzi and often Girolamo Odam to various sites inside and outside Rome in order to get information on new findings, purchase newly discovered engraved gems and other antiquities as well as to draw ruins and archaeological artifacts, which he later studied at home.⁵ Ghezzi and Odam, but also a few more artists, contributed to the illustrations of gems published in Stosch's book *Gemmae antiquae caelatae* too. This chapter is designed to be a gallery of artists who drew intaglios and cameos for Stosch and collaborated on his documentary and scholarly projects.⁶

It has been long disputed whether the drawing by Pier Leone Ghezzi in the Albertina (cf. book cover and fig. 4.1),⁷ of which another version is in the British Museum

---

1   Hansson 2021b, pp. 61–62. On the production of the so-called *dactyliothecae*, see: Kockel and Graepler (eds) 2006; Knüppel 2009.
2   Letter from Walton [Stosch] to Lord Carteret, dated 28 February 1722 (NA Kew SP 85/14 f. 9–12).
3   Zazoff and Zazoff 1983, p. 55; Hansson 2021b, pp. 61–62.
4   Stosch 1754, p. 50.
5   Ridley 2017, 85; Hansson 2021a, p. 116.
6   The list of the most important, but probably not all, draughtsmen working on gem illustrations for Philipp von Stosch is also briefly outlined in: Zazoff and Zazoff 1983, pp. 54–57. On this matter, see also: Eggers 1926, pp. 223–225, 229–230 and 232–233. Naturally, apart from the draughtsmen listed in this chapter, Stosch collaborated with some other artists, who might have drawn gems for him, however, no solid proof that they did so survives. It has been suggested that Edmé Bouchardon (1698–1762), a friend of Pier Leone Ghezzi, drew ancient engraved gems and other antiquities for Stosch (Kopp 2017, pp. 58–59). However, this seems to be a far-fetched hypothesis and a better example is that of Gaetano Piccini, an Italian artist active in Rome ca. 1702–1740. He worked as a draughtsman and illustrator for various collectors including Philipp von Stosch. He certainly contributed to his *Atlas* project. According to Stosch's letter to Paolo Maria Paciaudi dated Florence, 28 October 1755: '(…) *mi ricordo molto bene del disegnio che anni sono le feci vedere nel mio Atlante della pittura antica che fu scoperta l'anno 1724 negl' orti farnesiani, e che io feci disegnare sott' i miei occhi co' colori dell' originale da Gaetano Piccini coll' assistenza del cav. Girolamo Odam con ogni possibile diligenza*' ['I remember very well the drawing which years ago I showed her in my Atlas of an ancient painting which was discovered in the year 1724 in the Farnese Gardens, and which I had Gaetano Piccini drawn in front of my eyes in the original colours in assistance of the Cav. Girolamo Odam with every possible diligence']; (Justi 1871, pp. 28–29, no. XIV). Although it is not proven that Piccini drew engraved gems for Stosch, he did some for another notable gem collector Alessandro Gregorio Capponi (Ubaldelli 2001, pl. 2, nos 26 and 32). Piccini was introduced to Capponi by Pier Leone Ghezzi in 1728/1729 and he also worked for Francesco de'Ficoroni (Ubaldelli 2001, pp. 133–134 (esp. n. 496) and 138). According to Justi, Piccini specialised in etching of ancient coins as well and together with Ridolfino Venuti he elaborated collection of coins belonging to Cardinal Alessandro Albani (Justi 1871, p. 29; on this matter, see also: Ubaldelli 2001, p. 133, note 496). All of this suggests that he belonged to the circle of draughtsmen working for Stosch, although he was probably not involved in documentation of gems. It appears that in his collaboration with various artists Stosch was much in the footsteps of Cassiano dal Pozzo (1588–1657), who employed half a dozen of artists too to document antiquities for his *Paper Museum*, see: Heskell and Penny 1981, p. 43, and on the connection between Pozzo and Stosch, cf. Chapters 8 and 11 in this volume.
7   The Albertina Museum, inv. no.: 1266, pen and brown ink, 270 × 353 mm (described as: '*Baron Stosch, im Lehnstuhl sitzend und mit Ghezzi im Hintergrund, im Gespräch*').

(fig. 4.2),[8] depicts Stosch or Francesco de'Ficoroni giving a lesson on engraved gems and coins to some young gentlemen.[9] While the discussion focuses on the main figure seated in the chair and raising his hand and comparison of its head profile to the caricatures of both Stosch[10] and Ficoroni[11] by Ghezzi, one should also took into account the context of the presented scene and potential identities of other figures. The drawings are generally agreed to be dated to 1720s, which is the time when Stosch was in Rome surrounded by a few young artists including Ghezzi, Girolamo Odam, Johan Justin Pireßler (since 1726), Markus Tuscher (since 1728) as well as his brother Heinrich Sigismund Stosch (since 1727) and Christian Dehn (cf. discussion below). Assuming the key figure is Stosch, one proposes the following. Odam is absent as on the drawing of the gathering of antiquarians in Stosch's house by Ghezzi in the Biblioteca Apostolica Vaticana from 1728 (cf. chapter 2, fig. 2.5). This is probably because he was replaced in documentation of gems for Stosch by Preißler and Tuscher, so our drawings would date ca. after 1726 and before 1731 when Stosch exiled to Florence. The figure behind the chair is Ghezzi based on a comparison to his two self-portraits in Hamburg[12] and Stockholm.[13] The figure leaned against the table might be Tuscher (cf. fig. 4.18 below). The young, prominent man in the middle could be Preißler (cf. fig. 4.8 below) or an unidentified collector or buyer of gems whose portrait Ghezzi drew separately too.[14] The man in the background, on the left, examining gems or coins, remains a mystery (Stosch's brother or Dehn?). There is by no means certainty but the discussed drawings from London and Vienna could illustrate well Stosch and his studio where artists not just documented gems for him as drawings but were also educated by him, as contemporary sources suggest.

2 Pier Leone Ghezzi (1674–1755)

In the preface to *Gemmae antiquae caelatae* book, Stosch informs that Ghezzi was his artistic advisor to the project, at least in the beginning (Fig. 4.3).[15] In a letter to François Fagel dated 5 October 1715, Stosch calls Ghezzi: *'the foremost draughtsman in Italy'*.[16] Even though it is said that Ghezzi did not draw any plate in Stosch's book,[17] the research presented in Chapter 8 suggests otherwise. What is more, Ghezzi is attested to have drawn various kinds of antiquities from Stosch's collection.[18] Ghezzi's help in the book's creation must have been considerable since Stosch acknowledged him. Even though Ghezzi did not draw many gems for his book, he certainly helped Stosch a great deal during the process of preparation of illustrations and it is of crucial importance that all three: Stosch, Ghezzi and Odam, who contributed the most (cf. below), were close friends and connoisseurs of intaglios and cameos.[19] Micheli is certainly right in claiming that, apart from Fagel, Odam and Prince Antonio Farnese, Ghezzi

---

8   The British Museum, inv. no.: 1859,0806.93, pen and brown ink, 369 × 487mm.
9   Zazoff and Zazoff 1983, p. 17 (Ficoroni); Birke and Kertész 1994, no. 689 (Stosch); Spier and Kagan 2000, pp. 41–42 (Ficoroni); Ridley 2017, pp. 38–40 (Stosch). I am grateful to Isabella Chapman, the author of the entry on the version in the British Museum (https://www.britishmuseum.org/collection/object/P_1859-0806-93 – retrieved on 22 September 2024), who believes the main figure to be Ficoroni rather than Stosch, for a fruitful discussion on this and the Albertina drawing and directing my attention to the self-portraits of Ghezzi in Hamburg and Stockholm.
10 BAV, Cod. Ott. lat. 3112, fol. 131.
11 BAV, Cod. Ott. lat. 3113, fols 142 and 156.
12 The Hamburger Kunsthalle, Kupferstichkabinett, inv. no.: 21219, red chalk, 500 × 348 mm (sheet).
13 The Nationalmuseum Stockholm, inv. no.: NMH 654/1863, red chalk, 385 × 240 mm.
14 The Morgan Library Museum, inv. no.: 1978.28, pen and brown ink over black chalk, 190 × 130 mm.

15 Stosch 1724, p. V: *'J'ai aussi été beaucoup aide dans l'exécution de mon dessein par la presence & les conseils de M. le Chevalier Pierre Leon Ghezzi, Gentilhomme Romain, très-excellent Peintre.'*
16 Letter from Stosch to François Fagel, dated 5 October 1715 – NA The Hague inv. 2028, fol. 67, see: Hansson 2022, p. 58.
17 Justi 1871, p. 29 (but his statement is rather ambiguous); Reinach 1895, p. 156; Heringa 1976, pp. 77 and 79; Whiteley 1999, p. 183.
18 The lost Ms. Lanciani 104 at the Biblioteca di Archeologia e Storia dell'Arte in Rome, which was stolen in February 1989, included drawings by Ghezzi of a marble vase (fol. 29), a Parian marble head of Venus (fol. 43) and a terracotta sphinx (fol. 44) from Stosch's collection, see: https://manus.iccu.sbn.it/risultati-ricerca-manoscritti/-/manus-search/cnmd/86979? [retrieved on 13 September 2022]. The collection of Ghezzi's gem drawings now in the Biblioteca Apostolica Vaticana (Cod. Ott. lat. 3100–3101, 3103–3104 and 3106–3109) includes dozens of those reproducing Stosch's gems, which were made by Ghezzi for his own corpus rather than on Stosch's commission, see: Gołyźniak (Ghezzi – forthcoming). It also contains (3109, fol. 113) a drawing which depicts a *'Fragmento di marmo antico che si ritrova in casa del Signor Baron Stosch, il quale rappresenta Diogene dentro la tina con il cane simbolo dei filosofi cinici, vicino alla muraglia di Anete (sic.) Era alto palmi due e oncie 8 e largo palmi due e 3 oncie e lo ritrovò a Testaccio il di 8 maggio 1726 quando andava a bere e lo pagò scudo uno'* (this marble, with restorations and additions depicting Alexander, is now at Villa Albani, inv. no.: 161: see Jason M. Kelly's 19 November 2015 blog-entry on https://jasonmkelly.com/jason-m-kelly/2015/11/19/stosch-ghezzi-and-an-eighteenth-century-sculpture-restoration [retrieved on 8 August 2023]).
19 Justi 1871, p. 29; Heringa 1976, p. 77; Whiteley 1999, p. 183.

was one of the most influential people who encouraged Stosch to write his book on gems signed by ancient masters.[20] This is also confirmed by Ghezzi's diary notes, where he writes that just a day before Stosch exiled from Rome (15 February 1731) he gifted Ghezzi a terracotta and a plaster form of his own bust sculpted by Bouchardon in the presence of several close friends, including Odam.[21] Even though today a bit underestimated,[22] and known mainly from his outstanding caricatures illustrating *il mondo nuovo* (ca. 3000 surviving sheets and he is believed by some to be the inventor of that *genre*),[23] Pier Leone Ghezzi enjoyed a brilliant career and was one of the most talented and colourful Italian artists of the first half of the eighteenth century.[24]

He was trained, first, by his father Giuseppe Ghezzi (1643–1721), also a painter, and later by Carlo Maratta (1625–1713) and had established his reputation as an important portraitist by 1710.[25] He also received numerous commissions for altarpieces and wall decorations. Ghezzi served as court painter to the pope from 1708 to 1747, succeeding Giuseppe Passeri as painter of the apostolic chamber in 1714. He was one of the artists who worked on important projects of the nave paintings in San Clemente and St. John Lateran basilicas.[26] Ghezzi was knighted by Pope Clement XI (he belonged to the Order of Christ), and he also held a secretarial position at the Accademia di San Luca. He executed many official commissions for the Albani family of Clement XI, for the French Ambassador Cardinal Polignac (1661–1742) and for Cardinal Alessandro Falconieri (1657–1734), among others.[27] Throughout the 1740s, he continued to work for succeeding Popes Benedict XIII and Clement XII, under whose patronage he made not only religious paintings but he also produced a cycle of wall paintings in tempera for the gallery at Castelgandolfo in 1747.[28] He was multitalented; he also played several instruments and had a general interest in music.[29] Moreover, he studied medicine and anatomy and was an active painting and sculpture restorer.[30] He was even capable of engraving gems, and Justi says that he was a pupil of Flavio Sirleti in this art; however, his activity was probably never on a large scale.[31] Ghezzi notifies us about the serious problem of fake gem circulation, especially in Rome at Piazza Navona, although he claims to have not been involved in it.[32]

Ghezzi was also very much engaged in the study of archaeology. His passion towards Antiquity was born quite early, already during his education under the wing of his father.[33] It is said that Cardinal Falconieri strongly encouraged Ghezzi to develop his interest in antiquities and Antiquity.[34] As a result, Ghezzi participated in or visited excavation sites in Rome and its surroundings on a regular basis already in the 1720s, but he was particularly active in this matter from 1737 to 1744.[35] Regular visits to excavation

---

20 Micheli 1986, p. 41.
21 Dorati da Empoli 2008, pp. 68–69.
22 This is slowly changing, as the recent studies by Maria Christina Dorati da Empoli explore unknown archives and correspondence of Ghezzi, see: Dorati da Empoli 2008 and 2017.
23 Cazort and Percy 2004, no. 43. A part of his huge production of caricatures has been published, see: Rostirolla 2001. See also: Bodart 1976; Dorati da Empoli 2008, pp. 25–28 and 169–326; Dorati da Empoli 2009 and especially Dania (ed.) 2015, pp. 177–190 for a general discussion on them with a list of institutions holding major groups of Ghezzi's caricatures.
24 Hiesinger and Percy 1980, p. 23, no. 12. On Pier Leone Ghezzi and his career, see: Guerrini 1971; Bodart 1976; Lo Bianco 1985; Martinelli (ed.) 1990; Kieven 1991; Gallo 1999, p. 834; Lo Bianco (ed.) 1999; Loisel Legrand 1999; Lo Bianco 2010; Prosperi Valenti Rodinò 2014; Witte 2018.
25 Clark 1963; Cazort and Percy 2004, no. 43.
26 Cazort and Percy 2004, no. 43.
27 Olszewski 1983, p. 328; Lauterbach 1991; Cazort and Percy 2004, no. 43; Dorati da Empoli 2008, pp. 14–15; Coen and Fidanza (eds) 2011, pp. 41–42.
28 Cazort and Percy 2004 no. 43.
29 On Ghezzi as a portraitist, see: Clark 1963. On Ghezzi and his interest in music, see: Rostirolla 2010.
30 Hiesigner and Percy 1980, p. 23, no. 12; Giometti 2012, pp. 221–222.
31 Justi 1872, p. 334. On this matter, see also: Reinach 1895, p. 156; Bodart 1976, p. 13; Gasparri 1977, p. 27; Borroni Salvadori 1978b, p. 93; Zazoff and Zazoff 1983, p. 11. Moreover, Ghezzi himself in the manuscript catalogue of his *dactyliotheca* admits that he copied some gems, for example: Ghezzi 1734, I.L.no. 41 – '(...) copiato dal Meo'. In addition, the name of Sirleti and his works appear from the time in Ghezzi's diary suggesting a special connection between these two, for example: Dorati da Empoli 2008, pp. 69 (entry of 15 February 1731), 99 (entries of 18 and 20 December 1731). Furthermore, in his diary Ghezzi also registers some interesting transactions like that one from 8 January 1732: '*Compari un occhio di agata per legar in Anello, con una macchina in mezzo ben tonda, con altri Cerchietti attorno, e mela portò il. Cav. Odam, e mi disse che ne'era il Padrone il V. Eustachio Orefice al Pellegrino, e mi disse che ne voleva 15.pavoli, e che lui laveva pagata 12.e che ci voleva guadagniar trè Giulji, et Io Cav. Ghezzi consegnai al detto Cavaliere Giulji quindici.*' – could such a purchase of an unengraved piece of agate mean that Ghezzi intended to engrave it by himself? In other words, is this a purchase of a semi-finished product that he wished to make an intaglio of?
32 Zazoff and Zazoff 1983, p. 23 – Zazoff does not specify the source of this information.
33 Lo Bianco 2010, pp. 27–28.
34 Guerrini 1971, p. 10.
35 Guerrini 1971, pp. 18–26; Dorati da Empoli 2008, p. 10; Lo Bianco 2010, pp. 29–31; Maioglio 2011. Ghezzi would visit various archaeological sites in and around Rome and document what was discovered through his drawings. The best testimony of these activities are the two volumes of his drawings of marbles and inscriptions now preserved in the Biblioteca Angelica in Rome (Ms. 2136). Ghezzi describes them himself: '*Raccolta*

sites allowed him to examine, draw and cast many new finds.[36] He was familiar with all leading archaeologists and connoisseurs of antiquities of Rome, including Francesco de'Ficoroni (1664–1747) and Francesco Valesio (1670–1742). He acted as both a dealer in antiquities and agent working on commissions of important collectors, for example, Philipp von Stosch, Prior Anton Maria Vaini (1660–1737), Girolamo Odam (ca. 1681–1740) or Alessandro Gregorio Capponi (1683–1746).[37] Like his father Giuseppe Ghezzi, he was a passionate collector. He inherited a considerable collection of drawings from his father, who was able to create it due to his privileged position as the Secretary of Accademia di San Luca.[38] In 1734, Ghezzi recalled that 'since his childhood, together with Mons. Leone Strozzi', he had gathered 'with a lot of effort, impressions from the best museums of Europe', and that they were 'both amused by this hobby'.[39] Indeed, Ghezzi assembled 3710 sulphur gem impressions which were purchased, alongside to other Ghezzi's collections, particularly 26 codices of his drawings by Pope Benedict XIV in 1747, and deposited in the Biblioteca Apostolica Vaticana.[40] The catalogue of these impressions written by Ghezzi himself survived. According to it, his *dactyliotheca* project was also meant to include impressions taken after the papal coins (thus the number of 6669 items appears on the first page), however, this was never completed.[41] Ghezzi possessed a considerable library in his house as well.[42] Between 1731 and 1734 he wrote his *Diario*.[43] It is known that Ghezzi offered his service as a consultant for appraisals of antiquities.[44] After his death in 1755, his wife, Caterina Peroni Ghezzi (ca. 1694–1762), gradually sold the rest of his collections, drawings as well as a considerable library piecemeal and what still was left at the point of her death in 1762 was dispersed.[45] The legacy of Ghezzi, especially in terms of his drawings with particularly valuable didascalies reflecting his passion towards Antiquity, should be regarded as one of the most important testimonies of the evolution from traditional antiquarianism towards proto-archaeology.[46]

Ghezzi's network of contacts in Rome was impressive and quickly proved useful for Stosch, whom Ghezzi befriended in 1715 when the Prussian Baron came to Rome for the first time. Ghezzi drew his portrait in 1717 as well as some caricatures which are now among his numerous drawings in the Biblioteca Apostolica Vaticana collections.[47] Ghezzi regularly visited Stosch while in Rome since on the two famous drawings he executed in 1725 and 1728, Ghezzi presents himself among many antiquarians meeting in Stosch's house. These drawings are the best testimonies of Ghezzi's important position not only for Stosch but also within the whole antiquarian community of Rome.[48] Ghezzi acted as an agent to Stosch informing him about new interesting archaeological discoveries in Rome and its surroundings. He was certainly very close to him.[49] From Ghezzi's letter from 1723 to Alessandro Gregorio Capponi, one of the leading Roman antiquarians, it is known that he connected him with Stosch due to a deal on a marble statue ultimately sold by Stosch to Capponi in 1717. Most likely Stosch was kept up to date on the purchases and in general on Capponi's activities through Ghezzi, who worked incessantly to favour the studies and publications of Stosch. As a result, in 1731 Ghezzi sent a drawing to Stosch in watercolour of a cameo signed by Aulos from Capponi's collection which was meant to be published in Stosch's

---

di varie lapidi et inscriptioni, che io Cav. Pietro Leone Ghezzi sono andato a ricercarle nelle cave, dove o Saputo che vi erano, e le ò disegnate come le ò trovate con tutta esattezza.'

36 Carpita 2012, p. 123.
37 Lanciani 1882; Furtwängler 1900, vol. III, p. 411; Lo Bianco 1985, pp. 81–82; Ubaldelli 2001, pp. 132–134; Dorati da Empoli 2009, p. 155. On the correspondence between Ghezzi and Capponi, see: Martinelli (ed.) 1990, pp. 150–155.
38 Buttler 2011, p. 93. On the collecting practices and some items identified as from Ghezzi's collection of drawings, see: Witte 2018.
39 Ghezzi 1734; Pirzio Biroli Stefanelli 2006, p. 101.
40 Guerrini 1971, p. 47; Alteri 1987, pp. 8–12; Dorati da Empoli 2008, pp. 24–25; Gołyźniak (forthcoming – Ghezzi).
41 Ms. Vat. Lat. 14928. See also on this matter: Gasparri 1977, pp. 26–27; Maaskant-Kleibrink 1978, p. 33, n. 13; Ubaldelli 2001, 14–15. After Ghezzi's death in 1755, his wife sold the rest of his collections and drawings piecemeal, see: Buttler 2011, p. 93.
42 On Ghezzi's library, see: Dorati da Empoli 2008, pp. 401–487.
43 Guerrini 1971, p. 9.
44 Gasparri 1977, p. 27.

45 Bean and Griswold 1990, p. 83; Buttler 2001, p. 93. On Ghezzi's library, see: Dorati da Empoli 2008, pp. 401–402. The testament of Ghezzi's spouse still included some of Ghezzi's paintings and drawings (including those of gems) among others, see: Martinelli 1990, pp. 111–131. These will be commented on more broadly below. In 1762, an inventory of what still constituted Ghezzi's collections was made, which made it clear that some parts of Ghezzi's holdings were already missing, e.g. sold. The original inventory is kept in the Archivo di Stato di Roma: 30 Notai capitolini, Uff. 25, Notaio Placenti Petrus, 1762 ottobre 10, cc. 285r–330r and it is transcribed in Dorati da Empoli 2008, pp. 403–475. See also on this issue Witte 2018, p. 170.
46 Lo Bianco 2010, pp. 31–32.
47 Cod. Ott. lat. 3112, fols 115 and 131 and 3116, fol. 1. See also: Kagan 1985, p. 11.
48 For a thorough discussion on these drawings, see: Kanzler 1900; Zazoff and Zazoff 1983, pp. 9–11, Lo Bianco (ed.) 1999, pp. 174–176, no. 57; Lo Bianco 2010, p. 30. For a list of artists living in Stosch's house, see: Stosch 1754, p. 50.
49 Hansson 2014, p. 17.

unfinished supplement to the *Gemmae antiquae caelatae* book.[50]

Overall, Ghezzi was not only an accomplished artist, but also a very active member of the antiquarian society of eighteenth-century Rome. His connection to Stosch was indeed very special and close. Zazoff thought that Ghezzi's drawings of antiquities and gems preserved in the Biblioteca Apostolica Vaticana within the Codices Ottoboni latinarum 3100–3109 were made for Stosch. Additionally, he claimed that Ghezzi worked as Stosch's assistant because he also drew many drawings and plans of Rome for his *Atlas*.[51] While the latter might be true, the recent research suggests that the true purpose and fate of Ghezzi's drawings now in the Biblioteca Apostolica Vaticana was different, although many of them indeed reproduce Stosch's gems.[52] Ghezzi painted a scene of the meeting between Alexander the Great and Diogenes for Stosch.[53] He is said to have worked for Francesco Vettori (1692–1770), drawing, notably, a number of ancient oil lamps, many of which are now kept amongst the 26 volumes of drawings which the draughtsman sold in 1747 to the pope.[54] Maaskant-Kleibrink established that Ghezzi drew various kinds of antiquities and gems for the Dutch collector Frederick de Thoms (1669–1746),[55] so did he draw gems for Stosch too? This seems to be justified as another draughtsman employed by Stosch – Markus Tuscher – criticised Ghezzi's drawings claiming them to be of too artistic character and therefore inaccurate.[56] Furthermore, in his letter to Stosch from 11 September 1722, François Fagel says that Picart informed him that he made better drawings for the plates of *Gemmae antiquae caelatae* book than the ones by Ghezzi shown to him.[57] According to the research presented in Chapter 8, it is now clear that Ghezzi not only drew a few gems for Stosch's book project among others and but he also helped Odam to produce his drawings even though Stosch himself in the preface to *Gemmae antiquae caelatae* is misleadingly imprecise about Ghezzi's contribution.[58]

3   Girolamo Odam (1681–1741)

Girolamo Odam, like Pier Leone Ghezzi, was another multitalented Italian artist active in the Baroque epoch (Fig. 4.4). He was born in Rome to a family from Lorraine.[59] He trained first under Carlo Maratta (1625–1713) – drawing and painting, Carlo Fontana (1634 or 1638–1714) – architecture, and later Pier Leone Ghezzi (1674–1755) – drawing in pen and ink – as well as Domenico Marchi (ca. 1655–1737).[60] He was recognised and appreciated as a pastel portraitist and landscape artist, as well as wood engraver, sculptor and even architect and poet.[61] He was a member of the Accademia dell'Arcadia, where he was known as *Dorindo Nonacrino*, and similarly to Ghezzi or perhaps because of him, he was a recognisable figure within the circles of artists and musicians of Rome.[62] Like Ghezzi, he was educated well not only in art but also literature, philosophy and mathematics.[63] He lived in a house close to the *Chiesa Nuova*, which is today better known as Chiesa di Santa Maria in Vallicella in Rome.[64] His works are not well known and remain uncatalogued until today.[65]

Like Ghezzi, Odam was, in fact, another key figure in Roman antiquarian circles in the first half of the eighteenth century. He was well connected with a number of early archaeologists, artists, restorers, collectors and dealers.[66] He was close to Cardinal Pietro Ottoboni (1667–1740), a grandnephew of Pope Alexander VIII (1689–1691), who was a great patron of arts and music, but also an avid collector of engraved gems. Odam was a friend of Count Leone Strozzi as well as Pietro Andrea Andreini (1650–

---

50   Ubaldelli 2001, p. 85. This watercolour is not preserved among the drawings in the Princes Czartoryski collection but there is a copy of it made by Georg Abraham Nagel (Krakow No. 1670, cf. a discussion in Chapters 8 and 10 in this volume).
51   Zazoff and Zazoff 1983, p. 55; Lo Bianco 2010, p. 29.
52   Carpita 2012; Gołyźniak (forthcoming – Ghezzi). On Ghezzi's gem drawings in the Biblioteca Apostolica Vaticana, see also: Furtwängler 1900, vol. III, pp. 411–412.
53   Lo Bianco 1985, p. 72; Lo Bianco (ed.) 1999, pp. 30–31 and 143–144; Lo Bianco 2010, pp. 29–30.
54   Carpita 2012, pp. 118 and 122. Ghezzi's drawings of oil lamps are accumulated in Cod. Ott. lat. 3102.
55   Maaskant-Kleibrink 1978, p. 26.
56   Zazoff and Zazoff 1983, p. 55.
57   The relevant fragment of this letter is: '(...) *il me paroissoit estre bien entré dans le gout des pierres gravées, et de les avoir mieux representés, que ne l'avoit fait le chevalier Ghezzi dans les dessins que j'ai vu.*' – and it is reproduced in: Heringa 1976, p. 79.

58   Stosch 1724, p. V.
59   The earliest source for Odam's biography seems to be Pellegrino Antonio Orlandi but it lacks many key information like the dates of birth and death of Odam, see: Orlandi 1733, p. 261.
60   Füßli 1810, p. 475; Guerrini 1971, p. 41.
61   Lanzi 1809, vol. I, p. 232; Füßli 1810, p. 475; Cazort and Percy 2004, no. 27. Odam sculpted a funeral monument of the poet Alessandro Guidi which is now in the St. Onuphry Church in Rome, see: Dorati da Empoli 2008, p. 64, n. 42. For some general works on Odam, see: Orlandi 1733, p. 261; Clark 1962, pp. 150–151; Le Blanc 1854, p. 113; Ruysschaert 1964–1965 and especially the recent evaluation by Guerrieri Borsoi 2009.
62   Guerrieri Borsoi 2009, p. 162.
63   Cazort and Percy 2004, no. 27.
64   Dorati da Empoli 2008, p. 64, n. 41.
65   Hiesinger and Percy 1980, p. 22, no. 11.
66   Hiesinger and Percy 1980, pp. 22–23, no. 11.

1729). He was close to the Albani family as well, among which Cardinal Alessandro Albani (1692–1779) had a particular esteem for intaglios and cameos.[67] He advised on gems for Alessandro Gregorio Capponi.[68] Another important figure connected to Odam was Henry Howard, 4th Earl of Carlisle. Odam describes his friendly relationship with him in his letter sent on 14 June 1739 to Anton Francesco Gori, where he states that he met Lord Carlisle for the first time in 1719.[69] From another letter addressed to Gori (26 March 1740), one learns that Odam was instructed by Lord Carlisle to buy at any cost the burnt carnelian presenting Venus playing with Cupid signed by Aulos, which was owned at the time by Francesco Vettori (see below).[70] The best illustration of Odam's wide connections is the fact that he appears on a drawing by Ghezzi presenting a gathering of antiquarians in Philipp von Stosch's house from 1725.[71] Odam might have assembled a considerable number of sculptures, reliefs, fragments of sarcophagi and inscriptions from all the most fruitful excavations conducted at the time on the Palatine Hill, Caelian Hill, Aventine Hill, along the Via Appia and at Castel Gandolfo.[72] This was possible due to his appointment to the Order of Saint George at the court of Parma by Prince Antonio Farnese in 1723, which allowed him, for instance, to participate in the Farnese excavations on the Palatine.[73]

Odam was a passionate gem collector as well, nevertheless, there is virtually no knowledge about the scope and size of his collection and Odam's gems used to be incorrectly attributed to other collectors, like Johan Hendrik Graf van Wassenaer-Opdam (1683–1745).[74] The Florentine scholar Anton Francesco Gori (1691–1757) mentions that he was the owner of some gems and so does Francesco de'Ficoroni (1664–1747).[75] The recent analysis of the inventory list of a sulphur *dactyliotheca* composed by Ghezzi,[76] a brief summary given by Gori,[77] and in particular the collections of gem drawings from Krakow, Berlin and the Vatican facilitated identification of 121 of Odam's gems.[78] Maaskant-Kleibrink suggests that Count Frederick de Thoms purchased some of his gems from Odam, which are now in Leiden.[79] Single gems once owned by Odam can also be identified as now scattered among Italian collections.[80] Furthermore, a few of Odam's gems, according to a letter from Bellisario Ansidei from 6 February 1740 (close to Odam's death) to Henry Howard, 4th Earl of Carlisle, were acquired by the 3rd Duke of Marlborough.[81] The recently published reconstruction of the Marlborough collection of engraved gems confirms only two to have been indeed recorded in the archives with references to the name of Odam.[82] However, it is possible that these gems went to the Marlborough collection through marquis Giovanni Carlo Molinari (1715–1763), who according to Winckelmann, acquired some of Odam's gems.[83] Moreover, according to the analysis of gem drawings in Krakow, some of Odam's gems were also purchased by Philipp von Stosch.[84] The overall image of Odam's collection of gems suggests that Roman Republican and Roman Imperial examples clearly dominated and there are only single examples of Hellenistic, magical and early Christian gems within the assemblage. This is consistent

---

67 Hiesinger and Percy 1980, p. 22, no. 11; Cazort and Percy 2004, no. 27; Guerrieri Borsoi 2009, p. 168.
68 Ubaldelli 2001, pp. 83–84.
69 Epistolario di Anton Francesco Gori – volume BVII21, carte 12r–13r (https://sol.unifi.it/gori/gori – retrieved on 28 December 2022).
70 Epistolario di Anton Francesco Gori – volume BVII21, carte 27r–29bis: 'Milord Carlisle mi scrisse che averebbe comprato ad ogni prezzo la sua Venere col nome esso mi rispose che avendola pubblicata ex museo Victorio non pose a privarsene (...)' (https://sol.unifi.it/gori/gori – retrieved on 28 December 2022). Regarding the gem itself, it is now kept in London, the British Museum: inv. no.: 1913,0307.189, see: Vettori 1739, pp. 10–13; Raspe and Tassie 1791, no. 6320; Dalton 1915, no. 643; Rudoe 2003, p. 138. fig. 122.
71 Vienna, Albertina inv. 1263, see, a discussion on this drawing in: Zazoff and Zazoff 1983, pp. 9–11 and Chapter 2 here.
72 Guerrini 1971, pp. 40–41; Micheli 1986, p. 41; Guerrieri Borsoi 2009, p. 163; Carpita 2012, p. 109.
73 Micheli 1986, p. 41.
74 Platz-Horster 2012, p. 12, n. 29; Borbein, Kunze and Rügler 2019, p. 4.
75 Ficoroni 1730, pp. 29 and 100. Regarding Gori, see, a manuscript in the Biblioteca Marucelliana: MS. A.24, fol. 639 where there is also information that Odam possessed his own *museum*. Guerrieri Borsoi suggests that it included a *dactyliotheca* of gem impressions; however, the manuscript in question here does not make it explicit. I would like to thank Paolo Turcis from the Biblioteca Marucelliana for his kind help in my research on this issue.
76 Ms. Vat. Lat. 14928; Guerrini 1971, p. 41; Guerrieri Borsoi 2009, p. 177, n. 16.
77 Biblioteca Marucelliana: MS. A.24, fol. 639.
78 See a full discussion on Odam's collection of engraved gems among others in: Gołyźniak 2023b.
79 Maaskant-Kleibrink 1978, pp. 25 and 32–33, n. 13.
80 See, for example: Bruschetti 1985–1986, p. 35, no. 10.
81 Castle Howard Archives J 12/12/10, see: Scarisbrick 1987, p. 104, n. 101.
82 Boardman *et al.* 2009, nos 633 and 691 (bought by the Duke of Marlborough for 30 gns.).
83 Winckelmann 1760, class II, no. 1517, p. 243.
84 Krakow Nos 52, 171, 734, 2115 and 2253 and Berlin vol. II, pl. 117, vol. VI, pls 107–108 as well as: Biblioteca Apostolica Vaticana: Cod. Ott. lat. 3108, fols 43, 72, 88, 98, 104 and 108 depict gems once owned by Odam and later by Stosch, see a full discussion on this matter in: Gołyźniak (forthcoming – Odam).

with information about Odam's engagement into the excavations in Rome and surrounding area. It is fairly possible that he purchased many of his intaglios and cameos directly from the excavators and finders in the places he visited.[85] One more interesting issue is that Odam even commissioned copies of gems signed by ancient masters since Lorenz Natter claimed that he copied a gem with Venus signed by Aulos on his behalf turning the subject into Danae.[86]

Evidently, Odam enjoyed a brilliant career. There was one activity in which he was particularly successful, and which can tell us much about his work and interests – book illustrations. Odam was employed for several major publication projects. For example, he made the preparatory drawings to the accompanying tables of Gori's work *Monumentum sive columbarium libertorum et servorum Liviae Augustae Et Caesarum: Romae Detectum in Via Appia* published in Florence in 1727.[87] In 1729 Cardinal Melchior de Polignac organised a festival at Piazza Navona in Rome to celebrate the birth of the son of French King Louis XV. An illustrated volume commemorating this occasion entitled *Carlo Magno: festa teatrale in occasione della nascita del Delfino* was published, for which Odam provided the decorative drawings for the surrounds of the plates.[88] Furthermore, he illustrated Francesco Vettori's *Dissertatio glyptographica, sive Gemmae duae vetustissimae emblematibus et graeco artificis nomine insignitae quae exstant Romae in Museo Victorio explicatae, et illustratae. Accedunt nonnulla veteris elegantiae, & eruditionis inedita Monimenta ...*, published in Rome in 1739.[89] Apparently, Odam drew and produced leaflets for later advertisements of some particular gems, like the red jasper intaglio featuring the busts of Pupienus (AD 238), Balbinus (AD 238) and Gordian III (AD 238–244) on one side and the Capitoline triad on the other, once in the Francesco de'Ficoroni collection and now in Munich.[90] In 1744, Ficoroni used this illustration for his book entitled *Le vestigia e rarità di Roma antica ricercate e spiegate*.[91] He also conducted this activity with Philipp von Stosch (cf. Chapter 8). A comparison of Odam's drawings of antiquities (including engraved gems) with other contemporary artists like Gaetano Piccini (active in Rome between 1702–1740) clearly shows his accuracy and skill which derived from training with Pier Leone Ghezzi.[92]

As early as 1715, Odam started collaboration with Philipp von Stosch for whom he drew gems, usually from their impressions, for his celebrated book *Gemmae antiquae caelatae*.[93] He does not seem to be merely a draughtsman for the book since in the preface Stosch makes it clear that the book would not have been written without Odam's encouragement. There are other sources suggesting that Odam was an advisor to Stosch on many signed gems.[94] Stosch credits Odam for the preparation of many drawings for his book illustrations, and Justi says that Odam drew almost all plates before Picart transformed them into engravings.[95] One finds further confirmations of this in Stosch's correspondence.[96] Odam, who was engaged in excavations in Rome, apparently had a particular talent and interest in documentation of objects discovered during the fieldworks. Together with his unquestionable connoisseurship in terms of intaglios and cameos, his talents

---

85 Gołyźniak 2023b.
86 This copy is now in London, the British Museum collection, inv. no.: 1867,0507.12 (sold by Natter to Karl Maximilian, 6th Prince of Dietrichstein (1702–1784) as his own work, later in the collection of Louis Charles Pierre Casimir, Duc de Blacas d'Aulps (1815–1868)), see: Zwierlein-Diehl 2007, pp. 300–302.
87 Gori 1727; Guerrieri Borsoi 2009, p. 168.
88 Cazort and Percy 2004, no. 27.
89 Vettori 1739; Guerrieri Borsoi 2009, pp. 168–169.
90 Odam's original drawing and its engraving are now in the Biblioteca Apostolica Vaticana, Cod. Capponi I 24, fols 1–2, see: Ubaldelli 2001, pp. 55–56, n. 232. The original gem Odam reproduced is now in the Staatliche Münzsammlung in Munich, see: AGDS I.3, no. 2459.
91 Ficoroni 1744, p. 185. Odam's original drawing and its engraving are now in the Biblioteca Apostolica Vaticana, Cod. Capponi I 24, fols 1–2, see: Ubaldelli 2001, pp. 55–56, n. 232. The original gem Odam reproduced is now in the Staatliche Münzsammlung in Munich, see: AGDS I.3, no. 2459. Odam belonged to the circle of antiquarians related to Ficoroni, see: Ridley 2017, p. 240.
92 Guerrieri Borsoi 2009, p. 169.
93 Letter from Stosch to François Fagel, dated 10 August 1715 (quoted in Heringa 1976, p. 76, n. 23) – Archives of the Fagel family, Algemeen Rijksarchief, The Hague, inv. 2028 – Stosch expresses his intention of writing a book on ancient signed gems. He collected glass pastes taken from original intaglios and cameos and employed Girolamo Odam to draw them as illustrations for the forthcoming book.
94 Stosch 1724, p. III and also in his letter to François Fagel, dated 10 August 1715 (quoted in Heringa 1976, p. 76, n. 23) – Archives of the Fagel family, Algemeen Rijksarchief, The Hague, inv. 2028: 'C'est le Chevalier Odam qui a commence de m'en faire les desseins et je travaille deja depuis quelque tems a ramasser tout ce qu'on peut trouver dans Pline Junius et autres auteurs anciens et modernes.' Stosch makes it clear that he consulted his book with Cardinal Leone Strozzi and Girolamo Odam for his book (1754, p. 26). This is hardly surprising since the first possessed at some point 11 gems signed by ancient gem engravers and he was a very good friend to Odam, another gem connoisseur and collector.
95 Justi 1871, pp. 28–29 and 1872, p. 334.
96 For example, in a letter from Stosch to Henry Howard, 4th Earl of Carlisle, Stosch precisely says that the cameo with a bust of Phocion signed by Pyrgoteles was drawn by Odam for publication in Stosch's book and it was later engraved by Picart, see: Scarisbrick 1987, p. 104.

made a perfect mixture for Stosch's idea to faithfully reproduce ancient styles and techniques applied in gem carving to be visualised.[97] Odam is said to have produced at least 62 drawings for Stosch's book and his contribution to *Gemmae antiquae caelatae* will be discussed in detail in Chapter 9.[98]

In a letter to Anton Francesco Gori from 1738, Odam writes that when Stosch came to Rome for the first time, he had a chance to compare the impression of the famous so-called *Seal of Michelangelo* and some circulating prints of that gem. Because they proved to be inaccurate, he drew himself the gem anew.[99] This exceptional, large drawing by Odam is now in the Princes Czartoryski Museum collection (Krakow No. 74).[100] Odam also writes that he later produced 2700 drawings for Stosch, which were then redrawn by some German.[101] Indeed, some German draughtsmen like Johann Justin Preißler, Markus Tuscher and Georg Abraham Nagel lived and worked in Stosch's atelier first in Rome and after 1731 in Florence. According to the research presented in Chapter 8, all of them redrew some of Odam's works. Furthermore, the two collections of gem drawings rediscovered in Krakow and Berlin deliver more than 1900 examples attributed to Odam, so while writing to Gori, Odam does not make an empty boast.

4   Theodorus Netscher (1668–1728)

Theodorus Netscher was a painter born in Bordeaux, a son and pupil of Caspar Netscher (1639–1684) and the older brother of the painters Constantijn and Anthonie Netscher (Fig.4.5). He was a celebrated Dutch portrait and genre painter also known from his wall decorations. He worked mainly in The Hague but he also spent many years in Paris (1680–1699) and because of that he was often called the 'French Netscher'. Between 1715–1721, he worked in London until he moved to Hulst, where he died.[102]

He is the next artist acknowledged by Stosch in the preface to *Gemmae antiquae caelatae* book. He is said to have drawn just one gem for the book, the cameo featuring the marriage of Cupid and Psyche signed by Tryphon, the so-called *Marlborough Gem*.[103] This is confirmed by Picart, who acknowledged Netscher as a draughtsmen for the plate LXX in the book.[104] Stosch had seen this gem in London himself[105] and when embarking upon writing a book in which he wished to include it, he asked Mr van Borsselen (Dutch envoy extraordinary to the Court of Great Britain) for help via Fagel to obtain a drawing.[106] The drawing after the cameo was made by Netsher, who at the time was based in London, and sent by Fagel to Stosch together with a cast on 5 June 1716.[107] Stosch consigned the drawing to Picart, who then engraved the plate.

The Princeton University Art Museum claims to hold Netscher's drawing of the Tryphon cameo within its collections (formerly attributed to Edmé Bouchardon).[108] However, this drawing in red chalk should be certainly attributed to Bernard Picart, as it is explained in detail in Chapter 9. The real drawing produced for Stosch by Netscher remains unrecognised or is lost.

5   Anton Maria Zanetti (1679–1767)

Count Anton Maria Zanetti was a Venetian artist and engraver (Fig. 4.6).[109] He earned his living selling marine insurance, but he was also a successful art dealer and connoisseur of paintings, drawings, prints and engraved gems.[110] He studied in Bologna and travelled to Rotterdam,

---

97   Heringa 1976, p. 77; Guerrieri Borsoi 2009, p. 169.
98   Heringa 1976, p. 77; Whiteley 1999.
99   Letter from Odam to Anton Francesco Gori, dated Rome 21 December 1738 – Epistolario di Anton Francesco Gori (http://www.electronica2.unifi.it/gori/database.htm (volume BVII21, carte 8r–9v), retrieved on 4 February 2021).
100 Cf. also a discussion on this particular drawing in Chapter 5 in this volume.
101 Letter from Odam to Anton Francesco Gori, dated Rome 21 December 1738 – Epistolario di Anton Francesco Gori (http://www.electronica2.unifi.it/gori/database.htm (volume BVII21, carte 8r–9v), retrieved on 4 February 2021). The number of 2700 drawings of gems made for Stosch is also confirmed by Justi (1871, p. 29 and 1872, p. 334).
102 https://rkd.nl/en/explore/artists/59181 – retrieved on 4 February 2021.
103 Stosch 1724, p. V. On the cameo, which is now in the Museum of Fine Art in Boston (acc. no. 99.101), see: Boardman *et al.* 2009, no. 1 (with earlier literature).
104 Stosch 1724, pl. LXX; Justi 1872, p. 334; Heringa 1976.
105 Letter from Stosch to François Fagel, dated Paris 8 September 1713.
106 Letter from Stosch to François Fagel, dated Rome 17 August 1715.
107 Heringa 1976, n. 26.
108 Drawing no. x1966-15 (https://artmuseum.princeton.edu/collections/objects/10756 – retrieved on 4 February 2021).
109 On Zanetti in general, see: Lorenzetti 1917; Borroni 1956; Scarisbrick 1987; Scarisbrick 1990; Maggioni 1991; Bandinelli 1996; Sacconi 1996; Bettagno 2001; Bandinelli 2002; Toutain 2007; Magrini 2009; Piva 2012; Crosera 2013; Bortoluzzi 2014; Craievich 2018, Lucchese 2020; Favaretto 2021; Tassinari 2022.
110 Hindman 2020, p. 40. Many drawings from Zanetti's collection are now at the Museo Correr in Venice, see: Hansson 2021b, p. 64, n. 33.

Lyon, Paris, London and Vienna, among others, but lived his entire life in Venice. He worked as an agent to important British collectors of gems and other works of art.[111] He was also a friend and an agent of Pierre Crozat, Philippe II, Duke of Orléans, Pierre-Jean Mariette as well as Joseph Wenzel I, Prince of Liechtenstein, whom he assisted in forming and expanding their collections of paintings, drawings and prints.[112] He collected paintings, drawings and prints himself. Among his most successful purchases were drawings by Parmigianino, which were once owned by Thomas Howard, 2nd Earl of Arundel, and which he purchased from Gerhard Michael Jabach (1688–1751).[113] He was a friend and client of numerous celebrated painters of the Venetian Baroque and Rococo, such as Tiepolo, Sebastian and Marco Ricci, Canaletto, and Rosalba Carriera.[114] Furthermore, as a draughtsman, he offered to draw the gems of Henry Howard, 4th Earl of Carlisle.[115] Zanetti learnt the art of drawing and painting first from Niccolò Bambini (1651–1736) and later Antonio Balestra (1666–1740) and Sebastiano Ricci (1659–1734).[116] Like Pier Leone Ghezzi, he was a caricaturist drawing Venetian personalities in his album, sometimes nicknamed 'Venetian Bestiary'.[117] He published *Delle Antiche Statue Greche e Romane* between 1740 and 1743, a two-volume book illustrating ancient sculpture.[118]

Zanetti formed a considerable collection of engraved gems, which despite containing many modern pieces and fakes, was admired by his contemporaries, including Stosch himself.[119] It was published in 1750 as a book that contained 80 plates engraved from his own drawings while the Latin text was written by Anton Francesco Gori and translated in Italian by Zanetti's cousin, Girolamo Francesco Zanetti (1713–1782).[120] Zanetti's original drawings have circulated around the art market;[121] however, despite his will expressed in a testament to his heirs, most of his gems were dispersed almost 30 years after his death in 1795, when they were purchased by Baron Dominique Vivant Denon (1747–1825), the curator of gems for the Republic.[122] Some of his other gem drawings are now housed in the Museo Correr in Venice.[123] Zanetti's collection included some masterpieces, for example, the famous Althorp Leopard Cameo, which the collector purchased directly from the sole heir of the Prince Eugene de Savoy (1663–1736), Princess Anna Maria Vittoria of Soissons (1683–1763) in Vienna in 1736 (alongside to the paintings of Nicolas Poussin, Grechetto and Giuseppe Maria Crespi among others).[124] Prior to Eugene de Savoy, the cameo belonged to the Pope Clement XI who was advised by Stosch, as he was the first to notice this exceptional cameo in the cabinet of Marcoantonio Sabbatini (1637–1724), to buy it for 100 scudi. Later, Stosch told Cardinal Alessandro Albani, to take it for his diplomatic mission to Vienna in 1720 in order to gain Eugene de Savoy's favour.[125] In 1764, Zanetti sold it to John Spencer, 1st Earl Spencer (1734–1783) but it left the Althorp House in 1978 and it is now in a private collection.[126] In 1761, Zanetti sold four of his best gems to George Spencer, 4th Duke of Marlborough for the negotiated amount of £600 (1200 zecchini; 15 000 francs, according to Reinach; £1200 according to King).[127] Among

---

111 Scarisbrick 1987; Scarisbrick 1990.
112 For a comprehensive study of Zanetti's various antiquarian activities, see: Borroni 1956; Craievich 2018.
113 Matile 2018, p. 93.
114 Hindman 2020, p. 40.
115 According to a letter from Zanetti to Lord Carlisle dated Venice, 25 October 1740: '*Je me charge de en faire les desseins de tout les pieces, que vous m'envoyerez, et dessiner dans le totel goust de l'antique, sans aucun imaginable fraix; mais simplement pour vous temoigner la grande estime, et la veneration, que je vous ay concue*.', see: Scarisbrick 1987, p. 97.
116 Chennevières and Montaiglon (eds) 1859–1860, pp. 154–144.
117 Hindman 2020, p. 40.
118 Zanetti 1740–1743.
119 Furtwängler 1900, vol. III, p. 414; Zazoff and Zazoff 1983, pp. 113–114; Favaretto 2018; Tassinari 2022, pp. 115–133 (with more literature).
120 Gori and Zanetti 1750; Tassinari 2022, pp. 117–133. Zanetti started to draw his gems for the catalogue prior to 1744 (letter quoted in Bortoluzzi 2014, pp. 52 and 65 with conflicting dates). Zanetti himself drew each of the 80 plates: though it was erroneously indicated that '*Each of its 80 plates was engraved by the owner himself, from drawings by yet another of his relations, and his namesake, Antonio Maria Zanetti the Younger*' (Kagan 2006, p. 87). Zanetti himself wrote that '*io stesso di mia propria mano ho disegnato le* Gemme *tutte, con quanta diligenza per me si potè maggiore*' (introduction of Gori and Zanetti 1750) and this is also confirmed by one of his contemporaries, Pierre-Jean Mariette (1750, vol. I, p. 297): '*il est actuellement occupé à les faire graver, sur les Desseins qu'il en a fait*'.
121 Those 80 drawings, in pen and ink, were auctioned in New York on 29 October 2013 by Christie's (collection of Arthur and Charlotte Vershbow, lot 763, acquired in 1980 from Colnaghi, previously with the dealer Hans M. Calmann 1899–1982). Christie's mentioned that they had also previously belonged to the collector Erasmus Phillips, but the dates of life of Sir Erasmus Phillips (1699–1743) do not seem compatible. Recently, the drawings were sold again in Paris at Giquello (The Sale of Alain Moatti Library, 22 March 2024, lot 61) with the same provenance information.
122 Scarisbrick 1979; Kagan 2006, p. 87; Hindman 2020, p. 51; Tassinari 2022, p. 115.
123 Bandinelli 1996; Bortoluzzi 2014, pp. 63–83; Favaretto 2018.
124 Scarisbrick 1979; Boardman *et al.* 2009, no. 530; Craievich 2018, pp. 284–285; Hindman 2020, p. 39; Tassinari 2022, pp. 132–133.
125 Hansson 2021b, p. 66, n. 45 (letters nos 109 and 111).
126 Scarisbrick 1990; Hindman 2020.
127 Boardman *et al.* 2009, p. 206; Tassinari 2022, pp. 125–132.

them, there was the famous Sangiorgi black chalcedony intaglio with the bust of Antinous, now in the J. Paul Getty Museum.[128] Another significant gem purchased by the Duke of Marlborough from Zanetti was a head of 'Phocion' said to be an original carved by Alessandro Cesati.[129] Two other ones were a fine Sabina portrait and a shell cameo showing Horatius holding the bridge over the Tiber.[130] Another exceptional piece was the aquamarine intaglio depicting a giant with the spurious incomplete signature of Dioscurides (ΔΙΟC), which went to the collection of Sir Richard Worsley (1751–1805).[131] Zanetti was well connected which enabled him to buy gems of the finest provenance like 13 intaglios and cameos once in the collection of the noble Zaccaria Sagredo.[132]

Even though Stosch does not list Zanetti among the people who helped him to produce *Gemmae antiquae caelatae*, in the case of plates L and LIX Bernard Picart credited Zanetti as the author of drawings for these plates.[133] The pl. LIX reproduces a cameo featuring *Hercules Musarum* signed by Skylax at the time in possession of Domenico Tiepolo, a senator in Venice. Zanetti probably drew after the original gem and as Hansson writes, he must have done so between July 1717 when Stosch examined Tiepolo's original Hercules in Venice and decided to include it in his book, and 1724, when Bernard Picart engraved the plate based on Zanetti drawing in Amsterdam.[134] This is also confirmed by a letter sent by Apostolo Zeno to Anton Francesco Marmi, from Venice on 24 July 1724.[135] Regarding the second drawing delivered by Zanetti for Stosch's book, it was used for plate L, which depicts a carnelian intaglio with a hippocamp signed by Pharnakos, at the time in the Farnese collection in Parma. In this case, Zanetti must have delivered the drawing for the plate before 1723 as suggested by Picart on his plate, and he may have based it on an impression of the original, for example, the glass paste that belonged to Stosch or his own one.[136] The original drawings by Zanetti for Stosch's book remain lost.

The first half of the eighteenth century was the time of thriving correspondence exchange within the so-called *Republic of Letters*. Zanetti, like Stosch, is a perfect example of the transfer of knowledge at great distances using such a tool. In his letter sent from Venice on 24 March 1730 to his friend Hugh Howard, the art consultant to the Duke of Devonshire, Zanetti asks to send him impressions after the most famous gems he can find in London, including Duke's own cabinet. He often procured casts and impressions of gems like Stosch did from his friends in Rome, Florence, Parma, Bologna and Paris.[137] Stosch and Zanetti exchanged letters and impressions on a regular basis as well. They would discuss individual items like the famous Antinous intaglio (cf. Chapter 10).[138] Even though they seemed to be natural rivals on the art market for engraved gems, apparently, they did not compete much. On the contrary, they would discuss their transactions: new acquisitions as well as sales.[139] Having known that Zanetti was a great artist and enthusiast of intaglios and cameos, it was natural for Stosch to ask for his help with drawings of the two gems which were in Venice and which he needed for his book. In the context of complex relationships between the collectors of gems at the time, this could have also been a sort of appreciation of Zanetti's talents and connoisseurship. Furthermore, Zanetti cultivated the same ethics of research and publishing as Stosch. In the catalogue of his gem collection, he assures the reader that he made every effort for illustrations to be as faithful to the originals as possible, whether drawing his gems himself or through careful supervision of the work of the engravers of the plates.[140] Stosch seemed to pay much attention to

---

128 Acc. no.: 2019.13.17, see: Scarisbrick 1990, p. 413; Boardman *et al.* 2009, no. 753; Wagner and Boardman 2018, no. 151 (with full bibliography); Tassinari 2022, pp. 128–130. This gem was also discussed by Zanetti with Stosch through correspondence, see: Hansson 2021b, pp. 65–66 and cf. Chapter 10 here.
129 Boardman *et al.* 2009, p. 206 and no. 571, Tassinari 2022, pp. 128–130.
130 Boardnam *et al.* 2009, nos 509 (Horatius) and 773 (Sabina); Tassinari 2022, pp. 126–128 and 131.
131 Scarisbrick 1990, p. 414; Hansson 2021b, p. 66, n. 45; Tassinari 2022, pp. 120–122.
132 Tassinari 2022, 116.
133 Stosch 1724, pl. LIX.
134 Hansson 2021b, pp. 6–7. It is almost certain that Stosch had seen the Skylax *Herakles* cameo in person, according to a letter sent by Apostolo Zeno to Anton Francesco Marmi, from Venice on 24 July 1724 (FINA ID-12451): 'Il Sig. Stoschio ha molto tempo che si ritrova in queste parti, occupatissimo in vedere e studiare il celebre Museo Tiepolo; (…) Il suddetto Museo ha veramente ricevuto un nobile accrescimento da quello del famoso Sebastiano Erizzo, che era nella casa Cappello, copioso di rare medaglie, e di rarissimi medaglioni' (Zeno 1785, vol. 2, no. 398, pp. 371–372).
135 Zeno 1785, vol. 2, no. 398, pp. 371–372; Letter from Apostolo Zeno to Anton Francesco Marmi dated 24 July 1724 (Venice): 'Il Sig. Stoschio ha molto tempo che si ritrova in queste parti, *occupatissimo in vedere e studiare il celebre Museo Tiepolo; (…) Il suddetto Museo ha veramente ricevuto un nobile accrescimento da quello del famoso Sebastiano Erizzo, che era nella casa Cappello, copioso di rare medaglie, e di rarissimi medaglioni.*' – https://fina.oeaw.ac.at/wiki/index.php/Apostolo_Zeno_-_Antonfrancesco_Marmi_-_1717-7-24, retrieved on 6 August 2022.
136 Hansson 2021b, pp. 64–65.
137 Tassinari 2022, p. 116.
138 Hansson 2021b. On the Antinous intaglio, cf. n. 113.
139 Boardman *et al.* 2009, p. 209, n. 123.
140 Gori and Zanetti 1750, pp. 115–116; Tassinari 2022, p. 119.

the same qualities while producing his own book on gems and requesting artists to draw gems for him (see above). The fruitful cooperation between Stosch and Zanetti continued well into the 1730s. On 3 October 1733, Zanetti sent Stosch a letter in which he informed him about the very special amethyst he found and included into his cabinet, which depicted Hermaphrodite surrounded by Cupids, with a partial signature of the famous Dioscurides (ΔΙΟC). He believed it to be a genuine masterpiece after which many later ancient replicas and modern copies were made.[141] Stosch planned to publish this very gem in his second volume of *Gemmae antiquae caelatae* (cf. Chapter 10).

6 Bernard Picart (1673–1733)

Bernard Picart was a French draughtsman and engraver specialising in book illustrations (Fig. 4.7). He was a son of Étienne Picart (1631–1721) called *Le Romain*, also an engraver. Picart first trained in drawing and architecture at the Académie royale de peinture et de sculpture in Paris. He was taught by Charles le Brun, Benoît Audran the Elder, Sébastien Leclerc and Antoine Coypel. After the revocation of the Edict of Nantes in 1685, he went to the Netherlands for a few years, but he came back to Paris, where he married in 1702. After the death of his wife and children, he left for Holland. Ultimately, he settled in Amsterdam in 1711 where he got remarried to Anna Vincent (1684–1736) and founded a successful publishing house.[142] He was a reproductive engraver and book illustrator to the French dominated book trade there. He had much interest in cultural and religious habits and he was the author of the multivolume *Cérémonies et coutumes religieuses de tous les peuples du monde*, appearing from 1723 to 1743.[143]

The basic source on Picart's life and work is *Impostures innocentes ou recueil d'estampes d'après divers peintres illustrés tels que Rafael, le Guide ... et accompagnées d'un discours sur les prejuges de certains curieux touchant la gravure* published by his widow in 1734 in Amsterdam.[144] This publication includes Picart's biography written by his wife,[145] a treatise on the art of engraving as well as a list of his works. It is noteworthy that Anna Vincent would get proofs of all Picart's book illustrations from their publishers, which she collected.[146] It might be that because of that documentary activity that Picart made a series of counterproof drawings of his illustrations of gems published in the *Gemmae antiquae caelatae* book (cf. discussion in Chapters 8 and 9). After Picart's death, his own drawings were supposed to be divided among his three daughters after the youngest, Angélique, became an adult, unless there was a buyer who wanted to pay a good price for the complete collection.[147] However, these drawings were publicly auctioned together with all prints and drawings of French, Italian, Dutch etc., masters that Picart collected during his life in a sale organised in 1737 in Amsterdam and thus dispersed.[148] There are more than 1500 of his works preserved in the Teylers Museum in Haarlem, among which there are just a few prints of gems published in the *Gemmae antiquae caelatae* book.[149] The Rijksmuseum in Amsterdam holds around 2000 of his works too. Recently, there was a successful exhibition dedicated to Picart in the Musée national de Port-Royal des Champs, exhibiting a number of his previously unrecognised works.[150]

Picart published Stosch's book *Gemmae antiquae caelatae* in 1724 in Amsterdam and he was acknowledged by the author as the one who had engraved all the plates.[151] Although most scholars followed Stosch's suggestion that Girolamo Odam and others provided drawings of gems for the book after which Picart made the engravings, Picart's widow stated that most of the drawings were executed by her husband himself.[152] Indeed, Picart redrew all the drawings delivered to him, as he believed no one else could make better illustrations for Stosch's book than he himself. He had a decisive role at the end of the *Gemmae antiquae caelatae* project, giving the book its final shape and acting as the publisher. Picart's drawings and this issue will be fully discussed in Chapters 8 and 9.

7 Johann Justin Preißler (1698–1771)

Johann Justin Preißler was a German painter and draughtsman (Fig. 4.8). He was the son and pupil of Johann Daniel Preißler (1666–1737) and a brother of Georg Martin

---

141 Hansson 2021b; Tassinari 2022, p. 119.
142 Hiesinger and Percy 1980, p. 31, no. 19A–B.
143 Hunt, Jacob and Mijnhardt 2010; Hunt, Jacob and Mijnhardt (eds) 2010.
144 Vincent and Picart 1734, reprinted in: Dimier (ed.) 1928, p. 385 and *Nouvelles de l'Estampe* 10 (1973), 15–20.
145 Unless this was Picart's autobiography published posthumously.
146 Adams 2010; Marchesano 2010.
147 Auction Picart 1737, introduction.
148 Auction Picart 1737.
149 Stosch 1724, pl. I = Teylers Museum inv. no.: KG 12319; pl. XX = KG 12341; pl. XL = KG 12361; pl. LIX = KG 12381; pl. LXX = KG 12393.
150 Luez (ed.) 2019 (with more literature).
151 Stosch 1724, p. V.
152 Vincent and Picart 1734, pp. 4–5 and 8.

Preißler (1700–1754), who also worked for Stosch (see below).[153] He took a *grand tour* as a young man in 1724 and travelled extensively in Italy (Venice, Florence, Rome, Naples), but in 1726 he decided to stay in Stosch's house in Rome.[154] In 1731, he stayed in Rome for a while, drawing some gems for Capponi,[155] but he then followed Stosch in his voluntary exile to Florence and lived with him there alongside Markus Tuscher (1705–1751) and Christian Dehn (1696–1770).[156] In 1738, Preißler returned from Italy to his hometown Nuremberg and married Susanna Maria Dorsch (1701–1765), a successful glass-painter, jeweller and gem engraver.[157] In 1742, he became the director of the Nuremberg Academy of Arts (founded by his father), and in 1752, he became the director of the Drawing Academy in that city.

Preißler was praised by Stosch for his particular talent in drawing antiquities, especially gems.[158] In his memoirs, Preißler recalls that he delivered Stosch a considerable number of drawings of gems and other antiquities.[159] He wrote about his work for Stosch as follows: '*Soon after, I asked how I should start, and was given a large number of ancient engraved gems, as well as many ancient busts, which had not yet been sketched. I first attempted to draw a carnelian which was set in gold, that of Perseus and Andromeda;*[160] *when I completed the sketches, which were much larger than the original, a generous feast with different artists, both from France and Italy, took place.*'[161] Such passages demonstrate that there is still much to discover regarding Preißler's cooperation with Stosch. Stosch confirms that Preißler belonged to the circle of artists who drew gems for him.[162] Moreover, it seems likely that Preißler also produced drawings for Stosch's *Atlas*.[163] On the one hand, various sources suggest that Preißler was involved in preparations of the supplement to *Gemmae antiquae caelatae* book as he drew newly discovered signed gems.[164] This is confirmed by several drawings now in Krakow and Berlin (cf. Chapter 8). On the other hand, it seems very likely that like Ghezzi, Odam or Tuscher, he drew gems on Stosch's regular commissions that might have been related to his other documentary and scholarly projects as well.

One of the side effects of the friendship with Stosch was Preißler's collaboration with Edmé Bouchardon. The two cooperated on the documentation of the French royal collection of antiquities[165] and most importantly, Preißler drew Stosch's marble bust sculpted by Bouchardon in 1727.[166] This drawing is now in the Princes Czartoryski Museum in Krakow (Krakow No. 1665 and discussion in Chapter 5). Furthermore, with Bouchardon and his brother Georg Martin Preißler, Johann Justin published Stosch's collection of marble statues in 1732. The illustrations were drawn by Bouchardon, while Johann Justin made the engravings for the plates after them; and his brother was the publisher of the whole enterprise.[167]

Preißler benefited enormously from the friendship with Stosch, as the latter introduced him into the wide network of Roman artists, collectors, connoisseurs and

---

153 Michel 1999–2000, pp. 78–79.
154 Such a date is given by either Stosch (1754, p. 50) and Justi (1871, p. 29 and 1872, p. 337) but Leitschuh (1886, p. 16) and Sichelstiel (2012, p. 74) say that Preißler was connected with Stosch only in 1727 and Eggers claims that this happened not earlier than 1728 (1926, p. 229).
155 Letter from Stosch to Preißler, Florence 29 May 1731 (Leitschuh 1886, pp. 23–24); Ubaldelli 2001, p. 136.
156 Justi 1871, p. 29; Eggers 1926, p. 233; Borroni Salvadori 1978a, pp. 566–567; Hansson 2014, p. 17.
157 Klesse 1999; Klesse 2000; Klesse 2001; Sichelstiel 2012, pp. 75–76. A portrait of the couple, in the style of a medal, was engraved in 1803 by A.L. Möglich after P. Zwinger. On her, see Tassinari 1994, p. 56. She was recently widowed by the landscape painter Salomon Graf (1695/8–1737).
158 Heringa 1981, p. 63. Preißler is probably also the draughtsman Stosch praises while writing to William Cavendish, 2nd Duke of Devonshire in his letter dated Rome 24 July 1728 (Chatsworth, the Devonshire Archives, inv. no.: CS1/188.3). It is noteworthy that most likely because of the connection with Stosch, the Greffier of the States General of Holland, François Fagel (1657–1746/47) acquired a painting by Preißler in 1730 (Heringa 1981, pp. 62–69).
159 Sturm 1863, pp. 383–384; Leitschuh 1886, p. 20; Eggers 1926, pp. 230–231.
160 Winckelmann 1760, class III, no. 155, p. 342; Furtwängler 1896, no. 3101; Borbein, Kunze and Rügler 2019, no. III.155. There is a cameo of *Perseus and Andromeda* in the Hermitage, see: Rambach 2017.
161 '*Nachdem ich in kurzer Zeit mich recht comod eingerichtet, fragte ich bald womit meine Beschäftigung anfangen sollte: es Wurde mir eine grosse Menge von anticq geschnittenen Steinen nebst einer Menge antique busten so alle noch nicht gezeichnet ware andgewiessen u. machte meine erste Probe mit einem in Gold gefassten Carrniol, die von perseo befreute Andromada, Nachdeme solche Verferdigt v. zwar vielmal grösser war eben ein zimlich Convivinm von verschiedenen Künstlern so wol Franzosen als Italiener beysam*' (Sturm 1863, pp. 383–384; quoted in Eggers 1926, p. 230). We are grateful to Maike Messmann for her help in translating this passage. See also: Michel 1999–2000, pp. 78–79.
162 Stosch 1754, p. 50.
163 Sturm 1863, pp. 384–385; Eggers 1926, p. 229; Zazoff and Zazoff 1983, p. 56; Sénéchal 2000, p. 138.
164 Justi 1872, p. 337; Leitschuh 1886, p. 20.
165 Sturm 1863, p. 384.
166 Leitschuh 1886, pp. 20–21; Eggers 1926, p. 231; Rave 1957; Desmas et al. 2016, pp. 119–121. The drawing must have been made before 1732 as in the letter from 25 July 1732 Fagel thanks to Stosch for sending him an engraving of that drawing, see: Sénéchal 2000, pp. 143–144.
167 Preißler 1732; Kopp 2017, p. 58.

illustrious patrons.[168] One of them was Alessandro Gregorio Capponi, for whom Preißler worked in 1731. He is attested to have commissioned at least four watercolours from Preißler: *'I had the excellent draftsman Monsieur Gian Giustino Preißler of Nuremberg to make half-foglio size copies in watercolour of the recently obtained chalcedony cameo, of my cameo of Isis that was reproduced some years ago, of the carnelian engraving of Sallust purchased last month, and of the statue of the pig being sacrificed that I obtained last July, this being done on paper; and for these four pieces he wanted no less than six ecus, 6 whole ecus.'*[169] Another patron of Preißler, who requested from him to draw his gems and other antiquities, was William Cavendish, the 2nd Duke of Devonshire.[170]

Preißler also drew antiquities for Antonio Borioni and some of his works were used for Ridolfino Venuti's book *Collectanea Antiquitatum Romanarum: quas centum tabulis aeneis incisas et a Rodulphino Venuti Academico Etrusco Cortonensi notis illustratas exhibet Antonius Borioni*, published in Rome in 1736.[171] In a private collection in the USA, there are four drawings of engraved gems prepared by Preißler for this publication and signed by him in the bottom-left corner *JJ Preisler d.* (Figs 4.9–4.10).[172] These drawings were most likely made by Preißler ca. 1730–1736 (probably in 1731?) because according to Sturm: '(...) *after the departure of the baron* [Stosch from Rome for Florence mid-February 1731], *some works remained to be done: drawing of some ancient gems for a marquess and for an experienced connoisseur of ancient gems, the first was Marquess Caponi, the second a pharmacist named Antonio.*'[173] They are immensely important for our studies here because they help to establish techniques and style of Preißler regarding drawing of engraved gems (cf. Chapter 8). Borioni was one of the gem connoisseurs that appears in Ghezzi's famous group portrait, and there is also his individual portrait from 1737 by Ghezzi. This provides a link with Stosch, so it might be that the Baron sent his draughtsmen to Borioni to document his gems. But he was obviously a significant competitor of Stosch in his quest for engraved gems, succeeding in obtaining some new finds of significant quality such as: '*A very fine cameo, an inch and an half over, representing Bacchus and Ariadne, has fell into the hands of Sig*[re] [Antonio] *Borioni, of exquisite workmanship; it was lately found among some rubbish, in making the foundation of the convent of S. Augustia in Campo Marzo*';[174] '*I was at Sig*[re] [Antonio] *Borioni's to see a fine Cameo, found amongst some rubbish in a convent building: it represents Bacchus and Ariadne; a bit of the nose of the former, and an arm of the latter broke off; however the fore-mention'd old Gentleman, who has great skills in these sort of things, as well as Medals, did not scruple paying immediately for it seventy sequins; the workmanship is excellent, and of the best age.*'[175] Considering that Borioni occasionally acted as a dealer,[176] and that Venuti was also involved in commerce,[177] it is likely that this book, *Collectanea Antiquitatum Romanarum* (in which most gems are owned by Borioni) was meant to serve as a sale catalogue. Venuti was blamed,[178] supposedly on behalf of Francesco de'Ficoroni, for having included pieces that were not Borioni's in the book, leading him to publish a letter in self-defence.[179] But in fact, even the

---

168   Leitschuh 1886, pp. 16–19. It is noteworthy that Pier Leone Ghezzi put his name on the list of his friends, see: Dorati da Empoli 2008, p. 158.

169   '*Feci fare li disegni in acquerello della grandezza di mezzo foglio a monsieur Gian Giustino Preißler di Norimberga, ottimo disegnatore, del cameo preso ultimamente in calcidonia, della mia Iside in cameo già stampata anni sono, dell'intaglio in corniola di Salustio, comprato il mese passato, e della statua che sacrifice il porco havuta da me luglio passato, e questa fu fatta in foglio; e per questi quattro pezzi non volle meno di scudi sei, dico scudi 6*' (Ubaldelli 2001, pp. 136 and 414). These drawings are now lost.

170   Ubaldelli 2001, p. 136. '*Around 1724 the 2nd Duke of Devonshire commissioned sketches of gems in his collection from the French artist A. Gosmond (Gosmund) de Vernon, with a view to publication. Gosmond produced 99 drawings and these, along with several more made by a member of the Preißler family of Nuremberg artists, were engraved by the illustrator Claude Dubosc, another Frenchman. The best gems gained some fame as some of the prints circulated amongst the Duke's friends and they were soon gathered together and issued as a single publication (Collectio figuraria gemmarum antiquarum ex dactyliotheca Ducis Devoniae, drawn by A. Gosmond de Vernon and engraved by C. Du Bosc, London, 1730). This was the earliest example of an engraved publication of such a private collection in Britain,*' see: Kagan 2010, p. 111; Boardman, Kagan and Wagner 2017, p. 28.

171   Venuti 1736; Zazoff and Zazoff 1983, pp. 121–122.

172   Sold at Christie's, New York, on 22 January 2003, lot. 95, within a group of 26 drawings of gems and statuettes, the rest also attributed to Preißler and incorrectly connected to Philipp von Stosch.

173   '*Nach der Abreisse Hrn. Barons hatte noch einige Arbeit zu verfertigen in Nachzeichnen einiger antichen Steine für einen Marchise v. einen erfahrenen Kenner der antique Stein Marchise Caponi heist der erste Sign. Antonio der andere eine Apotheker*' (Sturm 1863, p. 387). We are grateful to Maike Messmann for her help in translating this passage.

174   Letter by James Russel to Ralph Howard, dated Rome 6 June 1752 – the National Library of Ireland, Wicklow MSS 38628/9; Kelly 2012, p. 136.

175   Letter by James Russel to Richard Russel, dated Rome 14 June 1752 – the British Library, Add. MSS 41169, fols 58v–60r; Kelly 2012, p. 137.

176   Coen 2010, vol. I, pp. 103–110, vol. II, pp. 418–444.

177   Venuti's publication of Albani's ancient coins, initiated in March 1735, led to their sale to the pope in 1738.

178   Scarfò 1739a.

179   Venuti 1740. On this subject, see Venuti's letters to Gori (Rome 25 April 1739 – BMF B VIII, 7, c. 110) and to his brother

gems that are not indicated to be in Borioni's possession, such as the Agathangelos intaglio, which *had* belonged to collector-dealer Marcantonio Sabbatini (1637–1724), might have been his (or at least consigned to him for sale).

After returning to Nuremberg in 1738, over the next years Preißler made good use of his skills in drawing of engraved gems. For example, he was the designer of the plates for the *Antike Steine des herzogl. Braunschweigischen Kabinets*.[180] Upon his return he brought about 2000 gem impressions in wax that were later used by his wife, as she presented them on an engraving by Valentin Daniel Preißler but they were sold after his death to the Painting Academy.[181] Furthermore, it is said that upon his return to Germany he brought back nine or ten volumes of drawings with him.[182] Their content is unknown, possibly Old Masters copies, which he had executed as training before arriving in Rome, but perhaps some of his gem drawings too. Moreover, in 1805, Schlichtegroll mentions that the publisher of his joint project Johann Fredrich Frauenholz had some drawings of Stosch's gems by Preißler and Schweickart that he used for his publication, '(...) *had a number of valuable drawings by the hand of Preißler and Schweickart which represented each stone* [in the Stosch collection] *about three times larger than the original.*'[183] Schlichtegroll makes it clear that after the death of Johann Adam Schweickart in 1787, in Nuremberg, Frauenholz purchased Schweickart's *dactyliotheca* of sulphur gem impressions as well as a few drawings by Preißler that Schweickart had taken himself to Nuremberg after Stosch's death.[184] Those drawings[185] are made according to the very same convention as the drawings attributed to Johann Justin Preißler, which were discovered in Krakow and Berlin. Apparently, they guided Schlichtegroll and Frauenholz on how to illustrate the gems in their publications.

In any case, there still might be some of Preißler's gem drawings made on the commission of Stosch stored in the public museums and libraries or circulating around the art market. For example, a group of four gem drawings, when catalogued in 1990, was attributed to Preißler by Mia Weiner[186] on the basis of other drawings in the same collection that were signed by him.[187] And she suggested that they were commissions from Stosch. Interestingly, when the Berlin auctioneer Max Perl sold a group of 24 drawings of gems in 1937, he had also assumed that they were Preißler's work for Stosch; but they cannot be the same group, as some of them were set within pre-drawn (pre-engraved?) frames.[188] What is more, the drawings auctioned by Max Perl in 1927 in Berlin were circulating on the art market since at least 1906 and some of them, unlikely for Preißler, were drawn on a bluish paper.[189] However, given the fact as evidenced above, Preißler having not worked exclusively for Stosch, one cannot assume that every surviving drawing of gems by Preißler was done for Stosch.

There is a tendency to ascribe to Preißler (as artist) and to Stosch (as commissioner) many gem drawing that appear on the market. As an example, this was the case when Sotheby's sold two drawings of gems (entitled *War*

(Naples 15 June 1739 – Biblioteca Apostolica Vaticana, Cod. Ott. lat. 3128, fol. 260).

180 Leitschuh 1886, p. 56, but we have not been able to trace this publication. His work on this commission is mentioned by Stosch in his letter to Paolo Maria Paciaudi dated Florence 28 October 1755, see: Justi 1871, pp. 28–29, no. XIV.

181 Leitschuh 1886, p. 59; Zwierlein-Diehl 2007, p. 294, ill. 919; Sichelstiel 2012, p. 75. He may possibly have brought back some gem books as well, such as La Chausse 1707, De'Rossi and Maffei 1707–1709, Stosch 1724, and Gori 1731–1732, which seem to have inspired his wife too as she changed her preferences after their wedding engraving subjects related to Classical Antiquity. It has been noticed that two female busts (Livia and Sabina) were engraved by both Lorenz Natter and Susanna Dorsch, and hypothesised that they were both inspired by casts originating from Stosch's house (Klesse 2000, pp. 28 and 37).

182 Leitschuh 1886, p. 59; Sichelstiel 2012, pp. 74–75.

183 Frauenholz: '(...) *avoit une certaine quantité de dessins précieux de la main de Preißler et de Schweickart, qui représentoient chaque pierre à peu près trois fois plus grande que l'original,*' (Millin 1805, p. 437). Schlichtegroll 1805, vol. I, pp. 12–13 and vol. II, p. 5. Supposing an average gem-height of 10 to 20 mm, a drawing '*trois fois plus grand que l'original*' would only be 30 to 60 mm high which seems rather small. The plates of Stosch 1724 do not reproduce the gems with a regular enlargement ratio, as all the gems are depicted ca. 120 mm high, *i.e.* six to twelve times larger than the originals.

184 Schlichtegroll 1805, vol. I, pp. 12–13, vol. II, p. 5. '(...) *und noch mehr eine vorhandene Anzahl schöner Zeichnungen von vorzüglichen Gemmen aus der Sammlung, die der verstorbene Stosch von dem berühmten Preißler in der Absicht zeichnen liess, um ein dem Picartischen ähnliches Werk herauszugeben, leiteten Hrn. Frauenholz, als den jetzigen Besitzer dieser Zeichnungen und der Schwefel, auf den Gedanken, das auszuführen, woran den Daron Stosch der Tod verhindert hatte.*' (Schlichtegroll 1805, vol. I, pp. 12–13); Michel 1999–2000, p. 82.

185 Schlichtegroll 1797, pls XI, XVII, XX and XXXI.

186 Weiner 1990, unnumbered pages, nos 41–42.

187 In an email exchange on 25 January 2011, Ms. Weiner wrote to me that '*There were a large group of these which were owned by Harry Bober. Some of them were signed and dated. Attribution is secure*'.

188 Auction Max Perl 1937, lot 642 (est. 30 Marks): '*24 Zeichnungen nach antiken Gemmen, in Florenz für Baron Stosch gezeichnet, z.T. in vorgestochenem Rahmen. Nach 1 Zeichnung liegt 1 Stich bei. Feder- u. Tuschzeichnungen. 8°*'. Their fate is unknown.

189 Auction Amsler & Ruthardt 1906, lot. 113: '*24 Blatt: Vergröserte Nachbildungen antiker Gemmen. 5,5/5,5 bis 13,3/15,8. Bleistift-, Tusch- und Federzeichnungen, einige auf blaues Papier.*'

and *Justice*) in 2018 (Figs 4.11–4.12).¹⁹⁰ But, unless one assumes that Preißler was a poor copyist,¹⁹¹ no gem of such iconography can be found in the Antikensammlung in Berlin (where Stosch's collection is preserved). Similarly, when Christie's had a group of 26 drawings of gems and statuettes for sale,¹⁹² the entire group was attributed to Preißler because four drawings were signed by him, despite differences in technique (black chalk/sanguine/pen and brown ink) and in style (some being obviously meant as book plates with *tabulae* for adding captions). Finally, there is a significant group of privately owned drawings in red chalk, all made by the same hand (Figs 4.13–4.16), which originates from the collection of the Avalon Professor of the Humanities at New York University, Harry Bober (1915–1988). How many thre were remains uncertain, but the 26, which have been located, can be classified into five groups:

Bober 'Group A': from the collection of Harry Bober (1915–1988), by whom were gifted in 1954 to Egbert Haverkamp-Begemann (1923–2017),¹⁹³ sold by his estate at Sotheby's, New York, 31 January 2018, lot 265.

Bober 'Group B': from the collection of Harry Bober (1915–1988), by whom were given to an unnamed friend in London. Sold by NYC dealer Paul McCarron (1933–2018) on 16 April 1990 to NYC dealer Mia N. Weiner.¹⁹⁴ Published: Weiner 1990, no. 41 (four heads listed at $10 000 together), which was sold in March 2018, and no. 42 (standing Venus listed at $3000).

Bober 'Group C': from the collection of Harry Bober (1915–1988), inherited by his son Jonathan Bober. Consigned to Mia N. Weiner in January 2011.

Bober 'Group D': from the collection of Harry Bober (1915–1988), by whom were gifted to a certain 'Paul' for his 75th birthday on 30 March 1967,¹⁹⁵ sold by Doyle, New York, rare books & autographs auction, 23 April 2013, lot 136.

Bober 'Group E': the property of a certain 'Robert' in October 1953; sold '*at a Long Island, NY estate sale years ago*'; sold on eBay on 9 March 2018 by seller 'forcatz' (i.e. Paul A. Larrabure).¹⁹⁶

The drawings from the last group were accompanied by a letter dated 19 October 1953 and indecipherably signed (supposedly by Bober himself), sent from the Fogg Art Museum to an unidentified 'Robert', who owned and brought these drawings to Harvard. It includes the enigmatic comment that: '*Not many people (who are not friends of the Bobers) own these rare Preislers*'. It has been recently established that the author of the letter was indeed the art historian Harry Bober who believed them to be by Johann Justin Preißler.¹⁹⁷ Nevertheless, given the four drawings of Borioni's gems signed by Preißler as well as hundreds of his rediscovered works made for Stosch, there is no solid proof to claim the drawings from Bober's collection to be indeed by Preißler.¹⁹⁸

8   Georg Martin Preißler (1700–1754)

Georg Martin Preißler was the son of Johann Daniel Preißler and brother of Johann Justin Preißler (Fig. 4.17). He was a painter, an accomplished portraitist, and like other members of the Preißler family, an engraver.¹⁹⁹ He is not listed among the draughtsmen working for Stosch but he published Stosch's collection of marble statues in 1732.²⁰⁰ Further proof of a connection between Stosch and Georg Martin Preißler is the fact that he made an engraving of Johann Justin Preißler's drawing of the marble bust

---

190   Sotheby's, New York, 31 January 2018, lot 265.
191   This hypothesis seems most unlikely, considering the praise given to his work by Stosch himself in 1727, when Preißler had just started working for him (Heringa 1981, p. 63).
192   Christie's, New York, 22 January 2003, lot 95.
193   Haverkamp-Begemann was Professor of art history at the Institute of Fine Arts (NYU) and Yale University, received the Guggenheim Fellowship, and was a member of the Institute of Advanced Study (Princeton).
194   We are grateful to Ms. Weiner for this information, provided by email on 16 March 2018.
195   By coincidence (?), this 30 March 1892 is the date of birth of Erwin Panofsky (1892–1968), whose book *Gothic Architecture and Scholasticism* Bober had reviewed in 1953 in *The Art Bulletin*, and in whose 1961 *Festschrift* Bober had published an article entitled 'In Principio: creation before time'.
196   Those were accompanied by a letter dated 19 October 1953: indecipherably signed (supposedly by Bober himself), sent from the Fogg Art Museum, this letter was addressed to an unidentified 'Robert' (who owned and brought these drawings to Harvard) and includes the enigmatic comment that '*Not many people (who are not friends of the Bobers) own these rare Preislers*'.
197   Miriam Stewart, Curator of the Collection at Harvard Art Museums, kindly emailed Hadrien J. Rambach on 26 March 2018 that: '*After some sleuthing, we have determined that the author of the letter was the art historian Harry Bober, who taught at Harvard at that time*', and she added that '*According to Harry Bober's son, Jonathan, who is a curator at the National Gallery in Washington, his father owned an album of dozens of these drawings by Preissler*'.
198   However, it is noteworthy that Preißler drew antiquities in various techniques and styles as evidenced by a small group of seven drawings of Egyptian antiquities (including two scarabs) attributed to him from the collection of the Brooklyn Museum in New York, inv. no.: N367.1 P91: https://www.brooklynmuseum.org/opencollection/archives/set/252 – retrieved on 26 July 2023.
199   His life and career are described together with a list of his works in: Leitschuh 1886, pp. 59–67.
200   Preißler 1732; Pietrzak 2018, p. 133.

of Philipp von Stosch sculpted by Edmé Bouchardon, certainly before 1732 (see above and Krakow No. 1666).²⁰¹ Nevertheless, the relationship between him and Stosch was not a direct one but rather due to an intermediary of Johann Justin Preißler. In 1737, like his father, he became a director of the School of Drawing at the Nuremberg Academy.

9   Carl Marcus Tuscher (1705–1751)

Carl Marcus Tuscher or more commonly known (and henceforth called) as Markus Tuscher was a German-born Danish polymath: portrait painter, printmaker, architect and decorator, as well as gem engraver (Fig. 4.18).²⁰² He was a celebrated artist working on the commissions of noble patrons in Italy but ultimately, he was employed at the Danish royal court in Copenhagen.²⁰³ He was born in Nuremberg, where he studied painting and drawing under Johann Daniel Preißler from 1719.²⁰⁴ As a young promising artist, he received a city scholarship to continue his education abroad. He set off for Rome in 1728 where he developed his skills in painting and architecture. His projects of church buildings earned him a Papal Knight's Cross. In Rome, he met his teacher's son, Johann Justin Preißler (see above) and due to his recommendation, he joined in the service of Baron Philipp von Stosch.²⁰⁵ Stosch introduced Tuscher to his wide circle of acquaintances – who commissioned drawings and prints from him.²⁰⁶ Among the illustrious antiquarians and artists he met in Rome, thanks to Stosch, Tuscher befriended Pier Leone Ghezzi, who might have had a considerable impact on the development of his talents as well as on his techniques and style of drawing, and who depicted him in one of his caricatures.²⁰⁷ Noack tells an interesting anecdote about these two, as during a festival organised by Cardinal Polignac at Piazza Navona in Rome to celebrate the birth of the son of French King Louis XV, Ghezzi prepared decorations and Tuscher organised fireworks, but due to some financial problems, Polignac paid the first with a diamond, whereas Tuscher had to wait for his payment for a long time.²⁰⁸ The story seems trivial, however, it may illustrate the master and the pupil relationship between Ghezzi and Tuscher at the time when the latter was in Rome. Ghezzi lists Tuscher amongst his friends,²⁰⁹ and Tuscher engraved an aquaforte depicting Ghezzi in 1743, which might not be a coincidence.²¹⁰ However, in the context of each other's work criticism, it seems rather habitual for Tuscher to complain about the quality of the gem drawings produced by none other but his own master – Pier Leone Ghezzi.²¹¹

In 1731, Tuscher left Rome for Florence with Stosch to help record the latter's enormous collection of gems and to assist with his *Atlas*.²¹² Tuscher drew tombs and Florentine churches for Stosch as archaeological-historical documentary studies.²¹³ Even though Stosch was not personally involved in archaeological excavations at the time, he was well-informed about the new discoveries because he had a habit of sending his draughtsmen (especially Tuscher) to document new findings for him at the very site.²¹⁴ Tuscher also received regular commissions from Gian Gastone de'Medici (1671–1737). For example, he executed a proposal for the facade of the church of Saint Lawrence in Florence.²¹⁵ By 1732, he was a member of the Accademia di Belle Arti in Florence, and in 1734 he left Stosch's atelier, establishing himself in Livorno. He stayed there until 1738 (travelling frequently, for instance to Cortona, Naples and Herculaneum), when he returned to Stosch's house, but he also joined the Accademia di San Luca in Rome.²¹⁶ He remained in Florence until 1741,

---

201 Leitschuh 1886, p. 66.
202 His self-portrait of 1731 is preserved in Oxford (ink, 360 × 230 mm, Ashmolean Museum, inv. A1935.112).
203 The most comprehensive biography of Tuscher so far has been presented in Borroni Salvadori 1978b.
204 Leitschuh 1886, pp. 25–27; Gialluca 2016, p. 59.
205 Justi 1872, p. 337; Leitschuh 1886, pp. 28–30; Eggers 1926, p. 232; Borroni Salvadori 1978b, pp. 85–86; Zwierlein-Diehl 2007, p. 275; Gialluca 2016, pp. 59–60.
206 Hiesinger and Percy 1980, p. 120, no. 107; Gialluca 2016, p. 60.
207 Cod. Ott. lat. 3116, fol. 120. He also gives a brief note on him on another drawing – Cod. Ott. lat. 3113, fol. 114.
208 Noack 1907, p. 41. See also: Bodart 1976, p. 12.
209 Dorati da Empoli 2008, p. 156.
210 Rostriolla 2001, p. 32, note 8. A print made after Tuscher's engraving is preserved, for instance, in the British Museum, inv. no.: 2006,U.407.
211 Zazoff and Zazoff 1983, p. 55. In this context, it is also interesting to notice that living with Tuscher might have not been especially enjoyable as, according to Nagler 1849, p. 171, '(...) *es wird als Sonderbarkeit erzählt, dass der Lehrling im Verlaufe von acht Jahren nicht mehr gesprochen habe, als man auf ein Quartblatt hätte schreiben können*'. The criticism of the work of others might have been also related to Tuscher's personality then.
212 Leitschuh 1886, p. 39; Hiesinger and Percy 1980, p. 120, no. 107; Eggers 1926, p. 233; Sénéchal 2000, p. 138; Hansson 2014, p. 17.
213 Borroni Salvadori 1978a, p. 568.
214 Borroni Salvadori 1978a, p. 582.
215 Borroni Salvadori 1978b, p. 99.
216 Tuscher is attested to live with Stosch in 1739 by a letter Stosch sent to Filippo Venuti (but addressed via Ridolfino Venuti) from Florence on 24 February 1739, in which he says: '(...) *Mon frère, Bonaccorsi, l'insigne Docteur Nagel et Marcus le peintre vous salient.*' – Cod. Cortonese 497, fol. 17 (quoted in *Engelmann* 1908, pp. 330–331).

when he left for Paris, Holland, and finally, London.[217] In 1743, he moved to Copenhagen, where he was made court painter and royal architect to King Christian VI, and in 1748 he became a professor at the Danish Academy of Painting and Drawing.[218] Tuscher was one of the leading architects of the Amalienborg Palace Square in Copenhagen, and he suggested a monument with a large fountain and Frederik V's statue at the centre (cf. Chapter 8, Fig. 8.53). At that time, he also proved useful in a variety of publishing projects. For example, he made copper plates out of original drawings to Frederik Ludvig Norden's *Voyage d'Egypte et de Nubie*, which was published only in 1755.[219] Many of Tuscher's paintings and other works were destroyed during the fire of the Christiansborg Palace in 1794.

Tuscher developed a special relationship with Stosch since he designed a medal for him in 1738 and another one for Stosch's close collaborator Francesco Valesio (1670–1742).[220] He also unfolded many talents under his wings and most likely was a gem collector on a rather small scale. According to a letter from Tuscher to Anton Francesco Gori sent from Livorno on 9 September 1735, Tuscher sent Gori a drawing and three prints of: '*An intaglio in chalcedony (...) currently in my possession*'.[221] Perhaps under the influence of Ghezzi or maybe later when Lorenz Natter joined Stosch's atelier (the two met in 1735), he learnt the art of gem engraving and cut intaglios, sometimes signing them with his name in Greek (ΜΑΡΚΟΣ).[222] In 1733, he made an intaglio with his own portrait and it is supposed that some modern gems from Stosch's collection were engraved by his hand.[223] Tuscher carved the dies for a self-portrait medal, ca. 1733, with his bare head right on the obverse, and a winged Apollo holding a palette, with the emblems of art and architecture on the reverse. But the motif of the owl (with brush, pen and compass) appears on the reverse of a 1751 medal by Magnus Gustav Arbien, in honour of the late Tuscher – here again maybe a sign of his association with Stosch. Tuscher was commissioned by the bookdealer Giuseppe Rigacci (fl. ca. 1765) to paint the portrait of Margaret Rolle d'Ayton, Countess Orford, Lady Walpole (1709–1781), which was then engraved in print by Carlo Gregori. Tuscher painted the profile of the sitter in the guise of Minerva and places it side by side in the exergue, with an owl, which is not only symbolic of Lady Walpole's wisdom, but which also symbolises her protector Philipp von Stosch.[224]

Tuscher's name appears on the list of draughtsmen working for Stosch.[225] He started working as such shortly after his arrival in Rome, as it is clear from his letter to Johann Justin Preißler written on 25 December 1728.[226] According to a letter from Stosch sent to Preißler from Florence on 29 May 1731, Tuscher appears to have drawn antiquities for Stosch extensively and the collector was so satisfied with his work so that he urged Preißler to take the drawings of Tuscher to Florence, since he left them in a hurry in Rome.[227] Indeed, Tuscher appears to have drawn a good number of Stosch's gems.[228] In the preface to his catalogue of Stosch's gems, Winckelmann notices that Tuscher executed several hundred of gem drawings for Stosch.[229] This is now confirmed by the drawings attributed to Tuscher found within the collections in the Princes Czartoryski Museum in Krakow and the Kunstbibliothek in Berlin (cf. Chapters 6–8). Furthermore, in the account of his rich collections, Stosch mentions in the section devoted to modern coins and medals that it also contained a volume of drawings after Stosch's modern medals of the Medicis, Sforza, Gonzaga, d'Este, Bentivoglio, Malatesta, etc., made by Markus Tuscher.[230] This volume is now considered lost; however, five of Tuscher's drawings of Stosch's medals were turned into engravings by Daniel Berger (1744–1824) and Johann Conrad Krüger (1733–1791),

---

217 Leitschuh 1886, p. 42; Borroni Salvadori 1978b, pp. 101–115.
218 Leitschuh 1886, pp. 44–45; Hiesinger and Percy 1980, p. 121, no. 107.
219 Norden 1755; Leitschuh 1886, p. 42.
220 Engelmann 1908, p. 336; Borroni Salvadori 1978b, p. 94; Arbeid, Bruni and Iozzo 2016, pp. 128–129, no. 38.
221 Letter from Markus Tuscher to Anton Francesco Gori dated Livorno 9 September 1735: '*il Disegno e tre impronti della Pietra (...) L'intaglio è in un calcedonio (...) presentemente trovasi nel mio possesso (...)*', see: Borroni Salvadori 1978b, pp. 104–105, nn. 102 and 105. Little is known on this matter, but noteworthy is also Furtwängler's remark that Tuscher owned an Etruscan scarab is noteworthy (1900, vol. III, p. 411, n. 1).
222 Tuscher's engraving skills are also testified by a sulphur impression made after one of his intaglios depicting Minerva in Ghezzi's *dactyliotheca* kept in the Biblioteca Apostolica Vaticana (Ghezzi 1734, cv.194).
223 Leitschuh 1886, pp. 36–38; Borroni Salvadori 1978b, pp. 90–91, 100 and 116; Jenkins and Sloan 1996, p. 95; Tassinari 2010a, pp. 23 and 31. It is still unclear whether Stosch encouraged Tuscher to copy ancient gems and whether this was a training practice or a deliberate action, see: Tassinari 2010b, p. 95.

224 Borroni Salvadori 1978°, p. 92; Borroni Salvadori 1982, p. 35; Borroni Salvadori 1983, pp. 83–84.
225 Stosch 1754, p. 50.
226 Leitschuh 1886, pp. 29–30.
227 Letter from Stosch to Johann Justin Preißler dated Florence 29 May 1731: '*les desseins de M. Marcus (...) que j'avois laissé a Rome.*' quoted in Leitschuh 1886, p. 23.
228 Arbeid, Bruni and Iozzo 2016, p. 129.
229 Winckelmann 1760, p. XXVII.
230 Stosch 1757, p. 268, no. 34. We are grateful to Agnieszka Smołucha-Sładkowska for her kind suggestion that the objects mentioned by Stosch are not coins but rather medals.

and published in 1773 by Johann Karl Wilhelm Möhsen (1722–1795) in his two-volume book entitled *Beschreibung einer Berlinischen Medaillen-Sammlung, die vorzüglich aus Gedächtnis-Münzen berühmter Aerzte bestehet.*[231] According to the author: 'The great treasure of drawings and other works of art by Baron von Stosch is now here in Berlin. His noble nephew, Baron Muzell-Stosch, a great connoisseur and admirable patron of scholars and artists, had the special goodness of giving the author a considerable stock of excellent drawings of the first modern medals and coins, in a very generous way to use. They are all drawn by the famous Marcus Tuscher; and since the drawing of this medal was among them, it was engraved on copper as it is, and attached to this sheet as its final vignette.'[232] Möhsen was the personal physician of Frederick II of Prussia, likewise was Friedrich Ludwig Hermann Muzell (1716–1784), brother of Heinrich Wilhelm Muzell-Stosch. It must have been due to their mutual contacts that Muzell-Stosch made Tuscher's drawings of Stosch's medals available to Möhsen.

Even though the five Stosch medals illustrated by Möhsen in his book probably constitute only a tiny part of the original collection, they say a great deal about its character and Stosch's extraordinary taste and ability to gather some of the rarest pieces. They are all examples of the early Renaissance medals.[233] The first one is a bronze medal attributed to Antonio Marescotti of Ferrara (active ca. 1444–1462), made ca. 1440–1443, depicting on the obverse side a portrait of Italian artist and medallist Pisanello (1395–1455), wearing a brocaded clothing and high, soft crumpled 'berretta' and inscription ·PISANVS· ·PICTOR·, while on the reverse side initials in two registers ·F(ides)·S(pes)·K(aritia)·I(ustitia)· and ·P(rudentia)·F(ortitudo)·T(emperamentia)· standing for the seven virtues (Faith, Hope, Charity, Justice, Prudence, Fortitude and Temperance), honouring Pisanello as a representative of the elite of his time, and a laurel branch below.[234] The second is a bronze medal by Nicholaus (perhaps Niccolo d'Alemagna, a medallist active in Ferrara ca. 1440–1454), made ca. 1445–1450, depicting on the obverse side a portrait of Pisanello (1395–1455) as well but without a cap, while on the reverse side a laurel branch and initials ·F·S·K·I· above and ·P·F·T· below.[235] The third specimen is one of the earliest struck signed bronze medals by Venetian medallist Marco Sesto, featuring a draped and laureate portrait bust of a Roman Emperor Galba to the left, sextant or a compass in front of his face,[236] inscription around: +MARCUS*SESTO*ME*FECIT:V: on the obverse side and a female figure standing on a wheel to the front with a banner of St. Mark (allegory of Venice), inscription around: *PAX*TIBI*VENETIA* and date in the centre 1393 on the reverse.[237] The fourth object is another rare Renaissance bronze medal likely executed by Niccolò Fiorentino (Niccolò di Forzore Spinelli, 1430–1514) ca. 1490–1499, presenting a portrait bust of Marsilius Ficinus (1433–1499) to the left surrounded by an inscription: MARSILIVS · FICINVS · FLORENTINVS on the obverse side and the standing female figure (Wisdom) gazing at a serpent which she is holding up that resembles the Roman goddess Salus on the reverse.[238] The

---

231 Möhsen 1773.
232 Möhsen 1773, p. 108: 'Der große Schatz von Zeichnungen und andern Kunst-Sachen des Freiherrn von Stosch, ist jetzt hier in Berlin befindlich. Dessen würdiger Greb, der Herr Baron Muzell-Stosch, ein großer Kenner und sehr zu schätzender Gdnerr der Gelehrten und Künstler, hat die besondere Gutigkeit gehabt, dem Verfasser, einen ansehnlichen Vorrats von vortrefflichen Zeichnungen der ersten neuern Medaillons und Medaillen, auf eine sehr edele Art zum Gebrauch mitzuteilen. Sie sind alle von der Hand des berühmten Marcus Tuscher, gezeichnet; und da die Zeichnung von dieser Medaille, mit darunter befindlich war, so hat man sie, so wie sie ist, in Kupfer stechen lassen, und diesem Bogen, al seine Schluß-Vignette beigefüget.'
233 These medals will be carefully studied and discussed alongside the coin collection of Philipp von Stosch in: Gołyźniak and Rambach (forthcoming).
234 Möhsen 1773, p. 88. The Münkabinett, Staatliche Museen zu Berlin holds a fine example of this medal (inv. no.: 18200127) which was acquired in 1869 from the collection of Benoni Friedländer (1773–1858), see: Börner 1997, p. 27, no. 36 (with discussion and parallels). For a discussion on the type, see: Hill 1930, no. 87 and Scher (ed.) 2019, no. 11.
235 Möhsen 1773, p. 104. This is a rare version of the first medal discussed above. An example can be found in the collection of the National Gallery of Art in Washington, DC, acc. no.: 1957.14.622 (once in the Gustave Dreyfus (1837–1914) and Samuel H. Kress Foundation, New York collections), however, without the initials of the Seven Virtues on the reverse, see: Hill and Pollard 1967, no. 30; Pollard 2007, vol. I, no. 53. For a discussion on the type, see: Hill 1930, no. 77.
236 See a discussion on the meaning of this symbol in: Stahl and Waldman 1993–1994, p. 170.
237 Möhsen 1773, p. 112. This medal is extremely rare, and it is known from only a few specimens: one is in the Museo Nazionale del Bargello in Florence (Hill 1930, no. 11), another in the collection of the American Numismatic Society in New York (inv. no.: 0000.999.71330), see also discussion in: Scher 2019, p. 35, fig. 13. According to Möhsen (1773, p. 112) and Schlosser (1897, p. 70), Stosch sent his medal to François Fagel in The Hague at some point and since then it remains lost (or unidentified). On the medals struck by the Sesto brothers in Venice, including the one discussed here, see: Stahl and Waldman 1993–1994, esp. pp. 168–171.
238 Möhsen 1773, p. 193. The version of this medal with Salus on the reverse is rare; an example can be found in the collection of the Metropolitan Museum of Art, acc. no.: 23.280.34. Much more popular was a variant with inscription PLATONE on the reverse;

last of Stosch's medals published by Möhsen is a bronze one made in 1508 by Vettor Gambello, called Camelio (ca. 1455/60–1537), depicting on the obverse artist's self-portrait surrounded by an inscription: VICTOR CAMELIVS SVI IPSIVS EFFIGIATOR MDVIII, while on the reverse a sacrificial scene in antique manner with the inscription FAVE FOR(tuna) above and SACRIF(icio) below.[239] While describing some other medals, Möhsen mentions a few more of Stosch's medals which were documented by Tuscher as drawings, however, he did not illustrate them.[240]

The volume of Markus Tuscher's drawings of Stosch's medals stayed with Muzell-Stosch until his death in 1782. It was offered for sale at the auction of the remaining of Stosch's collections organised by the Böhme on 22 April 1783 in Berlin. According to the lot's description, it included 84 *'drawings after medals mostly of the Medici family.'*[241] It is not known what happened to it after the sale in 1783, but since other drawings and prints from Muzell-Stosch's collection were dispersed widely,[242] including the drawings of gems, Tuscher's drawings of Stosch's medals were probably dispersed as well. In any case, it is clear that Tuscher was seriously involved in documentation of various collections of Stosch, not only intaglios and cameos.

10   Georg Abraham Nagel (1712–1779)

Georg Abraham Nagel was another German painter connected to Philipp von Stosch. So far, little was known about his activities in this matter. His self-portrait in the Uffizi Gallery in Florence (Fig. 4.19),[243] and his portrait as etching is also in the Österreichische Nationalbibliothek.[244] Stosch mentions Nagel as a famous painter in Rome among the artists working for him.[245] According to Engelmann, he spent six years in Stosch's house where he made many drawings and paintings for him, but it is not known when exactly this happened. Stosch's correspondence suggests that Nagel worked for him already in the late 1730s. For instance, in a letter from Stosch to Filippo Venuti addressed via his brother Rudolfino Venuti from Florence dated 24 February 1739, Stosch writes in the end *'My brother, Bonaccorsi, doctor Nagel and Markus the painter salute you.'*[246] This could have been a suitable time to start a cooperation with Stosch, who, around this date or even a bit earlier, probably sought an artist to replace Johann Justin Preißler in his service and who would help Markus Tuscher to work on his commissions.[247] In 1741, Nagel became a member of the Florentine Art Academy. Moreover, Stosch's correspondence confirms that Nagel was a sort of an agent working for the collector in the 1740s. In his letter to Henry Howard, 4th Earl of Carlisle, written most likely in 1743, Stosch writes about the Phocion cameo signed by Pyrgoteles (purchased by Cardinal Albani) and he mentions Nagel whom Stosch '(…) *asked to examine the cameo.*' Nagel sent him reports from Rome on this gem, ascertaining that it was much more beautiful than the illustration in Stosch's own book (1724) engraved by Picart after a drawing by Odam because the latter was made after an impression which could not present to Odam all its beauty (he never seen the actual cameo), while the original is absolutely dazzling.[248]

At some point in the 1740s, Nagel travelled to London, Copenhagen, Lubeck, Schwerin, Hamburg and Vienna, but he came back to Rome in 1750 where he worked on

---

see, for instance, the National Gallery of Art in Washington, DC, acc. no.: 1957.14.862 (once in the Gustave Dreyfus (1837–1914) and Samuel H. Kress Foundation, New York collections), see: Hill and Pollard 1967, no. 268; Pollard 2007, vol. I, no. 305.

239   Möhsen 1773, p. 273. This medal is well represented in various public collections, for example: the National Gallery of Art in Washington, DC, acc. no.: 1957.14.741 (once in the Gustave Dreyfus (1837–1914) and Samuel H. Kress Foundation, New York collections), see: Hill and Pollard 1967, no. 148; Pollard 2007, vol. I, no. 170 or The Frick Collection in New York (acc. no.: 2016.2.141). For a discussion on the type, see: Hill 1930, no. 446; Scher 2019, no. 44.

240   Möhsen 1773, pp. 110–111, 118–119 and 133.

241   Auction Muzell-Stosch 1783, lot 917: *'Zeichnungen nach Medaillen, mehrentheils aus der Medicaischen Familie'*. The catalogue is not listed on the Getty Provenance Index Databases. The only copy known to me is in the collections of the UCLA Library Special Collections (Rare Book Stacks Z1015.S88 1783). We are grateful to Agata Pietrzak and especially Kenneth Lapatin for their kind help in accessing it. See also: Pietrzak 2018, p. 135.

242   Pietrzak 2018, p. 131.

---

243   Inv. no.: A630, painted in 1742, oil on canvas, 74,5 × 58 cm, see: Berti (ed.) 1979, p. 941.

244   https://onb.digital/result/BAG_4034652 – retrieved on 6 February 2021.

245   Stosch 1754, p. 50.

246   Cod. Cortonese 497, fogl. 17: *'Mon frère, Bonaccorsi, l'insigne Docteur Nagel et Marcus le peintre vous saluent.'*

247   Since Johann Justin Preißler left Stosch's house in Florence and came back to Nuremberg in 1738 and Markus Tuscher left Stosch's atelier in 1741, could Nagel have settled in Florence in the early 1740s.? It is known that Johann Adam Schweickart came to Stosch's house in 1742 and stayed there until Stosch's death, but as one knows, sometimes two or even three artists worked for Stosch at the same time as it was the case of Johann Justin Preißler, his brother Georg Martin and Markus Tuscher.

248   Letter from Philipp von Stosch to Henry Howard, 4th Earl of Carlisle dated probably 1743? '(…) *donne commission de examiner ce Cammee*' – reproduced in Scarisbrick 1987, p. 104.

some commissions from Cardinal Alessandro Albani.²⁴⁹ In the 1750s, Nagel probably still executed some special commissions for Stosch. In January 1755 Stosch was gifted from a fellow academician Count Vicenzio Ansidei from Perugia the *Tydeus* gem.²⁵⁰ It was probably shortly after that when Stosch published a special flyer to advertise it among his peers and it was also subsequently published in the illustrated edition of Winckelmann's catalogue of Stosch's gems in 1760. The original flyer was engraved by Johann Adam Schweickart (1722–1787) after a drawing by Nagel.²⁵¹ However, it cannot be excluded that Nagel drew this gem for Stosch during an earlier his stay in his house (cf. drawing Krakow No. 1182 and discussion in Chapter 8).

It is noteworthy that Winckelmann came across Nagel while in Rome.²⁵² At that time, Nagel was busy with drawing gems for various collectors, not only for Stosch. An important group of six gem drawings, which appeared for sale in New York in 2020,²⁵³ had apparently been removed from an album that was inscribed '*Georgius Nagel Noricus del. Roma 1754*' on the first page (Figs 4.20–4.23).²⁵⁴ Each of them depicts an engraved gem with the 'actual size' tracing in the lower left corner, and the caption field below inscribed with a title and the material of the stone.²⁵⁵ The cataloguer from Eddie's auction indicated that '*The artist is not known as signed, but it has been suggested he may be a German Goldsmith, George Norwich*' – this was a misunderstanding of the Latin word *Noricus*, meaning 'from Noricum (Southern Germany)', i.e. 'from Nuremberg.' The signature is therefore clearly: 'drawn by Georg Nagel from Nuremberg in Rome in 1754.' Georg Abraham Nagel had indeed studied in Nuremberg (like the Preißler brothers and Johann Adam Schweickart) and he is attested to have signed as '*G. Nagel Noricus*' on a 1770 portrait of Stosch's former assistant Christian Dehn (1696–1770), whom he knew from his stay in Stosch's house.²⁵⁶ There are two more known drawings of the same size from the same group. They were sold online, and the auctioneer attributed them to Nagel and described as '*Reportedly after Roman stones in Cardinal Carlo Rezzonico's collections.*'²⁵⁷ The second gem is the only one providing a clue to the owner of

---

249 Engelmann 1908, p. 338.
250 AGDS II, no. 238; Hansson 2014, p. 23.
251 Schweickart's engraving after Nagel's drawing is reproduced in AGDS II, fig. 3, Jenkins and Sloan 1996, p. 96; Rügler in Winckelmann 2013, p. XLIX and Hansson 2018, p. 86.
252 Justi 1956, vol. II, pp. 25–26; Zazoff and Zazoff 1983, p. 57.
253 Eddie's auction, New York, 24 May 2020, lot 72: '*Six Old Master Drawings by George Nagel Noricus in Ink on paper of enlargements of Cardinal Rezzonico's collection of carved Roman Intaglio Gems. From a now disbursed album inscribed on the first page, "Georgius Nagel Noricus, del. Roma 1754"* (with stamped copy of inscription); *each image with an "actual size" tracing of the size of each gem in lower left corner, a subject title in Latin under gem, and the kind of stone: HARPOCRATES in Corneola, MINERVA STANS in Carneola, VENATOR in Onycvlo, MVSA in Sardonyche, HERMAPHRODITVS in Onycvlo, VENUS IN COLLVDENS CUM CVPININE in Plasma. The artist is not known as signed, but it has been suggested he may be a German Goldsmith, George Norwich. Each drawing mounted on a uniform larger antique sheet of gray paper and now in acid free archival book mats. Height of antique gray paper mounts 8 3/4 inches (22.5 cm.) X width of antique gray paper mounts 7 3/4 inches (19.9 cm.)*'. Condition report: '*old stains, small tears, wear and trim to the original drawings before the gray paper mounting which is uniform and in good condition*'.
254 The mount of each drawing was stamped with a copy of this inscription.
255 Drawings ca. 150 × 127 mm each: No. 1 '*Harpocrates. in Corneola*' (Fig. 4.20): Harpocrates standing to the front in contrapposto with the right hand raised to his mouth and cornucopia in the left arm supported on a column next to him. A cloak around his arms and lotus flower on the head. Ground line (gem ca. 12 × 9 mm); No. 2 '*Minerva stans in Carneola*' (Fig. 4.21): Athena/Minerva standing next to a column to the front in contrapposto, head turned right. She is dressed in a chiton and has a himation around her waist that she is grasping with the right hand, a Corinthian helmet on her head. She is holding a spear in the left hand, a shield at her feet. Ground line (gem ca. 22 × 14 mm); No. 3 '*Venator. in Onycvlo*' (Fig. 4.22): a hunter dressed in exomis and cloak walking to the left and shouldering a staff with a bird (partridge?) and a hare attached (gem ca. 15 × 11 mm); No. 4 '*Musa. in Sardonyche*': Terpsichore, the muse of dance and chorus, standing in profile to the right, dressed in a chiton and himation, playing a lyre. A staff (?) in front of her and a naked boy blowing an aulos (?) on a column behind her. Ground line (gem ca. 18 × 12 mm); No. 5 '*Hermaphroditvs. in Onycvlo*': Hermaphroditus standing in contrapposto in three-quarter to the left with a cloak in his hands (gem ca. 12 × 9 mm). This same gem, or a nicolo of identical iconography, is depicted on a drawing in Krakow; No. 6 '*Venus Collvdens cum Cvpinine. in Plasma*': Venus, with a garment around her left arm and leg, seated on a rock under a tree, playing with Cupid (gem ca. 11 × 8 mm).
256 Drawn by Nagel, this portrait was engraved by Domenico Cunego and used as frontispiece of Dolce 1772. Dehn had become manufacturer of glass and sulphur casts of engraved gems, which provides another link between Nagel and glyptics. He left Stosch's house in Florence in 1739, which supports the hypothesis that Nagel was employed by Stosch already in the late 1730s unless these two met only when Nagel returned to Rome in 1750. On the side note, it is noteworthy that Johann Justin Preißler was also called as 'Noricus', for example, see the full title of Preißler 1732. Moreover, Johann Adam Schweickart, who like Nagel studied in Nuremberg, signed one of the plates designed for Stosch's second book on ancient signed gems as 'J.A. Schweickart Norieg: sc. Florent' (see: Rügler in Winckelmann 2013, p. XLV) which is similar to the term 'Noricus' used by Nagel and Johann Justin Preißler.
257 26 November 2019 by Stockholms Auktionsverk (lot 703091): No. 7 '*Diomedes cum Paladio in Carneola*': Diomedes, helmeted, the lower part of his body covered by a robe, seated on a cuirass to the right. In his right hand a sword, on the left, outstretched one Palladion; a shield decorated with a star in front of him; No. 8 '*Fœmina sacerdos on Onycula*' (Fig. 4.23): a woman (Amymone?)

the gems when Nagel drew them. Winckelmann already commented that on this gem the woman seems to be collecting water from a fountain, whilst another intaglio[258] depicts a tombstone instead, the marble monument being without a female mask.[259] This[260] intaglio belonged in the 1750s to the marquis Giovanni Carlo Molinari (1715–1763) and was reproduced in plaster impressions (Fig. 4.17).[261]

After the death of Stosch in 1757, Nagel apparently stayed in touch with his nephew and heir Heinrich Wilhelm Muzell-Stosch (1723–1782).[262] Indeed, when Muzell-Stosch reduced the price of his uncle's *Atlas* to 15 000 scudi,[263] in order to attempt to sell it to Cardinal Alessandro Albani (1692–1779), he tried to gain Albani's favour by sending him a cameo as a gift. In Florence, he consigned the gem to a British traveller who was about to leave for Rome, and it was then entrusted to Nagel to bring it to Albani.[264] The cardinal was disappointed, so Muzell-Stosch offered to send another gem, and begged him to return to Nagel the inventory of the *Atlas*, which he had sent him several weeks earlier.[265] Therefore, one assumes that Nagel was involved in the attempt to sell the *Atlas* (to which he had contributed).[266]

Despite those close links between Nagel and Stosch as well as his heir Muzell-Stosch, the group of drawings from 1754 discussed above seem to have been commissioned by another – unidentified? – collector. The (unseen) first page of the dismembered album apparently mentioned that those drawings depicted a selection from '*Cardinal Rezzonico's collection of carved Roman Intaglio Gems.*' Did indeed Carlo della Torre di Rezzonico (1693–1769), Cardinal-Priest of Santa Maria in Aracoeli since 1747, own a collection of engraved gems in 1754? His relative count Antonio Giuseppe della Torre di Rezzonico (1709–1785)

---

dressed in a chiton and himation standing with a vessel next to a fountain.

258 London, British Museum inv. 1867,0507.39, formerly in the collections of Leone Strozzi and the Duke of Blacas, see: Lippert¹ I², p. 111, no. 445; Walters 1926, no. 561. Also illustrated in the Krakow drawing No. 605 (cf. Krakow gem drawings catalogue in Appendix 2). Winckelmann mistakenly wrote that the Strozzi gem is a carnelian intaglio '*semblable à une Sardoine du Cabinet de l'Empereur à Florence,*' but the gem illustrated in Gori 1731–1732, vol. II, p. 120, pl. LXXIII.2 is clearly mentioned to be the same one: '*Inscalptum Sardae ex Museo Strozzio.*' But there are, in fact, at least three other intaglios of this type: one in sard which is lost (formerly in the collection of cardinal Girolamo Verospi (1599–1652), see: Lippert¹ III², p. 45, no. 388; Zwierlein-Diehl 1986, no. 374); a carnelian in Berlin, see: AGDS II, no. 386; and one banded agate in Vienna, see: Furtwängler 1900, vol. I, pl. XXXIX.26, vol. II, p. 188; Zwierlein-Diehl 1973, no. 295.

259 The iconography has been identified as that of *Elettra alla Tomba di Agamennone suo Padre* (Pirzio Biroli Stefanelli 2007, p. 127, no. II.88).

260 Or another intaglio with an identical iconography and the same material (sardonyx).

261 Lippert¹ III², p. 45, no. 389 (mentioned in Winckelmann 1760, class II, pp. 310–311, no. 1864 = Borbein, Kunze and Rügler 2019, no. II.1864). The fate of this particular gem is unknown. Molinari's attractive portrait in pastel by Rosalba Carriera (1675–1757) was sold at Christie's Milan on 28 May 2008, lot 151, and it might be that Giovanni Paolo Panini painted the scene of his nomination as Archbishop of Damascus in front of the pope (cf. Artcurial, Paris, 8 November 2011, lot 18). Three *post-mortem* auctions of his belongings were organized in Brussels: on 4 July 1763 sqq. (Lugt 1308: '*Dessins 4, Estampes 13, Livres 760, Cartes 32*', 52 pp.), on 15 July 1763 (Lugt 1311: '*Tableaux 86, Tapis Tapisseries Etoffes Meubles 159, Bijoux 92, Porcelaines 147, Divers 129*', 19 pp.), and on 27 July 1763 sqq. (missing in Lugt who conflates its content with the previous one: '*Tapis Tapisseries Etoffes Meubles 159, Bijoux 92, Porcelaines 147, Divers 129*', 53 pp.). The last sale contained '*Une superbe Collection d'Antiques en agate, carniole, onyx, &c. montées en or, dont plusieurs sont enrichies de brillans*' with the precision '*Ces articles se vendront à la main & pas à l'encan*'.

262 The 'Stosch' who was caricatured by Thomas Patch in 1765 (D'Amelio 2006, pp. 65, 69, no. 6, fig. 31), is probably Muzell.

263 Hansson 2022, p. 57: '*At the time of Stosch's death in 1757, the Topographical Atlas consisted of 334 large folio volumes with 31.500 purchased or specifically commissioned drawings, prints and maps of cities, fortifications, palaces, churches and monuments from around the world.*' This remarkable achievement attests that Stosch was not afraid to commission, own, and classify, large numbers of documents.

264 On Nagel and Albani, see Anon. 1781, pp. 117–118 (*non vidi*); Borchia 2019, pp. 5, 156–157. See the letters of Muzell-Stosch to Albani, one undated and the other from 7 February 1758 (KA, Fasz. 170, ff. ss. nn.), and their replies on 11 and 18 February.

265 The cardinal was disappointed, as he found the cameo too worn: '(…) *J'ai recu hier le Camé, que Vous Vous étes donné la peine de m'envoyer, quoique par les traces, quon y remarque ce soit une piece digne du recueil, dont il a été tiré, je l'ai neanmoins trouvé si delabré, qu'il n'est aucunement propre à l'usage, au quel étoit destiné, c'est pourquoi je l'ai rendu à M. Nagel de qui le recevrez de retour avec les assurances de l'estime infinie, avec laquelle je ne cesserai jamais d'étre*' (letter from Albani to Muzell-Stosch dated 18 February 1758 – KA, Fasz. 170, f. s. n.; quoted in Borchia 2019, p. 56). Muzell-Stosch apologised, and asked if Albani was rather looking for a head or a figurative scene, small enough to be set a ring or larger: '*Le Sieur George Nagell m'a ecrit que Votre Eminence desiroit avoir un beau Cameé de ma Collection. Je la supplie de me faire savoir de quelle espece, ou téte ou historieé et si ce de grandeur de bague, ou plus grand. Quant aux pierres graveés en crems, avant que je n'aye perdu toute esperance de les vendre en gros je ne voudrois rien separer de la Collection. En cas que Votre Eminence ait encore le Catalogue de l'Atlas que j'ai eu l'honnuer de lui envoyer, il y-a quelque tems, je la supplie de le donner à Nagell qui le lui remettera lorsqu'elle l'ordonnera. Et je ne manquerai pas d'informer Votre Eminence lorsque je trouverai occasion de m'en defaire. Je ne crois cependant pas que cela sera avant la paix. Quoique Votre Eminence n'ait pas reussie à me faire vendre cet Atlas, je la supplie d'etre persuadeé que, je ne suis pas moins, avec un tres profond respect*' (undated letter from Muzell-Stosch to Albani – KA, Fasz. 170, f. s. n.; quoted in Borchia 2019, p. 157).

266 Winckelmann 1952–1957, vol. III, p. 382; Borroni Salvadori 1978b, p. 88, n. 12.

did own at least one very important cameo, the so-called *Bulla of Maria*,[267] but he had acquired it from Felice Caronni (1747–1815) and he is not known to have inherited any gem. In fact, cardinal Rezzonico, who is better known under the name of Pope Clement XIII since 1758 when he was elected as the 248th pontiff, is not known to have ever been a collector, which renders these drawings precious (and intriguing) documents. They are also valuable because they give us priceless insight into Nagel's techniques and styles applied for visual documentation of gems and because of that a good number of drawings found in Krakow and Berlin can be attributed to his hand.

11 Johann Adam Schweickart (1722–1787)

Johann Adam Schweickart was a German draughtsman and printmaker from Nuremberg. He specialised in book illustrations, as his father Wolfgang Schweikart had a publishing house. On 1 June 1735, he began his five-year apprenticeship with the engraver Georg Daniel Heumann (1691–1759).[268] Schweickart was then a student of Georg Martin Preißler. In 1742, being only twenty years old, he migrated to Florence, where, together with Georg Abraham Nagel, he replaced the Preißler brothers and Markus Tuscher in the service of Baron Philipp von Stosch.[269] In 1756, Schweickart was nominated a member of the Accademia dell'Arte del Disegno in Florence. This was due to his invention of aquatint, a method for printing tonal gradations. Schweikart's particular variation of aquatint was popular in Florence from the late 1750s.[270]

Schweickart was a long-term collaborator and he stayed with Stosch until his death in 1757.[271] When the Baron died, he personally brought his body to the city port of Livorno in a boat on the Arno River, because Protestant burials were not allowed in Florence.[272] In 1760, he returned to Nuremberg, visiting Venice, Trieste and Vienna on his way.[273] He later devoted himself primarily to the execution of engravings after paintings by famous old masters.[274] Indeed, Stosch mentions him among the artists working for him and furthermore, he says that Schweickart was selected to prepare illustrations for the supplement of the *Gemmae antiquae caelatae* book.[275] He produced engravings of the two most famous gems in Stosch's collection: an Etruscan scarab presenting five out of Seven against Thebes and another one with Tydeus scraping his leg.[276] Some further engravings of Stosch gems and glass pastes depicting gems with signatures and apparently inscriptions taken as such have been published in the luxurious edition of Winckelmann 1760 catalogue. These seem to be illustrations originally intended for Stosch's supplement to the *Gemmae antiquae caelatae* book (cf. Chapter 10).[277]

Even though Schweickart is said to have produced many more gem engravings for Stosch,[278] surprisingly only those mentioned above are known. In fact, he could have been more involved in Stosch's *Atlas* project rather than in gems.[279] Zazoff claimed that coming back to Nuremberg from Florence, Schweickart brought with him gem impressions and engravings after Stosch's intaglios and perhaps his own drawings too.[280] This is confirmed by Schlichtegroll, who says that after Schweickart's death in 1787, his collaborator Johann Fredrich Frauenholz purchased in Nuremberg Schweickart's cabinet of sulphur gem impressions as well as a few drawings by Preißler that he had taken with himself to Nuremberg after Stosch's death.[281] Still, the drawings by Schweickart may not be as numerous as they were originally thought to be. It seems a more likely scenario that at the time Schweickart worked for Stosch he focused on the engravings, while he was supplied with drawings made by Georg Abraham Nagel, whose works have been recently discovered (see above). In any case, it appears that some of Schweickart's drawings and subsequent engravings were used for his own publication on Stosch's gems entitled *Description Des Pierres Gravées Du Feu Baron de Stosch, Par Feu l'Abbé Winckelmann, Dessineés D'Après Les Empreintes Et Graveés En Taille-Douce Par Jean Adam Schweikart*, published in 1775.[282] The rest remains unknown or was to some extent reused by Frauenholz and Schlichtegroll, since the former

---

267 A cameo inscribed with the names of the family members of Maria, wife of Honorius (AD 384–423), set in a gold pendant with emeralds and garnets, which was discovered in February 1544 in the chapel of Saint Petronilla, Saint Peter's (Rome), and is nowadays preserved in Paris (Musée du Louvre, inv. no. OA 9523, anonymous gift of 1951). At Rezzonico's death, the *bulla* had passed into the collection of Don Carlo Trivulzio (1715–1789), see Rambach 2017, pp. 266–267, pl. 1.
268 Anon. 1791, pp. 250–251.
269 Müller 1864, p. 506.
270 Wiebel 2007, pp. 98–101.
271 Schlichtegroll 1805, vol. I, pp. 12–13; Zwierlein-Diehl 2007, p. 275.
272 Anon 1791, p. 251; Rée 1891, p. 330.
273 Rügler in Winckelmann 2013, p. XXV.
274 Anon 1791, p. 254; Müller 1864, p. 506; Rée 1891, p. 330.
275 Stosch 1754, p. 50. This is also suggested by Anon 1791, p. 251.
276 Hansson 2020 p. 61.
277 Anon 1791, p. 251; Schlichtegroll 1805, vol. I, pp. 11–12; Zazoff and Zazoff 1983, p. 57; Rügler in Winckelmann 2013, pp. XLII–LII.
278 Zazoff and Zazoff 1983, p. 181.
279 Anon 1791, p. 251.
280 Zazoff and Zazoff 1983, p. 57.
281 Schlichtegroll 1805, vol. I, pp. 11–13.
282 Schweickart 1775; Michel 1999–2000, p. 81.

is said to have purchased them together with some drawings by Johann Justin Preißler.[283]

Regarding Schweickart's *dactyliotheca*, Zazoff claimed that artists working in Stosch's atelier on his projects created *dactyliothecae* of his gems, and one of them was made by or for Schweickart, while the others are kept in the Biblioteca Apostolica Vaticana.[284] Zazoff's suggestion does not stand, since the Biblioteca Apostolica Vaticana holds only one *dactyliotheca* composed by Pier Leone Ghezzi, as well as a full set of 2061 impressions and casts made by Stosch's collaborator in this matter – Christian Dehn.[285] While the first was an entirely private initiative of Ghezzi (see above), the second might be connected to Stosch; however, there is no other *dactyliotheca* composed by any other draughtsman working for Stosch.[286] In conclusion, although Schweickart spent much of his career in Florence working for Stosch, not many of the works he made for him survived and are known today.

---

283 Schlichtegroll 1805, vol. I, pp. 12–13, vol. II, p. 5.
284 Zazoff and Zazoff 1983, p. 181, especially n. 172.
285 Alteri 1987.
286 We are grateful to Federica Orlando and Eleonora Giampiccolo from the Gabinetto di Manoscritti and Gabinetto delle Medaglie della Biblioteca Apostolica Vaticana (respectively) for their kind help in investigating this issue.

PLATE 20

FIGURE 4.1

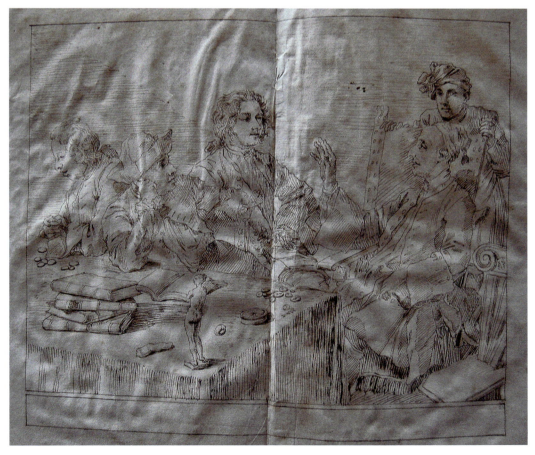

FIGURE 4.2

FIGURE 4.3

FIGURE 4.4

FIGURE 4.5

FIGURE 4.6

PLATE 22

FIGURE 4.7

FIGURE 4.8

FIGURE 4.9

FIGURE 4.10

FIGURE 4.11

FIGURE 4.12

FIGURE 4.13

FIGURE 4.14

FIGURE 4.15

FIGURE 4.16

PLATE 24

FIGURE 4.17

FIGURE 4.18

FIGURE 4.19

FIGURE 4.20

FIGURE 4.21

FIGURE 4.22

FIGURE 4.23

PART 3

Philipp von Stosch and His Paper Museum of Gems

∴

CHAPTER 5

Stosch's Corpus of Gem Drawings in the Archives

Paweł Gołyźniak

1 Stosch Commissions a Large Number of Gem Drawings

Chapter 4 presents all the known artists testified to work for Stosch, either throughout many years or just for specific projects and tasks producing gem drawings for him among others. Their production must have been of considerable size and started in early stages of Stosch's career. Already on 19 December 1722 Stosch, who settled permanently in Rome in January that year, wrote to Carl Gustav Heraeus (1671–1725) a letter in which he reported that: '*I am having all my ancient pastes* [e.g. ancient glass gems or modern glass pastes]¹ *drawn here, the number of finished ones has already risen to 270, but when they are completed it will pass one thousand and even more.*'² This is the earliest record to indicate that he indeed commissioned a large number of gem drawings. Apparently, the 270 ancient (?) glass gems were documented from his own collection, which was already at the time of substantial size, since the work eventually reached more than 1000 drawings at least. The very same year, Stosch informs Lord Carteret that he had earned a good reputation in Rome by having trained young artists in the difficult art of making accurate visual documentation of ancient engraved gems and other antiquities.³ This is not an empty boast because indeed, Pier Leone Ghezzi, one of Stosch's very close collaborators and friends, as well as a passionate collector and documentalist of gems and other antiquities, wrote in one of the caricatures dedicated to him, preserved in the Biblioteca Apostolica Vaticana, as follows: '(…) *and a very good friend of mine, a man knowledgeable in everything, and very erudite in antiquities, and I learned a great deal from him.*'⁴ Stosch had an impressive ability to enter into fruitful cooperation with artists whom he clearly inspired. For example, Ghezzi is believed to have documented around 1000 of gems (including many of those from Stosch's collection) for his own corpus of drawings of antiquities, following in the footsteps of Stosch.⁵

At that time, Stosch's book, *Gemmae antiquae caelatae*, was being produced. During realisation of that project, which started as early as 1715, Stosch cooperated with Girolamo Odam, among others, who originally prepared drawings for the plates. Interestingly, in 1738, Odam, in his letter to Anton Francesco Gori, recalls that when Stosch came to Rome for the first time (1715), he had a chance to compare the impression of the famous so-called *Seal of Michelangelo*, a carnelian intaglio featuring a celebration or sacrifice in honour of Bacchus during the grape harvesting, at the time in the French royal collection, and some circulating prints of that gem (certainly those by Élisabeth Sophie Chéron (1648–1711)). Because they proved to be inaccurate, he drew himself the gem anew.⁶ However, he also says that he produced a large number of gem drawings for Stosch, which were later redrawn by a German: '*So I made an exact drawing of it which is in the hands of Baron Stosch as well as two thousand and*

---

1 Stosch probably refers here not only to ancient glass gems from his collection but also glass pastes he sometimes took after originals to complement his cabinet. On the discovered gem drawings as well as in his correspondence, the term '*pates Antiques*' stands for either genuine ancient pieces in glass and glass pastes made after original intaglios and cameos. Stosch owned at least 379 of the latter at the end of his life. Most likely, Stosch initially manufactured them himself, as he learnt their production while in Paris in 1713 under the guidance of a teacher of physics and chemistry and a private physician to the Duke of Orléans, Wilhelm von Homberg (1652–1715). Later, he was assisted by his manservant Christian Dehn. They were of such good quality that Winckelmann often took them as ancient pieces while cataloguing Stosch's gem collection in 1760, see: Furtwängler 1896, pp. V–VIII. These glass pastes are now considered lost during the Second World War, but they might be in the State Historical Museum in Moscow, see: Zwierlein-Diehl 2007, p. 275.
2 The translations are all mine unless otherwise stated. The original text sounds as follows: '*Je fais desiner icy toutes mes pates Antiques dont le nombre des achevees est dejà monte a 270 quand ils seront achevé cela passera les milles et plus.*' Schneider 1907, pp. 346–347; Hansson 2022, p. 63, n. 73.

3 Letter from Walton [Stosch] to Lord Carteret dated 28 February 1722 (NA Kew SP 85/14 fols 9–12); Hansson 2021b, p. 62.
4 The Biblioteca Apostolica Vaticana, Cod. Ott. lat. 3112 fol. 115 – '(…) *e molto mio amico, Uomo Letterato in tutto, et eruditissimo nelle antichita, et io vi o'imparato assai.*'; Hansson 2021b, p. 62.
5 Pier Leone Ghezzi's gem drawings are now mostly preserved in the Biblioteca Apostolica Vaticana: Cod. Ott. lat. 3100–3101, 3103–3104 and 3106–3109. On that issue, see: Gołyźniak (forthcoming – Ghezzi).
6 Letter from Odam to Gori dated Rome 21 December 1738 – Epistolario di Anton Francesco Gori: no. 11123, volume BVI121, carte 8r–9v. I am grateful to Hadrien J. Rambach for referring me to this letter and identification of the prints mentioned by Odam as of Élisabeth Sophie Chéron, cf. Chapters 8 and 9 in this volume.

seven hundred drawings of gems made by my hand, which then lost their character of antiquity because he had them redrawn by a German, who put his own character on them, but that is said with my friendly seal of secrecy.'[7] The number of 2700 drawings of gems made by Odam alone for Stosch seems shocking at first glance, but Justi confirms that exact number.[8] Moreover, even though Stosch did not tell Heraeus explicitly, who drew gems for him in 1722, considering the numbers given in both letters and Stosch's later cooperation with other draughtsmen like Johann Justin Preißler (between 1726–1738) or Markus Tuscher (between 1728–1741) and Georg Abraham Nagel (in the late 1730s and early 1740s), Odam seems to be a suitable candidate to start documenting gems for Stosch. The fact that, as Odam says, his drawings were later redrawn by a German artist only prove that the visual documentation of gems commissioned by Stosch started early and continued expanding as the time went by.

This is confirmed by Stosch himself, who admitted that he had all his gems documented as drawings by artists like Johann Justin Preißler, Markus Tuscher, Georg Abraham Nagel and Johann Adam Schweickart.[9] Moreover, in his memoirs, Preißler recalls that he delivered to Stosch a considerable number of drawings of gems and other antiquities, and he mentions in particular a carnelian intaglio presenting Perseus and Andromeda mounted in a gold ring.[10] Furthermore, it is said that upon his return to Germany, he brought back nine or ten volumes of drawings with him, among which there could be drawings of gems.[11] Indeed, it was and it is still habitual for artists to collect and keep their drawings, usually in their studios, because they functioned as records of works made or sold. They were also often kept as inspiration for future projects. In this respect, the example of Pier Leone Ghezzi who used to keep hundreds if not thousands of his drawings that he later put into albums is the best illustration of that phenomenon.[12] However, in the case of the draughtsmen working for Stosch, this is a different situation, since all the drawings they produced were commissioned and accumulated by Stosch for his corpus. Apart from Bernard Picart, none of the artists working for Stosch is known to have produced counterproofs of their drawings or copies which they could keep for themselves or sell.

There is further proof of Stosch commissioning many gem drawings during his lifetime. For example, in the preface to his catalogue of Stosch's gems, Winckelmann justifies himself that he made every effort to compensate for the lack of illustrations, writing erudite commentaries whenever possible. At the same time, he claims that if the times had been better, the catalogue would have been published fully illustrated because Stosch had most of his gems drawn and Markus Tuscher alone produced hundreds of them: *'We have already informed the reader what we have done to make up for the figures that are missing in this work. In better times, one could have anticipated the wishes of the Curious; for the deceased owner of this cabinet had the vast majority of his gems drawn enlarged by skilful artists, who lived for many years in his house. Among the drawings he had made, there are a few hundred by the hand of the famous Marcus Tuscher.'*[13] To conclude, those gem drawings must have existed because, in his letter to Antonio Baldani written in Florence 26–30 September 1758, Winckelmann admits that while writing the catalogue of Stosch's gems, he used a large number of already prepared drawings of gems to facilitate his work.[14]

2 More Than Twenty Volumes of Gem Drawings – Stosch's *Paper Museum of Gems*

The production of gem drawings on Stosch's various commissions was ongoing throughout his whole career, but can the archives be more specific than that? Stosch left little autobiographical material and even in his correspondence he appears to say little about his affairs, how he built and managed his various collections, book project documentation and his studies.[15] It is sometimes suggested that he gained new items in ways that were not

---

7   The same letter as above: '*Io poi ne feci un disegno esatto che è nelle mani del Baron Stosch siccome si ritrova fatti di mia mano due mila e settecento disegni di gemme che esso poi gli hà levato il gusto del suo carattere antico con farle ridisegnare da uno tedesco che vi hà posto il suo carattere ma questo sia detto con il mio sigillo di segretezza di amicizia.*'
8   Justi 1871, p. 29 and 1872, p. 334.
9   Stosch 1754, p. 50 – although his list of draughtsmen working for Stosch is incomplete as it does not include Odam and Ghezzi.
10 Sturm 1863, pp. 383–384; Leitschuh 1886, p. 20; Eggers 1926, pp. 230–231. Preißler's drawing of an intaglio with Perseus and Andromeda might be Berlin vol. V, pls 54, 55 or 56.
11 Leitschuh 1886, p. 59; Sichelstiel 2012, pp. 74–75.
12 Witte 2018.

13 Winckelmann 1760, p. XXVII: '*On a déjà prevenu le Lecteur sur ce qu'on a fait pour suppléer aux figures qui manquent à cet Ouvrage. Dans de meilleurs tems on auroit pu prévenir les souhaits des Curieux; car le défunt Posseßeur de ce Cabinet en avoit fait déssiner en grand la meilleure partie par d'habiles Artistes qui ont vécu plusieurs années dans sa maison. Parmi les Desseins qu'il avoir fait faire, on en compte quelques Centaines de la main du célébre Marc Tuscher.*'
14 Winckelmann 1961, p. 105, no. 31: '(...) *a facilitarmi il lavoro ho soltanto i disegni fatti in grande.*'
15 Lewis 1961, p. 50; Pietrzak 2018, pp. 128–129.

always transparent, thus one knows so little.¹⁶ However, as far as his transactions, exchanges, etc., are concerned, he may have simply not been in the habit of recording them because he sold things directly to visitors of his house in Florence. Moreover, it might be that much of his documentation, correspondence and archives is lost. For example, once Stosch left Rome, he still exchanged letters with Cardinal Albani on a regular basis, mostly on the subject of Antiquity. This correspondence is now almost certainly lost during the unsuccessful transfer of Albani's papers and archives, which were purchased in 1863 by Mommsen for the Prussian government but sank with the capsized ship that was transferring them to Germany.¹⁷ Furthermore, in his letter to Antonio Baldani dated Florence 26–30 September 1758, Winckelmann says that: '*In addition to the collection of gems, Baron von Stosch possessed a collection of sulphur impressions, which he often used, that were taken from engraved gems from all collections in Europe. They were sold [?] after his death, but during the transport by sea from Florence to Hamburg, the 28 000 were reduced to 17 407, ordered in 151 boxes.*'¹⁸ Another source, the auction catalogue of the sale of the remaining parts of Stosch's rich collections that took place in 1783 in Berlin after the death of his heir Muzell-Stosch (see below), confirms that Stosch's collection of sulphur gem impressions was badly damaged during the transfer at the sea as well as due to other accidents: '*A collection of fine impressions in sulphur after ancient engraved gems, in 210 matching boxes, each respectively contains 50, 60, 70, 80, 90, 100, 110, up to 120 pieces, to be sold together. One can only say that this cabinet includes impressions of gems formerly possessed by the Baron von Stosch in Florence, and those which are the remnants of the large Stosch's collection of impressions of antiquities from all the cabinets* [e.g. impressions of gems from all European cabinets], *which, however, have been broken in a shipwreck and ruined by other incidents, yet they survived.*'¹⁹ After Stosch's death,

jede resp. zu 50, 60, 70, 80, 90, 100, 110, bis 120 Stuck enthält, und die zusammen verkauft warden soll. Man kann davon nur so viel anzeigen, daß solche das Cabinet von antiken Gemmen u. so ehemals der Baron von Stosch in Florenz besessen enthalte, auch aus Ueberbleibseln der großen Stoschischen Sammlung aller Antiken aus allen Kabinettern, die aber durch Schiffbruch und andere Vorfälle verdorben und zersteuer worden, bestehe.' There is a difference in the number of boxes with gem impressions mentioned by Winckelmann (151) and put at auction in Berlin (210). This is due to the fact that in his letter to Baldani Winckelmann refers only to the surviving part of Stosch's collection of sulphur gem impressions (17 407 in 151 boxes), while at the auction in Berlin, the original and complete *Dactyliotheca Stoschiana* – a collection of 3444 sulphur impressions of Stosch's own gems and glass pastes in 59 boxes, was put up for sale as well. Indeed, a great cabinet of gem impressions in sulphur numbering ca. 28 000 items was formed by Stosch over his life, which is confirmed by Winckelmann (1760, p. xxix). According to Winckelmann (1961, pp. 104–105, no. 35), they were already sold in 1758 and dispatched to Hamburg but this is unclear, and, in fact, Winckelmann probably meant that they were sent to Hamburg like Stosch's collection of drawings and prints to be sold there, but a considerable part of this cabinet was lost at sea during the transport (cf. above). Apparently, the sale in Hamburg was unsuccessful because the fourth auction of Stosch's collections organised in London in 1764 by *Langford and Son* included lot 40: '*A large collection of impressions in sulphur, from antique gems; with a catalogue of them*' (Auction Stosch IV). The impressions did not find a buyer and stayed with Muzell-Stosch until his death, and they were subsequently offered at the auction in Berlin in 1783. At that point, Stosch's remaining gem impressions attracted attention of Adelheid Amalie von Schmettau, Princess Gallitzin (1748–1806), who, in her letter to François Hemsterhuis (1721–1790) sent from Münster on 14 March 1783, said that Franz Friedrich Wilhelm von Fürstenberg (1729–1810) would like to acquire the sulphurs for the local Academy: '*Voici un catalogue de feu Stosch qu'il faut me renvoyer avec le retour du courier. Lisez y seulement les articles derniers concernant les souffres. Une collection d'environ 20 000 des plus beaux cabinets que Mr. de Furstenberg auroit envie d'acquerir pour l'academie d'ici, et il vous prie de nous dire tout d'abord jusqu'où on peut aller pour le prix.*', ['Here is a catalogue of the late Stosch which must be sent back to me with the return of the courier. Read there only the latest paragraph about sulphurs. A collection of about 20 000 from the most beautiful cabinets that Mr. de Furstenberg would like to acquire for the Academy here, please tell us how far we can go with the price.'] – FINA Wiki Database (ID 8849), https://fina.oeaw.ac.at/wiki/index.php/Adelheid_Amalia _von_Schmettau_-_Fran%C3%A7ois_Hemsterhuis_-_1783-3-14 [retrieved on 15 August 2022], see also: Sluis 2015, pp. 149–150, vol. II, letter 19. According to a letter from François Hemsterhuis to Adelheid Amalia von Schmettau, sent from The Hague on 28 September 1783, they were of exceptional quality and Stosch was credited as contributing a great deal to the development of production of *dactyliothecae* in the eighteenth century, see: FINA Wiki Database (ID 8801), https://fina.oeaw.ac.at/wiki /index.php/Fran%C3%A7ois_Hemsterhuis_-_Adelheid_Amalia _von_Schmettau_-_1783-9-28 [retrieved on 15 August 2022]; Sluis 2010, pp. 174–176, letter 4/68. However, neither Hemsterhuis nor Fürstenberg managed to buy Stosch's gem impressions at the auction in Berlin. They were acquired by Johann Friedrich

---

16 For example, while acting as an agent to Fagel in the purchase of a collection of drawings created by Joachim von Sandrart, he probably kept the best pieces for himself, sending his patron less accomplished pieces, see: Pietrzak 2018, pp. 128–129.

17 Lewis 1967, pp. 325–326; Francisci Osti 2000, p. 100; Dorati da Empoli 2008, p. 62, n. 22.

18 Winckelmann 1961, pp. 104–105, no. 31: '*Oltre alla collezione di gemme, il Barone von Stosch possedeva una raccolta di impronte in zolfo, come allora usava, delle pietre incise di tutte le raccolte d'Europa. Venduti dopo la sua morte, durante il transport, via mare, da Firenze ad Hamburg, i 28.000 si ridussero a 17.407, ordinati in 151 casse.*'

19 Auction Muzell-Stosch 1783, pp. 76–77: '*Eine Sammlung schöner Abdrücke in Schwefel von alten geschnittenen Steinen und Gemmen, in 210 auf einander passenden Schachteln, deren*

his collections, were often transported from one place to another by Muzell-Stosch in an attempt to sell them in Florence, Venice, London and Hamburg among others,[20] and apparently, during these travels, various incidents took place, resulting in destruction of some vulnerable parts like the cabinet of gem impressions. One imagines that the same could have happened to the gem drawings and other archives (for example, a lost manuscript of his own catalogue of his gem collection), which makes investigation of Stosch's life and his collecting, documentary and scholarly activities a great challenge.

In any case, Stosch himself in the 10th volume of *Das neue gelehrte Europa* published in 1757 provides us with a general overview of the rich *Museo Stoschiano*. It consisted of 11 collections: I. Cabinet of antiquities, II. Cabinet of ancient coins, III. Cabinet of modern coins and medals, IV. Collection of engraved gems, V. Drawings and copper plates by Old Masters, VI. Engravings and woodcuts, VII. Codices and manuscripts, VIII. Library, IX. Cabinet of natural history and curiosities, X. Armoury and XI. Geographical and topographical *Atlas*.[21] Stosch's most precious collection of engraved gems is only very briefly described,[22] let alone his other assemblages. However, Stosch's account includes information on the enormous collection of 28 000 sulphur gem casts and impressions that he amassed throughout his life,[23] and there is also a particularly valuable notice on gem drawings which accompanied the gems: '*The Baron had all his gems drawn by various people living in his house. The drawings were put in 20 volumes. In addition to this, he also had a large volume with a number of drawings and engravings of gems from various European cabinets.*'[24]

According to Stosch's will, apart from a few minor antiquities which went to Horace Mann, Ottaviano Bonaccorsi and Cardinal Albani, Heinrich Wilhelm Muzell (1723–1782), who took Stosch's name, and since then was called Muzell-Stosch, became the sole heir of Stosch's vast collections, an estate in Florence as well as some debts.[25] In his letter to Cardinal Albani from 18 November 1757, Muzell-Stosch describes the inherited collections and he mentions '20 *volumes of drawings after ancient engraved gems*' among them.[26] This information, although imprecise, since it is not specified whether the drawings reproduced only Stosch's own gems or also those from other collections, still seems to confirm what Stosch reports in *Das neue gelehrte Europa*. As a result, it appears that during his lifetime, Stosch, in cooperation with several Italian and German draughtsmen, built a large corpus of gem drawings apparently originally organised in about 20 volumes.

Frauenholz (1758–1822), a dealer from Nuremberg, who almost immediately wanted to re-sell them – the sulphur gem impressions in 151 boxes for 450 and the *Dactyliotheca Stoschiana* for 350 Reichsthalers, as evidenced from two announcements, first published in January 1784 in *Teutsche Merkur* (1. Viertelj. 1784/45), VI–VIII (112–114) and later also in *Journal zur Kunstgeschichte und zur allgemeinen Literatur* 13 (Nuremberg 1784, p. 73), with a summary catalogue by Johann Adam Schweickart on pp. 73–89 (Winckelmann 1952–1957, vol. I, p. 608; Borbein, Kunze and Rügler 2019, p. 32; Zwierlein-Diehl 2023, pp. 462–463). Ultimately, Stosch's sulphur impressions after gems (17 406 in 151 boxes) ended up with James Tassie (1735–1799) in London (Raspe and Tassie 1791, p. LXIV), who is said to have bought them in 1784 (Eppihimer 2016, p. 195), but Tassie's letter to Alex Wilson (first son of the astronomer Alexander Wilson (1714–1786)) sent from London on 29 March 1785 (the previous letter sent to Wilson dates 11 July 1784) suggests that he bought them in 1784 or early 1785 in London: '*My going to Paris and the bustle I have been in ever since, made me for a time give up the transparent medals I mentioned in my last letter to you. And not long after my return, I purchased a large Collection of sulphur impressions above 17 000 in number, Collected by the late Baron Stosch.*' (Smith 1995, p. 29, no. 20; Thomson 2003, p. 20, no. 20). The purchase of Stosch's sulphur impressions is also mentioned in another letter from Tassie sent to Wilson from London on 9 July 1785: '*I do not remember if I mentioned to you, That lately fell into my hands a Collection of above 17 000 sulphur impressions of Gems. Collected by Baron Stosch. which enables me to make very large additions to my former Collection. Having reported this acquisition to St Petersburg Her Imperial Majesty has ordered two supplements one to stand on each side of the great Cabinet, to correspond in Ornaments &c.*' (Smith 1995, p. 29, no. 21; Thomson 2003, p. 21, no. 21). An early description of Tassie's collection of impressions published by Raspe in 1786 mentions 12 000 of them among which, there was '(…) *the greater part of those that were collected by the Elder Baron Stosch*', see: Raspe 1786; Miller Gray 1894, pp. 21–22; Smith 1995, pp. 12–13. The various incidents that happened to the collection of Stosch's sulphur gem impressions are also confirmed by Raspe and Tassie (1791, p. LXIV). Tassie subsequently reproduced them in various materials to considerable success (Hansson 2021a, p. 119). The impressions of Stosch's own gems (*Datyliotheca Stoschiana*) was apparently not sold by Frauenholz but remained with him for the sake of his publication projects only partially realised with Johann Friedrich Schlichtegroll (1765–1822), see: Schlichtegroll 1805, vol. I, pp. 12–13.

20 Auction Stosch I–IV; Hansson 2021b, pp. 68–69.

21 Stosch 1757, pp. 257–287.
22 Stosch 1757, pp. 268–270.
23 Stosch 1757, pp. 269–270.
24 Stosch 1757, p. 269: '*Alle diese hat der Frenherr auch durch geschickte Leute, so er in seinem Hause unterhalten, abzeichnen lassen, und diese Zeichnungen in zwanzig Theken verlegt. Hiezu kommt eine Theke mit Zeichnungen und Kupferstichen aller solcher Bildarbeiten von ausserordentlicher Größe, so man in den verschiedenen Cabinetten in Europa findet.*'
25 Cf. Chapter 1 here. On Stosch's debts, see: Lewis 1961, pp. 50–51, 56–61, 63–64, 70–72, 78, 82, 85 and 188; Lewis 1967, p. 326.
26 Noack 1928–1929, p. 69: '20 *Mappen mit Zeichnungen nach antiken geschnittenen Steinen*'.

3   Stosch's Corpus of Gem Drawings after His Death

Even though Stosch himself wished otherwise, his nephew wanted to sell everything he inherited as quickly as possible.[27] Repayment of Stosch's debts and estate taxes combined with his plans for long-term travels across the Ottoman Empire and the Near East generated a need for money. The original plan of selling everything immediately to the Holy Emperor Francis I or any other potential buyer did not work out as Stosch's legacy was simply unbearably expensive even for the Emperor.[28] As a result, Muzell-Stosch split the lot into more sellable pieces and put it under the hammer (or at least tried to).[29] He began publishing catalogues of individual collections and cabinets as he hoped to increase their value and to boost the interest of potential buyers.[30] This was the case of Stosch's gems, whose catalogue was published by Johann Joachim Winckelmann in 1760.[31] Ultimately, Muzell-Stosch sold most of Stosch's legacy at a number of public auctions organised in Florence, Venice, London, Hamburg and elsewhere, and some pieces were also sold privately like the collection of engraved gems, which was purchased by Frederick the Great, King of Prussia in 1764 for 30 000 ducats.[32] Nevertheless, one does not find any specific clue that the gem drawings were sold during his lifetime (but cf. a discussion on the drawings now in Berlin in Chapter 7).[33] It was certainly not easy to monetise them. They had a great value when combined with his collection of gems and were useful if treated as a scholarly aid during collector's studies or the completion of Winckelmann's catalogue. Nevertheless, their large number, as well as the fact that they were unsigned and presented a series of gems in a documentary rather than artistic way, made them probably troublesome to sell. What is more, one does not know precisely what their condition at that time was, so they might have been problematic from the art market perspective, unless they found a very specific buyer.[34] On the top of that, Muzell-Stosch may have simply been asking a high price for them.[35]

Shortly after Muzell-Stosch's death in 1782, his family decided to sell what remained after him at a public auction organised by the Böhme on 22 April 1783 in Berlin.[36]

---

27 Zazoff and Zazoff 1983, p. 132.
28 Hansson 2021a, p. 119.
29 Muzell-Stosch cut even homogenous collections into smaller, sellable pieces. The case of the recently rediscovered so-called *Codex Stosch* now in the RIBA Library in London is a good illustration of this, see: Campbell and Nesselrath 2006, pp. 17–18. The majority of Stosch's Library was purchased by Cardinal Passionei in 1759 and went to the Biblioteca Apostolica Vaticana. However, the rest was sold piecemeal at a public auction in Florence, parts of these are now in the Riccardiana and Marucelliana Libraries, see: Lewis 1961, p. 194; Lewis 1967, p. 326. Finally, he offered 50 volumes with drawings of Rome selected from Stosch's *Atlas* to Cardinal Albani as one reads in a letter from Muzell-Stosch to the Cardinal dated 15 November 1757, but this offer could not be accepted (Noack 1928–1929, pp. 67–68).
30 The catalogue of Stosch's Library was published in 1758 and Winckelmann published his catalogue of Stosch's gems in 1760. On the dispersal of Stosch's legacy cf. Chapter 1 here and: Justi 1872, p. 345; Noack 1928–1929, p. 68; Lewis 1961, pp. 192–194; Lewis 1967, p. 326; Borroni Salvadori 1978a, pp. 613–614; Pietrzak 2018, pp. 126–131. Sometimes it is unclear how some parts of Stosch's legacy were sold. For instance, even though the majority of Stosch's gems were purchased in 1764 by Frederick the Great, King of Prussia, Christian gems left the collection much earlier as they were sold to Francesco Vettori (Justi 1871, p. 24; Rügler in Winckelmann 2013, pp. XII–XIII; Hansson 2014, p. 26, n. 86), the 'Persian' ones together with Etruscan and Egyptian scarabs as well as some valuable Near Eastern cylinder seals were sold to Giovanni Caraffa, Duke of Noja, but maybe these were sold earlier by Stosch himself (Schlichtegroll 1805, vol. I, p. 9; Winckelmann 1952–1957, vol. II, pp. 4–5, no. 274 and 6–7, no. 279; Zazoff and Zazoff 1983, p. 132, n. 216; Hansson 2014, p. 26, n. 86; Eppihimer 2016, p. 15) and about 100 cameos listed in Muzell-Stosch's letter to Cardinal Albani dated 18 November 1757 also disappeared (Justi 1872, p. 344).
31 Winckelmann 1760.
32 Hansson 2014, p. 29.
33 Stosch's collection of graphics was largely dispersed in a London sale on 24 March 1764 at Langford & Son and its brief inventory prepared by Winckelmann in 1758 does not include any gem drawings, see: Auction Stosch IV; Blunt and Schilling 1971, p. 13; Prosperi Valenti Rodinò 1993, p. 28; Sapori 2010, p. 104. Any other sale of Stosch's collections organised by Muzell-Stosch in London did not offer gem drawings for sale, see: Auction Stosch I–III. Other parts of Stosch's rich collection of drawings were auctioned in Hamburg but prior to this they were also shown to Anton Maria Zanetti in Venice, a gem enthusiast, collector and connoisseur, see: Hansson 2021b, pp. 68–69. Still, neither Zanetti nor anyone else seem to be interested in Stosch's gem drawings (if they were offered at all for sale at the time).
34 It would not be the first time when a part of Stosch's rich collections exceeded the capacity of the art market. For example, his collection of engraved gems was regarded as superior even to that of the Kings of France (Winckelmann 1952–1957, vol. I, pp. 444–445, no. 262), which made it very attractive, but also expensive and problematic to sale (cf. below).
35 It should be recalled that it took seven years to sell the collection of engraved gems itself. It was first offered to the Prince of Wales and then to the Duke of Parma and King of Spain, who all declined acquisition due to the high price asked, before it was purchased by Frederick the Great of Prussia. Muzell-Stosch's brother Friedrich Ludwig Hermann (1716–1784), the physician-in-ordinary to the king was involved in the negotiations which took at least two years (Zazoff and Zazoff 1983, p. 132; Hansson 2014, p. 29; Hansson 2021a, p. 119).
36 Auction Muzell-Stosch 1783. The catalogue is not listed on the Getty Provenance Index Databases. The only copy known to me is in the collections of the UCLA Library Special Collections

The files I–VI of the auction catalogue contained 918 lots referring to 4000 drawings in total that Muzell-Stosch did not manage to sell after Stosch's death. The file VI on pages 63–64 with lots 886–907 included ca. 2200 drawings of ancient gems (usually put in the form of sets of around 100 sheets, but it is unclear whether bound in volumes or organised in folders of some sort) described as *'Drawings of ancient gems from the cabinet of Baron von Stosch, by various, mostly Italian masters.'*[37] Among these, lot 907 included 100 drawings annotated as *'partially damaged'*.[38] The way this information is given suggests that the drawings in question were in a bad condition in 1783. In addition, in the same section VI, lot 918 includes '*39 drawings of ancient gems*'.[39] It is almost certain that all those gem drawings put at the auction in Berlin, in total 22 lots, originally belonged to the 20 volumes of drawings of Stosch's gems and perhaps even some more of those from other European cabinets briefly mentioned in Stosch's 1757 list, as well as in Muzell-Stosch's letter to Cardinal Albani (see above).

At that very same auction the remnants of his enormous cabinet of sulphur gem impressions, originally numbering 28 000 pieces, was offered in addition to a few remaining gems (see above). They attracted the attention of Adelheid Amalie von Schmettau, Princess Gallitzin (1748–1806), who in her letter to François Hemsterhuis (1721–1790) sent from Münster on 14 March 1783 also notices that: *'There is, moreover, a superb collection of drawings, engravings, portraits, etc. etc., but all this will sell collectively, do not think about it.'*[40] It is not explicit if she meant gem drawings only or also the other ones, but given the fact that in her letters exchanged with Hemsterhuis at the time she focuses on gems and their impressions specifically, it is likely that she refers to lots 886–907, which included exclusively gem drawings. According to her judgement, the collection should be sold *en bloc* and the gem drawings were considered of great value but extremely expensive, clearly beyond the budget: *'We shall be happy to obtain the sulphurs for the Academy, and if you think it is fine, some engraved gems, if we can have them for a reasonable price.'*[41] This helps us to understand why they remained unsold until Muzell-Stosch's death. This is the last trace of Stosch's huge number of important gem drawings to be found in the archives. No precise information as to their overall number, types, specific authors and so on has been available so far.

(Rare Book Stacks Z1015.S88 1783). I am grateful to Agata Pietrzak and especially Kenneth Lapatin for their kind help in accessing it. See also: Pietrzak 2018, p. 135.

37 Auction Muzell-Stosch 1783, lots 886–907: *'Zeichnungen von antiquen Gemmen aus dem Cabinet des Baron von Stosch, von verschiedenen großtentheils italiänischen Meistern'*.

38 Auction Muzell-Stosch 1783, lot 907: *'zum Theil schadhaft'*.

39 Auction Muzell-Stosch 1783, lot 918: '*39 Zeichnungen von antiken Gemmen*'.

---

40 Letter from Adelheid Amalie von Schmettau to François Hemsterhuis dated Münster, 14 March 1783, FINA Wiki Database (ID 8849), https://fina.oeaw.ac.at/wiki/index.php/Adelheid _Amalia_von_Schmettau_-_Fran%C3%A7ois_Hemsterhuis _-_1783-3-14 [retrieved on 15 August 2022]: *'Il y a au reste come vous verrez une collection superbe de desseins, gravures, portraits etc. etc., mais tous cela se vendra collectivement, il n'y faut pas penser'*.

41 The same letter as above: *'Nous serons trop heureux d'attraper les souffres pour l'Academie, et si vous les jugez bonnes, quelques pierres gravés si on peut les avoir pour un prix tolerable.'*

CHAPTER 6

Pierres gravees par Stosche in the Princes Czartoryski Museum in Krakow

Paweł Gołyźniak

1 The History of Collection – the Exile, Purchase and Donation

The Princes Czartoryski Museum in Krakow[1] preserves a substantial collection of 2246 drawings and 22 prints of engraved gems of various kinds arranged in 28 folio volumes (Fig. 6.1). It has never been a subject of scientific research and remains unpublished. Very little is known about its history, provenance and purpose. It is not known who executed these drawings, where and when exactly they were made and bought. Its structure has never been thoroughly analysed either and the gems presented on them remain unidentified. However, almost all the volumes have a clue – « *Pierres gravees par Stosche* » embossed in gold on the spines,[2] provoking inquiry of the connection between them and Philipp von Stosch.

The museum's archives are not very specific about the entrance of the albums to the Czartoryski collections, but their history traces back to the very early nineteenth century and it is interconnected with foundations of the Princes Czartoryski Museum.[3] They arrived together with a peculiar copy of Stosch's book, *Gemmae antiquae caelatae* (1724), and a luxurious edition of Winckelmann's catalogue of Stosch's gem collection (1760), which are now both kept in the Princes Czartoryski Library.[4] The albums and the books are unrecorded in the old inventories of the collections and the library of the Czartoryski Family prior to 1801. Between the years 1801 and 1830, the inventories of Czartoryskis' holdings, at that time kept in the family seat in Puławy (Central Poland), were updated very irregularly and a new general inventory was written only in 1830. This was due to the threat to the collections because of Russian repercussions after the unsuccessful November Uprising, supported by the Czartoryskis. The gem drawings were recorded in those inventories between 1801 and 1830 several times but without a precise date of their arrival. They are also described very briefly as *Collection de Pierres gravees de Stosch, fol. 28*.[5] Stosch's book, *Gemmae antiquae caelatae*, as well as Winckelmann's catalogue, *Description des pierres gravées du feu Baron de Stosch* from 1760, that arrived with the drawings, are also recorded between 1801 and 1830 in the inventories of the Czartoryski Library.[6] However, it is possible to suggest a more specific date of their purchase through scrutinising the correspondence between Adam Jerzy Czartoryski (1770–1861) and his parents Izabela Czartoryska (1746–1835) and Adam Kazimierz Czartoryski (1734–1823) during the exile of the young prince to Italy at the turn of the eighteenth and nineteenth centuries.

The Princes Czartoryski Museum was officially opened in 1876, but in fact it has much more ancient roots.[7] As early as 1801, Izabela Czartoryska founded her 'museum' in Puławy where various collections assembled by the Czartoryski family were exhibited in the so-called 'Gothic

---

1 The status of the Princes Czartoryski Museum remained unclear after 1945 when this originally private institution was nationalised by the communist government ruling in Poland and became a part of the National Museum in Krakow in 1950. In 1989, Prince Adam Karol Czartoryski recovered the Czartoryski Museum and its library to his family, and in 1991, he created the Foundation of XX. Czartoryski for its management, however, formally, the institution was still a part of the National Museum in Krakow. On 27 December 2016, the Polish government decided to purchase the collections belonging to the Princes Czartoryski and subsequently the Princes Czartoryski Museum in Krakow officially and fully became a branch of the National Museum in Krakow. After the reorganisation, the drawings and prints in question here belong to the Cabinet of Engravings and Drawings, which is a part of the Department of the Collections of the Princes Czartoryski Museum. To avoid misunderstandings, I apply here the short name 'the Princes Czartoryski Museum' because it seems to be the most suitable and will be easily recognised by the readers.
2 Only the last two volumes, XXVII and XXVIII, have no text on the spines. Their covers look exactly the same as in the case of the other volumes though.
3 Unless specific purchases are mentioned in Czartoryskis' correspondence or they are documented by surviving invoices, etc., up to 1830 the purchases are only sporadically noted in overall catalogues, which were updated only from time to time.
4 The Czartoryski Library, inv. no. 1237 IV and 1836 II respectively.
5 For instance, Rkps 12232, p. 176 and Rkps 12181, vol. 10, p. 162.
6 Rkps 12232, pp. 611 and 862 (with a wrong date of 1790) respectively; Rkps 12214, p. 200 and Rkps 12154, p. 65: '*Winckelmann* Description des pierres gravees 1760 – *Bookstand 2, shelf 8 at the back*'.
7 Chwalewnik 1926, p. 229. For the origin of the Princes Czartoryski Museum, see: Zamoyski (ed.) 2001, pp. 10–17; Górska 2021. For the most recent general overview of the Princes Czartoryski Museum and its collections, see: Płonka-Bałus and Koziara (eds) 2021.

© PAWEŁ GOŁYŹNIAK, 2025 | DOI:10.1163/9789004712553_007
This is an open access chapter distributed under the terms of the CC BY-NC-ND 4.0 license.

House' and the 'Temple of Sibyl', the latter modelled after the monopteral Temple of Vesta at Tivoli (Fig. 6.2).[8] The outstanding energy, taste and management skills of Izabela led to the beginnings of the Princes Czartoryski Museum, which was at the time an entirely private institution, but open to the public.[9] As a matter of fact, Poland did not exist as an independent country at that time, but the founder of the museum intended to preserve and cherish works of art and objects of material culture for the future generations of Poles.[10] Izabela Czartoryska also wanted her place to be friendly and inspirational for various kinds of visiting artists and she had some passion for antiquities as well. In realisation of her vision, she was strongly supported by her son Adam Jerzy Czartoryski, who was a passionate draughtsman and collector of drawings and prints (Fig. 6.3).[11]

The prince was well-educated and showed interest in art already at young age. In the years 1786–1788, he set off on a *grand tour* and visited places such as: Krakow, Bohemia, Germany, Paris, Switzerland, the Netherlands, England, Scotland and France.[12] However, after the Kościuszko Uprising in 1794, which the Czartoryskis supported, he was sent together with his brother Konstanty Adam Czartoryski (1774–1860) to St. Petersburg, officially to protect Polish heritage, but in fact they were political hostages.[13] There, the prince pursued a military career by the side of Alexander Pavlovich (1777–1825), the later Tsar Alexander I of Russia (1801–1825). They became friends, but it has been suggested to the current Tsar Paul I (1796–1801) that Czartoryski engaged in an affair with Alexander's wife, the Grand Duchess Elizabeth Alexeievna (1779–1826), which resulted in a childbirth. To quell these rumours, the prince was exiled to Italy, where he was appointed as an ambassador by the King of Sardinia – Charles Emmanuel IV of Sardinia (1796–1802). This ruined his promising military career, although he was summoned back by Alexander in 1801 and appointed as a member of the Ministry of Education shortly afterwards. Anyway, while on his exile to Italy, the prince's main task was to keep in contact with Russian field-marshal Alexander Suvorov (1729/1730–1800) and report to Tsar Paul I of Russia (1796–1801) about the current situation there.[14]

On 24 September 1799, Adam Jerzy departed St. Petersburg for Italy. He stopped in Vienna for a few days and then after travelling through Venice, Verona, Mantua and Bologna, he reached Florence on 28 or 29 December 1799 where Charles Emmanuel IV was then stationed.[15] He did what was expected from him obediently exchanging letters with Suvorov.[16] The times were still peaceful since Napoleon (1804–1814) had taken power in France not long before, but he had not started conquering Europe yet. Therefore, Adam Jerzy spent winter and early spring of 1800 mostly in Florence, but he also travelled around Italy a bit. He visited ancient ruins and cities, as well as art galleries, where he purchased antiquities and works of art. This was the time when, for example, the most valuable painting in the Czartoryski collection – the *Lady with an Ermine* by Leonardo da Vinci – was purchased by the prince from an unknown seller and sent to his mother as a gift.

While in Italy, Prince Czartoryski met some influential people. For instance, he was invited to a private audience by Pope Pius VII (1800–1823) and encountered such individuals as Cardinal Ercole Consalvi (1757–1824), Franciszek Rzewuski (1730–1800), the writer Count Vittorio Alfieri (1749–1803), Princess Louise of Stolberg-Gedern (1752–1824) – commonly called Countess of Albany, and a famous Italian adventurer, writer and envoy of the last King of Poland Stanislas August Poniatowski – Filippo Mazzei (1730–1816).[17] According to a letter he sent to his mother from 18 January 1800, the prince also met 'the best gem engraver in Italy', who might be Giovanni-Antonio

---

8   Technically speaking, Izabela Czartoryska never regarded her institution as a regular museum but rather a private collection open to the public. However, her initiative fits very well the formative period of European museums, see a discussion on this matter and more literature in: Betlej 2021, p. 9.
9   Dębicki 1887, vol. II, pp. 76–102; Dębicki 1888, vol. III, pp. 3–21; Kseniak 1998, pp. 17–20.
10 For a more detailed history of this museum and its collections and the founder, see: Haskell 1993, pp. 279–281; Aleksandrowicz 1998; Zamoyski (ed.) 2001, pp. 17–87; Żygulski jr. 2009; Betlej 2021. Its later history has also been presented in: Hyży (ed.) 1998; Zamoyski (ed.) 2001; de Rosset 2005, pp. 40–47; Górska 2021.
11 The prince was the son of Izabela Czartoryska and Adam Kazimierz Czartoryski; however, it is assumed that his real father was Nicholas Repnin (1734–1801) – a Russian envoy and Izabela Czartoryska's lover. For a detailed biography of Prince Adam Jerzy Czartoryski and study of his political activities, see for example: Czartoryski 1904; Handelsman 1948–1950; Kukiel 1955; Skowronek 1986; Zawadzki 1993; Skowronek 1994; Dziewanowski 1998. For the paintings and the involvement of Adam Jerzy Czartoryski in creation of the Princes Czartoryski Museum, see: Zamoyski (ed.) 2001, pp. 58 and 78–79; Czepielowa 2008, p. 170; Żygulski jr. 2009, pp. 240–241.
12 Skowronek 1986, pp. 7–8.
13 Czartoryski 1904, pp. 120–121; Zamoyski (ed.) 2001, p. 58.
14 Kukiel 1993, pp. 30–35; Skowronek 1994, p. 53; Zamoyski (ed.) 2001, p. 58.
15 Skowronek 1986, p. 15 gives the date 29 December 1799, while Skowronek 1994, pp. 55, 249–250 and 257–261 the date 28 December 1799.
16 Czartoryski 1904, p. 131.
17 Skowronek 1994, pp. 15 and 263–264.

Santarelli (1758–1826), indeed, one of the leading gem engravers and sculptors at the turn of the nineteenth century (see below).[18]

The prince undertook some attempts to study classical art too. He is even reported to have conducted his own amateur archaeological excavations at the Forum Romanum and attempted to write a guidebook on ancient ruins and monuments of Rome.[19] However, his passion and enthusiasm towards ancient culture cannot be compared to that of his mother.[20] During his stay, Adam Jerzy exchanged letters with his parents on a regular basis, at least once or twice a month. While writing to them, he often complained about the very slow pace of life practised by the local people, but his mother continued to encourage him to sightsee the ruins, cities, libraries and galleries and to make drawings wherever he was.[21] Because of his education in drawing and painting, these forms of art met his particular interest and appreciation.

Apparently, Izabela took advantage of the situation and turned her son into an agent.[22] She would send requests for specific objects of art (not necessarily ancient ones). For example, in a letter sent from Lviv on 23 February 1800, she writes as follows: '*I am extremely pleased with the hovels you have chosen for me and with those you promise me. Nothing has given me so much pleasure for a long time: Scipio's urn and the obelisk are very beautiful things. You wonder why I do not give you orders for pictures and statues. They are expensive and, besides, I don't like them much. However, speaking of a statue, I would like a bust of a faun or a panther, one or the other, big enough to exhibit it outside.*'[23] In her letter sent from Puławy on 25 June 1800, Izabela repeats her request: '*My Adam, please, could you buy me a nice statue? It does not have to be ancient*, a l'antique *is good enough. It could be a bust of a faun or a Satyr (…) or a marble lion or a panther or a sphinx. Whatever you find but please, let it be not small.*'[24] The prince delivered her only a head of Sappho, which did not meet expectations: '*I have already written you about Sappho's head, thank you for it, but I prefer a bust of a faun, a panther or a sphinx.*'[25] Overall, she required from the prince to inform her about anything interesting he came across while travelling which could fit into her collection, especially souvenirs from Rome and other places, e.g. in a letter sent on 17 December 1800: '*I am also asking you, very much, so that with those marbles that will come for me one day, to order putting some souvenirs of Rome on a ship; from the Capitoline Hill; from the Pantheon. I do not need anything extraordinary: let it be a piece of a building corner or of the Capitoline Palace or a relief – my Adam, I am asking you for this so much.*'[26] Those Roman souvenirs and antiquities were installed into one of the facades of the so-called 'Gothic House' in Puławy and they were meant to illustrate an idea fashionable at the time of the noble connection between the Roman Empire and the Polish nation.[27] In the correspondence exchanged between Izabela Czartoryska and her son, as well as prince's father Adam Kazimierz Czartoryski, one does not find detailed reports and only very few passages about specific purchases, which are still imprecise and ambiguous. Nevertheless, their letters shed some light on the history and provenance of the albums with gem drawings entitled *Pierres gravees par Stosche*.

There is some evidence from the correspondence suggesting that while in Italy Adam Jerzy Czartoryski was creating a valuable collection of drawings and prints. In his letter to his mother sent from Florence on 10 March 1800, the prince writes that his stay in Italy is

---

18 Rkps. 6097 II, p. 133 – letter from Adam Jerzy Czartoryski to Izabela Czartoryska dated Florence 18 January 1800.
19 Żygulski jr. 2009, pp. 240–241.
20 Zamoyski (ed.) 2001, p. 58.
21 See: letter from Izabela Czartoryska to Adam Jerzy Czartoryski dated Lviv 1 March 1800 and another one dated Krasnystaw 4 April 1800 – Duchińska 1891, pp. 52–56. See also another letter from Izabela Czartoryska to Adam Jerzy Czartoryski dated Sieniawa 16 January 1800 – Duchińska 1891, p. 43; letter from Izabela Czartoryska to Adam Jerzy Czartoryski from Lviv (undated) – Duchińska 1891, pp. 52–55.
22 His activity in this field is documented by many letters he exchanged with his mother in those days, see: Duchińska 1891, pp. 41–56. See also: Skowronek 1994, pp. 56 and 262–265; Zamoyski (ed.) 2001, p. 58; Żygulski jr. 2009, pp. 240–241 and some letters evoked here.
23 The translations are all mine unless otherwise stated. Rkps 6288/1 III, pp. 307–308: '*Ekstra jestem kontenta z ruderów, co mi wybrałeś, y z tych, co mi obiecuiesz. Il y a long temps que je n'ai eu quelque chose qui m'auye fait plus de plaisir. Scypiona urna y Obelisk y reszta co mi obiecasz to arcy piękne rzeczy (…) Dziwisz się, że ci nie daię poleceń na obrazy ani na statuy. Po pierwsze drogie, a ia nie mam pasyi zdecydowanie do nich. Statuy, ia cię prosiła o buste fauna albo o Pantherę, iedno lub drugie, dość duże aby na dworze mogły stać.*'
24 Rkps 6288/1 III, p. 338: '*Proszę cię moy Panie adamie żebyś mi się wystarał o iaką statuę ładną. Ja nie chcę żeby była Koniecznie antique, byle d'apres l'antique, chciała bym albo un buste de faune ou de Satyre (…) albo Lwa marmurowego, albo une Panthere, albo un Sphinx. Cokolwiek będzie żeby nie zanadto małe.*'
25 Rkps 6288/1 III, p. 352 – letter from Izabela Czartoryska to Adam Jerzy Czartoryski dated Puławy, 10 October 1800: '*Je ai deja rependue sur la tete de Sapho: ia ci za nią dziękuję, y wolę un bust de faune ou une panthere ou un Sphinxe.*'
26 Rkps 6288/1 III, p. 356: '*Też ciebie proszę bardzo, ale bardzo, żebyś z temi marmurami co dla mnie kiedyś przyjdą, żebyś mnie kazał na okręt wsadzić quelques souvenirs de Roma; soit du Capitole; soit de Pantheon. Ja niekoniecznie potrzebuję co wielkiego: niech będzie Kawałek rogu czy Kapitolu, czy basreliefu – moy Panie Adamie proszę cię o to bardzo.*'
27 Górska 2021, p. 20.

a perfect opportunity to do that: '*For a long time, I have had a desire to create a collection of drawings and prints, not in the sense of those who wants to possess, but only as much as it can help to those who want to improve drawing and composition, by putting under their eyes the most important works of great masters. I have started to implement this project and I hope that it will be easier* [for me to accomplish it] *in this country, although, so far, it does not meet my expectations in this respect.*'[28] He also informed his father about that project. In one of the letters Adam Jerzy received from him, one reads as follows: '*My dearest Adam, I have received your letter from 10 March. (…) In my opinion, the way you want to collect the drawings is very reasonable. However, great collections are generally created only in big libraries where an artist searches for some examples and draws inspiration that he needs; regarding a private cabinet, if one wants to gather everything, one will end up enjoying nothing; anyway, these are very expensive things.*'[29]

The correspondence gives us not only clues about the prince's motivations – his primary goal was to assemble the material that could be a source of inspiration for artists (certainly including Adam Jerzy himself) – but it also helps to establish the potential sources of his purchases of drawings and prints. In a letter sent from Florence on 29 March 1800 to his mother, the prince informs her that he was kindly guided by and apparently purchased many drawings from a painter named Fabre, a pupil of David: '*I believe I have told you already that I had started to build a collection of drawings and prints, to which very few great masters would have the honour of being admitted. It is not for profit, nor searching for what is rare, but only the perfection of the drawing, the perfection of the composition, of the expression that I seek to. A painter named Fabre, a pupil of David, very skilful in his art, helps me to find what I need because he himself has a collection of the same kind, which he praises. It is nice to meet him because he gave me what he already had. I am careful so that it does not cost much, though. That is the first condition.*'[30] The mentioned Fabre is certainly the French painter François-Xavier Fabre (1766–1837), the second pupil of the famous artist Jacques-Louis David (1748–1825) (Fig. 6.4). It is noteworthy that both Fabre and his patron Philippe-Laurent de Joubert (1729–1792) were avid art collectors, mostly focusing on paintings and drawings. Fabre built up a collection of sixteenth and seventeenth century Italian paintings and drawings as well as paintings by his French contemporaries. His collection was enriched by that of his friends, the poet Vittorio Alfieri and his companion the Countess of Albany. Fabre's collection was the basis of the Fabre Museum in Montpellier. Fabre was a very active art dealer while in Florence (1793–1824).

In the summer of 1800, Adam Jerzy Czartoryski departed from Florence to Rome. He visited Franciszek Rzewuski and he continued his journey to Pisa only to later come back to Rome, where he purchased more antiquities, books and various works of art commissioned by his mother.[31] He did not return to Florence because Napoleon defeated the Austrians in the battle of Marengo and the King of Sardinia decided to fall back deeper into Italy.[32] Prince Czartoryski stayed in Rome until April 1801, when he left for Naples. There, the information about Alexander I being crowned a tsar reached him and he

---

28 Rkps. 6097 II, p. 147 – letter from Adam Jerzy Czartoryski to Izabela Czartoryska dated Florence 10 March 1800: 'Depuis longtems j'avois le desir de faire une collection d'estampes, nullement dans le sens de ceux qui en ont, mais uniquement autant que cela peut aider au prefeetionnement du dessin et de la composition, en mettant sous les yeux les chefdoeuvres des plus grands maitres. J'ai commencé à executer ce projet et j'espere qu'j'y aurai plus de facilité dans ce pays, quoique jusqu'afresant il ne reponde pas à cet égard à mon attente.' The text is original as in the letter.

29 Rkps. 6285 II, pp. 111–112 – letter from Adam Kazimierz Czartoryski to Adam Jerzy Czartoryski dated Lviv 9 April or May? 1800: 'List twój 10go Marca pisany moy Adamie Kochany odbieram. (…) je trouve que la mecuilera (?) dout vous voulez essaire une collection d' (?) tangres est vrayement avoir de place qu (?) dans les grandes Bibliotheque, ou l'artiste se l'azuateur (?), vont chercher ce qui peut satisfaire leur goret (?); ou des niddelles en tout genre, mais un partieulier en voulant tout avoir, finit par ne jouir de rien, d'aillieu (?) c'est un gout tres dissendieux (?).' The letter has no precise date (only the number of the day, which is 9, is legible). The year 1799 added by the later cataloguer of the prince's correspondence is clearly incorrect.

30 Rkps. 6097 II, pp. 155–156 – letter from Adam Jerzy Czartoryski to Izabela Czartoryska dated Florence 29 March 1800: 'Je vous ai dit, je crois, que j'avois commencé une espéce de collection d'estempes, à laquelle fort peu de grands maitres auront l'honeur d'etre admis. Ce n'est pas le busin, ni ce qui est rare, mais uniquement la perfection du dessein, la perfection de la composition, de l'expression que je cherche. Un peintre nommé fabre, eleve de Dawid, et trés habile dans son art, m'aide à trouver ce qu'il me faut, lui même a une collection dans le même genre, qu'il complette; c'est une bonne rencontre, car il me cede ce qu'il a deja. Mam baczność największą, żeby to niewiele kosztowało; c'est la premiere condition.'

31 Rkps. 6097 II, pp. 181–184; Duchińska 1891, p. 88. For instance, in the letter dated 16 August 1800 sent to his mother, the prince informs her that he acquired for her an ancient bust of Sappho for her (cf. above). Izabela Czartoryska took advantage of the current situation and commissioned her son to buy various antiquities and objects of art on her behalf. An interesting example of this practice is the letter sent from Puławy in September 1800. She asked him to travel to Tivoli because she was informed that in the tavern near to the sanctuary the innkeeper used an altar from an ancient temple as his speakeasy (Duchińska 1891, pp. 67–68).

32 Skowronek 1994, p. 266.

was immediately called back to St. Petersburg.[33] He was travelling there for several months visiting his aunt Izabela Lubomirska (1733/1736–1816) in Vienna and his family in Puławy. Already in 1801, the prince arrived in St. Petersburg, where his political career started to flourish once again.

It must have been during his stay in Puławy in 1801 when Prince Czartoryski donated his collection of drawings and prints created in Florence to the museum of his mother. The assemblage, apparently built with the help of François-Xavier Fabre, included not only 28 volumes of *Pierres gravees par Stosche* but also drawings and prints of views of Italian cities, ancient ruins, etc., as well graphic reproductions of paintings. Even though there is no direct record of Fabre selling the collection of gem drawings to the prince,[34] there seems to be no better occasion for them to be bought by the prince and subsequently brought to Puławy. Prince Czartoryski may have had some general appreciation for engraved gems, since during his *grand tour* through Germany in 1786 he became acquainted with Johann Wolfgang Goethe (1749–1832), an enthusiast and passionate collector of intaglios and cameos.[35] Fabre was certainly interested in gems and antiquities in a general sense. He was an advisor to Pierre-Louis Jean Casimir, Count of Blacas d'Aulps (1771–1839), a famous collector of intaglios and cameos, who purchased some of Leone Strozzi's (1657–1722) gems in 1817.[36] Moreover, the Musée Fabre in Montepellier holds a series of Fabre's drawings of antiquities and especially engraved gems, many of which reproduce the same gems as documented on the drawings found in Krakow (could they be a source of inspiration for Fabre?) (cf. Chapter 3, Figs 3.13–3.14).[37] From some of those drawings, it is clear that Fabre studied specific aspects of Antiquity creating typologies of, for instance, ancient masks, and engraved gems were his main sources.[38] Furthermore, Fabre's master, Jacques-Louis David is attested not only to have taken inspiration from intaglios and cameos while composing some of his works, but he also executed about 1000 of drawings of various kinds of antiquities, including engraved gems (cf. Chapter 3, Figs 3.17–3.19).[39] Finally, Giovanni-Antonio Santarelli, a gem engraver whom Prince Czartoryski mentions in his letter (see above), established himself in Florence in 1797 and became a good friend of Fabre. He cut several medallions with cameos bearing portraits of Fabre and his father doctor Henri Fabre as well as a marble bust of François-Xavier Fabre – all now housed in the Musée Fabre in Montepellier.[40] In return, Fabre painted a portrait of the famous gem engraver twice. He was also a teacher to Santarelli's son – Emilio Santarelli (1801–1889) in Florence.[41] Last but not least, perhaps it is of significance that in 1811 Fabre painted a portrait of the Princess Barbara Czartoryska, née Jabłonowska (1760–1834), as this could be an echo of his earlier friendship with Adam Jerzy Czartoryski.[42]

Fabre was prominent in Florentine society and shared many friends with Prince Czartoryski, like Vittorio Alfieri or Princess Louise of Stolberg-Gedern, the Countess of Albany. The first was most likely also a fan of engraved gems and knew Giovanni-Antonio Santarelli. The Museo d'Arte Civica in Turin preserves a portrait of Vittorio Alfieri and Countess of Albany painted by Fabre in 1796, on which Alfieri has a ring on his finger with a portrait of Dante Alighieri engraved by Santarelli.[43] Among the mutual friends was also Franciszek Rzewuski, whose portrait was engraved upon an intaglio by Giovanni Pichler.[44] It is clear then that within the circle of Prince Czartoryski's friends in Italy, engraved gems were admired and their drawings could be much appreciated as well. One should not also underestimate the Czartoryski family's cultural aspirations, their current high esteem for everything related to the glyptic art, and the enduring importance and authority of Philipp von Stosch. The books and drawings related to him that were brought to Puławy by Prince Adam Jerzy Czartoryski were certainly a valuable addition to the Czartoryski collections. In Poland, a country in which the access to original antiquities was very limited, such

---

33 Skowronek 1994, p. 273.
34 In the archives of the Musée Fabre in Montepellier, there is no trace of a transaction between Fabre and Prince Czartoryski recorded.
35 On Goethe and his collection of gems, see: Femmel and Heres 1977.
36 Zwierlein-Diehl 2023, p. 446. For more information on this issue, see: Rambach (forthcoming – Baron von Schellersheim).
37 For example: Musée Fabre in Montepellier inv. nos: 837.1.414, 837.1.431, 837.1.438, 837.1.443, 837.1.442, 837.1.450, 837.1.579, 837.1.581, 837.1.582, 837.1.584, 837.1.585, 837.1.587.
38 The series of ancient masks studies by Fabre is Musée Fabre in Montepellier inv. no.: 837.1.431.
39 Cf. Chapter 3 here. On David and his interest in Antiquity, see also: Haskell 1993, pp. 394–400.
40 The medallions with cameos from the Musée Fabre in Montepellier: portrait of François-Xavier Fabre – inv. nos: 837.1.1163, portrait of doctor Henri Fabre, father of François-Xavier – inv. no.: 837.1.1112. For the marble bust of Fabre, see: Pellicer and Hilarie 2008, pp. 412–413. I am grateful to Florence Hudowicz, curator in the Musée Fabre in Montepellier for her kind assistance in investigating this issue.
41 Pellicer and Hilarie 2008, pp. 372–375, no. 196.
42 Pellicer and Hilarie 2008, p. 424, no. 211.
43 Pirzio Biroli Stefanelli 2009, p. 175, fig. 2.
44 Tassinari 2012, pp. 236–237, no. II.17.

albums were priceless.⁴⁵ It is noteworthy that according to the inventories and catalogues of the Czartoryski holdings written both, before 1801, and the outbreak of the November Uprising in 1830, the family possessed all the most valuable books on engraved gems like: Lorenz Berger's *Thesaurus Brandenburgicus Selectus: Sive Gemmarum, Et Numismatum Graecorum, In Cimeliarchio Electorali Brandenburgico* published in Cologne in 1696,⁴⁶ Abraham Gorlaeus' *Dactyliotheca seu Annulorum sigillarium quorum apud priscos tam Græcos quam Romanos usus ...* from 1707,⁴⁷ Francesco de'Ficoroni's *Gemmae antiquae litteratae aliaeque rariores etc.* published in 1737 in Rome,⁴⁸ two volumes of *Recueil de pierres gravées antiques* published in Paris in 1732 and 1737 by Michel-Philippe Lévesque de Gravelle,⁴⁹ Lorenz Natter's *Traité de la méthode antique de graver en pierres fines, comparée avec la méthode modern* published in 1754 in London,⁵⁰ Anton Francesco Gori's *Dactyliotheca Smithiana* published in Venice in 1767,⁵¹ Johann Joachim Winckelmann's *Monumenti antichi inediti spiegati ed illustrate* published in Rome in 1767,⁵² Josiah Wegwood's *Catalogue de camées, intaglios, médailles, bustes, petites statues, et bas-reliefs* published in London in 1774,⁵³ Géraud de La Chau and Gaspard Michel Le Blond's, *Description des principales pierres gravées du cabinet de M. le duc d'Orléans* published in Paris in 1780⁵⁴ and Richard Dagley's *Gems: selected from the antique, with illustrations* published in London in 1804.⁵⁵ Although not recorded in old inventories, Rudolph Erich Raspe and James Tassie's *A descriptive catalogue of a general collection of ancient and modern engraved gems, cameos as well as intaglios: taken from the most celebrated cabinets in Europe ...* published in 1791 can be found in the holdings of the Czartoryski Library today as well.⁵⁶ Most likely it entered the Library in the late eighteenth or early nineteenth century like the books listed above. The Czartoryski Library was considered one of the best if not the best of all those created by Polish aristocracy at the time. It was particularly strong in the subject of Antiquity because of a considerable interest in this matter of Adam Jerzy Czartoryski's father, Adam Kazimierz Czartoryski, who was also a passionate collector of books.⁵⁷ Prince Adam Jerzy Czartoryski collected books and manuscripts on a great scale as well.⁵⁸

After the collapse of the November Uprising in 1831, the Czartoryski family assets were confiscated due to their involvement in this political and military affair, but thanks to the help of Karol Sienkiewicz (1793–1860), the Czartoryskis managed to hide majority of their collections in Sieniawa, Klemensów and Krasiczyn among others. In 1835, they began transferring them to Paris, where they made Hôtel Lambert their residence.⁵⁹ In 1870, Prince Władysław Czartoryski decided to transfer the collections to Krakow, but this process dragged on until 1876. In the same year, the Czartoryski family created the Czartoryski Library – a place where their very precious collections of books and manuscripts have been made available to the public.⁶⁰ The assemblage of drawings and prints in question is mentioned in the *Spisy druków i sztychów J.O.Xcia Władysława Czartoryskiego przysłanych do Kórnika w roku 1872 oraz nabytków późniejszych w Krakowie*, so it was certainly back in Poland already in 1872.⁶¹ Throughout all these years, it survived in one piece and is now housed in the Princes Czartoryski Museum in Krakow.

According to the research of Czepielowa, the *Pierres gravees par Stosche* albums were not displayed during the rearrangement of the fixed exhibition, which took place in 1901 until 1950.⁶² In July 1941, Pelagia Potocka (1909–1994) – a former curator of the Princes Czartoryski Museum – wrote a few short notes about the collection

---

45 The interest of Adam Jerzy and Izabela Czartoryski in gem drawings fits a more general trend. Many Polish aristocratic families aspired to create collections of art, but regarding antiquities, these were often substituted with collections of casts and regarding engraved gems – *dactyliothecae*. On this matter, see: Laska 1986, pp. 9–31; Mikocki 1990; Laska 1994.
46 Rkps 12232, p. 796.
47 Rkps 12232, p. 329.
48 Rkps 12232, p. 281.
49 Rkps 12232, pp. 658 and 659.
50 Rkps 12232, p. 558.
51 Rkps 12232, p. 329.
52 Rkps 12232, p. 826.
53 Rkps 12232, p. 147.
54 Rkps 12232, pp. 216 and 217.
55 Rkps 12232, p. 313.
56 The Czartoryski Library: Sygn. 269 III/1–2.
57 Górska 2021, pp. 14–15.
58 Wierzbicki 2021, p. 238.
59 Kseniak 1998, p. 24; Żygulski jr. 2009, pp. 263–267; Górska 2021, pp. 22–28.
60 Czepielowa 2006, p. 87. It would take a lot of space to list the numerous precious books, prints and manuscripts located in the institution, but what is noteworthy is the fact that the Czartoryskis incorporated a part of the famous set of books and manuscripts once belonging to Tadeusz Czacki (1765–1813). Among his collection there were archives of the last King of Poland – Stanisław August Poniatowski (1732–1798). These were taken over by the Czartoryski family, while the rest of the Czacki library ended up firstly in Krzemieniec Lyceum and later at the University of Kiev, see more in: Szyndler 1997; Danowska 2006.
61 This document is now preserved in the Czartoryski Library. The record related to the collection is: XI.949.
62 Czepielowa 2006. It was not exhibited prior to 1901 as well since this year marks the appearance of the first ever selection of the best drawings and prints from the rich Czartoryski collection to be put on display.

that have never been published.[63] She assumed that the collection was the unpublished album for Winckelmann's catalogue of Philipp von Stosch's engraved gems (1760), basing her assumption on the drawings mentioned by Winckelmann in the preface to his book on pages IV and XXVII. She thought that most of them were made by Markus Tuscher and she even started to identify the drawings with gems but abandoned that project quickly.[64] She briefly summarised that the collection contains 23 (surely a typo) volumes of drawings in various techniques with descriptions added by Princess Izabela Czartoryska.[65] Whenever she believed a drawing to represent a gem from Stosch's cabinet, she gave a reference to a relevant record from Winckelmann's catalogue of Stosch's gems in pencil.[66] The drawings were inventoried for the first time in July 1941[67] and later, in 1957 they were inventoried again with numbers Krakow MNK XV Rr. 2500–4746 and subsequently in 1959 the prints were also given their ultimate inventory numbers (Krakow MNK XV R. 24430–24451).

2 The Provenance

In all probability, the *Pierres gravees par Stosche* albums of gem drawings and two related books (copies of Stosch's *Gemmae antiquae caelatae* and Winckelmann's *Description des pierres gravées du feu baron de Stosch*) now in Krakow were purchased in Florence in 1800 by Prince Adam Jerzy Czartoryski, perhaps with the help of or directly from François-Xavier Fabre. The investigation of their provenance is difficult due to limited archives, but identification of their original owner and investigation of the connection with Stosch is possible.

Let us recall the auction catalogue of Muzell-Stosch's remaining collections sold at the Böhme on 22 April 1783 in Berlin. It included 23 lots with 2239 gem drawings originally from Philipp von Stosch's corpus (cf. Chapter 5). This is very close to the number of drawings and prints from the Princes Czartoryski Museum – 2268 pieces. As reported in 1757, Stosch was said to have had probably 20 volumes of drawings of his own gems and a good number of those from other collections.[68] In 1783, the sale of Muzell-Stosch's remaining collections included 23 lots with Stosch's gem drawings. The different numbers of volumes between Stosch 1757 and the Berlin auction catalogue from 1783 is acceptable, as simply both sources describe them very briefly and they are in fact imprecise. Nevertheless, in both cases, this is much less than the current 28 volumes in Krakow, in which the number of drawings spans from 42 to 157.[69] However, one must take into account the reorganisation of the collection in the early nineteenth century by Izabela Czartoryska (see below). Thus, one should only compare the number of the drawings and they are, again, indeed very close. This fact and the description of the drawings offered at the auction in Berlin, according to which, most of them were made by 'Italian masters', while the vast majority of those discovered in Krakow are attributed to Girolamo Odam among others, suggest them to be the same collections.[70]

Moreover, the gem drawings under discussion entered the Princes Czartoryski collection together with a peculiar copy of Stosch's book, *Gemmae antiquae caelatae* (1724), and a luxurious edition of Winckelmann's catalogue of Stosch's gem collection (1760).[71] The latter might be identified in the auction catalogue of Muzell-Stosch's posthumous sale in Berlin.[72] There was also a rather luxurious copy of Stosch's book on ancient signed gems put up for sale as well,[73] but the copy in Krakow is different and its size (44,8 × 29 cm) suggests it to be one of the 'large folio' special copies which were made for prestigious clients like Louis XV, King of France.[74] This copy was rebound, probably when in Berlin, in a bluish paperbound trimmed *in crudo*. The plates, normally within the volume's text, had been relocated at the very end of the book. However, its peculiar feature is that it has a different design and

---

63 These documents are now preserved in the Department XV of the National Museum in Krakow – The Cabinet of Engravings and Drawings. I am grateful to Ewa Nogieć-Czepiel for allowing me to study these notes.
64 Some references to Winckelmann's catalogue of Stosch's gems in pencil appearing on the drawings are by her hand.
65 Notes of Pelagia Potocka (uncatalogued), the Princes Czartoryski Museum in Krakow.
66 Many of her identifications are incorrect since she had only Winckelmann's unillustrated catalogue at her disposal.
67 According to the notes of Pelagia Potocka.
68 Stosch 1757, p. 269.
69 Vol. I – 72 drawings, vol. II – 96, vol. III – 48, vol. IV – 71, vol. V – 65, vol. VI – 70, vol. VII – 50, vol. VIII – 98, vol. IX – 60, vol. X – 74, vol. XI – 127, vol. XII – 42, vol. XIII – 87, vol. XIV – 68, vol. XV – 74, vol. XVI – 75, vol. XVII – 137, vol. XVIII – 61, vol. XIX – 54, vol. XX – 80, vol. XXI – 78, vol. XXII – 77, vol. XXIII – 95, vol. XXIV – 49, vol. XXV – 77, vol. XXVI – 92, XXVII – 133, vol. XXVIII – 157.
70 For a discussion on the attribution, cf. Chapter 8 here.
71 The Czartoryski Library, inv. no. 1237 IV and 1836 II respectively.
72 Auction Muzell-Stosch 1783, p. 10, lot 45: '*Descriptions des pierres gravées du feu Baron de Stosch, par l'Abbé Winkelmann. Florent. 760. Papbd.*'
73 Auction Muzell-Stosch 1783, p. 3, lot 1: '*Philippi de Stosch Gemmae antiquae caelatae et aeri incisae per Bernhardum Picart. Pierres antiques gravées par B.P. expliqués, par Ph. De St. Amsterd. 724. vergold. Marmbd. mit gold. Schnitt ganz auf Rojalpap. gedruckt.*'
74 For a discussion on various editions of Stosch's books and their sizes, cf. Chapter 9 here.

numeration of the sheets in the bottom of the pages than the final edition published by Bernard Picart in 1724. Is this a pre-final-printing copy of Stosch's book made by Bernard Picart, who tested various arrangements of text and illustrations?

On the recto of the front cover endpaper, there are at least five references: N°. 11 or N°. 11 (the rest is covered by the paper note) – in black pen, ~~VI_8~~ – in black chalk, ~~VII.A.8~~ – in black chalk, 256i6/128 or 25616/128 – in black chalk and 877 – in red chalk. Only ~~VI_8~~ and ~~VII.A.8~~ are identified as references in old catalogues of the Czartoryski Library. There is also a paper note glued there, written in French, which reads as follows: *'This book was sold by Bourdeaux & Fils Libraires du Roi & de la Court in Berlin, where there is a complete assortment of books of all kinds & of the best Greek, Latin, French, English & Italian authors, all original & precious editions worthy of adorning the most distinguished Libraries. As for the acquisition, they offer them at the lowest possible prices, and on very favourable conditions, which can be agreed with the buyer.'*[75] There are also: *P* (top) and *N° 11. cz & oo &* (bottom) inscribed on it in black pen; the latter might be a lot number from the auction at which the book was sold (Fig. 6.5). The note suggests that this volume was in Berlin in the late eighteenth century and was sold there by a book shop run by Etienne-Laurent de Bourdeaux (active 1736–1793), who settled in 1736 in The Hague, where he worked for the bookseller Jean II Néaulme (1694–1780), then worked in Berlin between 1743 and 1749 with him, and then since before 1777 in partnership with his son Pierre Bourdeaux, who worked alone after 1786.[76] The name *Bourdeaux & Fils* on our note then suggests that the book was sold between 1777 and 1786.

In conclusion, it is assumed that the vast majority of the gem drawings from Krakow were sold in Berlin in 1783 at the auction organised by Böhme, but their later history up to 1800 is particularly difficult to reconstruct. The most valuable engravings offered at that auction were bought by Ernst Peter Otto (1724–1799), an antiquarian from Leipzig, while many drawings were acquired by Carl Rost (1742–1798) also from Leipzig. Later, they usually ended up in the most important art museums in the world like the British Museum, The Harvard Art Museum and the Bibliothèque nationale de France in Paris, one way or another.[77] It is clear that the majority of the collection was dispersed among numerous buyers, and it was later sold on and on by dealers. As a result, individual parts re-emerged in various countries.[78] Nevertheless, it is crucial that some old master drawings from Stosch's original collection put at the auction in Berlin in 1783 ultimately re-emerged in Italy.[79] This seems to be the case also for the *Pierres gravees par Stosche* albums. Apparently, they circulated around the art market and some additions to the original core were added until they were purchased in 1800 in Florence by Adam Jerzy Czartoryski.

In the absence of archives, it is impossible to say who bought them in 1783 in Berlin, but perhaps of importance is the fact that at that auction the remaining part of Stosch's collection of gem impressions in sulphur and the complete *Dactyliotheca Stoschiana* were also offered for sale, and they were purchased by Johann Friedrich Frauenholz from Nuremberg, the leading dealer in prints and drawings in Germany at that time.[80] He quickly announced the sulphurs for resale in the early 1784, so that in the second half of 1784 or in the early 1785 they were purchased by James Tassie in London.[81] Frauenholz was very much interested in Stosch in general, which is evidenced by the fact that he also acquired Johann Adam Schweickart's complete *dactyliotheca* of Stosch's gems and '(...) *an existing number of beautiful drawings of excellent gems from the collection, which the late Stosch had had drawn by the famous Preißler*' in 1787.[82]

Indeed, after Stosch's death, Schweickart tried to publish Stosch's gem collection illustrated using his own plates, which included several, only slightly enlarged,

---

75 The original text: *'Ce livre a été vendu par Bourdeaux & Fils Libraires du Roi & de la Cour à Berlin, chés lesquels on trouve un afforiment complet de Livres en tout genre & des meilleurs Auteurs Grecs, Latins, François, Anglois & Italiens toutes Editions originales & dignes d'orner les Bibliothéques les plus distinguées. Quant à l'acquisition, ils les offrent aux prix les plus modiques possibl, & à des Conditions très favorables, don't on pourra convener avec l'Acheteur.'*

76 http://www.idref.fr/124723934/id [retrieved on 6 July 2023]. I am grateful to Hadrien J. Rambach who helped to identify the book seller.

77 Pietrzak 2018, p. 133.

78 Pietrzak 2018, pp. 131 and 137–140.

79 For instance, a famous Polish art collector and Winckelmann's commentator Stanislas Kostka Potocki (1755–1821) purchased three drawings by Leonardo da Vinci in Italy, which were earlier in the Philipp von Stosch collection, see: Pietrzak 2018, p. 138.

80 On Frauenholz and his instrumental role in the dealing in prints and drawings in Germany in the last quarter of the eighteenth and first quarter of the nineteenth century, see: Luther 1988.

81 On this cf. Chapter 5, n. 19 here.

82 Schlichtegroll 1805, vol. I, pp. 12–13: '(...) *und noch mehr eine vorhandene Anzahl schöner Zeichnungen von vorzüglichen Gemmen aus der Sammlung, die der verstorbene Stosch von dem berühmten Preißler in der Absicht zeichnen liess*'; Zazoff and Zazoff 1983, p. 181; Michel 1999–2000, p. 82. This is also confirmed by other sources, see: Luther 1988, p. 93.

gems on one page.⁸³ Nevertheless, he managed to publish only 36 gems from the first class in Winckelmann's catalogue because the project turned out to be a financial failure.⁸⁴ In any case, his illustrations are much different than Preißler's drawings. Schweickart worked for Stosch primarily as an engraver and he prepared some plates for Stosch's unfinished supplement to *Gemmae antiquae caelatae* book based on drawings of other draughtsmen, like Tuscher and Nagel, so he may have left Florence with some of Preißler's drawings as well. Although some sources suggest him to have had a considerable number of Preißler's drawings in Nuremberg,⁸⁵ in fact, he probably had only a few.

In the years following acquisition of Schweickart's belongings, Frauenholz sponsored a series of publications discussing a selection of best Egyptian, Greek and Roman gems from Stosch's collection authored by Johann Friedrich Schlichtegroll (1792, 1794, 1797 and 1798).⁸⁶ Frauenholz had a much better understanding of the market than Schweickart, and thus, he started from these series to raise interest in Stosch first.⁸⁷ For the sake of the first one published under the title *Auswahl vorzüglicher Gemmen aus derjenigen Sammlung die ehemahls der Baron Philipp von Stosch besass, die sich jetzt aber in dem Kön. Preussischen Cabinette befindet*, Frauenholz and Schlichtegroll used four drawings made by Preißler but no more.⁸⁸ This confirms that Schweickart had only a few of Preißler's drawings, hence, the other illustrations were made anew from gem impressions that Frauenholz also bought in 1787.⁸⁹ In 1805, Frauenholz and Schlichtegroll published a larger two-volume edition, launching a complete, illustrated publication of Stosch's gems. Ultimately, this project failed financially like Schweickart's 30 years ago.⁹⁰

In conclusion, if by any chance Frauenholz had bought gem drawings offered for sale in 1783 in Berlin, he would have probably re-sold them quickly like he did with the Stosch's sulphur impressions and the *Dactyliotheca Stoschiana*. Frauenholz used to deal with sizeable and important collections of drawings, which he often sold abroad. For example, in 1801, he purchased the famous Praun drawings collection, numbering around 1800 works by various artists, which he later reorganised in 1804 and sold *en bloc* to the Hungarian Prince Nicholas II Esterházy de Galantha (1765–1833).

In any case, at some point, the gem drawings now in Krakow were sold outside Germany, perhaps directly to Italy like other drawings from Stosch's collection (see above). One can make only some more or less educated guesses about who could have owned them there, but it was probably a person living at the time in Florence who had a serious interest in engraved gems and Philipp von Stosch combined. For example, Augusto Domenico Bracci (1717–1795) fits the profile. He was a draughtsman himself and he was fascinated by Stosch, his study of gems with engravers' signatures and the ability to tell the difference between genuine ancient pieces and modern works as well as contemporary forgeries. He was in a fierce rivalry with Winckelmann, and he lost, for instance, in a competition to write the catalogue of Stosch's gems, but he published his own study of ancient signed gems between 1784 and 1786, expanding the corpus published by Stosch in 1724 with 44 new objects.⁹¹ The collection of gem drawings in Krakow includes early-state engravings of two plates published by Bracci in his two-volume study (cf. discussion in Krakow Nos 1382 and 1620). They must have been made prior to 1784, but it is unknown when exactly and under which circumstances they joined the gem drawings collection from Krakow.⁹² Likewise, what is quite mysterious is the presence of 30 sketches of the

---

83 Schweickart 1775.
84 On Schweickart's as well as other unsuccessful projects aiming at publication of illustrated catalogue of Stosch's gems, see: Luther 1988, pp. 94–95; Rügler in Winckelmann 2013, pp. XXIV–XXVI.
85 For example, in the 12th volume of the journal *Museum für Künstler und für Kunstliebhaber: oder die Fortsetzung der Miscellaneen artistischen Inhalts* edited by Johann Georg Meusel and published in 1790 there is mentioned a considerable number of Preißler's drawings which Frauenholz bought after Schweickart's death: 'Er besizt dazu eine beträchtliche Anzahl von Zeichnungen, die Stosch selbst von dem nun auch verstorbenen J.J. Preissler nach den Originalen verfertigen lies, vermutlich in der Absicht, sie in Kupfer stechen zu lassen, welches sein Tod hinderte.'
86 For a detailed account on this, see: Luther 1988, pp. 93–108 (with more literature).
87 Luther 1988, pp. 95–96.
88 Schlichtegroll 1792b, pls XI, XVII, XX and XXXI. The other plates published in these projects were made after the drawings supplied by Giovanni Battista Casanova (1730–1795) as well as a painter Schrazenstaller.
89 Additionally, the catalogue of copperplates produced by Frauenholz & Comp. published in 1809 lists 28 presenting engraved gems but only four were made after drawings by Preißler, see: Luther 1988, pp. 237–238.

90 Schlichtegroll 1805; Luther 1988, pp. 96–108; Rügler in Winckelmann 2013, pp. XXIV–XXVI.
91 Bracci 1784–1786; Zazoff and Zazoff 1983, pp. 122–126; Fileti Maza 1996. Out of those 44 newly published gems, only 14 were truly ancient (Zwierlein-Diehl 2007, p. 280).
92 These two engravings are particularly interesting because Bracci, in his book (1784–1786, vol. I, p. XV and vol. II, p. VII), informs that the preliminary drawings and some engravings he collected in regard to his study of ancient signed gems were stolen from him in 1767. Ten years later he managed to find most but not all of them.

gems published by Stosch in 1724, mostly in red chalk, which once belonged to Anton Francesco Gori, which somehow did not end up in the Biblioteca Marucelliana in Florence (cf. discussion in Chapter 8). Also, two works by Picart (Krakow Nos 391–392) are unlikely to be in the assemblage prior to 1783. These groups are likely to have been added to the core collection between 1783 and 1800, which would explain the difference in the current number of gem drawings and prints in Krakow and those put up for sale in 1783 in Berlin.

After Stosch's death, Winckelmann remained close with Muzell-Stosch, so Bracci could not get the gem drawings (if he knew about them at that time in the first place, but he was close to Stosch during his lifetime, so it is possible). Then, he moved to Florence while Muzell-Stosch was out of Italy. Could he somehow have learnt about the auction in Berlin in 1783 and purchased what was still left of Stosch's corpus of gem drawings or did he buy them from another dealer shortly after the auction? Let us remember that the auction must have been widely advertised and sparked much interest inside and outside Germany, as proves the correspondence and discussion on Stosch's gem drawings and sulphur impressions offered at it between Adelheid Amalie von Schmettau (Münster) and François Hemsterhuis (The Hague).[93] Could Bracci have purchased the collection from Frauenholz? Unless new archival sources emerge, this remains a speculation, but Bracci died in Florence in 1795 and his papers and collections were sold at a public auction there.[94] François-Xavier Fabre lived in Florence since 1793, so he potentially could have bought the gem drawings at that auction. It is perhaps not a coincidence that some of Fabre's gem drawings reproduce the same intaglios and cameos as the ones from Krakow's drawings.[95] In conclusion, what can be said with certainty is that the *Pierres gravees par Stosche* albums should be identified with the volumes of drawings once owned by Heinrich Wilhelm Muzell-Stosch that were auctioned in Berlin in 1783, which, consequently, were once owned by Philipp von Stosch himself.

3 Reorganisation of the Collection around 1801

The difference in the number of volumes indicated by Stosch (1754) and in the auction catalogue of the Berlin sale from 1783 compared to the current number of volumes housed in the Princes Czartoryski Museum suggests that originally the collection had a different structure and organisation. A careful examination of each volume reveals that the gem drawings and prints were manipulated at some point, e.g. cut out from the original sheets, transferred onto new paper and bound or rebound.

Every single volume in the collection has a hardcover made of thick cardboard and leather (on the spines and corners). As already mentioned, on the spine of 26 of them, « *Pierres gravees par Stosche* » is embossed in gold (Fig. 6.6).[96] Dimensions of individual sheets vary from 362 × 255 mm to 359 × 250 mm but only volumes XV and XVI are considerably smaller: 327 × 222 mm. The average number of drawings in one volume is 90, however there are smaller (vol. XII-42) and bigger (vol. XXVIII-157) ones depending on the number of gems fitting the same subject matter area. The covers are of the casual type used by Izabela Czartoryska to bind her books while in Puławy (up to 1831).[97] Each volume has on the recto of the endpaper written an old signature II.A.9 and a consecutive number of the volume. Some of them have also indicated the class and section of Winckelmann's catalogue of Stosch's gems to which they refer in pencil, most likely added by Pelagia Potocka.

The endpaper is always made of a different kind of paper than inner-folios of the volumes. It is laid paper of creamy-yellowish colour. In the case of volumes I–XXVII, its watermark is a legend: *Koten Schlos* and coat of arms: Strasbourg's lily (*Fleur-de-Lis*) at the top and a coat of arms with a bend (Fig. 6.7). This paper is said to have been used frequently to print Italian books in the years 1802–1803, or maybe around these dates, and may be a variation or German imitation of the paper produced by the famous Dutch Honigh family.[98] The members of the Honigh fam-

---

93 Cf. Chapter 5 here.
94 Gamba 1836, pp. 172–173. Unfortunately, no sale catalogue of that auction seems to have survived, which makes impossible to verify the hypothesis that Bracci could have owned Krakow gem drawings at some point.
95 Check out in particular Musée Fabre in Montepellier inv. nos 837.1.438, 837.1.442, 837.1.443, 837.1.450. On the other hand, there are also many different ones, but as 837.1.438 and 837.1.450 prove, he was clearly interested in those accompanied with signatures and inscriptions.

96 Only volumes XXVII and XXVIII have no text on the spine. Their covers look exactly the same as in the case of the other volumes though.
97 I am grateful to Ewa Nogieć-Czepiel, Bożena Chmiel and Bożena König from the Czartoryski Museum in Krakow for sharing this observation with me.
98 I am grateful to Ewa Nogieć-Czepiel, Bożena Chmiel and Bożena König from the Czartoryski Museum in Krakow for their suggestions regarding the paper in question. Compare also with Churchill 1935, no. 429 which has identical composition but differs in the name of the producer. See also a very similar design reproduced in Heawood 1950, nos 64 and 1824.

ily were one of the most famous papermakers in Europe and they owned mills first in Wormer and then in Zaandyk for more than two centuries (1675–1902). Their paper was considered amongst the finest obtainable and was often falsified.[99] In the case of the volume XXVIII, a different kind of endpaper was used, one with a watermark consisting of letters only, L.T.F.v.T N, and it remains unidentified (Fig. 6.8).[100] The observations on the covers and endpaper suggest that the gem drawings were bound or rebound shortly after the Prince Adam Jerzy Czartoryski brought them to Puławy in 1801.

Regarding the inside folios of all volumes, they are all numbered so that the lower number is the number of the drawing, while the second is the number of the folio, which is usually higher by 3, as each volume has several blank unnumbered flyleave folios at the beginning. These numbers are written in pencil, and they correspond to inventories made while the drawings were already in the museum. Consequently, the current inventory numbers are given in the bottom-left corner of each drawing and are written as, for example *XV/rys/52*. The new sheets onto which the drawings were transferred are made of two kinds of paper. The first distinctive type is laid Dutch paper with the watermark presenting Strasbourg's lily in a coat of arms with a crown in the upper part and the initials WR in the bottom. On the side, there is a countermark IV (Jean Viledary) and C & I Honig below (Fig. 6.9). This paper was produced by Jean Villedary II, a French papermaker, who worked for Dutch factories (including the one run by the Honigh family) between 1758–1812. It was extremely popular throughout the whole of Europe, especially in Holland and England.[101] The other folios are made of laid Dutch paper that usually has only a portion of a watermark visible, and it features an appendage of the coat of arms in the form of Honigh family's beehive mark accompanied with the name of the factory J Honig & Zoonen (Fig. 6.10). Most likely the full version of the watermark in question presents a crowned coat of arms with a horn inside and the mentioned appendage in the form of the Honigh family's beehive mark at the bottom. The name J Honig & Zoonen suggests the paper to have been produced between 1737–1787, but it was in use for many years after the production ceased.[102] The *Gravell Watermark Archive* documents the use of the paper bearing this watermark mostly between 1783–1809.[103]

Overall, the condition of the drawings vary since some are well-preserved, while others are in a relatively bad condition. However, all of them were cut out of the original sheets and transferred onto new paper, and in many cases only the enlarged gem drawing and the real-size gem drawing survived from the original sheet, unless the latter was drawn anew based on the original. A few drawings were transferred twice.[104] Many of them miss some parts that were sometimes later filled in with the use of pen or pencil, or they are torn and frayed, and some are faded. It is noteworthy that already in 1783 at least some (if not all) drawings are recorded as being in poor condition.[105] All the prints have survived almost untouched, though. Two fragments of original sheets related to the drawings Krakow Nos 171 and 1497 survived, loosely inserted in two volumes (Figs 6.11–6.16). The drawings were sometimes cut out, and therefore some of their important parts with potentially original commentaries or information on the provenance of the depicted piece are now missing. To sum up, paper analysis supports the conclusions drawn from the binding inspection – the reorganisation of the collection took place around 1801, certainly shortly after the drawings were brought to Puławy.

During that process, many of them received sometimes rather extensive commentaries. These texts are mostly written in brown ink by the same hand as the gemstone type information given in the recreated real-size gem drawings (Figs 6.17–6.18). The comparative analysis with letters and other archives from the Czartoryski Library makes it clear that they were written by Izabela Czartoryska.[106] It seems that she was working with the drawings for a longer period of time because sometimes her initially short descriptions of the objects illustrated by the drawings are later supplemented with additional texts (Figs 6.19–6.20). Moreover, she received some help from an assistant who, from time to time, extended Czartoryska's short comments into long

---

99   Voorn 1960, p. 554.
100 The same sequence of letters but with a crown above is illustrated by Heawood (1950, no. 1078).
101 Churchill 1935, pp. 21–22, no. 408 – which illustrates a slightly different version of the watermark in question. See also: Voorn 1960, pp. 132 and 153.
102 Churchill 1935, pp. 9 and 15, no. 322; Heawood 1950, no. 2748 – full version of the watermark in question.

103 See: http://www.gravell.org/results.php?search=SUBMIT&select =p&EnDescriptor=&FrDescriptor=&GrDescriptor=&SpDescrip tor=&secondaryDesc=&useYear=&origin=Netherlands &papermaker=&mill=&collector=&repro=&NameNo=&FiliNo =&comments=&useCountry=&repocountry=&reponame =&shelfmark=&format=&artifact=&author=&adddate = [retrieved on 15 October 2018].
104 These are the following: Krakow Nos 463, 3534, 1042, 1412, 1421, 1552 and 1674.
105 Auction Muzell-Stosch 1783, pp. 63–64, lot 907.
106 I am grateful to Janusz Pezda from the Institute of History, Jagiellonian University and The Czartoryski Library for confirming the handwriting appearing on the drawings to be that of Izabela Czartoryska.

elaborations using black ink (Fig. 6.21).¹⁰⁷ In some cases, there was no previous commentary given by Czartoryska, but her assistant supplied one (Fig. 6.22).¹⁰⁸

Because some of Czartoryska's and her assistant's texts are quite long and elaborate, including references to ancient literature, coins, sculpture, wall paintings discovered in Herculaneum, etc., one speculates that whenever the drawing has a long description including such references or explicit explanation of gem's iconography, it might have had an original text, which was later directly copied or rewritten with some changes. This is suggested by two fragments of original paper related to the drawings Krakow Nos 171 and 1497. The first has original text, the second does not. A comparison of the commentary from Krakow No. 171 with Czartoryska's later text makes it clear that she rewrote considerable parts of the original comment, and she was likely not inspired by another source, for example, a relevant record in the Winckelmann's catalogue of Stosch's gems.¹⁰⁹ It is difficult to judge if there were many cases like this.

Izabela Czartoryska is otherwise unknown to have much interest in intaglios and cameos. Her knowledge about Antiquity in general was superficial, definitely not at the level to provide such detailed analyses and references to various kinds of antiquities, e.g. ancient gems. In other words, it is difficult to imagine that she wrote such detailed commentaries entirely on her own. Theoretically, she may have found some help in the copies of Stosch's book, *Gemmae antiquae caelatae*, as well as Winckelmann's catalogue of Stosch's gems from 1760 that arrived in Puławy alongside the drawings. The Czartoryski library was also well equipped with books on engraved gems already at the time (see above). Some commentaries written by Czartoryska demonstrate considerable similarities or they are identical to the entries of specific gems in Winckelmann's catalogue, which could suggest her extensive usage of relevant literature.¹¹⁰ The surviving references to specific gems of Stosch catalogued by Winckelmann in 1760 on several hundred of drawings could be also suggestive.¹¹¹ For example, the drawing Krakow No. 2047 has a text by Czartoryska: '*Cupidon enchainé avec une houe, sur laquelle il s'appuye dans l'attitude de se reposer après le travail auquel il est condamné. Il y avoit anciennement au Capitole la statue d'un jeune homme rémuant la terre avec le meme instrument. Pompée l'avait apporté à Rome, et elle venoit du palais du Roy de Bithynie*' is strikingly close to the one appearing in Winckelmann's catalogue of Stosch's gems in the entry related to a glass paste reproducing the same gem: '*Cupidon enchainé & s'appuyant sur une houe, dans l'attitude de se reposer après le travail auquel il est condamné. Il y avoit anciennement au Capitole la Statue d'un jeune homme remuant la terre avec un tel instrument; Pompée l'avoit apportée à Rome, & elle sortoit des Galeries du Roy de Bithynie*'.¹¹²

Interestingly, one notices that in some cases, even though the drawing reproduces a gem not from Stosch's own collection, an analogy can be found among the gems published in 1760 by Winckelmann in his catalogue with

---

107 For example: Krakow Nos 473, 476–477, 483, 489, 661, 912, 1016, 1338 and more can be checked in the catalogue of Krakow drawings in Appendix 2. The hand of that assistant remains unidentified.

108 For example: Krakow Nos 62, 344, 1219, 1335, 1922, 2137, 2233 and more can be checked in the catalogue of Krakow drawings in Appendix 2. The Princess Czartoryska's assistant also sometimes corrected and improved gemstone type information given in the real-size gem drawings made by her, see: Krakow Nos 66, 235, 262 and 497. A potential assistant of Czartoryska could be Franciszek Kozłowski, whose handwriting is similar and who used to help the princess in organization of some of her manuscripts and studies in Puławy, apart from being the keeper of the Czartoryski collection at the time.

109 The original commentary from the drawing sounds as follows: '*Ceres coeffé d'un Voile, tenant d'une main un flambeau allumé, de l'autre une coupe. Devant elle un modius avec des epics de bleds et un cheval deriere un animal entre la chevre ou la chevreuil. Modius est une measure usité pour les grains chez les anciens.*', whereas Czartoryska described the gem as: '*Ceres assise avec un flambeau, pour rapeller qu'elle en avoit un en cherchant Proserpine: elle tient une Patere de l'autre main. Le Modius ou mesure de bled se voit a ses pieds avec des Epics. Devant est un cheval deriere un autre animal resemblant un chevreuil.*' Winckelmann's relevant record (class II, no. 235, p. 69) is different: '*Cérès voilée assise, tenant de la main droite un grand flambeau allumé, & de la gauche une coupe; devant elle on voit un Modius avec épis de bled & un Cheval, & derriére elle un autre Cheval. Les Etrusques représentoient aussi Cérès avec la patère, comme on remarque dans deux petites figures de bronze de la Galerie de l'Empereur à Florence.*'

110 This is the case of the following 208 drawings: Krakow Nos 2, 60, 79, 83–85, 120, 153–154, 172, 174–175, 177–178, 184, 188, 201–202, 208, 210–211, 228, 231, 256, 278–279, 281, 284–285, 298, 307, 326, 331, 349, 359, 397, 407, 417, 430, 436, 442, 449, 470, 475, 479, 495, 500, 566, 568–570, 584–585, 615–616, 627–628, 636, 662–663, 676, 678, 695, 705, 723, 730, 732, 748, 760, 783, 799, 805, 807, 811, 813–814, 830, 847, 870, 912, 921–922, 925–926, 955, 963, 991, 1001, 1042, 1119–1120, 1135, 1146, 1154, 1175, 1178, 1194, 1200, 1224, 1231, 1235, 1237, 1240, 1250–1251, 1259, 1273–1274, 1277, 1286, 1295–1296, 1306, 1308, 1316, 1344, 1401, 1475, 1491–1492, 1494, 1514, 1517–1518, 1523, 1529, 1555, 1564, 1573–1575, 1577, 1583–1584, 1594–1595, 1602, 1609, 1615, 1618, 1621–1622, 1628, 1632, 1634–1635, 1642–1643, 1650, 1652, 1662, 1752, 1776, 1780, 1791, 1840–1841, 1845, 1849, 1907, 1912, 1914, 1920, 1922, 1931, 1955, 1957, 1961, 1972, 1988, 1990, 1995, 2000, 2003, 2005–2006, 2014, 2016, 2023, 2047, 2052–2053, 2055, 2066, 2089, 2092, 2105, 2107, 2111, 2115, 2121, 2124–2125, 2137, 2145, 2162, 2164, 2166–2167, 2169, 2175, 2197, 2210, 2212, 2225, 2240, 2255 and 2261.

111 For a thorough discussion on those references, cf. Chapter 8 here.

112 Winckelmann 1760, class II, no. 820, p. 147.

an entry that sounds very close to the commentary that the drawing has. A good example of that is the commentary to the drawing Krakow No. 912: 'Tete de Satyre trouvé sur une piece ronde de Bronze au revers de la quelle etoit l'inscription: ΚΑΙ ΔΡΥΜΟΥΣ ΑΝΘΡΑ ΦΙΛΟΥΜΕΝ la meme tete se trouve dans le recueil du Commendeur del Pozzo. Et l'homme des bois nous aimons.', which refers to a glass paste in Stosch's collection.[113] In this case, the text is much closer but not identical to the one appearing in Winckelmann's catalogue of Stosch's gems: 'Tête d'un Satyre. Je trouve dans le Recueil des désseins du Commendeur del Pozzo une Tête de Satyre qui étoit sur une piece ronde de bronze, au revers de laquelle étoit l'Inscription: ΚΑΙ ΔΡΥΜΟΥΣ ΑΝΘΡΑ ΦΙΛΟΥΜΕΝ, Nous nous plaisons dans les buissons & dans les caverns.'[114]

In many cases, the commentaries to individual gems by Winckelmann in his catalogue are comparable or longer (more precise or include elaborate descriptions) to the ones appearing under the relevant gem drawings.[115] There is also a substantial group of drawings which have elaborate commentaries to the depicted gems, but they are not similar to the ones one finds in the relevant entries in Winckelmann's catalogue of Stosch's gems.[116] This means

---

113 Furtwängler 1896, no. 9822; Borbein, Kunze and Rügler 2019, no. II.1538 (with full bibliography).

114 More examples like this one can be consulted in the catalogue of Krakow drawings in Appendix 2. Winckelmann's entries to individual gems may vary from the descriptions accompanying the drawings of relevant gems from Stosch's corpus or Stosch's own inventory because as Winckelmann writes himself, while he worked on the catalogue of Stosch's gems, sometimes he had to reject original ideas and explanations of the collector (for example, a letter from Winckelmann to Hieronymus Dietrich Berendis dated 5 February 1758, see: Winckelmann 1952–1957, vol. I, p. 330; Décultot 2012, p. 169). As a result, even though considerable parts of Winckelmann's catalogue may be based on Stosch's earlier research, there might be differences between the original texts (including those on the drawings) and Winckelmann's entries.

115 This is the case of the following 235 drawings (WC – Winckelmann's comment is comparable, WL – Winckelmann's comment is longer, WS – Winckelmann's comment is shorter): Krakow No. 91 (WL), 94 (WL), 126 (WL), 129 (WL), 140 (WC), 143 (WC), 145 (WC), 147 (WL), 149 (WC), 156 (WL), 159 (WL), 162 (WC), 164 (WC), 173 (WL), 183 (WL), 219 (WL), 225 (WL), 241 (WL), 242 (WL), 250 (WL), 272 (WL), 273 (WL), 305 (WL), 314 (WL), 339 (WL), 343 (WL), 346 (WC), 347 (WC), 352 (WS), 360 (WL), 367 (WL), 370 (WL), 374 (WL), 375 (WS), 381 (WL), 384 (WL), 385 (WL), 387 (WC), 400 (WC), 413 (WL), 414 (WC), 418 (WL), 421 (WL), 457 (WC), 462 (WC), 463 (WC), 465 (WC), 469 (WC), 471 (WC), 474 (WC), 481 (WL), 488 (WL), 497 (WL), 517 (WC), 519 (WS), 520 (WL), 521 (WL), 536 (WL), 545 (WL), 548 (WC), 549 (WC), 554 (WL), 560 (WC), 607 (WS), 617 (WL), 640 (WC), 643 (WL), 679 (WL), 683 (WL), 696 (WL), 700 (WL), 701 (WL), 703 (WL), 707 (WL), 714 (WL), 721 (WL), 731 (WL), 734 (WL), 736 (WL), 737 (WL), 771 (WL), 772 (WL), 777 (WL), 824 (WL), 844 (WL), 853 (WL), 855 (WL), 863 (WL), 866 (WL), 867 (WC), 878 (WL), 879 (WL), 884 (WL), 889 (WL), 890 (WC), 907 (WC), 920 (WL), 940 (WL), 948 (WC), 977 (WL), 1034 (WL), 1050 (WL), 1053 (WC), 1093 (WL), 1101 (WL), 1103 (WL), 1110 (WL), 1112 (WC), 1113 (WL), 1122 (WL), 1129 (WC), 1133 (WC), 1139 (WL), 1145 (WL), 1148 (WL), 1153 (WL), 1157 (WC), 1169 (WL), 1170 (WL), 1193 (WC), 1205 (WL), 1217 (WL), 1223 (WL), 1225 (WL), 1228 (WL), 1230 (WL), 1233 (WL), 1236 (WL), 1239 (WC), 1244 (WC), 1264 (WL), 1291 (WL), 1298 (WC), 1319 (WL), 1320 (WL), 1332 (WL), 1353 (WL), 1395 (WL), 1396 (WL), 1399 (WL), 1407 (WL), 1443 (WL), 1451 (WL), 1452 (WL), 1460 (WC), 1462 (WC), 1463 (WL), 1466 (WL), 1467 (WL), 1472 (WL), 1486 (WL), 1497 (WC), 1499 (WL), 1513 (WL), 1545 (WL), 1624 (WL), 1630 (WC), 1631 (WC), 1638 (WL), 1781 (WL), 1838 (WL), 1858 (WL), 1859 (WL), 1866 (WL), 1870 (WL), 1891 (WL), 1892 (WL), 1905 (WS), 1906 (WL), 1919 (WL), 1923 (WL), 1925 (WC), 1932 (WL), 1934 (WL), 1936 (WL), 1938 (WL), 1940 (WC), 1942 (WC), 1943 (WL), 1946 (WL), 1947 (WL), 1949 (WL), 1950 (WC), 1952 (WL), 1958 (WL), 1959 (WC), 1965 (WL), 1968 (WC), 1970 (WL), 1973 (WC), 1985 (WC), 1989 (WC), 1992 (WL), 2012 (WL), 2015 (WL), 2020 (WL), 2030 (WC), 2031 (WC), 2045 (WL), 2046 (WL), 2051 (WL), 2057 (WC), 2070 (WC), 2072 (WC), 2083 (WC), 2126 (WC), 2128 WC), 2132 (WC), 2134 (WL), 2135 (WL), 2140 (WC), 2142 (WC), 2150 (WC), 2155 (WS), 2156 (WC), 2173 (WL), 2187 (WC), 2189 (WC), 2248 (WC), 2249 (WC) and 2250 (WC).

116 This is the case of the following 188 drawings (WC – Winckelmann's comment is comparable, WL – Winckelmann's comment is longer, WS – Winckelmann's comment is shorter): Krakow No. 3 (WC), 12 (WL), 13 (WL), 30 (WL), 41 (WC), 43 (WL, reference to coins), 52 (WL), 53 (WL), 54 (WL), 57 (WL), 58 (WC), 59 (WL), 62 (WC), 69 (WL – reference to bronze figures), 70 (WL), 73 (WL), 74 (WC), 86 (WL), 87 (WL – reference to literature on gems), 90 (WC), 102 (WC), 112 (WC), 114 (WL), 120 (WS), 121 (WL – reference to literature on gems), 124 (WC), 149 (WL), 167 (WL – reference to coins), 171 (WL – reference to bronze figurines), 181 (WS), 186 (WS), 187 (WS), 209 (WL – reference to coins), 212 (WL – reference to ancient literature), 214 (WL – reference to coins), 290 (WS), 322 (WS), 323 (WS), 422 (WS), 454 (WL), 478 (WS), 484 (WC), 506 (WL), 509 (WL), 510 (WL), 534 (WL), 540 (WC), 541 (WS), 562 (WC, reference to coins), 574 (WL), 578 (WL), 586 (WC), 588 (WL), 602 (WL), 606 (WL), 613 (WL), 641 (WL, reference to original gem in Florence), 642 (WL), 652 (WL), 654 (WL), 655 (WL, reference to coins), 657 (WC), 661 (WS), 682 (WS), 686 (WC), 689 (WC), 690 (WC), 706 (WS), 780 (WS), 781 (WL), 790 (WL), 801 (WL), 814 (WL), 836 (WS), 845 (WL), 846 (WC), 862 (WC), 868 (WL – reference to ancient literature), 873 (WS), 880 (WL), 888 (WL), 931 (WL), 1011 (WL), 1015 (WC), 1058 (WL – reference to coins), 1059 (WL), 1092 (WL), 1130 (WC), 1136 (WL), 1173 (WL – reference to ancient literature), 1174 (WS), 1176 (WC), 1179 (WS), 1180 (WL), 1182 (WL), 1188 (WC), 1196 (WL), 1202 (WL), 1203 (WL), 1204 (WC), 1212 (WL), 1227 (WL), 1257 (WS), 1275 (WC), 1278 (WS), 1279 (WS), 1282 (WL), 1283 (WL), 1288 (WL), 1294 (WL), 1297 (WC), 1303 (WL), 1304 (WL), 1329 (WL), 1330 (WC), 1334 (WC), 1355 (WL), 1365 (WL), 1371 (WS), 1372 (WL), 1381 (WC), 1387 (WL), 1390 (WC), 1397 (WL), 1398 (WL), 1427 (WC), 1428 (WC), 1430 (WL), 1431 (WC), 1439 (WL), 1441 (WC), 1449 (WL), 1450 (WL), 1454 (WL), 1469 (WC), 1476 (WL), 1479 (WL), 1480 (WS), 1487 (WC), 1488 (WL), 1489 (WC), 1490 (WC), 1499 (WL), 1509 (WL), 1512 (WC), 1519 (WL), 1522 (WL), 1524 (WL), 1535 (WL), 1536 (WS), 1540 (WL), 1542 (WS), 1559 (WS), 1562 (WL), 1582 (WL), 1585 (WL), 1586 (WL), 1587 (WL), 1647 (WC), 1648 (WC), 1649 (WS), 1660 (WC), 1735 (WC), 1765 (WL), 1786 (WL), 1787 (WL), 1793 (WL), 1814 (WL), 1857 (WL), 1888 (WL), 1894 (WL), 1904 (WL),

that probably Czartoryska took inspiration from somewhere else and the only reasonable suggestion seems to be original texts accompanying the drawings beforehand. At the same time, there are drawings within the collection with no commentaries whatsoever.[117] As evidenced by Krakow No. 1497, some of them originally had no comments and apparently, while there is no source of inspiration for Czartoryska, she would write nothing, or she described the subject matter of the gem but very briefly. One should also take into account that there is lack of extensive original commentaries on several hundred drawings found in Berlin which are preserved intact, on the original paper. Furthermore, the letter from Johann Joachim Winckelmann to Antonio Baldani, dated 26–30 September 1758, suggests that originally, a small number of gem drawings had extensive commentaries.[118]

To conclude, the analysis of the commentaries accompanying a good number of drawings discovered in Krakow suggests that they were mostly rewritten by Izabela Czartoryska from the original sheets. Their complexity and quality imply their author to be someone directly from Philipp von Stosch's circle or Stosch himself. The references to various kinds of antiquities, sculpture, coins, etc., bearing similar motifs, as well as wall paintings discovered in Herculaneum[119] and the Paper Museum (*Museo Cartaceo*) of Cassiano dal Pozzo (1588–1657)[120] were certainly beyond the skill of Izabela Czartoryska and they might mirror specific aspects of Stosch's life and career. The potential authorship and meaning of these commentaries will be fully discussed in Chapter 8. It seems that the gem drawings were treated in Puławy not only as a source of inspiration for the warmly welcomed artists, but they also helped Czartoryska to develop her passion towards ancient art and Antiquity in general. They were perfect tools to expand her knowledge of ancient mythologies, history, arts and crafts. To some extent, Winckelmann's catalogue of Stosch's gems was for Czartoryska a sort of a guidebook which helped her to reorganise the drawings according to the subject matter areas. One must keep in mind that in the early 19th century it was habitual to organise a collection according to a sort of a system.[121] It is not known how the collection was originally organised but taking into account that the drawings were believed to present, exclusively, Stosch's gems and glass pastes, Izabela Czartoryska could have learned from Winckelmann's catalogue how the collection should be organised, and thus tried to follow suit with the gem drawings she received, deciding to sort them according to the classes created by Winckelmann himself. As a result, the drawings regardless of their techniques and styles and previous sorting were bound into 28 folio volumes so that each includes specific thematic groups.

It remains unclear why Princess Czartoryska decided to cut the drawings out of the original sheets even if, as evidenced by the fragments related to the drawings Krakow Nos 171 and 1497 (see above), they were in good condition.[122] The transfer resulted in a considerable loss of important information because assuming the original gem descriptions to have been most of the time even partially copied or rewritten, most of them as well as provenance information etc. was lost. Moreover, apart from Stosch's gem drawings, the collection which Prince Czartoryski brought to Puławy also included some additional sheets with gem drawings and prints excerpted from books (see discussion on individual groups in Chapter 8). At the point of reorganisation of the collection by Izabela Czartoryska, all of them were mixed together.

Finally, the analysis of folio numbers proves that the reorganisation of the collection was not easy. Currently, each drawing within a volume is consequently numbered in the top-right corner but originally the numbering of folios was different and survived only in the case of four volumes. In volume XI, the original numbering starts from 43 and consequently raises up to 138 when it is broken as no. 140 goes first, before 139, then it continues up to 142 when it is broken again to 146, after which goes a sequence 145, 144, 143, 147, 149, 148, 150, 152, 151, 153, 154, 155, 162, 161, 160, 159, 158, again 158, 156, 163, 164, 165, 166,

---

1910 (WL), 1913 (WL), 1926 (WL), 1928 (WL), 1929 (WL), 1953 (WL), 2024 (WL), 2035 (WC), 2062 (WC), 2157 (WS) and 2247 (WL).

117   Check out the catalogue of Krakow drawings in Appendix 2.
118   Winckelmann 1961, p. 105, no. 31: '*Non ho altri amminicoli per schiarirmi e facilitarmi il lavoro che i disegni fatti in grande, ma senza veruna spiegazione.*'
119   According to Stosch (1754, pp. 22–23), during his early travels through Italy, he visited the excavations on Prince Elbeuf's property at Portici, inspecting the earliest sculpture finds surfacing from the buried city of Herculaneum, decades before excavations officially began.
120   Stosch had access to Pozzo's famous Paper Museum through Cardinal Alessandro Albani, who owned it at the time. Cassiano dal Pozzo is also regarded as a forerunner and inspiration for Stosch in developing his *Atlas* project (cf. Chapter 1 here).

121   I am grateful to Bożena Chmiel and Barbara König for sharing this observation with me.
122   However, it should be stressed that she would cut drawings from original sheets and paste them into the correspondence or manuscripts she worked on, like the study entitled *Melanges pour la Maison Gothique*, which includes several reused gem drawings from another source than *Pierres gravees par Stosche*, see: Rkps 6070/3 III (also available online: http://polona.pl/preview/30923f1f-605b-4633-855f-2036b1e2c4ff – retrieved on 29 October 2023).

167, 168 and 169. The rest of the drawings in this volume do not have these numbers. The total number of drawings in volume XI is 127, and they represent masks and their combinations. Volume XIII is another case like this. This time, the original numbering starts like the current one from 1 but only until 13 when it is breached by 15 after which goes 14, 17–36 (no. 16 is absent), 38, 39–62 (no. 37 is absent), 63, 64, 65 again (!), 66–83 and 85–87 (no. 84 is absent). Volume XIII includes drawings featuring gems with Dionysus and his *thiasos* and there are 83 of them. Volume XIV consists of 68 more drawings also presenting Dionysus and his companions and they also have original numbering given in the top-right corner: 85–87 again (!), 88–150. Finally, volume XXVII also has original folio numbering written consecutively from 1 to 133. It is noteworthy that some drawings in these volumes have no original numbering. Could this be related to the drawings' transfer onto new paper? The numbers listed above are written in brown ink by the same hand which wrote the new commentaries, i.e. Izabela Czartoryska.

Volumes XIII and XIV clearly show that the first attempts of sorting were unsuccessful, and that the drawings were once completely disorganised or one should say, they arrived in Puławy in 1801 as such. This is also reflected in the artificial organisation of the collection at the sale in 1783 in Berlin (although, the catalogue descriptions are brief and vague) as well as analysis of the part of Stosch's gem drawings corpus now preserved in the Kunstbibliothek in Berlin. Furthermore, ca. 566 drawings and prints combined have some numbers in pencil written in their fields.[123] No such numbering appears on the drawings found in Berlin, thus it is suggested that they were added after the auction in 1783. The new owner of the Krakow drawings or Izabela Czartoryska tried it seems to organise the drawings. The analysis of those numbers shows that a slightly different but still subject matter organisation was applied. The drawings with numbers 2–288 depict Amor/Cupid and Psyche, nos 289–483 mythological figures and subjects including the Trojan War episodes, nos 484–519 are mostly drawings depicting philosophers, 520–525 present warfare scenes, 526–545 bucolic themes and 546–591 are studies of Athena/Minerva and related matters. It seems that systematisation of the collection was unfinished, or the drawings were decided to be organised differently.

---

123 See relevant drawings in the catalogue. The number 566 refers only to those cases where the numbers are readable, in fact, there would be many more but the numbers in pencil have faded away.

FIGURE 6.1

FIGURE 6.2

FIGURE 6.3

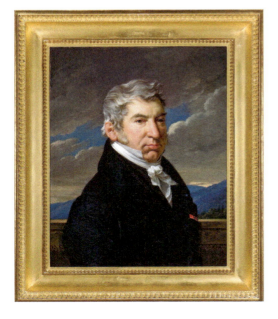

FIGURE 6.4

PLATE 27

FIGURE 6.5

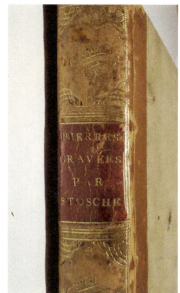

FIGURE 6.6

FIGURE 6.8

KOTEN SCHLOS

FIGURE 6.7

FIGURE 6.9

FIGURE 6.10

FIGURE 6.11

FIGURE 6.12

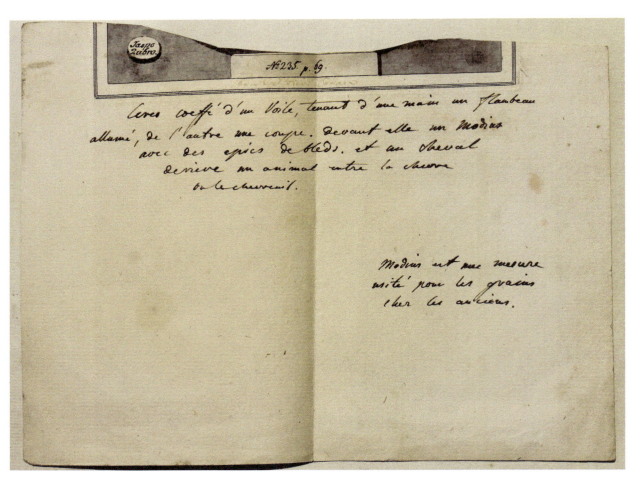

FIGURE 6.13

PLATE 29

FIGURE 6.14

FIGURE 6.15

FIGURE 6.16

FIGURE 6.17

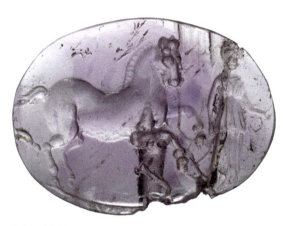

FIGURE 6.18

FIGURE 6.19

FIGURE 6.20

FIGURE 6.21

FIGURE 6.22

CHAPTER 7

Pierres gravées du roi avec figures in the Kunstbibliothek in Berlin

Paweł Gołyźniak

1   Introduction

In the Ornamentstichsammlung of the Kunstbibliothek, Staatliche Museen zu Berlin – Preußischer Kulturbesitz there is a unique edition of Winckelmann's catalogue of Stosch's gems in six 4° volumes entitled *Pierres gravées du roi avec figures* (Figs 7.1–7.2).[1] Each volume contains a part of Winckelmann's text accompanied by a series of relevant drawings of gems displayed as plates at the end. In the first one, there is an introduction and text of the First Class and the Second one up to the section of gems presenting Minerva (pp. 1–66) and 142 drawings. The second volume contains the text from Winckelmann's catalogue Second Class up to the section of Mercury (pp. 67–159) and 177 drawings. In the third volume, there is Winckelmann's text from the Second Class up to the section on Aesculapius (pp. 160–227) and 104 drawings. The fourth volume has Winckelmann's text up to the end of the Second Class (pp. 228–313) and 122 drawings inside. The fifth volume contains Winckelmann's text of the Third Class (pp. 314–403) and 130 drawings. The sixth volume includes Winckelmann's text of the Fourth, Fifth, Sixth, Seventh and Eighth Classes (pp. 404–569) and 155 drawings. While Winckelmann's text is the one officially printed but cut into six parts, the total number of 830 drawings is utterly unique.[2]

2   Provenance and History

In the preface to the catalogue of Stosch's gems, which was published in 1760 by Johann Joachim Winckelmann, the German scholar writes as follows: '*We have already informed the reader what we have done to make up for the figures that are missing in this work. In better times one could have anticipated the wishes of the Curious; for the deceased owner of this cabinet had the vast majority of his gems drawn enlarged by skilful artists who lived for many years in his house. Among the drawings he had had made, there are a few hundred by the hand of the famous Marcus Tuscher.*'[3] This account suggests that he was aware of the defect of the unillustrated book he was producing for Philipp von Stosch's sole heir Heinrich Wilhelm Muzell-Stosch, even though there were many drawings of Stosch's gems at their disposal, which could have been used for production of illustrations.[4] Ultimately, the catalogue was published without illustrations because Stosch's heir did not want to invest much in it. After all, his primary goal was to make a sale catalogue advertising the collection to the prospective buyers rather than a fully scholarly book.

According to the recent research though, a limited special edition, including 11 plates displaying some of the

---

1   Kunstbibliothek – Ornamentstichsammlung, inv. no.: os 4270 a kl 1–6. I am grateful to Joachim Brand, Jana Hettmann and Elke Blauert (emeritus) from the Kunstbibliothek in Berlin for their kind help in my research on these volumes and assistance during my visit in Berlin.
2   This is the current total number of drawings according to the most recent research conducted by me in 2022. However, the total number of drawings counted from the handwritten notes on the first inner-folios of all volumes is 846. This number is also recorded in the oldest inventory note of the Antikensammlung from 1816 (cf. below). In the online catalogue of the Kunstbibliothek in Berlin one finds information about 826 drawings in total (https://opac.spk-berlin.de/DB=2/SET=1/TTL=5/SHW?FRST=6 – retrieved on 18 November 2022), however, this seems to be a typo. The difference between the current, lower number and the old, higher one can be explained by the fact that some drawings were removed or fell out the volumes between 1816 and 2022. Some folios were clearly removed since fragments of torn folios are observable, for example, in volume I, between pls 22 and 23, 71 and 72, 82 and 83, vol. II, pl. 1 and 2, 50 and 51, 76 and 77 (?), 115 and 116, 117 and 118,

vol. IV, pl. 57 and 58, vol. V, pl. 37 and 38. In addition, the volumes, especially V and VI are preserved in relatively bad condition, including some folios that are now just loose sheets (note the turbulent history of the volumes during the Second World War). Finally, the drawings could have originally been incorrectly counted too which is suggested by the fact that in the case of vol. II, on the page with information of the book including 185 plates (*Ce volume renferme 185 dessins de planches*); in the corner another hand in another ink inscribed *184*, probably referring to the actual number of the plates. Similarly, vol. III has written '*Ce Volume contient 105 dessins*', while in the corner there is *106*.
3   The translations are all mine unless otherwise stated. Winckelmann 1760, p. XXVII: '*On a déjà prevenu le Lecteur sur ce qu'on a fait pour suppléer aux figures qui manquent à cet Ouvrage. Dans de meilleurs tems on auroit pu prévenir les souhaits des Curieux; car le défunt Posseßeur de ce Cabinet en avoit fait déssiner en grand la meilleure partie par d'habiles Artistes qui ont vécu plusieurs années dans sa maison. Parmi les Desseins qu'il avoir fait faire, on en compte quelques Centaines de la main du célébre Marc Tuscher.*'
4   Stosch (1754, p. 50) also claimed that he had all his gems documented as drawings by artists like Johann Justin Preißler, Markus Tuscher, Georg Abraham Nagel and Johann Adam Schweickart.

© PAWEŁ GOŁYŹNIAK, 2025 | DOI:10.1163/9789004712553_008
This is an open access chapter distributed under the terms of the CC BY-NC-ND 4.0 license.

gems and glass pastes from Stosch's assemblage was also published. Only a few copies are known to exist today,[5] but the richly illustrated edition like the one discovered in the Kunstbibliothek in Berlin is unique and already its decorative title folio suggests it to be tailored as a gift to Frederick II the Great, King of Prussia. In the second volume of his publication of Stosch's gem collection released in 1805, Schlichtegroll mentions many gem drawings to be housed in Berlin. He even suggests that these drawings were sold together with Stosch's gems to the King of Prussia: *'This collection of drawings came into the possession of the King of Prussia at the same time as the gems, and one still finds them in the Museum in Berlin.'*[6] Stosch's gems were sold in 1764 to him for 30 000 ducats and the king deposited them in his Antikentempel in Sanssouci Park in Potsdam alongside his collection of ancient coins.[7] They stayed there until 1798 when they were transferred to the Berlin Kunstkammer and recorded for the first time by Henry in 1805.[8] Only in 1816 did they enter the Royal Museum in Berlin (Antikensammlung) under Ernst Heinrich Toelken's (1785–1864) supervision.[9] During the transfer of the gems in 1816, Toelken also recorded in the *Altes Inventarium der Königlichen Gemmensammlung* (Inv. 5, part A): *'Finally, a considerable collection of drawings after the most excellent gems of the same 846 sheets bound together in 6 quarto volumes. Three hundred of them are by Markus Tuscher, and all were made under Stosch's eyes.'*[10] Henry's and Toelken's descriptions of the drawings, especially attribution of three hundred of them to Markus Tuscher sound very much like the words of Winckelmann from the preface to his catalogue evoked above – there were six volumes including multiple drawings, among which hundreds by Tuscher. That similarity cannot be merely a coincidence, and Henry's and Toelken's reports confirm the words of Schlichtegroll. Moreover, the six volumes including 846 plates with gem drawings listed by Toelken must be the very same volumes now rediscovered in the Kunstbibliothek in Berlin – the numbers of volumes and drawings fit (almost) perfectly.[11] Their presence in the Antikensammlung is confirmed by a stamp put at the bottom of the title folio of each volume, with the coat of arms of the Antikensammlung and text around – *Koenigliche Museen* (Fig. 7.3). It is noteworthy that on the recto side of the title folio in each volume there is a stamp of the Königliche Bibliothek zu Berlin – *Ex Biblioth Regia Berolinensi* (Fig. 7.4), which means that at some point the volumes must have been transferred from Antikensammlung to the Royal Library (since 1918 called Preußische Staatsbibliothek). This is also suggested by several inventory numbers written on the front folio, which must have been changed during the transfer of the volumes. They also appear on the spines – C 322; Mag 1907 and the current ones (OS 4270 a kl 1–6) (Fig. 7.5). Given the history of the collections of the Preußische Staatsbibliothek evacuated from Berlin during the Second World War, the volumes belong to those fragments of the collection, which after 1945 returned to Berlin. Most likely shortly after that date they were incorporated to the holdings of the Kunstbibliothek in Berlin.[12]

Because the volumes with the gem drawings in question were recorded by Henry and Schlichtegroll in 1805 and then by Toelken in 1816 together with Stosch's gems after their ultimate transfer to Antikensammlung in Berlin, it seems probable that they were kept together earlier as well. The volumes must have been made after 1760 and the title of the whole series, *Pierres gravées du roi avec figures*, suggests that they were composed once Stosch's gems were already negotiated to be sold to the King of Prussia. They were not put at auction following Muzell-Stosch's death organised in Berlin in 1783, so they must have left Stosch's corpus of gem drawings earlier.[13]

---

5   The only known copies are known to be in Rome, Fano, Berlin, Weimar, New York and Krakow, see: Rügler in Winckelmann 2013, p. XXIII, n. 88 and Krakow, The Czartoryski Library, inv. no.: 1836 II.
6   Schlichtegroll 1805, vol. II, p. 23: *'Diese Sammlung von Zeichnungen ist mit den Steinen zugleich in den Besitz des Königs von Prussed gekomen, wo sies ich jetzt noch im Museum zu Berlin findet.'*
7   Rave 1957, p. 26; Hansson 2014, p. 29.
8   Henry 1805, pp. 16–17: *'Von der ganzen Sammlung sind Schwefel abgüsse vorhanden, und von dem grösten Theile derselben vortreffliche Zeichnungen in sechs Bänden, welche in Florenz unter Stoschens Aufsicht von guten Meistern verfertigt worden, und zu einem Prachtwerk bestimmt waren.'*
9   Furtwängler 1896, pp. V–VIII; Zwierlein-Diehl 1969; Dmitrieva 2022a, p. 128. Hansson (2014, p. 29) claims that the gems were transferred to the City Palace in Berlin only in 1801.
10 The original text: *'Endlich eine ansehnliche Sammlung von Zeichnungen nach den vorzüglichsten Steinen derselben, 846 Blätter, in 6 Quartbände zusammengebunden. An 300 derselben rühren von Marc Tuscher her, und alle sind unter Stoschens Augen verfertigt.'* I am grateful to Hadrien J. Rambach who shared with me the discovery of that record by the late Gertrud Platz-Horster. The underlining follows original text.
11 On the issue of the current different number (830) of drawings than 846 reported by Toelken, cf. n. 10 above.
12 The inventories of the Kunstbibliothek in Berlin do not give us a precise date of the arrival of the volumes. I am grateful for confirming that to Jana Hettmann and Elke Blauert (emeritus) from the Kunstbibliothek in Berlin.
13 Auction Muzell-Stosch 1783. In the sale catalogue of that auction, there is no lot with such drawings or books including them.

3 The Albums and the Drawings

The six volumes of *Pierres gravées du roi avec figures* are all bound in cardboard and red leather (235 × 190 mm). On the spines, embossed in gold letters, is *Pierres gravees du Roi* and TOM I, II, III etc., respectively. The spines also bear old inventory numbers – 243, C 322 and *Mag 1907*. The sheets inside are made of laid paper measuring 225 × 180 mm, on average, while some of the drawings used as illustrations are a bit bigger (cf. the catalogue). The outer edges of the sheets are painted in gold and the endpaper is decorated with Morocco design in marine blue. Inside each volume, on the first inner-folio, the number of plates is given in brown ink in French written by hand, like: 'Ce volume renforme 146 dessins de planches' in the first volume.[14] The front folio is occupied with a decorative full title *Pierres gravées du roi avec figures* and the number of the volume – TOME I, II, III etc. and stars in the bottom in a number from 6 (vols I and V) to 10 (vols II–IV and VI). The decorative design of the letters in each case is different, but clearly by the same hand. In the case of each volume, these first folios are made of the Dutch laid paper bearing two types of watermarks. The first one is the Garden of Holland/Magdalene the Dutch within a circular fence or palisade (symbol of Dutch independence), a crowned lion with a sword and bunch of arrows in its paws, standing on its hind-legs in front of her, inscription *Pro Patria* in the field (in opposite direction to the images).[15] The *Pro Patria* watermark was one of the most popular ones after 1700 among the Dutch paper mills (and their imitators) and remained in use until the very end of the eighteenth century, which reflects the growing importance of Holland in paper production and trade over that century.[16] The second watermark type is the British royal cipher G R, surmounted with a crown and flanked by two palm branches. It is applied on the paper produced by various Dutch papermakers from the late seventeenth century till the end of the eighteenth century, which was made for the British market, thus the British royal ciphers appear as countermarks.[17]

Many of the drawings used as plates in the volumes were cut out of the original sheets so that only the enlarged gems survived, and they were subsequently transferred onto new paper during their production, but 378 are preserved on original sheets that were only trimmed to fit the format of the books. As far as the paper on which the drawings were transferred is concerned, one observes two types of watermarks – the initials *HR*, which is the Dutch royal cipher,[18] and the name of unidentified, apparently Dutch papermaker *I BASVET*.[19] The original sheets with the following types of watermarks observed are much more interesting. The first one is a monogram composed of the letters *C* and *R*.[20] The second is a lily in a circle with the letter *C* or *B* at the bottom, testifying the paper to be of Italian origin, which was often used around 1750.[21] The third is a Strasbourg lily in a crowned coat of arms, which according to Headwood, was in use at least since 1670.[22] The fourth type is the name of the French papermaker Jean Villedary I (1668–1758) – *I VILLEDARY*.[23] He founded a dynasty of papermakers active in Angoumois (with later branches in Vraichamp, Beauvais and La Couronne) between 1668 and 1758 and later also in Gelderland (Hattem) 1758–1812. The paper with this watermark in the collection of drawings in question was used in the first half of the eighteenth century.[24] The fifth type is an eight-rayed sun, which appears on Italian paper already at the end of the sixteenth century.[25] The sixth type is the most popular one and it is composed of a lily in a double circle with *V* above. According to Churchill and Headwood, it was used for Italian paper at least since 1690.[26] Finally, the seventh type is a *Fleur-de-Lys* alone, the type, according to Headwood, in use since ca. 1670.[27] Overall, the analysis of the paper confirms that the original sheets are much older than the ones on which some drawings were transferred

---

14 Volume 2: 'Ce volume renforme 185 dessins de planches' but corrected to *184* in the corner of the page by another hand in another ink; Volume 3: 'Ce volume contient *105* dessins' but corrected to *106* in the corner of the page by another hand in another ink; Volume 4: 'Ce volume renforme 122 dessins'; Volume 5: 'Contient *130* dessins & planches'; Volume 6: 'Contient *158* dessins & planches.'
15 It appears in the case of the volumes 1, 5 and 6 and is the most similar to Heawood 1950, no. 3699.
16 Heawood 1950, p. 26.
17 Churchill 1935, pp. 46–47. This type appears in the volumes 2, 3 and 4. It is the most similar to Churchill 1935, no. 255 and it cannot be precisely dated.
18 For instance, Berlin vol. I, pl. 1. For a similar watermark, see: Heawood 1950, p. 52, nos 328, 378? and 2747.
19 For instance, Berlin vol. II, pl. 167 and vol. IV, pl. 20. The closest parallel of that name seems to be: Headwood 1950, no. 407.
20 For instance, Berlin vol. I, pls 27 and 28.
21 For instance: Berlin vol. I, pl. 34 and vol. II, pls 50 and 119. For a similar watermark, see: Headwood 1950, no. 1573 (Naples, 1752).
22 For instance: Berlin vol. I, pls 13, 18, 40, 52, 56, 71 and vol. III, pl. 3. For parallel examples, see: Headwood 1950, nos 1725 (London, 1670) and 1734 (Paris, 1677).
23 For instance: Berlin vol. I, pl. 53, vol. III, pl. 41 and vol. V, pl. 11.
24 Churchill 1935, p. 21.
25 For instance: Berlin vol. I, pl. 84 and vol. II, pl. 118 and 177. For a similar type, see: Headwood 1950, no. 3902.
26 For instance: Berlin vol. I, pls 9, 15, 37 and 139, vol. II, pls 27, 120 and 147, vol. III, pls 43 and 55 and vol. V, pl. 48. Churchill 1935, no. 368; Headwood 1950, no. 1591 (Venice, 1690).
27 For instance: Berlin vol. VI, pl. 63. Headwood 1950, no. 1477 (London, ca. 1670?).

to. Furthermore, they are products of Italian, and perhaps in a few cases also French, papermakers, while during the production of the volumes of *Pierres gravées du roi avec figures* only later Dutch paper was used.

Concerning the drawings themselves, none of them have extensive commentaries like in the case of the drawings discovered in the Princes Czartoryski Museum in Krakow. Nevertheless, many of those surviving almost intact have short texts in pencil, judging by the style of the handwriting, written by Philipp von Stosch himself. They are corrections and confirmations of the subject matter, as well as brief descriptions appearing usually in the caption fields below the enlarged gems, like in the case of the drawing vol. 5, pl. 112 (Figs 7.6–7.7). Sometimes they also provide information about the gemstone type used for an intaglio or cameo (Figs 7.8–7.9).[28] Twenty-three drawings have original provenance information preserved (Figs 7.10–7.11),[29] however, there were originally many more as suggested by the fragments of the texts preserved in the case of the drawings that were cut out of the original paper (Fig. 7.12).[30]

All the drawings used as illustrations in the volumes have references to Winckelmann's catalogue of Stosch's gems of the same type added by Joannon de Saint Laurent, also like the 177 drawings in Krakow (cf. an extensive discussion on this issue in Chapter 8). A particularly valuable observation is that many drawings discovered in Berlin have 'offprints' of other drawings on the recto side. Among them, some are those after the drawings now in Krakow, which proves that both groups were once kept together (Figs 7.13–7.14).[31] Moreover, in some cases one notices that the same drawing left its impression on the recto side of another one twice in two different places or two different drawings left their 'offprints' (Fig. 7.15).[32] Sometimes the 'offprints' on the recto side show much better-preserved originals. For example, in the case of vol. 1, pl. 22 on the recto side there is an 'offprint' of a drawing from the next plate, but when it was not cut out of the original paper and beneath the caption field there was provenance information – *Ex Thesauro Ducis Etruriae* (Figs 7.16–7.17). Similarly, vol. 1, pl. 51 was once more complete, including provenance information (illegible), as one learns from its original 'offprint' on pl. 50. All of this proves that originally the drawings were not bound as volumes; however, they were put into an order according to the subject matter.[33] Furthermore, the 'offprints' sometimes are after drawings which are now lost, which proves the existence of many more gem drawings than those discovered in Krakow and Berlin.[34] Some 'offprints' remain unidentified too.[35] In conclusion, a thorough analysis of the drawings collected in the six volumes of *Pierres gravées du roi avec figures* reveals that, like the drawings discovered in the Princes Czartoryski Museum in Krakow, they once belonged to Philipp von Stosch's rich corpus of gem drawings.

---

28 This short information from Stosch is observed in the case of the following drawings: Berlin vol. I, pls 13, 18–19, 36, 39, 44, 53, 56, 84, 101 and 139; vol. II, pls 50, 61, 87, 94, 116 and 177; vol. III, pls 2, 28, 36, 41, 55, 70, 72, 76 and 79–82; vol. 4, pls 25–26, 40, 71, 73, 77, 83, 88–89 and 92; vol. v, pls 1, 5, 9–10, 13–14, 23, 25–27, 30, 32, 36, 44, 65, 68, 78, 88, 96, 102, 108, 112, 114; vol. VI, pls 24, 42–43, 52, 61, 100 and 143–144.

29 These are the following examples: Berlin vol. I, pls 23, 40, 46 and 138; vol. II, pls 20, 117 and 140; vol. III, pls 37, 44, 53–54 and 57; vol. VI, pls 107–108.

30 For example: Berlin vol. I, pls 51 and 123; vol. II, pls 4, 10, 15, 88, 91 and 111; vol. IV, pls 44 and 85.

31 This is the case of, for example: Berlin vol. I, pl. 5 = Krakow No. 1763, pl. 28 = Krakow No. 1803; vol. II, pl. 4 = Krakow No. 188, pl. 69 = Krakow No. 327, pl. 85 = Krakow No. 16; vol. III, pl. 47 = Krakow No. 639, pl. 54 = Krakow No. 467, pl. 55 = Krakow No. 468, pl. 70 = Krakow No. 677, pl. 72 = Krakow No. 704; vol. IV, pl. 23 = Krakow No. 591, pl. 39 = Krakow No. 1024, pl. 50 = Krakow No. 987, pl. 92 = Krakow No. 1065, pl. 96 = Krakow No. 1129, pl. 98 = Krakow No. 1073; vol. V, pl. 98 = Krakow No. 1915, pl. 111 = Krakow No. 1301; vol. VI, pl. 110 = Krakow No. 979, pl. 144 = Krakow No. 621.

32 For example: vol. I, pls 16, 22, 38, 41, 43, 44, 54, 87, 90, 101; vol. II, pls 1, 8, 21, 69, 85, 90, 92, 100, 108, 112, 120, 132; vol. III, pls 64, 72; vol. IV, pls 23, 34, 59, 63, 67, 69, 77, 78, 83, 90, 91, 113; vol. v, pls 2, 20, 42, 89, 94, 111, 112; vol. VI, pls 44, 50, 63.

33 For example, originally, after Berlin vol. I, pl. 41 was the drawing of the same kind from pl. 43. Inserting the drawing from pl. 42 separated pl. 41 and pl. 43. Berlin vol. I, pl. 81 was originally put after pl. 82. Berlin vol. I, pl. 112 was originally put directly after pl. 109. Berlin vol. I, pl. 31 was originally after pl. 128. Berlin vol. I, pl. 140 was originally after pl. 134. Berlin vol. II, pl. 18 was originally after pl. 15. Berlin vol. II, pl. 88 was originally after pl. 75. Berlin vol. II, pl. 97 was originally after pl. 95. Berlin vol. III, pl. 3 was originally after pl. 1. Berlin vol. IV, pl. 96 was originally after pl. 83. Berlin vol. IV, pl. 120 was originally after pl. 118. Berlin vol. V, pl. 100 was originally after pl. 101. Berlin vol. VI, pl. 63 was originally after pl. 61. Berlin vol. VI, pl. 70 was originally after pl. 68. Berlin vol. VI, pl. 71 was originally after pl. 69. Berlin vol. VI, pl. 97 was originally after pl. 98. Berlin vol. VI, pl. 104 was originally after pl. 105.

34 For example: Berlin vol. I, pls 73, 139, 141 and 142; Berlin vol. II, pl. 8, 17, 24, 25, 29, 61, 75; Berlin vol. III, pls 86, 92; Berlin vol. IV, pl. 8, 9, 34, 38, 90, 91; Berlin vol. V, pls 2, 20, 56, 63, 89, 108; Berlin vol. VI, pl. 62.

35 For example: Berlin vol. II, pls 27, 72, 90, 92, 100, 108, 112, 120, 132; Berlin vol. III, pl. 64; Berlin vol. IV, pls 8, 9, 34, 38, 63, 67, 69, 77, 78, 113, 115; Berlin vol. V, pls 2, 20, 56, 63, 89, 108, 112; Berlin vol. VI, pls 44, 62, 72, 85, 121.

PLATE 31

FIGURE 7.1

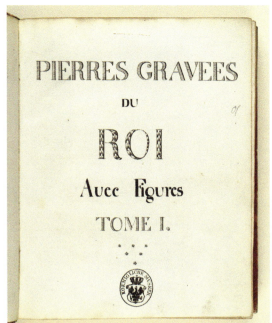

FIGURE 7.2

FIGURE 7.3

FIGURE 7.4

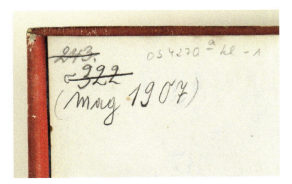

FIGURE 7.5

FIGURE 7.6

FIGURE 7.7

FIGURE 7.8

FIGURE 7.9

PLATE 33

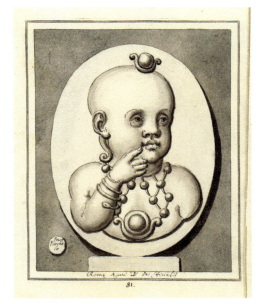

FIGURE 7.10

FIGURE 7.11

FIGURE 7.12

FIGURE 7.13

FIGURE 7.14

FIGURE 7.15

FIGURE 7.16

FIGURE 7.17

CHAPTER 8

Stosch's *Paper Museum of Gems* Rediscovered

Paweł Gołyźniak

1 Drawings' Analysis – Introduction

The 2268 objects in the collection housed in the Princes Czartoryski Museum are classified within 28 volumes according to the subject matters, which are the following: 1. Venus and related matters; 2. Zeus-Jupiter and related myths; 3. Ceres and Artemis/Diana; 4. Mercury; 5. Roman Gods (Saturn, Juno) and personifications; 6. Mars; 7. Nike/Victory; 8. Military subjects (helmets, casques, soldiers etc.); 9. Military subjects, objects and their configurations (cornucopiae, etc.) and pantheistic deities; 10. Apollo and Muses; 11. Masks and their combinations; 12. Actors and pygmies; 13. Dionysus/Bacchus and his *thiasos*; 14. Dionysus/Bacchus and his *thiasos*; 15. Heracles; 16. Heracles and related subjects (his attributes etc.); 17. Mythological figures (Oedipus, Meleager etc.); 18. *Grylloi/Baskania* and history of Rome (including portraits of prominent Romans and emperors); 19. Philosophers; 20. Symposia scenes and related subjects (vessels etc.); 21. Sport activities; 22. Animals; 23. Portraits (mixed: Hellenistic kings, Roman emperors etc.); 24. Egyptian deities and related subjects; 25. *Grylloi/Baskania* and objects; 26. Trojan War circle (mainly Greek heroes); 27. Amor/Eros/Cupid; 28. Amor/Eros/Cupid. This classification does not exactly follow the system of Winckelmann, but it is clearly inspired by it and as has been proved in Chapter 6, during the rearrangement of the drawings, Izabela Czartoryska was stimulated by Winckelmann's catalogue of Stosch's gems, very often copying descriptions and interpretations of gems' iconography quite directly from it.

The drawings in Berlin are grouped according to the system of classes based on the subject matters applied by Winckelmann in his catalogue of Stosch's gems published in 1760. In the previous chapter, it was proven that the drawings one finds in the albums *Pierres gravees par Stosche* now in Krakow as well as the six volumes of *Pierres gravées du roi avec figures* in Berlin were once kept together. All of them are executed in various techniques and styles, clearly by several different hands. Throughout his whole career, first in Rome and later in Florence, Stosch collaborated with a number of Italian and German artists drawing antiquities, especially gems, architecture and topographical views, among others, for him.[1] Abandoning the subject matter classifications and focusing on the techniques and styles makes it possible to distinguish several major groups consisting of the works from both Krakow and Berlin alike, that can be, not without challenges,[2] attributed to artists working for Stosch like Girolamo Odam, Pier Leone Ghezzi, Johann Justin Preißler, Markus Tuscher, Georg Abraham Nagel or Johann Adam Schweickart. Moreover, some groups (for example type 8, see below) indicate that there were more artists working for Stosch than those listed above, but they remain unidentified. Furthermore, a thorough analysis of all the drawings helps to reconstruct the original structure and nature of Stosch's rich gem drawings corpus and investigate his documentary and scholarly activities. It is also possible to show how the drawings were used after Stosch's death. Finally, in the case of the collection now in Krakow, one can determine its original part and identify

---

1 Regarding other antiquities than gems, for example, Markus Tuscher is said to have drawn Stosch's ancient coins, see: Stosch 1757, p. 268, no. 34.

2 On the problems with attribution of drawings to specific artists, who, like in the case of Girolamo Odam used to draw gems differently depending on the commission, project, commissioner and surely payment, see Chapter 3 in this volume. A small collection of seven drawings of Egyptian antiquities (including two scarabs) attributed to Johann Justin Preißler from the collection of the Brooklyn Museum in New York makes one aware about different approaches, techniques and styles applied by this artist alone for his various projects (https://www.brooklynmuseum.org/opencollection/archives/set/252 – retrieved on 26 July 2023). In the case of Stosch and the gem drawings he commissioned, we have direct evidence that the style of the drawings could be tailored for a specific customer, expressed by him in his letter to William Cavendish, 2nd Duke of Devonshire, sent from Rome on 17 February 1729 (Chatsworth, the Devonshire archives, inv. no.: CS1/188.8). Moreover, Stosch may have also expected the artists working in his studio one after another to draw the gems in a similar style to their predecessors for the sake of coherence of his *Paper Museum of Gems*. Given all those troubles, it might seem pointless to suggest any specific artist to produce a certain group of drawings. However, there are some clear differences in the applied techniques and styles, as, for instance, the documentary drawings by Odam are much different than those by Preißler, Tuscher and Nagel. On the other hand, the drawings attributed to the last three draughtsmen are close to each other. As a result, the distinguished groups are only attributed to specific artists which leaves room for the future discussion on them, should more explicit evidence in this matter appear.

© PAWEŁ GOŁYŹNIAK, 2025 | DOI:10.1163/9789004712553_009
This is an open access chapter distributed under the terms of the CC BY-NC-ND 4.0 license.

the objects which were added in the course of time by its next owners.

2 Type 1 – Girolamo Odam and Pier Leone Ghezzi (*Gemmae antiquae caelatae* Book Project)

There is a series of 21 drawings in Krakow and 35 more in Berlin drawn in black chalk, pen and brown ink (measuring on average ca. 120 × 100 mm), usually with a hatched background within an engraved frame – the type that was used in Stosch's book, *Gemmae antiquae caelatae* (full size of 265 × 185 mm). Except for one specimen,[3] they all depict gems signed by ancient artists that were selected for this remarkable publication. Regarding the style of these drawings, it is characterised by washy lines of warm, brown ink. The contours are delicate and thin with limited shading in the form of short, crossed lines as well as numerous, small dots made with a stipple (pointing). The portrait gems reproduced on these drawings are particularly rich in pointing. Noteworthy is the accurate and neat design of the hair and that the heads are smoothly accomplished by leaving the face and neck almost plain except for delicate dots marking the muscles and wrinkles (Figs 8.1–8.2). The drawings with figural scenes have quite vivid compositions. The subject is usually achieved by the use of strong and clear lines of brown tone. There is more use of shading, and this is done mostly by crossed lines, stippling is less applicable here. Most of these drawings still have some traces of the original sketch in black chalk, but they are barely visible (Figs 8.3–8.4).

The condition of these drawings varies from examples having only some small tears to severely chipped ones with considerable parts missing. Sixteen of them (out of which 13 from Krakow and 3 from Berlin) are preserved with complete or nearly complete frames, while others lack them or only their fragments have survived due to their transfer onto new paper. The drawings with complete frames have descriptions of gems' devices and gemstone type as well as provenance information given inside of the caption fields. These are handwritten in brown ink and sometimes differ in detail to the texts ultimately published in Stosch's book. Sometimes they were incomplete and later completed with the use of slightly darker brown ink but by the same hand (Krakow No. 50 and 1029). Judging by the completely or more completely preserved cases, most of them had a real-size gem drawing on the bottom-right side inscribed *gem. mag.* or *Gemmae magnitude*.

None of those drawings bear artist's signature; however, it turns out that they are made in the same technique and style, and consequently by the same hand as some individual works signed by Odam, also representing ancient engraved gems with the artist's signature but not meant for Stosch's book. One of them is a superbly executed drawing in pen and brown ink signed by Girolamo Odam that appeared in 2013 at the art market in London and is now kept in the Ashmolean Museum in Oxford (Fig. 8.5).[4] It depicts a sardonyx intaglio set in ancient gold ring featuring Diomedes ascending from an altar with the Palladion and sword in his hands, signed by Gnaeus (ΓΝΑΙΟΥ) now in the Devonshire collection at Chatsworth.[5] Beneath the gem there is Cupid holding a caption field inscribed: '*DIOMEDES PALLADIO · POTITVS · GNAII ADMIRABILE · OPVS SARDONYCHI · INCISUM LONDINI · APVD · HENRICUM · D'AVENANT*'. At his knees, there is a ring either in profile and to the front depicted and in the bottom one reads: *Hier. Odam Eques Romanus delineabat Romae An: 1722*. The drawing was certainly made for Stosch, and it seems likely that he owned the gem and sold or gave it to Henry Davenant, the British Envoy Extraordinary in Florence, who came to Rome in 1722 to discuss diplomatic matters with him. Subsequently, the intaglio went to the Devonshire Collection, while Stosch kept a glass paste copy for himself.[6] The drawing is set in an extraordinarily rich mount suggesting a sole publication as a print even though no such a print has been found yet. The drawing of the gem itself looks exactly like Odam's drawings made for Stosch's book and found in Krakow and

---

3 Berlin vol. IV, pl. 41.

4 Art market – Sotheby's, 5 July 2013 'Galleria Portatile' – the Ralph Holland Collection Sale, lot 346 (sold for 4.375 GBP with buyer's premium). The drawing was purchased from G. Norman ca. 1958 by the owners who put it up for auction. In 2013, it was purchased by Stephen Ongpin Fine Art, an art gallery in London, from which it was acquired by the Ashmolean Museum (the Art Fund, Russell Fund and private donations) in honour of Jon Whiteley, on his retirement as Senior Assistant Keeper in 2014 (acc. no.: WA2014.49). I am grateful to Angelamaria Aceto, the Research Assistant (Anonymous Drawings Project) in the Ashmolean Museum in Oxford for providing detailed information on the purchase of the drawing by the museum.

5 Gołyźniak 2020, no. 10.5 (with earlier literature). According to an unpublished letter from Stosch to William Cavendish, 2nd Duke of Devonshire, dated Rome 24 July 1728 (Chatsworth, the Devonshire Archives, inv. no.: CS1/188.3), the gem was taken out from the ring in order to examine if it was made of solid gold and then reset again afterwards.

6 The glass paste was published by Winckelmann (1760, class III, no. 318, p. 391) and was later in Berlin (Furtwängler 1896, no. 9897) but its current whereabout is uncertain.

Berlin under discussion here. In 1722, it could be too late to add it to the forthcoming book.[7] The letter from Stosch to William Cavendish, 2nd Duke of Devonshire, dated Rome 24 January 1728, suggests that the gem was later meant to be published by Stosch in the second volume of *Gemmae antiquae caelatae*.[8]

Another similar project by Odam is now preserved in the Philadelphia Museum of Art (Fig. 8.6).[9] It reproduces the famous Strozzi Medusa, a chalcedony intaglio signed by Solon discovered between ca. 1700 and 1709 in a vineyard on the Caelian Hill in Rome, now housed in the British Museum.[10] As Hiesinger and Percy write, this drawing is unique since even though clearly made for a print, it does not follow standard rules, which means schematic, stiff and dry execution. On the contrary, it offers a lively and elaborate treatment with some cross-hatching in the background, imitating the gemstone's curves and shadowing.[11] The proportions of the head and neck are perfect and both face elements as well as hair with numerous snakes intertwined are done with the utmost care. The drawing is strikingly close to the original gem, even though made after an impression, which is suggested by its orientation (Medusa faces left instead of right). One finds the following text in the caption field: '*MEDVSAM / A · SOLONE · IN CHALCEDONIO · INSCVLPTAM / ALTERAM · VELVTI · POLYCLETI · NORMAM / ADMIRANDAM · IMITANDAMQ · EXHIBET / ROMAE · EX · MVSEO · STROZZIO / EQVES · HIER · ODAM*' and below: '*ab eodem inventam et deliniatam*'. The drawing reveals itself then to be the work of Odam, who also made two engravings after this drawing known in two states, the earlier dated 1715 and the later 1717.[12] Both are very faithful to the original drawing in terms of style and stippling was used to mimic silverpoint on Medusa's face, which gives the profile an unusual and softly modelled appearance. Odam put his drawing into a wildly elaborated frame, which was his speciality, particularly if the drawing was intended to be published as a single item.

An interesting comment about some early drawings of individual gems commissioned by Stosch (including Strozzi Medusa by Odam in Philadelphia) is provided by Pierre-Jean Mariette, who in his book published in 1750 says: '*What M. de Stosch had begun to engrave in Italy, and which has not been made public, was, in my opinion, much better. I have only seen two plates of it, of which he gave me proofs in 1718, at the time when I was in Vienna with Prince Eugene of Savoy, and I do not know if he had had some engraved in greater numbers. The one executed on the drawing of Chevalier Ghezzi, represents Méléager, and the stone, which is of singular beauty, but without the name of the engraver, belonged to M. de Stosch; the other is the famous head of Medusa, from the Cabinet of Strozzi, drawn by Chevalier Odam.*'[13] Stosch is known to distribute drawings and prints of the most interesting gems he encountered among his friends and visitors of his house. The drawing by Odam from Philadelphia was made for such a purpose shortly before 1715, when Stosch became fascinated by gems signed by ancient masters under the influence of Charles César Baudelot de Dairval (1648–1722), among others whom he met in Paris and who wrote a dissertation on that intaglio.[14] Regarding the second drawing depicting the intaglio with Diomedes stealing Palladion by Gnaeus, it was probably discovered relatively late by Stosch, so that it could not be included into his study and consequently it was or was meant to be published as a separate print.[15]

---

7   Although, apparently as Rambach notices in Chapter 9 in this volume, some plates were cancelled and consequently some Odam's drawings may have been withdrawn.

8   Chatsworth, the Devonshire Archives, inv. no.: CS1/188.0.

9   Acc. no.: 1978-70-373. It entered the museum in 1978 at a bequest of Anthony Morris Clark, who in turn received it as a gift from Andrew Ciechanowiecki in 1975. The earlier provenance of this drawing is unknown, see: Hiesigner and Percy 1980, pp. 22–23, no. 11; Cazort and Percy 2004, no. 27.

10 London, the British Museum, inv. no.: 1867,0507.389 (once in the Cardinal Alessandro Albani, Leone Strozzi and Blacas collections), see: Gołyźniak 2020, no. 8.11 (with earlier literature).

11 Hiesigner and Percy 1980, p. 22, no. 11; Guerrieri Borsoi 2004, p. 168.

12 Both are now in the Gabinetto Nazionale delle Stampe in Rome, vol. 35.H.13, 1715 version – inv. no.: 37319, 1717 version – inv. no.: 37318. An example of the edition from 1717 is also included into one of the volumes of *Pierres gravées du roi avec figures* in Berlin (Berlin vol. V, pl. 52). Guerrieri Borsoi 2009, p. 168. The drawing in Philadelphia was made for the version from 1715 – Cazort and Percy 2004, no. 27.

13 The translations are all mine unless otherwise stated. Mariette 1750, vol. I, p. 332: '*Ce que M. de Stosch avoit commencer de faire graver en Italie, & qui n'a point été rendu public, valoit selon moi, beaucoup mieux. Je n'en ai vû que deux Planches, dont il me donna des épreuves en 1718. dans le tems que j'étois à Vienne auprès de M. le Prince Eugène de Savoie, & j'ignore s'il en avoit fait graver un plus grand nombre. L'une exécutée sur le Dessin du Chevalier Ghezzi, représente Méléagre, dont la Pierre qui est d'une singulière beauté, mais qui est sans nom de Graveur, appartenoit à M. de Stosch; l'autre est la fameuse tête de Méduse, du Cabinet de Strozzi, dessiné par le Chevalier Odam.*'

14 Baudelot de Dairval 1717. Prints made after that drawing exist and one of them recently appeared on the Austrian Ebay: https://www.ebay.at/itm/114671739234?hash=item1ab2f7e162:g:m-8AAOSwR5lgD83d [retrieved on 2 February 2022].

15 The drawing was made in 1722 and at that time the book production process was already quite advanced plus probably Stosch had little control over the project so that no more gems could be added. Moreover, as Rambach notices in Chapter 9 in this

A comparison of the two above-described drawings signed by Odam with the group of those under discussion here leaves no doubt that they should be attributed to this Italian artist. It is noteworthy that within the gem drawings collection of the Princes Czartoryski Museum there is another example featuring the Strozzi Medusa intaglio made in the same technique and style as Odam's drawing in Philadelphia (Krakow No. 1254). This version was a preparatory drawing for a plate in Stosch's book, *Gemmae antiquae caelatae* (Figs 8.7–8.8). The differences between the two works are minor, for example, in the drawing in Philadelphia there are three snake heads above Medusa's right shoulder, while in the case of Krakow there are two and a thick curl instead. Also, Solon's signature is written on the drawing in Philadelphia as ΣΟΛΩΝΟΣ with a sigma at the end, while on the one in Krakow the signature terminates with a sigma of a different type (C). The version from Krakow is more accurate to the original gem. In both cases, Odam used stippling to a great extent, especially for the face elements and the neck, and there is cross-hatching used for shadowing, especially in the field of the gem to give a sense of its shape and curves. The drawing in Krakow was drawn within a mount designed for the *Gemmae antiquae caelatae* book. There is a real-size gem drawing inscribed *Gemmae magnit*. On the side and a caption filed beneath with a text: MEDVSA · / SOLONIS · OPVS · / *Chalcedonio incisum / ex Dactyliotheca* ~~Strozziana~~ *Romae* written in brown ink by the hand of Odam as reveals a comparison to his handwriting from the drawing in Philadelphia and to Odam's text under his drawing of two gems made before 1709 preserved in the Biblioteca Apostolica Vaticana.[16]

The drawing of the Strozzi Medusa intaglio from Krakow was certainly made after 1715 and most likely before 1718 when Stosch himself reports to have already 62 gem drawings ready for his book,[17] and surely not later than 1722, as this date appears on the relevant plate made by Picart, so the drawing must have been delivered to him by this year.[18] A comparison between the drawing from Philadelphia and Krakow helps us to establish the techniques and style applied by Odam for documenting portrait and head studies on gems selected for Stosch's book. On the other hand, the drawing now in Oxford helps to prove that the drawings presenting figural scenes from the group under discussion here are by Odam too, as it is clear from a comparison of technique and style. Moreover, almost all these drawings share the same concept for the background which is hatched horizontally with the use of silverpoint like in the case of the individual drawing presenting Diomedes with Palladion by Gnaeus.

A further confirmation for attribution of most of the drawings forming this group to Odam comes from the analysis of plates in Stosch's book. For 10 of them, the publisher and ultimate illustrator Bernard Picart directly indicates that Odam made the preparatory drawings (*Girolamo Odam Eques Romanus delineavit*), out of which nine are now in Krakow and Berlin.[19] Moreover, Heringa suggested that whenever a star appears on the plate, it refers to Odam as the author of the original drawing for the plate.[20] Indeed, for the plates labelled with a star one identifies Odam's drawings from the collections in Krakow and Berlin. However, Stosch himself says that whenever the plate is labelled with a star, this means that Picart was provided with an impression or cast of the original gem.[21] According to Rambach, this information is misleading because the gems without a star mean that Picart had to rely *exclusively* on the drawing that he was supplied with, but the presence of a star means that he was able to check the *'veracity of the drawings, and not that he drew them himself directly from the cast'*.[22]

So, Picart redrew probably all of Odam's drawings during production of the book,[23] and apparently, the plates with a star were made after his own drawings. Nevertheless, he was supplied with Odam's drawings for those too, as evidenced. Only, the 10 plates listed above for which Picart directly credits Odam could be made not after Picart's own drawings but after Odam's. Nevertheless, there are five problematic cases for which Odam's drawings exist, but they are credited neither directly nor indirectly (e.g. with a star) by Picart. One of them is Krakow No. 1063 referring to pl. LIX in Stosch's book because, according to Picart, his engraving was based on a drawing delivered by Anton Maria Zanetti, not Odam.[24] The second is Krakow No. 1678 (pl. XXXIX), which is described by Picart as *B. Picart sculp.*

---

volume, some plates were cancelled and consequently some of Odam's drawings may have been withdrawn.
16 The Biblioteca Apostolica Vaticana, fondo stampati, Capponi I 24, tav. 1, 2 – reproduced in Ubaldelli 2001, p. 56, fig. 23a–b.
17 Letter from Stosch to François Fagel dated, Dresden 4 May 1718 – archives of the Fagel family, Algemeen Rijksarchief, The Hague, inv. 2031.
18 Stosch 1724, pl. LXIII.

19 Stosch 1724, pl. XIV = Krakow No. 77, pl. XVII = Berlin vol. II, pl. 9, pl. XXI = Berlin vol. III, pl. 1, pl. XXVI = lost drawing, pl. XXXII = Krakow No. 1384, XLII, pl. XLIII = Berlin vol. I, pl. 113, pl. LVII = Krakow No. 319, pl. LX = Krakow No. 910, pl. LXVII = Krakow No. 1220.
20 Heringa 1976, pp. 83–84.
21 Stosch 1724, p. v*.
22 Cf. Chapter 9 here.
23 Cf. Chapter 9 here.
24 Stosch 1724, pl. LIX is described *A.M. Zanetti del. B. Picart sculp. 1724*.

with the date 1723. The same cases are Krakow Nos 1384 (pl. IV) and 2141 (pl. VI), which Picart describes just as *B. Picart sculpsit 1719*. Finally, the last problematic drawing is Berlin vol. V, pl. 31 (pl. LI) because it is described as *B. Picart del. et scupl. 1722* but a star is present.

Heringa was right in claiming that when Picart rejected Odam's drawings, in some cases he asked for new ones; therefore, Zanetti is credited with two (pls L and LIX) and Netscher with one drawing (pl. LXX).[25] Odam's drawing Krakow No. 1063 referring to pl. LIX would be such a rejected case redrawn by another artist. The drawing Krakow No. 1678 (pl. XXXIX), was rejected by Picart too and instead he probably drew the gem after its illustration in Fulvio Ursinus' book.[26] In the case of Berlin vol. V, pl. 31 (pl. LI) apparently Picart is more explicit than in other plates marked with a star as to referring to an impression and possibly Odam's drawing as a resource for his own, but still, the plate is made after Picart's drawing. Considering the drawings Krakow Nos 1384 and 2141, they are made in a darker brown ink and their style is somewhat different than that of their peers. The strokes of brush are more expressive, as one notices analysing Socrates' beard and hair in the drawing Krakow No. 1384 as well as females' dresses from the drawing Krakow No. 2141. Also noteworthy is the lack of use of stippling, especially for Socrates' head, a feature typical of Odam's style (Figs 8.9–8.12).[27] Could they have been drawn by a different hand than Odam's and for this reason Picart does not credit them as related to him? The only person who drew in a very close technique and style and cooperated with Stosch at the same time as Odam did was Pier Leone Ghezzi. Both Ghezzi and Odam worked in pen and brown ink and Odam's techniques and style are close to Ghezzi's because they were both disciples of Carlo Maratta. What is more, Odam was also a pupil of Ghezzi from whom he learnt drawing in pen and ink with wash. In the preface to his book, Stosch explains that Ghezzi was his advisor and helped with the project: '*I was also greatly helped with the execution of my plan by the presence and the advice of Mr. Chevalier Pierre Leon Ghezzi, a Roman gentleman, and, a very excellent Painter.*'[28] Based on these words, Lewis suggested that Ghezzi may have commented on Odam's work or even drew with him.[29] Ghezzi and Odam clearly collaborated while working for Stosch, which is best illustrated by an individual gem illustration featuring the famous Stosch's Meleager gem, made in 1725 as the result of a joint effort of Pier Leone Ghezzi, who drew it, Girolamo Odam, who created the richly decorated mount and Vincenzo Franceschini, who made an engraving out of it.[30]

The drawings by Odam, and apparently Ghezzi, for Stosch's book, *Gemmae antiquae caelatae*, discussed here were produced between 1715 and 1718. This is suggested, on the one hand, by Stosch's letter to Gijsbert Cuper and his first report to François Fagel about embarking on the research project devoted to engraved gems signed by ancient masters in which he mentions Odam to be an artist delivering drawings for future plates.[31] On the other hand, in a letter to Fagel dated 4 May 1718 sent from Dresden, Stosch writes that he had already 62 drawings made for his book, which he sent to Bernard Picart, who started production of the plates already in 1719.[32] It is noteworthy that Odam's drawings are made within the frames which were ultimately used in the final edition of the book printed by Picart. Giving Odam's particular talent for design of frames, for instance those in which his drawing of the Strozzi Medusa in Philadelphia and Diomedes in Oxford are set, as well as his handwritten text in the caption fields, it is likely that he was the designer of the frames here too.

The selection of gems for the book was a challenging task due to the high number of existing forgeries and copies of ancient gems. This is best illustrated by the drawing Berlin vol. VI, pl. 55, which features an amethyst with a draped bust of Cicero that Stosch had in his cabinet, and which is a modern copy of a slightly earlier copy, also in amethyst, of an original, indeed possibly ancient and signed by Dioscurides. Stosch decided to publish in his

---

25   Heringa 1976, p. 84.
26   Ursinus 1606, pl. 75.
27   Similar techniques and styles are observed in the case of a few more drawings in the Princes Czartoryski Museum collection that are unrelated to the *Gemmae antiquae caelatae* book, but they are evidently by Ghezzi, see: Krakow Nos 75, 395, 1259, 1362, 1385, 1393, 1588 and 1612.
28   Stosch 1724, p. v: '*J'ai aussi été beaucoup aide dans l'exécution de mon dessein par la presence & les conseils de M. le Chevalier Pierre Leon Ghezzi, Gentilhomme Romain, très-excellent Peintre.*'

29   Lewis 1961, p. 61.
30   Rügler in Winckelmann 2013, p. XLVII.
31   Letter from Stosch to Gijsbert Cuper dated Rome, 8 August 1716 – the Koninklijke Bibliotheek, The Hague, inv. 72H25 – Stosch says that he has been collecting drawings for his book on signed gems already for a couple of years; Letter from Stosch to François Fagel dated 10 August 1715 – Archives of the Fagel family, Algemeen Rijksarchief, The Hague, inv. 2028 – Stosch expresses his intention to write a book on ancient signed gems, he collected glass pastes taken from original intaglios and cameos and employed Girolamo Odam to draw them as illustrations for the forthcoming book.
32   Letter from Stosch to François Fagel dated Dresden 4 May 1718 – archives of the Fagel family, Algemeen Rijksarchief, The Hague, inv. 2031. Cf. Chapter 9 here.

book the older copy, which was in the French royal collection at the time.[33]

3 Type 2 – Bernard Picart (*Gemmae antiquae caelatae* Book Project)

This group consists of only two items (Krakow No. 391 and 392), a counterproof and a preliminary drawing, both in red chalk evidently made by the same hand, measuring 127 × 87 and 120 × 100 mm, respectively. While the second is set in an engraved frame – the type used by Bernard Picart for Stosch's book – the first one lacks it. They are both of superb quality and represent gems published in Stosch's book *Gemmae antiquae caelatae* (1724) – Picart's plates X and XXXIV, respectively (Figs 8.13–8.16). None of them is signed, however, the technique, style and the subjects are distinctive enough to attribute them to Bernard Picart and to link them with other drawings by him discovered in The Hague, Philadelphia, London, Harvard, New York and private collections, all related to the production of the *Gemmae antiquae caelatae* book.[34] Indeed, Picart made his preparatory drawings and their counterproofs in red chalk and they are very skilful drawings reflecting his close study and attention to the condition of the objects he was documenting since, for instance, on Krakow No. 391 the crack in the gem's surface is suggested. What is notable is also Picart's proficiency in the very accurate reflection of gem engravers' signatures with rendering of the letters so that they look almost three-dimensional. Although later criticised,[35] there is no doubt that Picart tried to faithfully convey information about the original gems he was illustrating in Stosch's book. This was most likely the reason he drew some gems more than once before making the final plates. In The Hague, there are two study/preliminary drawings by Picart of the gems published as pls VII and LV in Stosch's book and Krakow No. 392 discussed here appears to be a preliminary drawing as well. This is suggested by some very small differences between this drawing and the final plate. For example, the fingers of the hand put on the chest are arranged differently and the positioning of the helmet on Minerva's head is at a slightly different angle. It seems that the final plate was made after another (lost) drawing by Picart, while this one was discarded.

After submitting the book manuscript and drawings by Odam to Amsterdam where Picart was supposed to take care of the publishing process, Stosch probably lost much of his control over the project. He never received Picart's drawings that ultimately replaced Odam's ones. Instead, it appears that many (if not all?) of them were later owned by François Fagel and while Picart kept some preliminary studies and a series of counterproofs for himself too because his wife got the proofs of all Picart's book illustrations from their publishers, which she collected.[36] A motivation for making the counterproofs could be François Fagel, who, in his letter to Stosch written on 3 January 1719, clearly stated that he did not intend to pay for the engravings but for drawings (of which he was a passionate collector).[37] Should Picart's wife have kept records of his gem drawings, she would have needed a series of counterproofs. In any case, it remains unclear when these counterproofs were made.[38]

According to Rambach, 85 of Picart's gem drawings, including mostly the preparatory ones for Stosch's book, were once bound into a single volume, which was sold as a part of Fagel's estate in 1801. According to the description in the auction catalogue, there were duplicates among them as well, seemingly some study drawings too, like in the case of pl. XI, of which there was a drawing of the whole gem as well as a sole cow, but there could also have been some non-gem drawings too.[39] Another even more numerous group (108 examples) of gem drawings by Picart existed, among which there could be counterproofs of original drawings as well as study projects, and less likely some original drawings made for the *Gemmae antiquae caelatae* project. These were dispersed in 1737 at auction in Amsterdam shortly after Picart's death and they were described as: '*Cent & huit contre-épreuves des Cornalines par B. Picart*'.[40] The term '*contre-épreuves*' probably refers

---

33 For a discussion on the original and these copies, cf. Appendix 1, pl. XVII here.

34 On those drawings cf. Chapter 9 here.

35 Mariette 1750, pp. 332–333.

36 Adams 2010; Marchesano 2010.

37 Heringa 1976, p. 78, n. 78. In the eighteenth century it was habitual for artists to make counterproofs of their drawings, which often served as records of the unfinished or finished jobs. From the technical point of view, they were a sort of convergence between drawing and printmaking. For example, Edmé Bouchardon, a friend of Stosch, made counterproofs to his drawings of antiquities on a regular basis, some of which he kept for himself, see: Kopp 2017, pp. 188–189.

38 In the internal catalogue of the Royal Library in The Hague, all Picart's drawings and counterproofs are given simply the date 1724.

39 Auction Fagel 1801, lot 128. Cf. full discussion in Chapter 9 in this volume.

40 Auction Picart 1737, lot 15: '*Cent & huit contre-épreuves des Cornalines par B. Picart.*' It is fairly possible that this group contained Picart's gem drawings (including those prepared for Stosch's book) that are now in The Hague and which once

to counterproofs. Because Prince Adam Jerzy Czartoryski left Italy with the collection of gem drawings in April 1801 and the sale of Fagel's estate and collections took place at the end of May 1801, the two drawings by Picart from the collection of the Princes Czartoryski Museum in Krakow must have come from the earlier dispersed group once owned by Picart and after his death by his wife and heirs. The drawing Krakow No. 391 is a counterproof after the original that is now in a private collection.[41]

Picart started production of his plates for the *Gemmae antiquae caelatae* book in 1719. The plate XXXIV to which the drawing Krakow No. 392 refers was made in 1723, so the drawing from Krakow must have been made between 1719 and 1723, apparently from a cast of the gem supplied by Stosch.[42] The counterproof Krakow No. 391 is related to the plate X, which, according to Picart, he made himself in 1722,[43] so it was apparently made between 1722 and Picart's death in 1733. Krakow Nos 391 and 392 were added to the corpus of Stosch's gem drawings auctioned in 1783 in Berlin between 1783 and 1800. This is suggested by the real-size gem drawing of Krakow No. 391 inscribed *Pat. de Verre*, written by a person who owned the collection after the auction in Berlin in 1783 and added some items before Prince Czartoryski bought it in Florence.

4 Type 3 – Girolamo Odam (Documentary Drawings)

This type of drawings is by far the most popular one. The collection in Krakow includes 1856 examples, while the one in Berlin has 77 of them. These drawings are made in pen and brown or dark grey ink with grey wash, and, as the two surviving fragments of original sheets from Krakow (Krakow Nos 171 and 1497) and some better-preserved examples (especially those in Berlin) suggest, the frames and some other elements like the caption fields under the enlarged gems were stuck down onto laid paper (Figs 8.17–8.18). Sometimes they are framed in a series of black ink borders. Occasionally, the artist drew the gem's surface in wash of a different colour (black, brown, marine blue, violet, red and yellow), which reflects the gemstones' layers, if the original was a cameo or apparently a glass paste. What is also noticeable is the different treatment of various kinds of gems; those in bright colours are put onto a dark setting in grey wash, while the dark ones are set onto a contrasting bright background in order to reflect differences in the gemstones. These drawings are well accomplished in terms of their composition and design. Pen is often used to highlight the contours of the figures, but in a very delicate way. Shadowing is limited and usually made with wash (Figs 8.19–8.20).

The vast majority of the drawings have a very simple, rectangular-shaped caption fields below the gem, where a brief description of the object was intended to be written, though, there are a few cases that instead have more elaborated fields resembling ancient altars (Krakow Nos 102, 444 and 1237 and Berlin vol. I, pl. 64 and vol. II, pl. 18). Actually, only two examples indeed have their subject matter described in the caption field (Krakow Nos 982 and 1596). Usually on the bottom-left side (much rarer on the right side), there is a real-size gem drawing with the type of gemstone indicated; however, that is not always the case. The names of the gemstones are generally written in French, but there are a few cases when they are given in Italian or even in Latin.[44]

The drawings of this type generally reproduce gems from Stosch's own collection, but a great deal also those from other contemporary cabinets. Among the 1933 drawings in total, a few dozen are preserved with provenance information, which appears at the bottom of the whole composition, under the caption field. In the case of 38 of them, it is possible to read that information and the following collections are mentioned: Pietro Andrea Andreini (Krakow Nos 630, 680, 1812, 1921 and 2231 and Berlin vol. II, pl. 20), Filippo Buonarroti (Krakow Nos 571 and 1339), Farnese collection (Krakow No. 5), Francesco de'Ficoroni (Krakow Nos 612 and 2221), French Royal collection (Krakow No. 578), Michel Ange de la Chausse (Krakow No. 283), Girolamo Crispi (Krakow No. 1291), Medici collection (Krakow Nos 650 and 1229), Girolamo Odam (Krakow Nos 171, 250, 274, 306, 569, 904, 995, 1651 and 1881 and Berlin vol. I, pl. 138, vol. VI, pl. 85, 107–108), King of Prussia collection (Krakow No. 1235), Leone Strozzi

---

belonged to Frederick de Thoms ('Thoms' portfolio' 72A20 3rd series). The so-called 'Thoms' portfolio' was purchased by The Royal Library of the Netherlands in The Hague at auction in 1901 but no more precise information about their provenance is available. I am grateful to Hein Maassen and Jeroen Vandommele who kindly shared information on the 'Thoms' portfolio'. It is noteworthy that all the gem drawings representing gems selected for Stosch's book which are now in The Hague are counterproofs – 'Thoms' portfolio' 72A20 3rd series, nos 1–3, 5–7, 9, 13 and 16–18.

41 Cf. Appendix 2, Picart (Stosch 1724, pl. X) here. I am grateful to Hadrien J. Rambach and Crispian Riley-Smith for a discussion on Picart's original drawings and their counterproofs.

42 Stosch 1724, pl. XXXIV – *B. Picart del. et sculp. 1723* and a star.

43 Stosch 1724, pl. X – *B. Picart del. et sculp. 1722* and a star.

44 Italian names appear on the following drawings: Krakow Nos 100, 616, 1351, 1363, 1372 and 1772. The Latin ones on two drawings: Krakow Nos 233 and 1811.

(Krakow Nos 131, 1375, 1483 and 1707 and Berlin vol. III, pl. 54), Duke of Stiualis (?) in Rome (Berlin vol. I, pl. 40), Prior Anton Maria Vaini (Krakow No. 1687) and Leone Vitelleschi-Verospi (Krakow No. 444) (Figs 8.21–8.24).[45] Originally, there were many more drawings with provenance information provided, as can be judged from those which were cut out of the original sheets so that fragments of texts are still visible but impossible to read.[46] None of the drawings from this group is signed.

The large number of nearly 2000 gem drawings clearly made by the same hand makes us to recall a letter sent in 1738 by Girolamo Odam to Anton Francesco Gori, where he writes that when Stosch came to Rome for the first time, he had a chance to compare the impression of the famous so-called *Seal of Michelangelo* and some circulating prints of that gem, certainly those by Élisabeth Sophie Chéron (1648–1711).[47] Because they proved to be inaccurate, he drew himself the gem anew.[48] This exceptional drawing by Odam is now in the Princes Czartoryski Museum collection (Krakow No. 74 – Figs 8.25–8.26) and it belongs to the group in question here and it also helps to establish Odam's techniques and styles implemented in a serial production of gem drawings for Stosch.[49] The technique and style of Odam is also deduced from illustrations in Gori's book *Monumentum sive columbarium libertorum et servorum Liviae Augustae Et Caesarum: Romae Detectum in Via Appia* published in Florence in 1727, for which Odam was solely responsible. Among them, on page XXV, there is a plate including a fragment of a cameo representing Livia as Ceres, of which the original drawing executed in pen, brown ink and grey wash by Odam is still preserved in the Biblioteca Marucelliana in Florence.[50]

This drawing is made in the same technique and style as the ones under discussion here. Furthermore, in his letter to Gori, Odam also says that he produced 2700 gem drawings for Stosch, which were later redrawn by a German: '*So I made an exact drawing of it which is in the hands of Baron Stosch as well as two thousand and seven hundred drawings of gems made by my hand which then lost their character of antiquity because he had them redrawn by a German who put his own character on them but that is said with my friendly seal of secrecy.*'[51] It appears that the drawings under discussion constitute a large number of those which Odam reported to have produced for Stosch in his letter to Gori.

The attribution of the drawings of this type to Odam is also supported by the fact that they are similar in terms of techniques and style to the series of gem drawings produced by Pier Leone Ghezzi on his own account and which are now preserved in the Biblioteca Apostolica Vaticana.[52] It should be recalled that Odam was a pupil of Ghezzi in drawing in pen and ink. Comparing both groups, one observes that the techniques used are almost the same – pen, brown or dark grey ink and grey wash in most of the instances. The style of these drawings is close, which reflects the same school of Ghezzi, even the size of the drawings is usually comparable (although, Ghezzi drew a bit more enlarged gems), and the scheme applied for the pictorial documentation of intaglios and cameos is very similar too, although in the case of Ghezzi's own

---

45   Krakow No. 1848 also has provenance information but illegible. On these collections and collectors, cf. Chapter 2 here.

46   This is observable on dozens of drawings from Krakow and Berlin alike, cf. relevant catalogues in Appendix 2.

47   Élisabeth Sophie Chéron was a well-known and appreciated painter, but she also documented a series of ancient gems from the most important French cabinets, see: Chéron 1728; Zazoff and Zazoff 1983, pp. 45–46.

48   Letter from Girolamo Odam to Anton Francesco Gori dated Rome 21 December 1738 – Epistolario di Anton Francesco Gori, no. 11123, volume BVII21, carte 8r–9v. I am grateful to Hadrien J. Rambach for referring me to this letter and identification of the prints mentioned by Odam as of Élisabeth Sophie Chéron, cf. Chapter 3 here.

49   The so-called Michelangelo seal with its extraordinary subject matter was often discussed in the eighteenth century and drawn also by, for example, Edmé Bouchardon, see: Kopp 2017, pp. 138–140, fig. 105. Stosch had it copied by Lorenzo Massini, see: Kagan 2006, p. 96, figs 22–23.

50   Guerrieri Borsoi 2004, p. 173, fig. 197. I am grateful to Hadrien J. Rambach for tuning my attention to this drawing and Oscar van Ditshuizen for noticing the gem inv. 1867,0507.486 = 1913,0307.10 in the British Museum (Dalton 1915, no. 1044): this post-classical cameo from the Blacas collection is identical to that depicted on the figure, with the crack in the exact same location, but it is complete in two fragments: might it be a later (completed) copy, or is it the cameo drawn by Odam with the lower section having been found afterwards and reunited to the upper one? One assumes that Gori had obtained this drawing from a regular client of Odam, Francesco Vettori (1692–1770), who '(…) *inviava regolarmente al corrispondente fiorentino* [i.e. Gori] *le novità editoriali uscite sul mercato romano, nonché un gran numero di calchi di gemme e disegni di ogni sorta di reperto antico (iscrizioni, camei, medaglie, dittici, lucerne, oggetti e vetri sacri)*' (Carpita 2012, pp. 108–109).

51   Letter from Girolamo Odam to Anton Francesco Gori dated Rome, 21 December 1738 – Epistolario di Anton Francesco Gori, no. 11123, volume BVII21, carte 8r–9v: '*Io poi ne feci un disegno esatto che è nelle mani del Baron Stosch siccome si ritrova fatti di mia mano due mila e settecento disegni di gemme che esso poi gli hà levato il gusto del suo carattere antico con farle ridisegnare da uno tedesco che vi hà posto il suo carattere ma questo sia detto con il mio sigillo di segretezza di amicizia.*'

52   The Biblioteca Apostolica Vaticana: Cod. Ott. lat. 3100–3101, 3103–3104 and 3106–3109. On the Pier Leone Ghezzi and his gem drawings in the Biblioteca Apostolica Vaticana among others, see: Gołyźniak (forthcoming – Ghezzi).

drawings there are much longer and more elaborated commentaries provided by the draughtsman himself. What is more, among Ghezzi's gem drawings there are many representing intaglios from Philipp von Stosch and Girolamo Odam's collections (Figs 8.27–8.34). It is evident that all of them closely collaborated as far as collecting, documentation and research on engraved gems is concerned. This is also confirmed by Stosch himself, who mentions both Odam and Ghezzi as primary advisors and assistants in writing and publishing his book on signed gems *Gemmae antiquae caelatae*.[53]

Further proofs for attribution of the drawings from the group under discussion to Odam come from the analysis of texts appearing on some elements of the drawings like information on the gemstones or provenance. Their comparative analysis with documents written by Odam and especially the drawing of a fragment of a cameo with Livia as Ceres now in Biblioteca Marucelliana in Florence reveals that they were clearly written by him. Moreover, even though made in a completely different technique and style, Odam's drawings of gems designed for Stosch's book *Gemmae antiquae caelatae* (cf. Type 1 above) also bear some texts in the caption fields evidently by him (see above).

It is also of importance that among the drawings with provenance information preserved, the most numerous by far are those representing intaglios from Odam's own collection.[54] Considering the fact that they are otherwise unknown, not reproduced in other media except for a few as plaster impressions once owned by Pier Leone Ghezzi,[55] one presumes that they would not have appeared in the drawings made for Stosch so often if had not been owned by Odam and the drawings had not been made by him as well. In conclusion, even though neither Stosch directly himself nor Winckelmann suggests that Odam lived in Stosch's house and produced numerous drawings after gems for him, the material discovered in Krakow and Berlin alike confirms the testimony of Odam, who apparently does not make an empty boast, stating that he produced 2700 gem drawings on Stosch's commission. The discovered pictorial documentation makes it clear that he was in fact the most prolific draughtsman in his service and his involvement was much beyond documentation of gems for Stosch's *Gemmae antiquae caelatae* book project.

Odam started to work for Stosch in 1715. According to the letter from Odam to Gori from 1738, Odam drew the so-called *Seal of Michelangelo* when Stosch came to Rome for the first time (cf. above). That year, Stosch also informed Fagel that he embarked upon the *Gemmae antiquae caelatae* project.[56] Many of Odam's documentary drawings of gems should have been made in the late 1710s and early 1720s. In his letter to Carl Gustav Heraeus from 19 December 1722, Stosch reports that: '*I am having all my ancient pastes* [e.g. ancient glass gems or modern glass pastes] *drawn here, the number of finished ones has already risen to 270, but when they are completed it will pass one thousand and even more.*'[57] This very early record of Stosch commissioning documentation of hundreds of his own gems must be related to the drawings made by Odam discussed here (among which indeed hundreds depict Stosch's gems and glass pastes) and mentioned by the artist in his letter to Gori.[58]

The suitable terminal date for production of those documentary gem drawings for Stosch seems to be the collector's voluntary exile to Florence in 1731. This is supported by the analysis of provenance information given by Odam on his drawings. A number of gems reproduced are referenced to the collections which existed in the 1710s and 1720s but were taken over by other collectors or dispersed in the late 1720s and early 1730s. For example, Pietro Andrea Andreini's collection of gems was purchased *en bloc* by Gian Gastone de'Medici in Florence in 1731 from Andreini's heirs. Prior Anton Maria Vaini's (1660–1737) collection of intaglios and cameos was also largely bought out by the Grand Duke of Tuscany in 1731. Even though

---

53 Stosch 1724, p. v.
54 13 out of 37 cases: Krakow Nos 171, 250, 274, 306, 569, 904, 995, 1651 and 1881 and Berlin vol. I, pl. 138, vol. VI, pl. 86, 108–109. It is also noteworthy that among the drawings of this type but without direct provenance information preserved, 20 more gems are identified as from Odam's collection (Krakow Nos 18, 171, 189, 250, 274, 306, 344, 415, 480, 483, 569, 904, 995, 1201, 1288, 1651, 1842, 1881 and 2238). In fact, there could be many more, but provenance information is not always given by the draughtsmen and the drawings probably lost a substantial number of commentaries and provenance information due to their rearrangement around 1801 (cf. Chapter 6 here). For more information on Odam's collection of engraved gems, see: Gołyźniak 2023b.
55 Ms. Vat. Lat. 14928. See also on this matter: Gasparri 1977, pp. 26–27; Maaskant-Kleibrink 1978, p. 33, n. 13; Ubaldelli 2001, pp. 14–15.

56 Letter from Stosch to François Fagel dated 10 August 1715 – Stosch expresses his intention to write a book on ancient signed gems. He collected glass pastes taken from original intaglios and cameos and employed Girolamo Odam to draw them as illustrations for the forthcoming book.
57 The original text sounds as follows: '*Je fais desiner icy toutes mes pates Antiques dont le nombre des achevees est dejà monte a 270 quand ils seront achevé cela passera les milles et plus.*' Schneider 1907, pp. 346–347; Hansson 2022, p. 63, n. 73.
58 Letter from Girolamo Odam to Anton Francesco Gori dated Rome 21 December 1738 – Epistolario di Anton Francesco Gori, no. 11123, volume BVII21, carte 8r–9v.

Girolamo Odam's own collection was dispersed most likely shortly after his death in 1741, some pieces could be sold to Stosch and other buyers earlier. For example, the provenance information on the drawing Krakow No. 306 proves that the gem was once in the Odam collection, but according to Gori. in 1731, it was already in Francesco Vettori's cabinet.[59] One more important case is the Michel Ange de la Chausse collection, dispersed after the collector's death in 1724. In the drawings made by Odam for Stosch, some gems are referenced as belonging to it, which means that they were probably made prior to 1724.

Finally, in his letter to Gori, Odam complains that a German artist redrew some of his drawings.[60] Johann Justin Preißler entered the circle of artists working for Stosch in 1726 and Markus Tuscher in 1728. At that time, Odam became more and more involved in his own projects or worked on new commissions (not Stosch's ones). For example, he was engaged in publication of Gori's *Monumentum sive columbarium libertorum et servorum Liviae Augustae Et Caesarum: Romae Detectum in Via Appia* published in Florence in 1727, for which he produced illustrations. In conclusion, it is quite possible that they replaced Odam in documenting gems for Stosch around these dates, and consequently, Odam's documentary gem drawings should be dated between 1715 and 1726 or 1728, but clearly not later than 1731. Furthermore, these two artists and Georg Abraham Nagel indeed sometimes drew the same gems as Odam (see drawings attributed to them – types 4, 5 and 6 below), but according to the number of redrawn examples (294), the scale of this phenomenon was apparently greatly exaggerated by Odam and probably coincidental (see below).

5 Type 4 – Johann Justin Preißler (Documentary Drawings)

While producing documentary drawings of gems for Stosch, Odam used pre-prepared templates. It appears that his followers also used such templates to speed up and facilitate their work. This could have been the idea of Stosch himself, and apparently two types of such templates were in use. They were identical in their composition to the ones used by Odam, but they had some minor differences in the technique and style. The first one has a line engraving background and a frame in black ink stuck down onto laid paper. The gem is enlarged approximately ten times and below it there is a caption field, which often includes description of the device in capital letters in brown ink. These fields also often bear gemstone type information but handwritten in black ink. On the left, there is always a drawing in real size inscribed *gemma magnitudo*, usually in an abbreviated form of *gem. mag.* or in a few cases lines inscribed *Gemae Altitudo/Gemae Latitudo* or *Camei Altitudo/Camei Latitudo*, illustrating the gem's size (Figs 8.35–8.36). The second type of the template basically differs in the background, which is made entirely in wash instead of line engraving. Except for that, all other elements are the same (Figs 8.37–8.38).

Those templates were used for a number of drawings, either from the Krakow or Berlin assemblages by various artists working for Stosch. Since they did not change over time, only analysis of the drawings of enlarged gems themselves makes it possible to form groups which can be attributed to specific artists. The first distinctive type are those executed in very dark grey or black pen and ink with grey wash. The artist who made those drawings expertly used pen to produce thin and delicate, curved lines, which are often short and do not connect with each other. As a result, the contours of the figures, their robes or elements of nature (trees, rocks etc.) are subtle and give the impression of dimmed edges; they are not clearly and strongly separated from the background, sometimes they are bloated by some shadowing in black or very dark grey wash. The treatment of body parts and faces is also based on very delicate, thin lines and sometimes cross-hatching, but major parts are left blank or they are textured with short strokes of brush in light grey wash to reflect muscles and flesh. This technique gives an impression of clean and delicate bodies, which are not overly muscled and particularly strong; their beauty is reflected by ideal proportions and smooth shapes. Moreover, the artist skilfully accentuates details like folds of garments or texture of the rocks and trees. His groundlines are rather thick and usually textured with a few thin parallel, horizontal lines in pen. There is usually some shadowing in dark grey wash beneath them. Noticeable is also his preference to reflect the structure of architectural elements like columns, altars or fountains with rather thick parallel lines in grey wash. He also uses grey wash of various tones of grey for shadowing bigger parts of his compositions. This is especially noticeable regarding reflection of the convex and concave shapes of the whole gemstone, e.g. if the gem is convex or has bevelled edges like, for example, most of Roman Imperial nicolos. This is finely mirrored by the shadowing gradually darkening towards deeper parts of the stone on the edges. He also expertly marks shadows cast by

---

59 Gori 1731–1732, vol. II, pl. 40.3.
60 Letter from Girolamo Odam to Anton Francesco Gori dated Rome 21 December 1738 – Epistolario di Anton Francesco Gori, no. 11123, volume BVII21, carte 8r–9v.

the figures on the ground and usually also alongside the right side of the figures, which gives a three-dimensional effect to the whole composition. The artist also makes a clear distinction between the intaglios and cameos he documented because, in the case of the latter, the relief engraving of the figures is in pale grey or even white wash, while the background in a greatly contrasting one of dark grey colour. Overall, the style of the drawings in question is expressive but delicate and even subtle.

There are 323 drawings of this type set in the templates with a hatched background and 16 more in the ones with a background made in wash in the combined collections from Krakow and Berlin.[61] Nearly all of those which are preserved with a full frame or on original sheets have the gemstone type information provided at the bottom of the caption field or below it usually by the same hand, but not always, while in most cases the short descriptions of subject matters are provided in capital letters in the caption fields. As far as can be judged, except for two cases (Krakow Nos 1798 and 1799), none of these drawings have provenance information added, which is written by a different hand than other texts on the drawings in this group (Figs 8.39–8.41).

In 1787, Johann Friedrich Frauenholz acquired Johann Adam Schweickart's complete *dactyliotheca* of Stosch's gems and a few drawings of Stosch's gems by Johann Justin Preißler. Together with Johann Friedrich Schlichtegroll, he launched a project to publish a selection of the best of Stosch's gems, which started in 1792 under the title *Auswahl vorzüglicher Gemmen aus derjenigen Sammlung die ehemahls der Baron Philipp von Stosch besass, die sich jetzt aber in dem Kön. Preussischen Cabinette befindet*. The plates XI, XVII, XX and XXXI in this brochure were made after Preißler's drawings (Fig. 8.42).[62] It is striking that these four plates are made in the very same design, technique and style as drawings under discussion here. They have the same size, real-size gem drawings on the bottom-left side, a caption field beneath the enlarged gem, as well as a hatched background and thick, single-line frame in black pen all around. This similarity cannot be a mere coincidence. The template from Preißler's drawings was then adopted for all plates by Schlichtegroll, including those appearing in the next publications.

The ultimate proof for the claim that the drawings from this group should be attributed to Johann Justin Preißler comes from a small group of four gem drawings signed by him *J.J. Preißler d.* (*d.* standing for *delineavit*), which were offered by Christie's at an auction in 2003 and are now in a private collection. Although sketched in red chalk, they are made in the same technique (pen and ink with grey wash) and style. Rambach is right claiming that these four gem drawings signed by Preißler were commissioned by Rodolfino Venuti (1705–1763), among which two, featuring gems from the Antonio Borioni collection, were selected as preparatory works for plates depicting them in a book published by Venuti in 1736.[63] The other two signed drawings by Preißler from the group are the carnelian intaglio signed by Agathangelos presenting a portrait of Sextus Pompey, which belonged to the collector and dealer of antiquities, including gems, Marcantonio Sabbatini (1637–1724), and the last drawing was made after an intaglio with a portrait of Agrippina the Elder. These drawings should have been made between 1730 and 1736 (possibly in 1731?) and it is known that Preißler received commissions to draw gems not only from Stosch and Venuti but also other collectors like Alessandro Gregorio Capponi.[64]

The drawing of a carnelian with Sextus Pompey's portrait by Agathangelos signed by Preißler is particularly valuable because the artist documented that gem also for Stosch (Berlin vol. VI, pl. 47), which makes it possible to compare the technique and style in detail. One observes the very same delicate modelling of each face element and skilful drawing with use of thin, short lines in pen. The shape of the nose, ear, eye as well as the beard are identical. The locks of hair are arranged in the very same way too. This drawing should be compared to Krakow No. 1749, depicting the garnet intaglio engraved with a head of a Roman and signed by Skopas, because, as proved in Chapter 10, it was certainly made by Preißler too, ca. 1727–1728. Both drawings give us an idea of how

---

61 Because the distinction of this and two following types is largely based on the technical and especially stylistic criteria, in some cases it is difficult to attribute a drawing to specific group and consequently artist. Nevertheless, such cases are not numerous, and they do not distort the general trends much.
62 Schlichtegroll 1792b, pls XI, XVII, XX and XXXI. On the publication project of Frauenholz and Schlichtegroll cf. Chapter 6 here.
63 Borioni and Venuti 1736, nos 42 and 49; cf. Chapter 3 here.
64 Cf. Chapter 4 here and Ubaldelli 2001, pp. 136 and 414. Besides, as Schlichtegroll and Zazoff write after Stosch's death Schweickart took his drawings with him as well as his gem impressions to Nuremberg (Schlichtegroll 1805, vol. I, pp. 12–13; Zazoff and Zazoff 1983, p. 181). He probably took all of them since none of his drawings can be securely identified among those now in Krakow or Berlin and he could take a few more by Preißler by accident or he get them from his master Georg Martin Preißler, brother of Johann Justin Preißler. The drawings from this group were certainly not made by Pier Leone Ghezzi, Girolamo Odam or Bernard Picart since their contributions to Stosch's scholarly projects known from other groups of drawings discussed in this book clearly show that they worked in different techniques and styles.

Preißler approached portrait gems. The other drawings signed by Preißler featuring figural scenes are also helpful to attribute the group discussed here to this artist. For example, a comparison of a drawing with a Nereid riding a hippocamp with similar studies from our group (Krakow No. 1293, Berlin vol. II, pls 63, 64 and 66) reveals identical elaboration of garments or the bodies of creatures (Figs 8.43–8.44), while the drawing presenting an intaglio with a Cupid riding a biga drawn by butterflies exposes how Preißler drew small but corpulent bodies, chariots and animals. His very same approach is observable in the case of many drawings from this group, for example: Krakow No. 2184, 2208 and Berlin vol. II, pls 139, 173 and 175 (Figs 8.45–8.46).

A similar technique and style, although sometimes in different mediums (pencil and red chalk), are also applied by Preißler in the case of a small group of seven drawings of Egyptian antiquities (including two scarabs) attributed to him from the collection of the Brooklyn Museum in New York.[65] The Egyptian scarab with a procession of deities on the *elytra* and head of Zeus engraved on the base belongs to the same project as four drawings signed by Preißler discussed above.[66] One observes the same way of rendering figures' bodies, expert use of short brushes of pen and ink, and rich texturing as well as attention to detail like in the case of many drawings from the group discussed here.

In conclusion, attribution of the drawings in question to Johann Justin Preißler seems reasonable and his drawings for Stosch should have been made between 1726, when he arrived in Rome and met Stosch for the first time, and 1738, when he left him and came back to his hometown – Nuremberg. Preißler's collaboration with Stosch was the most intense between 1726 and 1732, as evidenced by his drawing of Stosch's marble bust sculpted by Edmé Bouchardon and his engagement for the supplement of *Gemmae antiquae caelatae* as well as the *Atlas* project (cf. Chapter 10).

6 Type 5 – Markus Tuscher (Documentary Drawings)

The next group of drawings, like the previous one, consists mostly of objects put into the type of a template with a line hatched background, whereas only a few are made within frames with background in grey wash. They are executed in pen and black ink with grey wash. Their typical feature is extremely extensive use of lining in pen and ink so that all elements, whether bodies of the figures, flesh parts of portraits or rocks are structured with numerous, usually cross-hatched and curved lines. As a result, in contrast to the previous group, figures and other elements of the gems' iconography have much more distinctive and stronger contours, making the depictions more vivid and clear. Moreover, the artist who produced the drawings uses wash to a considerably lower degree than the previous, one which is especially the case of bodies as well as architectural elements which are textured with thin parallel lines in pen and ink rather than those with thick wash. Another contrasting feature to the previous group is that here no shadows on the ground are marked. Moreover, his groundlines are thick and usually textured with numerous thin cross-hatched lines in pen, although some are rendered with parallel lines as well. His compositions are dynamic but well balanced, and the level of detailing is high. Another typical feature is the artist's approach towards elements of nature like rocks, trees and groundlines, for which he combined wash and pen, so that the latter left zigzags and streamer lines, reflecting texture of those elements. Convex stones are marked with the use of darkening and shadowing of deeper parts. What stand out are the stylised hatched border decorations of some of the gems. Similarly to Preißler, this artist also makes a distinction only between intaglios and cameos, drawing the latter with white or very bright colour of the figures, while the background of the gem is considerably darker (Figs 8.47–8.52).

There are 240 drawings of this type set into the templates with a hatched background and 26 of those set in the templates with the background in wash. Among them, 15 are in Krakow, whereas 225 are in Berlin. Nearly all of those which are preserved with a full frame or on original sheets have the gemstone type information provided in the bottom of the caption field or below it usually by the same hand but not always as in the case of the previous group, while in most cases the short descriptions of subject matters are provided in capital letters in the caption fields. As far as can be judged, none of these drawings have provenance information added. Even though none of the drawings from this group is signed, it is striking that they are to some degree similar not only in terms of technique but also style to the previous group securely attributed to Johann Justin Preißler. It should be recalled that in 1728 Markus Tuscher joined Preißler in Stosch's atelier to document gems as well as other antiquities for

---

65 See, the Brooklyn Museum in New York, inv. no.: N367.1 P91: https://www.brooklynmuseum.org/opencollection/archives/set/252 – retrieved on 26 July 2023.

66 Relevant drawings by Preißler from Krakow are: Krakow Nos 1789 and 1808.

the collector. Moreover, he trained under Johann Daniel Preißler, father of Johann Justin Preißler.[67] Since both Tuscher and Preißler shared their master and worked together in the same studio for Stosch for many years at the same time, they are likely to have developed similar techniques of gem documentation.

Although no securely attributed or signed gem drawing by Tuscher is known, it still seems reasonable to attribute the group discussed here to him. This is evident if one compares the gem drawings with some of his other drawings and projects; for example, his proposal for an equestrian monument to King Frederick V in Amalienborg Square, drawn by Tuscher in 1750, now in the Royal Collection of Graphic Art, Statens Museum for Kunst in Copenhagen (Fig. 8.53).[68] From this project one learns that Tuscher indeed drew in pen and ink with grey wash in the same manner as the gem drawings discussed here. One observes the same lining and cross-hatching technique with the use of pen for elaboration of body parts. The contours of the figures, although built out of short, curved lines, give a clear effect. There is also a similar treatment of the robes as well as texture of the rocks. The application of sketchy zigzag lines for some detailing is also noticeable, like in the case of his gem drawings produced for Stosch. Moreover, the extensive use of lining and cross-hatching for texturing of various elements of compositions and shadowing, like it is observed on the discussed group of gem drawings is typical for Tuscher, as evidenced by his drawings of columns' capitals and other architectural elements in red chalk in a private collection attributed to him.[69]

Finally, according to Toelken, among the gem drawings that were recorded by him in 1816 in the Antikensammlung in Berlin, out of 846 works, about 300 should be by Tuscher. The current research confirms only 225 drawings in Berlin attributable to him, but this number might be underestimated due to the similarities in technique and style to the drawings already attributed to Preißler (see above) or the number of 300 was overestimated by Toelken for the same reasons. Toelken's record is largely imprecise. Because the drawings are not signed and his description very laconic, it is not known on which criteria he attributed the 300 drawings to Tuscher. Could this information come from an older, lost source? In conclusion, the group of drawings discussed here should be most likely attributed to Markus Tuscher. He worked for Stosch between 1728 and 1741 and because no specific dates for some of his documentary gem drawings can be proposed, the whole group should be dated to this broad time span.

7 Type 6 – Georg Abraham Nagel (Documentary Drawings)

The third group of drawings set in both templates, the one with a hatched background and that with a background in wash of the same types as two previous groups, includes drawings made in black pen and black ink with grey and black wash. They are made in a distinctive style characterised by the heavy use of pen and black ink and strongly emphasised contours as well as shadowing in black wash alongside them. The shadowed parts make a strong contrast to the lightened ones, which gives a sense of very clearly drawn figures to the viewer. At the same time, the texture of garments and bodies, etc., is elaborated with relatively thick brushes of pen, usually of slightly lighter grey tone. Rocks and water are often suggested by rather thick and numerous brushes of grey wash, which are dense, and details like face elements are also often done in the same way. Another very typical feature of many drawings in this group is reflection of the shapes of the gemstones with numerous, usually thick parallel, oval lines in wash. That lining is also often applied for architectural elements like columns, bases, altars, etc. Like in the case of two previous groups, here, the artist also makes a distinction between intaglios and cameos, drawing the latter with white or very bright colour or sometimes a mix of brown and white ones for the figures, while the background of the gem is considerably darker (Figs 8.54–8.60).

Among the drawings made in this technique and style found in Krakow and Berlin combined, there are 380 set in the template with a hatched background and 19 in the one with the background in grey wash. In contrast to the two previous groups, the drawings from this one are never accompanied by captions in capital letters. Texts like the gemstone type are specified in the caption field under the enlarged gem and provenance information below the frame is handwritten by the same hand. The gemstone types are always specified, while the provenance is not. Among the collections mentioned are: Pietro Andrea Andreini (Krakow No. 1289), Baron Georg von Bentinck (Berlin vol. III, pl. 37), Henry Howard, 4th Earl of Carlisle (Krakow No. 1668), Farnese collection (Krakow No. 659), French Royal collection (Berlin vol. III, pl. 44), Medici collection (Krakow No. 1298 and Berlin vol. III, pl. 57 and vol. V, pl. 13), Gabriel Medina (Krakow Nos 224, 304 and Berlin vol. I, pl. 46), Girolamo Odam (Krakow No. 637 and Berlin vol. III, pl. 53), Paul von Praun (Krakow

---

67 Leitschuh 1886, pp. 25–27.
68 The Royal Collection of Graphic Art, Statens Museum for Kunst in Copenhagen, inv. no.: KKSgb695, 355 × 472 mm.
69 Gialluca 2016, pp. 90–93, figs 18–25.

No. 1775), Philipp von Stosch (Krakow No. 1773) and Frederick de Thoms (Krakow No. 1357) (Figs 8.61–8.62).[70] In the case of five drawings, instead of a real-size gem on the left side there are lines inscribed *Gemae Altitudo/Gemae Latitudo* or *Camei Altitudo/Camei Latitudo* illustrating actual gem's size (Figs 8.63–8.64).[71] Ninety-nine drawings are observed to have the initial *N.* in the bottom-right corner just outside the drawing and frame (Figs 8.65–8.68).[72]

Exactly the same techniques and style applied in the drawings in question here are observed in the case of a small group of six gem drawings said to be works of Georg Abraham Nagel from 1754, and two more originating from another source but clearly in the same technique and style, now all in a private collection.[73] The similarities are striking; the format of the drawings, techniques including usage of thick parallel lines for the reflection of gems' shapes, as well as style – all match each other (Figs 8.69–8.72). Those drawings and the group from Krakow and Berlin are all indeed made by the same hand, although for different projects and commissioners.

It is noteworthy that many of the drawings from the group under discussion here have the initial *N.* in the bottom-right corner just outside the frame, which in all likelihood stands for Nagel. It is a substitute for a full signature. It remains unclear why only a portion of the drawings received it. The initial is clearly written by the same hand as the gemstone type and provenance information. Finally, attribution to Nagel makes sense if one analyses the prints Krakow Nos 1183 and 1184, which are reproductions of one of the masterpieces of Etruscan glyptics from Stosch's own collection – a carnelian scarab bearing Tydeus pulling a thorn out of his leg and inscription: TVTE – referring to hero's name (Figs 8.73–8.74).[74] According to the illustration published in the luxurious edition of Winckelmann's 1760 catalogue, the drawing for this print was made by Georg Abraham Nagel, while Johann Adam Schweickart made the engraving after it (*G.A. Nagel del.* and *I.A. Schweickart sculp.*). The original drawing by Nagel survived within the collection in the Princes Czartoryski Museum in Krakow – Krakow No. 1182 (Fig. 8.75).[75] According to the technique and style, it belongs to the group discussed here and it helps to prove that those drawings should be indeed attributed to Nagel.

Georg Abraham Nagel is said to have worked in Stosch's atelier for six years, most likely since the late 1730s and he left it in the early 1740s.[76] This is confirmed by the provenance information he left under his drawings. For example, in the case of Krakow No. 1289, he informs that the gem is in the Medici collection in Florence, but he also mentions that it once belonged to Pietro Andrea Andreini. Indeed, Andreini's cabinet of engraved gems was purchased *en bloc* by Gian Gastone de'Medici in Florence in 1731 from Andreini's heirs two years after his death. It appears that when the drawing was finished the memory of Andreini's collection was still strong. Furthermore, there are two drawings representing gems from the collection of Girolamo Odam, which means they should have been made prior to 1741 – the date of dispersal of Odam's collection. Based on the observations on techniques and styles applied by the artist producing these drawings, the handwritten information on the gemstone types and provenance, as well as other presented arguments, it is proposed that the drawings within that group should be attributed to Georg Abraham Nagel.

8   Type 7 – Pier Leone Ghezzi (Individual Works)

According to Philipp von Stosch himself, Pier Leone Ghezzi helped him grately during production of his book, *Gemmae antiquae caelatae*, and as discussed above, h he is likely to have drawn two gems for this project.[77] He was certainly very close not only to Stosch but also Odam and

---

70   There were certainly more examples with provenance information as evidenced by fragments of texts visible at the bottom of the drawings: Krakow Rr. 73, 115, 204, 277, 386, 398, 403, 416, 544, 579, 894, 909, 914, 963, 972, 1190, 1315, 1373, 1388 and Berlin vol. I, pls 51 and 123, vol. II, pls 4 and 10, vol. IV, pls 44, 85 and 114.

71   Krakow Rr. 304, 386, 403, 413 and 963.

72   These are the following: Krakow Nos 19, 27, 45, 73, 105, 119, 137, 155, 169, 204, 224, 244, 265–266, 288, 301, 304, 379, 389, 393, 416, 425, 458, 544, 587, 624–625, 637, 648, 659, 666, 887, 914, 967, 972, 1128, 1214, 1287, 1289, 1310, 1357, 1361, 1374, 1446, 1448, 1548, 1576, 1578, 1668, 1751, 1773, 1775, 1975, 1980, 2025 and Berlin vol. I, pls 17, 39, 46–47, 66, 71, 96 and 108, vol. II, pls 44, 47, 136, 151 and 174, vol. III, pls 37, 44, 53 and 57, vol. IV, pls 71, 73, 82–83, 87–88, 90, 92, 105 and 109, vol. V, pls 11, 13–14, 16–18 and 39, vol. VI, pls 9, 33, 36, 63, 90, 114, 127 and 138.

73   Cf. Rambach in Chapter 3 in this volume.

74   AGDS II, no. 238; Zwierlein-Diehl 2007, ill. 317 (with more literature).

75   Even though the hatched border decoration looks different than on the original gem and Schweickart's engraving, the very precise study of hero's body, his position and details like only three fingers of his left hand visible, his coiffure and perfectly mirrored inscription, make it clear that the drawing indeed depicts Stosch's own gem rather than its ancient replica, some of which are known to exist, see, for example: Zazoff 1968, p. 54, no. 61, pl. 17. Nagel drew the gem from an impression since it is reversed to the original scarab, and he apparently did so many years before the scarab entered Stosch's collection in the early 1750s (Hansson 2014, p. 23). This may explain the unfaithful hatched border decoration on his drawing.

76   Engelmann 1908, p. 338.

77   Stosch 1724, p. v.

all three were introduced to each other around 1715, when Stosch arrived in Rome for the first time. They remained friends and collaborators for many years. Even though Ghezzi is not recorded in the correspondence, or any other archival source as selected by Stosch to be an illustrator of his next various projects involving documentation of intaglios and cameos like Girolamo Odam, Johann Justin Preißler, Markus Tuscher and Georg Abraham Nagel, he certainly supplied him with individual gem drawings. This is confirmed by a letter sent by Ghezzi to Stosch on 17 May 1731, to which he attached his watercolour drawing of a cameo said to have depicted Lucius Licinius Murena, which was meant to be published in Stosch's unfinished second book (cf. Chapter 10).[78]

Among the gem drawings discovered in the Princes Czartoryski Museum in Krakow, there is a group made in pen and brown ink, of which the technique and style should be recognised as those of Pier Leone Ghezzi. This is evident in the case of the following drawings: Krakow Nos 75, 395, 1253, 1362, 1385, 1393, 1588, 1612 and perhaps also Krakow Nos 1724, 1754–1756. Some exhibit a dry, sketchy manner similar to Ghezzi's caricatures now preserved in the Biblioteca Apostolica Vaticana (Krakow Nos 395, 1385 and 1612) (Fig. 8.76–8.77),[79] and the other ones are made in a quite expressive manner but still very much in the style of Ghezzi (Krakow Nos 75, 1253 and 1588) (Figs 8.78–8.79). The others are made in a technique close to his and Odam's preparatory drawings for the *Gemmae antiquae caelatae* book (Krakow Nos 1362 and 1393), while others form a small but homogenous group made in the technique close to Ghezzi's one, but the style is a bit different than his usual works (Krakow Nos 1724, 1754–1756).[80]

Regarding the gems represented on those drawings, some of them are Stosch's own, like Krakow Nos 1588 and 1612. Particularly interesting is the drawing Krakow No. 1588, depicting a late sixteenth-century cameo with head of a lion to the front, cut in the tiger's eye probably in the workshop of the famous Miseroni family in Milan, most likely gifted by Stosch to Lorenz Natter and later in the Marlborough collection (Figs 8.78–8.79).[81] The richly elaborated frame and altar basis below suggests an individual project for a leaflet, one of those Stosch used to commissioned from Ghezzi and Odam; for example, for his famous Meleager intaglio (cf. below). Krakow No. 75 reproduces an amethyst intaglio once in the Carlisle collection, Krakow No. 395 represents a carnelian intaglio from Girolamo Odam's collection, Krakow Nos 1724 and 1756 depict two cameos from the Medici collection, now in Florence, Krakow No. 1253 bears an unknown, Hellenistic glass cameo of which Ghezzi had a sulphur impression in his *dactyliotheca*, while Krakow Nos 1362, 1385, 1393 and 1754–1755 represent unidentified gems. Taking into account that Stosch himself might have supplied Lord Carlisle with the amethyst intaglio (Krakow No. 395) and that the other identified gems belonged to him or his close collaborators, attribution of these drawings to Ghezzi is even more certain.

These drawings were not commissioned by Stosch for a specific project; they are individual works. It appears that from time to time Stosch asked Ghezzi to draw individual gems perhaps for his personal archive or simply to see how good Ghezzi was in documenting intaglios and cameos as he used to do with other draughtsmen.[82] Perhaps some of these drawings were in fact sort of experiments, e.g. Ghezzi tested his techniques and styles, trying to find the most suitable one which would satisfy his commissioner and Stosch, who boasted to have trained artists in Rome in the difficult art of documentation of gems and may have helped him to develop his skills.[83] Ghezzi was a prolific draughtsman of engraved gems and he reproduced hundreds of them for his own corpus of drawings of antiquities, which is now largely in the Biblioteca Apostolica Vaticana.[84] It is unclear if all the drawings included in the group under discussion were originally within Stosch's vast corpus. For example, they might be some of those listed in Ghezzi's *quadreria* accompanying the testament of Ghezzi's spouse, Caterina Peroni Ghezzi (ca. 1694–1762). Under no. 77 on the list, one finds a reference to 68 drawings of gems estimated for 12 scudi.[85] Unless they went to

---

78 Ubaldelli 2001, p. 85.
79 The Biblioteca Apostolica Vaticana, Cod. Ott. lat. 3110–3119.
80 For more general remarks on Ghezzi's techniques and styles developing over many years of his career, especially in reference to his caricatures, see: Bodart 1976.
81 This cameo recently re-emerged on the art market. It was offered by Sotheby's at the auction *Small Wonders: Early Gems and Jewels* on 16 December 2020: https://www.sothebys.com/en/buy/auction/2020/small-wonders-early-gems-and-jewels-2/italian-probably-milan-circa-1600-cameo-with-the [retrieved on 26 November 2022].
82 Zazoff and Zazoff 1983, p. 55.
83 Technically and stylistically, most of the drawings discussed here correspond to the early steps of Ghezzi's career, see: Bodart 1976, pp. 14–23. For Stosch on training artists in Rome in documentation of engraved gems, see: Letter from Walton [Stosch] to Lord Carteret dated 28 February 1722 (NA Kew SP 85/14 fols 9–12); Hansson 2021b, p. 62.
84 The Biblioteca Apostolica Vaticana, Cod. Ott. lat. 3100–3101, 3103–3104 and 3106–3109. On Ghezzi and his documentation of various kinds of antiquities, including gems, see: Gołyźniak (forthcoming – Ghezzi).
85 Martinelli (ed.) 1990, p. 131.

the Cardinal Alessandro Albani collection,[86] their fate is unknown, so that they could have circulated around the art market in Rome. Maybe they were added to the collection, which is now in Krakow, between 1783 and 1800.

9 Type 8 – Group of Red Chalk Drawings (Unattributed)

Only 15 works belong to this group and they are all in the collection of gem drawings in Krakow; none was included into the volumes from Berlin. They are executed in dark red chalk, clearly by the same hand. They are fully accomplished with all details highlighted, quite skilfully drawn. The artist managed to highlight shadowing with a complex series of cross-hatching, although their quality is inferior, for example, to the works attributed to Bernard Picart (see above). Only one example (Krakow No. 974) is preserved with fragments of the original frame, which was of square shape and consisted of simple lines in black ink (Figs 8.80–8.81). From the drawings which survived with some original background (Krakow Nos 23 and 974), it is clear that the real-size gem drawings accompanied them on the bottom-left or right and they were originally uninscribed (Figs 8.82–8.83). None of these drawings is signed.

The drawings from this group were almost certainly made by one of the numerous artists working for Philipp von Stosch, since seven out of fifteen represent original intaglios from his own collection or glass pastes he had made after mostly now lost gems.[87] In addition, 12 out of 15 drawings represent gems of which Stosch had their sulphur impressions.[88] Sulphur impressions were certainly used in Stosch's atelier to produce documentary gem drawings, which is suggested, for example, by a drawing by Georg Abraham Nagel (Krakow No. 1773) under which one reads *Ectyp: in Sulph: B: de Stosch* and some works which real-size gem drawings are inscribed *Sulphur magnitudo*.[89] Within the group discussed here, only one drawing reproduces a gem published by Stosch in the *Gemmae antiquae caelatae* book – this is a red jasper intaglio signed by Karpus, now in Florence (Krakow No. 898).[90] Concerning the remaining drawings, two (Krakow Nos 898 and 971) represent intaglios which are now in the collection of the Museo Archeologico Nazionale in Florence, Krakow No. 333 features an intaglio now in the Museo Archeologico Nazionale in Naples, Krakow No. 420 reproduces a gem now in the Bibliothèque nationale de France in Paris, while Krakow Nos 134, 141, 372, 946 and 1012 depict unidentified, most likely lost gems (some of which – Krakow Nos 134, 372 and 946 – could have been drawn from Stosch's sulphur impressions). The high proportion of Stosch's gems, his glass pastes and perhaps also sulphur impressions reproduced in the drawings in question means that their author must have accessed Stosch's considerable resources.

One excludes Ghezzi and Odam since as discussed above, their techniques and styles are very different regardless of the kind of a project they worked on with Stosch. The comparative analysis with drawings attributed to Bernard Picart (see above) also reveals that those under discussion here were not drawn by him. Among other draughtsmen identified as working for Stosch, according to the groups of drawings discussed above, none seems to draw in a similar technique and style. There are a number of gem drawings in red chalk that scholars tend to attribute to Johann Justin Preißler; however, none of them seems to be correct.[91] Furthermore, among the gem drawings in the Princes Czartoryski Museum in Krakow, there is a drawing of Philipp von Stosch's marble bust sculpted by Edmé Bouchardon in red chalk (Krakow No. 1665, see below for a discussion). That drawing is indeed attributed to Preißler, although the technique and style is different than the ones observed within the group of gem drawings under discussion here. They are made in a red-brownish chalk, a bit darker than the one applied for the drawing of Stosch's bust by Preißler, which is of a much higher quality too.

Finally, little is known about the techniques and styles applied by Georg Martin Preißler, the brother of Johann Justin Preißler, who joined him in Stosch's atelier before 1732, and Johann Adam Schweickart, who worked for Stosch from 1742 until the collector's death. Nevertheless, as explained in Chapter 4, Georg Martin Preißler does not seem to draw gems for Stosch on a regular basis, in contrast

---

86 Gołyźniak (forthcoming – Ghezzi).
87 Krakow Nos 23, 132, 134, 420, 898, 1114, 1232 and 1902.
88 Krakow Nos 23, 132, 134, 333, 372, 420, 898, 946, 974, 1114, 1232 and 1902.
89 For example, Krakow Nos 544 and 1773 both drawn by Nagel.
90 Florence, Museo Archeologico Nazionale: red jasper intaglio inv. no.: 14776 (early 18th century).
91 One such a group are red chalk drawings after engraved gems once in the collection of Harry Bober (1915–1988) and now in a private collection, which were attributed by Mia N. Weiner (1990, lots 41–42) to Johann Justin Preißler, who also suggested a commission from Stosch. There are also several other groups traditionally attributed to Preißler, however, the recent study by Rambach proves that only very few of them can be securely attributed to the artist and those are drawings which were not commissioned by Stosch but Preißler's other clients like Alessandro Gregorio Capponi or Rodolfino Venuti, cf. Chapters 3 and 4 in this volume.

to his brother, as he worked more as a printmaker rather than a draughtsman. Therefore, one should probably exclude him from the list of potential authors of the drawings under discussion. Regarding Schweickart, according to Schlichtegroll and Zazoff, while coming back to Nuremberg from Florence, Schweickart brought with him gem impressions and engravings after Stosch's intaglios, and perhaps his own drawings too, which remain lost.[92] As a result, it is impossible to securely attribute the drawings in question to any artist known to work for Stosch and it might be that they were produced by someone outside this group. It is noteworthy that *Das neue gelehrte Europa* and other sources one must rely upon give us incomplete lists of draughtsmen working for Stosch, and, as demonstrated by Rambach, there were many artists drawing gems in the course of the eighteenth century.[93]

10 Type 9 – Sketches of Gems Published in Stosch's Book *Gemmae antiquae caelatae*

The collection of gem drawings in the Princes Czartoryski Museum in Krakow also includes a group of 30 sketches of gems published in Stosch's book, *Gemmae antiquae caelatae*.[94] This kind of drawing is absent in the volumes from Berlin. With only one exception (Krakow No. 1360), which is drawn in pen and ink, all of them are executed in red chalk and they are all made by the same hand. They are all cut out of the original sheets except for one item (Krakow No. 1360), which suggests that the gemstone type information was originally given in a brief commentary below the enlarged gem. They are not framed except for one specimen stuck down onto a simple square frame in black pen, most likely made after transfer of the drawing onto new paper around 1801. Some of them have signatures of gem engravers corrected in dark brown ink (Figs 8.84–8.85). They are so imprecise that they look amateurish or were quickly produced sketches. It turns out that they are a part of a bigger collection originally related to Anton Francesco Gori (1691–1757). The second part, including identical drawings and representing other signed gems published in Stosch's book, is now preserved in the Biblioteca Marucelliana in Florence.

The Biblioteca Marucelliana holds a number of manuscripts on glyptic subjects by Gori. Among them is one (inv. no. A.194.1) entitled *Excerpta. Ex libro cui titulus est Gemmae Antiquae Caelatae ...* ('Excerpt from the book entitled *Gemmae Antiquae Caelatae ...*'). Dated 15 May 1726, it states that it had been copied from a volume in the library of Maria Nicolò Gabburri (1676–1742), as a favour for Pietro Andrea Andreini (1650–1729).[95] The library also possesses a group of 32 drawings of gems copied from Stosch's book *Gemmae antiquae caelatae*, which Micheli links to that manuscript on the basis that the drawings have annotations and comments written by Gori.[96] She suggests that all are by the same artist apart from inv. nos CIV.213 and CIV.79. The drawing inv. no. CIV.79, which is in pencil, indeed might have been added later to the collection, but CIV.213 does not differ much from, for instance, CIV.208 that Micheli attributes to Gori. Apart from CIV.208 and CIV.213, which are in pen and ink, all the drawings are drawn in red chalk. Only inv. no. CIV.79 is drawn more skilfully, whereas the rest are sketches like in case of their peers from Krakow. The drawings have annotations and numbering in brown ink, some evidently by Gori, some perhaps not by him (CIV.208 and CIV.213).[97] Although almost all drawings from Krakow have been cut out of the original paper, so they lost their comments. However, also like those from Florence, they have corrections made, for instance, engravers' signatures and annotations on the gems themselves are in brown ink. The drawing Krakow No. 1360 has been preserved with a complete commentary below the gem, which was evidently added by the hand of Gori and its technique and style is the same as two drawings in Florence, CIV.208 and CIV.213.

To sum up, the drawings from Krakow and Florence form a group of 62 objects among which three are in pen and ink, one in pencil and 58 in red chalk. It seems reasonable to put the drawing from Florence inv. no. CIV.79 (in pencil) aside because even though it alsso presents a gem published in Stosch's book, it is much different than the rest and it repeats the subject matter of inv. no. CIV.140. Two drawings in red chalk from Florence (CIV.201 and CIV.206) present gems that were not published in the *Gemmae antiquae caelatae* book. If one combines the rest of Florence drawings with those from Krakow, the result is the following sequence of Stosch's 1724 book plates: I, II, III, V, VII, VIII, IX, XI, XII, XV, XVI, XVI, XVII, XVIII, XIX, XX, XXI, XXII, XXIII, XXIV, XXV, XXVI (pen and ink), XXVII, XXX, XXXI, XXXI, XXXII (pen and ink), XXXIII, XXXV,

---

92 Schlichtegroll 1805, vol. I, pp. 11–12; Zazoff and Zazoff 1983, p. 57.
93 For example, Stosch does not mention Odam to have drawn gems for him (1754, p. 50); Rambach, Chapter 3 in this volume.
94 The refer to the following plates in Stosch 1724 book: I, II, III, V, VII, VIII, IX, XI, XII, XV, XVI, XVII, XVIII, XIX, XX, XXI, XXII, XXIII, XXIV, XXV, XXVI, XXVII, XXX, XXXI, LIII, LVI, LVII, LVIII, LIX and LXII.

95 Micheli 1986, p. 38.
96 Micheli 1986, pp. 42–50.
97 Micheli 1986, pp. 38–39.

XXXVI, XXXVII, XXXIX, XL, XLI, XLII, XLIII, XLIV (pen and ink), XLV, XLVI, XLVII, XLVIII, XLIX, L, LII, LIII, LIV, LVI, LVII, LVIII, LIX, LX, LXI, LXII, LXIII, LXIV, LXV, LXVI, LXVII, LXVIII, LXIX. Stosch's plate XXXI is reproduced twice in red chalk by the same hand – one drawing is in Florence (inv. no. CIV 215), the second in Krakow (Krakow No. 1124) (Fig. 8.86). Plates IV, VI, X, XIII, XIV, XXVIII, XXIX, XXXIV, XXXVIII, LI, LV, LXX are missing their drawings, either in red chalk or pen and ink or even pencil.

The authorship of the drawings in question has not been ascertained. Micheli noticed a close collaboration between Gori and Odam who drew most of the gems for Stosch's book and therefore, she suggested Odam as the author.[98] However, having established how Odam's drawings for the *Gemmae antiquae caelatae* project looked like (see above), it is impossible for those poor red chalk sketches to be by him. The drawings in Micheli's catalogue nos 3 (CIV.193/Stosch LXI); 4 (CIV.194/Stosch LX); 11 (CIV.201/Stosch XXXII); 12 (CIV.202/Stosch XXXIX); 17 (CIV.207/Stosch XLIX); 19 (CIV.208/Stosch L); and 28 (CIV.218/Stosch LXVII) are inscribed 'Je nay poin(t) denprinte' ('I have no impression'), in incorrect French, not by Gori, nor by Odam, neither by Stosch.[99]

Between 1726 and 1734, Gori's interest in engraved gems reached its culminating point, mostly due to the encouragement of Filippo Buonarroti (1661–1733), but the influence of Stosch ought not to be underestimated.[100] In 1727, Gori – certainly inspired by Stosch – published in Florence with Anton Maria Salvini (1653–1729) his *Inscriptionum antiquarum graecarum et Romanarum quae exstant in Etrutiae urbibus vol. I, in quo LXII antiquae gemmae literatae aere incisae explicantur*. In 1731–1732, he devoted the first two volumes of his *Museum Florentinum* to gems, *Gemmæ antiquæ ex Thesauro Mediceo et privatorum dactyliothecis Florentiæ*. Moreover, starting in 1742, Gori contributed to the *Giornale de' Letterati*, a journal financed by Stosch.[101] However, Stosch and Gori discussed gems already much earlier and the evidence of that comes from a letter that Stosch sent to Gori on 16 September 1720 from The Hague. He informed Gori that he was shipping him six freshly made prints for his forthcoming book and he asked Gori to look at them but to not show them to anyone.[102] The mentioned prints were certainly those which Stosch distributed as an advertisement for his forthcoming book due to the subscription of the book set to run from 1 August 1721 until 31 January 1722.[103] Could Stosch also have sent Gori some simple sketches like the ones discussed here to consult on a selection of the gems for his book and the signatures?

A question arises whether the red chalk sketches could have been drawn by Stosch himself as an aid in organisation of his work on the *Gemmae antiquae caelatae* book project, and perhaps for its consultation with Gori? Lewis claims that Stosch was capable of drawing and composed some, for instance, during his cooperation with Ghezzi and Odam (perhaps under their influence?) on the illustrations to obscene passages from the ancient authors, a project promised to Lord Carteret.[104] On the other hand, in Stosch's correspondence, no drawings of gems or other antiquities are to be found, only transcribed inscriptions, mostly from coins and medals.[105]

The description of the manuscript inv. no. A.194.1 in the Biblioteca Marucelliana in Florence *Excerpta. Ex libro cui titulus est Gemmae Antiquae Caelatae ...* sounds like it was transcribed from a copy of the original book, but why did Gori have Stosch's book text copied by hand, when in 1726 he could simply have purchased a printed copy, especially if he expressed his interest in the book many years before it was published (he may have even subscribed for a copy, see above)? It remains equally puzzling what the purpose was of having copies of illustrations. Gori's

---

98 Micheli 1986, p. 41. This view was also accepted by Kagan (2006, p. 83, n. 9). Indeed, Gori and Odam frequently exchanged letters, especially in the last years of Odam's life. A research in the Epistolario di Anton Francesco Gori returns 46 letters sent from Odam to Gori from Rome between 1738 and 1741, see: https://sol.unifi.it/gori/gori?cmd=40&sid=456950039:0&startrec=1 [retrieved on 6 April 2022].
99 Micheli 1986, p. 38.
100 Micheli 1986, p. 40; Kagan 2006, p. 83. On Gori's interest in engraved gems in general, see: Kagan 2006.
101 Cristofani 1983, p. 79; Micheli 1986, p. 41.
102 Letter from Philipp von Stosch to Anton Francesco Gori dated The Hague 16 September 1720: '*Profitto della occasione della partenza dei Sig.ri Cavallucci e Dereham per Firenze per mandare a V.S. le sei prime stampe del mio libro, pregandola di fare in modo che non eschino di mano sua, affidandomi in questo sopra di lei e de' Cavallucci.*' – Epistolario di Anton Francesco Gori, no. 19476, volume BVIII4, carte 326R–326v.
103 Leclerc 1721, pp. 229–231. In an undated letter to Bernard de Montfaucon (1655–1741), Jacques Clermont, a close friend to Bernard Picart, writes that six plates would be published to advertise Stosch's book: '*On va publier six planches pour tâcher d'avoir des souscriptions des curieux, et on est assuré qu'on n'en manquera pas pour acheter tout l'ouvrage.*' (FINA Wiki Database (ID 2657), https://fina.oeaw.ac.at/wiki/index.php/Jacques_Clemont_-_Bernard_de_Montfaucon_- [retrieved on 16 November 2022]).
104 Lewis 1961, pp. 67–68, a view based on information Stosch passed in his letter Lord Carteret dated 28 February 1722 (NA Kew SP 85/14 fols 9–12). According to a letter from Horace Mann to Horace Walpole dated 13 May 1758, these drawings and prints were bought by Frederick the Great of Prussia (Walpole 1927–1983, vol. V, p. 202), who also purchased Stosch's collection of engraved gems in 1764.
105 I am grateful to Ulf R. Hansson for confirming this.

growing interest in gems might have simply result in an attempt to revise Stosch's work, which must have made a great impact on him.[106] As evidenced by some drawings from Krakow (Krakow Nos 1256, 1354 and 1679) and Florence (CIV.199, 201, 210, 214, 216 and 220), Gori would correct gem engravers' signatures according to his own reading (Fig. 8.87). Moreover, among the red chalk drawings now in Florence, there are two (inv. no. CIV.201 and CIV.206) presenting gems that Stosch ultimately did not publish in his book in 1724, but which Gori apparently did not exclude from his own studies. Do those drawings and their improvements evidently by Gori prove the discussion on the signed gems between Stosch and Gori through their correspondence? Maybe one should attribute the simple red chalk sketches to Gori, who is credited authorship of three drawings in pen and ink (CIV.208 and CIV.213 from Florence and Krakow No. 1360 from Krakow) by Micheli, as well? It is noteworthy that Gori occasionally drew gems himself, like the one in a letter to Odam dated 25 November 1739.[107] The sketches attributed to him and discussed here may have been used in preparation for a large encyclopaedic work on engraved gems, which Gori was already preparing but never finished.[108]

The very simple style of these sketches makes their attribution troublesome. It also remains unclear how half of the original collection of the sketches discussed here ended up in the Biblioteca Marucelliana, while the rest is now in Krakow. Most of the large archive of Gori was purchased by Angelo Maria Bandini (1726–1803), the first librarian of the Biblioteca Marucelliana, for his institution in 1761. In 1783, Bandini organised Gori's papers and the Marucelliana Library drawings collection. Between the acquisition and the reorganisation, no thefts or missing parts were reported; thus, it is believed that the drawings which are now in Krakow must have left Gori's archive prior to 1761.[109] Most likely, they were added to the original collection of drawings inherited from Stosch by Muzell-Stosch between 1783 and 1800; however, it might be that the group from Krakow are the drawings which Gori resent (if one accepts the hypothesis that they were drawn by Stosch) or simply sent (if one believes they are by the hand of Gori) to Stosch during their mutual discussion on the subject of ancient signed gems.

11 Type 10 – Illustrations for the Luxurious Edition of Winckelmann's Catalogue from 1760

Winckelmann's catalogue of Stosch's gems was published in 1760 unillustrated. However, a special luxurious edition in a limited number of copies was also released and it included 11 plates that originally were meant to be published in the second, never finished volume of Stosch's book, *Gemmae antiquae caelatae*.[110] It is extremely rare, since the only known copies are known to be in Rome, Fano, Berlin, Weimar and New York, and now also one more that arrived with the collection of gem drawings for the Czartoryski collection. It is now preserved in the Czartoryski Library in Krakow.[111] An illustration of a bust of Philipp von Stosch introduces this book. It was engraved by Georg Martin Preißler after the drawing by Johann Justin Preißler, who based his work on the bust sculpted by Edmé Bouchardon in 1727.[112] Both the original drawing in red chalk (Krakow No. 1665) as well as the print in the line engraving technique produced after that drawing are to be found in Krakow's assemblage (Krakow No. 1666) (Figs 8.88–8.90). The 11 prints of gems published in the luxurious edition of Winckelmann's catalogue bear various subjects, but their common feature are inscriptions. Not all of them are signatures; sometimes the inscriptions refer to the gems' possessors or can be explained in another way. In any case, the collection from the Princes Czartoryski Museum includes all 11 published prints. The illustrations of a crouching satyr holding an oak wreath by Teukros and Tydeus scraping his leg are represented twice, while the illustration of Stosch's famous onyx intaglio with Meleager is represented as engraved by Vincenzo Franchesini.[113] As a result, the collection contains 15 prints and one drawing related to that luxurious

---

106 Stosch's book must have made a great impact on Gori. The attention he paid to filing and annotating each piece means that he understood the innovative value of *Gemmae antiquae caelatae*, see: Tassinari 2010a, p. 31.
107 See its reproduction in: Ubaldelli 2001, appendix 2, p. 376, no. 1b. The original chalcedony intaglio is now in the National Museum in Krakow, see: Gołyźniak 2017, no. 215.
108 Kagan 2006, p. 91.
109 The research on provenance of these drawings now in the Biblioteca Marucelliana brought no more results. The library also does not hold any gem drawings like those from Krakow (other classes). I am grateful to Paolo Turcis for his kind assistance in the research and all the information he shared.

110 For a discussion on this issue, cf. Chapter 10 here.
111 The Czartoryski Library, inv. no. 1836 II. Regarding the other known copies, see: Rügler in Winckelmann 2013, p. XXIII, n. 88.
112 This 85cm high marble bust is now in Berlin, Staatliche Museen, see: Sénéchal 2000, pp. 136–148; Arbeid, Bruni and Iozzo 2016, no. 33; Kopp 2017, pp. 54–59. Interestingly, in his diary, Pier Leone Ghezzi writes that Stosch gifted him a terracotta and plaster forms of Stosch's bust sculpted by Bouchardon on 14 February 1731, see: Dorati da Empoli 2008, pp. 68–69.
113 This gem is also drawn by Markus Tuscher, see: Krakow No. 1215.

edition in total.[114] The six volumes of *Pierres gravées du roi avec figures* in Berlin include eight plates from that edition.[115]

Additionally, the authorship of some of the drawings and engravings made after them is known. For instance, the glass gem bearing a Bacchant by Solon was engraved by Johann Adam Schweickart in 1745 (Krakow No. 874). The garnet representing a naked athlete standing frontally, apparently pouring oil from an alabastron into his lowered hand with a hydria standing beside him on a table, was drawn by Markus Tuscher (1705–1751) and later engraved by Johann Adam Schweickart (1722–1787). The gem is signed by Gnaios and now kept in the Walters Art Museum in Baltimore.[116] Schweickart also engraved the gem with a crouching satyr holding an oak wreath, signed by Teukros (Krakow Nos 936 and R. 937). Another example of the work from this set is the famous *Gemma Stosch* – an Etruscan scarab bearing five out of seven heroes fighting against Thebes (Krakow No. 1180).[117] According to the signature in the bottom of the engraving, Johann Adam Schweickart is its author, and as the text on the print presents, he produced it in 1756, shortly after Stosch got it from Count Vicenzio Ansidei. Furthermore, the famous Tydeus gem from Stosch's collection was drawn by Georg Abraham Nagel and was later engraved by Johann Adam Schweickart. Two engravings by the latter are in the collection (Krakow Nos 1183–1184). The head of a horse with the inscription MIΘ from a carnelian intaglio in Stosch's collection (Krakow No. 1593) was also engraved by Schweickart.

12 Type 11 – Varia

Finally, the *Pierres gravees par Stosche* in the Princes Czartoryski Museum in Krakow and the six volumes of *Pierres gravées du roi avec figures* from Berlin contain a few dozen of various kinds of objects (drawings, sketches and prints), which escape any reasonable sorting. They are all executed in different techniques (engraving, red and black chalk drawings, pen and ink with grey wash drawings, even pencil, etc.). Among them, some subgroups can be formed. The first one consists of three drawings (Krakow Nos 338, 1325 and 2058) made in the same technique (pen and ink with brown and grey wash) and style. The contours are clearly highlighted with the use of pen. In the case of Krakow No. 2058 (Fig. 8.91), Cupid stands to the front with a torch and the background is suggested by numerous horizontal lines, a technique typical for Odam's works known from his preparatory drawings for the *Gemmae antiquae caelatae* book (cf. Type 1 above). Moreover, this drawing also has a highly elaborated and decorative frame, since the gem is encircled by a laurel wreath. This was another specialty of Odam, as one knows from the frames he designed for some individual drawings like the one representing Stosch's Meleager intaglio (see below) or another representing Diomedes ascending from an altar with Palladion signed by Gnaeus, discussed above. However, the other examples, like Krakow No. 338, have a sort of a frame which simply reflects the ancient, hatched border of the gem itself, while Krakow No. 1325 presenting *lupa romana* is surrounded with zodiacal signs. These drawings are of high artistic level, but they cannot be securely attributed to Odam and their dates cannot be firmly established as well.

The next distinctive group is formed by two drawings – Krakow Nos 459, 1343 and a print Krakow No. 1806. Although they are not made according to one convention, they are clearly drawn in the same technique, which is pen and ink with grey wash, and the same style, which to some degree resembles those applied by Markus Tuscher (cf. Type 5 above). These objects were evidently made on individual commissions of Stosch rather than for a specific project. Krakow No. 459 is particularly interesting because it represents a terracotta relief, and it has some text in pencil written by the hand of Stosch (*p.l.onr.3*; *p.l.onr.7* and *in terra cotta*). Moreover, Krakow No. 1343 represents not the original intaglio but its impression in unknown material (probably sulphur or glass), evidently a part of a *dactyliotheca*, which is suggested by the frame and the background reflecting a wooden box the impression was set into. A very interesting case is also Krakow No. 1806, where the text *Dedicata al. Bel Sesso della Citta di Cortona* suggests that this was a special flyer designed to be disseminated during one of the meetings/sessions at the Accademia Etrusca di Cotona, the so-called *Notti Coritane*, which Stosch often attended, and which served as a platform through which local antiquarians exchanged knowledge (Fig. 8.92). The handwritten text *Cicada intaglio antico in Carneola nella Dactyliotheca Stoschiana* is undoubtedly added by Stosch himself. Any secure attribution of those drawings cannot be made, and dates of their production remain unknown as well, however, the engraving Krakow No. 1806 could have been made by Johann Adam Schweickart.

---

114 Krakow No. 71, 117, 286, 874, 936–937, 1180, 1183–1184, 1221, 1444, 1516, 1593 and 1665–1666.
115 Berlin vol. I, pl. 94; vol. III, pl. 69; vol. IV, pls 24 and 37; vol. V, pl. 64; vol. VI, pls 86, 111 and 136.
116 Boardman *et al.* 2009, no. 429.
117 Now in Berlin, see: AGDS II, no. 237.

Another group consists of three drawings (Krakow No. 1061, 1219 and 1557) made in black chalk and black ink, which depict gems published by Stosch in his book *Gemmae antiquae caelatae*. They are much bigger than any type distinguished so far and of simple technique and rather primitive style. They refer to the following plates from Stosch's book: Krakow No. 1061 – pl. LIX, Krakow No. 1219 – pl. LXVII and Krakow No. 1557 – pl. XVI. They have captions written in black ink, which provide information about the gems' provenance and material they are made of. It remains a mystery who made these drawings and when, but it is possible that they joined the collection from the Princes Czartoryski Museum in Krakow between 1783 and 1800.

There are also single drawings that were probably added to the collection from the Princes Czartoryski Museum in Krakow after its sale in 1783 in Berlin. Among them, there is Krakow No. 61, a drawing in black chalk, red chalk and black ink featuring two regular gems, one probably ancient depicting the goddess Ceres, and the other probably modern depicting Three Graces. However, one must keep in mind that Stosch received gem impressions from various collectors for examination and consultation, but he was also sent drawings of gems. The perfect example of this is the drawing in pen and ink with grey wash (Krakow No. 1800) depicting a Hellenistic cameo with a griffin combating a serpent once in the Comte de Caylus collection. As one reads in the first volume of Caylus' *Recueil d'antiquités égyptiennes, étrusques, grecques, romaines et gauloises*, the collector sent a drawing of his cameo to Stosch in order to support his work on the second volume of *Gemmae antiquae caelatae* book (cf. a full discussion on this issue in Chapter 10).[118] Moreover, Krakow No. 393 is most likely authored by Lorenz Natter, a gem engraver whom Stosch instructed to copy ancient gems between ca. 1732–1735 when he worked for him in Florence.[119] That is a documentary or study drawing of the original gem of Eutyches, while apparently later, Natter also drew Krakow No. 394 (Fig. 8.93), a project of his own copy of this gem in pale amethyst (?).[120] Some other drawings like Krakow No. 1379, made in red chalk, pen, ink and grey wash, depicting a cameo with draped bust of Phocion signed by Pyrgoteles and finally Krakow No. 1715, made in black chalk, reproducing a sard intaglio with a Roman Imperial couple, now in the Beverly collection at the Alnwick Castle, could be also sent to Stosch for inspection or support of his documentary efforts and research. It is not known who might have produced those drawings as the techniques and styles are different than those applied by draughtsmen working for Stosch, and they are not distinctive enough to attribute them to any other specific artist.

Finally, both the collection from the Princes Czartoryski Museum in Krakow and the six volumes of *Pierres gravées du roi avec figures* in Berlin contain some prints. Some of them, like Krakow Nos 223,[121] 438, 1340, 1346, 1382,[122] 1620,[123] 1753 (Fig. 8.94) and 2073, are illustrations of gems excerpted from various books, which were evidently added to the original core of the collection now in Krakow in the course of time. Similarly, the six volumes from Berlin include two illustrations excerpted from the books (Berlin vol. I, pls 21–22), which were mixed with original drawings during composition of the volumes. Furthermore, the collection from Berlin includes several prints that apparently were individual projects of leaflets that Stosch used to distribute among other collectors and connoisseurs of gems (Berlin vol. V, pl. 52 and vol. VI, pls 16, 45 and 73?).[124]

---

118 Caylus 1752–1767, vol. I, p. 144.
119 The technique and style are comparable to the drawings from his album of the unfinished project *Museum Britannicum*, compare: Boardman, Kagan and Wagner 2017, pp. 253–272.
120 The technique and style are comparable to the preliminary sketches and drawings from his album of the unfinished project *Museum Britannicum*, compare: Boardman, Kagan and Wagner 2017, pp. 273–294. There is a copy in Baltimore, the Walters Art Museum, inv. no.: 42.1028, amethyst intaglio, 37 × 28 mm (once in the Bessborough and Marlborough collections), attributed to Natter, see: Scarisbrick 1981, pp. 54–55, fig. 8; Boardman *et al.* 2009, no. 410. However, in contrast to the final work, the drawing in Krakow does not have the inscription, only its transcription with explanation below added by the hand of Stosch, surprisingly finished with 'Roma'. This most likely means that the gem was in Rome (found by Natter there?). Was then Natter indeed the author of this copy which he would have made outside Stosch's studio, and he just sent his preliminary drawing to Stosch or did he discover that copy in Rome, which was at that point uninscribed, and he sent his drawing to Stosch? In the case of the copy in Baltimore, Boardman's (*et al.* 2009, no. 410) argument in favor of Natter's authorship is the fact that it has λ and another (illegible) letter on the side of Minerva's bust, which he suspects to be Natter's initials.
121 Gori 1731–1732, vol. I, pl. 69.2.
122 Bracci 1784–1786, vol. I, pl. VI.
123 Bracci 1784–1786, vol. I, pl. XXV.
124 For example, the print Berlin vol. VI, pl. 45 was made after a drawing from Krakow (Krakow No. 1343). It remains unclear if the sketches of gems published in *Gemmae antiquae caelatae* book (*Type 9*) joined the collection in the Princes Czartoryski Museum in Krakow after Muzell-Stosch's death as well, but it is likely and so is an addition of preliminary engravings (Krakow Nos 1382 and 1620) for two plates published by Augusto Domenico Bracci in his *Memorie degli antichi incisori che scolpirono i loro nomi in gemme e cammei con molti monumenti inediti di antichità statue bassorilievi gemme opera di Domenico Augusto Bracci della Società reale antiquaria di Londra* in 1784.

13   Two Collections – One Corpus

As discussed in Chapter 5 various archival sources and correspondence suggest that Philipp von Stosch built a large pictorial corpus of engraved gems from contributions of various artists like Girolamo Odam, Johann Justin Preißler, Markus Tuscher and Georg Abraham Nagel, who collaborated with him during his whole career. The evidence discussed in Chapters 6 and 7 and here proves that large parts of that original corpus survived. First, as *Pierres gravees par Stosche* albums in the Princes Czartoryski Museum in Krakow. Second, as illustrations to the unique edition of Winckelmann's catalogue of Stosch's gems in six volumes entitled *Pierres gravées du roi avec figures*, now preserved in the Kunstbibliothek in Berlin. The fact that these two collections were once put together is proved, among others, by the 'offprints' of some of the drawings from Krakow on the backsides of the drawings in Berlin and by the references to records from Winckelmann's catalogue of Stosch's gems of the same type (clearly added by the same hand) that appear on all drawings in Berlin and almost two hundred of those now in Krakow (cf. discussion below). Moreover, as demonstrated in this chapter, focusing on the techniques and styles rather than subject matters makes one realise that both collections largely consist of groups of the same types of drawings, which can be further attributed to specific artists working for Stosch. The information found in the archive is confirmed then; Stosch indeed organised an atelier for draughtsmen, including Pier Leone Ghezzi, Girolamo Odam, Johann Justin Preißler, Markus Tuscher and Georg Abraham Nagel, among others, who created visual documentation of a vast number of engraved gems. They worked in a truly archaeological spirit focusing not only on accuracy of their drawings, but they also delivered information on the gemstone types (material), size, state of preservation, provenance of the reproduced pieces and even commented on the gems' iconography from time to time. As a result, Stosch's original corpus of gem drawings has been largely rediscovered and recreated and it can be also re-evaluated. The ca. 3200 gem drawings from Krakow and Berlin combined deliver a large dataset that gives us great insight into Stosch's ambitious collecting, documentary and scholarly enterprises.

Stosch and his collaborators created a sort of a system for documentation of such a large number of intaglios and cameos. Regardless the techniques and styles applied by various draughtsmen, they drew gems for Stosch according to specific standards. The gems were usually drawn within pre-prepared frames stuck onto sheets of laid paper. This is especially true in the case of the drawings attributed to such artist as Johann Justin Preißler, Markus Tuscher and Georg Abraham Nagel (Fig. 8.95), while those produced for Stosch by Odam usually have the frames drawn by hand and only some stuck down (Fig. 8.96).[125] There was a gradual advancement of techniques applied in Stosch's studio regarding serial documentation of gems over time then. Perhaps the reason for that was to prepare such drawings which could be later easily turned into engravings if intended as illustrations for some kind of a study or book project.

Every single gem is considerably enlarged, usually ten times its original size so that all details of the devices appearing on gems could be entirely legible. Generally, the scale of the gems is reflected, which means the smaller stones are a bit less enlarged and vice versa and their shapes are carefully drawn too. The state of preservation of individual pieces is suggested by chips and breaks drawn with a dotted line or cracks by wash. Their shapes are suggested either by darkening and shadowing of the convex or bevelled edges of the gemstones. Cameos can be easily distinguished due to the various colours of wash applied by the draughtsmen reflecting different layers of the multicoloured gemstones, whereas intaglios were usually drawn with the same tones of grey wash as the backgrounds. The drawings were mostly made after gem impressions, not the original stones, since it was easier to read details of iconography this way and the drawings could be as accurate as possible.

All the drawings originally had real-size gem drawings on the bottom-left or -right side. This was primarily made to give a sense of the real dimensions of intaglios and cameos reproduced. However, some differences between the draughtsmen working for Stosch are noticeable. For example, Odam would put information there on the type of gemstone the object was made of or whether it was an intaglio, cameo, glass gem or a glass paste. Even though this information is not always accurate, an important observation is that it is written by him, which proves his considerable knowledge in the field of mineralogy. Some drawings lack this kind of information though, which means that Odam drew an object from an impression, cast or another drawing (although this is rarely directly indicated), so he did not know or see the original, and subsequently did not know the gemstone it was made of (Fig. 8.96). Regarding the drawings made by Odam for Stosch, their caption fields appearing beneath the enlarged gems intended

---

125   For instance, Krakow Nos 171 and 1497 and Berlin vol. I, pls 15, 40, 48, 57 are clearly made within the pre-stuck down frames, while Berlin vol. I, pls 5, 8, 14, 19, 38, 64 and 138–139 have the framing drawn by hand.

for short texts specifying gems' subject matters, except for two cases (Krakow Nos 982 and 1596), are all left without text.

Nevertheless, Odam often gives provenance information (Fig. 8.96). He was a collector and connoisseur of engraved gems himself and his profound knowledge of mineralogy, intaglios and cameos as well as connections with other collectors of gems must have been an important asset for Stosch in choosing him to document so many gems.[126] In the case of the documentary drawings attributed to Johann Justin Preißler and Markus Tuscher, the information on the gemstone type, material or the form (intaglio, cameo, glass gem, glass paste or sulphur paste) is provided in the caption field or below it usually by them (?), although sometimes also by another unidentified hand (Figs 8.97–8.98). It should be recalled that Stosch's brother Heinrich Sigismund (1699–1747) arrived in Rome and lived with Stosch from 1727 until his death. He is said to have helped him to organise his collection of engraved gems (cf. below). In any case, Stosch clearly supervised and controlled production of gem drawings since he would correct and confirm the captions, or sometimes provide information on the gemstone type or material of the reproduced gem if it remained unknown. His short texts are written in pencil (Figs 8.99–8.100).[127] Georg Abraham Nagel in turn certainly specified gemstone types and provenance on his drawings himself, like Odam, although (and again, similarly to Odam), his drawings lack capitalised descriptions of the subject matters.[128] There is evidence that Nagel acted not only as a draughtsman documenting gems for Stosch like was in the case of Preißler and Tuscher, but he was also his agent travelling across Italy to gather information for Stosch about some particularly important pieces like the cameo depicting Phocion with signature of Pyrgoteles.[129] His close collaboration with Stosch while drawing the gems is attested by the fact that the latter would discuss gemstone types of the reproduced gems with him, which is testified by his texts in pencil added to some of Nagel's drawings (Figs 8.101–8.102).

Stosch was very much concerned not only about the accuracy and faithfulness of the drawings he commissioned but apparently also information about the gemstone types and interpretations of the subject matters. One finds evidence for that in his correspondence (cf. for instance, many examples evoked in Chapter 11) and in the drawings discussed above. The artists he hired were first tested before they were given a series of gems to be drawn for sure.[130] This is probably why they would draw a few signed gems that were already published by Stosch in the first volume of *Gemmae antiquae caelatae* in the first place. For example, Johann Justin Preißler is attested to have drawn the aquamarine intaglio depicting Neptune on a biga of hippocamps to the front, inscribed with the name Quintilius (Berlin vol. II, pl. 56)[131] and carnelian with head of Maecenas to the right with a fake signature of Solon (Berlin vol. VI, pl. 56).[132] Markus Tuscher drew the carnelian engraved with a draped bust of Socrates to the right signed by Agathermos (Krakow No. 1383)[133] as well as the agate or nicolo intaglio depicting Marsyas seated on a panther skin, pipes between his crossed legs with the inscription ΝΙΣΟΛΑΣ (Berlin vol. IV, pl. 28).[134] Finally, Georg Abraham Nagel reproduced as drawings for Stosch the fragmentary modern amethyst intaglio with draped bust of a young man with scanty beard to the right (a Hellenistic prince?) with a fake signature of Dioscurides (Krakow No. 1672),[135] the cameo dated to the second half of the seventeenth century presenting a draped bust of Phocion to the left with the inscription behind the head: ΦΩΚΙΩΝΟϹ and fabricated signature of Pyrgoteles at the bottom of the bust: ΠΥΡΓΟΤΕΛΗΣ ΕΠΟΙΕΙ (Krakow No. 1378), which he might have drawn during his inspection of that piece around 1743 in Rome.[136] He also drew the sixteenth-century cameo featuring Atalanta seated on the rock with a quiver at her feet and Meleager presenting her the slayed Calydonian Boar with the fake signature of Sostratos (Krakow No. 1222).[137]

---

126 Gołyźniak 2023b.
127 These short information from Stosch are observed in the case of the following drawings: Krakow No. 1809 and Berlin vol. I, pls 13, 18–19, 36, 39, 44, 53, 56, 84, 101 and 139; vol. II, pls 50, 61, 87, 94, 116 and 177; vol. III, pls 2, 28, 36, 41, 55, 70, 72, 76 and 79–82; vol. IV, pls 25–26, 40, 71, 73, 77, 83, 88–89 and 92; vol. V, pls 1, 5, 9–10, 13–14, 23, 25–27, 30, 32, 36, 44, 65, 68, 78, 88, 96, 102, 108, 112, 114; vol. VI, pls 24, 42, 44, 53, 62, 101 and 144–145.
128 Krakow Nos 224, 304, 637, 659, 1289, 1357, 1668, 1773, 1775 and Berlin vol. I, pl. 46, vol. III, pls 37, 44, 53, 57, vol. IV, pl. 88, vol. V, pl. 13 and some examples with only fragmentary preserved provenance information: Krakow Nos 19, 73, 115, 204, 251, 277, 386, 398–399, 403, 416, 894, 909, 3679, 1190, 1991 and Berlin vol. I, pls 51 and 123, vol. II, pls 4, 10, vol. IV, pls 44, 85. Consult also the catalogues of Krakow and Berlin gem drawings in Appendix 2.
129 Letter from Philipp von Stosch to Henry Howard, 4th Earl of Carlisle dated probably 1743? – reproduced in Scarisbrick 1987, p. 104. On Stosch's brother, see: Zazoff and Zazoff 1983, pp. 54–55.
130 Letter from Walton [Stosch] to Lord Carteret dated 28 February 1722 (NA Kew SP 85/14 fols 9–12); Hansson 2021b, p. 62.
131 Stosch 1724, pl. LVII.
132 Stosch 1724, pl. LXII.
133 Stosch 1724, pl. IV.
134 Stosch 1724, pl. XLIV.
135 Stosch 1724, pl. XXVI.
136 Stosch 1724, pl. LVI.
137 Stosch 1724, pl. LXVII.

Stosch was famous for training his draughtsmen in the difficult art of visual reproduction of antiquities, notably gems. His obsessive perfectionism is evident because in some cases he was apparently dissatisfied by the drawing made by one artist, so he would ask another draughtsman to make a new, better reproduction. In his letter to Anton Francesco Gori sent from Rome in 1738, Girolamo Odam claimed that his drawings were redrawn by some German and because these were less accurate, they lost their character of antiquity.[138] The analysis of all discovered drawings in Krakow and Berlin reveals that indeed some of Odam's drawings were redrawn by German artists working in Stosch's studio after him. Preißler, Tuscher and Nagel alike drew some of the same gems as he did, but the scale of that phenomenon is not as great as one may suppose reading Odam's letter where he speaks about 2700 sheets. It is confusing to find out that some gems were drawn differently. For example, Odam drew them as of oval shape horizontally, while another draughtsman vertically, or they differ considerably in details. For instance, while Odam omitted the hatched border, it appears in the drawing by Nagel or another draughtsman (Figs 8.103–8.106).[139] The reason for making new drawings of the same gem could be Odam's mistakes or perhaps Stosch obtaining better gem impressions that would make it possible to see some additional details, like the hatched border. In addition, for sure the other draughtsmen simply sometimes drew the same gems unconsciously.[140]

A few gems are attested to be drawn by even three different draughtsmen as well (Figs 8.107–8.110).[141] This can be explained by heavy use of gem drawings in Stosch's correspondence (cf. discussion below) – he simply sometimes needed multiple drawings, one for his archive and others to be sent to other collectors. Among the documentary drawings of Odam, there are four works duplicating the images of signed gems published by Stosch in 1724.[142] In any case, the accusations of redrawing all of Odam's original works are probably exaggerated and mostly coincidental rather than purposeful.

14   The Purpose of Stosch's *Paper Museum of Gems*

The large number of more than 3000 gem drawings discovered in Krakow and Berlin originating from Philipp von Stosch's corpus was certainly made on purpose. The correspondence and archival sources combined with the drawings suggest that the primary one was to document Stosch's own collection of engraved gems in visual form. Stosch's intention to have his gems documented as drawings is best illustrated by him reporting to Carl Gustav Heraeus on having 270 of his glass gems (or glass gems and glass pastes) drawn already in 1722 and hundreds more scheduled for pictorial documentation.[143] Among the discovered drawings in Krakow and Berlin, more than 1500 indeed reproduce Stosch's own gems and glass pastes (Figs 8.111–8.114). Even though the number is substantial, it is still just a fraction of the whole collection, which ultimately consisted of ca. 3500 objects. However, one must keep in mind that the rediscovered materials are a major part, but nevertheless only a part, of the original corpus. For example, as far as Odam and his documentary gem drawings made for Stosch alone are concerned, several hundred of his works appear to be missing.[144] Stosch's

---

138   Letter from Girolamo Odam to Anton Francesco Gori dated Rome 21 December 1738 – Epistolario di Anton Francesco Gori, no. 11123, volume BVI121, carte 8r–9v.
139   For example: Krakow Nos 412 and 413 and 664 and 665.
140   There are only 121 drawings by Preißler, Tuscher and Nagel presenting the same gems as Odam's drawings, cf. catalogues of Krakow and Berlin gem drawings in Appendix 2.
141   For example, a carnelian intaglio featuring a naked, kneeling soldier with a shield feeding his horse was drawn by Odam (Krakow No. 488), Preißler (Berlin vol. III, pl. 7) and Tuscher (Krakow No. 487). A glass gem with Cleobis and Biton drawing a chariot with their mother abord to the Temple of Hera was drawn by Odam (Krakow No. 1308), Preißler (Berlin vol. VI, pl. 9) and Tuscher (Krakow No. 1309). A carnelian presenting young athletes jumping over each other was drawn by Odam (Krakow No. 1545), Tuscher (Berlin vol. VI, pl. 95) and Preißler (Krakow No. 1510). A green chalcedony intaglio bearing Diomedes feeding his horses was drawn by Odam (Krakow No. 1970), Preißler (Krakow No. 1969) and Tuscher (Berlin vol. IV, pl. 78) too.

142   One finds a reproduction of an intaglio with a Persian satrap's head signed by Aethion (Krakow No. 1888) referring to Stosch 1724, pl. III (for which Odam made a drawing, see Berlin vol. V, pl. 72); the drawing of the lost intaglio presenting standing Cupid with the signature of Solon – Krakow No. 2066, referring to Stosch 1724, pl. LXIV (for which he made a drawing, see Berlin vol. II, pl. 102); the drawing of sard intaglio depicting a female Sphinx scratching its head with her leg signed by Thamyras (Krakow No. 1194), referring to Stosch 1724, pl. LXIX (for which Odam made a drawing, Berlin vol. V, pl. 15) and finally, the drawing of the cameo presenting the wedding of Cupid and Psyche signed by Tryphon (Krakow No. 2228), referring to Stosch 1724, pl. LXX (for which the drawing was made by Theodorus Netscher).
143   Schneider 1907, pp. 346–347; Hansson 2022, p. 63, n. 73.
144   Regarding gem drawings by Johann Justin Preißler, there could be more of them than those discovered in Krakow and Berlin as well. This is confirmed by several drawings bought by Schlichtegroll after the death of Johann Adam Schweickart (Schlichtegroll 1805, vol. I, pp. 12–13; Zazoff and Zazoff 1983, p. 181) as well as a group of 24 drawings attributed to Preißler made in pen, ink and wash measuring ca. 55 × 55 mm and 133 × 158 mm, which circulated on the art market in the twentieth century and whose fate is unknown, see: Auction Amsler and Ruthardt 1906,

collection of gems could have originally had more complete visual documentation. Based only on the available evidence alone – the statements of Stosch and Winckelmann that Stosch had had all his gems drawn – seem to hold much truth.[145] It has been proven that documentation of Stosch's gems started shortly after his arrival in Rome in 1715 and the first few hundreds of gems were documented by Odam. It is testified that the project was continued by all the draughtsmen hired by Stosch later down to, at least, Georg Abraham Nagel, who worked in the studio for sure in the early 1740s. This correlates well with organisation and classification of the collection, which apparently, according to Stosch's vision, should have had pictorial documentation. Stosch had also all his gems documented as sulphur impressions.[146]

Stosch was one of the very first collectors in history to systematically catalogue their assemblages of gems. Winckelmann made it known that when he started to write the catalogue of Stosch's gems, he was in a very privileged position because the material was already inventoried by Stosch himself and his brother – Heinrich Sigismund Stosch, at least to some extent.[147] His brother joined Stosch in 1727 in Rome and stayed with him in Florence until his death in 1747.[148] In 1731, Pier Leone Ghezzi presented him in one of his caricatures, preserved now in the Biblioteca Apostolica Vaticana, as seated in a chair examining coins brought by some man.[149] Stosch notices that his considerable geographical knowledge helped him to build his *Atlas*. It appears that, indeed, Heinrich Sigismund helped Stosch to organise the many gems, pastes and impressions in the collection, sorting them thematically and compiling Stosch's basic inventory list with brief descriptions of subject matter, information on provenance, reflections on iconography, analogies, etc. Together with Christian Dehn, Heinrich Sigismund assisted his brother in the production of impressions and casts of gems from various other collections that Stosch needed for reference purposes as well.[150] It is impossible to assess how considerable the help of Stosch's brother was in the classification of the collection, but the cooperation must have been fruitful because by 1747 ca. 2500 gems were already inventoried.[151] This is suggested by the description of Stosch's collection by Stosch himself and by a letter from Winckelmann to Christian Ludwig von Hagedorn; both sources confirm that ca. 2500 gems were already classified when Winckelmann was embarking on his own catalogue project.[152] It is highly possible that Heinrich Sigismund also helped a lot with organisation of the gem drawings, at least those produced by Johann Justin Preißler, Markus Tuscher and Georg Abraham Nagel (see above).

Stosch's own catalogue of his gem collection is now considered lost.[153] However, the information passed by Stosch and Winckelmann says much about its character. It appears to be an inventory list, surely helping to keep the gems in order. Most likely, it was written in French.[154] The intaglios were classified according to subject matters with mythological and historical sections and various subclasses. This basic structure has been preserved by Winckelmann while producing his *catalogue raisonné* of Stosch's gems, and thus, one more or less knows how the original Stosch's catalogue was designed.[155] It appears that it included little information about the engraving

---

lot 113: '*24 Blatt: Vergröserte Nachbildungen antiker Gemmen, 5,5/5,5 bis 13,1/15,8. Bleistift-, Tusch- und Federzeichnungen, einige auf blaues Papier.*' and Auction Max Perl 1937, lot 642: '*24 Zeichnungen nach antiken Gemmen, in Florenz für Baron Stosch gezeichnet, z. T. in vorgestochenem Rahmen. Nach 1 Zeichnung liegt 1 Stich bei. Feder- u. Tuschzeichnungen. 8°*.

145   Stosch 1757, p. 269; Winckelmann 1760, p. XXVII.
146   Which were sold at the auction in 1783 in Berlin following Muzell-Stosch's death, cf. Chapter 5, n. 19 here.
147   Winckelmann 1760, pp. I–II.
148   Stosch 1754, p. 6; Eggers 1926, p. 223; Borroni Salvadori 1978a, p. 606. Zazoff states that Heinrich Sigismund Stosch lived with his brother in Rome from 1722, which is rather a misunderstanding as no other source gives such an early date in contrast to 1727 (Zazoff and Zazoff 1983, p. 54).
149   The Biblioteca Apostolica Vaticana, Cod. Ott. lat. 3116, fol. 81.
150   Stosch 1754, p. 49; Hansson 2014, p. 21. Wilton and Bignamini (1996, p. 300, no. 262) even claim that Christian Dehn also contributed to the original catalogue of Stosch's gems, but there is no information supporting this claim in Stosch's or Winckelmann's correspondence and other archives. Of course, Stosch consulted his gem collection (especially impressions of gems) with Dehn, who probably helped with ordering the *dactyliotheca*, which apparently was classified according to subject matters, e.g. the same way as Stosch's gems were, see: Zazoff and Zazoff 1983, pp. 55–56.
151   Zazoff and Zazoff 1983, pp. 74–75.
152   Stosch 1757, pp. 268–270; Letter from Winckelmann to Christian Ludwig von Hagedorn dated 13 January 1759 – Winckelmann 1952–1957, vol. I, pp. 444–449, no. 262. These numbers are also confirmed by another source, a *Description of Stosch museo in Florence by Winckelmann to Mr. L.R.v.H.* in *Bibliothek der schönen Wissenschaften und der freyen Künste* 5, 1759, pp. 23–33 (reproduced in: Winckelmann 2013, pp. 363–365).
153   Borroni Salvadori 1978a, p. 612; Rügler in Winckelmann 2013, p. XVII. Stosch's own documentation, correspondence and archives were largely lost at sea during the unsuccessful transfer of his papers in 1863, see: Lewis 1967, pp. 325–326; Francisci Osti 2000, p. 100; Dorati da Empoli 2008, p. 62, n. 22.
154   Rügler in Winckelmann 2013, p. XVII.
155   Letter from Winckelmann to Muzell-Stosch dated 11 August 1759 – Winckelmann 1952–1957, vol. II, pp. 78–79, no. 292; Letter from Winckelmann to Muzell-Stosch dated 16 June 1759 – Winckelmann 1952–1957, vol. II, pp. 6–7, no. 279.

techniques and styles of gem engravers.[156] Stosch's manuscript catalogue is referred to in the following entries of Winckelmann's catalogue of Stosch's gems: class II, nos 534, 909 and 1768; class III, nos 226 and 247; class IV, nos 22, 26 and 83.[157]

As far as the drawings are concerned, it remains unclear if they were originally meant to be used later for production of illustrations as suggested by Winckelmann,[158] but they certainly could have been, which fact testifies to Stosch's outstanding ambitions. Even if the number of potential illustrations was enormous, one should recall that even bigger collections of drawings were originally conceived with a view to publication, like in the case of Cassiano dal Pozzo's gigantic *Paper Museum* or the Farnese gem collection was catalogued around 1730 with the prospect of being published as fully illustrated (cf. Chapter 3, p. 37), and some even were partially published, like that of Bernard de Montfaucon.[159] Moreover, the later efforts of, for instance Schlichtegroll, show that the drawings could be used to illustrate Stosch's gems in printed format.[160] The drawings originally put into simple line frames stuck down onto sheets of paper look like book illustrations ready to have some explanatory text to be added below them (which actually happened in many cases). However, the chosen format may be due to Stosch's considerable efforts to accurately display gems for their later analysis. His own book published in 1724 discussed 70 intaglios and cameos displayed on individual plates of incredible quality in order to present selected gems with attention to detail, showing also their imperfections and to reflect Stosch's idea that each gem engraver developed his own individual style. He possibly had the same idea in mind while commissioning visual documentation of his own gems. For sure, the drawings were very helpful in Stosch's studies of various techniques, styles and iconography.

The visual documentation of Stosch's own collection of engraved gems was one aim for building a substantial corpus or rather a *Paper Museum* of gem drawings. Another one was documenting intaglios and cameos from other contemporary cabinets. This was a vital part of Stosch's research and documentary practices. It was as important as amassing 28 000 sulphur gem impressions and casts, which were taken after intaglios and cameos from all major and minor European collections.[161] It is noteworthy that Stosch's impressions and drawings do not document as many of the same gems as would be expected, so they were complementary sources to each other.[162]

A list of collections Stosch accessed and used to reproduce their gems as drawings is long and can be recreated from either provenance information surviving on several dozens of drawings discussed above, as well as from the study of the depicted gems that could be identified today using various sources (catalogues of public and private collections, *dactyliothecae*, publications on engraved gems from the sixteenth to nineteenth centuries and those just including illustrations of intaglios and cameos, among others). Identification of the gems is a challenge due to a considerable loss of information because of the drawings' transfer onto new paper by Izabela Czartoryska around 1801 (in the case of the ones from Krakow) and composition of *Pierres gravées du roi avec figures* (in the case of those from Berlin). As a result, over 500 drawings represent gems identified as from other than Stosch's own collection, the majority of which are now lost. They belonged to the following, more or less contemporary to Stosch, cabinets (in alphabetical order), (Figs 8.115–8.118):[163] the Accademia Etrusca di Cortona,[164] Leonardo Agostini,[165] Alessandro Albani,[166] Baron Konrad Adolf

---

156 Rügler in Winckelmann 2013, p. XVII.
157 Justi 1956, vol. II, p. 309. Justi suggests that in the record Winckelmann 1760, class II, pp. 299–300, no. 1823 there is a reference to Stosch's original catalogue, but no such reference is noticed there. He also suggests that such a reference is provided in the record Winckelmann 1760, class IV, p. 444, no. 214 but it includes only a reference to Stosch's opinion through Gori's publication. I am grateful to Hadrien J. Rambach for the discussion on this issue.
158 Winckelmann 1760, p. XXVII.
159 On Cassiano dal Pozzo's *Paper Museum* and its potential publication, see: Herklotz 1999, pp. 262–265; Vaiani 2016, pp. 46–49. Bernard de Montfaucon's (1655–1741) enormous collection of ca. 30 000–40 000 prints and drawings of antiquities was partially used to illustrate his fifteen volumes of *L'antiquité expliquée et représentée en figures* between 1719 and 1724, see: Montfaucon 1719–1724.
160 Schlichtegroll 1805, vol. I, pp. 11–12.
161 On Stosch's sulphur impressions, cf. Chapter 5 n. 19 here.
162 Among the surviving drawings from Krakow alone (2268), only 328 have their twins among Stosch's sulphur impressions. The number of gems from collections other than Stosch's own is higher assuming that the unidentified gems did not permanently belong to him but were in other cabinets. After all, one only knows how many and what kind of gems Stosch possessed at the end of his life, but it is not known (except for a few exceptions) how many and what kind of gems passed through his hands during his lifetime.
163 For some general information and literature on the listed collectors and collections, cf. Appendix 2.
164 Krakow Nos 589, 674, 972 and 1996.
165 Krakow Nos 631 (1674), 686 (Berlin vol. III, 74; Picart (Stosch 1724, pl. XLV)), 1010 (Berlin vol. IV, pl. 41; Picart (Stosch 1724, pl. XLIX)), 1179, 1205, 1724, 1788 and 2111.
166 Krakow Nos 455, 1254 (Berlin vol. V, pl. 52/Picart (Stosch 1724, pl. LXIII)), 1377 ((1378–1380)/Picart (Stosch 1724, pl. LVI)), 2047? and Berlin vol. VI, pl. 63.

von Albrecht in Vienna,[167] Pietro Andrea Andreini,[168] Count Vicenzio Ansidei,[169] August II the Strong, Elector of Saxony,[170] Urbano III Barberini, Prince of Palestrina,[171] Giovanni Pietro Bellori,[172] the Bentinck collection,[173] William Ponsonby, 2nd Earl of Bessborough,[174] the Beverley collection,[175] the Boncompagni-Ludovisi collection,[176] Antonio Borioni,[177] Claude de Bourdaloue,[178] the Brühl collection,[179] Filippo Buonarroti,[180] James Byres,[181] Alessandro Gregorio Capponi,[182] Giovanni Carafa, Duke of Noia,[183] the Carlisle collection,[184] Giovanni Battista Casanova,[185] Anton Maria Castiglioni,[186] Anne Claude de Tubières-Grimoard de Pestels de Lévis Comte de Caylus,[187] Holy Roman Emperor Charles VI,[188] the Cerretani collection,[189] Michel Ange de la Chausse,[190] Francesca Cheroffini (née Gherardi),[191] the Chesterfield collection,[192] the Colonna collection,[193] Galeotto Ridolfino Corazzi,[194] Clayton Mordaunt Cracherode,[195] Girolamo Crispi,[196] Pierre Crozat,[197] Sir Edward Dering,[198] the Devonshire collection,[199] the Esterházy collection,[200] the Farnese collection,[201] Francesco de'Ficoroni,[202] Mr. De Franz collection at Vienna,[203] the French Royal collection,[204] Baron Thomas von Fritsch,[205] Niccolò Galeotti,[206] Sir John Germain,[207] the Gesura collection,[208] Guido, Duca della Gherardesca,[209] Pier Leone Ghezzi,[210] Baron Karl Heinrich von Gleichen-Rußwurm,[211] Anton Francesco Gori,[212] Sir William Hamilton,[213] Robert Harper,[214] Thomas Hollis,[215] Charles François Hutin,[216]

---

167 Krakow No. 1194 (Berlin vol. V, pl. 15).
168 Krakow Nos 13, 84, 253, 630, 680, 686 (Berlin vol. III, pl. 74/ Picart (Stosch 1724, pl. XLV)), 1029 (1045/Picart (Stosch 1724, pl. XXIII)), 1289 (Krakow No. 2165), 1812, 1921, 2078 (2144/Picart (Stosch 1724, pl. LIII)), 2231, Berlin vol. II, pls 20, 140, Berlin vol. IV, pl. 104 (Picart (Stosch 1724, pl. LXVIII)), Berlin vol. V, pl. 117 and Berlin vol. VI, pl. 48.
169 Krakow No. 1180.
170 Krakow Nos 80, 996 and 1758.
171 Krakow No. 391 (Picart (Stosch 1724, pl. X)).
172 Krakow No. 1520 (Berlin vol. VI, pl. 93).
173 Krakow Nos 111 and Berlin vol. III, pl. 37.
174 Krakow Nos 58, 245? 286 (Berlin vol. III, pl. 69), 304, 963, 1018 (1019), 1511 (1539), 1699, 1857? 1947, Berlin vol. II, pl. 54 and vol. V, pls 80, 83.
175 Krakow Nos 268, 1202, 1223, 1590, 1715, 2118 and 2266.
176 Krakow Nos 319 (320/Berlin vol. II, pl. 56), 1351, 1357 (Picart (Stosch 1724, pl. LXII)) and 1671 (Berlin vol. II, pl. 9).
177 Krakow Nos 327, 1516 (Berlin vol. VI, pl. 86) and 2158.
178 Krakow No. 122.
179 Krakow Nos 245? 1701, 2105, 2159 and Berlin vol. VI, pl. 153.
180 Krakow Nos 11, 253, 470, 571, 1339, 1798, 2212 and Berlin vol. IV, pl. 97.
181 Krakow No. 1548 and 2222.
182 Krakow Nos 152, 1003, 1670, 1759, 1784 and Berlin vol. I, pl. 21.
183 Krakow Nos 1151, 1202, 1790 (1809), 1792, 1794–1795, 1798–1799, 1807? and 1808?
184 Krakow Nos 75, 277, 633, 669, 841, 1002, 1136 (Berlin vol. IV, pl. 75), 1219 (1220, 1222), 1255, 1291, 1546 (1556–1557/Picart (Stosch 1724, pl. XVI)), 1668, 1745, 1991, 2141 (Picart (Stosch 1724, pl. VI)), Berlin vol. II, pl. 12 (Picart (Stosch 1724, pl. XXXVI)), Berlin vol. III, pl. 35, Berlin vol. IV, pl. 85, Berlin vol. V, pl. 53, Picart (Stosch 1724, pl. LXVI) and Berlin vol. VI, pl. 58.
185 Krakow No. 1904.
186 Krakow No. 1377 ((1378–1380)/Picart (Stosch 1724, pl. LVI)).
187 Krakow Nos 542 1607 (1800) and Berlin vol. V, pl. 93.
188 Krakow Nos 501, 1113, 1194, 1278, 1757, 1909 and Berlin vol. I, pl. 57 and Berlin vol. V, pl. 31 (Picart (Stosch 1724, pl. LI)).
189 Krakow Nos 910, 2066 (Berlin vol. II, pl. 102/Picart (Stosch 1724, pl. LXIV)) and 2247.
190 Krakow Nos 43–44, 91, 202, 278 (Berlin vol. III, pl. 67), 283, 298? 384 (Berlin vol. I, pl. 130), 430, 585, 627, 663 (Berlin vol. III, pl. 68), 1225 (Berlin vol. V, pl. 35), 1320 (Berlin vol. II, pl. 24), 1492, 1840, 1864, 1884, 2070, Berlin vol. III, pls 40, 100, Berlin vol. V, pl. 129 and Berlin vol. VI, pl. 118.
191 Krakow Nos 1055, 2047? and Berlin vol. VI, pl. 63.
192 Krakow Nos 58–59 and 286 (Berlin vol. III, pl. 69).
193 Krakow Nos 392 (393).
194 Krakow No. 1340.
195 Krakow Nos 1238 and 1548.
196 Krakow Nos 1136 (Berlin vol. IV, pl. 75) and 1291.
197 Krakow Nos 627, 1590? 2054 and Berlin vol. III, pl. 44.
198 Krakow No. 455.
199 Krakow Nos 1132 (Berlin vol. IV, pl. 76/Picart (Stosch 1724, pl. IX)), 1354 (Berlin vol. VI, pl. 65/Picart (Stosch 1724, pl. II)), 1382 (1383–1384/Berlin vol. VI, pl. 16/Picart (Stosch 1724, pl. LIV)), 1558 (Berlin vol. III, pl. 1), 1619 (1620/Berlin vol. VI, pl. 140/ Picart (Stosch 1724, pl. XI)), 1888 (1889/Berlin vol. V, pl. 72), 2183, Berlin vol. III, pls 35? and Berlin vol. V, pl. 72.
200 Krakow No. 1725 (Berlin vol. VI, pl. 66).
201 Krakow Nos 3, 5, 60, 116 (117 and Berlin vol. I, pl. 4), 296 (Berlin vol. II, pl. 14/Picart (Stosch 1724, pl. XII)), 333 (335), 416, 659, 664 (665), 1228, 1256 (Picart (Stosch 1724, pl. XXX)), 1257, 1458, 1938 (Berlin vol. V, pl. 124), 1997, 2087, 2146, Berlin vol. I, pl. 101, Berlin vol. III, pl. 32 and Berlin vol. VI, pl. 56.
202 Krakow Nos 50 (55), 612, 671, 809, 1003, 1518 (Berlin vol. VI, pl. 102), 1520 (Berlin vol. VI, pl. 93), 1933, 2221, Berlin vol. V, pl. 57 and Berlin vol. VI, pl. 73.
203 Krakow No. 288.
204 Krakow Nos 69, 74, 578, 1168, 1237, 1347 Picart (Stosch 1724, pl. XXXIII), 1350 (Picart (Stosch 1724, pl. XXVII)), 1669 (Berlin vol. VI, pl. 13), 1884, Berlin vol. II, pls 36 and 145, Berlin vol. III, pl. 44, Berlin vol. IV, pl. 52 (Picart (Stosch 1724, pl. XL)), Berlin vol. V, pl. 82 and Berlin vol. VI, pl. 55.
205 Krakow No. 453.
206 Krakow No. 1340.
207 Krakow No. 2228 (Picart (Stosch 1724, pl. LXX)).
208 Krakow No. 276.
209 Nos 398? 1799 and Berlin vol. IV, pl. 15?
210 Krakow Nos 377, 458, 635, 709, 723, 727, 729 and 776.
211 Krakow No. 2047.
212 Krakow Nos 274, 278 (Berlin vol. III, pl. 67) and 565.
213 Krakow Nos 1151, 1790 (1809), 1792, 1794–1795 and 1798–1799.
214 Krakow No. 391 (Picart (Stosch 1724, pl. X)).
215 Krakow Nos 2098 and 2137.
216 Krakow No. 1343 (Berlin vol. VI, pl. 45).

Józef Aleksander Jabłonowski,[217] the Museo Kircheriano in the Collegio Romano collection,[218] the City of Leipzig collection,[219] Giovanni Pietro Lucatelli,[220] Hendrik Adriaan van de Mark *heer* van Leur,[221] the Marlborough collection,[222] the Massimo collection,[223] the Medici collection,[224] Gabriel Medina,[225] Giovanni Carlo Molinari,[226] Henry Mordaunt, 2nd Earl of Peterborough,[227] August Moszyński (1731–1786),[228] Lorenz Natter,[229] Girolamo Odam,[230] the Odescalchi collection,[231] William IV, Prince of Orange,[232] Philippe II, Duke de Orléans,[233] Cardinal Pietro Ottoboni,[234] Francesco Palazzi,[235] Onofrio Pini,[236] a private collection in England,[237] the Prussian Royal collection,[238] Carlo della Torre di Rezzonico,[239] the Riccardi collection,[240] Cardinal Ferdinando de Rossi,[241] Marcoantonio Sabbatini,[242] Lothar-Franz von Schönborn,[243] Reginaldo Sellari,[244] François Sévin,[245] Duke of Stiualis (?) in Rome,[246] Philipp von Stosch,[247] Cardinal Leone Strozzi,[248] Frederick de Thoms,[249] Giovanni Domenico Tiepolo,[250] Prior Anton Maria Vaini,[251] Ridolfino Venuti,[252] Francesco Vettori,[253] Count Mihály Viczay of Hédervár,[254] the Vitelleschi-Verospi

---

217 Krakow Nos 433–434?
218 Krakow No. 925.
219 Krakow Nos 582, 872, 880, 1749, 2032, 2089 and Berlin vol. III, pl. 39.
220 Krakow No. 1346.
221 Krakow Nos 446 and 1382 (1383–1384/Berlin vol. VI, pl. 16/Picart (Stosch 1724, pl. IV)).
222 Krakow Nos 2, 58, 123, 245? 286 (Berlin vol. III, pl. 69), 304, 444, 455, 559, 569, 684, 903, 957 (Berlin IV, pl. 28), 963, 1018 (1019), 1167 (Berlin vol. IV, pl. 99/Picart (Stosch 1724, pl. I)), 1511 (1539), 1588, 1699, 1743, 1857? 1947, 2019, Krakow No. 2228 (Picart (Stosch 1724, pl. LXX)), Berlin vol. I, pl. 22, Berlin vol. II, pl. 54, Berlin vol. V, pls 80 and 83.
223 Krakow No. 1673 (Berlin vol. VI, pl. 54/Picart (Stosch 1724, pl. XXV)) and Berlin vol. III, pl. 39.
224 Krakow Nos 3, 13, 63, 78, 84? 145 (Berlin vol. I, pl. 121), 149 (Berlin vol. I, pl. 122), 175, 212, 223, 253, 274, 282, 294, 300, 333 (335), 386, 399, 403–404, 416, 424 (425), 538, 544, 565, 576, 630–631 (1674), 641, 644, 646, 650 (651), 659, 663 (Berlin vol. III, pl. 68)–664 (665), 680, 686 (Berlin vol. III, pl. 74/ Picart (Stosch 1724, pl. XLV)), 898 (1023/Berlin vol. IV, pl. 11/Picart (Stosch 1724, pl. XXII)), 905, 912, 959, 965, 971 (974), 976, 1010 (Berlin vol. IV, pl. 41/Picart (Stosch 1724, pl. XLIX)), 1012? 1065, 1103, 1130 (Berlin vol. V, pl. 13), 1133, 1179, 1229, 1266 (Berlin vol. III, pl. 12), 1289 (Krakow No. 2165)? 1306 (Berlin vol. V, pl. 46), 1315, 1329, 1575, 1582, 1664, 1668, 1674, 1678–1679 (Berlin vol. VI, pl. 48), 1724, 1754–1756, 1780, 1782, 1788, 1812, 1921, 1936, 1997, 2046, 2077, 2078 (2144/Picart (Stosch 1724, pl. LIII)), 2111, 2146, 2151, 2212? 2231? Berlin vol. I, pls 23, 48? 59, Berlin vol. II, pls 20, 91, Berlin vol. III, pls 12, 32, 57, 83, Berlin vol. IV, pls 64, 88, 104 (Picart (Stosch 1724, pl. LXVIII)), Berlin vol. V, pl. 91 and Berlin vol. VI, pls 26, 48.
225 Krakow Nos 220? 224, 245? 304, 456, 744? 871, 1511 (1539), 1857? Berlin vol. I, pls 22, 46, Berlin vol. V, pl. 83 and Berlin vol. VI, pl. 7.
226 Krakow Nos 957 (Berlin IV, pl. 28) and 1167 (Berlin vol. IV, pl. 99/ Picart (Stosch 1724, pl. I)).
227 Krakow No. 2228 (Picart (Stosch 1724, pl. LXX)).
228 Krakow No. 137.
229 Krakow Nos 1588 and 1699.
230 Krakow Nos 18? 52, 171, 250, 274, 306, 395, 454, 473, 569, 635, 637, 670, 734, 904, 957 (Berlin IV, pl. 28), 995, 1104, 1210, 1277, 1288, 1515, 1651, 1881, 1885, 2115, 2163, 2168, 2253, Berlin vol. I, pl. 138, Berlin vol. II, pl. 117, Berlin vol. III, pls 51, 53, Berlin vol. IV, pls 16, 114 and Berlin vol. VI, pls 85, 107–108.
231 Krakow Nos 32, 419, 887, 1546 (1556–1557/Picart (Stosch 1724, pl. XVI)), 1590? and 2058.

232 Krakow Nos 102, 189, 251, 1262, 1540, 1673 (Berlin vol. VI, pl. 54/ Picart (Stosch 1724, pl. XXV)), 1893 and Berlin vol. I, pl. 39.
233 Krakow Nos 91, 627, 987, 1236, 1590? 1678, 2054, Berlin vol. II, pl. 68 and Berlin vol. III, pl. 100.
234 Krakow Nos 641, 646, 1002, Berlin vol. V, pl. 53 and 1219 (1220, 1222), Picart (Stosch 1724, pl. LXVI).
235 Krakow No. 1893 and Berlin vol. VI, pl. 32.
236 Krakow No. 1759.
237 Krakow No. 157.
238 Krakow Nos 608, 1107, 1124 and 1234 (1235).
239 Krakow No. 20.
240 Krakow Nos 114, 910 and 1195 (Berlin vol. V, pl. 17).
241 Krakow No. 1885.
242 Krakow Nos 102? 189, 321, 442, 1254 (Berlin vol. V, pl. 52/Picart (Stosch 1724, pl. LXIII)), 1372, Berlin vol. II, pl. 141 and Berlin vol. VI, pls 47–48.
243 Picart (Stosch 1724, pl. LV).
244 Krakow No. 1627.
245 Krakow No. 1132 (Berlin vol. IV, pl. 76/Picart (Stosch 1724, pl. IX)) and Picart (Stosch 1724, pl. XXIX).
246 Berlin vol. I, pl. 40.
247 But left his collection prior to 1760 – Krakow Nos 760, 823, 1018 (1019), 1066, 1151, 1298, 1453, 1516 (Berlin vol. VI, pl. 86), 1588, 1619 (1620/Berlin vol. VI, pl. 140/Picart (Stosch 1724, pl. XI)), 1699, 1790 (1809), 1792, 1794–1795, 1798–1799, 1807? 1808? 2202, Berlin vol. III, pl. 35 and Berlin vol. VI, pl. 13.
248 Krakow Nos 131, 309 (Berlin vol. III, pl. 99/Picart (Stosch 1724, pl. XVIII)), 321, 605, 679, 711, 916 (Berlin vol. IV, pl. 33/Picart (Stosch 1724, pl. LVIII)), 954 (Berlin vol. IV, pl. 27/Picart (Stosch 1724, pl. XX)), 1029 (1045/Picart (Stosch 1724, pl. XXIII)), 1191, 1205, 1254 (Berlin vol. V, pl. 52/Picart (Stosch 1724, pl. LXIII)), 1348, 1374 (1375), 1483, 1629, 1707, 1786 (Berlin vol. I, pl. 45), 2139, Berlin vol. I, pl. 42, Berlin vol. III, pls 54, 73 and Berlin vol. VI, pl. 51.
249 Krakow Nos 18, 102? 189, 251, 324, 1262, 1357, 1540, 1673 (Berlin vol. VI, pl. 54/Picart (Stosch 1724, pl. XXV)), Berlin vol. I, pl. 39, Berlin vol. II, pl. 141, Berlin vol. V, pl. 93 and Berlin vol. VI, pls 7, 32.
250 Krakow No. 1061 (1062–1063).
251 Krakow Nos 161? 1687 and Berlin vol. I, pl. 59.
252 Krakow Nos 1340, 1892? and (Berlin vol. V, pl. 74).
253 Krakow Nos 306, 597, 1277, 1310, 1524, 1554, 1581, 1730, 1874, 1911, 1986 and Berlin vol. II, pl. 89.
254 Krakow No. 1234 (1235).

collection,[255] Friedrich Vitzthum von Eckstädt,[256] Joseph Anton Gabaleon von Wackerbarth-Salmour,[257] Johan Hendrik Graf van Wassenaer-Opdam,[258] Joseph Wenzel I, Prince of Liechtenstein,[259] Jacob Benedict Winckler,[260] Anton Maria Zanetti[261] and Apostolo Zeno.[262]

The identification and provenance studies of the gems documented in the drawings reveal Stosch's impressive network of contacts which was of a large scale.[263] The gem drawings prove useful for the reconstruction of a much more in-depth image of collecting of engraved gems in Stosch's times than was previously known. Like in the case of his sulphur impressions, over the years, Stosch accessed thousands of gems, not only from the well-known cabinets, which were often accessible only to the best connoisseurs of ancient art, but he also documented gems from small, even more challenging to access, scarcely known cabinets. Due to his reputation as the best connoisseur of intaglios and cameos, Stosch often received impressions and other reproductions of gems from fellow collectors, but all the names listed above also reflect Stosch's extensive travelling and visits in many major European cities, where he met collectors and enthusiasts of intaglios and cameos like himself. Finally, the list confirms the high importance of Stosch's contacts with Cardinal Alessandro Albani and all major English collectors. Stosch worked as an agent for some of them and the numerous gems documented as drawings in his corpus suggest that he supplied the collections of Lords Bessborough, Carlisle, Devonshire and Marlborough, among others, with intaglios and cameos. In the case of the Duke of Devonshire, Stosch sold him many gems, as documented by his letters preserved at Chatsworth.[264] Furthermore, perhaps it should be postulated that many of the drawings document gems which once were in Stosch's possession, but they were later re-sold to his clients. For example, the list above includes such names as August II the Strong, Elector of Saxony and those from the Elector's circle, like Friedrich Vitzthum von Eckstädt, Baron Thomas von Fritsch, Charles François Hutin and Count Heinrich von Brühl. While Stosch was appointed the royal antiquary at the court in Dresden,[265] he may have supplied the monarch (and his circle) with gems. Likewise, Stosch's work as an art advisor to the Emperor in Vienna may have resulted in the supply of gems for his collection, but also establishment of valuable contacts and selling gems and other antiquities to the local collectors in Vienna, like Baron von Albrecht and Mr. De Franz. For sure a portion, maybe even a substantial one, of the unidentified gems reproduced in the drawings constitutes intaglios and cameos Stosch once might have owned but later sold, exchanged or gifted to others.

The provenance study of gems documented in the drawings also reveals that many of those now housed in a variety of public museums have illustrious pedigree reaching at least the eighteenth century. Thanks to the gem drawings, it is also possible to determine the fate of some collections dispersed in the times of Stosch, and they facilitate the discovery of some cabinets from which Stosch incorporated gems into his own assemblage (Figs 8.119–8.122). For example, regarding the Michel Ange de la Chausse collection of intaglios and cameos,[266] its fate after the collector's death can be now much better reconstructed. So far, it was believed that ca. 200 of La Chausse's gems were bequeathed in his will to Pierre Crozat.[267] However, recently Zwierlein-Diehl has discovered that this applies only to a major part of the collection, while some gems were dispersed on the art market, surely shortly after his death in 1724.[268] Indeed, Stosch managed to buy some intaglios once owned by La Chausse, while the others were purchased by the Duke of Orléans, Pierre Crozat and some even ended up in the French royal collection (cf. above). Another interesting case is Marcoantonio Sabbatini, who was one of the most important connoisseurs and collectors of gems at the time of Stosch's activities in Rome. As evidenced by the identification and provenance studies, he frequently traded gems with Stosch. Some of those from his collection were documented as drawings by Stosch, and they ultimately entered Stosch's cabinet, most likely after Sabbatini's death and dispersal of his gems in 1727 (cf. above).[269] Another famous connoisseur of

---

255 Krakow No. 259, 444, 1167 (Berlin vol. IV, pl. 99/Picart (Stosch 1724, pl. I)) and 1185.
256 Krakow No. 1153, 1278 and Berlin vol. II, pl. 7.
257 Krakow No. 1055.
258 Krakow No. 446.
259 Krakow No. 50 (55).
260 Krakow No. 252? 880, 982, 1749 and Berlin vol. III, pl. 39.
261 Krakow Nos 71, 1263, Berlin vol. IV, pl. 104 (Picart (Stosch 1724, pl. LXVIII)).
262 Krakow No. 1516 (Berlin vol. VI, pl. 86).
263 On Stosch's network of contacts, see: Lang 2007 and chapters 1–2 in this volume.
264 For example: Stosch's letters to William Cavendish, 2nd Duke of Devonshire dated 13 March 1728 (CS1/188.1 13), another dated 24 July 1728 (CS1/188.3), the one dated 18 September 1728 (CS1/188.5) and 17 February 1729 (CS1/188.8).

265 Hansson 2014, p. 16.
266 On that collection, cf. Chapter 2 here.
267 Kagan and Neverov 2000, pp. 64–69.
268 Zwierlein-Diehl 2023, p. 448.
269 Ubaldelli 2001, p. 80. Or shortly afterwards as suggested by Stosch in his letter to William Cavendish, 2nd Duke of Devonshire, dated Rome 5 February 1729 (Chatsworth, the Devonshire Archives, inv. no.: CS1/188.7), where he says that he was waiting

gems and antiquities from whom Stosch purchased gems and consulted them was Francesco de'Ficoroni (Krakow No. 1518).[270] As to the collection built by Girolamo Odam, one of Stosch's closest collaborators during his two stays in Rome, while Stosch may have exchanged gems with him on a regular basis, it seems likely that after Odam's death in 1740 he bought some of his intaglios as well, while the other part of that cabinet was overtaken by Stosch's rival Frederick de Thoms.[271]

Finally, around 1000 drawings commissioned by Stosch depict gems that remain unidentified among contemporary public and private collections. Most of them are probably lost gems that circulated on the art market in the times of Stosch. In most of the cases, their drawings are the only testimonies to their existence, which makes Stosch's visual documentation of gems an even more valuable source of information, and it proves his documenting activities to be of crucial importance not only for him but also future generations (Figs 8.123–8.126).

All in all, documenting gems from various cabinets as drawings was an important aspect of Stosch's collecting and scholarly activities. The drawings could have been used as references to the gems from Stosch's own cabinet, e.g. analogies. Moreover, Stosch was also consulted on intaglios and cameos by various collectors at his house and through constant correspondence. Thus, the gem drawings of his own gems as well as those from other collections constituted a database in which he gathered useful information that he later used for meetings with his clients and their inquiries as well as for his personal studies.[272] This is well illustrated by his letter to Paolo Maria Paciaudi (1710–1785) dated Florence, 26 January 1743, in which Stosch replies to the inquiry of two intriguing gems: '*Among my drawings and gems I find nothing like the following two things which could serve the purpose. The first is a fragment of a beautiful ancient sardonyx cameo, as far as I can say, according to what the replicas of similar intaglios and cameos teach us, must have represented a sleeping Bacchus. A putto holds a fan to make wind, the other plays the lyre, etc. The other one is a copy of a part of a large design which I had before my eyes with the colours of ancient painting, discovered in the year 1724 in Rome in the Farnese gardens on the Palatine Hill.*'[273] Gem impressions, although sometimes more faithful, accurate and replicable, were still of very small size. The drawings presented what was engraved upon gems considerably enlarged – a far more useful and convenient way if one wanted to analyse techniques, styles and iconography of individual pieces and compare groups. Additionally, the fact that not many drawings, after all, depict the same gems as Stosch's sulphur impressions means they were made for documentary purposes in principle, but at the same time they could be easily transformed into a publication of some sort. Stosch was constantly expanding his knowledge about glyptics and the visual documentation of gems from his own and other collections certainly helped him to widen his horizons on this matter and make better observations and analyses during his studies.

Stosch commissioned drawings of gems not only for his personal use but also to send them attached to his correspondence. The drawings were less fragile than impressions and casts so they had better chances of surviving their transportation, even though they were certainly more expensive to produce and somehow less reliable, but probably sufficient enough to discuss the matters of particular iconographies or to ask if a client would like to buy a specific gem or not, etc. Several of 10 unpublished letters of Stosch sent to William Cavendish, 2nd Duke of Devonshire, which survive at Chatsworth, give us a unique insight into how the gem drawings were attached to the letters, either to discuss individual gems or advertise them

---

for the nephew and heir of Ottoboni to run out of money, which would force him to sell inherited collections for lower prices than currently asked.

270 Ridley (2017, p. 22) claims that Ficoroni was the main source of Stosch's Roman gems. These two were indeed close, since on his deathbed Ficoroni gave Stosch an admirable gem showing a man putting on a mask (Ridley 2017, p. 150). On the relationship between Stosch and Ficoroni, see: Ridley 2017, pp. 261–262.

271 For a reconstruction and comprehensive study of Odam's cabinet of engraved gems, see: Gołyźniak 2023b.

272 They were certainly often used in the same way as his gem impressions in sulphur, wax and glass. For example, in his letter to William Cavendish, 2nd Duke of Devonshire, dated Rome 28 August 1728 (Chatsworth, the Devonshire Archives, inv. no.: CS1/188.4), Stosch states that he keeps a number of impressions of gems with inscriptions to show his visitors and clients the difference between those with signatures and those inscribed with the names of their owners or informing about the identity of the depicted figure.

273 Letter from Stosch to Paolo Maria Paciaudi dated Florence 26 January 1743: '*Fra li miei disegni e gemme non trovo altro delle due seguenti cose che servir po tranno al suo intento. Il primo è un frammento d'un bellissimo cammeo antico di sardonica del mio studio che, secondo che ci insegnano le ripetizioni di simili gemme intagliate e intere, doveva rappresentare un Bacco dormiente. Un putto tiene in mano un ventaglio per farli vento; l'altro suona la lira etc. L'altro è copia di parte d'un gran disegno ch'io feci sotto li miei occhi fare colli colori della pittura antica, che fu scoperta l'anno 1724 in Roma nelli orti farnesiani sul monte palatino.*', (FINA Wiki Database (ID 7224), https://fina.oeaw.ac.at/wiki/index.php/Philipp_von_Stosch_-_Paolo_Maria_Paciaudi_-_1743-1-26 [retrieved on 16 November 2022]; Justi 1871, pp. 15–16.

for sale.²⁷⁴ For example, in his letter sent from Rome on 24 July 1728, Stosch writes that he has a print of a gem featuring a head of a satyr signed by Lucius of the same size as the drawing he had attached to this letter, and he thinks the gem to be a forgery.²⁷⁵ The drawing in question must have depicted the same gem as Krakow No. 1023, which testifies that Stosch had multiple drawings of the same gem made either for the sake of his personal archive and to use them in correspondence for business purposes as well. In another letter sent from Rome on 9 October 1728 to the Duke, Stosch actually acts as his agent. He claims that no interesting antiquities had been recently found in Rome except a sardonyx cameo, of which Stosch attached a drawing of the same size and colour as the original. He also says that the Grand Prior Anton Maria Vaini offered 150 scudi for it, but the current owner was asking for at least 200 since he paid 130 himself.²⁷⁶ These letters show that Stosch's employment of numerous artists to draw gems and other antiquities for him was not only for the sake of his private archive, but it was also a business decision. Sending images of what he had to offer certainly stimulated his success in dealing in antiquities a great deal. Stosch acquired particular appreciation for having his drawings to be exceptionally accurate, which helped him to build his position as a trustworthy art seller.

In a similar vein, Stosch distributed prints presenting particularly important gems, which is proved by the very special drawing of Strozzi Medusa by Girolamo Odam discussed above after which prints were made. This is confirmed by one of them which survives in the fifth volume of *Pierres gravées du roi avec figures* in Berlin.²⁷⁷ One more such case was a publication of a sard intaglio from Stosch's collection depicting Meleager with two spears presenting the head of the Calydonian Boar at the shrine of Artemis, with dogs at his feet (Krakow No. 1221) (Figs 8.127–8.128). Adolf Furtwängler, believed that the gem was in fact cut in the eighteenth century after an ancient prototype from 2nd–1st century BC, which remains lost.²⁷⁸ According to the captions on the print, the drawing of that gem was made by Pier Leone Ghezzi (*Eques Petrus Leo Ghezzius desin.*), while Vincenzo Franchesini later engraved it (*Vincentius Franceschini sculp*). The very rich and elaborate mount was drawn and engraved by Girolamo Odam (*Hier. Eques Odam inci. et scul.*). An interesting commentary of Pierre-Jean Mariette related to that very print appears in his book published in 1750. Mariette says: '*What M. de Stosch had begun to engrave in Italy, and which has not been made public, was, in my opinion, much better. I have only seen two plates of it, of which he gave me proofs in 1718, at the time when I was in Vienna with Prince Eugene of Savoy, and I do not know if he had had some engraved in greater numbers. The one executed in the drawing of Chevalier Ghezzi represents Méléager, and the stone, which is of singular beauty, but without the name of the engraver, belonged to M. de Stosch; the other is the famous head of Medusa, from the Cabinet of Strozzi, drawn by Chevalier Odam.*'²⁷⁹ Mariette certainly refers to the print with the Meleager gem under discussion here, which must have been made prior to 1718. His commentary demonstrates that Stosch commissioned illustrations of individual pieces that he later distributed among his peers.²⁸⁰

Once exiled to Florence, Stosch still gifted such special flyers to numerous visitors of his house-museum. What is more, Stosch was an active member of *Società Colombaria*, Accademia Etrusca in Cortona and *Società del Museo Fiorentino*, among others. He also financed the journal *Giornale de' Letterati*.²⁸¹ He sent drawings, engravings, prints, impressions and casts of the objects from his collections to discuss them at the meetings, especially the well-known *Notti Coritane* of the Accademia Etrusca in Cortona.²⁸² In the holdings of the Princes Czartoryski

---

274   I am very much indebted to Kenneth Lapatin for the introduction to Sash Giles, who informed me about those unpublished letters that proved to be very helpful and illuminating on many aspects regarding Stosch and his gem drawings, as well as the gems he discussed and sold to the Duke of Devonshire.
275   Chatsworth, the Devonshire archives, inv. no.: CS1/188.3. Stosch also attached to this letter a drawing of a very beautiful bas-relief in '*Marmo Palombino*', about a foot tall, representing Apollo and Marsyas as well as drawings of two antique vases in '*pietra dura*'.
276   Chatsworth, the Devonshire archives, inv. no.: CS1/188.6.
277   Berlin vol. V, pl. 52. Especially after his exile to Florence, where Stosch entered the learned circles of local antiquarians, see: Chłędowski 1935, pp. 674–675; Bruschetti 1985–1986, pp. 10–11; Borroni Salvadori 1978a, pp. 575, 587–588 and 604; Hansson 2014, p. 22; Hansson 2020, p. 61.
278   Furtwängler 1896, no. 9296.
279   Mariette 1750, p. 332: 'Ce que M. de Stosch avoit commencer de faire graver en Italie, & qui n'a point été rendu public, valoit selon moi, beaucoup mieux. Je n'en ai vû que deux Planches, dont il me donna des épreuves en 1718. dans le tems que j'étois à Vienne auprès de M. le Prince Eugène de Savoie, & j'ignore s'il en avoit fait graver un plus grand nombre. L'une exécutée sur le Dessin du Chevalier Ghezzi, représente Méléagre, dont la Pierre qui est d'une singulière beauté, mais qui est sans nom de Graveur, appartenoit à M. de Stosch; l'autre est la fameuse tête de Méduse, du Cabinet de Strozzi, dessiné par le Chevalier Odam.'
280   Indeed, such practices made some of Stosch's gems famous and his Meleager intaglio is the best example of that, as stated by Winckelmann in his letter to Christian Ludwig von Hagedorn dated Florence 13 January 1759: 'Ich könnte den berühmten Meleager anführen, welcher in Kupfer gestochen und bekannt ist.' – Winckelmann 1952–1957, vol. I, p. 446, no. 262.
281   Cristofani 1983, p. 79; Micheli 1986, p. 41.
282   Chłędowski 1935, pp. 674–675; Hansson 2014, p. 22.

Museum in Krakow, there are several engravings illustrating this phenomenon. For example, Krakow No. 1180 represents – considered the best of all Stosch's gems, a true masterpiece – an Etruscan scarab carved around 500–480 BC in carnelian with a scene of a meeting of Five out of Seven against Thebes (Figs 8.129–8.130). It was discovered before 1742 in a burial near Perugia and received much attention due to its exceptional quality and intriguing inscriptions referring to the names of the depicted heroes, which were disputed to be in the Etruscan, Greek or Pelasgian languages.[283] The gem is now in the Antikensammlung, Staatliche Museen zu Berlin.[284] The engraving was made on Stosch's commission by Schweickart who, according to the information at the bottom of the page (*I.A. Schweickart fc.*), might have also been the author of a drawing prepared for print. The very elaborate format of his work with a long, learned commentary suggests that it was made as an individual project executed in 1756, shortly after the scarab entered Stosch's collection as a gift of the Count Vicenzio Ansidei, and was called *Gemma Stosch* since then.[285] Similarly, another masterpiece of Etruscan glyptic art in Stosch's collection, the carnelian scarab bearing Tydeus pulling a thorn out of his leg and inscription: TVTE – referring to hero's name – was clearly advertised in the same way (Figs 8.73–8.74).[286] The idea was to publish a sort of flyer introducing these exceptional pieces to the members of the learned societies in Florence and beyond.[287]

Last but not least, it ought to be believed that such a considerable production of gem drawings as commissioned by Stosch, especially of gems from collections other than his own, was also done to realise some potential publishing projects. For example, in the preface of his book, *Gemmae antiquae caelatae*, he informs about his plans to write a study on glass pastes for which he would need some illustrations for sure.[288] He also offered his services in publishing to other collectors of gems. Particularly valuable evidence in this matter comes to us from Stosch's letter sent from Rome on 5 February 1729 to William Cavendish, 2nd Duke of Devonshire.[289] Judging from his previous letters to the Duke, Stosch established an important bond with him acting as his agent in Rome, discussing gems and other antiquities and offering them for sale among others. In this letter, though, Stosch says that if one has spent a lot of money on wonderful gems, one should publish them in a manner fitting with the refined taste of the century. He attached to the letter a drawing made in haste in just one morning but if it pleases His Grace, Stosch asks to send him impressions of other gems he owns so that he could have them drawn by the same artist (Johann Justin Preißler – cf. below) under his own watchful eye. In addition, Stosch adds that if His Grace wishes, he could get them engraved to a good standard for a relatively small cost compared to that in England. He would himself, with pleasure, take on attaching concise explanations.

In his next letter to the Duke of Devonshire sent from Rome on 17 February 1729,[290] one learns that the drawing sent before was made by Johann Justin Preißler and it depicted a red jasper intaglio with a bust of '*la Ruffine*'.[291] Stosch attached here a drawing of another gem, featuring Nike sacrificing a bull, of which he had a good impression in his collection of sulphurs. He then asks if His Grace likes this style of drawing because, if that is the case, he may continue with it once he receives from the Duke

---

283   Gori 1742, p. CXXVIII; Justi 1872, pp. 341–342; Zazoff 1974; Zazoff and Zazoff 1983, pp. 58–63; Micheli 1984; Kagan 2006, pp. 89–90; Harloe 2013, pp. 81–82; Hansson 2014, pp. 23–24.
284   AGDS II, no. 237; Zwierlein-Diehl 2007, ill. 311 (with more literature).
285   Hansson 2014, p. 23.
286   AGDS II, no. 238; Zwierlein-Diehl 2007, ill. 317 (with more literature). Winckelmann (1760, class III, no. 174, pp. 348–350) thought that the hero is removing a spear from his leg and he believed the gem to be the most beautiful of all Etruscan gems and comparable to the best works of Greek artists, engraved in the 'high style' of great perfection, which meant it could be regarded as one of the oldest gems in the world. The engraving of the *Tydeus Gem* by Schweickart is undated, but it is likely to be executed alongside the one of *Gemma Stosch* in 1756. It was surely made prior to 1759 as both engravings are mentioned by Winckelmann in his letter to Christian Ludwig von Hagedorn dated Florence, 13 January 1759 (Winckelmann 1952–1957, vol. I, p. 446, no. 262): '*Die seltensten Steine sind überhaupt die hetrurischen: Mann kann von deren Werth urtheilen, aus dem, was über ein einziges Stüdt von einem hetrurischen Steine im königl. Französischen cabinet gesaget ist. Unter diesen aber sind die vornehmsten zween Carniole: der eine stellet fünfe von den Sieben Helden vor, die den ersten Zug wider Theben thaten, nämlich den Tydeus, Polynices, Amphiaraus, Udrastus und Parthenopäus; zu jeder Figur ist der Name in der ältesten hetrurischen oder pelasgischen Schrift geschnitten. Der andere zeiget den Tydeus mit dessen Namen, wie er sich einen Pfeil aus dem Fuße zeihet. Beyde warden zum erstmal in Kupfer gestochen auf mef meiner angeführten Schrift erscheinen.*'
287   Hansson 2014, p. 23. According to Justi: '*of every gem [Stosch] bought, of every coin and bronze, he sent impressions, drawings, descriptions to the Academy of Cortona*' – Justi 1871, p. 25: '*Von jeder Gemme, die er kaufte, von jeder Münze und Bronze sandte er Abdrücke, Zeichnungen, Beschreibungen [an die Academie von Cortona]*'.
288   Stosch 1724, p. XIX: '*Mais je parlerai plus au long de ces Pâtes de Verre dans un autre Ouvrage que je medite sur ce sujet!*' ['But I will speak more about these Pâtes de Verre in another book that I intend on this subject.']. However, this project was never realised and except this one mention, no other source or Stosch's correspondence informs about it.
289   Chatsworth, the Devonshire archives, inv. no.: CS1/188.7.
290   Chatsworth, the Devonshire archives, inv. no.: CS1/188.8.
291   Chatsworth, the Devonshire collection, inv. no.: IRN 5034.

accurate impressions of his gems so that they could be later engraved with utmost accuracy, if His Grace orders them for a reasonable price. The testimony from these two letters allow us to understand that the discovered gem drawings, although they seem to be primarily made for Stosch's personal archive, could have been used for different purposes as well. Among the drawings in Krakow and Berlin, just a few document gems from the Devonshire collection (let alone those drawn by Odam and Picart for Stosch's book published in 1724).[292] The last letter from Stosch to William Cavendish, 2nd Duke of Devonshire, was sent from Rome on 7 May 1729, but it does not include any discussion on gems. The Duke died on 4 June 1729, and as a result the potential project of publication of the Devonshire gems was never realised.

All in all, Stosch's corpus of gem drawings could have served multiple purposes, starting from personal studies, publishing his book projects (including the catalogue of his collection of gems and the never-finished second volume of *Gemmae antiquae caelatae*), helping in day-to-day transactions and building his authority as a connoisseur of glyptic art in the learned circles of gem enthusiasts in Rome, Florence and beyond. Many more drawings than the ones discovered in Krakow and Berlin were made and Stosch sent them to other collectors and scholars attached to his correspondence on a regular basis. However, Stosch's project of building a pictorial documentation of gems on paper, given its scale and scope, somehow recalls the efforts of Cassiano dal Pozzo and his visionary project of *Museo Cartaceo*, embracing all kinds of knowledge with the use of drawings as visual platforms for information about Antiquity, the natural world and beyond.[293] In the case of Stosch, this was focused primarily on Antiquity and glyptics in particular. Whether Stosch planned to publish his numerous drawings as a sort of general overview of glyptic art cannot be verified, but again it should be recalled that even projects as big as Pozzo's *Paper Museum* were originally conceived with the plan to publish.[294] Furthermore, Bernard de Montfaucon's (1655–1741) enormous collection of ca. 30 000–40 000 prints and drawings of antiquities were partially used to illustrate his fifteen volumes of *L'antiquité expliquée et représentée en figures*.[295] Although Mariette suggested that already in 1718 Stosch started to have had his drawings of gems engraved seemingly for some kind of publication (not the book *Gemmae antiquae caelatae*) as plates, he admits that he was not aware if the numbers were significant, as Stosch showed him just two examples (which probably were just individual prints, see above).[296] In any case, Stosch's enormous corpus of gem drawings gives us valuable insight into his encyclopaedic approach to both collecting original gems and documenting their vast numbers on paper, which fits in the ongoing transformation of the antiquarianism movement into more scientifically oriented early archaeological research. This issue is more broadly commented on in Chapter 11.

15   Stosch's *Paper Museum of Gems* and Production of a Catalogue of Stosch's Gems by Winckelmann and Others (1760)

Shortly after Stosch's death, his heir Heinrich Wilhelm Muzell-Stosch started to complete Stosch's manuscript catalogue, adding 1000 gems that were not inventoried between 1747 and 1757. Tried as he might, he put those gems within the already existing classes, but the results were unsatisfactory, and thus he asked Winckelmann for help, who was in fact designated to catalogue Stosch's gems by the collector himself earlier.[297] Muzell-Stosch wanted to sell the collection as quickly as possible. For this reason, he probably tried to convert the original inventory list into a sale catalogue, but Winckelmann, once realising the great potential of the collection itself and probably of Stosch's manuscript catalogue too, decided to write a regular *catalogue raisonné*.[298] He arrived in Florence in

---

292   Krakow Nos 1260 and 2182 and Berlin vol. I, pl. 128.
293   The *Museo Cartaceo/Paper Museum* of Cassiano dal Pozzo, is a collection of more than 7000 watercolours, drawings and prints, assembled during the seventeenth century by the famous Roman patron and collector, Cassiano dal Pozzo, and his brother Carlo Antonio dal Pozzo (Herklotz 1999 – with extensive bibliography). See the project on this subject realised at The Warburg Institute in London, resulting in a series of 37 volumes publications being the *catalogue raisonné* of all identified drawings and prints once belonging to *Museo Cartaceo/Paper Museum* of Cassiano dal Pozzo and more: https://warburg.sas.ac.uk/research-projects/archived-research-projects/paper-museum-cassiano-dal-pozzo-1588-1657 [retrieved on 3 February 2023].
294   Herklotz 1999, pp. 262–265; Vaiani 2016, pp. 46–49.
295   Montfaucon 1719–1724. See also critical examination of this work in: Poulouin 1995 and Burke (2003, p. 286) on Montfaucon's collection of prints and drawings.
296   Mariette 1750, vol. I, p. 332.
297   Zazoff and Zazoff 1983, pp. 71–76; Rügler in Winckelmann 2013, p. XIV; Hansson 2014, p. 27; Lang 2017, pp. 204–205. Just two months after Stosch's death Muzell-Stosch invited Winckelmann to discuss Stosch's collections in Florence. According to Winckelmann's letter to Angelo Michele Bianconi, dated Rome 10 December 1757, Muzell-Stosch offered to host him for six months: '(…) *Il Nipote del defunto Baron di Stosch à Firenze mi esibisce un ospizio per 6 mesi, senza veruna spesa, per avere con chi raggionare sopra la famosa Raccolta Stoschiana, prima che vien ad essere dispersa: una offerta da farne gran caso, se fosse da accettarla senza parere di far poco conto dell'intercessione d'un gran Principe (…)*' (Winckelmann 1961, p. 75, no. 15).
298   Cristofani 1981, p. 24; Rügler in Winckelmann 2013, p. XIV; Harloe 2013, p. 80; Lang 2017, pp. 204–205. According to a letter

1758 and spent eight months working with Stosch's gems there; he continued writing the catalogue in Rome later. It is doubtful that he actually did much work directly from the original gems.[299] From his letter to Walther dated 26 September 1758, it is clear that he also worked from a limited number of sulphur and wax impressions of the most interesting gems.[300] Moreover, in his letter to Antonio Baldani written in Florence 26–30 September 1758, Winckelmann admits that while writing the catalogue of Stosch's gems, he used already prepared drawings of gems presenting their greatly enlarged images to facilitate his work.[301] This letter is of extreme importance because Winckelmann must have been referring to the gem drawings by Odam, Preißler, Tuscher, Nagel and others made for Stosch and rediscovered in Krakow and Berlin. They must have been as valuable in his research on Stosch's gems as Stosch's original inventory and Winckelmann's testimony reveals their primary asset – Stosch's gem drawings were of utmost importance in the research of iconography, techniques and styles of gems because they offered enlarged images, and as discussed above also a lot of valuable information about the gemstones, provenance and maybe even interpretations of the subjects depicted on them, as can be now judged from the drawings themselves, although, Winckelmann suggests that they had little explanatory text.[302]

The rediscovery of Stosch's corpus of gem drawings helps to clarify why Winckelmann thought it necessary to improve Stosch's organisation system of his collection. He considered his ideas conservative. Many times, Winckelmann claims that he should avoid writing what Stosch had already written about specific gems and present his own innovative commentaries.[303] One presumes that Stosch's catalogue entries were much in the antiquarian vein. This is somehow suggested by the brief captions accompanying most of the drawings from his pictorial corpus discovered in Krakow and Berlin, which focused mostly on the subject matters and interpretation of iconography, as well as the types of gemstones.[304] In other words, the gem drawings from Stosch's corpus offer better insight into the production process of the catalogue of Stosch's gems by Winckelmann because, in the absence of other sources, they help to evaluate that Stosch's and his close collaborators' thoughts on gems from his own and other collections were merely restricted to the description of iconography and offered little information on their chronology, meaning, functions, interconnections with other branches of ancient art, etc.[305]

The discovered drawings also help to advance research on the contribution of Joannon de Saint Laurent (1714–1783) to the catalogue of Stosch's gems and his legacy overall. He was a French mineralogist, naturalist, physician, antiquarian and collector (including engraved gems).[306] He was born in Lyon but he later moved to Italy, where he offered his services to some collectors regarding the description of their cabinets.[307] He also helped Stosch to organise his collection of engraved gems in Florence.[308] Like him, he was a member of *Società Colombaria*,[309] and apparently of Accademia Etrusca in Cortona as evidenced by the letters he wrote to the members of that community, as well as some short essays and dissertations he publicly read during its meetings, which were later published in the series *Saggi di dissertazioni accademiche: pubblicamente*

---

from Winckelmann to Giovanni Lodovico Bianconi (1717–1781), dated Florence 30 September 1758, Winckelmann wanted to comment on the artistic aspect of gems, among others, because once the collection was sold, the catalogue could be still consulted with the collection of Stosch's gem impressions, making it a valuable scientific tool: '*Io sto qui alloggiato in casa del Sig^{re} de Stosch con tutto il comodo e in mezzo de' suoi tesori superiori al grado d'un privato. Ho dato mano, all'istanze di questo Sig^{re}, ad un catalogo degl'Intagli suoi, ma volendo evitare la secchezza d'un Semplice Indice e farvi qualche rifflessione intorno all'Arte, al disegno e all'Antichità, mi sono ingolfato in un mare dove non mi mancherà per lungo tratto acqua da navigare. Le pietre stanno per vendersi come le altre raccolte: ma il Catalogo può essere proseguito sopra gli impronti e i Solfi.*' (Winckelmann 1961, p. 112, no. 34).

299 Furtwängler 1900, vol. III, p. 416; Winckelmann 1961, pp. LIV–LV; Zazoff and Zazoff 1983, p. 74; Hansson 2014, p. 27.
300 Winckelmann 1952–1957, vol. I, pp. 415–417, no. 236.
301 Leitschuh 1886, p. 36; Winckelmann 1961, p. 105, no. 31: '(…) *a facilitarmi il lavoro ho soltanto i disegni fatti in grande.*'
302 Letter from Winckelmann to Antonio Baldani, dated 26–30 September 1758: '(…) *ma senza veruna spiegazione.*' (Winckelmann 1961, p. 105, no. 31).

303 For example, in a letter from Winckelmann to Hieronymus Dietrich Berendis dated 5 February 1758, see: Winckelmann 1952–1957, vol. I, p. 330, no. 202; Décullot 2012, p. 169; Lang 2017, pp. 205–206.
304 It is also noteworthy that in his letter to William Cavendish, 2nd Duke of Devonshire, dated Rome, 5 February 1729, Stosch encourages the Duke to publish his gems for which he could make illustrations in his atelier. He offered to write *concise* explanatory texts for each gem, cf. Chatsworth, the Devonshire archives, inv. no.: CS1/188.7.
305 For a thorough discussion on the differences between Stosch and Winckelmann, cf. Chapter 11 here.
306 Barocchi and Gallo 1985, p. 176.
307 For example, he wrote a catalogue of the collection of natural history specimens, minerals, precious and semi-precious stones and fossils of Johann de Baillou (1679–1758), which comprised 30 000 objects and was acquired in 1748 by the Holy Roman Emperor Francis I (1745–1765) for the Naturhistorisches Museum in Vienna (Saint Laurent 1746).
308 Rosenberg and Clary (eds) 2018, p. 141.
309 Harloe 2013, p. 80.

lette nella nobile Accademia Etrusca dell'antichissima città di Cortona.[310] He also wrote about the glyptic activities of the gem engraver Louis Siries (ca. 1686–1766).[311] Since he was in contact with Stosch before his death, it is supposed that once Muzell-Stosch had to compile the gem catalogue he hired him to determine gemstone types wherever they were not determined by Stosch himself (mostly 1000 uncatalogued gems).[312] However, his contribution must have been more substantial. Some scholars believe that he is the author of the text for classes V–VIII in the catalogue published by Winckelmann,[313] while others think that indeed Saint Laurent elaborated the gems with ships and also those presenting vases, but later Winckelmann probably re-wrote these sections on his own.[314] Moreover, Saint Laurent is also said to have produced an introduction essay to the section with gems bearing various symbols, but ultimately it was not included into Winckelmann's catalogue of Stosch's gems. Moreover, he might have translated or just proofread Winckelmann's manuscript.[315] Even though Winckelmann disregards Saint Laurent's contribution,[316] the most recent research established that during the production of the catalogue of Stosch's gems, Winckelmann focused on the three first classes (I – Egyptian and Persian gems, II – *Mythologie sacrée* and III – *Mythologie historique*), while Cardinal Alessandro Albani helped him with portrait gems from the fourth class entitled *Histoire ancienne,* and the remaining classes (V – Jeux, Festins, Vases &c, VI – Vaisseaux des Anciens, VII – Animeaux and VIII – Abraxas, Gravures avec des Caractéres Orientaux & Gravures Modernes) were elaborated by Joannon de Saint Laurent.[317]

The gem drawings from Krakow and Berlin provide a great deal of new insights. Joannon de Saint Laurent's help in organisation of Stosch's various collections of original gems, sulphurs, and especially gem drawings is confirmed by the drawing Krakow No. 171, which presents one of Stosch's own gems that survived with a substantial fragment of the original sheet on which there is an extensive commentary written by him in black ink.[318] The described gem belongs to the second class of Winckelmann's catalogue published in 1760. The commentary varies from the text published by Winckelmann. It sounds as follows: '*Ceres coeffé d'un Voile, tenant d'une main un flambeau allumé, de l'autre une coupe. Devant elle un modius avec des epics de bleds et un cheval deriere un animal entre la chevre ou la chevreuil. Modius est une measure usité pour les grains chez les anciens.*' The text in Winckelmann's catalogue sounds like this: '*Cérès voilée assise, tenant de la main droite un grand flambeau allumé, & de la gauche une coupe; devant elle on voit un Modius avec épis de bled & un Cheval, & derriére elle un autre Cheval. Les Etrusques représentoient aussi Cérès avec la patère, comme on remarque dans deux petites figures de bronze de la Galerie de l'Empereur à Florence.*'[319] Both commentaries focus on the iconography and basically describe what is engraved upon the gem, but an important difference is that Winckelmann added his observation on the Etruscan bronze figurines, which bear a similar motif.

In the context of this finding, Décultot seems right suggesting that apart from collaboration there might have also been rivalry between Saint Laurent and Winckelmann during the elaboration of Stosch's gem collection.[320] The evidence from drawing Krakow No. 171 illustrates that indeed Saint Laurent was seriously involved in cataloguing Stosch's gem collection and perhaps he commented not only on those from classes V–VIII of the final catalogue.[321] It appears that he used Stosch's gem drawings to a far greater extent than Winckelmann, probably commenting

---

310 BCAE Joannon de Saint Laurent 1748, vol. V; Saint Laurent 1751.
311 Saint Laurent 1747.
312 Zazoff and Zazoff 1983, p. 80; Rügler in Winckelmann 2013, pp. XVI–XVII.
313 Zazoff and Zazoff 1983, p. 79; Arbeid, Bruni and Iozzo 2016, pp. 133–134, no. 42.
314 Rügler in Winckelmann 2013, pp. XVI–XVII. However, it might be that Laurent's parts of the catalogue were largely based on what Stosch had written earlier or what they both established during their potential cooperation, which is suggested by Stosch's letter to Paolo Maria Paciaudi dated Florence 28 October 1755, see: Justi 1871, pp. 28–29, no. XIV.
315 Zazoff and Zazoff 1983, p. 75; Rügler in Winckelmann 2013, pp. XVI–XVII. Décultot (2012, p. 186) raises an interesting issue that Winckelmann knew French himself quite well and even though his text was indeed proofread by Laurent, he must have checked and decided which version would be finally published to be sure that Laurent did not change his ideas.
316 In his letter to Muzell-Stosch dated Rome 2 January 1760, Winckelmann says: '*St. Laurents Arbeit wird als ein geflickter Bettel-Mantel hinten anhängen, und das Ende des Wercks wird, wie wenn die Affen den Hinteren zwigen, lächerlich seyn.*'

317 Zazoff and Zazoff 1983, p. 79; Rügler in Winckelmann 2013, pp. XIII–XXIII; Hansson 2014, p. 28.
318 The comparative analysis of the text from the Krakow No. 171 drawing and Joannon de Saint Laurent letters preserved in the in the Biblioteca del Comune e dell'Accademia Etrusca di Cortona (for example, BCAE Joannon de Saint Laurent 1748, vol. V, fol. 29) proved that the handwriting matches in both cases.
319 Winckelmann 1760, class II, no. 235, p. 69.
320 Décultot 2012, p. 186.
321 Although, the 21st volume of *Pierres gravees par Stosche* in Krakow, which includes drawings of gems representing ships and other maritime subjects, has seemingly many examples with extensive commentaries.

not only Stosch's own gems but the other ones documented on drawings as well. In Chapter 6, it has been mentioned that in some cases of the drawings from Krakow the later commentaries written by Izabela Czartoryska are clearly not inspired by the records from the catalogue of Stosch's gems published by Winckelmann in 1760. They were written by a person with a considerable knowledge of glyptic art and Antiquity in general. It is unlikely they were written by Izabela Czartoryska on her own. In fact, they sound in a very similar way to the one from the drawing Krakow No. 171 – explanatory, even encyclopaedic, in scope. A good example of that is the drawing Krakow No. 2573 reproducing a carnelian intaglio from Stosch's collection engraved with an eagle surrounded by a variety of symbols.[322] The commentary to the drawing sounds as follows '*Les attributs des Dieux: L'aigle de Jupiter posé sur la foudre tenant daus son bec les Emblemes de la Victoire: a coté de l'aigle l'astre du Soleil: En haut le baton de Pan, le Thyrse de Bacchus: En bas la Massue de Hercule, L'Arc d'Apollon, a droitte le Haste de Mars, l'Epi de Ceres, le Pigeon de Venus; a gauche la tete d'un Elephant Simbole de l'Afrique, et une tete d'une Simbole de l'ancienne Dacie.*' The text sounds like an explanation of the iconography for a potential reader. All the symbols are carefully listed, analysed and attributed to specific deities and mythological figures. To compare, let us have a look at the description of that very gem in Winckelmann's catalogue: '*Une Aigle planant dans l'air, tenant la Foudre dans ses serres, & dans son bec un Rameau de plame avec une couronne. Autour de l'Aigle on voit sans aucun ordre un Thyrse, un pedum, un oiseau, une étoile, une fléeche, un arc, une massue, on coq & un papilloni..*'. As one can see, the original commentary was not only longer but also much more precise and explanatory. Winckelmann's text is merely a description of what is engraved upon the intaglio. Such cases engender the thought that more drawings from Krakow could originally have had added texts by Joannon de Saint Laurent.[323] Moreover, it is likely that, similarly to Winckelmann, Saint Laurent wrote texts exceeding simple descriptions of gems' iconography.

Indeed, many supposedly originally his commentaries constitute long subject matter descriptions, but they also include encyclopaedic explanations of iconography, even single elements like the case of the preserved original commentary for Krakow No. 171 illustrates (cf. Chapter 6, Fig. 6.13). These texts also convey reflections on the history, customs, life and mythology of ancient Egyptians, Etruscans, Greeks and Romans.[324] Sometimes, references to individual elements of a gem's iconography are explained as reflecting specific myths. In the case of the drawing Krakow No. 236 featuring a carnelian intaglio engraved with a standing Mercury with the caduceus and a money bag, and a cockerel and a tortoise at his feet, the tortoise is said to reflect the history of the invention of the lyre by the god: '*Mercure. La tortue qui est a ses pieds est relative a l'invention de la Lyre*'. The cameo reproduced in the drawing Krakow No. 416 is correctly interpreted as featuring the contest of Athena and Poseidon: '*Neptune et Minerve cette gravure a raport au dessi de ces deux divinites a qui produiroit un plus bel ouvrage. Neptune fit sortir d'un coup de trident donné a la terre un cheval, Minerve fit naitre l'Olivier.*' (Figs 8.131–8.132) and Krakow No. 1182 is rightly said to depict: '*Tydée un des Sept Chefs qui vinrent au Siége de Thébes qui étant blessé retire le Javelot de sa Jambe. Son nom est gravé en Etrusque.*' (Fig. 8.75).

The symbolism of the depictions from gems is often explained in detail, like the one from the drawing Krakow No. 301, where the Tyche-Fortuna figure is correctly recognised as a personification of a city and the head of elephant as a reference to Africa: '*Sujet Simbolique pour marquer les succes de quelque Ville: La tete d'Elephant designe qu'elle etoit en Affrique, Le gouvernail qu'elle etoit Maritime.*' In the drawing Krakow No. 490, representing a Graeco-Persian gem with a soldier next to his horse, the commentary includes an observation on the outfit, which suggests the man to be a Macedonian warrior: '*Un Soldat dans l'attitude de monter a cheval: on croit que c'est un Soldat Macedonien a cause de ses casque en cuir qui servoit de bonet.*' It has also been observed that some animals may stand for a specific personification and deities, which is clear from the commentary to the drawing Krakow No. 623: '*La cigogne dans les monuments antiques acompagnoit la Pieté: il est probable qu'elle est représenté sous cette figure.*' A similar case is Krakow No. 634, where the griffin is taken as a symbol of Apollo and Pan: '*Apollon. On voit un Griffon a ses pieds. On le regardoit comme le simbole d'Apollon et de Pan*' and Krakow No. 637, where the raven is said to be another sacred animal of Apollo: '*Apollon: a ses pieds est le corbeau qui lui est consacré*'. In the drawing

---

322 Furtwängler 1896, no. 7882; Pirzio Biroli Stefanelli 2007, no. IV.171; Borbein, Kunze and Rügler 2019, no. II.102 (with full bibliography).
323 Cf. Chapter 6 here for more examples illustrating this phenomenon.
324 This is clear from the following 116 examples: Krakow Nos 73, 87, 91, 97, 114, 171, 174, 176, 180, 185–187, 190, 227, 229, 236, 243, 247, 256, 264, 282–284, 290–291, 299, 301, 310, 323, 341, 350–351, 407, 416, 422, 424, 430, 442, 452, 464, 476, 489–490, 510, 525, 530, 534, 557, 574, 579, 581–583, 586, 592, 598, 614, 623, 634, 637, 658, 678, 846, 868, 1000, 1002, 1015–1016, 1019, 1092, 1173–1174, 1179, 1202, 1229, 1306, 1365, 1372, 1429, 1441, 1475–1476, 1478–1479, 1482, 1485, 1488, 1491, 1496, 1502, 1514, 1519–1520, 1522, 1564, 1574–1575, 1577, 1582, 1596, 1637, 1639, 1752, 1780, 1793, 1813, 1824, 1846, 1856, 1875, 1970, 1988, 2039, 2120, 2157 and 2233.

Krakow No. 658, the lion is believed to be another symbol related to Apollo or Sol as it stands for the Sun: '*Apollon ou le Soleil dans son char. Au bas le Signe du Lion au dessus du quel passe le Soleil*'. However, it was noted that sometimes the iconography of the gems is obscure and difficult to explain, like the one from the drawing Krakow No. 625: '*Figure Panthée, composé du buste d'Apollon, attache a un corp de Bouc, sur lequel est une Minerve armé d'un Bouclier et d'un gouvernail: L'Apollon tient une balance et une Palme: le tout ensamble est une allegorie qui ne se trouve point expliquer.*' or Krakow No. 1563: '*Ce vaisseau sous la forme d'un Coq est un simbole ou une allegorie qu'on ne peut deciner. Le Papillon qu'on voit audessus est l'embleme du Zephir, qui etoit un veut dans et favorable a la navigation.*'

In the case of the drawing Krakow No. 579, the female seated in front of a burning altar is interpreted as a woman examining the burning fire looking for omens, an activity called in Latin *ingnispicium* related to the pyromancy: '*Une superstition fort comunne chez les Anciens c'etoit la Pyromantie, en latin ignispicium: c'est a dire une maniere de chercher des augures dans le mouvement du feu, de la flamme, de l'eclat. Cette femme assise au miliu de la nuit est occupé a examiner le feu qui brule devant elle. L'en faut sur la Colonne represente le genie de la personne ou de la maison. Ces divinités moyenaes sont souvent representés avec cette espéce de corne.*' (Fig. 8.133). Krakow No. 1000 features three gems on one drawing, all of which, according to the commentary appearing beneath, are related to the cult and mysteries of Bacchus: '*Ces trois differenttes emprintes sont relatives aux misteres de Bacchus. Touttes les trois representent la Corbeille mistique de ce Dieu, surmonté de differens emblemes*' and Krakow No. 1002 features: '*Ceremonies relatives au Culte de Bacchus*'. However, if the scene on the gem was believed to be taken from the everyday life, this is also indicated, for instance, on Krakow No. 1429: '*Ce sujet n'est ni mythologique ni historique et paroit simplement representer deux ouvriers.*'

Another group of drawings should be singled out due to the fact that their commentaries include references to ancient coins, sculpture, reliefs, literary sources, other gems and wall paintings in Herculaneum.[325] Interestingly, these commentaries very often appear in the case of the gems from collections other than Stosch's. For example, in the commentary to the drawing Krakow No. 169 (Fig. 8.134), the goddess inside the temple is identified as Ceres, but it is said that similar depictions are taken as Isis because on the coins of Emperor Macrinus, the goddess holds a sistrum rattle in her hand: '*Ceres dans un Temple. D'autres voyent que cette figure represente Isis: parce qu'on voit une Isis avec un timon a la main sur une medaille de Macrin.*' In the case of the drawing Krakow No. 245, the depiction from the gem is explained in detail clearly by someone who possessed considerable knowledge of ancient culture and art as the specific names of the types of Mercury representations are evoked (Agonaios, Enagonaios and Palestrite) and was familiar with nomenclature of the Greek world, since he uses the names/concepts like '*Poedotribe*' – a trainer in gymnastics often represented in ancient Greek art as supervising the exercises of young athletes – as a comparison to the figure of Mercury depicted on the intaglio. There is also a reference to a similar representation that appears on the coins minted by the Annia family: '*Mercure. Apellé, Agonios, Enagonius, ou Palaestrite, c'est a dire qui preside aux jeux Publics: tel on le voit dans une medaille de la famille Annia: debout devant une colonne, avec ses attributs, tenant son caducée renverssé, comme pour corriger les athlettes et ayant l'attitude d'un Progymnaste ou Paedotribe.*' The drawing Krakow No. 697 presents an intaglio engraved with the figure of the Muse Polymnia, which is, according to the commentary, a type that is also often used for sculptures and reliefs: '*Polymnie on voit dans les statues et bas reliefs anciens plesieurs pareilles statue de cette Muse*'. Krakow No. 1907 features an unidentified intaglio engraved with Achilles and Penthesilea, a subject which, according to the commentary, was also painted by Panaenus, brother of Phidias in the portico of the Temple of Jupiter of Olimpia: '*ACHILLE & PENTHESILÉE. Le même Sujet avoit été fait par Panem, frére du célébre Phidias qui l'avoit peint sur un des Portiques du Temple de Jupiter Olympien*'. Interestingly, one of Stosch's gems is commented on by Winckelmann in his catalogue in a very similar way but a bit more accurately: '*Penthésilée Reine des Amazones soutenue par Achille qui vient de la tuer; elle est sur ses genoux, & Achille la soutient sous les bras. Le même sujet se trouve sur deux Pierres gravées du Museum Florentinum, & c'en étoit un des*

---

325 31 drawings in total: Krakow Nos 14 (reference to wall painting in Herculaneum), 169 (reference to coins), 190 (reference to another gem – signed by Apollonios, 231 (reference to coins), 2742 (reference to coins), 245 (reference to sculpture), 310 (reference to coins), 322 (reference to sculpture), 489 (reference to ancient literature), 569 (reference to ancient literature), 649 (reference to sculpture), 661 (reference to ancient literature), 697 (reference to sculpture and relief), 723 (reference to relief), 1022 (reference to a wall painting in Herculaneum), 1057 (reference to coins), 1064 (reference to coins), 1173 (reference to ancient literature), 1224 (reference to another gem, seal of Commodus), 1306 (reference to coins and sculpture), 1485 (reference to ancient literature), 1518 (reference to literature on gems), 1529 (reference to ancient literature), 1574 (reference to ancient literature), 1575 (reference to ancient literature), 1584 (reference to coins), 1782 (reference to coins), 1824 (reference to literature), 1907 (reference to wall painting), 2164 (reference to coins) and 2175 (reference to coins).

Peintures don't Panéne frére du célèbre Phidias, avoit orné une espéce de Portique du temple de Jupiter Olympien à Elis.'[326]

As far as inscriptions on gems are concerned, they were interpreted from various angles as signatures of gem carvers, names of gems' owners as well as collectors. The language of the inscription attracted attention too, plus sometimes careful explanations of Greek words were offered.[327] For example, the LAV.R.MED. is correctly interpreted as proof that the carnelian intaglio depicted in the drawing Krakow No. 664 once belonged to Lorenzo de'Medici: *'Le Char du Soleil: lui meme tient un Flambeau et passe par dessus le Nil qu'on voit audessus avec une Nayade. Le nom de Lau: de Medicis prouve que la pierre lui a apartenau'* as well as Krakow No. 1668: *'L'arche de Noe pierre moderne: apartenant a Laurent de Medici.'* The provenance information is also sometimes provided,[328] as are observations on engraving techniques, styles and chronology, although the latter are usually limited to the statements that the piece is Etruscan, Egyptian or *'de la plus hautle antiquité'*.[329]

In conclusion, Joannon de Saint Laurent is thought to have added some commentaries to the drawings now housed in Krakow, and he probably did so when Stosch's gems were being catalogued between 1757 and 1760, although the lack of his commentaries on the drawings selected for *Pierres gravées du roi avec figures* suggests that they could have been added later,[330] unless this is merely a coincidence, as many more drawings from Krakow did not receive his commentaries either. In any case, the process of writing the catalogue must have been complicated and management of Stosch's extensive collections of original gems, sulphur impressions and casts and drawings difficult too. All of this required cooperation from various angles. For instance, the rich correspondence between Muzell-Stosch and Winckelmann after the latter's return to Rome in May 1759 suggests that Muzell-Stosch played a very active part in coordinating the work on the catalogue of Stosch's gems, sending Winckelmann gem impressions, looking up references, translating and editing text, etc.[331] Joannon de Saint Laurent could indeed have prepared the text for some sections and done the language editing. In any case, both Winckelmann and Saint Laurent are attested to have used gem drawings from Stosch's rich corpus during production of the catalogue of his gems, but the latter was clearly much more interested in them. Even though, as Winckelmann laments, there were gem drawings ready to be used as illustrations for the catalogue, Muzell-Stosch did not intend to publish the book illustrated.[332] However, once the catalogue was printed and the gems agreed to be sold to Frederick II the Great, King of Prussia, apparently he decided to use at least a portion of the existing drawings in order to give the buyer a unique edition of the illustrated catalogue of Stosch's gems.

16 Stosch's *Paper Museum of Gems* and the Sale of Stosch's Gems to the King of Prussia in 1764

The *Pierres gravees par Stosche* albums of gem drawings in the Princes Czartoryski Museum in Krakow were traditionally identified with Stosch, and they were actually believed to depict exclusively his gems (cf. for instance the view of Pelagia Potocka discussed in Chapter 6). This view was probably coined shortly after Stosch's death because

---

326 Winckelmann 1760, class III, no. 272, pp. 379–380.
327 Krakow Nos 77 (*'ΠΡΟΝΟΙΑ en grec veut dire prevoyance ΘΕΟΛΟ ... est le comencement d'un mot qui a raport aux Dieux'*), 85 (*'Tete de Jupiter Serapis avec l'inscription qui veut dire Serapis est unique'*), 583 (*'les initiales du nom du Proprietoire'*), 664 (name of Medici proves the gem to belong to them), 880 (*'le mot Ampeli qui veut dire en grec sep de vigne'* – Ampeli, which means in Greek vine stock/vineyard/grapes/vinery), 1182 (TUTE – name is engraved in Etruscan language), 1194 (le nom du graveur), 1458 (*'Le meme avec le nom de graveur'*), 1540 (*'(...) avec le nom du graveur au bas'*), 1668 (Medici), 1735 (*'le nom de graveur'*), 1845 (*'l'inscription veut dire – Marcus Virrius, a qui apartenoit la pierre'*), 1888 (*'le nom du graveur'*) and 2066 (*'avec le Nom du Graveur ϹΟΛΩΝΟϹ'*).
328 Krakow Nos 282 (*'(...) cette pierre est au cabinet du Gr: Duc: a Florence'*), 442 (*'Cette Paste apartenait a Sabatini celebre Antiquaire'*), 459 (*'cette pierre se trouve a Florence'*), 578 (*'Roy de Francia'*), 1194 (*'L'Original est dans la Cabinet de Vienne'*), 1229 (*'Museum Florentinum'*), 1793 (*'et se trouvoit dans la collectioné de me* [or monsieur?]*: le Baron Stosch'*) and 1986 (*'il est d'un Cabinet du Chevalier Vettori a Rome'*).
329 Krakow Nos 150 (*'gravure Etrusque'*), 197 (*'cette gravure est de la plus hautte antiquité'*), 570 (*'gravure Etrusque'*), 1033 (*'C'est une des plus belles pierres de l'antiquité.'*), 1089 (*'gravure Etrusque'*), 1092 (*'gravure Etrusque'*), 1156 (*'gravure Etrusque'*), 1182 (*'grave en Etrusque'*), 1365 (*'Etrusque'*), 1752 (*'graveure tres antique'*), 1792 (*'gravure Egiptienne'*), 1793 (*'cette pierre est veritablement persanne est de la plus hautte antiquité'*), 1801 (*'Pierre Egiptienne'*) and 1910 (*'Cette Pierre est superbe'*).

330 It would have been pointless to write different texts on the illustrated gems or repeat Winckelmann's entries under the drawings.
331 Rügler in Winckelmann 2013, pp. XIV–XV; Hansson 2014, p. 28.
332 Winckelmann 1760, p. XXVII. One should also consider if another reason for publishing the catalogue of Stosch's gems unillustrated was the problem with identification of the gems on the drawings. Still, Saint Laurent succeeded in the case of several hundred, which could have served as a good selection of illustrations. Thus, abandoning illustrations for the printed catalogue was probably due to economic reasons.

Stosch's heir and his collaborators – Winckelmann and Saint Laurent, did not fully understand what Stosch's *Paper Museum of Gems* was, at least not at the beginning.[333] As suggested above, certainly when Winckelmann's catalogue was already published (1760), and most likely around the date of the purchase of Stosch's collection of engraved gems by the King of Prussia, Joannon de Saint Laurent identified several hundreds of Stosch's gems on the drawings from Stosch's archive he apparently worked on. Those references are written in dark brown ink, the same one as Saint Laurent's commentary to the drawing Krakow No. 171.

As far as the drawings from Krakow are concerned, they appear in the following formats: *N. xxx. p. yyy.*[334] (the most popular one) or *n. xxx. p. yyy* or *No. xxx. p. yyy.* or *p. yyy. No. xxx* or *xxx.* (very popular) or *xxx. p. yyy.* or *N. xxx. yyy* or *n. xxx. p. yyy.* or *xxx. yyy* (Figs 8.135–8.142). They were written in various places, usually at the bottom of the enlarged gem, in the caption field or at the bottom of the drawing.[335] Had the drawings not been transferred onto new paper, more of those references would have survived.[336] The number of 53 out of 177 references (30%) is incorrect, e.g. in fact the drawing reproduces a different intaglio or cameo from Stosch's own or another contemporary collection.[337] In the case of a few examples, the suggested gems from Stosch's collection are indeed very close (for instance: Krakow Nos 380, 610, 1318, 1321, 823 and 1766), sometimes even identical but made of glass instead of a hardstone as, for example, Krakow No. 361. However, Saint Laurent also suggested two different gems from two different drawings to reproduce the same gem in Stosch collection – Krakow Nos 1318 and 1321, 764 and 765, 775 and 776, 705 and 787.

All the drawings used as illustrations in *Pierres gravées du roi avec figures* in Berlin have references to Winckelmann's catalogue of Stosch's gems of the same type added by Joannon de Saint Laurent. They are written in the same formats: *N. xxx. p. yyy.*[338] (the most popular one) or *n. xxx. p. yyy* or *No. xxx. p. yyy.* or *p. yyy. No. xxx* or *xxx.* (very popular) or *xxx. p. yyy.* or *N. xxx. yyy* or *n. xxx. p. yyy.* or *xxx. yyy* (Figs 8.143–8.144), in the same ink and writing style. Some of them are incorrect – 68 examples out of 830 drawings (8%), so the ratio of the incorrect identifications to the correct ones is much lower than in the case of the drawings in Krakow (30%). During the preparation of *Pierres gravées du roi avec figures* in the first two volumes, Saint Laurent initially added only inventory numbers without pages in pencil or light dark brown ink. However, later, he confirmed them using dark brown ink, usually giving a full version of a reference with a page number.[339] In the case of the first volume, sometimes the short reference to specific number of the record in Winckelmann's catalogue written at the bottom of the gem drawing is repeated in the upper-right corner of the drawing in dark brown ink in its full form with the number of the page as well (Figs 8.145–8.146). Later on, Saint Laurent was less careful, and he simply crossed out and replaced incorrect identifications with the new ones (Fig. 8.147).[340] It is crucial to observe that those references also appear on illustrations published in the luxurious edition of Winckelmann's catalogue of Stosch's gems published from 1760, so they must have been written after that date (Fig. 8.148).[341]

Overall, it is noteworthy that on the illustrations printed in the luxurious edition of Winckelmann's catalogue similar references to ours appear in the top-right corner of the pages.[342] Only the engraving of Stosch's Meleager gem is missing it, but analysing the rest, one distinguishes two types: first, where the format is *Pag yyy No xxx* and the second *P. yyy n. xxx*. They were added by two different hands and none of them is of similar style to those appearing on the drawings from Krakow and Berlin.

To conclude, Joannon de Saint Laurent tried to identify as many gem drawings with Stosch's gems as possible, but the task was challenging because Stosch's *Paper Museum of Gems* included many drawings of gems from all contemporary collections too. He managed to select only over 800 examples which were used for the six volumes of *Pierres*

---

333 This is suggested, among other things, by the way Winckelmann refers to Stosch's gem drawings, claiming that Stosch had his all gems drawn (Winckelmann 1760, p. XXVII).

334 XXX – refers to the number of a gem in Winckelmann's catalogue of Stosch's gems while YYY – refers to the page from that publication.

335 Cf. the catalogue of Krakow gem drawings in Appendix 2.

336 This is clear from fragmentary preserved references cf. the catalogue of Krakow gem drawings in Appendix 2.

337 53 drawings in total: Krakow Nos 223, 237, 250, 351, 361–362, 380, 504, 518, 610, 684, 738, 747, 750, 764–765, 775–776, 779, 787, 796, 819, 823, 846, 853, 1027, 1064, 1121–1122, 1281, 1292, 1305, 1318, 1321, 1393, 1401, 1478, 1535, 1715, 1758, 1766, 1824, 1829, 2065, 2075, 2123, 2154, 2162, 2187, 2189, 2214, 2232 and 2262.

338 XXX – refers to the number of a gem in Winckelmann's catalogue of Stosch's gems while YYY – refers to the page from that publication.

339 As a matter of fact, already in the second volume, many drawings have just the final references, but some also the preliminary numbers, cf. the catalogue of Berlin drawings in Appendix 2.

340 For example: Berlin vol. VI, pl. 10.

341 Berlin vol. I, pl. 94; vol. III, pl. 69; vol. IV, pls 24 and 37; vol. V, pl. 64; vol. VI, pls 86, 111 and 136.

342 Rügler in Winckelmann 2013, pp. XLII–LII.

gravées du roi avec figures. His insufficient understanding of the gem drawings from Stosch's corpus is the best illustrated by the fact that he cut out nearly half of the selected ones from original sheets and transferred them onto new paper, sometimes ignoring provenance information, which suggested the gem to be from a different collection than Stosch's.[343] Everything suggests that the special illustrated edition of Winckelmann's catalogue entitled *Pierres gravées du roi avec figures* was made as a gift for the prospective buyer of Stosch's collection of engraved gems – the King of Prussia. One recalls how hard it was for Muzell-Stosch to sell the gems, since several offers were made prior to 1764 and all were declined.[344] Apparently, this unique publication accompanied the original gems like a complete set of their impressions in sulphur did.[345]

Regarding the rest of Stosch's *Paper Museum of Gems*, it remained with Muzell-Stosch until his death, and it was auctioned in 1783 in Berlin and finally purchased by Adam Jerzy Czartoryski in 1800. In between 1764 and 1800, some of them received new references to Stosch's gems published by Winckelmann, which were certainly not written by Joannon de Saint Laurent or Izabela Czartoryska and her assistant.[346] It is likely that the new owner who bought them in 1783 believed that he purchased drawings depicting Stosch's own gems and he attempted to identify them by adding new references to Winckelmann's catalogue. They are written in black ink, and they appear on 295 drawings from Krakow in the following formats: *No. XXX. p. YYY.* or *p. YYY. No. XXX.* or *pag. YYY. No. XXX.* or *No. XXX. pag. YYY* (Figs 8.135–8.137 and 8.149–8.152). It is very likely that they originally appeared on an even larger number of drawings because the new owner also indicated the gemstone type if this information was absent or sometimes, he overwrote the already existing one if the original faded considerably, or because he had thought that the drawing depicts one of Stosch's gems, he took the type of the gemstone from Winckelmann's catalogue and overwrote the original information.[347] While his references are sometimes missing due to the transfer of the drawings onto new paper, the real-size gem drawings often survive, indicating which ones could be identified by him as representing Stosch's gems.[348] These new references always appear in the caption fields or very close to them. They were sometimes controlled and corrected but by the same hand.[349] The new identifier often improved, corrected, crossed out and replaced or repeated the already existing references added by Joannon de Saint Laurent.[350] Even though his identifications are more numerous (295 cases), many more of them are incorrect (115 out of 295–39%).[351]

---

343 For example, this is clear in the case of Berlin vol. I, pl. 22 which represents a gem from the then Medici, now Museo Archeologico Nazionale in Florence collection that bears indeed an identical subject matter as one of Stosch's gems.

344 The gems were first offered to the Prince of Wales and then to the Duke of Parma and King of Spain, who all declined acquisition due to the high price asked, before it was purchased by Frederick the Great of Prussia, see: Zazoff and Zazoff 1983, p. 132; Hansson 2014, p. 29; Hansson 2021a, p. 119 and Chapter 1 in this volume.

345 Schlichtegroll 1805, vol. I, pp. 11–12.

346 This type of reference does not appear on the drawings preserved in *Pierres gravées du roi avec figures* in Berlin.

347 This is the case of the following drawings: Krakow Nos 17, 20, 69, 112, 129, 135, 161, 167, 273, 387, 390, 397, 418, 627–628, 661–662, 1027, 1102, 1105, 1178, 1224, 1229, 1236, 1239, 1243, 1247, 1250, 1276, 1278, 1309, 1337, 1371, 1428, 1582, 1616, 1745 and 1892.

348 Cf. the catalogue of Krakow gem drawings in Appendix 2. Moreover, analysis of the following gemstone type information clearly written by the new owner suggests that it was taken from relevant records in the Winckelmann's catalogue of Stosch's gems, and subsequently it is assumed that these drawings had also references to that book but they did not survive: Krakow Nos 406, 1225, 1247, 1261, 1274, 1398, 1548 and 1961. Nevertheless, there are also cases where the identifier indicated the gemstone type, but he did not provide relevant reference to Winckelmann's catalogue of Stosch's gems, see: Krakow Nos 17, 369, 523, 1085, 1229, 1360 and 1368.

349 This is evident on the drawings: Krakow Nos 69, 217, 311, 446, 488, 1214, 1578 and 1919. Also, a comparative analysis of the gemstone information provided on the drawings Krakow Nos 285 and 1398 suggests another two mistakes resulting from incorrect referencing to a record in Winckelmann's catalogue of Stosch's gems.

350 There are 116 cases like that: Krakow Nos 39, 44, 175, 250, 273, 339, 347–348, 360, 362, 380, 469, 471, 628, 667, 679, 705–706, 721, 723, 736, 738, 747, 750, 760, 764–765, 771, 775–776, 779–781, 783, 796, 801, 805, 813, 819, 823, 829, 846–847, 853, 869–870, 995, 1027, 1056, 1064, 1112, 1121–1122, 1136, 1141, 1145, 1157, 1182–1187, 1190, 1202–1203, 1206, 1237, 1250, 1281–1282, 1292, 1295, 1308–1309, 1401, 1430, 1442, 1467, 1497, 1541, 1577, 1585, 1632, 1662, 1715, 1766, 1786, 1806, 1812, 1824, 1844–1845, 1849, 1914, 1924, 1992, 2000, 2045, 2065, 2075, 2083, 2092, 2145, 2150, 2154, 2156–2157, 2160, 2162, 2173, 2175, 2189, 2210–2211, 2214, 2232 and 2256.

351 115 cases: Krakow Nos 20, 27, 71, 92, 119, 137, 148, 197, 203, 217, 224, 233, 236, 242, 245, 250, 277, 285, 311, 313, 327, 334, 340–341, 346, 353, 377, 399, 401, 434, 439, 441, 443–444, 447–448, 464, 467–468, 472, 477, 480, 483, 486, 585, 631, 638–639, 659–661, 670, 687, 697, 779, 880–881, 885, 895, 909, 914–915, 917, 929, 962–963, 996, 1021, 1033, 1105, 1142, 1156, 1208, 1284–1285, 1303, 1543, 1578, 1588, 1622, 1630–1633, 1637, 1640–1641, 1650, 1659–1660, 1697, 1788–1789, 1798–1799, 1857, 1860, 1879, 1901, 1908, 1915, 2047, 2184 and 2231. Regarding the drawings identified with the same gem from Stosch collection, see: Krakow Nos 447–448.

PLATE 35

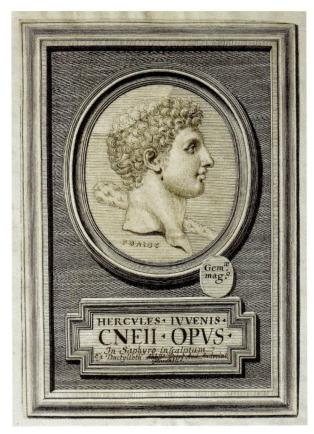

FIGURE 8.1

FIGURE 8.2

FIGURE 8.3

FIGURE 8.4

FIGURE 8.5

FIGURE 8.6

FIGURE 8.7

FIGURE 8.8

PLATE 37

FIGURE 8.9

FIGURE 8.10

FIGURE 8.11

FIGURE 8.12

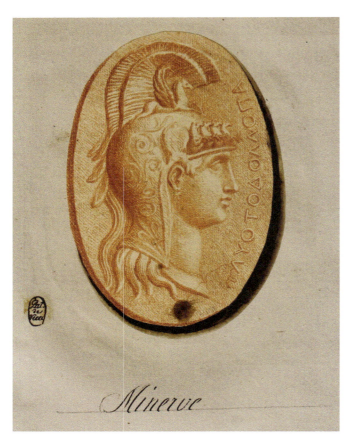

FIGURE 8.13

FIGURE 8.14

FIGURE 8.15

FIGURE 8.16

FIGURE 8.17

FIGURE 8.18

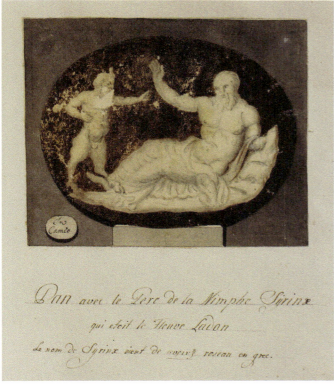

FIGURE 8.19

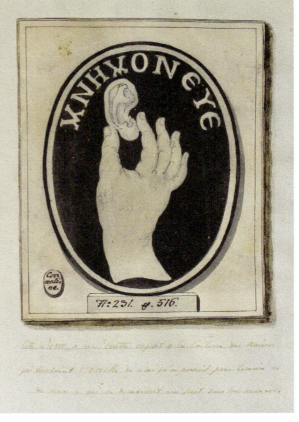

FIGURE 8.20

FIGURE 8.21

FIGURE 8.22

FIGURE 8.23

FIGURE 8.24

PLATE 41

FIGURE 8.25

FIGURE 8.26

FIGURE 8.27

FIGURE 8.28

FIGURE 8.29

FIGURE 8.30

PLATE 43

FIGURE 8.31

FIGURE 8.32

FIGURE 8.33

FIGURE 8.34

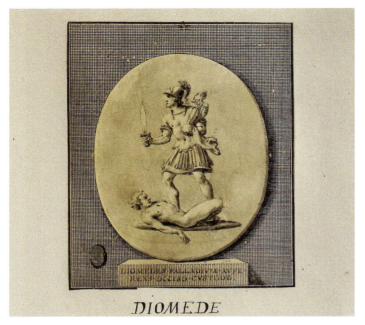

FIGURE 8.35

FIGURE 8.36

FIGURE 8.37

FIGURE 8.38

PLATE 45

FIGURE 8.39

FIGURE 8.40

FIGURE 8.41

FIGURE 8.42

FIGURE 8.43

FIGURE 8.44

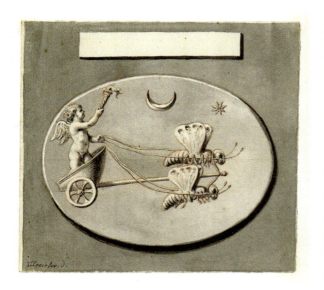

FIGURE 8.45

FIGURE 8.46

FIGURE 8.47

FIGURE 8.48

FIGURE 8.49

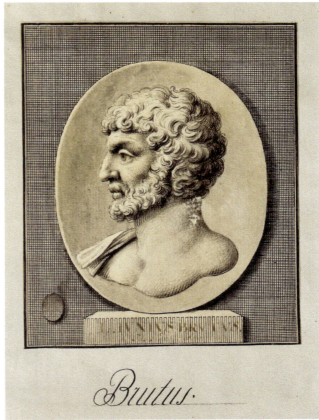

FIGURE 8.50

FIGURE 8.51

FIGURE 8.52

FIGURE 8.53

PLATE 49

FIGURE 8.54

FIGURE 8.55

FIGURE 8.56

FIGURE 8.57

FIGURE 8.58

FIGURE 8.59

FIGURE 8.60

PLATE 51

FIGURE 8.61

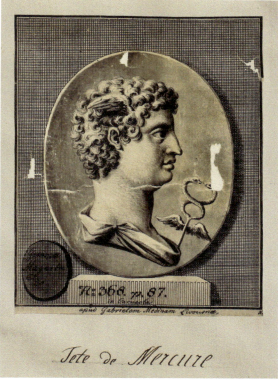

FIGURE 8.62

FIGURE 8.63

FIGURE 8.64

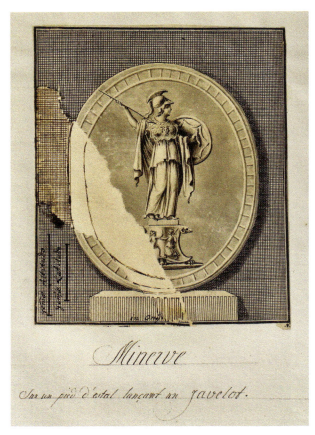

FIGURE 8.65

FIGURE 8.66

FIGURE 8.67

FIGURE 8.68

PLATE 53

FIGURE 8.69

FIGURE 8.70

FIGURE 8.71

FIGURE 8.72

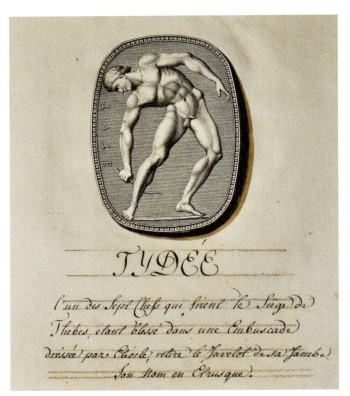

FIGURE 8.73

FIGURE 8.74

TYDÉE
l'un des Sept Chefs qui firent le Siège de Thèbes, étant blessé dans une Embuscade dressée par Etéocle, retire le Javelot de sa jambe. Son Nom en Etrusque.

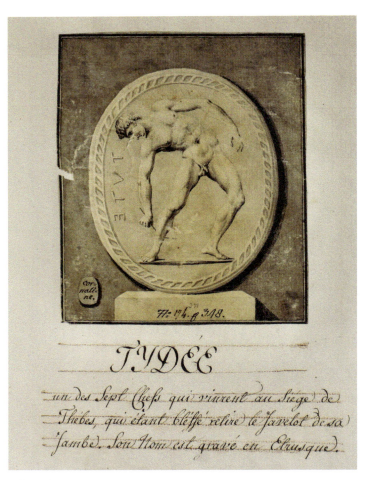

FIGURE 8.75

TYDÉE
un des Sept Chefs qui vinrent au Siège de Thèbes, qui étant blessé retire le Javelot de sa jambe. Son Nom est gravé en Etrusque.

PLATE 55

FIGURE 8.76

FIGURE 8.77

FIGURE 8.78

FIGURE 8.79

FIGURE 8.80

FIGURE 8.81

FIGURE 8.82

FIGURE 8.83

PLATE 57

Persée avec le nom du graveur

FIGURE 8.84

Tête d'un Empereur

FIGURE 8.85

Hercule attachant Cerbere

FIGURE 8.86

Tête de Marc aurele

FIGURE 8.87

FIGURE 8.88

FIGURE 8.89

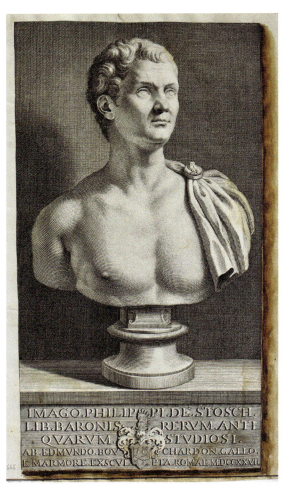

FIGURE 8.90

PLATE 59

FIGURE 8.91

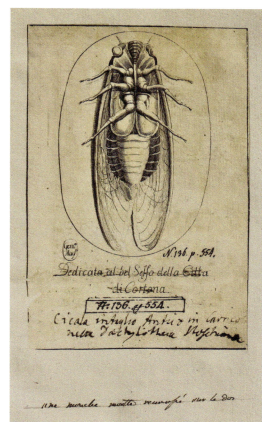

FIGURE 8.92

FIGURE 8.93

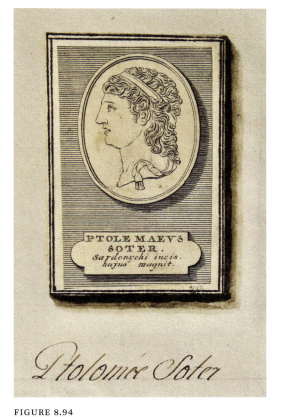

FIGURE 8.94

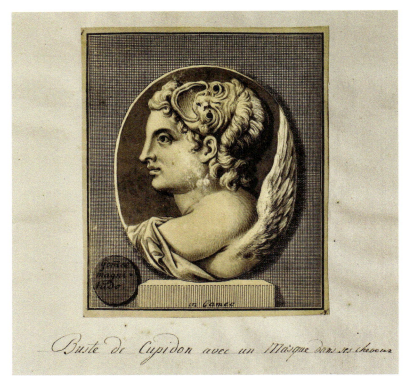

FIGURE 8.95

FIGURE 8.96

FIGURE 8.97

FIGURE 8.98

PLATE 61

FIGURE 8.99

FIGURE 8.100

FIGURE 8.101

FIGURE 8.102

FIGURE 8.103

FIGURE 8.104

FIGURE 8.105

FIGURE 8.106

PLATE 63

FIGURE 8.107

FIGURE 8.108

FIGURE 8.109

FIGURE 8.110

FIGURE 8.111

FIGURE 8.112

FIGURE 8.113

FIGURE 8.114

PLATE 65

FIGURE 8.115

FIGURE 8.116

FIGURE 8.117

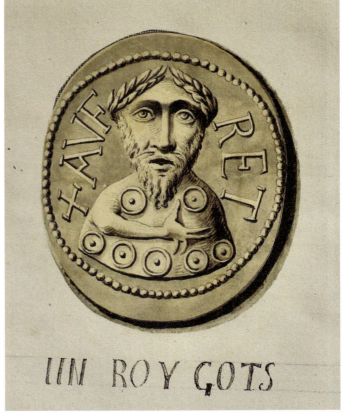

FIGURE 8.118

La victoire sur un globe

pour prouver qu'elle est mobile. elle tient un trophée et reçoit des signes de victoire de deux hommes a genoux qui les lui presentent. Cette Paste apartenoit a Sabatini celebre Antiquaire: Maffei croit qu'elle a apartenu au Vainqueur de quelques nations, designé par les deux figures agenouillés.

FIGURE 8.119

FIGURE 8.120

FIGURE 8.121

Un homme conduisant un Lion: Maffei pretend y trouver Androclès qu'un Lion qu'il avoit guéri d'une blessure, reconnut dans un combat et caressa au milieu de l'arene.

FIGURE 8.122

PLATE 67

FIGURE 8.123

FIGURE 8.124

FIGURE 8.125

FIGURE 8.126

FIGURE 8.127

FIGURE 8.128

FIGURE 8.129

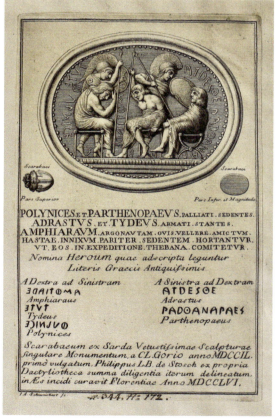

FIGURE 8.130

PLATE 69

FIGURE 8.131

FIGURE 8.132

FIGURE 8.133

FIGURE 8.134

FIGURE 8.135

FIGURE 8.136

FIGURE 8.137

FIGURE 8.138

FIGURE 8.139

Mercure
berger des troupeaux d'Admette.

FIGURE 8.140

FIGURE 8.141

L'Esperance

FIGURE 8.142

PLATE 73

FIGURE 8.144

FIGURE 8.143

FIGURE 8.145

FIGURE 8.146

FIGURE 8.147

FIGURE 8.148

FIGURE 8.149

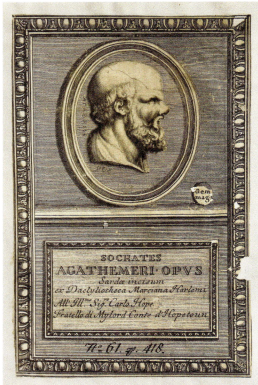

FIGURE 8.150

FIGURE 8.151

FIGURE 8.152

PART 4

Philipp von Stosch and His Studies of Engraved Gems

∴

CHAPTER 9

Stosch's *Magnum Opus* – *Gemmae antiquae caelatae* 1724 in the Context of His Life, Collecting and Studying Engraved Gems

Hadrien J. Rambach

1   Baron von Stosch, the Baron of Gems

Winckelmann wrote on 5 February 1758 that *'with the death of Mr von Stosch, I have lost a great friend and an endless amount of news. For although he never got to know the beauty in art, because the plague of the other antique dealers spoiled him too early, he had nearly the largest cabinet in the world'*.[1] In 1827, Goethe wrote that Stosch *'was for his time an eminently remarkable person'*,[2] rightfully commenting that he had left at his death an *'extremely valuable collection'*.[3]

The importance of Stosch in the world of antiquarianism, and in particular of gem-collecting, is well-known and has already been acknowledged. But his association with the drawings rediscovered in Krakow and Berlin justify for him to be presented in depth, and notably to summarise what is known about the conception and realisation of his book *Gemmæ antiquæ cœlatæ*[4] *scalptorum nominibus insignitæ/Pierres antiques gravées, sur lesquelles les graveurs ont mis leurs noms ... et traduites en François par M. de Limiers*, published in Amsterdam in 1724 by Bernard Picart (1673–1733),[5] which is a volume *in folio* containing (3), (2), xxi, 97, (1) pages, and 70 plates[6] (Figs 9.1–9.2).

'By reading him you learn nothing, but you become something'[7] – those words written by Goethe (about Winckelmann) apply perfectly to Stosch's *magnum opus*, which is perhaps the most attractive of all illustrated books on gems published in the eighteenth century,[8] and undoubtedly the most famous.

Some bibliographical questions about this book still need solving, such as that of paper-sizes. Indeed, a contemporary source mentions that the publication *'was made on three kinds of paper of different sizes, the average kind of which can match and serve as a continuation of the Book of l'*Antiquité expliquée par Dom Bernard de Monfaucon,

---

1   Letter from 5 February 1758 (see transcription hereafter in the Appendix).
2   Goethe 1827, p. 563 (quoted in Kashcheev 1999, p. 17): *'Er war zu seiner Zeit ein höchst merkwürdiger Mann'*.
3   Goethe 1851, vol. XXIV, p. 24 (quoted in Kashcheev 1999, p. 25): *'Kein geringer Vorteil für ihn war sein Verhältnis zu dem Erben der großen Stoschischen Besitzungen. Erst nach dem Tode des Sammlers lernte er diese kleine Kunstwelt kennen und herrschte darin nach seiner Einsicht und Überzeugung. Freilich ging man nicht mit allen Teilen dieser äußerst schätzbaren Sammlung gleich vorsichtig um, wiewohl das Ganze einen Katalog, zur Freude und zum Nutzen nachfolgender Liebhaber und Sammler, verdient hätte. Manches ward verschleudert; doch um die treffliche Gemmensammlung bekannter und verkäuflicher zu machen, unternahm Winckelmann mit dem Erben Stosch die Fertigung eines Katalogs, von welchem Geschäft und dessen übereilter und doch immer geistreicher Behandlung uns die überbliebene Korrespondenz ein merkwürdiges Zeugnis ablegt.'*
4   Despite the similarity in its title, George Ogle's book *Gemmae antiquae caelatae, or a Collection of gems wherein are explained many particulars relating to the fable and history, the customs and habits, the ceremonies and exercises of the ancients, taken from the classics by George Ogle Esq.; engraved by Cl. du Bosc* (London 1741) covers a completely different subject. It is actually a second edition of the book entitled *Antiquities Explained. Being a collection of figured gems illustrated by similar descriptions taken from the classics by George Ogle, Esq.; vol. I* (London 1737).
5   On Bernard Picart, see: Faliu 1988; Te Rijdt 1993; Preaud 1996; Bartelings 2001; Henry 2002; Hunt, Jacob and Mijnhardt 2010a; Hunt, Jacob and Mijnhardt 2010b; Wyss-Giacosa 2006; Chapter 4 in this volume.

His earliest identified work is *Jesus dit au Paralytique: mon fils confiance vous pechez* (Mathew 9.2.6), 'Inventit pinx B. Picart romanus ex cum Pri regis 1685', possibly after a 1944-destroyed painting by Jean Jouvenet (1644–1717); copy in the Getty Research Institute's Library (Los Angeles), inv. 2003 PR 48, reproduced in Jacob 2005.

The Louvre, the Bibliothèque nationale de France, and the Teylers Museum (Haarlem) possess large groups of drawings by Picart, but none has drawings after gems.
6   Brunet 1863, vol. V, p. 552; Cohen and de Ricci 1912, no. 959; Cicognara 1821, vol. II, p. 86, no. 3016; Ebert 1937, vol. IV, p. 1783, no. 21801; Hoefer 1865, XLIV, cols 524–526, Levine 1898, no. 516; Quérard 1838, vol. IX, p. 273; Sinkansas 1993, vol. II, 996–997, no. 6379.
7   Eckermann 1884, vol. I, p. 244 (misquoted in Kashcheev 1999, p. 14 as being the words of Johann Peter Eckermann, who was instead the destinatory of Goethe's comment): *'Man lernt nichts, wenn man ihn liest, aber man wird etwas'*.
8   Picart 1734, pp. 8–9: *'De tous les Ouvrages de Gravure qui ont paru jusqu'à ce jour, on peut bien dire qu'aucun n'a jamais été exécuté si magnifiquement que celui là; non seulement par rapport à l'exactitude du Dessein & de la Gravure, mais aussi par rapport à l'impression des Planches & du Discours, & eu égard au papier qu'on a pris d'une beauté extraordinaire, & qui outre cela a été choisi feuille à feuille pour les Planches. Tellement que cette Edition sera toujours recherchée, & deviendra rare, puisque toutes les épreuves, qui avoient le moindre petit défaut, ou une petite tache de rouille, ont été rebutées.'*

© HADRIEN J. RAMBACH, 2025 | DOI:10.1163/9789004712553_010
This is an open access chapter distributed under the terms of the CC BY-NC-ND 4.0 license.

being of the same size'.⁹ Montfaucon's monumental work of 1719–1724 in 15 volumes, including supplements, was an *in folio* of 45,5 × 29,5 cm¹⁰ (i.e. printed on sheets of at least 59 by 46 cm). An analysis of copies of Stosch's book uncovers several sizes: some were indeed printed on ca. 63 × 46 cm sheets,¹¹ whilst others were apparently printed on ca. 48 × 37 cm sheets.¹² Those would, therefore, be the small and medium paper copies, and no large copies of Stosch 1724 have yet been documented. Regarding such luxury copies,¹³ the Muzell-Stosch auction of 1783 contained a copy of the *Gemmae antiquae caelatae* described as '*printed on royal paper*',¹⁴ and an individual plate (plundered during WWII) is attested as having been printed on pink paper.¹⁵

By modern standards, Stosch's short introduction and general comments for each gem would not suffice to save it from the coffee-table-book category, but in the context of its time the readers did indeed end up changed men: possibly with a better feeling of what ancient glyptic masterpieces might look like, but certainly with new perspectives, including an interest in the carvers (and the dating) of gems, rather than simply for their iconography. Stosch surpassed the illustration of Antiquity by the use of artefacts, and instead cared about the items themselves, paying special attention to their provenance, their location, their material, etc.

As noted by Gołyźniak, '*Rejecting typical subject matter organisation,* [Stosch in 1724] *listed the objects in alphabetical order of engravers, which allowed several works attributed to one artist to be observed at the same time. Moreover, Stosch provided full information on the published gems for the first time, not only discussing their subject matters but also provenance, the gemstones they were made of and individual styles.*'¹⁶ Stosch was a precursor of art history, like Winckelmann (cataloguer of his gems in 1760)¹⁷ would later be.¹⁸

2 Stosch and the Context of His Book

In order to appreciate the phenomenon of Stosch and his book on ancient signed engraved gems, one needs to also consider his antiquarian activities and network, his personal and professional connections, including cooperation with gem engravers and draughtsmen, his considerable skills in producing and procuring of gem impressions,

---

9   Picart 1734, 9: '*a été faite sur trois sortes de papier de différentes grandeurs, dont la moyenne sorte peut assortir & servir de suite au Livre de l'*Antiquité expliquée par Dom Bernard de Monfaucon, *étant de même grandeur.*'

10 Figure provided by Alain Maes in Krings 2021, vol. I, p. 243. Stosch's is not the only book destined to fit the series, as this would also be the case of a numismatic publication – Mangeart 1763.

11 The binding of the copy of John Kyle Wood, sold by Kolbe & Fanning (10 June 2023, lot 114), measures 47 by 35 cm. The copy sold by Galerie Bassenge on 20 October 2011, lot 1066, measures 46,5 × 31,5 cm (**sheet > 63 × 47 cm**). The copy of Silvio Zipoli, H.D. Lyon (in 1983) and Arthur and Charlotte Vershbow, sold by Christie's on 20 June 2013 (lot 642), measures 46,2 × 30,9 cm (**sheet > 62 × 46 cm**). The copy of Ivan Nagel (1931–2012), sold by Galerie Bassenge on 29 November 2012, lot 5900, measures 46 × 30 cm (**sheet > 60 × 46 cm**). The copy of king Louis XV (1710–1715–1774), Jean-Louis de Viefville des Essarts (1744–1820), and Roger Peyrefitte (1907–2000), measures 45 × 29,5 cm (**sheet > 59 × 45 cm**). The copy of William Blakiston Bowes and the Kufa Gallery, sold by Sotheby's in October 2000, (lot 344) measures 45 × 28,5 cm (**sheet > 57 × 45 cm**). The copy recently sold by Le Feu Follet measures 43,5 × 28 cm (**sheet > 56 × 44 cm**). The copy of David Garrick (1717–1779), of Edward Smith-Stanley, 13th Earl of Derby (1775–1851), of Raphaël Esmerian (1903–1976), measures 42,7 × 28 cm (**sheet > 56 × 43 cm**). The copy of princess Izabela Czartoryska (1746–1835) measures 44,8 × 29 cm (**sheet > 58 × 45 cm**), and deserves specific mention, as its quiring is distinct from that of the other copies we have handled, e.g. the page XXI is numbered ** ** ** 2 (instead of *** 3), and the page 3 is numbered A 2 (instead of A). I am grateful to France Huyard for her assistance.

12 The copy of Mathias Benzelstierna (1713–1791), for sale in September 2023 by InLibris Gilhofer Nfg., measures 36,8 × 24 cm (**sheet > 48 × 37 cm**). The copy sold by Koller on 24 March 2021, lot 250, measures 36 × 24 cm (**sheet > 48 × 36 cm**). The copy for sale in September 2023 by Antiquariaat A. Kok & Zn, measures 36,5 × 23 cm (**sheet > 46 × 37 cm**).

13 The watermarks found on the (small) Koller 2021 copy are the same as those of the (medium or large) French royal copy.

14 Lot 1: '*Philippi de Stosch Gemmae antiquae caelatae et aeri incisae per Bernhardum Picart. Pierres antiques gravées par B.P. expliqués, par Ph. De St. Amsterd. 724. vergold. Marmbd. mit gold. Schnitt ganz auf Rojalpap. Gedruckt*'.

15 Online database of art objects kept at the Jeu de Paume in Paris, inv. Zu MA-B 1224 Kiste Nr. MA-B 74: '*Folioband mit 252 eingeklebten Kupferstichen von Bernard Picart*' (the fate of this album is unknown). One of these (item #43) is described as '*Nach rechts gewandte Profilbürte der Minerva im Oval. Nach einer Gemme. Darunter Tafel mit Inschrift. Rechts Grössenangabe der Vorlage-Gemme. Rahmenartige Umrandung. Sign. B. Picart del. et sculpsit 1719. Auf rosa Papier. 27,2 × 18,7 cm.*' Identifying this plate is proving difficult, as there are three Minerva gems in Stosch 1724, but pl. X is signed '*B. Picart del. et sculp. 1722*', pl. XIII '*B. Picart sculp. 1719*', and pl. XXXIV '*B. Picart sculp. 1723*'.

16 Chapter 10 in this volume.

17 Winckelmann catalogued all of Stosch's 3444 gems (amongst which 887 modern glass pastes), and this enormous task led to the comment that '*Achilles had found his Homer*' (Femmel and Heres 1971, p. 65).

18 Winckelmann is '*souvent considéré comme le premier historien de l'art et comme le précurseur des développements de l'archéologie moderne*' according to Blanc 2018.

and his collecting of both original gems as well as drawings of gems. Various stories about him have been circulating, both positive and negative ones, of which some are related here below in order to present a more global picture of Stosch, who was undoubtedly a complex figure. What is certain, though, is that his book reflects a genuine passion for collecting and studying engraved gems.

Stosch was a multifaceted figure. He employed Johann Lorenz Natter (1705–1763) to copy several ancient gems,[19] as well as Lorenzo Masini (b. 1713),[20] so he did commission artists to engrave *all'antica* gems, or even replicas of ancient ones. It would, nevertheless, seem unfair to accuse him of having owned or handled 'false gems'. He may well have been the inspiration of Alexander Pope (1688–1744), when he wrote his satire: '*But Annius, crafty Seer, with ebon wand, and well-dissembl'd Em'rald on his hand, false as his Gems and canker'd as his Coins, came, cramm'd with Capon, from where Pollio dines*'.[21]

As a young man, Stosch travelled from 1709 until 1717 for an extended Grand Tour. Back in Rome in 1722, in order to finance his collections, he became both an antique dealer and a British spy.[22] His activity as a dealer remains to be studied in detail, but one finds occasional mentions of gem sales. In 1739, Ficoroni noted that Stosch provided him with a satyr in topaz at a cost of 16 *scudi*.[23] Ca. 1743 (?), Stosch himself wrote to the Earl of Carlisle, mentioning that the Englishman had acknowledged receipt of '*the engraved gems and cameos which I had sent you*' and that he had paid him 100 pounds.[24] Stosch also occasionally acted as advisor and/or broker, acquiring engraved gems on behalf of other collectors, such as the now lost carnelian intaglio of a young Hercules, which Caylus described as '*a carnelian sent to me from Florence by the Baron of Stosch, whom I had asked to choose an engraved gem for an acquaintance*' (Fig. 9.3).[25] Stosch valued this gem highly, which he believed to be engraved by Dioscurides, though unsigned, and he commissioned a copy for his own collection, as well as its drawing by Georg Abraham Nagel (Krakow No. 1066) (Fig. 9.4).[26]

Stosch was particularly good at networking with important collectors (such as Carlisle), talented scholars and artists, to whom he proved instrumental. However, he obviously did not only have friends, and the editor of the letters of Horace Walpole (1717–1797) described him as '*a Prussian, virtuoso, and spy for the court of England on the Pretender. He had been driven to Rome, although it was suspected that he was a spy on both sides; he was a man of the most infamous character in every respect*'.[27] Nevertheless, Walpole was a client of Stosch, acquiring, for example, a gold coin of Galla Placidia in 1749.[28] Might his resentment be explained as a collector's frustration, having been

---

19   Stosch 1724, pl. IV was copied (= Nau 1966, no. 52), as well as pl. XIII (= Nau 1966, nos 5–7), pl. XLVI (= Nau 1966, no. 18), pl. XXII (= Nau 1966, no. 35), pl. XXIII (= Nau 1966, no. 19), pl. XXIV (= Nau 1966, no. 48), pl. XXXV (= Nau 1966, no. 41), pl. LXV (= Nau 1966, nos 27–28), pl. LXIII (= Nau 1966, no. 29), and pl. LXVII (= Nau 1966, no. 69).

20   The ancient Gaios' garnet engraved with the dog star Sirius, then in the Bessborough collection (Boardman *et al.* 2009, no. 293), was copied by Natter in garnet, which is now in the British Museum – inv. no.: 1978,1002.1069, 22 mm (with bezel) and Masini cut another replica in rock crystal, which is now in the Antikensammlung in Berlin, inv. no.: FG 9243 (Winckelmann 1760, class II, no. 1240, p. 206: '*Cette copie a été faite par Laurent Masini, qui y a mis son nom, sous les yeux du feu Baron de Stosch, & a très-bien réussi*'; Furtwängler 1896, no. 9243; Borbein, Kunze and Rügler 2019, no. II.1240). For a discussion on the original gem and its replicas, cf. Chapter 10 here.

21   *The Dunciad*, book IV, quoted in Middleton 1891, p. XXIV, n. 1.

22   For a biography of Stosch, see: MacKay Quynn 1941, Lewis 1967, Borroni Salvadori 1978b and Chapter 1 here. Research on Stosch is never-ending, and the British Library has recently (2016–2017) acquired the '*William Capel Correspondence. This is a collection of diplomatic correspondence preserved by William Capel, King George II's ambassador to the court of Turin. Included is one volume of approximately 70 letters by Baron Stosch (John Walton), secret agent for the English Government at Rome and Florence. The collection includes a considerable quantity of autograph material and several portions in diplomatic cipher*'.

23   Scarisbrick 1987, p. 95.

24   Scarisbrick 1987, p. 104.

25   Caylus 1752–1767, vol. II, p. 143, pl. 48.3: '*Une cornaline qui m'a été envoyée de Florence par M. le baron de Stosch, que j'avoie prié de me choisir une pierre gravée pour une personne de ma connoissance*'. The gem was later in the collection of M*** [Joseph-Hyacinthe-François-de-Paule de Rigaud de Vaudreuil (1740–1817)], 26 November 1787, lot 252 ('*Thésée avec la dépouille du Minotaure*'), acquired by Jean-Baptiste-Pierre Le Brun (1748–1813) for 610 livres = collection of Le Brun, Paris, 11 April 1791 and following days, lot 829, purchased back by the vendor for 612 livres. See also: Dehn/Dolce Vatican F.38 (19 × 11 mm, carnelian); Raspe and Tassie 1791, no. 5909; Furtwängler 1900, vol. I, pl. XXXIX.20, vol. II, 187.

In the same 1791 auction, the lot 828 (carnelian intaglio of a military sacrifice with three figures, set in a gold ring with diamonds, acquired by Alexandre-Joseph Paillet (1743–1814) for 931 livres, formerly from the Saint-Maurice auction, lot 1051, when it had fetched 1104 livres) is indicated '*vient ci-devant du célèbre cabinet de Stosch*.'

26   Caylus 1752–1767, vol. II, p. 143, pl. 48.3: '*Je crois la gravure être de Dioscoride, et [je crois] que vous approuverez mon choix. Depuis dix ans on ne m'a offert aucune gravure [i.e. intaille] d'indubitable Antiquité plus belle que celle-ci*.' Stosch's copy is now in the Antikensammlung in Berlin, inv. No.: FG 9293 – Furtwängler 1896, no. 9293.

27   Toynbee 1903, vol. I, p. 103, n. 4; Walpole 1937–1983, vol. XVII, p. 164, n. 5.

28   In a manuscript entitled *Note delle Medaglie falsificate, e loro Autori*, by Bernardo Sterbini (fl. 1718–1751) – Spier and Kagan 2000, pp. 68–73; FINA ID-2824 – one reads that Stosch had

unable – like Barthélemy would later be – to acquire all the objects of his lust, such as an intaglio with a gladiator and a vase for which he was willing in 1749 to pay £100, but which Stosch gave instead the next year to William Ponsonby, 2nd Earl of Bessborough (1704–1793)?[29]

The French Royal curator, Abbot Barthélemy, wrote to Caylus in 1755 to relate a visit to Stosch at home.[30] In that letter, he did not only mention the wealth of his cabinets (*'twenty-five thousand sulphurs, prints, engraved stones, antiques, medals, manuscripts, maps and drawings. He has robbed Italy'*), but also how difficult it was to handle him: *'he has shown me everything and given me nothing. I have stooped to the point of prayers; they have hardened a heart that is naturally not tender. I triumphed over the resistance of Abbé Boule and a few other second-hand dealers; but I did not triumph over the most powerful of them all.'* Nevertheless, the list of Stosch's many correspondents and contacts suggests that he was probably not unlikeable: he was in fact even described (posthumously) as a *'pleasant man'*,[31] and had been close to many of the greatest collectors – such as Albani and Caylus.[32]

It is in this context that *'Stosch left Rome suddenly in January, 1731. According to his own story, he was ordered to leave Rome by a member of the Pretender's suite. Four masked men attacked his carriage as he left a party at the palace of Cardinal Bentivoglio on the night of January 21, 1731. The leader, at the point of a gun, threatened his life if he would not leave Rome within a week'*.[33] Being an infidel[34] or being a homosexual were possible reasons for this ejection from the Papal State, but the most likely reason is that his employment by Sir Robert Walpole's government had been uncovered. Stosch therefore left his large apartment in Vicolo Merangolo in Rome[35] (he had previously stayed 1722–1725 at Via de' Pontefici[36]), and fled to Florence, where he took residence in the Palazzo Ramirez-Montalvo.[37]

Living in Florence provided him a new, additional source of income: he acted occasionally as *cicerone*. Joseph Spence (1699–1768), professor of Poetry at Oxford, who *'visited with Stosch in Florence (...) records a number of anecdotes'* about archaeology, literature, etc.[38] And Stosch was well surrounded, as *'he took with him his brother, his man-servant Christian Dehn (1696–1770), and the two artists Johann Justin Preißler (1698–1771) and Karl Markus Tuscher (1705–1751), who had belonged to his Roman household'*.[39] Whilst *'Odam did not follow Stosch in exile*[40] *(...) Georg Adam Nagel (1712–1779) and Johann Adam Schweickart (1722–1787) joined the household in Florence'*.[41] He can, therefore, be described as having lived with an artistic court, as seen on the two drawings by Pier Leone Ghezzi (1674–1755), in which he is depicted amongst an assembly of antiquaries.[42] This is not his only portrait, and sev-

---

acquired the tools of the Florentine forger Nicolo Dervieux. On Stosch and numismatics, see: Burnett 2020.

29 Walpole writes: *'I find I cannot live without Stosch's intaglia of the Gladiator with the vase'* – letter from Walpole to Sir Horace Mann, 26 November 1749, quoted in Toynbee 1903, p. 131; Walpole 1927–1983, vol. XVII, pp. 232–233 as well as *'I still think it one of the finest things I ever saw and am mortified at not having it'* – in another letter to Mann written once he learnt the gem had been given to William Ponsonby, 2nd Earl of Bessborough, see: Walpole 1927–1983, vol. XX, p. 157. The gem is now in Baltimore, The Walters Art Museum, inv. no.: 42.109, garnet intaglio, 18 × 15 mm and it was apparently considered to be published by Stosch in a supplement to his book, cf. Chapter 10 here for a full discussion and bibliography.

30 Letter from 23 October 1755 (see transcription hereafter in the Appendix).

31 Letter from 28 September 1783 (see transcription hereafter in the Appendix).

32 Letter from 23 April 1784 (see transcription hereafter in the Appendix).

33 MacKay Quynn 1941, pp. 337–338. She continued: *'Whatever the cause of his departure, Stosch reached Florence before the end of January, and was welcomed by resident scholars and antiquarians, as well as by the ruling prince. His house became the Mecca of distinguished travelers, English visitors, and learned Italians.'*

34 'Peccato che sia un eretico, ateista (...)', as noted in Rave 1965, p. 26.

35 Via dell'Arancio, next to the Collegio Liegese (Eggers 1926, pp. 223–224).

36 At nr. 57 of which was the entrance of the Mausoleum of Augustus.

37 Borgo degli Albizi 26–50122 Firenze FI, which is now the siege of Pandolfini auctioneers. On Stosch's addresses in Rome and then Florence, see: Hansson 2022a, p. 52.

38 Spier and Kagan 2000, p. 84, n. 76. See also: Spence 1966, vol. I, pp. 578–582, nos 1548–1555.

39 Hansson 2014, p. 17.

40 A sign of a possible falling out between 1725 and 1728 between Odam and Stosch is to be found in the absence of the artist from Ghezzi's second group portrait, cf. Chapter 4 here.

41 Hansson 2014, p. 21.

42 *Versammlung römischer Antiquare um den Baron Stosch* dated 1725 (chalk and ink, 270 × 395 mm, Albertina, inv. 1265) and *Barone Stosch e alcuni antiquari romani* dated 10 October 1728 (ink, Biblioteca Apostolica Vaticana, Cod. Ottob. Lat. 3116, fol. 191), see: Zazoff and Zazoff 1983, pp. 9–18, Kunze (ed.) 1998, pp. 139–140, and Chapter 2 here. *'The event depicted has been plausibly interpreted as a coin auction (Justi 1872, p. 301), but many of the people present were also important collectors and experts on engraved gems. The Albertina drawing from 1725 depicts Sabbatini, Stosch, Valesio, Andreoli, Fontanini, Ficoroni, Vitri, Palazzi, Odam, Bianchini, Grazini, Marsili, Strozzi, and Ghezzi himself. The later Vatican version, dated 1728, depicts Stosch, Ghezzi, Sabbatini, Valesio, Fontanini, Marsili, Bianchini, Viti, Strozzi, Borioni, Campioli, Forier, Ficoroni, Grazini, Andreoli, and*

eral ones issued on medals (Figs 9.5–9.6)⁴³ and carved on gems survive.⁴⁴

Stosch was a significant collector of drawings, as well as the commissioner of many new works. Pietrzak recently discovered that 26 Old Master drawings which had belonged to Stosch, *'including works by Raphael, Michelangelo, Correggio, Parmigianino, Annibale and Lodovico Carracci and Rubens'*,⁴⁵ were acquired by Stanisław Kostka Potocki (1755–1821).⁴⁶ In this context, considering his passion for both gems⁴⁷ and drawings, it is no surprise that Stosch would have owned drawings of gems. But those were not mentioned in his will (written in 1754).⁴⁸ Most of them were kept until his death and inherited by his nephew.⁴⁹

After his death, Stosch's library was offered for sale with a fixed-price catalogue entitled *Bibliotheca Stoschiana, sive catalogus selectissimorum librorum*: *'A sale catalogue was issued in Lucca, 1758, for the sale to take place in Florence, 16 January 1760, offering nearly 8000 lots. An* Index codicum manuscriptorum *(96 pp.), of 571 manuscripts was appended to a few copies, such as the Newberry Library copy. These manuscripts were sold en bloc to the Vatican Library. The sale of the printed books never took place and was therefore not the first Italian book auction as has been asserted; their catalogue was re-issued* [in 1759], *this time with printed prices, the books for sale at Stosch's house during February, 1760. The two catalogues are extremely rare.'*⁵⁰

Then, his paintings and drawings were consigned to four auctions in London on 6 February and 12 March 1760, 21–23 and 24 March 1764,⁵¹ and in Berlin on 22 April 1783 and following days.⁵² There were some 16 files containing drawings and engravings in the latter auction, the six first ones of which numbering some 918 items, including almost 4000 drawings of which over 2200 drawings of gems. Such a large number of 'documentary' drawings of gems is understandable since Stosch had *'acquired*

---

43 Fig. 5: François-Joseph Marteau (d. 1757), *Portrait of Philipp von Stosch (1691–1757)*, 1727, bronze medal (reverse with Diogenes), 40,72 mm diameter – Staatliche Kunstsammlungen Dresden Münzkabinett, inv. no.: 1991/A5545.
   Fig. 6: Johann Karl von Hedlinger (1691–1771), *Portrait of Philipp von Stosch (1691–1757)*, 1728, bronze medal (reverse with inscription: VIRI · GENEROSISSIMI · AC · DE· REB · ANTIQUS · OPTIME · MERITI · EFFIGIEM · AMICO · ADFECTU · AETERNITATI · DICARUNT · N · KEDER · NOBIL · SVEC · ET · I · C · HEDLINGER · EQUES · MDCCXXVIII), 41,5 mm diameter – Staatliche Kunstsammlungen Dresden Münzkabinett, inv. no.: 1991/A5546.

44 Stosch's portrait was engraved on gems in 1717 by Francesco Ghinghi (1689–1766); in around 1730 by Hieronymus/Girolamo Rossi (1682–1762); before 1731 by Carlo Costanzi (1705–1781); in around 1733, 1735 and 1739 by Lorenz Natter (1705–1763); and twice in around 1758 by Lorenzo Masini (b. 1713) on whom see: Pirzio Birolli Stefanelli 2006b, vol. II, pp. 890–897. On these, see: Kagan 1985; Gennaioli 2007, p. 441; Tassinari 2010a, pp. 94–95; Tassinari 2010b, p. 32; Gennaioli 2010, p. 281; Zwierlein-Diehl 2007, pp. 274 and 480. On his 1727 marble bust by Bouchardon, which was to be reproduced by Georg Martin Preißler in an engraving, see: Metz and Rave 1957 and Sénéchal 2000.

45 Pietrzak 2018.

46 Pietrzak 2018, pp. 127–128: *'From the enigmatic description in Des Neuen Gelehrten Europa* [Stosch 1757], *we learn that in this section, drawings including works by Michelangelo and his pupils were kept. There were also Raphael sketches and engravings based on them, and works by Perino del Vaga and Giulio Romano and other students of the Master of Urbino and contemporaneous artists. These were adjacent to sketches of ancient arabesques and bas-reliefs used by Raphael as sources of inspiration for his own works. There was also a group of works by famous Florentine artists including Giorgio Vasari, Santi di Tito, Antonio Tempesta and Jean de St. Jean, Pietro da Cortona, Livio Mehus, Volterrano. Certainly among the most interesting drawings were by Giulio Parigi and Baccio del Bianco, presenting masquerades and ceremonies at the Medici court. The description also mentions drawings by Stefano della Bella, Guido Reni, Joseph d'Arpino, Ciro Ferri, Carlo Maratta and Salvator Rosa. Work by von Stosch's friend Pier Leone Ghezzi could not be missed, as well. In addition to numerous Italian artists, a group of Dutch artists including Lucas van Leyden is also mentioned. Among German masters, Albrecht Dürer holds the eminent position. French painters included Claude de Lorraine, Jacques Callot, Simon de Vouet, Nicolas Poussin, Charles Le Brun. The collection concluded with architectural drawings as well as coats of arms, theater set design and drawings of occasional buildings. In* the context of research on the provenance of drawings from the collection of Stanisław Kostka Potocki, most interesting is the fact that among the many artists are Agostino, Ludovico and Annibale Carracci, Correggio, Titian, Parmigianino, Gaspard Poussin, Edmé Bouchardon and Ottavio Leoni'. Supposedly acquired by Potocki in Leipzig (from Carl Rost?), in the 1790s. Some of these drawings had been auctioned in Berlin in 1783. This is an additional – unexpected – link between Stosch, drawings and Poland.

47 Four of the seventy gems illustrated in Stosch's book (1724, pls XI, XIX, XXVIII and XXXVI) were from his own collection, cf. Appendix 1.

48 Published in Morelli Timpanaro 1996, pp. 425–428.

49 Cf. Chapter 5 here.

50 Entry from Christie's, catalogue of the Bibliotheca Bibliographica Breslaueriana, New York, 22–23 March 2005, lot 790.

51 Auction Stosch I – 8 pages, 278 lots (146 drawings and 132 prints); Auction Stosch II – unknown number of pages (catalogue *vidi* through a modern typescript), 81 lots; Auction Stosch III – 12 pages, 224 lots – not all of which were Stosch's. Pierce 1965, p. 209 had not seen a copy of this sale, and did not understand that Langford was the name of the auctioneer Abraham Langford (1711–1774) and tried vainly to identify a city with this name; Auction Stosch IV – 4 pages, 66 lots – not all of which were Stosch's.

52 Auction Muzell-Stosch 1783–78 pages, 1080 lots + some copperplates, sulphur gem impressions and varia. Only one copy is known of this catalogue, at the UCLA Clark Library, inv. Rare Books Z1015.S88-1783.

illustrations by Gaetano Piccini of wall paintings discovered during Bianchini's and the Duke of Parma's excavations on the Palatine, and Odam, Ghezzi and other artists were paid to carry out careful archaeological documentation around the city [i.e. Rome]'.⁵³ They were obviously scholarly witnesses as much if not more than just works of art, for him.

Since Wilhelm Homberg (1652–1715) improved their technique,⁵⁴ collecting casts and impressions of engraved gems had become a fashionable trend. The artist Pier Leone Ghezzi (1674–1755) recalled that '*since his childhood, together with Mons. Leone Strozzi*' (1657–1722), he had gathered '*with a lot of effort, impressions from the best museums of Europe*', and that they were '*both amused by this hobby*'.⁵⁵ The practice of making impressions of gems is well-attested, but also that of buying ready-made ones, even before the industrial enterprises of Dehn, Tassie, Paoletti, etc.: one knows for example that Dr Richard Rawlinson (1690–1755) bought twelve dozen paste copies of gems while he was staying in Paris in 1720.⁵⁶

Several of the gems illustrated and commented on in Stosch (1724) were lost at the time, or at least inaccessible, and Stosch and his draughtsmen used paste impressions of them.⁵⁷ Whilst staying at the court of the Duke of Orléans during his Grand Tour, Stosch had been taught by Homberg himself how to make good-quality impressions, and this had become his '*passion … main madness*'⁵⁸ as he admitted in 1714 in a letter addressed to François Fagel (1659–1746) (Figs 9.7–9.8),⁵⁹ leading him to visit numerous collectors around Europe, such as the princess Piombino in Rome (1715), Mario Piccolomini (1715), general Marsigli in Florence (1717), and the Elector of Saxony in Dresden (1718). It might be then, in order to look closely at gems, that he started to wear a monocle – a fashion which he is credited to have initiated. His ability was well-known, and he seems to have been willing to teach fellow amateurs. For example, Zanetti advised (in very poor French) the Earl of Carlisle to '*ask Monsieur the Baron Stosch in Florence, he will teach you, because he has an admirable way to make them*.'⁶⁰

Gifted at making them, and having employed as servant Christian Dehn (1696–1770),⁶¹ who became a casts-vendor in Rome, Stosch also owned an enormous documentation of modern paste impressions, which became the basis for the incredible group amassed by James Tassie (1735–1799), who acquired his '*above 17 000 sulphur impressions of Gems*' according to a letter from 9 July 1785.⁶² Unsubstantiated secondary sources cannot be fully relied upon, but it is worth noting that – according to Justi (1871), '*of every gem* [Stosch] *bought, of every coin and bronze, he sent impressions, drawings, descriptions to the Academy of Cortona*'.⁶³ This suggests indeed that he was a studious collector, a scholar even. Indeed, there are

---

53   Hansson 2022a, p. 58.
54   Homberg 1712. On him, see: Zwierlein-Diehl 1986, pp. 10–12; Welzel in Zwierlein-Diehl 1986, pp. 297–305, 301–303.
55   Manuscript catalogue of Pier Leone Ghezzi's *dactyliotheca* (1734) – Biblioteca Apostolica Vaticana Ms. 14928: '*Il valore, soprattutto documentario, di queste raccolte è sottolineato già nel 1734 da Pier Leone Ghezzi che ricorda di aver cominciato "sino da giovanetto assieme con Mons. Leone Strozzi" a raccogliere "con somma industria … solfi dalli migliori Musei di Europa" e che erano "tutti due burlati stimandosi che fosse una pazzia*". Strozzi was caricatured by Pier Leone Ghezzi in a drawing now in the Biblioteca Apostolica Vaticana, Cod. Ott. lat. 3112, fol. 66r (reproduced in Ubaldelli 2001, p. 81, fig. 38).
56   '*Bought of Madame Henrion, in the rue des Noyers, the intaglios or seals taken from the originals in the possession of the King of France, the Duke regent and his mother, in number 12 dozen. They are well done in a form of paste or glass and polished well to look good to the sight. They cost me 60 livres [i.e. 17.5 grams of fine gold], which is about 33 shillings English*' (Bodleian library, Oxford, Rawlinson MS D 1180–87).
57   On the difference between casts (*Abgüsse*) and impressions (*Abdrücke*), see: Zwierlein-Diehl 2007, pp. 326–329.
58   '*Ma passion …, ma folie dominante*'. This inevitably recalls the letter sent on 12 December 1758 by Caylus in which he declared: '*J'ai pris pour maîtresse l'antiquité: je la caresse, je la regarde, je l'étudie*' (Nisard 1877, vol. I, p. 19). And those words also remind of the March 1777 letter by the Marquis de Voyer d'Argenson: '*Les chevaux sont aujourd'hui mon gout dominant*' (Bibliothèque de l'université de Poitiers, P 130 mémoire à Bertin). This replacement of painting-collecting by horse-collecting, evokes the traditional opposition between shell-collecting and coin-collecting (Pomian 1976).
59   Letter from Stosch to Fagel, dated Paris 13 April 1714 (quoted in Heringa 1976, n. 5; and in Chapter 1 in this volume). Archives of the Fagel family, Algemeen Rijksarchief, The Hague, inv. 2027.
60   Letter from 4 June 1745 (see transcription hereafter in the Appendix).
61   Zwierlein-Diehl 1986, p. 12; Kockel and Graepler 2006, pp. 168–170; Knüppel 2009, pp. 67–69.
62   Glasgow City Archives, TD 68/1; quoted in Reilly 1994, pp. 95 and 396, n. 64. The number of Stosch's sulphur impressions of gems is variably recorded: over 30 000 impressions and casts according to Zazoff and Zazoff (1983, p. 75), Winckelmann mentions 28 000 '*empreintes en souffre*' (1760, p. XXIX), while Gurlitt says there were only 14 000 sulphurs in the Stosch collection (1798, p. 137) and a similar number is also mentioned by Winckelmann in his letter to Francke, 1 January 1759 – '*Herrn Lippert wünschte ich die große Sammlung von Schwefeln von allen Steinen in der Welt, so viel man hat haben können: es sind deren an 14 000*' (Winckelmann 1952–1957, vol. I, pp. 442–444). However, as established by Gołyźniak in Chapter 5 in this volume, originally Stosch collected indeed over 28 000 sulphur gem impressions of which almost half were lost in an accident during their transport to Hamburg in 1758, thus Tassie purchased only 17 000 of them.
63   Justi 1871, p. 25: '*Von jeder Gemme, die er kaufte, von jeder Münze und Bronze sandte er Abdrücke, Zeichnungen, Beschreibungen [an die Academie von Cortona]*' (noted in Chapter 8 in this volume too).

several mentions in Winckelmann (1760) that Stosch had written a (partial?) catalogue of his gems.[64] This manuscript has not survived,[65] and Gołyźniak argues that this catalogue was (co-)written by Stosch's brother, Heinrich Sigismund (1699–1747).[66]

A letter which Stosch sent to Johann Justus Preißler (1698–1771) on 29 May 1731 is sealed with a Greek (?) female bust,[67] but a glyptics-orientated study of his surviving correspondence remains to be done. Nevertheless, all that has been said above proves how much engraved gems were part of Stosch's daily life, on both the personal (collecting originals, impressions, drawings) and professional levels (antiquarian activities, networking, dealing, correspondence etc.). And when he died in 1757, Stosch bequeathed to his nephew a remarkable ensemble of 3444 ancient and modern gems. Most of these were then acquired in 1764 by Frederick the Great and are now in Berlin.[68] Some of those were spoliated by the French army in 1806,[69] but most were returned in 1871, and again by the Russian army after WWII. Amongst those, only a few glass pastes came back, while the rest might still be in Moscow at the Historical Museum.[70]

Stosch's Etruscan gems had a different fate, as most of them were sold shortly after his death to Giovanni Caraffa (1715–1768), Duke of Noia,[71] and were later acquired by Charles Francis Greville (1749–1809)[72] and are now in the British Museum.[73] It is by-the-way noteworthy that none was included in Stosch (1724), though many bear inscriptions. He might not have owned any himself by then, as the *Stosch'scher Stein*, a gem inscribed with the names Parthenopaios, Adrastos, Amphiaraos, Tydeus and Polyneikes,[74] was only acquired in 1755, but could certainly have had access to others in private collections. So, one must hypothesize that he understood their inscriptions to be the names of their original owners or of the figures depicted, rather than that of their engravers.

3 Preparing the *Pierres antiques gravées*

Stosch's book of 1724 is not a catalogue of a single collection, but a selection of signed gems from a number of cabinets worldwide, and the author paid unusual care to mentioning the present (and sometimes past) ownership of the gems which he was publishing.[75] The fate of some

---

64 Winckelmann 1760, p. 114, no. II.534 (*'C'est sous ce nom que cette tête a été marquée par le défunt Possesseur de notre Collection'*); pp. 159–160, no. II.909 (*'je me suis fondé sur l'ancien Catalogue de notre Collection'*); pp. 287–288, no. II.1768 (*'Je trouve dans l'Ancien Catalogue des Pierres Gravées de notre Collection, qu'on a cru voir ici (…)'*); pp. 367–368, no. III.226 (*'Feu le B. de Stosch l'a nommée ainsi, & dans ses Remarques il cite (…)'*); p. 374, no. III.247 (*'Dans l'ancien Catalogue des Pierres de notre Cabinet, je trouve (…)'*); pp. 411–412, no. IV.22 (*'Je trouve cette Pierre dans l'ancien Catalogue de notre Cabinet sous le nom (…)'*); p. 412, no. IV.26 (*'(…) que je trouve marquées par le Bar. De Stosch sous le nom de (…)'*); pp. 421–422, no. IV.83 (*'Dans l'ancien Catalogue de notre Cabinet je l'ai trouvée sous le nom (…)'*).
65 Many of Stosch's documents were lost at sea: *'Albani and Stosch never met after the latter left Rome, but they kept up a continual interchange of letters, mainly, it would appear, on the subject of antiquity. This correspondence is now almost certainly lost. In 1863 Alessandro's library in Rome was purchased through Mommsen for the Prussian government, but went to the bottom of the sea when the ship which was carrying it to Germany capsized. The consignment included 656 groups of miscellaneous papers.'* (Lewis 1967, pp. 324–326), but there is no reason to assume that Cardinal Albani (1692–1779) would have been given this manuscript, supposedly still in Muzell-Stosch's and Winckelmann's hands in 1760.
66 Chapter 8 in this volume. Wilton and Bignamini (1996, p. 300, no. 262) claim that Dehn also contributed to Stosch's original catalogue, but there is no information supporting this claim in Stosch's or Winckelmann's publications, correspondence or other archives.
67 The letter (in French!) is reproduced in Leitschuh 1886, pp. 23–24.
68 Platz-Horster 2012, p. 14. I am grateful to Ulf R. Hansson for informing me that the gem-cabinet, by Johann Heinrich Hülsemann, preserved at Sanssouci (ill. in Metz and Rave 1957, p. 25), is *not* Stosch's.
69 Overall, 538 intaglios and cameos from the Prussian cabinet were transported to Paris, see: Platz-Horster 2012, pp. 18–19.

  Their return started as early as 1815 but most were returned only in 1871, though Furtwängler claimed in a letter to Babelon that at least one gem was still missing (I am grateful to Ulf R. Hansson for mentioning this letter from the archives of the Bibliothèque nationale de France coin-cabinet, which he was shown by Mathilde Avisseau-Broustet).
70 Miller (ed.) 2005, pp. 311–325; Zwierlein-Diehl 2007, p. 275; Sena Chiesa, Magni and Tassinari 2009, pp. 175–176; Tassinari 2019, p. 82; Borbein, Kunze and Rugler 2019, pp. VII–VIII, n. 4.
71 Frans Hemsterhuis indirectly referred to this sale, in a letter from 8 December 1783 (see transcription hereafter in the Appendix), when he blamed Caraffa (on whom see Di Franco and La Paglia 2019) for having cheated *'our poor Stosch'*, meaning his heir Muzell-Stosch.
72 Schlichtegroll 1805, vol. I, p. 9. Nephew of Sir William Hamilton (1730–1803), whom his mistress Emma (1765–1815) married, he must not be confused with his homonym Charles Greville MP (1762–1832), husband of Charlotte Cavendish-Bentinck (1775–1862), who herself must not be confused with the coin- and gem-collector Charlotte-Sophie von Aldenburg Bentinck (1715–1800).
73 Gołyźniak 2023a, p. 9.
74 Winckelmann 1760, p. 344, no. III.172; Zazoff 1974; Zwierlein-Diehl 2007, pp. 82–84; Hansson 2014, p. 23, fig. 7.
75 Latteur 2012, p. 31: *'On notera la grande diversité des cabinets visités par von Stosch. Si la plupart des camées sont issus de différents cabinets italiens (41 sur 70), d'autres proviennent de France (6), d'Angleterre (5), d'Autriche (2), des Provinces-Unies (2), des principautés allemandes (2) ou encore des collections personnelles de*

of those are better known due to his private letters. For example, the Polykleitos gem (plate LIV) had been stolen from Pietro Andrea Andreini (1650–1729), but Stosch located it and wrote to him in 1720 that '*after much correspondence, I now know that your gem by Polykleitos is held by a certain Cavaliere di Rovigo, a.k.a. Count Carlo Silvestri. Do your best now to get it back*'.[76] Nevertheless, when Stosch's book was published four years later, the gem was described as '*formerly owned by Andreini*', which suggests that it had not yet been recovered.

Published, twenty-six years before Mariette's celebrated *Traité des pierres gravées*, and thirty-six years before Winckelmann's *Description des pierres gravées du feu Baron de Stosch*, Stosch's book on ancient signed gems helped to develop a general knowledge of engraved gems and an interest in them. The specific subject is an interesting evolution from earlier research devoted to portraits of *uomini illustri* (depictions of famous people), focusing instead on famous depicters.[77]

Stosch developed in the 1710s his taste for the – exceedingly rare – signed gems. He was not the first or only one, noting in his book that the abbot Pietro Andrea Andreini (1650–1729) had been '*le premier de tous qui ait recherché à grands frais & avec un travail immense les Pierres Gravées qui portent le Nom des Graveurs*' (plate V). But his passion was sincere, and not limited to buying originals, but also to obtaining casts of those which were not for sale. He was not searching for a 'niche' opportunity of a successful book, as he was still trying to acquire signed gems for his own collection long after publishing his work.[78]

Stosch was a real pioneer, if one considers that building an inventory of signed gems, carefully distinguishing genuine ancient ones from the later fakes, is still an ongoing task. '*Indefatigable, adventurous pioneers ...*'.[79]

Because of his modern art historical approach to gems, Stosch wanted to show that each carver has its own individual style. In order to escape additional bias by using several draughtsmen, Stosch chose to employ a single engraver – Picart – for all the plates, providing graphic uniformity.[80] An interest for signed gems was in the mood of time, as Charles César Baudelot de Dairval (1648–1722) published in 1717 a treatise on Solon's gems,[81] but Stosch had initiated his project before the publication of that booklet:[82] he had indeed started as early as 1715 to collect material for his forthcoming volume, commissioning drawings from Girolamo Odam (1681–1741).[83] Apparently one of the very first gems to be selected was the so-called Strozzi Medusa (plate LXIII), drawn at Stosch's request by Odam, and then engraved. Stosch sent a print of it to Fagel on 6 September 1715 and once approved, Odam drew it once again, this time, specifically for Stosch's book (Figs 9.9–9.12).[84] When his project

---

l'auteur (8)'. As opposed to this last figure, it should be noted that Stosch owned 'only' four of the seventy signed gems which he published in 1724: those illustrated on pls XI, XIX, XXVIII, and LIV. In the case of pls II, III and XXI, his pastes were used but he did not own the gems (cf. Appendix 1).

76 Letter from 16 September 1720 (see transcription hereafter in the Appendix). Andreini's amethyst by Teukros (Stosch 1724, pl. LXVIII) was also stolen, and he recovered it from Anton Maria Zanetti (1679–1767). It is not known how Carlo Silvestri (1690–1754) had obtained the carnelian by Polykleitos, nor therefore whether he knew that it was stolen-property. See: Zwierlein-Diehl 1986, p. 26 and Zwierlein-Diehl 2005, pp. 324–325.

77 This new fashion immediately led to the creation of new gems, and to the addition of new inscriptions on ancient gems, the extreme case being of course that of the collection of Prince Stanislas Poniatowski (1754–1833). Stosch 1724 was the first book solely devoted to these 'signed gems' (some of which, despite his efforts, were not genuine). He would be followed by Köhler 1851, Furtwängler 1913, and Vollenweider 1966. On the rise of the interest in gem-signatures, see: Zwierlein-Diehl 2007, pp. 279–280 and 300–304.

78 E.g., he acquired in 1739 Gnaios's intaglio of an *Athlete pouring oil* from Apostolo Zeno (now in Baltimore, The Walters Art Museum, inv. 42.109, see: Platz-Horster 1993, 11, who refers to Kent Hill 1975).

Gertrud Platz-Horster noticed that this gem's gold mount is very similar to that of another of Stosch's gems (Berlin, Antikensammlung, inv. FG 194 = AGDS II, p. 103, pl. 51.237). This suggests that they were mounted for Stosch with his design of choice. Too little attention is still being paid to the mounts of the gems, though it is not only an interesting aspect of the history of jewellery but also a potentially significant element of provenance-indication, and I must praise the efforts of Wagner and Boardman 2009. The study of Capponi's notes informs us that '*da 2 a 6 scudi erano necessary, a seconda del tipo di lavoro, per montare in oro una gemma antica*' (Donato 2004, p. 143).

79 '*Indefatigable, adventurous pioneers. O toiling hands of mortals! O unwearied feet, travelling ye know not wither! Soon, soon, it seems to you, you must come forth on some conspicuous hilltop, and but a little way farther, against the setting sun, descry the spires of El Dorado. Little do ye know your own blessedness; for to travel hopefully is a better thing than to arrive, and the true success is to labour*' wrote Robert Louis Stevenson, quoted in Wethered 1923, p. 108.

80 Reed 2010, p. 231. On the question of gem-illustrations, see: Stante 2006 and Chapter 3 in this volume.

81 Baudelot de Dairval 1717.

82 Hansson 2014, p. 18, referring to a letter from Stosch to Cuper on 8 August 1716 (quoted in Heringa 1976, p. 77).

83 See Stosch's letters to Fagel of 10 August 1715, and to Cuper of 8 August 1716 (see transcriptions hereafter in the Appendix).

84 Letter quoted in Heringa 1976, n. 25, *and Fagel forwarded it to Cuper on 21 March 1716* (letter quoted in Heringa 1976, n. 26). *Two states of the print exist, from 1715 and 1717, see*: Le Blanc 1854, p. 113 and Cazort and Percy 2004, no. 27, *which show some differences with Picart's 1724 plate*. Cf. also Chapter 8 in this volume for a detailed study of Odam's drawings.

neared completion, whenever possible, he supplied Picart with casts of the original gems, so that he could ensure the faithfulness of his plates. It seems that Picart had also done some of the impressions himself, according to a letter by Winckelmann: *'The alleged head of Alexander was engraved by* (sic!) *Mr. von Stosch*[85] *from a wax copy by Picart, which had been made by himself on the basis of this head, as large as half the size of the engraving'*.[86] Picart could therefore either correct the drawings that he was provided with the casts or draw directly from them.[87]

4 Writing the *Pierres antiques gravées*

The choice to publish bilingually was common at the time. For example, in 1729, Montfaucon wrote that he was forced to do so for his monumental *Antiquité expliquée*: *'the booksellers want me to put a Latin version at the bottom of the pages (…) They claim that this is necessary for many foreigners who don't understand enough French'*.[88] There is nevertheless a major difference: Montfaucon was writing in French, and this vernacular language was not (or so the publisher thought) read fluently by the entire erudite world. In Stosch's case, instead, the book was written in Latin, which suggests that he or Picart assumed that the French-speaking market was significantly large enough to justify the costs of a translation and of a thicker volume. The title indicates *Pierres antiques gravées … traduites en François par M. de Limiers*. Henri-Philippe de Limiers is a name shared by a father (d. 1728) and his son (d. 1758), both of whom were successively directors of the *Gazette d'Utrecht* – the translator is most likely the son, who had converted to Catholicism, acted as a spy, and was a correspondent of Fagel. The fact that it is translated from Latin into French, is noteworthy: *'Stosch knew very little Latin'*,[89] which gives weight to the rumours that Stosch was not the true author of the text.

Indeed, a drawn portrait of Stosch was annotated by its author Pier Leone Ghezzi (1674–1755), who knew him well, with the explanation that the sitter was: *'Baron Stoch, who published a book on gems with the names of the engraver, the explanations of which were made by the Abbot Valesio'*.[90] Stosch probably *did* write the introduction himself,[91] but he admitted that Francesco Valesio (1670–1742) was in fact the author of the commentaries.[92] Their closeness is confirmed by Stosch's commissioning in 1730 a medal from Markus Tuscher (1705–1751)[93] bearing Valesio's bust on the obverse, whilst the reverse bears the inscription BENE QVI LATVIT BENE VIXIT. PH. B. DE STOSCH AM. OPT. G.A.M.F.C. ROMAE MDCCXXX.V.T.XXV. Taken from Ovid's *Tristia*, the motto *'He lives well who lives unnoticed'* could be interpreted as a reference to Valesio's unsigned contribution to Stosch's book.

5 Publishing the *Pierres antiques gravées*

The writing and preparation of Stosch (1724) therefore lasted some nine years, starting with the choice in 1715 to collect drawings and impressions of all the signed gems that he could locate and examine. By August 1715, he owned casts of the Apollonides gem (pl. XI) and of four gems by Dioscurides (pls XXVI–XXXI); by September 1715, he owned 50 impressions, and Odam had finished eight drawings.[94] Already that year, in November, it was known in Rome that Stosch had prepared an *'excellent work'* about signed ancient gems.[95]

---

85   Stosch 1724, pl. LV.
86   Letter from 1 May 1762 (see transcription hereafter in the Appendix).
87   In the case of the following eighteen plates Picart did not have the casts, as they would otherwise be marked by a star in the bottom-right corner: IV, VI, XIV, XVII, XXI, XXVI, XXXI, XXXII, XXXIX, XLII, XLIII, L, LV, LVII, LIX, LX, LXVII and LXX.
88   '*Les libraires souhaitent que je mette une version latine au bas des pages … Ils prétendent que cela est nécessaire à beaucoup d'étrangers qui n'entendent pas assez le français*' (quoted in Le Gall 2019, pp. 176–177).
89   Hansson 2014, p. 20, who refers to Zazoff and Zazoff 1983, pp. 53–54 and n. 180.
90   Biblioteca Apostolica Vaticana, Cod. Ottob. lat. 3112, fol. 115: '*Baron Stoc, che publico un libro di gemme col nome dell'intagliatore, a cui fece le spiegazioni l'Abb. Valesio. Fu esiliato di Roma per la sua irreligiosità*'.
91   Cf. Chapter 1 here, as well as: Giovanni Lami in *Novelle Letterarie* 46, 18 November 1757, (pp. 720–723), and Hansson 2022, p. 48.
92   Letter from 16 August 1746 (see transcription hereafter in Appendix). Hansson 2014, p. 20: '*Justi (1872: 334) takes for granted that the real author was Valesio, as does Reinach (1895: 156). Zazoff assumes that Valesio wished to remain anonymous (Zazoff and Zazoff 1983: 24). Doubts on the truth of these allegations have been cast by Jan Heringa (1976: 82–83)*'.
93   Regarding Stosch and medals, see Hansson 2025b.
     Earlier in 1730, Tuscher had been working for cardinal Melchior de Polignac (1661–1742), but – upset not to have yet been paid – he stopped and chose to devote himself to Stosch's request, see: Borroni Salvadori 1978b, p. 94.
94   Letter from Stosch to Fagel, dated Rome 7 September 1715 (quoted in Heringa 1976, n. 29) – Archives of the Fagel family, Algemeen Rijksarchief, The Hague, inv. 2028.
95   Letter from Giusto Fontanini (1666–1736) to Gijsbert Cuper (1644–1716), Rome, 9 November 1715 (quoted in Heringa 1976, n. 21) – Koninklijke Bibliotheek, The Hague, inv. 72G23.

By May 1718, 62 drawings of gems had been completed, and Stosch did not plan to commission any more: '*My book on the sculpture of the ancients is finished. The sixty-two drawings have been finished in ink with the same exactitude as with the Minerva by Aspasius that I sent you*'.[96] But, because this entire book is a reflection on sculpture, all its beauty consists in being engraved under my eyes and direction, as otherwise the book and engravings would not fit together'.[97] In December, Stosch returned to Amsterdam, initiating his search for a capable engraver for the book. Collectors such as Lambert ten Kate (1674–1731) and Nicolaas Kalf (1677–1734) recommended Bernard Picart (1673–1733), whom Stosch immediately hired for sixty engravings, paying 60 Gulden each.[98]

From this point onwards, the progress of the book is more difficult to follow in the absence of correspondence – Stosch lived in The Hague for three years and could meet with (rather than write to) Fagel. In any case, publication of the book was announced in 1721,[99] with the precision that it contained the depictions of 65 gems (i.e. more than was considered in 1718 but less than would actually be printed in 1724). A public subscription started on 1 August 1721, running until 31 January 1722, with the promise that the book would be delivered no more than two years afterwards.[100] The *Republic of Letters* seems to have been awaiting it anxiously, with – for example – a *Kurmainzer Rat* from Mayence writing to Montfaucon that '*Mr baron von Stosch will publish a volume of 60 antiquities* [i.e. ancient engraved gems], *and has already had some of these engraved*'.[101]

The following year, Stosch's correspondence mentions his collecting activities but not the book project: '*I live here in great peace … just enlarging every day my library and collection of engraved gems, as this is my only joy*'.[102] But by 1723, he had sent several 'dissertations' (extracts from his book?) to Fagel, and begged him to accept to be the dedicatee of the volume. Fagel modestly declined the honour on 7 May, writing to Stosch that: '*your book is too beautiful to be dedicated to a stupid private person such as me. You shall easily find higher Lords to please*'.[103] So, in August 1723, Stosch wrote instead the book's final dedication to the Holy Roman Emperor, Charles VI (1711–1740). It is likely the same year that he wrote the preface, which cannot predate the book's printing by much, as it mentions an engraved diamond that was first published in 1723.[104]

In the absence of a colophon, the exact date of printing of the book remains unknown, but Picart sent the first copy to Fagel in March 1724,[105] whilst Stosch himself apparently did not receive copies until the end of the year. It had reached Vienna by then already, as Apostolo Zeno mentioned to his elder brother: '*reading the preface of the book entitled* Gemmae antiquae caelatae, Sculptorum (sic!) nominibus insignitae, *illustrated by the famous Bernard Picart, and published and explained by Philip of*

---

96   This information is noteworthy, considering that Stosch had not yet met Picart: those sixty-two drawings must therefore be attributed to Odam. *Picart* (1734, p. 8) mentions: '*Mr. Stosch avoit pris des Empreintes de toutes ces Pierres, à quelques-unes près, & en avoit fait faire des Desseins en Italie par Jerome Odam, & le Chevalier Ghezzi, dans l'intention de les faire graver d'après ces Desseins*'. This is the only source that ascribes such preliminary drawings to Ghezzi, but Chapter 8 in this volume discusses the possibility to attribute to him the drawings for plates IV and VI which are now in Krakow.

97   Letter from 4 May 1718 (see transcription hereafter in the Appendix).

98   Letter from Stosch to Fagel, dated Amsterdam, 1 January 1719 (quoted in Heringa 1976, n. 48). Archives of the Fagel family, Algemeen Rijksarchief, The Hague, inv. 2032. I am grateful to Ulf Hansson for informing me that Stosch and Picart had already met before, in the early 1710s, from the Chevaliers de Jubilation (see: Hansson 2025c). Sixty gulden amounted to 36.34 grams of fine gold (1.28 oz).

99   Leclerc 1721, pp. 229–231.

100 Heringa 1976, n. 55.

101 Letter from 18 October 1721 (see transcription hereafter in the Appendix). An undated letter addressed to Montfaucon informed him that '*Mr Picart has been busy for several months engraving the gems that Mr Stosch collected from the oldest engravers such as Praxiteles, etc., during a trip he made around Europe over several years. There will be sixty-six in all. Mr Picart is giving it all his attention. Several plates have already been produced, but they have been done with a master's hand. It has to be said that Picart has outdone himself. Six plates will be published in an attempt to obtain subscriptions from the curious*' (see transcription hereafter in the Appendix). Its author, the Amsterdam printer Jacques Clermont was '*intimement lié avec les deux Picart, le père et le fils, tous deux graveurs de grand talent, fort en vogue alors et également d'origine française. Ces deux artistes, qui surent, à ce que disent les contemporains, allier le culte des arts à celui de leur fortune, gagnaient beaucoup d'argent à graver des planches d'après les antiques. C'était, on le comprend, tout à fait l'affaire de dom Bernard, et Clermont lui écrit avec détails la suite et le progrès de ces publications qui l'intéressaient si fort*' (according to his letters' editor, Emmanuel de Broglie).

102 Letter from 19 December 1722 (see transcription hereafter in the Appendix).

103 Letter from 7 May 1723 (see transcription hereafter in the Appendix).

104 Attributed by Stosch to Giovanni Costanzi (ca. 1674–1754), this gem had been offered for sale in February 1723 by a Venetian, Andrea Cornaro, and later acquired by Anton Maria Vaini (1660–1737). It had been described as: '*un Diamant du poids de vingt-cinq grains* [i.e. about 8 carats], *d'une vilaine eau, plein de pailles, & mal poli*', cf. Appendix 1.

105 Letter from Fagel to Stosch, dated 24 March 1724 (quoted in Heringa 1976, n. 93) – Archives of the Fagel family, Algemeen Rijksarchief, The Hague, inv. 2038.

Stosch in Latin, with the French translation of Mr. de Limiers alongside, and printed in Amsterdam at the said Picart 1724. In-folio.[106]

6 Illustrating the *Pierres antiques gravées*

Bernard Picart (1673–1733) both published Stosch's book in Amsterdam[107] and engraved himself all of its seventy plates (which are signed '*Picart sculpsit*'), work which he carried out over several years.[108] He was the son of the engraver Etienne Picart *le Romain* (1632–1721), who engraved glyptic plates for a new edition of the *Images des heros et des grands hommes de l'Antiquité* by Giovanni Angelo Canini (1609–1666),[109] which was to be published by his son in Amsterdam in 1731. The son's taste for small-sized antiquities might have been transmitted from his teacher Sébastien Leclerc (1637–1714), who contributed to a number of numismatic books.[110]

The difficulty in choosing the right draughtsman was explained in 1747 by Caylus to Gori (who probably knew it well!). The Florentine had asked the Parisian for an engraving of an ivory, and Caylus replied that he had it redrawn, despite the difficulty finding an artist gifted enough, but also not so gifted that he added his touch to the result.[111] It has been noted that '*The question of the botanical drawing is essential, from the point of view of conservation: indeed, the material quickly deteriorates once harvested. Not all draftsmen are as talented as the Austrian brothers Franz and Ferdinand Bauer, who approach perfection, both in terms of technical precision and in terms of artistry*'.[112] The same issues about ability and fidelity arise for the drawings of antiques, even if there is not the same need for urgency. The choice of a draughtsman is complex, his ability not being the only criteria but also his faithfulness, as noted by the sculptor Etienne Maurice Falconet in 1711: '*Do not always rely on a design made from certain ancient works. The more the design will be made by a skilful Draftsman, the more the Draftsman will have reasons to show you the Antique as beautiful* [rather than a truthful depiction], *and the more his design should be suspect to you*'.[113] The same issue had been described in 1695 by the numismatist Andreas Morell: '*My engravers enrage me by always wanting to add to my designs and to embellish inappropriately*',[114] though in his case it was not about drawing from the antique (which he was doing himself), but rather about engraving from his drawings.

Very few plates in Stosch (1724) mention an artist's name as credit for the original drawing, though it is known that in 1721 Picart was provided with drawings of each gem.[115] The majority were by Odam,[116] but one was by Netscher,[117]

---

106 Letter from 2 December 1724 (see transcription hereafter in the Appendix).
107 Born in Paris, Picart travelled to the Low Countries in 1696–1697, and in 1711 moved permanently to Amsterdam, where he died.
108 The plates IV, VI, XIII, XXVIII, LV and LXX are dated 1719. The plates I, II, III, VIII, X, XV, XVI, XVIII, XIX, XXV, XXVII, XXIX, XXX, XXXVIII, XL, XLV, XLVI, LI, LII, LIII, LVI, LVIII, LXIII, LXIV, LXV and LXVI are dated 1722. The plates V, VII, IX, XI, XII, XIV, XVII, XX, XXI, XXII, XXIII, XXIV, XXVI, XXXI, XXXII, XXXIII, XXXIV, XXXV, XXXVI, XXXVII, XXXIX, XLI, XLII, XLIII, XLIV, XLVII, XLVIII, XLIX, L, LIV, LVII, LX, LXI, LXII, LXVII, LXVIII and LXIX are dated 1723. The plate LIX is dated 1724.
109 The book's preface mentions that Canini was gifted at drawing engraved gems, so it is a plausible hypothesis that the 1731 plates would be after 116 unpublished drawings that were not used for the original (1669) unillustrated edition.
110 On the quest for perfectly illustrated, typeset and printed books at the time, see Rambach 2008, about the 1723 edition of the *Médailles sur les principaux évènements du règne entier de Louis le Grand avec les explications historiques*, a book whose vignettes were often the work of Leclerc, whilst the majority of the medals were engraved by Charles-Nicolas Cochin (1688–1754).
111 Letter from 20 October 1747, (transcribed in *Revue* 1882; quoted in Griener 2010, p. 194: '*je vous envoye en même tems un dessein du même dyptique, tout autrement exact que l'estampe. (...) Il n'était plus question que de trouver un dessinateur exact, et rien n'est si difficile. Si c'est un peintre supérieur dans son art, il a ordinairement une manière faite à laquelle il ne manque pas de rapporter tout ce qui sort d'entre ses mains. Si, au contraire, on s'adresse à un dessinateur ordinaire, il s'en acquitte mal; et d'une ou d'autre manière, il arrive que l'imitation ne se fait que très imparfaitement.*').
112 Beaurepaire 2019, pp. 100–101: '*La question du dessin botanique est essentielle du point de vue de la conservation. En effet, une fois récolté, le matériau s'altère rapidement. (...) Tous les dessinateurs n'ont pas le talent des frères autrichiens Bauer, Franz et Ferdinand, qui s'approchent de la perfection, tant sur le plan de la précision technique que sur le plan artistique.*'
113 Falconet 1771, p. 76 (quoted in Meyer 2022, p. 37): '*Ne vous fiez pas toujours à un dessein fait d'après certains ouvrages antiques. Plus le dessein sera fait par un habile Dessinateur, plus le Dessinateur aura de raisons pour vous montrer l'Antique en beau, et plus son dessein doit vous être suspect.*'
114 Letter from 29 January 1695 (see transcription hereafter in the Appendix).
115 Cf. Chapter 1 here, after Stosch 1754, p. 38.
116 Only 10 plates are mentioned as being engraved after Odam (pls XIV, XVII, XXI, XXVI, XXXII, XLII, XLIII, LVII, LX and LXVII).
117 The 'Marlborough gem' (plate LXX) was kept in London, where Stosch saw it in person (according to a letter sent to Fagel, from Paris on 8 September 1713). Through Fagel, Stosch asked for help of the Dutch envoy extraordinary to the Court of Great Britain, Mr van Borsselen to obtain a drawing of it (letter from Rome 17 August 1715). Theodorus Netscher (1661–1728) was then commissioned and, through Fagel again, Stosch received a drawing and a cast in June 1716 (see: Heringa 1976, n. 28).

two by Zanetti,[118] two maybe by Ghezzi,[119] and seven by Picart himself.[120]

For some gems, Picart was also provided with an actual cast of the gem, otherwise he had to rely on the drawing only: '*The plates marked with a star are those for which Bernard Picart was given the pastes or prints; for the others, he followed exactly the drawings he was given.*'[121] But, in his preparation for the engravings, in order to achieve a coherent style, Picart redrew each gem – and this explains why the Spencer-Churchill album (see below) apparently contained drawings for each of the seventy plates – not just those that are also signed by Picart as draughtsman.

According to a publication which is part-obituary and part-retail-catalogue, of uncertain authorship,[122] Odam's drawings were '*neither in good taste, nor correct, and [Picart] could not find in them the fineness of expression of the heads that he could see in the stones. He therefore decided to draw them again from the impressions, with the exception of those for which Mr Stosch had not been able to obtain impressions, and which had to be engraved after the drawings that he had had made of them*'.[123] This opinion was apparently shared by others, such as the contemporary who wrote that: '*When M. Picart engraved the gems with the author's name, they sent him the badly done drawings by Cavalier Odam (...) Those who do not know the whole story cannot understand how Picart made such awful plates.*'[124]

I already mentioned an album which is significant about Stosch (1724) and the contribution of Picart. Indeed, there is a large number of drawings[125] in red chalk, with a common provenance (Spencer-Churchill), which are believed to be the works of Picart, preliminary to his engraving of the book's plates. Until recently, these were bound together in a volume which originally belonged to François Fagel (1659–1746). It was sold as part of his estate in 1801,[126] when it was bought by the auctioneer himself for £1/14/0. He was a book and print dealer, possibly bidding on behalf of a client. They were most likely acquired by Fagel directly from Picart because in a letter to Stosch of 3 January 1719, Fagel made it clear that he did not intend to pay for the engravings – presumably as opposed to the drawings (of which he was a passionate collector).[127]

---

118 Because they were in Venetian collections, it was drawings by Anton Maria Zanetti (1679–1767) that were used for the gems L and LIX, rather than by Odam (who nevertheless had a cast of the first one).

119 Heringa (1976, p. 84) ascribed two more drawings to Odam (pls IV and VI), but Golyzniak argues that they are after Ghezzi instead, cf. Chapter 8 here. Distinguishing Odam's drawings from Picart's is easy, as showed by those discovered in Krakow, and not only because Odam worked in pen and ink whereas Picart used red chalk (as noted in Whiteley 1999, p. 184). But Picart '*imitated so exactly the drawings [by Odam] that had been done in ink, that he rightly copied the brush-strokes line per line*' (Picart 1734, p. 8) that identifying the draughtsman on the basis of the engravings is difficult.

120 '*Picart delineavit et sculpsit*', plates II, X, XXVIII, XLVIII, LI, LV, LXII. Surprisingly, some plates are not attributed to any draughtsman, and four of these do not have a star either (plates IV, VI, XXXI, XXXIX), though an unsigned plate with a star would have been attributable to Picart. Did he forget to add a star and to sign as draughtsman, or did he forget to mention who the original artist was? Two of these in fact were certainly likely copied from book-illustrations: plate XXXI after Beger (1696–1701, vol. III, p. 192) and plate XXXIX after Orsini (1598, no. 75), as demonstrated by Heringa (1976, p. 86).

121 Stosch 1724, p. V: '*Les Planches marquées d'une Etoile sont celles dont on a communiqué les Pâtes ou les Empreintes à Bernard Picart; pour les autres, il a suivi exactement les desseins qu'on lui en a donné*'. The description in Auction Picart 1737, pp. 10–11 of '70. *Planches, Folio, dessinées, & gravées par B. Picart d'après des Pierres Antiques, (quelques unes on (sic) été gravées d'après des desseins du Chevalier Odam, ce sont celles qui n'ont pas de petite étoile au coin de la Planche en bas)*' seems misleading: the gems without a star mean that Picart had to rely *exclusively* on the drawing that he was supplied with, but the presence of a star means that he was able to check *the* veracity of the drawings, and not that he drew them himself directly from the cast.

122 Picart 1734 might be written by the artist's widow Anna Vincent, or by Prosper Marchand, see: Dury (ed.) 2019.

123 Picart 1734, p. 8: '*ni de bon gout, ni corrects, & [Picart] n'y remarqua pas non plus cette finesse des airs de Têtes, qu'il apercevoit dans les pierres. Il se resolut donc à les dessiner de nouveau d'après les Empreintes, à la reserve de quelques-unes, dont Mr Stosch n'a pu avoir d'Empreintes, & qu'il fallut graver d'après les Desseins qu'il en avoit fait faire.*'

124 Letter from 27 August 1748 (see transcription hereafter in the Appendix). The same writer '*remarked that he would like very much to see a list of the books Stosch had promised to write; another, of the things he claimed to have discovered; and a third, of the things he had stolen*' (MacKay Quynn 1941, p. 336).

125 Whiteley 1999, p. 186, n. 20 indicates that the Department of the History of Art (Oxford) holds photographs of the drawings for the plates III, XI (with a variant), XXIX, XXXV, XLVII, XLVIII and LXI. In the absence of any other information on the actual drawings (size, provenance or location), we did not judge it useful to include them here.

126 Sale by Thomas Philipe, London, 29 May 1801, lot 128: '*a small porte-folio, in vellum, containing the drawings made by Bernard Picart, from the gems, engraved by him in the celebrated work of Baron Stosch – elegantly and carefully designed in red chalk, and consisting of 85 pieces; some of them duplicates – a precious collection.*'

127 Heringa 1976, p. 78, n. 78: '*Stosch an Fagel, Amsterdam 1. January 1719. Merkwürdig ist es, dass Stosch schreibt, die Konditionen vereinbart zu haben in Ausfrträgen die ihm von Fagel gegeben wurden; Fagel distanziert sich aber in seiner Antwort vom 3. Januar: er habe nie vorgehabt, die Zeichnungen auf seine Kosten stechen zu lassen; er würde aber die Vollendung des Werkes schätzen und mit Freude ein Exemplar kaufen.*'

The volume reappeared at auction in 1965,[128] when Christie's dispersed the collection of the Northwick family. The main collector of the family had been John Rushout, 2nd Lord Northwick (1770–1859),[129] whose collections were inherited by his eldest nephew George John Rushout, 3rd Baron Northwick (1811–1887). His wife had a daughter from a previous marriage, Augusta Warburton (1854–1941), who married Edward Spencer-Churchill (1853–1911), and the auctions took place after the death of their first son, who was Edward George Spencer-Churchill (1876–1964).[130] It was then described as an early-nineteenth-century folio album entitled *Dissegne di Gemmi Antiche*, bound in red half morocco and containing '79 *fine sepia drawings*'. Having purchased it at the sale, Christopher Powney resold it to Sven Gahlin, who broke up the album and sold most of the drawings to Yvonne ffrench (all three were London print dealers). Unfortunately, the album was dispersed without a complete photographic record having been made of it.

The album, which had been rebound in-between, contained 85 drawings in 1801, but only 79 in 1965, whilst the book itself (Stosch 1724) contains only 70 plates. So, what happened to the six drawings that disappeared before 1965, and what were the fifteen 'extra' drawings? Some of the missing items must be the so-called 'duplicates' mentioned in the 1801 description, and Whiteley noted that the album contained two drawings for plate XI (one of the whole gem, the other of just the reclining bull).[131] The latter could be a study or preparatory drawing. It is also possible that some non-gem-related drawings had originally been included in the album and were removed,[132] and the album also likely contained some drawings of unsigned gems (Fig. 9.13).[133]

It is noteworthy to observe that a group of two original red chalk drawings[134] and 10 red chalk counterproofs ('offsets') of drawings by Picart on elaborate engraved cartouches, signed at the bottom *B. Picart delin.*, are preserved in The Hague.[135] They once belonged to Frederick de Thoms (1669–1746) and were acquired from his daughters, alongside his gems, in 1751 by William IV, Prince of Orange (1711–1751).[136] The two originals within this group (referring to plates VII and LV) are undoubtedly studies or preparatory drawings (Figs 9.14–9.15). Moreover, there is also a small group of two works by Picart in Krakow – No. 391 (a counterproof of pl. X) and No. 392 (a study or preparatory drawing for pl. XXXIV). Both groups, most likely originate from '*Cent & huit contre-épreuves des Cornalines par B. Picart*', an ensemble that was sold at Picart's estate

---

128   Christie's, London, 24 November 1965, lot 67.
129   Did Philipe in 1801 have a commission-bid of the second Lord Northwick? The family continued to acquire for many decades: e.g. two Marlborough intaglios (lots 59 and 61 of the Christie's, 7 December 1965 auction) were acquired at Christie's on 27 June 1899, and some of their coins were bought as recently as 1936.
130   Christie's held a number of sales from the collection in 1965. In the prints and drawings auction of 25 May 1965, lot 122 was '*Italian school. Studies after Old Masters, antique and other sculpture, of horses, flowers and other subjects, by various hands – in various media – (fifty-three)*' – could gems be amongst the '*antique sculptures*'?
  The Northwick/Spencer-Churchill book sale contained some gem books (Gori 1767, Le Blond and Le Chau 1780–1784, Wicar 1789–1807), and the November sale contained even more (Bartolozzi 1780–1791, Caylus 1775, Eckhel 1788, Mariette 1750, Marlborough 1845, Worlidge 1768), but neither contained a copy of Stosch 1724.
131   Whiteley 1999, p. 186, n. 26, without source.
132   When Christie's dispersed the Walter Lees collection in 2010, they sold as a group seven drawings by Picart: four were after gems (and with the Northwick-ffrench provenance) and three were not (the only one described was a *Study of a woman's sleeve*, and a ca. 140 × 200 mm *Study of a left foot* might be a free study after the fragmented colossal marble statue of Constantine in the Capitoline Museums).
133   A drawing of an unsigned gem by Picart, apparently from the Spencer-Churchill album, later in the collection of Burnet Pavitt (1908–2002), by whom bequeathed to the Royal College of Music, by whom sold at Christie's (London South Kensington) on 12 December 2003 as part of lot 544; later offered for sale at Artcurial (Paris) on 21 June 2010 as part of lot 1, and sold at Artcurial (Paris) on 4 February 2011 as part of lot 63, purchased by a London private collector by whom resold in May 2011, accompanied two drawings by Picart made for Stosch 1724 (pls LI and LXVIII).
134   Stosch 1724, pls VII and LV.
135   Stosch 1724, pls II, VII, IX, XII, XVI, XX, XXVII, XXIX, LXII and LXIII. These counterproofs are described in Appendix 2, along with the drawings by Picart which we could locate.
136   Now in the The Royal Library of the Netherlands in The Hague: 'Thoms' portfolio' 72A20 3rd series, pls 1–3, 5–7, 9–10, 13 and 16–18. They are accompanied by six more red chalk drawings attributed to Picart too, which, however, do not depict the signed gems but regular ones. Thoms is attested to have collected drawings of antiquities and even collaborating on documentation of antiquities and especially his own gems with a number of artists, some of whom were related to Stosch too, notably Ghezzi and Picart and he was preparing a publication of his collection of engraved gems as an illustrated catalogue (Maaskant-Kleibrink 1978, pp. 25–26 – who takes all Picart drawings as originals, not counterproofs). We are grateful to Hein Maassen and Jeroen Vandommele for informing us that the 'Thoms' portfolio' was acquired by the The Royal Library of the Netherlands in The Hague in 1901. It was described by Korteweg and de Heer (1988, p. 110) as '*Les antiquités du Cabinet du Comte de Thoms*', 2 volumes, 104 folios in 113, ca. 320 × 210 mm. Volume II, third series: '*Bernard Picart (1673–1733), Achttien tekeningen van gesneden stenen bevestigd binnen de cartouches van gegraveerde bladen*'.

auction in 1737.[137] As argued by Gołyźniak, it seems likely that Picart kept this (originally complete?) set of counterproofs, as well as sketches, and perhaps additional drawings of gems unrelated to Stosch's book (Fig. 9.16), whilst the original drawings were offered to Fagel.[138]

7 The Excluded Gems and the Second Volume of *Pierres antiques gravées*?

Over the nine years of preparation of his book, Stosch acquired his later widely acclaimed connoisseurship, especially regarding signed engraved gems. However, to choose which intaglios and cameos should be published in his study and which ones should not was undoubtedly a difficult task. As proved in our edition of Stosch (1724) (cf. Appendix 1), both modern imitations and gems with added signatures were already circulating at the time, as well as copies of genuine originals, which had been described or published in the sixteenth and seventeenth centuries – but have been lost since then. An example is an amethyst intaglio known since the sixteenth century.[139] Stosch believed at first that the original was a gem which he acquired and owned until his death,[140] and he commissioned its drawing to Odam (Fig. 9.17). He then decided that the original was rather a gem, which is now in the Bibliothèque nationale de France, and commissioned a new drawing, which was then used to engrave plate XXVII. Neither are the ancient stone – which remains lost to this day – and Odam's drawing remained unused.

The changing number of gems Stosch intended to publish in the book (cf. above) also proves that new discoveries were made whilst the book was being produced. For example, the counterproof of a lost drawing by Picart, in The Hague, depicts a gem with the portrait of Maecenas signed ϹΟΛΩΝΟϹ (Fig. 9.18).[141] It is related to the plate LXII, in which Stosch mistakenly illustrated a gem from the Riccardi collection, whereas the text mentions a gem in the Boncompagni-Ludovisi collection, both of which are copies of a lost original once owned by Caesare de Camei. Let us remember that not all Picart's drawings were done for Stosch, and that not all Picart's drawings that were done for Stosch relate to the book *Pierres antiques gravées*.[142] But this counterproof by Picart depicts the Boncompagni-Ludovisi copy (Fig. 9.19),[143] which suggests a change of heart by Stosch about which example to illustrate in his book.[144]

Those two examples do not only illustrate the ongoing research process of Stosch's research and book project, but also suggest the potential existence of even more drawings by Odam, Picart and other draughtsmen. Having organised a subscription, Stosch could not delay the book's publication indefinitely, but his research continued and he was working on the subject. He continued corresponding with Valesio, who was seemingly '*providing learned commentaries to the endless row of illustrations of gems that Stosch acquired*'.[145] Those might have been for Stosch's private use, such as preparing a catalogue of his collection, but it might also have been with the idea

---

137 His estate was sold at auction in Amsterdam by Philippe Van Der Land, 25 November 1737 and following days (Auction Picart 1737). The books included three copies of Stosch's book on large paper (lots 76, 77, 79) and one on regular paper (lot 85). Lots 133–135, of prints, contained '*22/15/14 Pieces cornalines de Madame Cheron*', probably groups of the 1709 print of the '*Cachet de Michel-Ange*'. Finally, the lot 15 included '*Cent & huit contre-épreuves des Cornalines par B. Picart*'.

138 Cf. Chapter 8 here. All rediscovered Picart's drawings made for Stosch (1724) originating from the Spencer-Churchill Album are catalogued in Appendix 2. After the Spencer-Churchill sale of 1965, the drawings were attributed to Edmé Bouchardon (1698–1762). It was Nadia Baalba in 1967 who realised what they were, and argued that the Spencer-Churchill album contained the 70 drawings, plus nine not connected to the book (Balbaa 1968, p. 166; Whiteley 1999, p. 184).

139 Orsini 1570, no. 146; Furtwängler 1900, vol. II, 241; Zwierlein-Diehl 1986, no. 859.

140 Berlin, Antikensammlung, inv. no.: FG 9198 – Winckelmann 1760, class IV, no. 215, p. 441; Furtwängler 1896, no. 9198; Borbein, Kunze and Rügler 2019, no. IV.215.

141 The Royal Library of the Netherlands in The Hague: 'Thoms' portfolio' 72A20 3rd series, pl. 6.

142 For example, the Spencer-Churchill album contained a few drawings of gems that are not signed (which therefore cannot be preparatory to the 1724 book) but which nevertheless were likely drawn for Stosch considering their shared provenance with the drawings for the *Pierres antiques gravées*.

143 Rome, Musei Capitolini, inv. no.: Med 6732, carnelian intaglio, 21 × 25 mm, see: Molinari et al. 1990, 61, no. 36. From the collection of Francesco Martinetti (1833–1885), discovered on 22 February 1933 when destructing his home on Via Alessandrina 101 in Rome. At the time, there were two more copies circulating, one in Vienna and the second in the Farnese collection. For a discussion on the original gem and its copies, cf. Appendix 1, pl. LXII.

144 Possible reasons would include doubts in the gem's authenticity, or at least in the age of the signature. Some plates were indeed apparently cancelled: were they re-engraved, or were these additional gems? In 1847, the London bookdealer Henry G. Bohn offered for sale '*Sixty-three Miscellaneous Proofs, Etchings, and Cancelled plates, of the preceding work* [Stosch, Pierres antiques gravées ...], *with Portrait, the engraver's own copy, unbound*' at the low price of £0.15.0 (it was still listed in the 1848 edition of Bohn's catalogue).

145 Quoted in Chapter 1 here by Ulf R. Hansson, who refers to a letter from Stosch to Venuti from 16 August 1747 (see: Engelmann 1909, pp. 333–335).

of writing a second volume: this is suggested by Ghezzi sending in 1731 of a watercolour drawing of an additional signed gem,[146] and this hypothesis is developed further in this volume.[147]

In his letter to the Duke of Devonshire, sent from Rome on 24 July 1728, Stosch had expressed his intention to 'engrave on one plate the different engraved gems with the names of the forged engravers, invented or copied in modern times',[148] and no such study of forgeries can be found in the 1724 publication, which suggests that the drawings of the gems which he decided not to include in his book might have been used instead in an additional volume.

8 Appendix: Original Letters Quoted or Mentioned Hereabove

29 January 1695, letter from Andreas Morell (1646–1703) to Nicolas Thoynard (1628–1706): '*Mes graveurs me font enrager en voulant toujours ajouter à mes dessins et embellir mal à propos*'.[149]

10 August 1715, letter from Philipp von Stosch (1691–1757) to François Fagel (1659–1746): '*C'est le Chevalier Odam qui a commence de m'en faire les desseins et je travaille deja depuis quelque tems a ramasser tout ce qu'on peut trouver dans Pline Junius et autres auteurs anciens et modernes*'.[150]

8 August 1716, letter from Philipp von Stosch to Gisbert Cuper (1644–1716): it was under his own eyes that had been drawn '*les empreintes des pieres gravees avec le nom des graveurs anciens (que j'ay ramassé avec une fatigue incroyable) en faisant observer exactement dans le desein le caractere de l'ouvrage d'un chacun … Dans les explication des gravures j'espere donner au public une idee non seulement des figures que les gemmes representent, mais de la beaute de la sculpture en quoi differe le style de l'un de celui de l'autre ouvrier*'.[151]

4 May 1718, letter from Philipp von Stosch to François Fagel: '*Mon ouvrage de la sculpture des anciens est achevé. Les soixante et deux desseins sont acheves a la plume avec la meme exactitude de celui de la Minerve de Aspasius que je vous ay envoyé. Mais comme tout cet ouvrage est un raisonnement sur la sculture et par consequence toute sa beaute consiste quil soye gravé sous mes yeux et sous ma direction sans quoy le livre et les tailles douces ne connecteront point ensemble*'.[152]

16 September 1720, letter from Philipp von Stosch to Pietro Andrea Andreini (1650–1729): '*A forza di scrivere so adesso, che la sua pietra di opera di Policleto sta in mano d'un certo cavaliere di Rovigo, chiamato il conte Carlo Silvestri. Faccia diligenze adesso per ritrovarla, affinché io possa inserirla nella mia opera sotto il nome di V.S.I e del suo celebra studio*'.[153]

18 October 1721, letter from Ludwig de Chanxe (d. 1735) to Bernard de Montfaucon (1655–1741): '*Ce bijoux a toujours été reconnu pour la figure d'Alexandre le G. et de la main de Pyrgothélès, le nom de ce fameux ouvrier y est gravé en très beaux caractères grecs au même endroit où il est écrit sur le buste moulé, l'original est d'une seule pierre quoique de différente couleur; l'empressement que Mr le Baron de Stosch qui va faire paraître un / recueil de 60 antiques, a eu pour avoir celle-ci et qu'il a déjà fait graver m'a fait naître le dessein de vous en offrir une copie, si vous trouvez Mon très Révérend Père qu'il puisse être du ressort de votre Supplément, je tâcherai pour lors d'engager S.A.E. à en faire mouler une qui représente moins mal l'inimitable original et m'estimerais très heureux si je pouvais par là vous marquer en quelque façon que je suis (…)*'.[154]

19 December 1722, letter from Philipp von Stosch to Karl Gustav Heräus (1671–1725): '*je vis ici d'un grand calme … en augmentant ma bibliotheque et recueil de pieres gravees touts les jours, en quoy consiste mon unique bonheur, ou pour mieux dire ma Dulcinée de Toboso*'.[155]

Undated, letter from Jacques Clermont to Bernard de Montfaucon: '*(…) j'ajouterai à cela un autre article. C'est que M. Picart est occupé depuis plusiers mois à graver les gemmes que M. Stosch a ramassées des plus vieux graveurs comme Praxitèle, etc., dans un voyage de plusieurs années qu'il a fait dans l'Europe. Il y en aura un nombre de soixante-six en tout. M. Picart y donne tous ses soins. Il y a déjà plusieurs planches de faites, mais faites d'une main de maître. Il faut avouer que Picart s'est surpassé. On va publier six planches pour tâcher d'avoir des souscriptions*

---

146 As noted in Ubaldelli 2001, 85: '*il Ghezzi inviò nel 1731 allo Stosch, che stave raccogliendo nuovo materiale per il progettato secondo volume delle* Gemmae antiquae caelatae, *un disegno in acquerello del cameo firmato da Aulos*' (Ghezzi's diary, Bibliotheca Casanatense – Rome, ms. 3745, fol. 7r, 17 May 1731).
147 Cf. Chapter 10 here.
148 Chatsworth, the Devonshire Archives, inv. no.: CS1/188.3.
149 Paris, Bibliothèque nationale de France, NAF 14823, f. 110r – Meyer 2022, p. 37; FINA ID-8542.
150 The Hague, Algemeen Rijksarchief, Archives of the Fagel family, inv. 2028 – Heringa 1976, p. 76, n. 23 (mention). Transcription kindly provided by Ulf R. Hansson.
151 The Hague, Koninklijke Bibliotheek, inv. 72H25 – Heringa 1976, p. 77, n. 41.

152 The Hague, Algemeen Rijksarchief, Archives of the Fagel family, inv. 2031 – Heringa 1976, n. 42.
153 Justi 1861, p. 4; Hansson 2014, p. 16, n. 19.
154 Paris, Bibliothèque nationale de France, Fonds français 17704, f° 104.
155 Schneider 1907, p. 347; Heringa 1976, n. 66b.

des curieux, et on est assuré qu'on ne manquera pas pour admirer tout l'ouvrage. M. préside à cet ouvrage, et j'y veille avec lui. On fera un discours court et nerveux sur l'ouvrage de chaque graveur dont les pierres sont gravées, et je crois que l'on nous en saura gré. Comme vous êtes le premier antiquaire de ce temps, je vous demande aussi instamment votre protection pour cet ouvrage. Enfin Monsieur, comme l'on ne vit pas pour soi, permettez-moi de vous demander si de part et d'autre on pourrait trouver son compte en troquant des livres d'ici contre ceux de France: par exemple, on a ici le Trésor de M. Sallengre, on a les Vetera Romæ par M. Overbeck, magnifique ouvrage en trois volumes in-folio. Si quelque libraire, qui tous vous ont tant d'obligation, voulait penser à ce troc contre votre Trésor, on pourrait s'être utile, car je dirigerai cela avec prudence (...)'.[156]

7 May 1723, letter from François Fagel to Philipp von Stosch: '*vostre ouvrage est trop beau pour estre dedié a un particulier idiot comme moy. Vous trouverez aisement de plus grand seigneurs a qui vous ferez par la un grand plaisir*'.[157]

2 December 1724, letter from Apostolo Zeno (1668–1750) to Pier Caterino Zeno (1666–1732): '*Prima che me ne scordi, vi dirò che i giorni passati leggendo la prefazione del libro intitolato* Gemmae antiquae caelatae, Sculptorum (*in realtà Scalptorum, ndr*) nominibus insignitae, *intagliate dal famoso Bernardo Picart, e pubblicate e spiegate da Filippo di Stosch latinamente, con la traduzione Francese a fianco del Sig. di Limiers, e impresse in Amsterdam presso il detto Picart 1724. in foglio, notai le seguenti parole (passage en latin, ndr). Ora questa testa di Nerone scolpita in diamante si è probabilmente la stessa, che già mi fu data costì a recare in questi parti, donde l'ho poi rimandata a chi me la diede, e che ne voleva molte centinaja di ungheri*'.[158]

4 June 1745, letter from Anton Maria Zanetti (1706–1778) to Henry Howard (1694–1758), 4th Earl of Carlisle: '*J'attendrai de tout mon Coeur les souffres de vos admirables Pierres, car les emproints en cire rouge sont assez mieux, que rien; mais en souffre ils vont bien beaucoup d'avantge, en vous faisant mon cusin ses tres humbles compliments, etant en joie d'avoir les siennes, car si la Persone, qui vous trouvera Monsieur Joli sera assez abile, elle formera aussi les emprointes de la Camèes, que de les pierres gravées, et si vous fairez ecrire à Monsieur le Baron Stosch à Florence, il vous apprendra, car il a la manière de les former admirablement*'.[159]

16 August 1746, letter from Philipp von Stosch to Ridolfino Venuti (1705–1763): '*Monsieur, In replica alla sua Lettera de 13. D. Le mando qui ingiunte 4 Stampe ragionevolmente male intagliate, che l'Ab^e Valesio mi dette un giorno, senza dirmi à che appartenavo Li Originali, ed io L'avrei ignorato, Se L'Ab^e Sellari non mi avesse detto, che Le gemme appartenavo all'Accad^a Etrusca di Cortona. Le spiegazioni in margine sono del mentovato Ab^e Valesio, Le quali io suppongo egli abbia fatte estemporaneamente*'.[160]

27 August 1748, letter from Giovanni Gaetano Bottari (1698–1775) to Bartolomeo Corsini (1683–1752): '*Quando M. Piccard intaglio le Gemme col nome dell'autore gli mandavano i disegni fatti molto male dal Cav. Odam, ma egli ch'era il primo bulino d'Europa, gli riduceva al suo buon gusto. Di qua aveva sempre delle doglianze, che provenivano dal detto Cav. Odam. Egli vinto dalla noia ne intaglio alcune secondo il disegno, che appetto all'altre paiano fatte con la scopa, e chi non sa questa storia, non capisce, come Piccard abbia fatto rami cosi scellerati*'.[161]

23 October 1755, Letter from the abbot Barthélemy (1716–1795) to the Count of Caylus (1692–1765): '*Nous avons fouillé aussi dans le cabinet du baron de Stosch. Je lui ai remis vos souffres qu'il a reçus avec plaisir, et votre livre qu'il a lu avec autant d'avidité que de satisfaction; son cabinet est immense: vingt-cinq mille soufres, des estampes, des pierres gravées, des antiques, des médailles, des manuscrits, des cartes de géographie, des dessins. Il a dépouillé l'Italie, et la tient encore asservie par ses correspondans; il m'a tout montré et ne m'a rien cédé. Je me suis abaissé jusqu'aux prières; elles ont endurci un cœur qui naturellement n'est pas tendre. J'ai triomphé de la résistance de l'abbé Boule et de quelques autres brocanteurs; mais je ne triomphe pas du plus puissant de tous*'.[162]

5 February 1758, letter from Johann Joachim Winckelmann (1717–1768) to Hieronymus Dieterich Berendis (1720–1783): '*Ich muß bekennen, ich habe mehr Glück, als Wiz; aber wer sein Glück erkennet und nuget, der ist es werth. Es fehlet nichts an meinem Glück, als Jemand von denen hier zu haben, die mir theils übels gewünschet, theils doch weissagen wollen. Durch den Tod des Herrn von Stosch habe ich einen großen Freund und unendlich viel Nachrichten eingebüßet. Denn ob er gleich niemals das*

---

156 Paris, Bibliothèque nationale de France, Fonds français 17704, fol. 172^v–173^r – Broglie 1891, pp. 275–276; FINA ID-2657.
157 Quoted in Heringa 1976, p. 81, n. 86.
158 Lost – Zeno 1752, vol. 2, p. 351; FINA ID-6827.
159 Castle Howard Archives, inv. no.: J12/12/21 – Scarisbrick 1987, p. 98.
160 Cod. Ott. lat. 3128, fol. 217 – Engelmann 1909, pp. 333–335.
161 BCR, Cors. 44E21, fols 222v–223v – Minor 2001, p. 415.
162 Lost – Barthélemy 1802, p. 26; De Callataÿ 2007, p. 563, n. 27.

Schöne in der Kunst kennen lernen, weil ihn die Seuche der übrigen Antiquitäts-Krämer zu zeitig verdorben, so hatte er das größte Cabinet fast in der Welt, und es ist nur 70,000 Scudi taxiret worden, d. i. gerichtlich wegen der Abgabe von Sachen, die etwa außer Florenz gehen werden. Sein Erbe ex asse ist ein Muzel aus Berlin, der vordem in französischen Diensten gewesen. Er war hier und ich bin mit ihm Rom ziemlich durchgefahren. Ich könnte, wenn ich nicht nach Neapel gehen müßte, mich ohne alle Kosten in Florenz divertiren; denn er hat mir Alles, was man zum Leben nöthig hat, angeboten. Einen einzigen Landsmann habe ich hier, einen jungen Maler aus Berlin, Reklam; sein Vater ist, glaube ich, Hofjuwelier gewesen. Weil er aber einige Jahre in Paris gewesen, so ist er verdorben, und wir sehen uns daher selten. Er wurde an mich von Paris' aus recommendiret, und ich habe ihm sogar freies Quartier bei mir angeboten'.[163]

1 May 1762, letter from Johann Joachim Winckelmann to Georg Conrad Walther (1710–1778): '*La presunta testa di Alessandro la fece incidere il Sig. di Stosch da una copia in cera di Picart, che era stata realizzata da lui stesso sulla base di questa testa, grande come la metà dell'incisione; ma sulla base di questa copia era difficile formulare un giudizio. Questo pezzo non si trova nel Gabinetto del Re di Prussia, come afferma Natter, ma nelle mani del Conte di Schönborn, il quale diede al Sig. Cardinale Aless. Albani, a Roma, la copia dello scritto e soprattutto il nome dell'artista, e si ritenne antica la scrittura. Non sono in grado di dare altri giudizi a proposito*'.[164]

28 September 1783, letter from Frans Hemsterhuis (1721–1790) to Princess Galitzin (1748–1806): '*Dans le moment, ..., je reçois ... le catalogue de feu l'aimable Stosch. Pour ce qui est des souffres, je suppose qu'ils sont assez bien conservés, qu'il y ait des catalogues joints à chaque caisse ou à chaque tiroir, et que la plus part soient bien attachés au fond des layettes. Dans ce cas la on peut en donner hardiment jusqu'à 250 ducats. On n'a pas fait de meilleurs souffres que du temps du vieux Stosch. Cet art d'en faire doit beaucoup à lui et à son ecole. Mais d'ailleurs Stosch avoit une reputation prodigieuse comme dactyliologue et par consequent commerce avec tous les cabinets de l'Europe, et on se faisoit un plaisir de lui fournir des empreintes, prises sur les originaux même. Il vendit ou fit vendre même des petites collections de ces empreintes originales, mais cela ne pouvoit pas durer long temps. Ainsi on fit des moules sur ces empreintes, qui devinrent mères d'autres qui ne valoient pas leur pères, mais qui se vendoient encore assez chers. Voila l'une des sources des mauvaises empreintes qui ne sont pas à fleur de coin. L'autre c'est que du temps de Stosch l'art de faire des pastes devint commun, et alors les possesseurs de pierres et les directeurs de cabinets aimoient mieux de faire une fois un paste sur une belle pierre, que de la risquer par cent fois plus en tirer des empreintes en souffre ou en cire. Ces pastes remplacerent les pierres, et les souffres qu'on en tira devoient être mauvaises, puisque le meilleur paste doit porter les marques des grains de la pierre ponce dans laquelle il a été jetté, quelque raffinés qu'elle pût être, ce qui donna lieu à une methode detestable. On retoucha ces pastes et on les polit soit au tourret, soit à la main, ce qui detruisit non seulement toutes les vives arrêttes qui se trouvoient encore plus ou moins dans ces pastes, mais même les contours des figures. Jugez des empreintes qu'on tira de ces pastes, et qu'on vend très bien en Italie en souffre et en Allemagne en plâtre aux amateurs apprentifs. Somme que les souffres de Stosch etant bien conservés sont les meilleurs qui existent. Si j'étois l'antiquaire du Roi de Prusse je les acheterois à tout prix pour servir à l'histoire des pierres gravées que le Roi a acheté de Stosch et où il a été horriblement trompé par l'addresse de Winckelman, qui en a donné le catalogue in quarto, infiniment curieux que vous avez et que vous devez garder avec soin. Notez que le Roi n'a pas été trompé par la friponnerie de personne, mais l'etourderie et l'ignorance de ceux qu'il a employé dans cette affaire. Pour les pierres gravées, ma Diotime, il est impossible d'en juger sur un tel catalogue. D'ailleurs je ne lui ai connu qu'une seule bonne pierre, c'etoit la tête d'un Silene en camée sardaine brun et blanc, qui valoit certainement deux cent ducats, mais il m'a dit ici, si je ne me trompe, qu'il ne l'avoit plus. Si vous aviez envie de risquer 6 ou 7 ducats, j'en ferai de même et alors nous risquerons à tout hazard sur les no. 5 Marquera et sur 13 Isis, ne fut ce que pour avoir quelque chose de cet homme vraiment aimable*'.[165]

8 December 1783, letter from Frans Hemsterhuis to Princess Galitzin: '*Le Duc de Noya Caraffa (…) a si horriblement triché notre pauvre Stosch*'.[166]

23 April 1784, letter from Frans Hemsterhuis to Princess Galitzin: '*Ce qui m'a paru remarquable, c'est qu'ayant connu grand nombre d'amateurs de presque toutes les nations, soit personnellement, soit par lettres, les Allemans sont mieux faits, sans comparaison, pour juger de l'art en general que les autres nations, et les François sans comparaison le moins. Lorsque je pense à cett illustre et digne Comte de*

---

163 Weimar, Landesbibliothek inv. no.: D.1805. Winckelmann 1952–1957, vol. I, pp. 330–331; quoted in Kashcheev 1999, p. 18.

164 Lost – Winckelmann 1952–1957, vol. II, p. 310 and 429T; Winckelmann 2002, vol. 4.1, p. 680; Tassinari 2019, p. 231.

165 Universitäts- und Landesbibliothek Münster, Gallitzin-Nachlaß Band 6 – Sluis 2010, vol. IV, pp. 174–176; FINA ID-8801.

166 Universitäts- und Landesbibliothek Münster, Gallitzin-Nachlaß Band 6 – Sluis 2010, vol. IV, pp. 235–236; FINA ID-8806.

Caylus, qui m'honoroit assez de son estime, j'ai dû repentir de ne lui avoir pas marqué ingenuement les bevues palpables et inportantes qu'il a fait dans ses beaux ouvrages. Le vieux Stosch de Florence et Caylus etoient fort liés et firent bien des trâcs ensemble. Jugez qui fut dupe de l'Allemand ou du François. Sur cet article je pourrois dire des nouvelles, sans la grande cloche de cette ville'.[167]

---

167 Universitäts- und Landesbibliothek Münster, Gallitzin-Nachlaß Band 7 – Sluis 2010, vol. V, pp. 126–127; FINA ID-8811.

Acknowledgements

I would like to dedicate this chapter to the memory of the late Jan Heringa (1919–2010), a specialist on Stosch and Fagel, on whom he did pioneering research: Heringa 1980 is a book of exemplary scholarship and clarity.

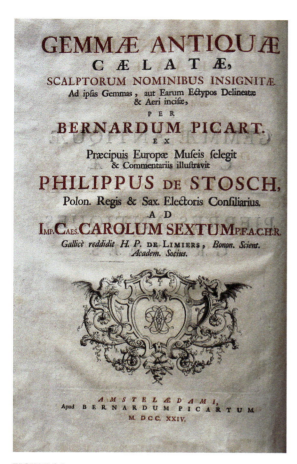

FIGURE 9.1

FIGURE 9.2

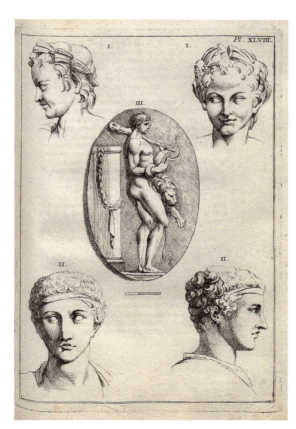

FIGURE 9.3

FIGURE 9.4

FIGURE 9.5

FIGURE 9.6

FIGURE 9.7   FIGURE 9.8

FIGURE 9.9

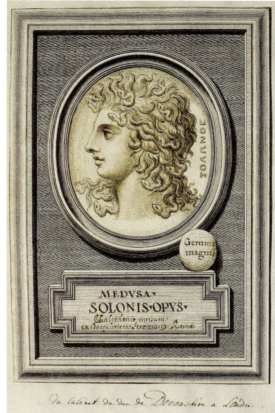

FIGURE 9.10

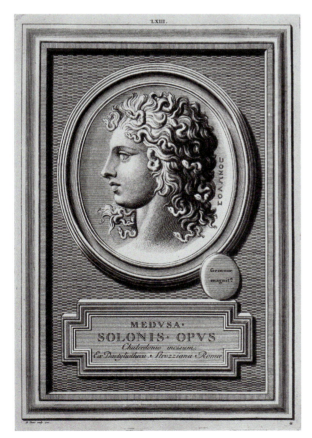

FIGURE 9.11

FIGURE 9.12

FIGURE 9.13

FIGURE 9.14

FIGURE 9.15

FIGURE 9.16

FIGURE 9.17

FIGURE 9.18

FIGURE 9.19

CHAPTER 10

Gemmae antiquae caelatae II

Paweł Gołyźniak

1 Stosch's Planned Second Book on Engraved Gems

Stosch's book *Gemmae antiquae caelatae* published in 1724 was largely successful establishing him as the foremost and widely respected authority in the field of engraved gems. It raised a great deal of interest in intaglios and cameos in general and in the signed ones in particular.[1] Even though it was not without flaws since it has been recently revealed that 21 intaglios and cameos published by Stosch were not genuine ancient works, nine more are ancient but with their signatures added in modern times, and another three bear the names of their owners rather than signatures of their makers (cf. Appendix 1 for a discussion on individual gems).[2] Still, it set outstanding standards not only in the field of glyptics but archaeology in general. This is because Stosch focused his research on the very peculiar problem. Rejecting typical subject matter organisation, he listed the objects in alphabetical order of engravers, which allowed several works attributed to one artist to be observed at the same time. Moreover, Stosch provided full information on the published gems for the first time, not only discussing their subject matters but also provenance, the gemstones they were made of and individual styles. But, above all, he published particularly accurate and faithful illustrations. All these aspects made the book a highly successful volume (cf. Chapter 11).

It is certain that Stosch continued his studies of *gemmae antiquae caelatae* – ancient engraved gems (translating the title literally) and planned to publish another book.[3] The rather vague mentions in the archives resulted in much confusion as to its subject, the character and the number of gems this new volume could cover. Some scholars claim that it was designed to discuss not only recently discovered and previously unpublished signed gems but also the regular ones.[4] Zazoff thought that the drawings of various gems made for Stosch by Tuscher, Preißler, Schweickart and others were all created with the intention to be published in that book.[5] It is also thought that because Stosch's first study, *Gemmae antiquae caelatae*, did not include any Etruscan gem, Stosch planned his next book to present the best pieces from his own collection, which was indeed strong in terms of Etruscan glyptics.[6] It is even believed that Stosch only heralded his new project but, in fact, he did little towards its realisation as he lost interest and became engaged in his *Atlas* project instead.[7]

As one could see in the previous chapter, the production process of Stosch's first book on gems was complex and involved a number of people, including artists, who made drawings for the plates as well as the publisher, Bernard Picart, who redrew them and made the final engravings. Dozens of drawings originally belonging to Stosch, now preserved in the Princes Czartoryski Museum in Krakow and in the Kunstbibliothek in Berlin and elsewhere, are important testimonies of those events. It turns out that a combination of the study of the archival sources, Stosch's correspondence, information from old, printed books on gems and most importantly the drawings from his corpus deliver information allowing to solve at least some mysteries. This chapter presents all the evidence regarding preparation of the new study by Stosch, whether archival, correspondence or visual (drawings) combined with a discussion on its potential subject, the gems that it could

---

1 Furtwängler 1900, vol. III, p. 410.
2 Not ancient are the following ones: Stosch 1724, pls II, VI, VII, XX, XXI, XXII, XXV, XXVI, XXVII, XXXV, XXXVII, XLII, XLIII, XLVIII, LII, LV, LVI, LVIII, LXII, LXIV and LXVII. In the case of Stosch 1724, pls III, XV, XVII?, XVIII, XIX?, XLIV, LIV?, LX, LXIX? their signatures were added in modern times. Regarding Stosch 1724, pls I?, X, LVII – their inscriptions may actually stand for gems sitters' names.
3 Actually, in the preface of his first book, Stosch explains that he will write a study on glass pastes – probably about their production, see: Stosch 1724, p. XIX: '*Mais je parlerai plus au long de ces Pâtes de Verre dans un autre Ouvrage que je medite sur ce sujet.*' ['But I will speak more about these Pâtes de Verre in another book that I intend on this subject.']. However, this project was never realised and except this one mention, no other source or Stosch's correspondence provides information about it.
4 Zazoff and Zazoff 1983, pp. 54–57; Weiner 1990, lot 41; Coen and Fidanza (eds) 2001.
5 Zazoff and Zazoff 1983, pp. 74–75.
6 Arbeid, Bruni and Iozzo 2016, pp. 158 and 174. One of the arguments in favour of this claim would be that among the illustrations appearing in the luxurious edition of Winckelmann 1760 catalogue of Stosch's gems one finds two famous Etruscan gems reproduced. However, in fact they were flyers that Stosch used to distribute among his correspondents and on the occasion of his lectures at the Accademia Etrusca di Cortona.
7 Micheli 1986, p. 51.

present and discuss, and finally the reasons why the project was ultimately unfinished.

2   The Early Stages of the New Book Project in Rome

The point of departure for investigations on the second book Stosch worked on is his unpublished correspondence with William Cavendish, 2nd Duke of Devonshire, preserved at Chatsworth.[8] There are 10 Stosch's letters there sent from Rome between 24 January 1728[9] and 7 May 1729 and some of them include valuable information on the subject, character and production process of Stosch's new book.[10] Of particular importance is the letter sent on 24 January 1728, from which one learns that Stosch was delighted to hear about four gems he published in the first volume (pls II, IV, IX and XXIX) to be in the Devonshire collection. Subsequently, he asks about the gemstone types of the ones signed by Aepolianus (pl. II) and Aetion (pl. IV), so that he could note this information in the appendix to his first book, if he ever publishes it.[11]

In the same letter, Stosch also informs the Duke about the sale to a collector from Leipzig, named Winckler, of three remarkable carved gems, almost at the same time as the discovery of the tombs of the Slaves ('*les Affranchis*') of Livia.[12] The first one was a dazzling cameo with a portrait of Marcellus, as had been commonly agreed by antiquarians, which Stosch greatly admired. The second gem was a magnificent hyacinth featuring a portrait of a Roman consul with the name of engraver ΣΚΟΠΑΣ and the third one presented a young laughing satyr with *nebris* on his shoulder. Behind his head, there are three Greek words in small, almost invisible, letters, which one reads ΥΛΛΟC ΔΙΟCΚΟΥΡΙΔΟΥ ΕΠΟΙΕΙ. According to Stosch, that inscription testifies that Hyllos, whose three works had been already published by him in 1724, was the son, or disciple, of Dioscurides. Winckler paid 340 scudi for those gems but Stosch believes that the cameo with a laughing satyr is worth three times as much alone. Later on, one reads that Stosch had the last two drawn accurately to have them engraved for the appendix of his book, together with two other gems – one was the '*Diomede de Gnaeus in Sardius*' belonging to '*Mr. Davenant*', and the second presented a head of a Roman consul, a work of Agathangelos in carnelian, which belonged to '*Antonio Sabatini*' and which Stosch identifies with Pompey. Finally, Stosch asks the Duke of Devonshire if he would do him the honour of sending impressions of engraved gems with the names of engravers from his collection, so that he could add them to the second volume of his book.[13]

This letter is packed with information about Stosch's second volume of *Gemmae antiquae caelatae* and it testifies that its subject was clearly focused on newly discovered signed gems. However, for the sake of this new volume, Stosch also collected information about the ones he had already published to update his first book. The work on this new volume started shortly after the first book was published, since while writing to the Duke of Devonshire, Stosch already mentions to have found four new signed gems and he immediately commissions accurate and faithful drawings that would serve for future engravings. His plans on publishing those gems are confirmed by other sources as well.

The mentioned Winckler who owned the two first signed gems mentioned in Stosch's letter is Jacob Benedict Winckler (1699–1779), a lawyer from Leipzig, who built a sizeable cabinet of engraved gems that he sold in 1742 to the City Council of Leipzig.[14] Among them, there was a garnet intaglio featuring a head of a Roman to the right signed by Skopas (ΣΚΟΠΑΣ), which is now in the GRASSI Museum in Leipzig (Fig. 10.1).[15] This must be the '*jacinth*' mentioned in Stosch's letter. Stosch had it drawn by Markus Tuscher in early 1728, shortly after Tuscher's arrival at Stosch's house and introduction by Johann Justin Preißler, close to the discovery of the columbarium of Livia's freedmen in 1727, and certainly prior to 24 January 1728 (Stosch's letter). His drawing is now in the Princes Czartoryski Museum in Krakow (No. 1749, Fig. 10.2). It was made within a frame of the same type as the frames used in Stosch's first

---

8 I am very much indebted to Kenneth Lapatin for the introduction to Sash Giles, who informed me about those unpublished letters, which proved to be very helpful and illuminating on many aspects regarding Stosch and his gem drawings, as well as the gems he discussed and sold to the Duke of Devonshire.

9 The first letter is a reply to the one sent to Stosch by the Duke of Devonshire on 30 November 1727.

10 Another subject that is often discussed in those letters are ancient coins and other antiquities found in Rome at the time. They are also crucial evidence for understanding how important a figure William Cavendish, 2nd Duke of Devonshire, was in securing the continued payment of Stosch's pension from the British government.

11 Chatsworth, the Devonshire Archives, inv. no.: CS1/188.0.

12 Stosch means here the discovery of the *Monumentum Liviae* on the Appian Way, a columbarium for the slaves and freedmen of the household of Livia, wife of Augustus, which took place in 1727.

13 Chatsworth, the Devonshire Archives, inv. no.: CS1/188.0.

14 For more on Winckler and his collection, see: Lang and Cain 2015, pp. 22–28; Zwierlein-Diehl 2023, pp. 465–466.

15 GRASSI Museum in Leipzig, inv. no.: 1952.055/501; Lang and Cain 2015, pp. 104–105 and 137, no. II.14 (with more literature).

book, stuck down on paper, which was also used later by Schweickart while preparing the final plates for the second book (cf. below). Soon, the gem gained much recognition, and its impressions were frequently made, including a glass paste by Stosch.[16] Due to its subject and signature of Skopas, the intaglio was widely discussed and there is a general compromise that it was cut in the first third of the 1st century BC and the inscription below the head is indeed a genuine signature.[17] As Lang and Gołyźniak recently claimed, the facial elements of the portrayed person are delicately engraved with a considerable amount of individualisation, though, Hellenistic influence is reflected by wide open eye, slightly open mouth, attention to details such as the eyebrow and delicate treatment of cheekbones. The proportions of the head as well as rendering of the haircut are impressive. Overall, this is an extremely well-accomplished study of someone's physical appearance testifying to the significant skilfulness of the engraver, who is otherwise unknown. He must have been a Greek though who worked somewhere in the east Mediterranean, which is suggested by the signature, type of the stone used, its form as well as the style. The gem proves the continuation of the trend that began in the 2nd century BC, when the Romans travelling to the East started commissioning portrait gems by Greek engravers. The person depicted on the Leipzig intaglio remains unidentified. Nevertheless, it is clear he must have been an important statesman, politician, general, province's administrator or consul, as suggested by Stosch.[18]

The second gem bought by Winckler in 1727 and mentioned by Stosch in his letter, the cameo by Hyllos (Fig. 10.3), was also drawn for the second volume of *Gemmae antiquae caelatae* but by Preißler, probably already in 1727. This is testified by Nagler who claimed that Schweickart engraved the plate after Preißler's drawing.[19] Both Preißler's drawing and Schweickart's engraving are now lost.[20] Curiously, the illustration of the cameo was not included into the series of engravings Schweickart made for Stosch, which were published in 1760 in the luxurious edition of Winckelmann's catalogue of Stosch's gems. This could be because Schweickart took it to Nuremberg, where he returned after Stosch's death. It is important to highlight that the cameo under discussion was also drawn by Pier Leone Ghezzi and his drawing is now in the Biblioteca Apostolica Vaticana (Fig. 10.4). Ghezzi confirms that it was purchased by Winckler who paid 100 scudi for it.[21] The comparison of Ghezzi's drawing with the original cameo reveals that Hyllos' signature is misplaced; it should appear above the arm, not behind the head. Platz-Horster hypothetised that the cameo was found much earlier and it was often copied already in the 16th and 17th centuries, thus, maybe Ghezzi drew from its copy.[22] The large number of copies indeed suggests a much earlier find date, but Ghezzi may have been slightly inaccurate while documenting it probably not because he drew a copy, but because he worked from an impression as he used to do with other gems. Moreover, in his letter to the Duke of Devonshire Stosch writes that it was difficult to read the inscription even from the original, let alone a cast. The cameo was not sold by Winckler to the City Council of Leipzig in 1742 like the garnet carved by Skopas. It is documented later to be in the von Bose and Electors of Brandenburg collections. Stosch's deduction from the inscription that Hyllos was the son of the famous Dioscurides proves to be right.[23] The cameo is dated ca. 10 AD and it is now in the Antikensammlung, Staatliche Museen zu Berlin.[24]

Regarding the other two gems Stosch claimed to have already collected their drawings for the supplement to the first volume of *Gemmae antiquae caelatae* in early 1728, he had the '*Diomede de Gnaeus in Sardius*', belonging to Henry Davenant, the British Envoy Extraordinary in Florence, drawn by Girolamo Odam already in 1722 in the same way Odam drew the gems published in the first book (cf. Chapter 8, Fig. 8.5). This drawing of Odam was ultimately not used back then. It is likely that Stosch

---

16 The earliest surviving cast seems to be in in the *dactyliotheca* of Pier Leone Ghezzi (Ghezzi 1734, I.I.no. 159 (21 × 15 mm)). In the introductory text of the manuscript catalogue of his *dactyliotheca* Ghezzi specifies that he collected gem impressions up to October 1734, see: Biblioteca Apostolica Vaticana, MS Vat. lat. 14928. On the Ghezzi's *dactyliotheca* itself, see: Alteri 1987, pp. 8–12. The other recorded casts of the gem are: Lippert[1] I[2], no. 316; Lippert[2] II, no. 337; Dehn/Dolce Vatican, Y.23 (21 × 15 mm, hyacinth); Raspe and Tassie 1791, no. 12192 (carnelian, city of Leipzig, convex); Cades Grande, IV.C.322; Pirzio Biroli Stefanelli 2007, no. III.159. On Stosch's glass paste, see: Borbein, Kunze and Rügler 2019, no. IV.324.

17 On Skopas and this gem in particular, see: Furtwängler 1900, vol. I, pl. XXXIII.8, vol. II, p. 161; Vollenweider 1966, pp. 25–27, pl. 15.1 and 3; Richter 1968, no. 676; Vollenweider 1972–1974, vol. I, pp. 87–89, vol. II, p. 40, pl. 59.4–6; Zazoff 1983, p. 285, pl. 79.9; Plantzos 1999, pp. 93–94, no. 618; Gołyźniak 2020, pp. 85–86, no. 7.50, fig. 132.

18 Lang and Cain 2015, pp. 104–105, no. II.14; Gołyźniak 2020, pp. 85–86.

19 Nagler 1846, p. 132, no. 8.
20 Platz-Horster 2012, no. 28.
21 Biblioteca Apostolica Vaticana, Cod. Ott. lat. 3106, fol. 38: '(...) *Le possede Monsieur Wincler tedesco il quale loe pagò scudi cento*.'
22 Platz-Horster 2012, no. 28.
23 On Hyllos, son of Dioscurides, see: Vollenweider 1966, pp. 69–73; Zwierlein-Diehl 2007, pp. 117 and 120–121.
24 Berlin, Antikensammlung, inv. no.: FG 11063; Platz-Horster 2012, no. 28 (with earlier literature); Lapatin 2015, pl. 114.

discovered this new signed gem as late as 1722 and it was too late to include it to the book, which was already being produced by Picart. However, it seemingly made him think about an appendix to his work. No other drawing of this gem has been found so far and no engraving by Schweickart is known to exist, but it seems that Odam's drawing is the one Stosch speaks about in his letter to the Duke of Devonshire.

Finally, Stosch also speaks about a carnelian signed by Agathangelos featuring a portrait of Pompey that belonged to 'Antonio Sabbatini'. This gem was one of the most extraordinary finds for the new volume of *Gemmae antiquae caelatae* (Fig. 10.5). It is said to have been found near the tomb of Caecilia Metella on the Appian Road.[25] Stosch's letter confirms that the very first owner of Agathangelos's gem was the prominent antiquary, Marcoantonio Sabbatini (1637–1724). He was born in Bologna but spent most of his life in Rome, where he became one of the most important connoisseurs and collectors of gems at the time of Stosch's activities. He was a papal curator to Pope Clement XI (1700–1721), art advisor to the Emperor Charles VI (1711–1740) and a central figure among the *cognoscenti* in Rome. He was a supervisor of Cardinal Alessandro Albani in his development of taste for antiquities and art.[26] His collection was dispersed a few years after his death, in 1727.[27] He was a friend of Stosch and the two are depicted examining a gem or negotiating a transaction involving one on a caricature by Pier Leone Ghezzi described as '*Due famosi Antiquari*', after which Arthur Pond made an engraving in 1739 (cf. Chapter 2, Fig. 2.3).[28] As Winckelmann explains, shortly after Sabbatini's death, the Agathangelos gem was sold for 200 scudi.[29] The next recorded owners were the Comtesse de Luneville in Naples and the painter Jacob Philipp Hackert (1737–1807). In 1834 the intaglio entered the Antikensammlung in Berlin.[30]

Stosch had the Agathangelos intaglio documented as a drawing by Preißler, apparently in 1727, like other gems mentioned in his letter to the Duke of Devonshire (Berlin vol. VI, pl. 47, Fig. 10.6).[31] The gem was first published in 1736 by Borioni and Venuti in *Collectanea Antiquitatum Romanarum* and Preißler made a preparatory drawing for the illustration that appeared in this book too.[32] That drawing is now in a private collection (Fig. 10.7). Stosch identified the portrayed man as '*Pompey*' and it is not known whether he meant Pompey the Great or his son Sextus Pompey. However, since its publication by Borioni and Venuti, it is almost entirely agreed that it depicts Sextus Pompey, mostly on the basis of the proximity to his portrait with characteristic curly hair spreading from one point on the top of the head in a rather untidy manner and a short beard, known from his coins minted between 42 and 40 BC.[33] There are quite a number of ancient replicas of this gem.[34] The authenticity of Agathangelos' signature was never doubted.

Over the next few months, the subject of engraved gems signed by ancient masters often appears in Stosch's letters sent to the Duke of Devonshire. In the one sent from Rome on 28 August 1728, Stosch thanks for the Duke's letter from 12 July, which enclosed an impression of a gem with the name NEICOV. He had much appreciation for its quality, and he thought the inscription stood for the name of a Greek engraver who cut this intaglio. Moreover, he remarked that the representation of Zeus on the gem is comparable to that of Vejovis. He also informs that the draughtsmen working in his studio speak highly of it, and should he receive a better impression, he would have published the gem in his forthcoming book.[35]

One identifies the gem described by Stosch as a carnelian intaglio dated to the 2nd century BC, presenting a Hellenistic ruler as Zeus with an inscription NEICOY, once in the collection of Pierre Crozat (1665–1740) and Philippe II, Duke of Orléans (1674–1723), now preserved in the State Hermitage Museum in St. Petersburg.[36] Furthermore, as discussed in Chapter 6, when Schweickart died in 1787 in Nuremberg, Johann Fridrich Frauenholz purchased his drawings of Stosch's gems as well as a few of those produced by Preißler. Later, Frauenholz together

---

25 AGDS II, no. 418; Winckelmann (1760, class IV, no. 186, pp. 437–438) says that it was found in a burial outside Rome. On Agathangelos, see: Vollenweider 1966, p. 39; Zwierlein-Diehl 2007, p. 123; Gołyźniak 2020, pp. 136–137.
26 On Marcoantonio Sabbatini, cf. Chapter 2 here.
27 Ubaldelli 2001, p. 80.
28 Now in Chatsworth, the Devonshire Collection, inv. no.: IRN 6637 Old Master Drawing 641, see: Jaffé 1994, vol. II, no. 194. For the later engraving by Arthur Pond, see, for example: London, the British Museum, inv. no.: 1979,U.844. On Stosch and Sabbatini, see: Justi 1872, p. 303.
29 Winckelmann 1760, class IV, no. 186, pp. 437–438.
30 AGDS II, no. 418; Borbein, Kunze and Rügler 2019, no. IV.186.

31 Preißler's drawing could have been made after a glass paste that Stosch had in his collection, see: Winckelmann 1760, class IV, no. 186, pp. 437–438; Borbein, Kunze and Rügler 2019, no. IV.186.
32 Borioni and Venuti 1736, p. 48, pl. 68.
33 RRC, no. 511/1 (aureus of Sextus Pompey, 42–40 BC). However, Zwierlein-Diehl suggests that the gem depicts a young Roman nobleman rather than Sextus Pompeius, see: AGDS II, no. 418; Zwierlein-Diehl 2007, p. 123.
34 Gołyźniak 2020, pp. 136–137, nos 9.13–22.
35 Chatsworth, the Devonshire Archives, inv. no.: CS1/188.4.
36 The State Hermitage Museum in St. Petersburg, inv. no.: Ж609; Neverov 1976, no. 53.

with Schlichtegroll used four of Preißler's gem drawings made for Stosch in their own publication entitled *Auswahl vorzüglicher Gemmen aus derjenigen Sammlung die ehemahls der Baron Philipp von Stosch besass, die sich jetzt aber in dem Kön. Preussischen Cabinette befindet* published in Nuremberg in 1792.[37] Among them, the plate XX (Fig. 10.8) presents the gem in question.

The drawing by Preißler published much later by Frauenholz and Schlichtegroll must have been made in 1728 then, and it was originally meant to serve as an illustration in Stosch's second book on ancient signed gems. Knowing the history of the gem and being aware of good relationships between Stosch, Crozat and Duke of Orléans, it is rather surprising that Stosch got to know the gem through the Duke of Devonshire (between late 1727 and early 1729) unless it surfaced at the art market around that time. The intaglio is first recorded much later in the descriptive catalogue of Crozat's cabinet of gems written by Pierre-Jean Mariette in 1741, who believed the intaglio to depict Emperor Augustus in the guise of Jupiter.[38] It is not known how it found its way to Crozat's collection. In any case, Preißler's drawing is then the earliest documentation of the gem of which Stosch also had a glass paste. Winckelmann's commentary on it supports the belief in the inscription to be a signature in the circle of Stosch, although there was much uncertainty about the identification of the figure depicted on the intaglio, as Winckelmann does not agree with Stosch and Mariette's proposal.[39]

The inscription continued to be taken as a signature by Bracci, Raspe and Tassie later on.[40] It was only Furtwängler who believed otherwise. He suggested dating the gem to the 4th or 3rd century BC and identified the figure depicted on it as Alexander the Great. He observed that the quality of the inscription is far lower than the gem itself, and he concluded that it must stand for the name of the owner who added it in the Roman period.[41] Over the twentieth century, the intaglio was widely discussed not only in terms of the inscription but also identity of the person depicted on it, usually taken as Alexander the Great but Zwierlein-Diehl's interpretation as one of the followers of Alexander seems the most certain. She dates the inscription to the 1st century AD or later, which is also acceptable due to the irregular, careless shapes of the letters and style.[42] As Plantzos observes, the type of representation may indeed originate from a statuary prototype.[43]

3   To Add or Not to Add – That Is the Question and More Contribution of Johann Justin Preißler to Stosch's New Book?

The unpublished Stosch's correspondence between Stosch and the Duke of Devonshire preserved at Chatsworth is particularly illuminating on the early stages of Stosch's new book, apparently already in preparation shortly after the first one was published. In his letters, Stosch is generally enthusiastic about a few new signed gems he discovered thanks to the help of the Duke, but this is not always the case. In his letter sent from Rome on 24 July 1728, Stosch writes that he has an impression of a gem featuring a faun's head with the name of the engraver Lucius of the same size as the drawing he has attached. He believes that this gem is modern (both the image and the signature) and it was made by the same notorious forger who also cut a portrait of a veiled Sabine with the name of Aspasios and several other similar stones.[44]

The gem mentioned by Stosch is probably that of which another drawing (unattributed), survived in Krakow (Krakow No. 1024, Fig. 10.9). The intaglio is now considered lost, but it was first published unillustrated by Canini in 1669 and republished in 1731 with an engraving by Bernard Picart.[45] However, its earlier illustration was published in 1695 by Jakob Gronovius (1645–1716), who described it as 'Head of Pan, with inscription ΛΟΥΚΤΕΙ' in

---

37 Schlichtegroll makes it clear that after the death of Schweickart in 1787, Johann Fredrich Frauenholz purchased in Nuremberg Schweickart's *dactyliotheca* of sulphur gem impressions as well as a few drawings by Preißler that Schweickart had taken with himself to Nuremberg after Stosch's death: '(…) *und noch mehr eine vorhandene Anzahl schöner Zeichnungen von vorzüglichen Gemmen aus der Sammlung, die der verstorberne Stosch von dem berühmten Preissler in der Absicht zeichnen liess, um ein dem Picartischen ähnliches Werk herauszugeben, leiteten Hrn. Frauenholz, als den jetzigen Besitzer dieser Zeichnungen und der Schwefel, auf den Gedanken, das auszuführen, woran den Baron Stosch der Tod verhindert hatte.*' (Schlichtegroll 1805, vol. I, pp. 12–13). These must be the drawings used in Schlichtegroll 1792b, pls XI, XVII, XX and XXXI.
38 Mariette 1741, no. 713; Kagan and Neverov 2000, no. 115/22 (with more literature).
39 Winckelmann 1760, class II, no. 48, pp. 39–41; Furtwängler 1896, no. 9727; Borbein, Kunze and Rügler 2019, no. II.48 (with more literature).
40 Winckelmann 1760, class II, no. 48, pp. 39–41; Bracci 1784–1786, vol. II, p. 284; Raspe and Tassie 1791, no. 962.
41 Furtwängler 1889, pp. 67–68 (with earlier literature); Furtwängler 1900, vol. I, pl. XXXII.11, vol. II, p. 156.
42 Zwierlein-Diehl 2007, ill. 269 (with more literature).
43 Plantzos 1999, pp. 67–68, however, dating it to the Augustan period is rather too late.
44 Chatsworth, the Devonshire Archives, inv. no.: CS1/188.3.
45 Canini 1731, pl. XCI.

a much-expanded re-edition of the catalogue of Abraham van Goorle's (or Gorlaeus) of Delft (1549–1608) collection of gems (Fig. 10.10).[46] Goorle published his cabinet of 196 rings with gems first in 1601, and an enlarged edition including 148 new pieces was published posthumously in 1609.[47] In 1695 and 1707, his book was republished by Gronovius, who included ca. 300 items from other unspecified collections originating from the Low Countries.[48] The intaglio under discussion here belongs to this bulk of unprovenanced gems. Goorle's collection and publication reflect the unprecedented outburst in passionate collecting of gems in the Low Countries, often found locally in the places occupied by Roman soldiers, who brought glyptics products of lower quality. However, the slowly growing understanding of glyptic art at the time also resulted in inclusion of many post-classical gems into the collections formed by Goorle and his contemporaries as well as down in the seventeenth century.[49] As remarked by Furtwängler, the quality of many of Goorle's gems was rather low and many were modern or at least of dubious antiquity. This is also the case of the gem discussed here, which, despite being poorly documented, is clearly a post-classical product of the late sixteenth or seventeenth century. Stosch was right that the signature was fabricated too, and it was perhaps indeed meant to stand for Lucius[50] or Leukios, a gem engraver known from a lost carnelian bearing Victory on a chariot he published in 1724.[51]

Stosch seems to be particularly proud of his ability to tell the difference between genuinely signed gems and the ones with inscriptions of other kinds and forgeries. In his letter to William Cavendish, 2nd Duke of Devonshire, dated Rome 28 August 1728, he not only writes about the gem signed ΝΕΙΟΟΥ discussed above, but also about another one with Diomedes ascending the altar with the Palladion and name 'Onesas', which he believes to be of little importance because it must stand for the name of the gem's owner, or the person depicted on it.[52] From his experience, there are numerous mediocre gems bearing such names in Greek or Latin. He has a large number of signed gems and those with other kinds of inscriptions, including forgeries, reproduced in sulphur, wax and glass impressions which he keeps in his house in Florence specifically to educate visiting antiquarians so that they could see the differences between them.[53] Furthermore, in the same letter in which Stosch mentions the gem with a faun's/satyr's head signed by Lucius, he says that in order to warn collectors ('*les curieux*') of the fraud and trickery, in his future book, he will have had one plate engraved with examples of gems bearing the names of the forged engravers invented or copied in modern times. He adds that this will be done as soon as he has the money.[54]

All of this makes one realise that not all signed gems of which drawings have been discovered in Krakow and Berlin were regarded by Stosch as genuine and suitable for publication in his second volume of *Gemmae antiquae caelatae* unless as in the appendix illustrating the most common forgeries. Given the relatively few archives and especially correspondence of Stosch that survived, it is very difficult to verify this. Nevertheless, it is noteworthy that the few gems discussed so far were almost all drawn by Preißler, who was particularly praised by Stosch for his outstanding accuracy in drawing selected gems faithfully. In general, Preißler is believed to have been especially prolific for the project of Stosch's new book,[55] which can be confirmed by a few more drawings of signed gems that were potentially meant to be published.

---

46   Gronovius 1695, vol. II, p. 44, no. 506, described as: '*Larva Panis, cui adscriptum* ΛΟΥΚΤΕΙ'. Abraham van Goorle was a Dutch antiquary of Flemish origin, a self-made humanist serving as a counsellor and treasurer to Adolf, Count of Nieuwenaar and Meurs, and Stadholder of Utrecht and Gelderland (1545–1589). He published his cabinet of 196 rings with gems first in 1601, and an enlarged edition including 148 new pieces was published posthumously in 1609 (Goorle 1601; Goorle 1609). Goorle's cabinet of gems was purchased *en bloc* in 1612 for £2200 by Hans von Dirbige on the behalf of James I, King of England (1603–1625) who gifted it to his son Henry, Prince of Wales (1594–1612). The prince died young and thus the collection was subsequently inherited by his younger brother, the future Charles I (1625–1649) and then eventually largely dispersed during the Cromwell's accession, while its remains were dispersed at the end of Charles II's (1660–1685) reign or they were destroyed during the Whitehall fire of 1698 (Strong 1986, p. 199; Boardman *et al.* 2009, p. 3; Henig 2008, pp. 269–271). However, some of Goorle's gems must have escaped the royal collection earlier as they were later in the Arundel collection, probably gifted by Henry, Prince of Wales or Charles I to Thomas Howard, 14th Earl of Arundel (1585–1646) as tokens of their friendship (Furtwängler 1900, vol. III, p. 404; Boardman *et al.* 2009, p. 6 and no. 56). For more information on Abraham van Goorle and his collection of engraved gems, see: Furtwängler 1900, vol. III, pp. 403–404; Maaskant-Kleibrink 1997, pp. 229–235; Zwierlein-Diehl 2007, p. 272; Henig 2008, pp. 269–271.

47   Goorle 1601; Goorle 1609.

48   Gronovius 1695; Furtwängler 1900, vol. III, pp. 403–404.

49   On Goorle, his collection and publications and their social meaning, see: Maaskant-Kleibrink 1997, pp. 229–236.

50   Canini 1731, pl. XCI.

51   Stosch 1724, pl. XLI.

52   This is rather surprising considering that Stosch earlier published two gems signed by Onesas, see: Stosch 1724, pls XLV and XLVI.

53   Chatsworth, the Devonshire Archives, inv. no.: CS1/188.3.

54   Chatsworth, the Devonshire Archives, inv. no.: CS1/188.3.

55   Justi 1872, p. 337; Leitschuh 1886, p. 19; Eggers 1926, p. 233; Metz and Rave 1957, p. 23; Rave 1965, p. 30; Kagan 1985, p. 10.

One of them could be an intaglio bearing Marsyas or his father seated to the front on a panther skin with two pipes and a vessel next to him with signature ΓΑΙΟC (Gaius) on the side, which appears to be drawn by Preißler (Krakow No. 668, Fig. 10.11). This gem has been relatively rarely documented as an impression in the *dactyliothecae* or discussed in glyptic literature; it is now considered lost (Fig. 10.12).[56] Nothing precise is known about its history and provenance. It is surprising that Winckelmann, while describing Stosch's glass paste in his catalogue, does not mention the signature at all.[57] Panofka considered both the gem and the inscription to be genuine. He believed the inscription to be the name of the gem's owner referring to the fact that Marsyas used to be called the '*Son of the Earth*' and he played the pipes of the Earth goddess Cybele.[58] However, the subject itself seems unrelated to the inscription and there are some uninscribed contemporary parallel stones.[59] Furtwängler believed the gem to be authentic and dated it to the 3rd or 2nd century BC, but he regarded the inscription as a signature of modern date.[60] Zwierlein-Diehl also thinks the intaglio itself to be original, an ancient work, probably made in the middle of the 1st century BC, but that the signature was forged, judging from the glass cast of the intaglio in Würzburg.[61] There is one more impression of that gem in Pier Leone Ghezzi's *dactyliotheca* in the Biblioteca Apostolica Vaticana, which I examined in autopsy and I agree with Zwierlein-Diehl's judgement as to both; the date for the intaglio and the signature seem to have been added in modern times.[62] Ghezzi's impression is a valuable testimony because it was certainly made prior to October 1734.[63]

The gem engraver Gaius is known from the exquisite garnet intaglio depicting the frontal head of the dog star Sirius, much admired by Stosch and which was certainly scheduled for publication in the second volume of *Gemmae antiquae caelatae* (cf. below).[64] It could be that the forger of the signature on the gem in question here modelled it on the authentic garnet indeed signed by Gaius. However, the quality of his work is very low; the letters are carelessly cut with considerable distance between them, and they have no small dots at the ends. An imitator of the genuine signature would have done better and there is no proof that the Gaius garnet with the head of the dog star Sirius was available to the public and well known prior to 1734. Stosch himself accessed it, most likely from Lord Bessborough in the 1740s or even 1750s, and Natter published it in 1754 (cf. below). In conclusion, the signature appearing on the intaglio discussed here was most likely invented independently, with no relation to the later famous Gaius garnet. After all, it might have been a similar case to the gem with a faun's/satyr's head signed by Lucius (according to Stosch, cf. above). Lucius and Gaius are very common Roman names, which could have been randomly applied by poorly educated gem forgers as suitable for their projects.

Another gem most likely selected by Stosch for his second book on ancient signed gems and apparently drawn by Preißler, was a fragmentary red jasper intaglio presenting a portrait bust of a bearded Roman wearing a drapery over his left shoulder to the right, inscribed at the bottom ΝΙΑΟC (Krakow No. 1745, Fig. 10.13). In this case, it seems not to be a mere coincidence that it is set in a frame of the same type as the frames used in Stosch's first book, which were also used later by Schweickart while preparing the final plates for the second book (cf. below). Preißler drew the intaglio after a glass paste or a sulphur impression that Stosch had in his cabinet.[65] Winckelmann, in his catalogue of Stosch's gems, says that the inscription beneath the bust is a name but he hesitates to decide whether it is a signature of the gem's maker or the name of its owner. At the end of the eighteenth century, Raspe and Tassie supposed the inscription to be a signature of a Greek gem engraver.[66]

The intaglio is now in the British Museum in London, where it arrived after the purchase of the Carlisle gems in

---

56 Panofka 1852, pp. 4–5, no. 2, pl. I.3 (obsidian); Furtwängler 1896, no. 9504; Zwierlein-Diehl 1986, no. 233; Borbein, Kunze and Rügler 2019, no. II.1136 (with full bibliography). On Gaius, see: Zwierlein-Diehl 1986, no. 147; Zwierlein-Diehl 2005, pp. 338–339; Zwierlein-Diehl 2007, pp. 77–78.
57 Winckelmann 1760, class II, no. 1136, p. 192.
58 Panofka 1852, p. 4, no. 2.
59 For example: Paris, Bibliothèque nationale de France, inv. no.: Pauvert.119, see: Richter 1971, no. 176.
60 Furtwängler 1888, p. 134, no. 15, pl. 3.
61 Zwierlein-Diehl 1986, no. 233.
62 Ghezzi 1734, III.C.43 (ca. middle of the 1st century BC, signature added in the 18th century).
63 In the introductory text of the manuscript catalogue of his *dactyliotheca* Ghezzi specifies that he collected gem impressions up to October 1734, see: Biblioteca Apostolica Vaticana, MS Vat. lat. 14928. On the Ghezzi's *dactyliotheca* itself, see: Alteri 1987, pp. 8–12.

64 Laptin (2015, pl. 91) mentions clay sealings found in an archive on Delos where the Gaius name appears, but in contrast to his view that these are also signed by Gaius, they seem more likely to bear names of the owners of the seals.
65 Winckelmann 1760, class IV, no. 310, p. 449; Raspe and Tassie 1791, no. 11626 (Stosch sulphur); Furtwängler 1896, no. 9951; Borbein, Kunze and Rügler 2019, no. IV.310 (with full bibliography).
66 Raspe and Tassie 1791, no. 11626 (Stosch sulphur).

1890 (Fig. 10.14).[67] Henry Howard, 4th Earl of Carlisle and founder of Carlisle collection of gems, was particularly fond of those bearing artists' signatures and he sought after them with much dedication through his agents like Francesco de'Ficoroni in Rome and Anton Maria Zanetti in Venice. It is likely then that at the time of Stosch, the inscription on our gem was taken as a genuine signature. Stosch is likely to have taken his glass paste and sulphur impression from the original already while in Rome because Pier Leone Ghezzi also had its impression in his *dactyliotheca*.[68]

Whatever the opinion in the eighteenth century, the inscription should not be taken as a signature anymore. Walters believed the intaglio to be dated to the 2nd century AD. Indeed, it depicts a private portrait of a Roman noble man, whose coiffure and beard are modelled after the imperial portraits of the members of the Antonine dynasty, particularly close to Emperor Hadrian. Moreover, the red jasper gemstone was the most popular material used in Roman glyptics in the 2nd century AD. The inscription is authentic, the letters are in the right size and have slightly careless shapes typical for the late Roman Imperial period (cf. for instance, the name NEICOY on the gem discussed above). The name of engraver Nilos is unregistered on any other intaglio or cameo. The inscription is, certainly the name of the gem's owner or the portrayed person (or both at the same time).

4   Continuation of the Project After Exile to Florence in 1731

In early 1731, Stosch was forced to leave Rome and he moved to Florence, where he continued his collecting of engraved gems signed by ancient masters for the second volume of *Gemmae antiquae caelatae*. This is testified by a record in Pier Leone Ghezzi's diary from 17 May 1731, in which he says that he sent Stosch his drawing of a portrait cameo of (possibly) Lucius Licinius Murena with the signature of gem engraver Aulos[69] in watercolour: '*I sent Baron Stosch a watercolour drawing made by me in the same size as those gems that he had printed by Picart, with the Greek names, whose drawing is from the cameo owned by the Marquis Capponi, with the Greek name, and he paid for it two zecchinis. Capponi says that it is the head of Antinoo, but he is wrong* [because it is not]'.[70] It is noteworthy that Ghezzi prepared his drawing in the same size as drawings of gems which Picart published in 1724. The cameo reproduced by Ghezzi for Stosch was made of sardonyx and it is now lost but it was at the time in the Alessandro Gregorio Capponi collection in Rome (and subsequently in the Museo Collegio Romano). Ghezzi, who collaborated with Capponi at the moment, had a sulphur cast of it in his *dactyliotheca*, which he probably used to make his drawing.[71] The recent profound analysis of this and other surviving casts of the cameo in question by Ubaldelli suggests it to be a work of probably the 17th century, including the signature.[72]

Ghezzi's drawing made for Stosch did not survive to our times; however, in the Princes Czartoryski Museum in Krakow, one discovers a drawing of this very cameo attributed to Georg Abraham Nagel (Krakow No. 1670, Fig. 10.15). As discussed in Chapter 8, the documentary gem drawings made for Stosch by Odam were sometimes later redrawn by Preißler, Tuscher and Nagel. The Ghezzi's drawing of the cameo in question could be a similar case, unless Stosch asked Nagel to draw the gem anew from a sulphur impression or a glass paste, but no such a reproduction is recorded among his rich collections. In any case, the discussed example illustrates that shortly after Stosch's exile to Florence, Ghezzi still acted as his agent in Rome and supplied him with drawings of ancient signed gems he discovered so that Stosch could publish them in the second volume of his study.[73] Indeed, it is said that

---

67   London, the British Museum, inv. no.: 1890,0601.126; Walters 1926, no. 2037.
68   Ghezzi 1734, I.K.no. 239 (carnelian (sic!), 12 × 12 mm).
69   On Aulos, son of Alexas and his works, see: Vollenweider 1966, pp. 40–43; Plantzos 1999, p. 91; Zwierlein-Diehl 2007, pp. 115–116; Gołyźniak 2020, pp. 127 and 215.
70   Biblioteca Casanatense Roma, Ms 3765 (diary of Ghezzi), c. 7r (17 May 1731): '*Al baron Stosch gli mandai il Disegnio fatto da mè in Acquarella nella medisima grandeza di quelle Gemme che fece stampare da Picart con i nomi Greci, il qual Disegnio è del Cameo comparato di novo dal Marchese Capponi con il nome Greco è lo pagò due Zecchini, et il detto Capponi dice che è una testa di Antinoo, mà sbaglia [perché non] è.*' See also: Ubaldelli 2001, p. 85, the gem illustrated on p. 250, no. 149 and its cast is in Paoletti (Pirzio Biroli Stefanelli 2007, no. IV.441); Dorati da Empoli 2008, p. 79. The break between the publication of the *Gemmae antiquae caelatae* in 1724 and the letter from Ghezzi from 1731 seems long; however, Stosch's own documentation and archives do not give us more clues. After all, only a tiny part of them were published and much of Stosch's archives and correspondence is probably lost (cf. discussion on this issue in Chapter 5 in this volume).
71   Ubaldelli 2001, no. 149; Ghezzi 1734, I.A.no. 84.
72   Ubaldelli 2001, no. 149. One more cast in glass paste is preserved in Leiden, Rijksmuseum van Oudheden, inv. no.: GS-11588 – https://www.rmo.nl/collectie/collectiezoeker/collectiestuk/?object=201690 [retrieved on 4 August 2023].
73   Stosch had a particularly close relationship with Ghezzi because according to Ghezzi's diary, just a day before he exiled from Rome (15 February 1731), he gifted him a terracotta and plaster

shortly after the transfer to Florence Stosch set a few goals ahead of himself. The main one was to enlarge his collection of gems but the work on his *Atlas* as well as on the second book about engraved gems was equally important to him.[74]

Pier Leone Ghezzi was not the only draughtsman engaged in the production of the first volume of the *Gemmae antiquae caelatae* book with whom Stosch continued his friendship and cooperation after his exile to Florence in 1731. Throughout the 1730s, Stosch intensively corresponded with Anton Maria Zanetti, who continued to help him find new ancient engraved gems with signatures of their makers, mostly by sending him their impressions in sulphur but in some cases also probably his own drawings. For example, on 3 October 1733, Stosch sent a letter in response to Zanetti's previous correspondence, discussing with him the authenticity and reproduction of some important gems. In particular, he thanked Zanetti for having sent him a sulphur impression of one of the most precious gems from his collection – the prized black chalcedony intaglio with the head of Antinous bearing the fragmentary inscription ANTO(...). Zanetti traced this gem for a long time, and he finally managed to buy it (Fig. 10.16). No drawing of it has survived to our times, suggesting its potential publication in Stosch's next book, but from Stosch's letter to Zanetti it is clear that he took the inscription as a signature. He also noticed that the intaglio captured his interest when he was still in Rome and he reported to have its impression made back then; however, not as good as the one sent by Zanetti.[75] Zanetti later sold the intaglio alongside his three other exceptional gems to George Spencer, 4th Duke of Marlborough for the negotiated amount of £600 (1200 zecchini; 15 000 francs, according to Reinach; £1200 according to King), on the occasion of his visit to Venice in 1761.[76] After the dispersal of the Marlborough collection in 1899, it belonged to Charles Newton-Robinson (1853–1913) and Giorgio Sangiorgi (1886–1965), among others. This exceptional and large (35 × 29 mm) gem is now in the J. Paul Getty Museum in Malibu. It was cut ca. 131–138 AD and it indeed depicts Antinous. The fragmentary vertical inscription written in retrograde Greek letters is generally believed to be the name of the gem engraver.[77]

The black chalcedony intaglio was not the only piece worth Stosch's attention. In the same letter, one learns that Zanetti also informed Stosch before about the very special amethyst he had recently found and added to his cabinet. It depicted Hermaphrodite reclining asleep on the rocks on a cloak under a tree attended by three Erotes – the first blowing a *syrinx*, the second fanning an ivy-leaf to cool Hermaphrodite and the third playing a lyre; it had a partial signature of the famous Dioscurides (ΔΙΟC).[78] Stosch now explicitly said that he would love to have a drawing of that gem and he asked Zanetti to pay particular attention to copy the letters of the signature as accurately as possible so that he could illustrate this piece in the supplement to his first book.[79] Zanetti's original drawing remains unknown, but in the luxurious edition of Winckelmann's catalogue of Stosch's gems published in 1760, one finds the engraving depicting that amethyst made by Schweickart, of which a copy is also in Krakow (Krakow No. 71, Fig. 10.17).[80] Stosch had no glass paste or sulphur made after this intaglio, which probably indicates that Zanetti sent him his drawing, which was meant for the production of the final engraving by Schweickart.

Zanetti believed the gem to be a genuine masterpiece, after which many ancient replicas and modern copies were made, and Stosch was of the same opinion.[81] Its current whereabouts remain unknown, but it is important to note that it once probably belonged to the collection of Fulvio Orsini (1529–1600) before him.[82] In contrast to the opinion of Zanetti, the signature is now regarded as certainly counterfeit. This was already discovered by Bracci, who claimed the whole gem to be the work of

---

forms of his own bust sculpted by Bouchardon in the presence of several close friends, including Girolamo Odam, see: Dorati da Empoli 2008, pp. 68–69.

74 Zazoff and Zazoff 1983, p. 54.

75 Letter from Stosch to Anton Maria Zanetti dated Florence 3 October 1733: '*Già fra il miei solfi racolti anni sono in Roma ne avevo una della stessa gemma ma non era così bien* (...)' (Magrini (ed.) 2021, letter no. 56).

76 Boardman *et al.* 2009, p. 206; Hansson 2021b, pp. 65–66; Tassinari 2022, pp. 125–132.

77 Malibu, J. Paul Getty Museum, acc. no.: 2019.13.17; Scarisbrick 1990, p. 413; Boardman *et al.* 2009, no. 753; Wagner and Boardman 2018, no. 151 (with full bibliography); Tassinari 2022, pp. 128–130.

78 On Dioscurides, see: Vollenweider 1966, pp. 56–64; Zwierlein-Diehl 1986, no. 145 (with a list of his works); Plantzos 1999, pp. 95–97; Zwierlein-Diehl 2005, pp. 339–341; Zwierlein-Diehl 2007, pp. 117–119; Gołyźniak 2020, pp. 215–217.

79 Letter from Stosch to Anton Maria Zanetti dated Florence 3 October 1733: '*Cossì avrei gusto di avere un schizzo d'un dissegno colli imitazioni estate de caratteri, per poterlo inserire nel appendice del mio libro.*' (Magrini (ed.) 2021, letter no. 56).

80 Rügler in Winckelmann 2013, p. XLIII.

81 Letter from Stosch to Anton Maria Zanetti dated Florence 3 October 1733: '*Questo è sincere lavoro di Dioscoride e di più belli che egli habbia fatto se ne vendono delle copie fatte da valenti artefici antichi* (...)', (Magrini (ed.) 2021, letter no. 56). Hansson 2021b; Tassinari 2022, p. 119. That amethyst intaglio was published with other Zanetti gems in: Gori and Zanetti 1750, pp. 115–116, pl. LVII.

82 Zwierlein-Diehl 1986, no. 887.

Flavio Sirletti, a gem engraver close to Stosch.[83] This is far-fetched, especially if one accepts the view that it once belonged to Orsini. The intaglio is difficult to judge from the surviving illustrations only, but it depicts a subject which was commonly copied since the Renaissance.

A piece of information about another gem that Stosch wanted to publish in his new book can be found in the letter dated 27 December 1738, in which Stosch thanks Zanetti for having sent him a sulphur impression of an aquamarine intaglio featuring a giant to the front, inscribed like his amethyst intaglio with Hermaphrodite, with a partial signature of the famous Dioscurides (ΔIOC), which as Stosch says will be drawn for him for his second book: '*I am very grateful for the beautiful sulphur you sent me of your other very rare intaglio with the name of the excellent craftsman Dioscorides, which is certainly and undoubtedly the work of this famous master. I will have it drawn with all possible accuracy to put it in my book.*'[84]

This gem was once owned by Prince Eugene de Savoy (1663–1736) and after his death Zanetti bought it directly from the sole heir, Princess Anna Maria Vittoria of Soissons (1683–1763) in Vienna in 1736. After Zanetti's death, in turn, it was purchased by Sir Richard Worsley (1751–1805) from Zanetti's heirs, probably during his visit in Venice (Fig. 10.18).[85] It could be that Zanetti sent his drawing or an impression of that intaglio to Stosch. Whatever the case, no drawing seems to have survived, but it is noteworthy that the original gem was closely copied in sard by an anonymous engraver, and this copy, once in the Blacas collection, is now in London in the British Museum.[86] Stosch had it drawn later by Georg Abraham Nagel for his *Paper Museum of Gems* (Krakow No. 119). Regarding the original aquamarine intaglio, Stosch and Gori thought it was a genuine piece.[87] Bracci suggested that it was a modern work of Flavio Sirletti.[88] Certainly, the partial signature ΔIOC on the aquamarine was counterfeited but the gem itself might be ancient.[89] The intaglio was well known at the time since Piranesi illustrated it in one of his preparatory drawings of the fifth plate for his publication entitled *Parere sull'architettura*.[90]

5 The Antiquarian World as a Stimulus for Stosch's Scholarly Activities

Another source mentioning Stosch's new book project and specifying its subject is Stosch's letter to Filippo Venuti (but addressed via Ridolfino Venuti) dated Florence, 24 February 1739. Stosch indicates that the visit of the new Grand Duke of Tuscany in Florence in 1739 resulted in the sumptuary costs borne by local aristocrats so that many had to sell some of their assets. Some important gems were put for sale and Count Frederick de Thoms (1669–1746) challenged Stosch and bought them: '*The visit of the Grand Duke, and the expenses of the aristocracy for this occasion, have led to the sale of many nice things. I bought quantities of excellent ancient bronze figures. (…) Bravely, Gori has sold some of his nicest things to a certain B. Thoms. (…) I did not want to sell anything to the said Thomas (sic!) and refused the offer of six hundred sequins for twelve of my rings. I refuse to swop diamonds, which surprised him greatly, as he had found Princes and Cardinals in Italy more willing to negotiate. He caught the nicest stones and cameos in the world. Some of these have engravers' names, which I had drawn to publish them in the supplement of my book. I recognise several of these as debris of the great Farnese cabinet, ruined by the deadly Jesuit and the barbarity of the Spaniards and the carelessness of the last Duke Antonio. (…) My brother, Bonaccorsi, the distinguished Doctor Nagel and Marcus the*

---

83 Bracci 1784–1786, vol. I, pp. 25–27 and vol. II, pp. 70–71, pl. 68.
84 Letter from Stosch to Anton Maria Zanetti dated Florence 27 December 1738: '*Io Le rendo infinite grazie del bellissimo solfo che mi ha mandato dell'altro Suo rarissimo intaglio col nome dell'eccellente artifice Dioscoride, il quale è sicuramente e indubitatamente opera di tal Famoso maestro. Ed io con tutta la possible esattitudine il farò disegnare per collocarlo nel mio libro.*' (Magrini (ed.) 2021, letter no. 112). On the gem, see: Gori and Zanetti 1750, pp. 66–68, pl. XXXIII.
85 Worsley 1824, vol. I, pp. 142–143; Scarisbrick 1990, p. 414; Tassinari 2022, pp. 120–122. Zanetti managed to buy more exceptional gems from the Savoy collection. In the *post scriptum* of his letter sent to Zanetti and dated 11 October 1738, Stosch congratulates him on the acquisition of the famous Althorp Leopard Cameo from Savoy's heiress too. Interestingly, it was Stosch who first noticed this exceptional cameo in the cabinet of Marcoantonio Sabbatini and he advised Pope Clement XI to buy it for 100 scudi. In 1720, Stosch advised Cardinal Alessandro Albani to take it for his diplomatic mission to Vienna in order to gain Eugene de Savoy's favour, see: Boardman *et al.* 2009, no. 530; Craievich 2018, pp. 284–285; Hindman 2020, p. 39; Tassinari 2022, pp. 132–133. In 1764, Zanetti sold the cameo to John Spencer, 1st Earl Spencer (1734–1783) and since then it was housed in the Althorp House. It left it in 1978 and it is now in a private collection in England, see: Scarisbrick 1990; Hindman 2020.

86 London, the British Museum: inv. no.: 1913,0307.43, once in the Blacas collection, see: Raspe and Tassie 1791, no. 996; Dalton 1915, no. 849; Tassinari 2022, pp. 120–122.
87 See the letter to Zanetti evoked above and Gori and Zanetti 1750, pp. 66–68, pl. XXXIII.
88 Bracci 1784–1786, vol. I, pp. 25–27.
89 Tassinari (2022, pp. 120–122) thinks that the gem and the signature are modern.
90 Scarisbrick 1990, p. 413.

painter salute you.⁹¹ This letter provides interesting information about the collecting habits of Frederick de Thoms, who apparently acquired some gems from the celebrated Farnese collection and who was a real threat to Stosch on the art market for gems.⁹² Moreover, it is illuminous about the reasons why some prestigious collections (such as the Farnese one) were dispersed in the 1730s. However, most importantly, it testifies that in the 1730s Stosch made considerable efforts to advance with the second volume of the *Gemmae antiquae caelatae* book and it confirms its subject – ancient engraved gems signed by their makers which were not published in the first volume.⁹³

The quoted fragment of Stosch's letter also testifies that he had had some signed gems bought by Thoms documented as drawings for his new book. There is a group of five intaglios and cameos now housed in the Rijksmuseum van Oudheden in Leiden that are identified as once belonging to Frederick de Thoms and it is very likely that Stosch referred to at least four of them in his letter to Venuti.

The first one is a garnet (almandine) intaglio presenting Mercury wearing a *petazus* and cloak, who is standing to the front-right holding little Dionysus and a roll of parchment in his hands. There is a crater at his feet and signature of Aulos (ΑΥΛΟΥ) in the field (Fig. 10.19).⁹⁴ This gem was documented for Stosch's new book by Nagel surely in 1739, apparently from an impression (Krakow No. 251, Fig. 10.20). At the time of Stosch, it was seemingly considered genuine. Later, only Janssen believed the gem to be genuine and while she had some doubts about the authenticity of the inscription, ultimately, she concluded it to be not the signature of otherwise well-known Aulos engraver but the name of the owner of the intaglio.⁹⁵ This view should be rejected because some elements of the gem's iconography are already incorrect. For example, the unwrapped roll of parchment in the hand of Mercury is a completely atypical attribute for this god and the form of his *petazus* is not right. Moreover, the relatively poor technique of engraving and style and particularly the way the signature of Aulos is carved suggest this intaglio to be a forgery from the late seventeenth century or first third of the eighteenth century.

The second gem once in de Thoms collection that Stosch probably had had documented for his forthcoming book was a banded agate intaglio with Perseus wearing a cloak and Phrygian cap, standing to the left with a harpa and raising the head of Medusa, while reflecting himself in a shield at his feet inscribed ΑΞΕΟΥ (Fig. 10.21).⁹⁶ According to Thoms' own notes, he bought the gem in Rome during one of his excursions to the city. The intaglio itself is authentic, cut in the *Republican Wheel Style* in the second half of the 1st century BC; however, the signature is by all means modern. Judging from the size and careless shapes of the letters, it was added in the 17th century.⁹⁷ Maaskant-Kleibrink is right to claim that the motif from the gem is fairly popular and an ancient engraver would not put his name on the shield where Perseus' reflection should be but rather in the field.⁹⁸ Furthermore, as already noticed by Janssen,⁹⁹ the name ΑΞΕΟΥ is a variation of Axeochos (ΑΞΕΟΧΟΣ), which appears on a genuine carnelian intaglio carved with a head of Heracles (cf. below) and on a modern amethyst depicting a Faun with panther skin on the head playing a lyre to young Bacchus

---

91 Cod. Cortonese 497, fol. 17: 'La venue du Granduc et les depenses que la Noblesse a faites a cette occasion, ont causé la vente de bien de belles choses. J'ay achette quantité de excellentes figures Antiques de bronze. (...) Gori a bravement vendu a un certain B. Thoms ses plus belles choses (...). Je n'ay rien voulu vendre au dit Thomas (sic) et j'ay refusé l'offre de sixcent sequins pour douze de mes anneaux. J'ay refusé le troc des diamants, dont il a été d'autant plus surpris, qu'il a trouvé de (sic) Princes et Cardinaux plus traitables en Italie. Il a attrapé les plus belles pieres (sic) et Camees du monde. Il y a parmi quelquesuns avec des noms des graveurs, que j'ai fait dessiner, pour le (sic) publier dans le supplement de mon livre. Je reconnais en plusieurs les debris du Gran Cabinet Farnesien ruiné par le fatal Jesuite et la barbarie des Espagnols et la nonchalence du Dernier Duc Antonio. (...) Mon frère, Bonaccorsi, l'insigne Docteur Nagel et Marcus le peintre vous salient.' (quoted in Engelmann 1908, pp. 330–331).

92 Frederick de Thoms (1669–1746) was a German art collector with various influential political ties. In 1719, he became secretary to King George I of Great Britain. In the 1730s he lived in Naples where he started to build his considerable collection of antiquities, often buying specimens from prominent dealers in Rome. In 1741 he settled in Leiden and tried to organise his private museum but after his death his holdings, including 1050 gems, were sold to Dutch stadtholder William IV, Prince of Orange (1711–1751). For more information on Frederick de Thoms and his collection of engraved gems, see: Maaskant-Kleibrink 1978, pp. 22–33; Zwierlein-Diehl 2023, p. 464.

93 The book was clearly not devoted to unsigned gems too as then presumed by Zazoff, Weiner, Coen and Fidanza, see: Zazoff and Zazoff 1983, pp. 54–57; Weiner 1990, lot 41; Coen and Fidanza (eds) 2001.

94 Leiden, Rijksmuseum van Oudheden, inv. no.: GS-11394; Maaskant-Kleibrink 1978, p. 27, figs 17a–b.

95 Janssen 1866, no. 10.

96 Leiden, Rijksmuseum van Oudheden, inv. no.: GS-00276; Maaskant-Kleibrink 1978, no. 276 (with full bibliography).

97 Zwierlein-Diehl (1989 and 2005, 326–328) observes that fabricated and fake signatures of such carless style were typically added to original ancient gems in the sixteenth and seventeenth centuries while more carefully carved ones even imitating the small dots usually appearing at the ends of the letters appear in the eighteenth century.

98 Maaskant-Kleibrink 1978, no. 276.

99 Janssen 1866, no. 5.

on a pedestal with a thyrsus, a crescent in the field, once in the Strozzi and Blacas collections, which Stosch published in the first volume of *Gemmae antiquae caelatae*.[100] These three gems together show some consequence of Stosch's thinking about the names of certain engravers. He must have strongly believed that Axeochos was indeed an ancient engraver, perhaps because he found that name on ancient coins, but it is likely that the forger came up with it because this was the name of the son of famous Alcibiades.[101] In any case, Stosch had had the gem in question drawn by Nagel in the late 1730s/early 1740s apparently after its impression, which he indeed possessed, made in sulphur (Krakow No. 1262, Fig. 10.22).[102]

The third gem once in the de Thoms collection that Stosch most likely had had documented for the supplement of *Gemmae antiquae caelatae* was the glass gem featuring four quadrigas racing in a circus around a spina on the left, with the inscription ΔΕΥΤΟΝΟC at the bottom (Fig. 10.23).[103] According to Winckelmann, in the circle of Stosch, the inscription from the gem was taken as a signature,[104] and this is also suggested by the text appearing under the drawing which was made for Stosch by Preißler (Krakow No. 1540, Fig. 10.24) certainly shortly prior to his departure from Florence in 1738 ('Quattre chars courants autour d'une borne avec le nom du graveur au bas'). According to the orientation of the drawing, it was made after an impression of the original gem. Later, Janssen incorrectly rejected the inscription and the whole gem as modern.[105] The style of engraving is distinctly the *Republican Extinguishing Pellet Style* suggesting the date of the second half of the 1st century BC and the inscription is original, although it stands for the name of the gem's owner rather than its engraver.

The fourth gem once in de Thoms collection that Stosch had had documented for his second book was a glass cameo imitating onyx depicting Triton with a rudder and Venus with Cupid stretching the bow riding on a three-headed-sea-Cerberus-like monster to the left (Fig. 10.25).[106] According to the drawing made by Nagel in the late 1730s or early 1740s (Krakow No. 324, Fig. 10.26), there is an inscription on Venus' leg: ΑΡΧΙΟΝΟΟ, suggested as a signature of some Archionos. However, this name or its variation does not appear on any other gem, and, in fact, there is no inscription or signature on our cameo too. Nagel (maybe after Stosch's advice) overinterpreted folds of the garment on which Venus sits as a series of letters forming a signature.[107] The cameo judging by the iconography, material, technique and style is ancient, made in the Augustan era (early 1st century AD), when similar depictions were extremely popular. Stosch had a sulphur cast of this gem which was used for preparation of the drawing.[108] This example illustrates some pitfalls in the research on ancient signed gems that Stosch and his collaborating artists encountered.

Finally, the last gem once in de Thoms collection that Stosch very likely had had documented for the second volume of *Gemmae antiquae caelatae* was a sardonyx cameo presenting a draped and laureate bust of Septimus Severus to the left. At the bottom of the bust, there is a signature: ΜΑΞΑΔΑC (Fig. 10.27).[109] The drawing was made for Stosch by Nagel and in his drawing the gem is specified to have belonged to Frederick de Thoms (Krakow No. 1357, Fig. 10.28). There must have been many controversies around this cameo already in the times of Stosch because in 1767 Anton Francesco Gori in his *Dactyliotheca Smithiana* judged it as fabricated in modern times.[110] Indeed, according to the technique and style this gem is modern, cut in the seventeenth century and the shapes and style of the letters suggest the signature to be contemporary to the cameo. Janssen also came to such conclusions.[111]

To conclude, the increasing accessibility of old collections, so far locked in private treasuries like that of Farnese, through sales on the art market resulted in discoveries of new ancient (or not) signed gems by Stosch. The growing interest in archaeology over the 1720s, 1730s and 1740s significantly contributed to the expansion of Stosch's corpus of new signed gems as well.

---

100   Stosch 1724, pl. XX. This gem is now in the British Museum in London, inv. no.: 1913,0307.111.
101   Janssen 1866, no. 5.
102   Raspe and Tassie 1791, no. 8864 (sulphur, Stosch).
103   Leiden, Rijksmuseum van Oudheden, inv. no.: GS-00258; Maaskant-Kleibrink 1978, no. 258.
104   Winckelmann 1760, class V, no. 55, p. 468.
105   Janssen 1866, no. 14.
106   Leiden, Rijksmuseum van Oudheden, inv. no.: GS-10225.
107   I could not examine the original by autopsy and my judgment is based on the analysis of the high resolution photograph available from: https://www.rmo.nl/collectie/collectiezoeker/collectiestuk/?object=198721 [retrieved on 7 January 2023] as well as a cast of the cameo in: Raspe and Tassie 1791, no. 2639.
108   The cameo was also replicated in the eighteenth century as glass pastes (perhaps originating from Stosch's studio?), see for example: London, the British Museum, inv. no.: 1923,0401.980 (once in the Townley collection), taken by Walters as ancient (Walters 1926, no. 3726) – https://www.britishmuseum.org/collection/object/G_1923-0401-980 [retrieved on 31 January 2023].
109   Leiden, Rijksmuseum van Oudheden, inv. no.: GS-10089.
110   Gori 1767, p. 34.
111   Janssen 1866, no. 29.

6 The Sequel to the First Volume Starts to Be Advertised

As a result of exchange of drawings and impressions between Stosch, the Duke of Devonshire, Ghezzi, Zanetti and others, the corpus of newly discovered signed gems expanded over time. The draughtsmen in Stosch's service tirelessly documented them for the sake of future illustrations, the research continued, and the new book was slowly taking shape. In the late 1730s, there were the first signs that its forthcoming publication started to be advertised. Confirmation of that comes from a notable antiquary Francesco Vettori (1692–1770).[112] In 1739, he published a treatise entitled *Dissertatio glyptographica*,[113] where he described Stosch as one of the foremost connoisseurs and a much respected scholar publishing an excellent book on the peculiar subject of ancient signed gems with illustrations made by Bernard Picart.[114] He also wrote that: '*Stosch, master of that field, will enrich this series of ancient engraved gems in a second edition of his work, which – we are told – should be more precise*'.[115] This short passage confirms that Stosch was working on the supplement to his first book and that it was already advertised at the time to other antiquarians. The subject of the book is made clear – new ancient signed gems and interestingly, that book should be more precise, which in the context of Stosch's letters exchanged with the Duke of Devonshire discussed above, means that it would include additional information on the gems Stosch already published in 1724.[116] The fact that Stosch advertised his forthcoming volume is no proof of the existence of an actual draft or a book manuscript at this point, though. However, he certainly continued to collect more gems for that study.

In his book, Vettori discussed two signed gems he owned, among others. The first one was the burnt carnelian intaglio presenting Venus seated on a rock, balancing a rod on her finger and thus playing with her son Cupid in front of her, signed by Aulos (Fig. 10.29).[117] The second gem was a fragmentary sardonyx intaglio featuring the legs of Mars with a signature of Quintus – ΚΟΙΝΤΟC ΑΛΞΑ ΕΠΟΙΕΙ (Fig. 10.30).[118] According to Vettori, the first intaglio entered his collection on 5 June 1735.[119] This is confirmed by Pier Leone Ghezzi, who drew it immediately after its discovery in June 1735.[120] His drawing is now in the Biblioteca Apostolica Vaticana (Fig. 10.31), and curiously Ghezzi drew the gem within a frame very similar to the ones Stosch published in the first volume of *Gemmae antiquae caelatae*. Ghezzi's drawing is as important as the laudable commentary on Stosch in Vettori's book because it demonstrates a considerable impact of Stosch's first volume of *Gemmae antiquae caelatae* at the time. Stosch had this gem documented as a drawing by Nagel, which is now in the Kunstbibliothek in Berlin (Berlin vol. II, pl. 89, Fig. 10.32). It was made for him in the late 1730s, so more or less contemporary to Vettori's book release. It is fairly

---

112 Francesco Vettori lived in Rome but he belonged to a noble family of Florentine origins. Ghezzi drew his caricature in 1744 and described him as a scholar of literature and connoisseur of antiquities, especially engraved gems and medals (The Biblioteca Apostolica Vaticana, Cod. Ott. lat. 3119, fol. 86; Carpita 2012, p. 107). Indeed, over the course of his life, Vettori accumulated a considerable collection of sculptures, engraved gems and ancient coins (Guerrini 1971, pp. 44–45). Apparently, he was a client of Girolamo Odam as far as gems are concerned (Guerrini 1971, pp. 44–45; Carpita 2012, p. 107). According to Justi (1871, p. 24), shortly after Stosch's death in 1757 he managed to buy the Christian and Persian gems from his heir Muzell-Stosch. He published extensively on aspects of Christian archaeology and he often used gems as illustrations and wrote about glyptic art eagerly. He built a cabinet of ca. 130 gems which he presented to Pope Benedict XIV receiving in return a post of Prefect of the newly created *Museo Cristiano* (now the *Museo Sacro*) in 1757. During the French occupation of the Vatican in 1798 the entire collection of gems was plundered and has disappeared almost without trace but in the Gabinetto di Medagliere of the Biblioteca Apostolica Vaticana there is a collection of wax impressions of Vettori's gems (Vettori Vatican; Gasparri 1977, p. 28; Alteri 1987, p. 25; Spier 2007, p. 5, pls 152–155; Guerrieri Borsoi 2009, pp. 168–169).

113 Vettori 1739. For a discussion on this book, see: Zazoff and Zazoff 1983, p. 121.

114 Vettori 1739, pp. 3–4.

115 Vettori 1739, p. 7: '*Augebit vero Stoschius, (cujus tota ea provincia est) hanc feriem veterum caelatorum gemmarum editione altera sui operis, quam parare compertum est elegantiorem.*'

116 Borroni Salvadori (1978a, p. 568) claims that Stosch also probably wanted to explore more thoroughly the matter of various, distinctive styles of individual engravers in this new book but this cannot be confirmed in his existing correspondence or on the discovered drawings.

117 Vettori 1739, pp. 74–77. It was later in the Charles Townley collection, and it is now in the British Museum in London and both, the intaglio and the signature are agreed to be genuine, see: Dalton 1915, no. 643; Zazoff 1983, pl. 80.6 (with full bibliography); Zwierlein-Diehl 2007, ill. 455.

118 Vettori 1739, pp. 108–118. This gem is now in a private collection. It appeared at auction at Christie's in 2003 (sale of the estate of Gavin Todhunter on 29 October 2003, lot 299) and it was suggested to have once belonged to Philipp von Stosch, which is not true. See a detailed discussion on these two Vettori gems and their history in: Zwierlein-Diehl 2005, pp. 325–326; Arbeid, Bruni & Iozzo 2016, no. 83. On Quintus, son of Alexas, see: Zwierlein-Diehl 2007, pp. 115–116.

119 Vettori 1739, p. 75.

120 Biblioteca Apostolica Vaticana, Cod. Ott. lat. 3108, fols 123–124 with a caption field in the bottom inscribed: '*VENUS · CUM · CUPIDINE AULI · OPUS In Sardoniche Incisum ex Dacthyliotecha Victoria*', and an extensive commentary.

possible that it was planned to be included in Stosch's forthcoming volume.

The case of the intaglio with Venus and Cupid from Vettori's collection is particularly interesting and important because it illustrates the climax of *gemmomania* in Rome at the time. The appearance of this new, genuine signed gem by Aulos resulted in an uncontrolled enthusiasm outburst among the antiquarians. According to Vettori, the finders took advantage of that and they quickly made some sulphur impressions, which they distributed to several potential buyers. One of these casts reached Stosch in Florence, who admired this excellent work by Aulos. Apparently, he made some impressions on his own, which he later sent further to his friends, including one who was a mutual friend of Stosch and Vettori. This was how Vettori learnt that impressions of the gem he had just bought were already circulating.[121] Regarding the other new signed gem owned by Vettori, there is no drawing of it in Krakow or Berlin, but it cannot be excluded that Stosch planned to publish it in his new book as well. Its drawing could be lost.[122]

7 Georg Abraham Nagel and His Contribution to the Second Volume of *Gemmae antiquae caelatae* in the Late 1730s and Early 1740s

The passage from Vettori (1739) suggests that the works on the second volume of *Gemmae antiquae caelatae* intensified towards the end of the 1730s. This is also suggested by a series of drawings of new signed gems attributed to Georg Abraham Nagel, who worked for Stosch in late 1730s and early 1740s. One of them documents a sardonyx cameo featuring a warrior with a female goddess crowning him and Victory behind him on biga to the right, signed ΑΛΦΗΟC (Alpheios) in the exergue (Krakow No. 455, Figs 10.33–10.34). At the times of Stosch, this gem was in the Cardinal Alessandro Albani collection, from whom Stosch could easily obtain a cast and a drawing by sending Nagel to visit him in Rome as he sometimes did. Later, the cameo went to Sir Edward Dering (1732–1798), from whom it was probably directly bought by George Spencer, 4th Duke of Marlborough (1739–1817).[123] Now it is preserved in a private collection.[124] Its ownership by Albani and later by the Dukes of Marlborough suggests that it was highly esteemed at the times of Stosch. The most recent analysis indeed suggests it to be genuine work of the 1st century BC/AD;[125] however, the signature, even though neatly incised in what seems to be a natural place, was probably added only in the early eighteenth century. In the State Hermitage Museum in St. Petersburg, there is an ancient cameo depicting Drusus and Antonia Minor with an inscription: ΑΛΦΗΟC | CΥΝ | ΑΡΕΘΩ also added in the eighteenth century.[126]

Another gem drawn by Nagel for Stosch very likely with the intention to publish in his new book was the onyx cameo engraved with Jupiter driving quadriga and striking giants, probably Typhon and Pophyrion, with his thunderbolts, bearing the signature of Athenion in Greek – ΑΘΗΝΙΩΝ (Krakow No. 116, Fig. 10.35).[127] Stosch had its cast,[128] and Nagel's drawing was later transformed into an engraving by Schweickart, which was published in the luxurious edition of Winckelmann's catalogue of Stosch's gems (Krakow No. 117, Fig. 10.36).[129] The cameo was once in the Orisini and Farnese collections and it is now kept in the Museo Archeologico Nazionale in Naples (Fig. 10.37).[130] It is an exceptional Hellenistic work probably made in the artistic milieu of Pergamon between the 3rd and the 2nd centuries BC. Furtwängler assumed that Athenion could be a royal gem engraver at the court of Eumenes II (197–159 BC).[131] Pannuti suggests that the subject for the cameo was inspired by a statuary group or a relief.[132] Indeed, the scene it represents could refer to the victories of the Attalid dynasty against the Galatians as much as contemporary sculptures and reliefs, for instance, from the famous Pergamon Altar.

---

121 Vettori 1739, p. 75.
122 As discussed in Chapter 8 in this volume, the gem drawings discovered in Krakow and Berlin certainly constitute a considerable part, but clearly only a portion of Stosch's original *Paper Museum of Gems*.
123 Borbein, Kunze and Rügler (2019, no. III.274) claim that Sir Edward Dering, 5th Baronet (1705–1762) was the owner, but he seems to early as suggested Boardman, Kagan and Wagner (2017, p. 225).
124 Lippert¹ II², no. 151 (cameo); Dehn/Dolce Vatican, T.18. (14 × 18 mm, cameo, Albani coll.); Raspe and Tassie 1791, no. 7823 (cameo, Duke of Marlborough); Cades Grande, 33.IV.A.69; Zwierlein-Diehl 1986, no. 862; Pirzio Biroli Stefanelli 2007, no. I.301.
125 Boardman *et al.* 2009, no. 506 (with full bibliography).
126 Neverov 1971, no. 73.
127 On Athenion, see: Zwierlein-Diehl 2007, p. 69.
128 On Stosch's glass paste reproducing this cameo, see: Furtwängler 1896, no. 9451; Borbein, Kunze and Rügler 2019, no. II.110.
129 Rügler in Winckelmann 2013, p. XLII.
130 Museo Archeologico Nazionale in Naples, inv. no.: 25848/16; Raspe and Tassie 1791, no. 986; Lippold 1922, pl. 3.4; Pannuti 1994, no. 71 (with more literature); Zwierlein-Diehl 2005, p. 322; Pirzio Biroli Stefanelli 2007, no. I.147.
131 Furtwängler 1900, vol. I, pl. LVII.2, vol. II, p. 259.
132 Pannuti 1994, no. 71.

The next gem which would have been included into Stosch's second study of ancient signed gems, as testified by relevant drawing by Nagel (Krakow No. 2047, Fig. 10.38), was a sardonyx cameo dated to the third quarter of the 1st century BC, featuring a chained Cupid leaning on his pickaxe to the right with a genuine signature of Aulos (ΑΥΛΟC) incised below the groundline (Fig. 10.39). The gem was once in the Baron Karl Heinrich von Gleichen (1733–1807) collection and is now considered lost.[133] Perhaps, it is not a coincidence that while describing a modern nicolo intaglio from Stosch's collection, which bears exactly the same subject but without the signature of Aulos, Winckelmann mentions that Countess Cheroffini in Rome possessed an exquisite cameo bearing the same motif.[134] Could it be the same gem as discussed here but later owned by Baron von Gleichen? Francesca Cheroffini (née Gherardi, 1709–1778) was a passionate art collector and the lover of Cardinal Alessandro Albani (1692–1779) by whom she bore two daughters. She received many gems from him as gifts.[135] If the cameo in question here was once in the hands of Cardinal Albani or Countess Cheroffini, it would explain how Stosch documented it for his second book since he was a close friend of the cardinal and he often sent Nagel to check upon his collections in Rome.

Regarding the gems with signature of Aulos, Stosch had also had documented by Nagel as a drawing an amethyst intaglio presenting Cupid seated on the ground tied to a trophy on his right with a large torch atop, signed in the field above in Greek ΑΥΛΟΥ (Krakow No. 1991, Fig. 10.40). Apparently, Nagel drew it after a sulphur impression that Stosch is attested to have had.[136] The intaglio is now housed in the British Museum in London but it was once a part of the Carlisle cabinet of gems (Fig. 10.41).[137] It was published by Lorenz Natter (1705–1763), who spent a few years in Stosch's house in Florence in the 1730s, in his treatise. He was fascinated by the quality of the stone and the engraving.[138] It is very likely that the gem was meant to be published in the second volume of *Gemmae antiquae caelatae*, despite later being a rather controversial piece. Brunn and Köhler considered this intaglio entirely modern, while Furtwängler thought that only the signature was added in the eighteenth century.[139] More recently, Vollenweider and Rudoe thought it to be an entirely genuine work, whereas Zwierlein-Diehl says that the surface of the stone was repolished.[140] As one can see, while the gem itself is accepted to be ancient (dated to the third quarter of the 1st century BC), it is still uncertain if the signature of Aulos is genuine.[141]

The next gem to be discussed here is a carnelian intaglio depicting the head of Heracles with the lionskin on his head to the left signed by Axeochos (ΑΞΕΟΧΟΣ), a drawing of which is attributed to Nagel and now in Krakow (Krakow No. 1055, Fig. 10.42). The gem dates to the late Hellenistic period (1st century BC) and it features a fairly popular type at the time.[142] It is now in a private collection (Fig. 10.43),[143] but it was first recorded by Lippert as early as 1755 and later also in 1767, the second time as in the collection of gems belonging to Joseph Anton Gabaleon von Wackerbarth-Salmour (1685–1761).[144] He was a Saxon minister and diplomat, as well as an envoy to Italy in 1730–1731. He met Stosch in 1717 in Vienna and he urged him to visit Dresden and offered him an attractive position on the court as royal antiquary. It is fairly possible that these two were in direct contact later too

---

133   Dehn/Dolce Vatican, I.37 (19 × 17 mm); Raspe and Tassie 1791, no. 6988 (cameo, Bar. Gleichen); Cades Grande, 14.II.B.200; Furtwängler 1900, vol. I, pl. LVII.9, vol. II, p. 260; Vollenweider 1966, pp. 41 and 103, pl. 31.5; Richter 1971, no. 652; Zazoff 1983, p. 286, pl. 80.5; Pirzio Biroli Stefanelli 2007, no. IV.255. Baron Karl Heinrich von Gleichen-Rußwurm (1733–1807) was a chamberlain at the Danish royal court and a companion of the Baroness of Bayreuth (Germany, Bavaria region) during her journey to Rome in 1755 and since 1756 he was her dedicated art dealer (Borbein, Kunze and Rügler 2019, no. II.737). His collection of engraved gems remains virtually unresearched, but it must have been a considerable cabinet. One finds at least 11 (mostly Roman) gems originating from it in Tassie's *dactyliotheca* (Raspe and Tassie 1791, nos 51, 750, 939, 1133, 1149, 1336, 1357, 1476, 1859, 1937 and 6988). Winckelmann met him in Rome in March in 1756 (Winckelmann 1952–1957, vol. I, p. 214, no. 136). For more information about Baron von Gleichen-Rußwurm, see: Zwierlein-Diehl 2023, p. 451.

134   Winckelmann 1760, class II, no. 819, p. 147.

135   For example, the fragmentary cameo with Orestes and Pylades grieving before the tomb of Orestes' father, Agamemnon, in Argos once in the Lewes House collection and now in the Museum of Fine Arts in Boston, acc. no.: 21.1221. Winckelmann, who personally knew Countess Cheroffini, in his catalogue of Stosch's gems mentions seven gems from her collection (Winckelmann 1760, class II, nos 413, 737, 819, 1513, 1683, class III, no. 246 and class IV, no. 241).

136   Raspe and Tassie 1791, no. 7114 (sulphur, Stosch).

137   London, the British Museum, inv. no.: 1913,0307.178; Dalton 1915, no. 659; Zazoff 1983, p. 286, pl. 80.3; Zwierlein-Diehl 2007, ill. 456 (with more literature); Pirzio Biroli Stefanelli 2007, no. III.483.

138   Natter 1754, pp. 38–39, pl. XXIV.

139   Dalton 1915, no. 659.

140   Vollenweider 1966, p. 41, pl. 33.1, 2 and 4; Rudoe 1996, p. 201, fig. 3; Rudoe 2003, p. 136, fig. 119; Zwierlein-Diehl 2007, ill. 456.

141   For a general study of Aulos's gems, see: Vollenweider 1966, pp. 40–43.

142   About the general type, see: Plantzos 1999, pp. 85–86.

143   The intaglio was recently sold at auction 'Small Wanders: Early gems and Jewels' on 9 July 2020, lot 15.

144   Lippert[1] I[1], no. 300; Lippert[2] II, no. 626.

and hence Stosch obtained a cast of the gem from him. However, according to Winckelmann, as well as Raspe and Tassie, the intaglio was in the Countess Cheroffini collection.[145] Because of the close relationship between Stosch and Albani, it is also possible that a cast of the gem in question or even its drawing was made by Nagel during one of his inspections of Albani's collections in Rome on the behalf of Stosch. In any case, selection of the gem for the second volume of *Gemmae antiquae caelatae* is very likely. Stosch already published one gem signed by Axeochos in 1724.[146] The banded agate intaglio with Perseus signed ΑΞΕΟΥ, once in de Thoms collection discussed above, was probably another work attributed by Stosch to this artist and selected for new publication. The one discussed here would be the third but in fact, the genuineness of Axeochos' gems is difficult to verify even for contemporary scholars. Furtwängler believed the intaglio in question here to be modern, although he thought that the gem engraver Axeochos was active in Antiquity and the amethyst intaglio with a Faun from the Strozzi collection that Stosch published in 1724, was his original and a genuine work.[147] Recently, Zwierlein-Diehl and Plantzos have convincingly argued that our intaglio and its signature are genuine, while the amethyst published by Stosch is a fake.[148] The gem from the de Thoms collection now in Leiden, as discussed above, seems to have a forged signature of this artist which continued to be added on modern gems as late as the 19th century.[149]

The name of Axeochos, although differently spelled as ΑΞΕΟΧ, appears on another intaglio drawn by Nagel, which depicts a dancing maenad with thyrsus and head of a man (Orpheus?) in her hands (Krakow No. 972, Fig. 10.44). The drawing was transferred by Princess Izabela Czartoryska so that the provenance information from the bottom was cut off and cannot be read now. The intaglio remains unidentified. The subject of a dancing maenad with thyrsus was common in Hellenistic glyptics,[150] but not with a male head in the other hand. They were often found dancing with a bunch of grapes instead. As a result, the iconography on our gem appears to be done according to a modern concept and it is a rather direct interpretation of an ancient myth. Moreover, the signature of Axeochos is clearly fabricated, most likely like the whole gem in the first half of the 18th century.

Nagel also documented for Stosch a carnelian featuring Faun sacrificing a goat under a tree, Silenus playing a lyre behind him seated on a rock and a young satyr playing pipes with partial signature of Dioscurides – ΔΙΟϹΚΟΙ (Krakow No. 1002, Fig. 10.45). One recalls the letters Stosch sent to Zanetti in which he discussed two other gems with similar fragmentary signatures of Dioscurides, which he believed to be genuine (cf. above). Thus, this piece was most likely selected for his new book as well. The intaglio has a distinctive pedigree, as it is said to be once in the Pope Alexander VIII, Cardinal Pietro Ottoboni and Carlisle collections and is now in the British Museum in London (Fig. 10.46).[151] The gem itself is ancient, probably from the early 1st century AD judging by its subject matter, technique of engraving and style. However, the fragmentary signature of Dioscurides (ΔΙΟϹΚΟΙ) was certainly added in the course of the eighteenth century, the letters are cut inaccurately, even a bit amateurish.

The first pictorial record of the gem was made by Pier Leone Ghezzi and it is now preserved in the Biblioteca Apostolica Vaticana in Rome (Fig. 10.47). On that drawing, the gem lacks the fake signature, but Ghezzi gives us its detailed provenance information: '*This rare carnelian intaglio representing a Faun playing the pipes appears with its usual panther skin and with Silenus playing the lyre, and with another man caressing an adorned dog in the field which means a festival in the countryside, was in the collection of Pope Alexander VIII, which then was passed*

---

145 Winckelmann 1760, class II, no. 1513, p. 242; Raspe and Tassie 1791, no. 5515.
146 Stosch 1724, pl. XX.
147 Furtwängler 1888, p. 72.
148 https://www.sothebys.com/en/buy/auction/2020/small-wonders-early-gems-and-jewels/greco-roman-1st-century-b-c-1st-century-a-d-or – retrieved on 8 January 2023. Having a chance to study the amethyst intaglio with Faun signed by Axeochos now in the British Museum (inv. no.: 1913,0307.111) in autopsy as well as the high-resolution photographs of the carnelian discussed here, I agree with the conclusions of Zwierlein-Diehl and Plantzos. Furtwängler's theory about existence of the original of the amethyst to have been published by Stosch in his first book and its later copy (now in the British Museum) cannot be straightforwardly rejected but it seems far-fetched.
149 See, for example: Henig, Scarisbrick and Whiting 1994, no. 823. The name of Axeochos but spelled in two different variants also appears on two Poniatowski gems, see: Poniatowski 1830–1833, no. II.239 – spelled ΑΞΕΟΧΟΣ (see also the Beazley Archive Gem Database: https://www.beazley.ox.ac.uk/record/DAB8AFDA-84DC-4696-BE82-9383AFB35E22 [retrieved on 8 May 2023]) and no. II.293 – spelled ΑΞΕΟΧΟΣ (see also the Beazley Archive Gem Database: https://www.beazley.ox.ac.uk/record/A579193C-3C1F-434B-B90F-3774DB867F9D [retrieved on 8 May 2023]).

150 Plantzos 1999, p. 87 – the Neo-Attic tradition of the late 2nd–early 1st century BC.
151 The British Museum, inv. no.: 1890,0601.77, see: Walters 1926, no. 1585. Lippert suggests that it also belonged to Joseph Anton Gabaleon von Wackerbarth-Salmour (Lippert[1] I[2], no. 454 (sard, C. a Wackerbarth Salmour)), however, he is probably mistaken because more contemporary sources like Ghezzi (see below), suggest a sequence the Pope Alexander VIII, Cardinal Pietro Ottoboni and Carlisle collections.

into the hands of his nephew Cardinal Pietro Ottoboni Vice Chancellor, and then was donated by him to My Lord Count of Carlisle, a peer in England, with other cameos bearing the names of the ancient craftsman which can be seen in the book published by Baron Stosch, and it is all carved in carnelian.'[152] Ghezzi does not specify when exactly he made his drawing but considering the fact that he mentions the intaglio to be already in the Carlisle collection, where it went alongside other most precious gems Cardinal Ottoboni had, including several pieces signed by gem engravers and published by Stosch in 1724,[153] the drawing must be dated shortly prior to 1739 and Ghezzi's commentary around this date or shortly after.

Indeed, Horace Walpole describes how Ottoboni sold some of his gems to Lord Carlisle in 1739 in his letter to Richard West dated 7 May 1740: *'I must give you an instance of his generosity or rather ostentation. When Lord Carlisle was here last year, who is a great virtuoso, he asked leave to see the Cardinal's collection of cameos and intaglios. Ottoboni gave leave, and ordered the person who showed them to observe which my Lord admired most. My Lord admired many and they were all sent to him next morning. He sent the Cardinal back a good fine repeater, who returned to him an agate snuff box, and more cameos of ten times the value. Voila qui est fini! Had my Lord produced more gold it would have been begging for more'.*[154] Ghezzi compiled albums out of his drawings between 1724 and 1740, which he ultimately sold in 1747 to Pope Benedict XIV,[155] so it is fairly possible that his drawing of the intaglio in question was made much earlier than 1739, when it has no signature at all, but he added the commentary later. Having known his extraordinary attention to detail while documenting antiquities, it is hard to imagine that he would have omitted the signature or at least did not mention it in his text. What is more, Stosch knew Ottoboni well and published several of his signed gems already in 1724. Had our gem been gifted by Pope Alexander VIII to Ottoboni, this would have been done prior to 1691 when the pope died. Consequently, if the intaglio had had the signature already prior to 1724 when Stosch collected gems for his first book, he would have published it with other signed pieces from Ottoboni's cabinet,[156] unless he thought it at that time unreliable but later changed his mind.

Interestingly, an impression of the intaglio is to be found in the Dehn/Dolce *dactyliotheca* in the Vatican, where there is no trace of a signature either.[157] Moreover, Stosch had a glass paste made after that intaglio which does not bear the problematic inscription either;[158] however, it appears on Nagel's drawing which was made in the late 1730s or more likely in the early 1740s. It looks then that the signature was added to the original gem after Ghezzi drew it and potentially after Dehn took his impression and Stosch made his glass paste, but before he had had it documented for his second book. Assuming that either Stosch's glass paste and Dehn's sulphur impressions were made prior or in 1739, when the carnelian under discussion was still in the Ottoboni's collection, it is concluded that the fake signature of Dioscurides was added to it in 1739 or shortly after that year. This is supported by the date until Nagel worked for Stosch (ca. 1744 or 1745? cf. Chapter 4) and it is perhaps noteworthy that Lord Carlisle had a special esteem for ancient signed gems, which were extremely valuable at the time and difficult to obtain. In one of his letters to Lord Carlisle, Ficoroni feared that the only way to get some signed gems for his client was to wait patiently until death led to a dispersal of some important collections.[159] It is not certain if our gem was given to Lord Carlisle by Ottoboni himself; it could have been on the art market after his death in 1740. In such circumstances, it is easy to imagine how profitable it was to add a signature to an otherwise ancient gem. In any case, in the early 1740s, Stosch apparently considered including this gem into his supplement of *Gemmae antiquae caelatae*, perhaps as an example of the fake signature being added to the genuine gem.

Finally, for his future book, Stosch also found two new gems signed by Sostratos. In the volume published in 1724, Stosch already discussed three gems attributed by him to

---

152　Biblioteca Apostolica Vaticana, Cod. Ott. lat. 3107, fol. 184: *'Questo raro intaglio in Corniola che rappresenta un Fauno sonando le tibbie pare con la sua solita Pelle di tigre e con un Sileno che suona la lira, e con un altro che accarezza un cane adornato il campo da un Alberto che significa festa in campagnia, era nella raccolta del Papa Alessandro Ottavo, che poi passò nelle mani del suo Nepote Cardinal Pietro Ottoboni Vice Cancelliere, eppoi donato dà esso a Milord Conte di Carlisle pari di Inghilterra, con altri Camei con il nome dell'antico artefice che veggonsi nel libro stampato dal Baron Stosch, ed è tutto ciò scolpito in corniola.'*
153　These were: a chalcedony intaglio of Medusa signed SOSOKLES (Stosch 1724, pl. LXV), an onyx cameo engraved with Eros leading the chariot of Dionysos drawn by two female panthers, signed by Sostratos (Stosch 1724, pl. LXVI) and a sixteenth-century cameo of Meleager and Atalanta which once belonged to Rubens (Stosch 1724, pl. LXVII).
154　Quoted in Scarisbrick 1987, p. 90.
155　Ghezzi's drawings were executed most likely between ca. 1724 and 1740, see: Guerrini 1971, pp. 48–49; Lo Bianco 1985, pp. 41–42; Fusconi 1994, p. 149; Lo Bianco 2010, p. 30; Coen and Fidanza (eds) 2011, pp. 11–12; Gołyźniak (forthcoming – Ghezzi).
156　Stosch 1724, pls XIII and LXV–LXVII.
157　Dehn/Dolce Vatican, N.40.
158　Borbein, Kunze and Rügler 2019, no. II.1534 (with full bibliography).
159　Scarisbrick 1987, p. 93.

this artist, all from Cardinal Pietro Ottoboni's collection.¹⁶⁰ The first new gem was an intaglio with Nike slaughtering a bull, which was drawn for him by Nagel (Berlin vol. III, pl. 35, Fig. 10.48). According to Winckelmann, the original gem was once owned by Stosch himself who sold it to the Duke of Devonshire; however, according to Zwierlein-Diehl, Winckelmann must have been mistaken since already in 1754 Natter had published this gem as belonging to Henry Howard, 4th Earl of Carlisle.¹⁶¹ In the unpublished letter from Stosch sent to the Duke of Devonshire from Rome on 17 February 1729, Stosch speaks about a drawing of a gem with a woman sacrificing a bull that he attached and of which he had a good impression in his collection.¹⁶² He is not explicit enough to identify that gem with the one signed by Sostratos, but this is likely given the fact that in his correspondence with the Duke he mostly discusses signed gems. Therefore, Winckelmann's testimony gets credibility, and the gem could be later sold to or exchanged with Lord Carlisle by the 3rd Duke of Devonshire. Ultimately, since 1890, the intaglio has been in the cabinet of gems of the British Museum in London and it was bought from the Carlisle collection (Fig. 10.49).¹⁶³

It is noteworthy that the gem was also drawn and commented on by Pier Leone Ghezzi for his albums including representations of various antiquities now deposited in the Biblioteca Apostolica Vaticana.¹⁶⁴ Ghezzi does not provide any clue in his commentary for the gem as to when he drew it and who the owner was, but he drew a number of Stosch's gems for his own corpus and had many impressions of Stosch's gems in his *dactyliotheca*.¹⁶⁵ It is not known when and how Stosch obtained the gem but, even if he sold it in 1729 to the Duke of Devonshire, he kept its impression which was used by Nagel to produce his drawing. Furthermore, the reason Nagel drew the gem could be because Stosch sent his earlier drawing (by Preißler?) to the Duke back then. In any case, the intaglio is widely accepted to be a genuine piece and a rather late work of Sostratos dated ca. 20 BC. Its subject probably refers to the widely promoted idea of Augustus symbolising his regaining of legionary standards from the Parthians.¹⁶⁶

The second gem signed by Sostratos discovered by Stosch and drawn for his new book by Nagel, was the onyx cameo depicting Eos or Victory riding a biga drawn by two horses, to the right inscribed at the top ΣΩΣΤΡΑΤΟΥ as well as LAV·R·MED·in the field, dated to the mid-1st century BC (Berlin vol. III, pl. 32, Fig. 10.50).¹⁶⁷ It has an illustrious provenance since it was once owned by Cardinal Pietro Barbo (1417–1471), who became Pope Paul II in 1464 and amassed the largest collection of engraved gems in the Renaissance numbering ca. 800 objects. A manuscript inventory of his assemblage, begun in 1457, lists this cameo. Once Pietro Barbo died his collection was dispersed among various noble collectors, among which there were the Medicis of Florence, the Gonzagas of Mantua, and the Grimani of Venice. This cameo was purchased by Lorenzo de'Medici as testified by the possession inscription added to the cameo and standing for LAVRENTIVS MEDICES or rather LAVRENTIVS REX MEDICES, which illustrates the high ambitions of the Florentine aristocrat to be perceived as a king.¹⁶⁸ The cameo was also registered in the inventory of Lorenzo's gems written in 1492.¹⁶⁹ After the death of Alessandro de'Medici (1510–1537), his widow, Margaret of Parma (1522–1586), daughter of the Holy Roman Emperor Charles V (1519–1556), married Ottavio Farnese, Duke of Parma (1524–1586), and the gems once owned by Lorenzo de'Medici went first to Rome, then to the Netherlands (1559–1567), next to Ortona and subsequently to Parma.¹⁷⁰ Later, they were transferred back to Rome by Alessandro Farnese (1545–1592), the son of Margaret of Parma, and they stayed there until the death of Antonio Farnese (1679–1731), the last Duke of Parma from the Farnese family, when the cameo was transferred with other Farnese gems to Naples.¹⁷¹ It is now kept in the Museo Archeologico Nazionale in Naples (Fig. 10.51).¹⁷²

---

160 Stosch 1724, pls LXV–LXVII.
161 Winckelmann 1760, class II, no. 1099, p. 187; Natter 1754, pp. 45–46, pl. XXIX; Zwierlein-Diehl 1986, no. 156. Raspe and Tassie 1791, no. 7760 probably took information about the current whereabouts of the gem from Winckelmann: '*carnelian, Duke of Devonshire, formerly in Baron Stosch's collection*'. Indeed, Zwierlein-Diehl seems right in her judgment because it is hard to imagine the gem moving from the Devonshire to Carlisle collection because the Duke of Devonshire and Lord of Carlisle competed for signed gems fiercely and both were Stosch's clients.
162 Chatsworth, the Devonshire Archives, inv. no.: CS1/188.8.
163 British Museum inv. no.: 1890,0601.50. For a discussion on this gem and literature, see: Dalton 1915, no. 770; Vollenweider 1966, p. 36, pl. 27.2 and 8; Zwierlein-Diehl 1986, no. 156; Borbein, Kunze and Rügler 2019, no. II.1099 (with full bibliography); Gołyźniak 2020, p. 215, no. 10.1.
164 Biblioteca Apostolica Vaticana, Cod. Ott. lat. 3106, fol. 87.
165 Gołyźniak (forthcoming – Ghezzi).

166 Gołyźniak 2020, p. 223 and no. 10.1.
167 Furtwängler (1889, p. 62) proposed that the source of inspiration for the depiction of such a female goddess driving a biga on gems was the statue by Pheidias. It remains disputable whether the goddess should be taken as Eos or Nike/Victory, see: Zwierlein-Diehl 1986, no. 16; Vollenweider 1966, p. 34; Borbein, Kunze and Rügler 2019, no. II.1087 (with full bibliography).
168 Gasparri (ed.) 1994, p. 64.
169 Giuliano 2009, p. 89, no. 7.
170 Neverov 1982, p. 2.
171 On the transfer of the Farnese gems to Naples, see: Dacos *et al.* 1980, p. 9; Rambach 2011, p. 274.
172 Naples, Museo Archeologico Nazionale, inv. no.: 25844/248; Lippert¹ II¹, no. 286; Lippert² I, no. 689; Bracci 1784–1786, vol. II, pp. 228–229; Raspe and Tassie 1791, no. 7774 (King of Naples);

Stosch had already published three gems from the Farnese collection in his first book.[173] He probably accessed the Farnese collection during his visit to Parma while on the road to Rome in 1714, and he had a glass paste cast made after the cameo in question here in his collection.[174] It remains a mystery why he did not publish the cameo in his first book but some Farnese gems were clearly inaccessible until the sale of a portion of them in 1739 as evidenced by Stosch's letter to Filippo Venuti discussed above. Regarding the authenticity of the gem, Winckelmann and Köhler, following him, claimed that no ancient cameo should have had the signature incised other than in relief, but this argument has been convincingly rejected by Zwierlein-Diehl.[175] Although some nearly perfect imitations of signatures of ancient gem engravers were carved, for example by Giovanni Pichler,[176] it appears that Stosch did not consider Sostratos name appearing on the cameo under discussion here as falsified and he planned to include it into the second volume of *Gemmae antiquae caelatae* which would have been the very first publication discussing this piece.[177]

8 Heading towards Publication of *Gemmae antiquae caelatae II*

The survey through the correspondence and gem drawings made for Stosch by various artists discovered in Krakow and Berlin reveals that Stosch collected dozens of new gems in the early 1740s suitable for his second volume of *Gemmae antiquae caelatae*. In his book *Traité des Pierres graveés* published in 1750, Pierre-Jean Mariette, while discussing some engravings of gems he once received from Stosch (cf. Chapter 8), wrote about Stosch as follows: '*I have recently been assured that this judicious writer will publish any day a sequel to his book, and that he already has a large quantity of material ready.*'[178] Moreover, according to Stosch himself, after the death of François Fagel in 1746 and his brother Heinrich Sigismund in 1747, he primarily focused on enlargement of his gem collection but he was also persistent in finishing his new book for which Schweickart was supposed to prepare the plates using the drawings prepared by other artists working for Stosch earlier: '*From then until now, the Freiherr of Stosch has lived in Florence and exclusively devoted his time to the commission of the British court regarding matters of the Catholic State. On the one hand, he uses his remaining time to broaden his different collections, which requires time and money, and to show them to foreigners who do not want to leave Florence without visiting him; on the other hand, to finally make headway with the publication of the second volume of his "Gemmarum antiquarum caelatarum sculptorum imaginibus insignitarum", which is why he now commissioned Mr Adam Schweichhard of Nuremberg, a very talented draughtsman and copperplate engraver, to complete the copper plate engravings. He has employed such artists in his house since 1726, namely Mr Johann Justin Preißler, who is now the director of the Academy of Painting in Nuremberg, Mr Tuscher of Nuremberg, who died as court painter and constructor for the King of Denmark, Mr George Nagel, also of Nuremberg, who is now a famous painter in Rome, and the above-mentioned Mr Schweichard.*'[179]

Furtwängler 1900, vol. I, pl. LVII.5, vol. II, pp. 259–260; Lippold 1922, pl. 34.4; Vollenweider 1966, p. 34, pl. 26.1–2; Richter 1971, no. 700; Zwierlein-Diehl 1986, no. 16; Pannuti 1994, no. 148; Gasparri (ed.) 1994, no. 29; Giuliano 2009, no. 7; Borbein, Kunze and Rügler 2019, no. II.1087 (with full bibliography).

173 Stosch 1724, pls XII, XXX and L.
174 Furtwängler 1896, no. 9791; Borbein, Kunze and Rügler 2019, no. II.1087 (with full bibliography).
175 Zwierlein-Diehl 1986, no. 16.
176 On this issue, see: Zwierlein-Diehl 1986, no. 3.
177 Borbein, Kunze and Rügler (2019, no. II.1087) claim that the cameo was first published by Michel-Ange de la Chausse in 1707 in his *Romanum Museum sive Thesaurus eruditae Antiquitatis* on plate 45. However, they refer to incorrect plate (a similar cameo appears on the plate 43 and the first edition of La Chausse book appeared in 1695) and the gem published by La Chausse is evidently one of many ancient replicas of Sostratos' work rather than the original from the Farnese collection. The goddess does not have wings but a scattered cloak behind her, the horses look different and, according to the plate description, the cameo is from the 'D. Devviti' collection, which remains unidentified.

178 Mariette 1750, vol. I, p. 334: '*On vient de m'assûrer que ce judicieux Ecrivain doit faire paroître incessamment une suite de son Ouvrage, & qu'il a déjà un grand nombre de matériaux prêts à être mis en œuvre.*'

179 Stosch 1754, pp. 49–50: '*Seit der Zeit bis anitzt lebet der Freyherr von Stosch zu Florenz, einzig und allein mit der Commission des großbritannischen Hofes, so die Sachen des Kirchenstaats betrifft, beschäfftiget. Alle übrige Zeit wendet er an, theils zur Vermehrung seiner verschiedenen Sammlungen, allerdings Mühe und Zeit kosten, theils um solche denen Fremden, so Florenz nicht verlassen würden, ohne ihn zu besuchen, zu zeigen; theils endlich um die Ausgabe des zweyten Theils seiner "Gemmarum antiquarum caelatarum sculptorum imaginibus insignitarum" zu befördern; wozu itzt Herr Adam Schweichhard, von Nürnberrg, ein sehr geschickter Rißmaler und Kupferstecher, die Kupferstiche zu verfertigen beschäffiget. Seit dem Jahre 1726 bis anitzt hat er dergleichen Künstler in seinem Hause unterhalten, nähmlich Herrn Johann Justin Preißler, itzigen Director der Malerakademie zu Nürnberg, Herrn Tuscher von Nürnberg, welcher als Hofmaler und Baumeister des Königes von Dännemark gestorben ist, Herrn George Nagel, gleichfalls von Nürnberg, anitzt berühmten Maler zu Rome, und obgemeldeten Herrn Schweichard*'.

Schweickart arrived in Florence in 1742 and he joined Nagel in the service of Stosch, with whom he stayed until the end of his life. Twelve engravings made by Schweickart for Stosch are known to exist and most of them indeed present gems with artists' signatures or at least inscriptions believed to be them, which Stosch owned himself or at least had glass pastes, sulphur impressions and drawings made after them. Eleven of those engravings were published in the luxurious edition of Winckelmann's catalogue of Stosch's gems in 1760.[180] It is extremely rare since the only known copies are known to be in Rome, Fano, Berlin, Weimar, New York and one more that arrived with the collection of gem drawings to the Czartoryski collection, and it is now preserved in the Czartoryski Library in Krakow.[181] The *Pierres gravees par Stosche* albums in Krakow include all the plates published in this luxurious edition, some even represented by two examples (Nos 936–937 and 1183–1184) and the six volumes of *Pierres gravées du roi avec figures* in the Kunstbibliothek in Berlin include eight plates from that edition as well.[182] Not all of Schweickart's surviving engravings were meant to be published in a supplement to the *Gemmae antiquae caelatae* book. Some of them, like the one depicting the famous *Gemma Stosch* (Krakow No. 1180) and another prized Etruscan scarab depicting Tydeus (Krakow Nos 1183–1184) and his beloved nicolo intaglio with Meleager (Krakow No. 1221), were made for publication of flyers distributed among Stosch's peers during the scientific meetings he participated in Florence (cf. Chapter 8).

Concerning those engravings which were made for the new book, they used the same type of frames as those published in 1724 by Picart. It is not precisely known when Schweickart made them but a hint is the plate reproducing the glass gem with a bust of a Bacchant or Maenad with a thyrsus on a shoulder to the right signed by Solon (ϹΟΛΩΝΟϹ), which was in the Stosch collection and ended up with his other gems in the Antikensammlung in Berlin (Fig. 10.52).[183] According to the information given by Schweickart himself on the plate, it was made in 1745 and this very plate was made after his own drawing (*J:A:Sveicart del; et Scul. 1745* appears in the bottom).[184] Both the collections of gem drawings from Krakow and Berlin include an example of this engraving (Krakow No. 874 and Berlin vol. IV, pl. 37, Fig. 10.53). It remains a mystery when and how Stosch added this piece to his cabinet of gems. Winckelmann had already taken the inscription to be the signature of the gem engraver; however, he had some doubts as to the genuineness of the gem itself. He also mentions that Schweickart executed a copperplate depicting it.[185] Today, there is a common agreement that this is an original work of Solon dated to the early Augustan times.[186] Schweickart's preliminary drawing was probably taken by him, like his *dactyliotheca* to Nuremberg after Stosch's death and it was later purchased by Johann Friedrich Frauenholz after Schweickart's death in 1787, but since then its whereabouts have remained unknown.

In the 1740s, Stosch owned some other signed gems of which Schweickart made engravings for the forthcoming book. One of them was the carnelian intaglio featuring a satyr crouching and plaiting an ivy wreath to the right, with a signature of Teukros (ΤΕΥΚΡΟΥ) on the side (Krakow Nos 936–937, Fig. 10.54 and Berlin vol. IV, pl. 24 – cf. Chapter 8, Fig. 8.148).[187] Schweickart indicated only his own authorship as the engraver (*J:A:Schweikart Noricg: Sc: Florent:*), not specifying if there was a drawing by another draughtsman he used. According to Winckelmann, Stosch sold that gem to the French gem engraver Jacques Guay (1711–1793).[188] This excellent artist employed at the French royal court of Louis XV (1710–1774), as well as teacher of this art to Madame de Pompadour (1721–1764), visited Stosch in Florence in 1742 during his study of the collection of gems owned by the Grand Duke of Tuscany. He cut a carnelian intaglio depicting an owl, which used to be perceived as a caricature of Voltaire, but the bird was also a favourite pet of Stosch, so it might allude directly to him.[189] Perhaps the carnelian intaglio with a satyr discussed here was sold by Stosch to Guy during this visit. It is also noteworthy that Schweickart arrived at Florence and started to work for Stosch the same year. In conclusion, this plate seems to be one of Schweickart's first assignments. The gem later went to the Carlisle collection and ultimately it

---

180 Zwierlein-Diehl 2007, p. 275; Hansson 2014, p. 28. These plates refer to the following records in Winckelmann 1760 catalogue: class II, nos 110, 434, 1240, 1494 and 1553; class III, nos 120, 172 and 174; class V, nos 9 and 122; class VII, no. 543.
181 The Czartoryski Library, inv. no. 1836 II. Regarding the other known copies, see: Rügler in Winckelmann 2013, p. XXIII, n. 88.
182 Berlin vol. I, pl. 94; vol. III, pl. 69; vol. IV, pls 24 and 37; vol. V, pl. 64; vol. VI, pls 86, 111 and 136.
183 Furtwängler 1896, no. 6269; Zwierlein-Diehl 2007, ill. 447 (with full bibliography); Borbein, Kunze and Rügler 2019, no. II.1553 (with full bibliography).
184 Rügler in Winckelmann 2013, XLVI. This is also confirmed in: Nagler 1846, p. 132, no. 13.
185 Winckelmann 1760, pp. XI–XII and class II, no. 1553, p. 251.
186 Zwierlein-Diehl 2007, ill. 447 (with full bibliography). On Solon and his works, see: Vollenweider 1966, pp. 47–56; Gołyźniak 2020, pp. 95–96 and 157–159.
187 On Teukros, see: Vollenweider 1966, pp. 43–44; Zwierlein-Diehl 1986, no. 157 (with a list of works); Zwierlein-Diehl 2007, p. 113.
188 Winckelmann 1760, class II, no. 1494, p. 240.
189 Borbein, Kunze and Rügler 2019, no. VIII.102.

ended up in the British Museum (Fig. 10.55), but Stosch kept its glass paste in his collection.[190] At some point, it must have been strongly repolished because now only the letters TE(...)KI(...) are visible.

How Stosch became the owner of the gem remains unknown, but in 1724 he had already published the amethyst with Heracles and Iole signed by Teukros and Winckelmann believed that the carnelian with a satyr was also signed by the same artist.[191] It was first Bracci who questioned the authenticity of the gem.[192] Furtwängler considered it genuine and dated to the 1st century BC.[193] Dalton rejected it as an eighteenth-century work and Zwierlein-Diehl claimed that the head type is not ancient, and thus suggested dating it to the 18th century. Indeed, the workmanship seems to be a bit too controlled and the body of the satyr too muscled for an ancient work although, this imagery exists on ancient intaglios and the overall effect is distorted by repolishing of the surface. Therefore, no secure judgement can be made.[194]

Another gem owned by Stosch at the time, which was selected for his second book, was a garnet intaglio depicting a naked athlete standing frontally and pouring oil from an alabastron into his lowered hand, beside him a hydria is standing on a table. On the side, in the field, there is a signature of Gnaeus (ΓΝΑΙΟΥ).[195] The intaglio dates to the second half of the 1st century BC and it has a distinctive provenance, as it probably belonged to Pope Clement V,[196] then it was owned by an apothecary and antiquarian Antonio Borioni (ca. 1690–after 1737), who published it with Rudolfino Venuti (1705–1763) in 1736 in *Collectanea Antiquitatium Romanorum*.[197] Later, it belonged to Apostolo Zeno (1668–1750), who sold it to Stosch in 1739.[198] Stosch had a great admiration for this piece, like many others, including Horace Walpole (1717–1797), who offered Stosch to buy it from him at any price. In his letters exchanged with Horace Mann (1706–1786), Walpole writes: '*I find I cannot live without Stosch's intaglia of the Gladiator with the vase*'.[199] Mann tried his best to secure it for his friend for 100 pounds, but in vain, as Stosch was still reluctant to sell. Instead, in 1750, he strategically offered the gem to William Ponsonby, 2nd Earl of Bessborough (1704–1793), in order to secure the continued payment of Stosch's pension from the British government.[200] Walpole was left gravely disappointed: '*I still think it one of the finest things I ever saw and am mortified at not having it*',[201] and this probably led him to spread unfavourable rumours about Stosch intended to undermine and harm his reputation as a collector, scholar and art expert.[202] Subsequently, the gem went to the celebrated Marlborough collection and is now preserved in the Walters Art Museum in Baltimore (Fig. 10.56).[203]

Furtwängler believed that the gem was repolished in modern times, which was more recently confirmed by Platz-Horster.[204] Indeed, repolishing of the intaglio's surface affected the signature, which led to its incorrect reading by Venuti as ΓΗΛΙΟΥ (Gaelius), but Stosch was more experienced with the works of Gnaeus and he recognised his hand correctly.[205] He planned to publish this gem in his second volume of *Gemmae antiquae caelatae* as a work of Gnaeus (ΓΝΑΙΟΥ), as evidenced by a plate prepared by Schweickart after Tuscher's drawing as the plate itself informs (*Mar. Tuscher del.* and *J.A. Schweickart fecit a Florentiae*).[206] In the collections of gem drawings in Krakow and Berlin, there are two engravings of this plate preserved (Krakow No. 1516 and Berlin vol. VI, pl. 86, Fig. 10.57); however, Tuscher's preparatory drawing remains lost, but it must have been made between 1739,

---

190 London, the British Museum, inv. no.: 1913,0307.150; Dalton 1915, no. 726; Zwierlein-Diehl 1986, no. 877. On Stosch's glass paste, see: Furtwängler 1896, no. 9817; Borbein, Kunze and Rügler 2019, no. II.1494 (with full bibliography).
191 Winckelmann 1760, class II, no. 1494, p. 240.
192 Bracci 1784–1786, vol. II, p. 235.
193 Furtwängler 1900, vol. I, pl. XLII.58, vol. II, p. 203.
194 Dalton 1915, no. 726; Zwierlein-Diehl 1986, no. 877.
195 On Gnaeus, see: Vollenweider 1966, pp. 45–46; Zwierlein-Diehl 1986, no. 148 (with a list of works); Plantzos 1999, pp. 94–95; Zwierlein-Diehl 2007, p. 121; Gołyźniak 2020, pp. 135–136.
196 Story-Maskelyne 1870, no. 621. However, Story-Maskelyne's attribution to Clement V may be from a misreading of '*Cl.V.*' (*clarissimus vir*) in the 1736 publication of Borioni and Venuti (pl. 75), see: Sieveking and Curtius 1913, p. 237, n. 3; Boardman *et al.* 2009, no. 429.
197 Borioni and Venuti 1736, pl. 75.
198 Platz-Horster 1993, p. 11.
199 Letter from Walpole to Sir Horace Mann, 26 November 1749, quoted in Toynbee 1903, p. 131; Walpole 1927–1983, vol. XVII, pp. 232–233.
200 Henig, Scarisbrick and Whiting 1994, p. XIV.
201 Walpole 1927–1983, vol. XX, p. 157.
202 Lewis 1961, pp. 54 and 61.
203 Baltimore, Walters Art Museum, inv. no.: 42.109; Lippert² II, no. 908; Raspe and Tassie 1791, no. 7931; Cades Grande, 43.IV.F.74; Furtwängler 1900, vol. I, pl. L.9, vol. II, p. 241; Lippold 1922, pl. 56.3; Vollenweider 1966, p. 45 and pl. 42.5; Richter 1971, no. 660; Platz-Horster 1993; Zwierlein-Diehl 2005, p. 341; Zwierlein-Diehl 2007, ill. 476; Boardman *et al.* 2009, no. 429 (with discussion and more literature).
204 Furtwängler 1888, p. 316; Platz-Horster 1993.
205 Stosch had already published a beryl intaglio with head of Heracles by Gnaeus (1724, pl. XXIII). Interestingly, Natter (1754, pp. 39–41, pl. XXV), probably instructed by Stosch, published the gem with a correct reading of the signature, while Winckelmann (1760, class V, no. 9, pp. 455–456) mentions it with the incorrect name of the engraver clearly taken from Venuti's publication.
206 This is also confirmed in: Nagler 1846, p. 132, no. 12.

when Stosch bought the gem, and 1741, when Tuscher permanently left Florence.

Another plate made by Schweickart for the second volume of *Gemmae antiquae caelatae* depicted the garnet intaglio engraved with the dog star Sirius with curving rays to the front, signed by Gaius on the collar as ΓΛΙΟC · ΕΠΟΙΕΙ (Krakow No. 286 and Berlin vol. III, pl. 69, Fig. 10.58). The early history of that gem is unclear. The earliest recorded owner is Philip Stanhope, 4th Earl of Chesterfield (1694–1773), who acquired his collection from the bequest of his younger brother, John Stanhope (1705–1748), who worked with him while he was an ambassador in The Hague. It is noteworthy that the brother travelled in Italy and a number of his gems have a 16th/17th-century Italian ancestry. The gem was later bought by William Ponsonby, 2nd Earl of Bessborough by 1754 as is published by Natter in his treatise as belonging to the Bessborough collection.[207] It went to the Marlborough collection in 1760 or 1761 when the Bessborough gems were acquired by George Spencer, 4th Duke of Marlborough (1739–1817). After dispersal of the Marlborough gems, the intaglio found its way to the Edward Perry Warren (1860–1928) collection and was subsequently purchased from him in 1927 by the Museum of Fine Arts in Boston, where it remains today (Fig. 10.59).[208]

It could be through the contact with Lord Bessborough that Stosch discovered this gem for his new study. Although no source suggests him to have had an impression of the gem, it is likely that he had it, or as Zwierlein-Diehl suggests, he asked artists in his service to copy the gem from an illustration published by Natter in 1754.[209] If that is the case, only Schweickart could have made a drawing for the final plate. It is noteworthy that Stosch ordered a copy of the gem in rock crystal from Lorenzo Masini (1713–?), which was later incorporated into his collection. According to Winckelmann, Masini, in the presence of Stosch, put his own signature (ΜΑCΙΝΟC ΕΠΟΙΕΙ) on the dog's collar in the very same place where Gaius' master put his own name.[210] Massini specialised in copying ancient signed gems for Stosch for academic purposes rather than for fraud.[211]

The Gaius garnet is a late Hellenistic work executed around 100 BC, extremely deeply cut so that on an impression the head is virtually in the round. Its antiquity was doubted by Raspe and Tassie: '*We observe that no work of this artist was known before the year 1724, when Baron Stosch published his book upon engraved Gems, with the names of the masters; and being of very singular merit, the antiquaries and connoisseurs would not have failed to have mentioned it if it had existed before that time. The ancients do not speak of that master: but since Lord Bessborough (at that time Lord Duncannon) purchased the Gem, and Natter gave an account of it in 1754, its celebrity has been spread all over the world, and some copies have been seen executed by very excellent masters.*'[212] Their judgement is unfair, though, because as evidenced by the gems collected by Stosch for the second volume of *Gemame antiquae caelatae* and discussed here, in the 1720s, 1730s and 1740s new signed gems were freshly discovered from the soil and others made their public appearance from some private collections that had remained inaccessible before. The Gaius garnet is a poorly documented and isolated example, with its signature on the actual object and not in the field which is indeed unusual compared to other ancient signed gems. Although the subject matter of the dog star Sirius appears on gems in Antiquity, it is rather captured as a forepart with legs shown rather than just a head. This makes it suspicious at the first sight.[213] Overall, the gem is not like, for instance, the carnelian with the portrait of Sextus Pompey signed by Agathangelos, which is unique and cut by an engraver, who is otherwise unknown from

---

207 Natter 1754, pp. 27–28, pl. XVI; Boardman *et al.* 2009, p. 126.
208 Boston, Museum of Fine Arts, acc. no.: 27.734; Furtwängler 1888, p. 139, no. 27; Furtwängler 1889, p. 57; Furtwängler 1900, vol. I, pl. L.4, vol. II, p. 240; Lippold 1922, pl. 163.4; Zwierlein-Diehl 1986, no. 147; Plantzos 1999, no. 709; Boardman (ed.) 2002, no. 114; Zwierlein-Diehl 2007, ill. 296; Lapatin 2015, pl. 91; Borbein, Kunze and Rügler 2019, no. II.1240 (with full bibliography).
209 Natter 1754, pp. 27–28, pl. XVI; Zwierlein-Diehl 1986, no. 147.
210 Winckelmann 1760, class II, no. 1240, p. 206; Furtwängler 1896, no. 9243; Borbein, Kunze and Rügler 2019, no. II.1240. Lorenz Natter (1705–1763), another famous gem engraver who worked for Stosch in Florence between 1732–1735, copied the Gaius gem with the dog star Sirius twice in garnet and topaz. He did that probably while in London in the early 1750s, where he may have had access to the original gem. He described his experiments to achieve the depth of cutting while retaining the minute details of the original and he illustrated the intaglio in his treatise on the art of gem engraving (Natter 1754, pp. 27–28, pl. XVI). The topaz copy was later sold to a Russian collector and it is now considered lost, but the garnet copy signed L.NATTH EII on the collar is now in London in the British Museum, inv. no.: 1978,1002.1069 (once in the Anne Hull Grundy and the Professor John Hull Grundy collection), see: Gere *et al.* 1984, no. 828.
211 Masini also copied for Stosch the famous amethyst with Diana of the mountains signed by Apollonides (Stosch 1724, pl. XII), see: Winckelmann 1760, class II, no. 295, p. 77. He also made a copy of the carnelian with portrait of Sextus Pompey signed by Agathangelos, which he signed as ΑΓΑΘΑΝΓΕΛΟΥ/ΜΑCΙΝΟC/ΕΠΟΙΕΙ, see: Tassinari 2022, pp. 153–154. On Stosch's collaboration with contemporary gem engravers, see: Gołyźniak (forthcoming – Stosch and forgeries).
212 Raspe and Tassie 1791, no. 3251.
213 For instance: Furtwängler 1896, nos 3271 and 7043; Richter 1956, no. 405; Zwierlein-Diehl 1973, no. 386; AGDS IV Hannover, no. 693.

any ancient written source as well, but the context of its find is known well, and the signature is in the right place (cf. above). The case of the Gaius garnet demonstrates that we still know too little about the history of some gems to understand them fully. It is noteworthy that for his forthcoming book, Stosch collected two gems inscribed with the name of Gaius – see above a discussion on the intaglio presenting Marsyas seated on a panther skin to the front playing pipes inscribed ΓΛΙΟΣ. He probably regarded them both as signed by the same artist, although in fact, there is no relationship between them whatsoever.

Apart from those, Schweickart prepared a few more plates for Stosch's second book on ancient signed gems. These included one presenting an amethyst with Hermaphrodite with a partial signature of the famous Dioscurides (ΔΙΟΣ) from Zanetti's collection – (Krakow No. 71, Fig. 10.17) and another depicting the onyx cameo engraved with Jupiter driving a quadriga and striking giants, bearing the signature of Athenion in Greek – ΑΘΗΝΙΩΝ (Krakow No. 117, Fig. 10.36), which was made after a drawing by Nagel (Krakow No. 116, Fig. 10.35) – both already discussed above. One more plate depicted the cameo featuring a bust of a satyr with *nebris* by Hyllos after the drawing by Preißler but both the drawing and the plate remain lost.[214]

Finally, two more plates were made by Schweickart for Stosch's unfinished book, with a rather surprising choice of gems. The first one is a banded agate intaglio, dated to the 1st century BC, carved with an urn decorated with a sphinx, two bearded masks and inscription: DIPHILI, flanked by two corn ears, which is now in the Museo Archeologico Nazionale in Naples.[215] The provenance of the gem remains unknown. The inscription appearing on it is the name of the gem's owner rather than a signature of an artist who made it. However, Winckelmann takes it as the latter and moreover, he explains that Stosch was going to discuss this piece in the second volume of *Gemmae antiquae caelatae* book: '*The late Baron von Stosch had this Paste engraved to talk about it in the II. volume of his book about engraved gems.*'[216] Indeed, Stosch had a glass paste made after this intaglio in his collection,[217] and he had it drawn by Georg Abraham Nagel in the late 1730s or early 1740s (Krakow No. 1458, Fig. 10.60). Was it already meant to be published by Stosch in the second volume of his new book back then? Interestingly, the commentary under the drawing written by Izabela Czartoryska (probably rewritten from the original sheet) also suggests the inscription to be the name of gem engraver.[218] Although this is not directly indicated by Schweickart, Nagel's drawing was surely used by him to produce a plate presenting this intaglio in the forthcoming book, of which examples are in Krakow and Berlin alike (Krakow No. 1444 and Berlin vol. VI, pl. 111, Fig. 10.61).

The last case is the plate depicting a carnelian intaglio engraved with head of a horse to the right and inscription in the field in Greek – ΜΙΘ – from Stosch's own collection, now in the Antikensammlung in Berlin (Fig. 10.62).[219] Winckelmann considered the inscription to be the name of intaglio's maker, which he read variably as ΜΙΘ (Mith) and ΜΥΘ (Myth).[220] However, most likely, the inscription stands for *tria nomina*, a shortcut of a full Roman name rather than a signature of the artist. Such inscriptions usually have the letters separated with dots, but in the Roman Imperial period this is not always the case. Schweickart engraved a plate representing this gem for Stosch's second volume of *Gemmae antiquae caelatae* (*J.A. Schweikart sculp.*), but he did not indicate the maker of the preparatory drawing for it. No such a preliminary drawing has been found so far. The collections in Krakow and Berlin each just include examples of the plate engraved by Schweickart (Krakow No. 1593 and Berlin vol. VI, pl. 136, Fig. 10.63). In the case of the one in Krakow, Izabela Czartoryska's commentary suggests that the inscription may be artist's name in full or an abbreviation of some sort, not exactly like Winckelmann thought that it was an abbreviation of his name.[221]

Last but not least, among the gems apparently meant to be published by Stosch in his second book on ancient signed gems, there was also a fragmentary Hellenistic agate cameo featuring a griffin fighting with a serpent

---

214 Nagler 1846, p. 132, no. 8.
215 Naples, Museo Archeologico Nazionale, inv. no.: 26141/303; Lippert¹ I², no. 533; Lippert² II, no. 1074; Raspe and Tassie 1791, no. 13706 (onyx); Cades Grande, 44.IV.H.47; Pannuti 1994, no. 265.
216 Winckelmann 1760, class V, no. 122, p. 490: '*Le feu Baron de Stosch avoit fait graver cette Pâte pour en parler dans le II. Tome de son Ouvrage des Pierres Gravées*'.
217 Furtwängler 1896, no. 9959; Borbein, Kunze and Rügler 2019, no. V.122 (with full bibliography).
218 Krakow No. 1458: '*Une Urne posé sur deux Epics avec le Nom de Graveur*'.
219 Berlin, Antikensammlung, inv. no.: FG 7051; Raspe and Tassie 1791, no. 13185 (carnelian, King of Prussia); Cades Grande 48.IV.O.1; Furtwängler 1896, no. 7051; Borbein, Kunze and Rügler 2019, no. VII.1 (with full bibliography). Glass pastes replicating this intaglio exist, for example: Leiden, Rijksmuseum van Oudheden, inv. no.: GS-Z 1892/11.15 – https://hdl.handle.net/21.12126/194750 [retrieved on 4 August 2023].
220 Winckelmann 1760, class VII, no. 1, p. 542; Borbein, Kunze and Rügler 2019, no. VII.1 (with full bibliography).
221 Krakow no. 1593: '*Tete de Cheval. Les trois lettres sont probablement le nom du graveur ou abrege. Cette cornaline est de la plus grande beauté*'.

entwined around its leg, signed ΜΙΔΙΟΥ in the exergue, of which a drawing is preserved in the Princes Czartoryski Museum in Krakow (Krakow No. 1800, Fig. 10.64). This drawing is relatively small compared to regular documentary drawings made by artists working for Stosch in his studio in Rome and Florence, and it differs in technique and style to any group distinguished from Stosch's corpus of gem drawings (cf. Chapter 8). A short text under the documented gem probably directly copied by Izabela Czartoryska from the original sheet describes that the cameo is of great beauty, and it belonged to Comte de Caylus.[222] The cameo was indeed in the Anne Claude de Tubières-Grimoard de Pestels de Lévis Comte de Caylus' (1692–1765) collection before it entered the French royal cabinet, later transformed into the Cabinet des Médailles of Bibliothèque nationale de France (Fig. 10.65).[223] Caylus published it in the first volume of his monumental work *Recueil d'antiquités égyptiennes, étrusques, grecques, romaines et gauloises* in 1752 on plate LIII no. 4, and there is a striking similarity between the drawing from Krakow and this illustration (Fig. 10.66).[224] Both are nearly identical in terms of composition, technique and style, even the contours of the surviving fragment of the cameo match almost entirely. The mystery unveils itself in Caylus' description of the cameo, since he says as follows: '*I have seen few cameos of such fine workmanship, nor of better taste. We read at the bottom* ΜΙΔΙΟΥ *in very well-done characters & engraved in hollow. I fear that the name of this engraver is incomplete; the layout and the space where the letters are placed persuades me that at least the first letter of the name may be missing. As much as one looks at this name, it seems to me to belong to a Greek engraver that is not yet known. This is what pushed me to send its drawing to M. Stoch* (sic!). *I will be delighted to contribute to the second volume of his book that he is going to give us, & to increase the number of stones on which we find the names of the artists; but I would be even more satisfied to have some appreciation from such a great connoisseur.*'[225] The rediscovered drawing Krakow No. 1800 must be that very drawing which Caylus mentions sending to Stosch and his account proves that Stosch was still working on the second volume of *Gemmae antiquae caelatae* in 1752. We do not know when exactly Caylus sent his drawing of the cameo, but it was certainly prior to 1752, when he published it himself, since he recalls that at the point of his discovery of the cameo that he urgently sent the drawing to Stosch because he believed it to have been unpublished.

The author of the drawing is probably Comte de Caylus himself. He was capable of drawing, and he was an active member of the *Académie royale de peinture et de sculpture* in Paris and an admirable and prolific etcher.[226] Alternatively, it was made by one of the draughtsmen he worked with, for example, on his multi-volume study of antiquities.[227]

As discussed in Chapter 9, there is strong evidence that Caylus and Stosch corresponded, exchanged gems, their drawings, opinions and ideas in general. Actually, Stosch acted as an agent of Caylus whom he used to send gems like the now lost carnelian with Heracles shouldering a club (cf. Chapter 9).[228] Moreover, some of Stosch's own gems, which were never published as illustrated, appear after his death in Caylus' *Recueil d'antiquités égyptiennes, étrusques, grecques, romaines et gauloises* most likely due to an exchange of drawings.[229] It is difficult to imagine that Caylus would get the images of the gems elsewhere than directly from Stosch. What is more, in his description of the cameo discussed here, Caylus clearly admires the connoisseurship of Stosch as far as engraved gems are concerned and by sending a drawing of his signed cameo, he hopes for some appreciation for its discovery. In fact,

---

222 Krakow No. 1800: '*Fragment d'une grande beauté, apartenant a Mon: le Comte de Caylus.*'
223 Paris, Biblithèque national de France, inv. no.: camée.182.
224 Caylus 1752–1767, vol. I, p. 144, pl. LIII.4; Bracci 1784–1786, vol. I, pl. 25.1; Cades Grande, 28.III.D.15; Chabouillet 1858, no. 16; Babelon 1897, no. 182, pl. 18 (with more literature); Furtwängler 1900, vol. I, pl. LVII.4, vol. II, p. 259; Pirzio Biroli Stefanelli 2007, no. III.496.
225 Original text from Caylus 1752–1767, vol. I, p. 144: '*J'ai peu vû de camées d'un aussi beau travail, ni d'un meilleur goût. On lit au bas* ΜΙΔΙΟΥ *en caractères très-finis & gravés en creux. Je craindrois que le nom de ce Graveur ne fût pas entier; cependant la disposition de l'espace où les lettres se trouvent placées me persuade qu'il ne peut manquer au plus que la premiére lettre du nom. De quelque façon qu'on regarde ce nom, il me paroît que le Graveur Grec n'est pas encore connu. C'est ce qui m'a engagé à l'envoyer à M. Stoch avec le dessein. Je ferai charmé de contribuer à la seconde partie qu'il va nous donner de son Recueil, & d'augmenter le nombre des pierres où l'on trouve les noms des Artistes; mais je ferai plus satisfait encore d'avoir le sentiment d'un si grand connoisseur.*'
226 On Caylus and his gem drawings, cf. Chapter 3 here.
227 Most of illustrations appearing in Caylus' are unsigned, no illustration is signed in the first volume where the cameo under discussion here appears, but some artist certainly cooperated on them with Caylus, see a list: https://www.royalacademy.org.uk/art-artists/book/recueil-dantiquites-egyptiennes-etrusques-grecques-et-romaines – retrieved on 9 January 2023.
228 Which fact was noticed by Furtwängler 1900, vol. I, pl. XXXIX.20, vol. II, p. 187. A drawing of that gem survived in the Princes Czartoryski Museum in Krakow (No. 1066), see: Chapter 9, Fig. 4.
229 For example, Stosch's carnelian intaglio presenting athletes training jumping above each other, trees on both sides and a laurel wreath in the field (Berlin, Antikensammlung, inv. no.: FG 6913) was published by Caylus in 1762 in the fifth volume of his *magnum opus*, see: pl. LXXXVI.3.

in Caylus' multi-volume publication, Stosch, alongside Anton Francesco Gori and Pierre-Jean Mariette, is the most frequently evoked authority on this subject.[230]

Regarding the cameo itself, Caylus claimed it was carved by a Greek artist and burnt,[231] while Babelon dated it to the Hellenistic period.[232] Furtwängler also concluded that the gem must have been burnt and thus the original colours changed, but he dated it to the Augustan times. Indeed, the discoloured layers of the cameo suggest its exposure to great heat. Although the explanation of its iconography as reflecting a fight between the griffin as a creature related to Apollo and thus Augustus with Evil represented by the serpent would fit the Augustan epoch indeed, the technique, dynamic composition and expressive style points more to the Hellenistic period and the date of 3rd or 2nd century BC. The subject matter may simply refer to a standard combat between good and evil, appropriate for Hellenistic rulers as well.[233] Caylus suggested the signature to be incomplete by at least one letter in the beginning due to a chip in the bottom of the cameo.[234] Babelon (inspired by Brunn and Chabouillet), proposed that the full name of engraver could be ΧΑΡΜΙΔΙΟΥ, but he doubted its authenticity in the first place.[235] Furtwängler seems right, though, taking the signature as it is, and he believed it to be genuine.[236] It is positioned in the very centre of the cameo so that a longer name in the beginning would ruin the composition and it is very carefully incised with little dots on the edges of the letters, which adds credibility.

9 Conclusions – Why Did the Project Collapse?

The analysis of various archival resources, including references to Stosch's second book being under preparation as well as the gem drawings discussed above, clearly demonstrates that this long forthcoming volume was designed to discuss newly discovered ancient signed gems that were not published by Stosch in his first book. In addition, Stosch planned to include some extra information about the gems he had already published in 1724 as an update. Finally, he also wanted to add an appendix illustrating the most common forgeries of ancient signed gems. As evidenced by his letters to William Cavendish, 2nd Duke of Devonshire, preserved at Chatsworth, Stosch started to work on this new volume shortly after the first one appeared in 1724. He quickly collected some new gems while in Rome and he continued his project after 1731 in Florence too. The future illustrations were prepared by many artists, including Girolamo Odam, Johann Justin Preißler, Markus Tuscher, Georg Abraham Nagel and finally Johann Adam Schweickart, who made at least nine final plates setting them in the mounts of the same design and style as Bernard Picart did for the first volume of *Gemmae antiquae caelatae*. Ultimately, counting only the gems whose drawings survived or which are mentioned in the archives, Stosch accumulated 33 new gems believed to be signed by ancient artists to publish in his forthcoming book.[237]

This number is much less than 70 gems published in the first volume of *Gemmae antiquae caelatae*. This may have been perceived by Stosch as insufficient for publication, and consequently it was probably one of the reasons why the project dragged on for so many years. Another one could be Stosch's perfectionism, since in his correspondence with William Cavendish, 2nd Duke of Devonshire, many times Stosch admits how difficult was to distinguish genuine ancient signed gems from the circulating forgeries; thus, selection of the suitable material took much time. This is the best illustrated by the fact that despite Stosch's great merits and experience, from a contemporary perspective, many of the gems which apparently were selected are problematic at the very least. Out of the examples discussed above, five: Krakow No. 1540, (Fig. 10.24), the carnelian intaglio presenting a Hellenistic ruler as Zeus with an inscription ΝΕΙϹΟΥ drawn by Preißler

---

230   See, for example: Caylus 1752–1767, vol. I, p. 124, vol. IV, p. 97, vol. V, p. XVIII, vol. VI, pp. 107–112 and vol. VII, p. 160.
231   Caylus 1752–1767, vol. I, p. 144.
232   Babelon 1897, no. 182.
233   Noteworthy is that the subject (only slightly modified – the creature trampling the serpent being goat-headed) appears on a probably glass gem documented by Girolamo Odam for Stosch earlier (Krakow No. 1607) and Pier Leone Ghezzi on his own (London, the British Museum volume, fol. 85).
234   Caylus 1752–1767, vol. I, p. 144.
235   Babelon (1897, p. XC and no. 182) clearly follows the judgment of Chabouillet (1858, no. 16).
236   Furtwängler 1900, vol. I, pl. XXXIX.20, vol. II, p. 187.

237   The visual evidence in the form of gem drawings and Schweickart's prints from the collections of the Princes Czartoryski Museum in Krakow as well as the Kunstbibliothek in Berlin gathered together in this chapter is the largest body of evidence related to Stosch's second book discovered so far. However, it is certainly incomplete. For example, it is also difficult to imagine that Stosch would have not included into his book the fragmentary sardonyx intaglio featuring legs of Mars with a signature of Quintus – ΚΟΙΝΤΟϹ ΑΛΞΑ ΕΠΟΙΕΙ that was published by Vettori in 1739. Furthermore, as evidenced by the two last Schweickart's plates discussed, it might be that there were more gems with inscriptions that Stosch could have incorrectly classified as suitable for his new study and of which he had drawings made, but without explicit suggestions one cannot identify them.

(Fig. 10.8), Krakow Nos 1745, (Fig. 10.13), 1458 (Fig. 10.60) No. 1593 (= Berlin vol. VI, pl. 136, Fig. 10.63) are the gems with the names of their owners rather than signatures of their makers. Next, 12 gems bear fake signatures on them: Krakow Nos 1670 (Fig. 10.15), 71 (Fig. 10.17), the aquamarine intaglio bearing a Giant with inscription ΔΙΟC (Fig. 10.18), 251 (Fig. 10.20), 1262 (Fig. 10.22), 1357 (Fig. 10.28), 972 (Fig. 10.44), 1002 (Fig. 10.45), 668 (Fig. 10.11), 1024 (Fig. 10.9), 1745 (Fig. 10.13) and 936–937 (= Berlin vol. IV, pl. 24, Fig. 10.54). Finally, Krakow No. 324 (Fig. 10.26) was believed to have a signature but this was due to a misinterpretation of a cast after which Nagel drew. Overall, only 13 out of 33 new signed gems amassed by Stosch for his future book were authentic. Many of those gems were regarded as controversial even in the times of Stosch, which might have been another reason why the project was never completed. The complexity of the subject of the study made it particularly difficult to judge whether the gems were genuine or not. Reinach made an interesting suggestion that Stosch lost interest in the subject of ancient signed intaglios and cameos at some point, not because he did not have the necessary financial means (although this was an issue too) but because the subject itself proved too complicated for him.[238] Stosch must have realised that publication of controversial material may cast a shadow on his reputation as the most knowledgeable connoisseur of ancient glyptics. While the first volume of *Gemmae antiquae caelatae* brought him fame and appreciation, the second one could have ruined it. Stosch was very critical towards the material he worked on, not like, for example, Domenico Augusto Bracci (1717–1795), who, between 1784 and 1786, published 44 more gems with signatures than Stosch in 1724, out of which only 14 turn out to be truly ancient.[239]

After the publication of the 70 signed gems in the first book, it was much harder for Stosch to evaluate whether the new gems he found had genuine signatures or not.[240] A side effect of the success of Stosch's first book was a considerable increase in production of modern fake gems with signatures as well as adding fake signatures to ancient pieces. This clearly happened even to intaglios and cameos from notable collections, like the carnelian with fragmentary signature of Dioscurides once in the collections of Pope Alexander VIII and Cardinal Pietro Ottoboni, and finally the Carlisle collection (Krakow No. 1002, Fig. 10.45). Aside from direct forgeries, there were multiple copies ordered by collectors from contemporary engravers, which made Stosch's studies complicated once the original was no longer traceable either. Over the many years of the second book's production, counterfeits of various kinds were delivered to the art market on a regular basis, making Stosch's research extremely challenging.[241] As evidenced above, tried as he might, Stosch still selected many intaglios and cameos with fake signatures, and he sometimes mistook signatures with the names of gems' owners. This is hardly surprising because even today, after hundreds of years of research, it is still challenging to say which gems are genuine and have authentic signatures.[242]

In conclusion, there were multiple reasons, from organisational, through economic, ethical and scholarly ones, which all contributed to the postponing of the project. The considerable engagement in documentation of his own collection of engraved gems (completed only after Stosch's death by publication of a *catalogue raisonné* in 1760 by Winckelmann, cf. Chapters 6, 8 and 11), supervision of his *Atlas* project (also incomplete)[243] and finally organisation and running of a sort of a house-museum all contributed to the fact that Stosch's second book was not finished, even though Mariette in 1750 and Caylus in 1752 still sound like there were chances for that. Stosch's collecting, documenting and research activities were simply too large scale for one lifetime.

Stosch had more unfinished book projects that are attested to have been in preparation in his correspondence. One of them was a secret volume on debaucheries of the ancients, their Bacchanals, priapic games and sacrifices, reported as being prepared in 1722 for Lord Carteret.[244] The project started, as always, with the collection of suitable illustrations from Ghezzi and Odam (Stosch even claims that he would have contributed some himself). Nevertheless, the book never reached Lord Carteret's

---

238 Reinach 1895, pp. 148–149.
239 Bracci 1784–1786. For a critical commentary on Bracci's work, see: Furtwängler 1900, vol. III, pp. 419–420; Zazoff and Zazoff 1983, pp. 122–127; Fileti Mazza 1996, pp. 240–246; Zwierlein-Diehl 2007, p. 280.
240 This was an issue Stosch must have tackled already during production of his first book, see: Zazoff and Zazoff 1983, p. 23.
241 Zwierlein-Diehl 2005, p. 326.
242 On the matter of ancient signed gems alone, considerable contributions were made by Furtwängler (1888, 1889 and 1900), Vollenweider (1966), Plantzos (1999, pp. 38–41) and Zwierlein-Diehl (1986, 2005 and 2007). Zwierlein-Diehl 2005 includes very useful references to earlier literature (including works from 16th–19th century) on the subject and a detailed history of the research on the phenomenon of ancient signed gems.
243 Stosch's considerable engagement in these other projects is suggested in the letter from Winckelmann to Raphael Mengs dated late September 1758 – Winckelmann 1952–1957, vol. I, p. 414, no. 234 as well as in the introduction of Winckelmann's catalogue of Stosch's gems (1760, pp. I–II).
244 Letter from Walton [Stosch] to Lord Carteret dated 28 February 1722 (NA Kew SP 85/14 fols 9–12).

hands, but the drawings which were already prepared are said to have been purchased by Frederick the Great of Prussia.[245] In the preface of his first book, Stosch writes about his plans to write a study on glass pastes, but this book never came to light either.[246]

Despite some failures, Stosch's efforts, reflected especially in the visual documentation of gems discussed in this chapter, help to illustrate some more positive phenomena. In the second quarter of the eighteenth century, important signed gems were continuously discovered during the fieldworks conducted in Rome and its surrounding area, like the carnelian with the portrait of supposedly Sextus Pompey by Agathangelos or the burnt carnelian depicting Venus playing with Cupid signed by Aulos. Other examples became known due to the increasing accessibility of various collections, so far, strictly treasured in private hands. This illustrates another dimension of Stosch's substantial contribution to the development of glyptic studies because the popularity of engraved gems as the subjects of collecting and research grew considerably over time.

---

245 Walpole 1927–1983, vol. V, p. 202 – a letter from Horace Mann to Horace Walpole dated 13 May 1758. Stosch's unfinished book projects unfortunately contributed to his later bad press. For example, the Florentine archaeologist Giovanni Gaetano Bottari (1689–1775) said: '(…) *simply sneered that he would like first of all to see a list of books von Stosch had promised to write, then a list of objects he announced he had discovered, and finally a list of items he had stolen.*' (Justi 1872, p. 337; Pietrzak 2018, p. 123).

246 Stosch 1724, p. XIX: '*Mais je parlerai plus au long de ces Pâtes de Verre dans un autre Ouvrage que je medite sur ce sujet.*' ['But I will speak more about these Pâtes de Verre in another book that I intend on this subject.'].

PLATE 80

FIGURE 10.1

FIGURE 10.2

FIGURE 10.3

FIGURE 10.4

FIGURE 10.5

FIGURE 10.6

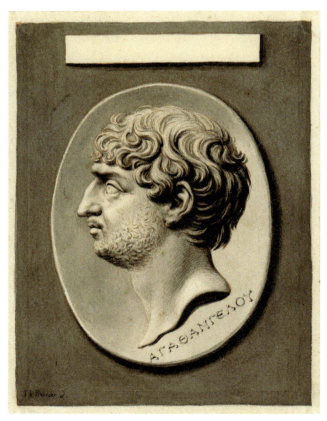

FIGURE 10.7

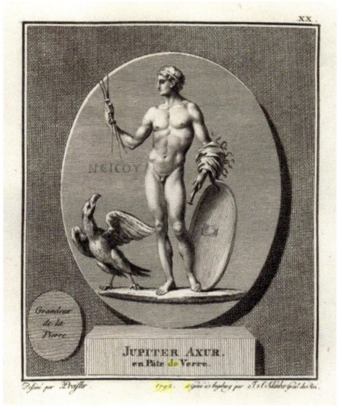

FIGURE 10.8

FIGURE 10.9

FIGURE 10.10

FIGURE 10.11

FIGURE 10.12

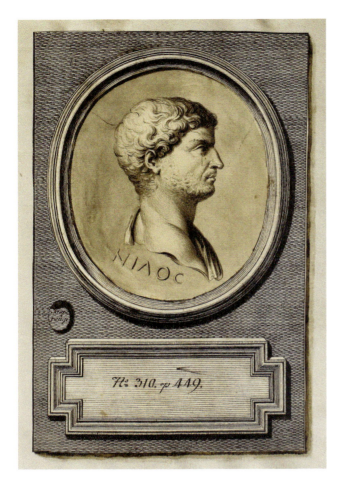

FIGURE 10.13

FIGURE 10.14

FIGURE 10.15

FIGURE 10.16

PLATE 84

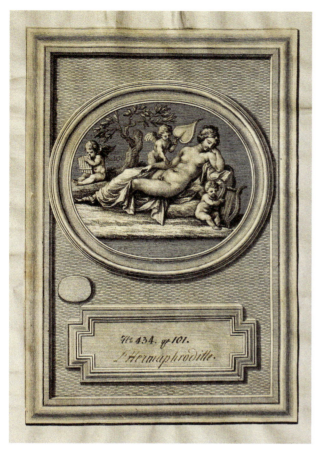

FIGURE 10.17

FIGURE 10.18

FIGURE 10.19

FIGURE 10.20

FIGURE 10.21

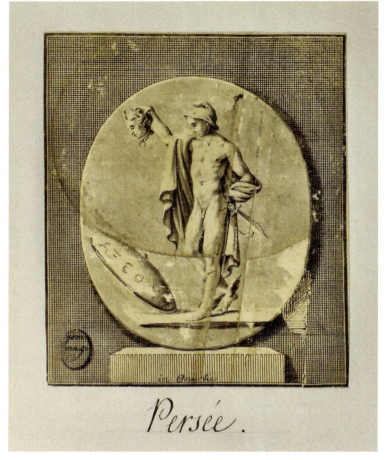

FIGURE 10.22

FIGURE 10.23

FIGURE 10.24

PLATE 86

FIGURE 10.25

FIGURE 10.26

FIGURE 10.27

FIGURE 10.28

FIGURE 10.29

FIGURE 10.30

FIGURE 10.31

FIGURE 10.32

PLATE 88

FIGURE 10.33

FIGURE 10.34

FIGURE 10.35

FIGURE 10.36

FIGURE 10.37

FIGURE 10.38

FIGURE 10.39

FIGURE 10.40

FIGURE 10.41

FIGURE 10.42

FIGURE 10.43

FIGURE 10.44

FIGURE 10.45

FIGURE 10.46

FIGURE 10.47

PLATE 92

FIGURE 10.48

FIGURE 10.49

FIGURE 10.50

FIGURE 10.51

FIGURE 10.52

FIGURE 10.53

FIGURE 10.54

FIGURE 10.55

PLATE 94

FIGURE 10.56

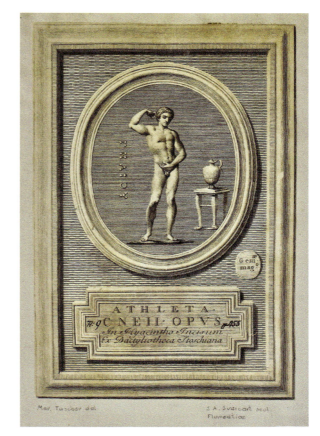

FIGURE 10.57

FIGURE 10.58

FIGURE 10.59

FIGURE 10.60

FIGURE 10.61

FIGURE 10.62

FIGURE 10.63

FIGURE 10.64

FIGURE 10.65

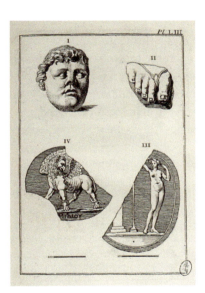

FIGURE 10.66

CHAPTER 11

Stosch and His Contribution to the Development of Gem Studies and Antiquarianism

Paweł Gołyźniak and Hadrien J. Rambach

1   The Matter of Illustration Quality in Antiquarian Studies of Engraved Gems

Since the Renaissance, engraved gems were the most desirable antiquities on the art markets in Europe, collected by the elites for the sake of both rare precious stones they were made of and most importantly artistic virtuosity, testifying to the exceptional craftsmanship and skills of the artists who cut images on them. They were some of the best indicators of high social status and refined taste in art overall. Moreover, they quickly started to be perceived as particularly useful in the exploration of Antiquity. In the second half of the seventeenth and the first half of the eighteenth century, gems, like coins, often became subjects of intensive discussions by the representatives of the *Republic of Letters* and their images started to be published for a wider circulation.[1] They became a part of ongoing developments in the antiquarianism movement, which resulted in the increasing role of illustrations. The illustrations became central for the collection and processing of data about antiquities and further dissemination of knowledge produced as a result of their careful analysis in general.[2] This included, in principle, comparative iconography and required combining literary rules such as presentation of the sources, internal criticism of the documents and delivery of proofs with philological analysis of the non-literary objects of study, regardless of their type.[3]

As a consequence of this, some ground-breaking projects were realised. For example, the encyclopaedic visual documentation of antiquities, architecture, natural history and beyond compiled by Cassiano dal Pozzo (1588–1657) and his younger brother Carlo Antonio dal Pozzo (1606–1689) within the project *Museo Cartaceo/Paper Museum* represents one of the most significant attempts ever made before the age of photography to embrace all human knowledge in visual form.[4] In 1697, Francesco Bianchini (1662–1729) decided to realise an ambition to write a true universal history of the world from its creation to the present day, using eclectic images of ancient statues, reliefs

---

1   The *Republic of Letters* was a self-proclaimed intellectual community of scholars and literary figures in the late seventeenth and eighteenth centuries in Europe, formed across national boundaries and communicating mostly through correspondence.
2   Naturally, this process was much more ancient and the first attempts of more scholarly treatment of illustrations in the books concerning antiquities date well to the Renaissance period. A good example of that is the case of Jacopo Strada (1507–1588) and his exemplary publishing of ancient coins in 1553 under the title of *Epitome Thesauri Antiquitatum*, which presented sober but still carefully supervised illustrations of coin obverses among which, for the first time, Strada did not copy already existing illustrations from other studies or invent the lacking ones as it was habitual at the time (Haskell 1993, pp. 14–16). On the other hand, the case of Fulvio Orsini (1529–1600), a scholar who was to make the first serious attempt to produce a major repertoire of ancient portraits published in 1570 under the title *Imagines et Elogia Virorum Illustrium*, is noteworthy for using variety of sources (including gems) while working on a very well-defined project and the illustrations that were of considerable frankness compared to other sixteenth-century studies (Haskell 1993, pp. 39–41). On the importance of illustrations for the development of antiquarianism and early archaeological research in general, see: Haskell 1993 (especially pp. 13–41, 88–101 and 112–127) – general use of images, including illustrations; Schnapp 1997, pp. 235–237; Burke 2003, pp. 279–280 and 291–296. On the development of antiquarianism and classical archaeology in general, see: Momigliano 1950; Haskell and Penny 1981; Piggott 1989; Trigger 1996, pp. 52–66 and 97–113; Schnapp 1997, pp. 179–324; Bickendorf 1998; Herklotz 1999, pp. 151–306 (with more literature for Cassiano dal Pozzo and collections of drawings of antiquities); Kaufmann 2001; Burke 2003; Sloan (ed.) 2003; Herklotz 2004; Miller 2013; Gould 2014; Miller (ed.) 2014; Williams 2017.
3   Haskell and Penny 1981, pp. 43–49; Schnapp 1997, pp. 182–198. Haskell (1993, p. 25) is right to point out that ancient coins were the earliest and the most significant category of antiquities involved in the evolution of antiquarian studies, especially the role of images due to the visual and literary nature of coins.
4   The *Museo Cartaceo/Paper Museum* of Cassiano dal Pozzo, is a collection of more than 7000 watercolours, drawings and prints, assembled during the seventeenth century by the famous Roman patron and collector Cassiano dal Pozzo and his brother Carlo Antonio dal Pozzo (Herklotz 1999 – with extensive literature). See the project on this subject which was realised at The Warburg Institute in London, resulting in a series of 37 volumes publications being the *catalogue raisonné* of all identified drawings and prints once belonging to *Museo Cartaceo/Paper Museum* of Cassiano dal Pozzo and more: https://warburg.sas.ac.uk/research-projects/archived-research-projects/paper-museum-cassiano-dal-pozzo-1588-1657 [retrieved on 3 February 2023].

© PAWEŁ GOŁYŹNIAK AND HADRIEN J. RAMBACH, 2025 | DOI:10.1163/9789004712553_012
This is an open access chapter distributed under the terms of the CC BY-NC-ND 4.0 license.

and other artefacts as sources for illustrations of early stages of history.[5] In 1704, Domenico de'Rossi (1659–1730), the entrepreneurial printer-publisher, published the first eighteenth-century art book, a collection of engravings of ancient and modern Roman sculptures under the title *Raccolta di statue antiche e moderne*.[6] He turned to the well-known antiquarian Paolo Alessandro Maffei (1653–1716) for a suitably learned descriptive text, while the illustrations were provided by several French artists.

These are only a few examples of broad and more focused projects realised by the antiquarians in their pursuit for knowledge about the past in which drawings/illustrations played a critical role as platforms transmitting valuable information about ancient beliefs, customs, institutions, historical and mythological figures and so on.[7] For all of them, a frustrating problem of inaccurate reproductions of antiquities was difficult to tackle and still remained largely unsolved in the first quarter of the eighteenth century. The best example of this is the unquestionably ambitious project of Bernard de Montfaucon (1655–1741) *L'antiquité expliquée et représentée en figures*, an enormous study in 15 volumes that became emblematic for the traditional antiquarian vein; however, it was rather poorly illustrated because it was largely based on the previously published materials, e.g. prints and drawings that de Montfaucon collected himself, while the illustrations presenting unpublished sources varied considerably in their degree of accuracy.[8] Still, what he accomplished was raising public awareness among the members of the *Republic of Letters* about the important role that accurate and faithful images can play in illustrating books on Antiquity.[9] For the antiquarians of the first half of the eighteenth century, it was becoming more and more clear that relying on primary sources rather than on literary traditions was crucial for making a step forward in their studies. The best illustration of this trend is Francesco Scipione Maffei (1675–1755) and his activities in Verona focused on creating a museum of sculptures and inscriptions there. Maffei should be also singled out for his ambition to rely only on the illustrations taken directly from the originals, not already existing images that could distort the perception of the researcher.[10] One later finds a similar approach to be practised by one of Maffei's direct continuators – Comte de Caylus.[11] Indeed, then high-quality execution, authenticity and faithfulness to the originals were the qualities that antiquarians sought to in the illustrations accompanying their studies.

Engraved gems were in the very centre of these developments because of the considerable interest of seventeenth- and eighteenth-century antiquarians in intaglios and cameos.[12] It was difficult to faithfully reproduce glyptic masterpieces due to their artistic virtuosity and small size, but even casual types of gems were illustrated unsuccessfully.[13] For example, Michel-Ange de la Chausse's (1660–1724) study of Roman antiquities entitled *Romanum museum sive thesaurus eruditae antiquitatis*, which included a separate section devoted solely to intaglios and cameos, as well as publication of his collection of gems *Le gemme antiche figurate di Michel Angelo Causeo dela Chausse* from 1700 have rather mediocre illustrations of gems.[14] Yet, La Chausse must be credited for his proclamation of gems as valuable sources for reconstruction of ancient religions due to the series of images of deities, religious rituals, priests and so on appearing on intaglios and cameos.[15] He saw great potential in the image studies of gems despite not having enough good tools for visualising this. Between 1707 and 1709, De'Rossi and Maffei published *Gemme antiche figurate*, an overview of 410 engraved gems from notable Italian collections (Sabbatini, Buonarroti, Strozzi, Borioni, Ficoroni, del Carpio, Albani, Piccolomini, Riccardi, Vanni, Ottoboni, Odam and so on) in four volumes, clearly inspired by the earlier work of Leonardo Agostini (1593–1676),[16] but

---

5   Bianchini 1697. On Bianchini in general, including his approach to Antiquity, see: Momigliano 1950, pp. 299–300; Schnapp 1997, pp. 182–188; Sölch 2007; Heilbron 2022.
6   De'Rossi 1704.
7   For a general discussion on the development of antiquarian methods, see: Schnapp 1997; Herkoltz 1999, pp. 151–306 (with more literature).
8   Montfaucon 1719–1724. See also critical examination of this work in: Haskell and Penny 1981, pp. 43–45; Haskell 1993, pp. 131–144; Poulouin 1995; Schnapp 1997, pp. 235–237.
9   Haskell 1993, p. 159.
10 On Maffei's role in the development of antiquarianism, see: Haskell 1993, pp. 174–180.
11 Caylus 1752–1767, vol. I, pp. 37–38 and vol. II, pp. 379–380.
12 Another type of antiquities that shared the considerable interest of antiquarians, also due to the importance of images appearing on them, were ancient coins. In their case, the images were easier to read due to accompanying explanatory inscriptions and their dates were easier to be established as well. It is, therefore, not a coincidence that they gained much more recognition than gems already in the Renaissance period and especially since ca. 1550 when major studies of ancient numismatics started to appear, see: Haskell 1993, pp. 13–25.
13 Zazoff and Zazoff 1983, p. 47.
14 La Chausse 1690, pp. 1–32, pls 1–55; La Chausse 1700.
15 La Chausse 1700, preface. For a more extensive discussion of La Chausse's research on gems, see: Zazoff and Zazoff 1983, pp. 40–42.
16 Agostini 1657 and 1669. For critical evaluation of Agostini's books, see: Furtwängler 1900, vol. III, p. 405; Zazoff and Zazoff 1983, pp. 37–38.

even though Maffei's commentaries were more erudite, testifying to some development of gems descriptions, the illustrations remained simple and unfaithful to the originals in many respects.[17] Slightly predating Stosch's book on ancient signed gems, the study of the works of gem engraver Solon by Baudelot de Dairval offered only very simplistic illustrations of analysed gems and coins.[18] Even notorious authorities like Anton Francesco Gori were often criticised for low quality of engravings illustrating their books, which were, in addition, in the case of Gori, of very small size.[19] Finally, at the time of Stosch there were also publications like *Pierres antiques gravées tirées des principaux cabinets de la France* by Élisabeth Sophie Chéron in which the gems were reproduced in an entirely artistic way that had little to do with an accurate, scientific approach.[20]

The eighteenth century in general experienced an unprecedented surge in the interest in engraved gems, which resulted in many studies and books (sometimes unfinished projects) realised by leading antiquarians, scholars and even artists or writers like Caylus, Ficoroni, Mariette, Natter, Winckelmann, Lessing and Goethe.[21] As rightly defined by Haskell and Penny, the interest of antiquarians in engraved gems was mainly due to three reasons: the precious and semi-precious gemstones used as materials in the production of artworks, the artistic virtuosity of the engravings and exceptionally rich iconography that posed many problems to understand what the engravings depict and mean.[22] For all these reasons, proper illustrating (and describing) of intaglios and cameos mattered. As observed by Burke, indeed, two predominant groups of illustrators of antiquities in the seventeenth century were artists and physicians, and as can be deduced from the long list of illustrators of intaglios and cameos provided in Chapter 3, this was also the case for the eighteenth century and later.[23] The artists, due to their talents could be easily trained to reproduce objects of the past and the cases of nearly all draughtsmen employed by Philipp von Stosch prove that they became interested in glyptic art, some like Girolamo Odam or Pier Leone Ghezzi to a considerable degree by collecting, cutting and studying intaglios and cameos on their own. Physicians like Jacob Spon (1647–1685) and Charles Patin (1633–1693) were numismatists and also successful because of their capabilities in direct observation, which was particularly useful in both historical and antiquarian research, especially when the production of book illustrations is concerned.[24]

Philipp von Stosch was neither an accomplished artist (cf. discussion in Chapter 8) nor a physician; however, the issue of faithful illustrations of gems was exceptionally important to him, which is clear from some of his letters. In the one sent in 1722 to Lord Carteret, Stosch writes that he had earned a good reputation in Rome by having trained young artists in the difficult art of making accurate visual documentation of ancient engraved gems and other antiquities.[25] In his letter to Anton Maria Zanetti sent from Florence on 3 October 1733, Stosch says that he would love to have a drawing of a discussed gem and he explicitly asks to pay particular attention to accurate copying the letters of the signature, so that he could illustrate this piece in the supplement to his book.[26] In another letter to Zanetti sent on 27 December 1738, Stosch assures the collector that he will have his amethyst intaglio with Hermaphrodite and Cupids drawn with all possible accuracy to put it in his new book.[27] The accuracy and faithfulness of the drawings Stosch commissioned to the artists working for him are highlighted multiple times in his letters to William Cavendish, 2nd Duke of Devonshire, as well.[28] In one of them, he boasts having an excellent

---

17 De'Rossi and Maffei 1707–1709; Furtwängler 1900, vol. III, pp. 405–406; Zazoff and Zazoff 1983, pp. 38–40.
18 Baudelot de Dairval 1717. For a critical examination of his work, see: Zazoff and Zazoff 1983, p. 33.
19 Gori 1731–1732; Kagan 2006, p. 82; Zazoff and Zazoff 1983, pp. 52–53. These are just a few examples, but see also a more extensive account on the literature about engraved gems pre-dating Stosch's book *Gemmae antiquae caelatae* in: Zazoff and Zazoff 1983, pp. 30–46. None of the published treatises offered high-quality images of the discussed gems.
20 Chéron 1728; Zazoff and Zazoff 1983, pp. 45–46.
21 Zazoff and Zazoff 1983, p. 19.
22 Haskell and Penny 1981, pp. 49–50. On the problems with reading iconography of antiquities by antiquarians, see: Burke 2003, p. 292.
23 Burke 2003, pp. 293–294.
24 Momigliano 1950, p. 300; Haskell 1993, p. 20. On the key role of numismatists in the development of archaeological thought and proper illustrating of antiquities, see: Haskell 1993, pp. 13–25.
25 Letter from Walton [Stosch] to Lord Carteret dated 28 February 1722 (NA Kew SP 85/14 fols 9–12); Hansson 2021b, p. 62.
26 Letter from Stosch to Anton Maria Zanetti dated Florence 3 October 1733: '*Cossì avrei gusto di avere un schizzo d'un dissegno colli imitazioni estate de caratteri, per poterlo inserire nel appendice del mio libro.*' (Magrini (ed.) 2021, letter no. 56).
27 Letter from Stosch to Anton Maria Zanetti dated Florence 27 December 1738: '*Io Le rendo infinte grazie del bellissimo solfo che mi ha mandato dell'altro Suo rarissimo intaglio col nome dell'eccellente artifice Dioscoride, il quale è sicuramente e indubitatamente opera di tal Famoso maestro. Ed io con tutta la possible esattitudine il farò disegnare per collocarlo nel mio libro.*' (Magrini (ed.) 2021, letter no. 112). On the gem, see: Gori and Zanetti 1750, pp. 66–68, pl. XXXIII.
28 Chatsworth, the Devonshire Archives, inv. no.: CS1/188.0, CS1/188.3, CS1/188.4, CS1/188.5 and CS1/188.8.

draughtsman in his service who draws things easily and accurately within just a morning under his watchful eye.[29] Stosch's perfectionism and attention to detail was obsessive, as he probably instructed Bernard Picart to pay particular attention for details of the gems he was going to illustrate in his book and as a result Picart '(...) *was said to have used a microscope to examine the particular manner of each master*'.[30] When one looks at this from a wider perspective, one realises that this particular attention to as faithful as possible reproduction of gems in the visual form was the result of the ongoing developments in the antiquarianism movement.

The antiquarian interest had initially focused mostly on subject matter and iconography,[31] whereas formal and stylistic aspects became increasingly important as the eighteenth century drew on. As a result, in every new book on glyptic art, the illustrations of earlier publications were habitually criticised for being inadequate in this respect.[32] Needless to say, it was a habit of the time to criticise previous publications in order to justify one's own. According to Stosch himself, his predecessors' works: '*swarm with mistakes, and are far from being in accordance with the originals, by the fault of those who drew them*'.[33] Yet what makes Stosch different from his antecedents is that he had a modern art historical approach. He wanted to show that the beauty of gem engraving varies with the style of the carvers. This is clearly expressed by him in his letter to Gijsbert Cuper sent from Rome on 8 August 1716: '*The impressions of the gemstones carved with the names of ancient engravers (which I collected with incredible fatigue) should demonstrate not only the designs, but also the character of each person's work ... In the explanations of the engravings I hope to give the public an idea not only of the figures that the gems represent, but also of the beauty of engraving which differs in style one from that of the other engraver*'.[34] Stosch's attitude was much different than the one of his predecessors because he no longer expected from the visual reproductions of gems made for him to conform to what they might have been expected from the written texts, whether more or less ancient. In this respect, Stosch belonged to a wider circle of scholars, who started to perceive antiquities not only as supplementary to ancient written sources but as sources of knowledge about Antiquity in their own right.[35]

Moreover, Stosch had ample experience with original intaglios and cameos and he treated them as regular archaeological artefacts, not only objects carrying images, like was the case of most of his predecessors and contemporaries.[36] Furthermore, in contrast to many of his peers, Stosch precisely knew most of the gems he had documented by the artists employed in his studio because these were mostly his own and he could control the faithfulness of their drawings with the originals, having them on hand. The fact that some gems are drawn several times by different artists may be due to his testing of artists' capabilities in reproduction and comparing their works, but maybe also because he was sometimes dissatisfied with the work of one and asked another to try to do a better job. In addition, his large number of documentary drawings of gems discussed in this book are made according to well-thought-out standards, concentrating not only on iconography, but also material, state of preservation, proper scaling of the documented gems and their provenance, among others.

Regarding the gems from other collections, Stosch must have often relied upon the efforts of others and

---

29 Chatsworth, the Devonshire Archives, inv. no.: CS1/188.7.

30 Vincent and Picart 1734, p. 8: '*C'est avec un soin & une application toute particulière, que B. Picart a exécuté ce bel Ouvrage : car non seulement il l'a gravé lui-même, mais il en a de plus fait les Desseins à l'aide du Microscope, & y a observé, autant qu'il a été possible, la manière particuliére de chaque Maitre*'. See also Smentek 2014, p. 205.

31 Especially as far as engraved gems are concerned. For example, the *Gemme antiche figurate* by De'Rossi and Maffei is organised as follows: vol. I – portraits, vol. II – deities and Heracles, vol. III – deities and vol. IV – various subjects.

32 Hansson 2014, p. 13. On the role of illustrations in eighteenth-century antiquarianism, see also: Miller 2013, pp. 81–82 and for a detailed description of development of glyptic studies prior to Stosch, see: Furtwängler 1900, vol. III, pp. 402–409; Zazoff and Zazoff 1983, pp. 30–46; Lang 2017, pp. 199–204; cf. Chapter 3 here.

33 Stosch 1724, p. III: '*fourmillent de fautes, & que, par la négligence de ceux qui les ont dessinées, il s'en faut bien qu'elles soient conformes aux Originaux*'.

34 Koninklijke Bibliotheek, The Hague, inv. 72H25 – letter from Stosch to Gijsbert Cuper dated Rome, 8 August 1716: '*Les empreintes des pieres gravees avec le nom des graveurs anciens (que j'ay ramassé avec une fatigue incroyable) en faisant observer exactement dans le desein le caractere de l'ouvrage d'un chacun ... Dans les explication des gravures j'espere donner au public une idee non seulement des figures que les gemmes representent, mais de la beaute de la sculpture en quoi differe le style de l'un de celui de l'autre ouvrier*' (quoted in Heringa 1976, p. 77, n. 41).

35 On this issue in a broader sense, see: Haskell 1993, pp. 88–101. A good example of an antiquary who also like Stosch investigated the matter of style as chronological indicator was Filippo Buonarroti (1661–1733), see: Haskell 1993, pp. 124–127.

36 On the clearly philological method of approaching images in publications devoted to antiquities, in which the illustrations had no value on their own, but they were made just to complement the text, see: Schnapp 1997, pp. 235–237; Burke 2003, pp. 295–296. It is noteworthy that Mariette, like Stosch, also used a scale for illustrations in his book and focused on gems as objects rather than offering erudite philological passages (Smentek 2014, p. 202).

their skills in taking accurate gem impressions (which were sent to him) since these were mostly sources from which gem drawings were made. In this instance, mistakes were more likely to occur. An interesting example is Stosch's Tydeus Etruscan scarab, which was drawn by Nagel (Krakow No. 1182) first from an impression, and thus inaccurately as far as the border decoration is concerned. The final print by Schweickart was made once the gem was in Stosch's collection, and hence the mistakes were corrected in his design (Krakow Nos 1183–1184). Still, an important conclusion is that Stosch made every effort to have the gems documented as faithfully as possible. He gained a profound understanding of glyptic art due to his encyclopaedic collection, observation of a vast number of gems from the originals and their impressions. Moreover, his exemplary cooperation with artists and so much focus put on the accuracy of the visual documentation of gems helped him to immerse in this kind of art too. The result was a widely-respected position of an 'Oracle for collectors'. However, his *Paper Museum of Gems* also demonstrates the systematic use of visual evidence to a much more advanced level than anyone else before him and in his own times.[37] Stosch firmly believed in the differences between ancient gem engravers' hands, and his focus on the technical and stylistic aspects of intaglios and cameos was unprecedented in the studies of glyptic art. This automatically pushed him to develop a new methodology of the research, with very accurate visual documentation as its key aspect. The best proof of effectiveness and approval for Stosch's unprecedented and ground-breaking methods is the critical reception of his book *Gemmae antiquae caelatae*.

2 The Critical Reception of *Gemmae antiquae caelatae*

Olivier Latteur's comment that Stosch's book '*was essentially aimed at a limited readership formed of wealthy scholars with an interest for glyptics*'[38] must be mitigated. Indeed, a folio volume with 70 plates was expensive, and this restricted its access to a certain wealthy class. But the number of surviving copies suggest that many were printed, and that its readers were numerous. Moreover, as noted by Philippe Sénéchal, artists and erudites realised in the eighteenth century that '*the coins*[39] *and the engraved gems give us an image of Greek statues, known or lost, which is occasionally more faithful or more complete than the plastic works that have survived*',[40] which justifies documenting and publishing them. So, the volume would be of interest to artists, as inspirations, and scholars of Antiquity in general. And indeed, despite the lack of illustration, Winckelmann's catalogue of Stosch's gem-collection several decades later was a widely-disseminated publication with a resounding commercial success.

Stosch was initially uncertain about the choice of language in which to publish his book. In 1719, Fagel encouraged him to have it printed in both French and Latin.[41] The translator into French was a Dutch heraldic expert, Henri Philippe de Limiers (d. 1725), who seems to have been selected and paid by Picart in 1723.[42] He was not a good choice and many readers found the French text disappointing. Nonetheless, by 1754, Stosch's book had made his name immortal in the world of erudition (Stosch was then still alive).[43] The success of his book was such that in 1784–1785 Jean-Charles de Poncelin de la Roche-Tilhac (1746–1828) published in Paris a two-volume folio book, *Chefs d'œuvre de l'antiquité sur les Beaux-Arts et les monuments précieux de la religion des Grecs et des Romains ... tirés des principaux cabinets de l'Europe; ouvrage orné d'un grand nombre de planches en taille-douce, dont*

---

37 On the relatively small ability to use images of antiquities as visual evidence, see: Schnapp 1997, pp. 235–237; Burke 2003, pp. 295–296.

38 Latteur 2012, p. 30: '*s'adressait essentiellement à un public restreint, constitué d'érudits aisés s'intéressant à la glyptique.*'

39 Picart played an important role in numismatics, having engraved the coins illustrated in the volume *Les Césars de l'Empereur Julien, traduit du grec par feu Mr le Baron de Spanheim, Avec des Remarques & des Preuves, enrichies de plus de 300 Medailles, & autres Anciens Monumens* (Amsterdam 1728).

40 Sénéchal 1986, p. 173: '*Le monete e le pietre intagliate ci trasmettano una rappresentazione delle statue greche, conosciute o scomparse, talvolta più fedele o più complete delle opera plastiche giunte fino a noi.*' See also: Gurlitt 1831, pp. 75–76 (after Hansson 2014, p. 13): '*These miniature artworks had many advantages. They had survived, often intact and in vast numbers, from all ancient cultures and time periods; the images they carried, either engraved into the surface of the stone (intaglio) or carved in relief (cameo), were soon recognized as one of the richest visual sources available to Greek and Roman mythology, portraiture, and ancient iconography in general.*'

41 Letter from Stosch to François Fagel, dated Amsterdam 1 January 1719 (mentioned in Heringa 1976, p. 78, n. 48 – Archives of the Fagel family, Algemeen Rijksarchief, The Hague, inv. 2032). Answer dated 3 January 1719 (mentioned in Heringa 1976, p. 78, n. 52).

42 Heringa 1976, p. 80, n. 79.

43 Stosch 1754, p. 41: '*Dieses prächtige und überaus gelehrte Werk, welches das einzige in seiner Art ist, machet allein den Namen unseres Freyherrn in der gelehrten Welt unsterblich.*'

soixante-dix ont été gravées par B. Picart, without, however, adding much to Stosch's work.⁴⁴

Ever since it was published, Stosch's book has been admired and sought after. As early as January 1725, a London publication could write that *'this Book is too curious to take no notice of it, and too well known already to enlarge upon it'*.⁴⁵ In the year of its publication, Jean Leclerc had encouraged his readers to buy the book, even those *'who would rather look at the engravings than read their commentaries. They should buy the book, which will please their eyes by the beauty of its plates.'*⁴⁶ Critics especially admired the elegance of the illustrations, but usually with a caveat: they were more attractive than accurate, a rather unfair criticism when they are compared to any earlier publication. One of the book's most severe critics was Mariette, who, having explained that he did not think a selection of signed gems to be important, admitted that Picart had engraved the plates *'with this neatness which has had so many admirers'*.⁴⁷ He then commented: *'after Mr de Gravelle's verdict,*⁴⁸ *I am less afraid to note that this artist [Bernard Picart], was not suitable for the serious task that was set him, as he is only able to engrave pretty things after designs of his own. His engraving, overworked, is unbearably peasant-like; the way he affects to give colour in engraving is in bad taste and inappropriate. This mannerist master (...) does not have the ease and purity which are so precious in the Antique: whatever he engraves looks as though it has been issued from the same mould, and therefore M de Stosch's main goal has not been achieved, i.e. to show the various degrees of skilfulness of the ancient engravers. Once more, it is not that Picart has no merit; his fault is to have worked in a field in which he was a complete beginner, and to have been influenced by the country to which he has been transplanted – where the art of drawing has never shown great taste.'* Mariette's only appreciative comments are for Stosch's Latin commentaries: *'the explanations accompanying the plates by Bernard Picart are such as could be expected from a scholar (...). How sharp, how precise is the work! His descriptions depict their subject with such bright and matching colours that it seems to be in front of us.'* Of the illustrations in Mariette's own book, it would be written a century later: *'There are in this book neither ancient stones nor modern stones, there are only Bouchardons, and he was an awful and peculiar interpret of Antiquity, this Bouchardon! (...) Let it be examined, and one shall see that – whether Antiquity or Renaissance – all under his pencil was turned into Pompadour'*.⁴⁹

It would be interesting to know how Stosch reacted to these negative comments – which he knew, since he had copies of the works in which they appear in his very extensive library (catalogue of 2920 + 4014 lots).⁵⁰ He would not live to read what Eckhel wrote in 1788 about Stosch's *'magnificent work'*.⁵¹ Furtwängler, writing in 1900 about Stosch's *'great work'*, follows the opinions of Lippert in 1767 and of

---

44   Vinet 1877, p. 199, no. 1639: '*Sous ce titre mensonger, se retrouvent les planches gravées pour l'ouvrage du baron de Stosch, avec l'adjonction d'un nouveau texte, des plus médiocres.*' Jacques-Charles Brunet was more restrained: '*ce sont les planches des Pierres gravées de Stosch, avec un nouveau texte qui n'est nullement estimé*' (Brunet 1863, col. 803).

45   Anon. 1725, pp. 282–283.

46   Leclerc 1724, pp. 381–390 (quoted in Heringa 1976, n. 100): '*qui aiment mieux voir les figures, que de lire ce qu'on en dit. Ils feront bien d'acheter le livre même, qui amusera agréablement leurs yeux, par la beauté des gravures.*'

47   Mariette 1750, vol. I, pp. 331–332: '*Avec cette propreté qui a eû un si grand nombre d'admirateurs (...) après le jugement qu'en a porté M. de Gravelle, je crains moins de remarquer que cet Artiste [Bernard Picart], uniquement fait pour graver de jolies choses d'après des Desseins de son invention, n'étoit point propre pour l'entreprise sérieuse dont on le chargeoit. Trop de travail rend sa Gravûre d'une pesanteur insupportable; cette affectation de colorier en Gravûre les objets, est de mauvais goût & déplacée. Le Dessein maniéré de ce Maître a le défaut d'être trop arrondi, & pour me servir des termes de l'Art, trop soufflé; il n'a point ce coulant & cette pureté si précieuse dans l'Antique: tout ce qu'il nous donne se ressemble, tout paroît sorti du même moule, & par conséquent le principal objet de M. de Stosch, qui étoit de montrer au doigt, pour ainsi dire, les divers dégrés d'habileté des anciens Graveurs, & d'enseigner à discerner les maniéres, n'est point rempli. Ce n'est pas, encore un coup, que Picart manquât de mérite; le mal vient de ce qu'il traitoit une matiére dans laquelle il étoit tout-à-fait novice, & que transplanté dans un Pays où l'on n'a jamais dessiné de grand goût, il s'est laissé entraîner au torrent de l'exemple*' (...) '*Les explications qui accompagnent les Planches de Bernard Picart, sont telles qu'on les pouvoit attendre d'un Sçavant (...). Quelle netteté, quelle précision dans le travail! Ses descriptions peignent avec des couleurs si vives & si bien assorties le sujet dont il doit rendre compte, qu'on croit l'avoir présent.*'

48   La Gravelle 1732–1737, p. VII: '*Il vient de paraître depuis peu en Hollande une suite dont le projet était nouveau et bien formé ... Mais les gravures de ce livre sont trop lourdes et trop finies et le dessin chargé et maniéré s'écarte trop de la grandeur et de la pureté des contnours des excellents originaux qu'il copie.*' Gravelle's work was widely read, and provided inspiration for draughtsmen: see, for example, the fifty-nine drawings, mounted on seventeen sheets, by Félix Boisselier (1776–1811) in the Musée de l'Hôtel de Vermandois (Senlis), on which see: Ottinger 1997.

49   Chabouillet 1858, pp. 315–316: '*Il n'y a dans ce livre ni pierres antiques, ni pierres modernes, il n'y a que du Bouchardon, et c'était un terrible et singulier interprète de l'antique que Bouchardon! (...) Qu'on l'examine, et on verra qu'Antiquité ou Renaissance, tout sous son crayon, devenait du Pompadour.*'

50   Stosch 1759, no. 855 (Mariette 1750) and no. 865 (La *Gravelle* 1732–1737).

51   Eckhel 1788, p. 42: '*(...) lors que M. le Baron de Stosch travailloit à son magnifique ouvrage (...).*'

Klotz in 1768,⁵² in his comment that *'the plates are some of the best plates of gems to be found'.*⁵³

Stosch, and his attempted exhaustive catalogue of signed gems, is a scientific precursor: Gabriella Tassinari mentions his *'revolutionary approach'*.⁵⁴ It was just a century earlier, when John Earle could ridicule the Antiquary, *'a man strangely thrifty of Time past, and an enemy indeed to his Maw, whence he fetches out many things when they are now all rotten and stinking. He is one that hath that unnatural disease to be enamoured of old age and wrinkles, and loves all things (as Dutchmen do Cheese) the better for being mouldy and worm-eaten. (…) A great admirer he is of the rust of old monuments, and reads only those characters, where time hath eaten out the letters. Hee will go you forty miles to see a* Saint's Well *or a ruined abbey (…). His estate consists much in shekels, and Roman Coynes; and he hath more pictures of Caesar, than James or Elizabeth. Beggars coozen him with musty things which they have rak'd from dunghills (…). His chamber is hung commonly with strange Beasts' skins, and is a kind of Charnel-house of bones extraordinary (…). He never looks upon himself till he is grey-haired, and then he is pleased with his own antiquity. His grave do's not fright him, for he ha's been us'd to Sepulchers, and he likes Death the better, because it gathers him to his Fathers'.*⁵⁵ With Stosch, one enters a new age of research, one leaves forever the time of humanists, to whom *'history was a rhetorical exercise. They used historical characters as ideal types, whether of moral virtue (or vice) or political* virtú. *They made politics depend on personalities, ascribed edifying or unedifying motives, and invented appropriate speeches. They set great store on an elegant Latin style. Indeed, they were more interested in style than in objective truth, for history to them had an ulterior purpose: it was "philosophy teaching by examples" and the examples were chosen, or adjusted, to fit the philosophy'.*⁵⁶ Amongst the distinctions of Stosch 1724 is that the restorations were differentiated from the original gems on the fragments they depict, with dotted lines: such practice was not commonly adopted, and in 1764 Winckelmann was still calling for it – so as to prevent misinterpretations – in his *History of the Art of Antiquity*.

In 1895, for the volume of the *Bibliothèque des monuments figurés grecs et romain* series dedicated to engraved gems, Salomon Reinach (1858–1932) published a volume entitled *Pierres gravées des collections Marlborough et d'Orléans, des recueils d'Eckhel, Gori, Levesque de Gravelle, Mariette, Millin, Stosch, reunies* (sic) *et rééditées avec un texte nouveau*. He devoted the eighth and last chapter to *'Pierres publiées par Stosch'*, with a ten-page introduction and lengthy descriptions of the gems (including research on their location and antiquity).⁵⁷ Although Reinach's work of research, compilation and reflection is admirable, this *'new'* edition of Stosch does not offer much of interest to today's readers: Reinach himself said of the 1724 edition, *'the text is nowadays completely negligible'*. Most interesting is his final comment: *'the comparison of these engravings with photographs of impressions has not shown a single inexactitude of importance'*. According to Furtwängler, *'even Stosch's choice of the gems is good: of the seventy pieces, only about a dozen are not ancient'*.⁵⁸

The most pertinent (and unfair) aspect of Mariette's criticism of Stosch's book is whether the gems illustrated in his book were genuine, or at least whether their inscriptions were authentic. *'In Mariette's opinion, antiquarians were not only too weeded to iconography, they were also too trusting of epigraphs. While he agreed with Stosch that*

---

52 Lippert² I, p. 54; Klotz 1768, p. 70.
53 Furtwängler 1900, vol. III, pp. 409–410: '(…) *von den Stichen, die zu den besten gehören, die von Gemmen gemacht worden sind, (…) Die feineren Eigentümlichkeiten und der Ausdruck des Kopfes sind freilich völlig verfehlt; das weichliche rundliche Gesicht entspricht dem Originale keineswegs; aber in solchen Dingen treue Stische von Gemmen sind überhaupt noch nie gemacht worden. Wo es weniger auf den Ausdruck ankommt, da sind die von Stosch gebotene Stiche zum Teil völlig befriedigend.*' On the evaluation of Stosch's book, see also: Zazoff and Zazoff 1983, pp. 48–50.
54 Tassinari 2010a, p. 31: '*L'impostazione rivoluzionaria del suo libro* Gemmae Antiquae Caelatae (*Amsterlodami 1724*) *aveva fatto di Stosch una delle maggiori autorità sulle gemme antiche.*'
55 Earle 1628, character 9 (extensively quoted in Piggott 1989, p. 16). According to Gent ((ca. 1690), s.v. 'antiquary'), an Antiquary was '*a curious Critick in old Coins, Stones and Inscriptions, in Worm-eaten Records, and ancient Manuscripts; also one that affects and blindly doats, on Relicks, Ruins, old Customs, Phrases and Fashions.*'
56 Trevor-Roper 1985, p. 137.
57 Reinach 1895, pp. 147–184, pls 132–137.
58 Furtwängler 1900, vol. III, p. 410. Since a number of the gems are lost, it is difficult to judge how many of the gems illustrated are authentically ancient. Some 40 years ago, it was estimated that the total number of genuine signed gems in existence was about 130 (Zazoff and Zazoff 1983, p. 27). According to Hansson (2012, p. 42): '*Some nineteenth-century scholars, notably H.K.E. Köhler (1765–1838), cast serious doubts on the authenticity of the preserved corpus, suggesting that many or even most "ancient" gems could well be modern. Köhler* [Köhler1833] *himself claimed that only five of the many surviving ancient gems with artists' names were in fact genuine, all other were modern. The only gems that one could be absolutely sure about were those found during archaeological excavations*'; this was obviously erroneous. But, of the 70 stones illustrated in Stosch 1724, it has been argued that seven are engraved with the name of their owner rather than that of their engraver: pls I, II, X, XXI, XXXVI, XLIV and LVII (Zazoff and Zazoff 1983, p. 28), now this number drops to three: pls I?, X, LVII (cf. Appendix 1 for a detailed analysis).

names engraved on intaglios almost[59] *always referred to artists, lettering was nevertheless to be treated with caution. They could as easily be added to engraved gems as they could to paintings and prints and to the same fraudulent ends.*[60] *Inscriptions on drawings (...) were in Mariette's view added solely to increase their financial value.*[61] *So it was with intaglios. For this reason, epigraphs provided no basis for "induction". Unless the name on a gem could be matched with documentary evidence from other sources, its usefulness was limited. It was also no guarantee of quality: "The names that one sees on engraved gems are ... nothing but pure curiosities. One can induce from them nothing with certainty regarding the quality of an intaglio and one cannot hope for clarification of the history of art".*[62] *Similarly, although the kind of gemstone used, its shape, and its subject matter provided useful supplementary information – Mariette devoted a section of his treatise to a discussion of stones suitable for engraving – they were all equally uncertain guides to quality or authenticity.*[63] *Relying on such factors was akin to pronouncing on the authorship or authenticity of a painting or drawing on the basis of its support; it was dubious at best.*[64] *Instead, it was through the analysis of style – the goût de nation – that gems could be most accurately classified and assessed'.*[65] It is in fact to Stosch's honour that so few of the gems in his book were forgeries,[66] though it is interesting to note that the publication of his book contributed to a heightened interest of collectors for signed gems, which led to the multiplication of straightforward forgeries and of name additions to ancient stones, culminating in the extreme case of the Poniatowski collection.[67]

Overall, the book had a lasting effect on neoclassical art and design. Its inspiration can be traced in Georgian architectural decoration (for example, the dining room at Burton Constable Hall), marquetry furniture (such as a square piano of the 1770s in the Lady Lever Art Gallery in Port Sunlight), gold jewellery, and Grand Tour souvenirs.[68]

---

59 The Felix gem in Oxford, or rather its copy (Stosch 1724, pl. XXXV) is an example of a name that is the owner's rather than the engraver's.
60 Mariette 1750, vol. I, pp. 99–101.
61 Mariette 1851, vol. IV, p. 3.
62 Mariette 1750, vol. I, pp. 264 and 330.
63 Mariette 1750, vol. I, pp. 96 and 103–104.
64 Mariette 1750, vol. I, p. 96.
65 Smentek 2014, pp. 205–206.
66 Stosch's ability is also confirmed by the fact that, '*of 3442 items* [*Stosch's gems that entered the Berlin collection, only*] *887 originals and pasts were found to be modern*' (Hansson 2014, p. 30 referring to the calculations by Adolf Furtwängler and Erika Zwierlein-Diehl). Stosch's expertise was recognised at the time, and he was consulted by amateurs wishing to know his opinion of their gems, for example, on 16 April 1746, the cardinal Albani wrote to Friedrich de Thoms: '*Je presse M. le Baron de Stosch, en envoyant la letter que vous m'avez addressee pour lui, de vous satisfaire, dans la recherche, que vous lui avez faite de son avis sur vos pierres gravées avec le nom de l'auteur, savoir quelles il croit antique et quelles non, et je me flatte de vaincre sur ce chapitre son opiniatreté*' (quoted in Noack 1928–1929, p. 44). Another example of Stosch acting as a judge of authenticity and quality is when he was sent a gem by Joachim Rendorp (1728–1792) for his advice (Tassinari 2019, p. 230; the gem being a carnelian depicting head of Theseus with a bovine headdress and inscribed ΓΝΑΙΟΣ, now in the Beverley collection at Alnwick Castle, see: Scarisbrick, Wagner and Boardman 2018, no. 99 (dated 19th century)). Filippo Buonarroti, on 6 June 1717, wrote about having met Stosch who: '*began to show me some of his intaglios, and I saw the Meleager and the Bacchante that he had set in rings, and I could see by our discussion during the evening spent at my home that he is very expert in the subject of Antiquity*' ('*mi ha cominciato a far vedere de suoi intagli ed ho veduto il Meleagro e la Baccante che ha legati in anelli e potei vedere dalla veglia che fece da me che è molto esperto di materia d'antichità*' – ASF, Mediceo del Principato, carte strozziane, serie III, 63, carteggio Filippo Buonarroti – Leone Strozzi, fol. 31r, 11 maggio 1717, cited in Guerrieri 2010, p. 104).
67 Rambach 2014 (with more literature).
68 We are most grateful to David Connell for informing us that the plasterer William Collins (1721–1791) modelled a number of free-standing and relief pieces of plaster sculpture for the dining room at Burton Constable (*East Yorkshire, England*) in 1768–1769. The fireplace *overmantel plaque* with *Bacchus & Ariadne* copies the gem Stosch 1724, pl. XXII and the room contains a set of four relief vases, one of which shows *Cupid playing a harp and riding on a lion* (which copies the gem Stosch 1724, pl. LIII), and another the *Putto holding a thyrsus over his shoulder* (which copies the gem Stosch 1724, pl. LXX). On the casts of engraved gems at Burton Constable Hall (where a copy of Stosch's book remains in the library), see: Connell 2009a. Moreover, examples of ca. 1820 porcelain vases by the manufacture of Ginori, illustrated with gems published by Stosch in his book in 1724, can be found in Gennaioli 2010, p. 79. Furthermore, there exists a square piano, the outer case of which was done by Christopher Fuhrlohg (ca. 1740–after 1787), which copies the gem Stosch 1724, pl. XLV, published in Wood 1994, pp. 115–119, figs I–XI (referred to in Sotheby's, *Important English Furniture*, London, 10 July 1998, lot 78). In addition, George Michael Moser (1706–1783) created a number of jewels after engraved gems. For example: an enamel étui of ca. 1760 in the Museum zu Allerheiligen – Schaffhausen, which copies the gem Stosch 1724, pl. VII (Edgcumbe 2000, no. 59); a 1774 gold plaque for a box in the Gilbert collection, which copies the gem Stosch 1724, pl. VI (Edgcumbe 2000, no. 38); a 1775 enameled watch case, which copies the gem Stosch 1724, pl. XLVII (Edgcumbe 2000, no. 39); and another enameled watch case and its chatelaine, which copies the gems Stosch 1724, pls VI and LXV (Edgcumbe 2000, no. 38 note). In 1768 Moser drew a copy of the gem Stosch 1724, pl. XLVII (ink, 146 × 119 mm, British Museum inv. 1902,0606.160, H.J. Ellis donation). Finally, it should be noted here that Giovanni Battista Pozzi (ca. 1670–1752) carved a number of small ivory plaques for Roman visitors, and that he made a portrait of Stosch (German National Museum), but the plaque sold by Bonhams with the Sextus Pompey's (?) head (Howard Neville collection, London, 9 December 2009, lot 240), copying the carnelian intaglio by

A large number of copies of the book survive, some very attractive.[69]

3   The Encyclopaedic Approach – between Antiquarianism and Proto-archaeology

Publication of *Gemmae antiquae caelatae* by Stosch in 1724 positioned him very well in antiquarian circles of the *Republic of Letters*. He became a widely appreciated expert in the field of glyptics at the time when intaglios and cameos gained particular popularity as collecting items and as the subject of antiquarian studies.[70] As Justi says, Stosch became the '*Oracle for collectors*',[71] who would send him impressions and drawings of their gems for consultation like, for instance, Anton Maria Zanetti (cf. Chapter 10). Stosch is generally appreciated for steering the studies of glyptic art on a very innovative course. The discovery that the names carved on gems could refer to artists rather than the figures portrayed on them redirected interest to gem engravers, some of whose names were already known from Pliny's *Natural History* (37.8).[72] His contribution greatly stimulated later discussion on this peculiar topic and also inspired others to study intaglios and cameos of this kind.[73] Stosch's prominent figure was critical for dissemination of knowledge about engraved gems not only through his valuable book but also the flyers he distributed and lectures delivered at the meetings of the *Società Colombaria* in Florence and Livorno and *Accademia Etrusca* in Cortona that he eagerly participated in, among others (cf. Chapters 2 and 8).

Stosch was a familiar figure in the antiquarian and art market circles across Europe, also because of his diverse and voluminous collections that were more widely known outside Italy only shortly after his death by the publication of their list and descriptions in *Das neue gelehrte Europa* (1757).[74] While in Florence, though, his *Museo Stoschiano* was as Anton Francesco Gori described, '*one of the greatest jewels of the city and a compendium of the most select museums*'.[75] However, the poor documentation of Stosch's collections and their imminent dispersal by his heir Heinrich Wilhelm Muzell-Stosch resulted in only fragments of Stosch's wide-ranging activities as a collector, dealer, agent and scholar to be reconstructed and known today. As rightly observed by Hansson, the complexity of Stosch's various activities involving antiquities, notably engraved gems, remains little understood

---

Agathangelos (AGDS II, no. 418) was not based on Stosch's book (this gem was first published in 1736 in Borioni and Venuti 1736, pl. 68).

69   For example, a specimen bound in full contemporary red morocco has been on display at Strawberry Hill House 24 March–24 July 2022 in the *The Grand Tour: the two Horaces and the Court of Florence* exhibition. From the library of the playwright David Garrick (1717–1779), sold at his auction by Mr Saunders on 23 April–3 May 1823, lot 1880 ('*large paper, red morocco*'), sold to the bookdealer William Clarke (active 1802–1830) for £5 7s. 6d. Later in the library of the Earls of Derby, who added their arms on the binding, probably an acquisition of Edward Smith-Stanley, 13th Earl of Derby (1775–1851), listed in the 1893 catalogue of his collection (vol. IV, p. 843), but not included in any of the auctions by Christie's of the books from Knowsley Hall (19–20 October 1953, 17–18 December 1953, 23–24 March 1954, and 3–4 May 1954). Later in the library of Raphaël Esmerian (1903–1976), sold Paris 6 June 1973, lot 96, sold for FFr. 2200, in whose auction catalogue the binding was described as the work of Antoine-Michel Padeloup (1685–1758). Later in a private library dispersed at auction by Me Galateau, Montignac sur Vezere, 27 August 2008, lot 1214; offered by Cahn Auktionen (Basel, 9 November 2009, lot 306). Another exceptional specimen is bound in dark blue morocco with the large arms of the French King Louis XV (1710–1715–1774), also ascribed to Padeloup, bears the printed ex-libris of the Président de Viefville, supposedly Jean-Louis de Viefville des Essarts (1744–1820); and the printed ex-libris of an unidentified Marchal. From the library of Roger Peyrefitte (1907–2000); lot 142 of his sale by Loudmer & Poulain on 20 December 1976 (sold for FFr. 2200); later sold by Sotheby, Monaco; 12 December 1984, lot 3194; later sold by Anne Lamort Livres Anciens (Paris), catalogue XXXI, 2019, lot 56. '*Exemplaire en grand papier, dans lequel ont été ajoutés les tirages à part de la grande vignette de titre, d'un bandeau en-tête, d'une grande initiale et d'un grand cul-de-lampe*' (Peyrefitte catalogue). Large-paper copies would always sell at very high prices, in the eighteenth century especially, but also in the first half of the nineteenth century, as confirmed by auction catalogues and dealer-lists: £3.3.0 for an undescribed copy in 1794 (library of Rev. John Pitts – lot 501), £5.5.0 for a '*very well bound*' copy on large paper in 1770 (library of the Duke of Newcastle and others – lot 114), £9.9.0 for a green morocco copy on large paper in 1813 (library of Col. Stanley – lot 79), etc. In France too, very high prices were recorded for morocco-bound copies on large paper: 50 fr. (de Cotte library), 59 fr. (Barthélémy library), 80 fr. (Trudaine library) and even more at earlier auctions (see: Brunet 1810, p. 514). For comparison, the monthly salary in 1823 of the writer Alexandre Dumas as '*surnuméraire*' for the Duke of Orléans was only 100 francs.

70   Hansson 2021a, p. 113. On the studies of gems predating Stosch, see: Zazoff and Zazoff 1983, pp. 30–46.
71   Justi 1956, vol. II, pp. 283–284: '*Vor allem aber war er ein Orakel für Sammler, denn er hatte mehr gesehen, mehr erworben oder prüfend durch seine Hände gehen lassen, als irgendein Lebender*'.
72   Reinach 1895, pp. 156–157; Furtwängler 1900, vol. III, pp. 409–410; Zazoff and Zazoff 1983, pp. 48–50; Hansson 2014, p. 13; Lang 2017, p. 202; Hansson 2020, p. 59.
73   Furtwängler 1888; Furtwängler 1889; Zazoff and Zazoff 1983, pp. 27–29; Zwierlein-Diehl 1989 and 2005; Hansson 2014, pp. 18–21.
74   Stosch 1757, pp. 257–301. For a broader commentary on Stosch's various collections, see: Hansson 2021a, pp. 118–122.
75   Gori 1742, pp. CCXXXVII–CCXXXVIII; Hansson 2021a, p. 113.

also because even the surviving fragmentary information is obscured by the dense mythology that was created around Stosch already during his life due to his involvement in spying or masonic movement.[76] As a result, his contribution to the history of collecting and development of proto-archaeology is not fully understood.[77] Yet, even the incomplete bits of documentation and correspondence and especially some widely appreciative comments about Stosch's holdings from his contemporaries certainly make an impression that Stosch's various contributions should have been of much greater scale than just a book on ancient signed gems.

This led to creation of some rather far-fetched theories. For example, Stosch is sometimes believed to have been working on a sort of a large project or study of the so-called *universal history*.[78] However, there is virtually no information in Stosch's correspondence or in any other archival source about his unfinished or even planned book on this subject. According to Lewis, Stosch's greatest project should have been encyclopaedic in scope and it started from collecting maps and other pictorial works for his *Atlas*.[79] The *Atlas* project was indeed gigantic and Justi confirms that Stosch's efforts in this matter began as early as 1721, which is, in fact, more or less contemporary to his studies of engraved gems.[80] It was further developed under Stosch's guidance and supervision by all the draughtsmen working in his house. At the time of Stosch's death, it comprised 334 folio volumes encompassing ca. 31 500 maps, architectural and topographical drawings and prints, but it was never fully accomplished.[81] Now, the discovery of Stosch's *Paper Museum of Gems* created under the watchful eye of Stosch in his studio in Rome and Florence by several Italian and German artists allows a fuller understanding of his collecting, documentary and research activities, which were of a great scale. It turns out that, indeed, Stosch kept working on the supplement to his famous book until the end of his life and he was also preparing a catalogue of his gem collection, which perhaps could have been illustrated at least to some degree. But above all, the character of his corpus of gem drawings illustrates the ongoing transformation of the antiquarianism movement rather than to be strictly goal-oriented on some kind of ultimate and universal book project.

Justi says that for every gem or coin Stosch bought he made an impression, drawing or a note that he sent to the Accademia Etrusca in Cortona.[82] For sure he did the same for the sake of his own archive. The discovery in Krakow and Berlin of the gem drawings he commissioned proves that he created what seems to be the largest ever made and very carefully designed pictorial database of intaglios and cameos. It is a unique phenomenon, not only in terms of the scale of the project but also its quality.[83] It was certainly inspired by such encyclopaedic visual documentations of antiquities as the *Museo Cartaceo* of Cassiano dal Pozzo, among others (cf. Chapters 1 and 3). The collection of drawings assembled by Pozzo in the seventeenth century was later acquired by Pope Clement XI, who, in 1714, gave it to his nephew Cardinal Alessandro Albani. Because Stosch and Albani were good friends, during his visits and longer stays in Rome from 1715 until 1731, Stosch had many occasions to consult Pozzo's *Paper Museum* in Albani's villa and to take it as inspiration for his own documenting and publishing practices regarding engraved gems and the topographical *Atlas* project.[84] Pozzo's *Paper Museum* did not include many illustrations of engraved gems,[85] but its

---

76 Hansson 2021a, pp. 114 and 122.
77 Hansson 2021a, p. 122.
78 Borroni Salvadori 1978a, p. 574. According to Borroni Salvadori (1978a, p. 567; 1978b, pp. 64–65), Markus Tuscher and Johann Justin Preißler were the two artists meant to produce illustrations for it.
79 Lewis 1967, p. 323. On Stosch's *Atlas*, see: Eggers 1926; Kinauer 1950; Zazoff and Zazoff 1983, p. 66.
80 Justi 1871, p. 11.
81 Sénéchal 2000, p. 138; Hansson 2014, pp. 21–22.
82 Justi 1871, p. 25.
83 Some contemporary gem collectors and researchers created visual records of gems too. For example, Filippo Buonarroti created a notebook with hundreds of simple sketches reproducing intaglios and cameos from Florentine collections, see: Quartino 1978. Pier Leone Ghezzi produced hundreds of gem drawings which are now preserved in the Biblioteca Apostolica Vaticana ((Cod. Ott. lat. 3100–3101, 3103–3104 and 3106–3109, see: Gołyźniak (forthcoming – Ghezzi)). Alessandro Gregorio Capponi often asked artists to draw gems for him, see: Ubaldelli 2001, pp. 129–149. Francesco Valesio produced a manuscript on gems with their sketches, impressions and drawings, which was purchased by Onofrio Baldelli (1677–1728), the first director of the Accademia Etrusca in Cortona, see: Bruschetti 1985–1986, p. 8. Finally, the gem engraver Lorenz Natter formed a sketchbook of his own projects and he worked on a publication of the most valuable gems in British collections (*Museum Britannicum*), for which he made hundreds of drawings, see: Boardman, Kagan and Wagner 2017. Nevertheless, none of them can compete with Stosch, not only in terms of visual documentation of intaglios and cameos but also collecting, reproduction as impressions and research.
84 Lewis 1967, p. 326.
85 Vaiani 2016, no. 67. See also some examples made in pen and brown ink with grey wash preserved in London, the British Museum: 2005,0927.87 – seven studies of ancient intaglios and one cameo (including: no. 427 – refers to a gem published in De'Rossi and Maffei 1707–1709, vol. IV, fig. 8; no. 429 – refers to De'Rossi and Maffei 1707–1709, vol. IV, fig. 40; no. 430 – refers to De'Rossi and Maffei 1707–1709, vol. IV, fig. 4; no. 431 – refers to

structure and overall scope may have guided Stosch on how to build his own *Paper Museum of Gems*.

It was certainly uneasy to design and manage such an ambitious project as visual documentation of all important collections of intaglios and cameos over one's whole life in collaboration with several different artists. The case of the never-finished second volume of *Gemmae antiquae caelatae* book illustrates numerous obstacles to be tackled in the case of a research on a very specific topic, let alone a broad survey through all kinds of gems imaginable, as will be shown below. One would also probably expect some measurable results, not just an enormous collection of images. Certainly, Lewis sounds disappointed saying that, even though Stosch indeed might have been working on a sort of a general project devoted to the history of Antiquity and ancient art, he left nothing but a number of collections.[86] However, by saying this, he underestimates the value of Stosch's lifetime achievements, which these collections actually were. Stosch's rediscovered corpus of gem drawings provokes a closer look at his collecting, documentary and scholarly activities from another perspective. His almost obsessive collecting of everything related to engraved gems, whether the original intaglios and cameos, their impressions and casts in sulphur and glass paste, as well as commissioning thousands of documentary drawings, was driven by his holistic, encyclopaedic approach. Gems, impressions and drawings were intrinsically connected and complemented each other, and they were probably also interconnected with Stosch's other holdings.[87] For example, perhaps it is not a coincidence that the description of the *Atlas* appears at the very end of Winckelmann's catalogue of Stosch's gems. The gems and this visual album were connected, they complemented each other by bringing up visual records (images appearing on the gemstones and pictorial records of ancient ruins among others) of Antiquity from various angles as was clear to Winckelmann, the 'spiritual heir' of Stosch's projects and visions.[88] Looking at it from such a perspective, one agrees with Hansson who thinks that Stosch's activities were not restricted to any category of art or a specific subject, but in fact Stosch's house-museum full of antiquities, maps, drawings, gems, coins, etc., constituted a sort of encyclopaedia to numerous visitors of all kinds, whom Stosch warmly welcomed first in Rome and later in Florence.[89] It is noteworthy that, again, the analogue collection of drawings and prints of Cassiano dal Pozzo, was also broadly famed as a general archival resource, from which scholars not only in Rome but throughout Europe might have hoped to obtain reference material for their research and illustrations for their publications.[90] One would expect that Stosch's corpus of gem drawings worked the same way and it actually did as evidenced by numerous gem drawings attached to Stosch's letters sent to William Cavendish, 2nd Duke of Devonshire.[91]

Stosch's encyclopaedic approach originates from the antiquarian tradition of evidence accumulation, in some respects recalling Cassiano dal Pozzo's approach to his *Museo Cartaceo*.[92] Already Zazoff noticed that the classes I–IV in Winckelmann's catalogue of Stosch's gems are in fact organised as a sort of encyclopaedia of ancient history and mythology.[93] Indeed, one gets the same impression looking at the structure of Stosch's collection of original gems. At the time of his death in 1757, it was the largest cabinet of its kind in existence. In 1760, Winckelmann published 3444 original gems and glass pastes in his *catalogue raisonné*.[94] This was the cabinet purchased in 1764 by Frederick the Great of Prussia for his Antikentempel in the garden at Sanssouci, Potsdam.[95] However, Stosch's

---

Gori 1731–1732, vol. I, pl. C.6–9; no. 432 – refers to De'Rossi and Maffei 1707–1709, vol. IV, fig. 10 and no. 433 – refers to De'Rossi and Maffei 1707–1709, vol. IV, fig. 15); 2005,0927.69 – no. 396 – a gem depicting scene of combat between Roman heroes, perhaps the Horatii and the Curatii; 2005,0927.113 – a gem featuring a crane drinking from a long-necked vase at which a dog is sniffing; 2005,0928.68 – a gem once in the Albani collection presenting Eros trying to catch a bird in a tree; 2005,0928.70 – an intaglio with Eros asleep, leaning on a pole; 2005,0928.70.bis – a gem showing Nessus and Deianeira; 2005,0928.69 – a gem (cameo?) presenting Eros seated on his cloak and playing a *kithara*.

86 Lewis 1961, p. 49.
87 Hansson 2021a, p. 122.
88 Winckelmann 1760, pp. 571–596. While for Winckelmann such a juxtaposition was valuable in showing the interconnections between Stosch's holdings, one must keep in mind that at the same time his catalogue was an advertisement for the cabinet of gems which Muzell-Stosch wanted to sell as much as it was for the *Atlas*, also destined for sale. Depending on the perspective, Stosch's collections may have been inspirational from both the scholarly and art trade points of view. On Winckelmann as the 'spiritual heir' of Stosch, see: Winckelmann 1760, p. 95.
89 Hansson 2021a, p. 119.
90 Vaiani 2016, p. 7.
91 The following six out of 10 letters sent by Stosch to the Duke had gem drawings attached: Chatsworth, the Devonshire Archives, inv. no.: CS1/188.1, CS1/188.3, CS1/188.5, CS1/188.6, CS1/188.7 and CS1/188.8.
92 On Pozzo and seventeenth-century antiquarian/early archaeological research, see: Herklotz 1999, especially pp. 261–262 – for encyclopaedic projects in the circle of Pozzo.
93 Zazoff and Zazoff 1983, p. 79.
94 For a critical study of this publication, see: Zazoff and Zazoff 1983, pp. 71–105; Lang 2017, pp. 204–210.
95 Rave 1957, p. 26; Hansson 2014, p. 29.

original gem collection was even bigger and more diversified because perhaps already at the end of his life Stosch himself, or more likely shortly after his death, his heir Heinrich Wilhelm Muzell-Stosch sold the Christian gems to Francesco Vettori,[96] while Egyptian and many Etruscan scarabs as well as some important Near Eastern cylinder seals went to Giovanni Carafa, Duke of Noia,[97] both friends of Stosch. According to Muzell-Stosch's letter to Cardinal Albani from 18 November 1757, Stosch's collection also included about 100 cameos but they disappeared before the purchase of the King of Prussia and nothing precise can be said about them.[98] It is reported that the 600 best gems were mounted in gold, while the rest in silver rings and the collection was kept in 30 large chests with 10 drawers each, ordered thematically according to their subject matter. As Justi and Hansson notice, Stosch's collecting was not governed primarily by aesthetic considerations; he wanted his collection to be representative of gem engraving as a whole, encyclopaedic in scope and a source of knowledge about the life and customs of the Ancients.[99] As a result, as Winckelmann remarks, Stosch's collection of gems: '*contains almost the entire mythology of the Egyptians, Etruscans, Greeks and Romans, their main uses, the representations commemorating many memorable events of antiquity and portraits of the most famous characters*'.[100]

Whether Stosch's collection of original engraved gems or his documentary gem drawings are concerned, one does not observe a selection of more or less suitable materials. Stosch collected both masterpieces, like the two exceptional Etruscan scarabs, the so-called *Gemma Stosch* and the one depicting Tydeus scraping his leg, as well as ordinary products of Roman Republican and Roman Imperial glyptics.[101] He gathered regular hardstone intaglios made of a great variety of gemstones as well as glass gems. He did not discard chipped or broken gems. With his impressive network of contacts, Stosch certainly could have created a much more selective and better, in terms of quality, collection of gems. After all, he owned three signed gems already at the time of publishing his book (pls XI, XXVIII and LIV) and provenance studies confirm that he was in possession of at least several very important and valuable gems like, the garnet intaglio presenting an oiling athlete signed by Gnaeus currently in the Walters Art Museum in Baltimore,[102] the carnelian featuring the standing figure of Mercury signed by Dioscurides now in the Fitzwilliam Museum in Cambridge,[103] a fragment of a carnelian intaglio with a reclining cow signed by Apollonides and bust of Socrates signed by Agathermos, sold by Stosch to William Cavendish, 2nd Duke of Devonshire (1672–1729),[104] and a turquoise cameo presenting Livia with head of Augustus now in the Museum of Fine Arts in Boston.[105]

His focus was set not only on quality or quantity but most importantly on diversity of the gems he owned, and therefore the subject matter issue was the main driving force in building his cabinet of originals, *dactyliotheca* and gem drawing corpus. From a letter from Johann Joachim Winckelmann to Heinrich Wilhelm Muzell-Stosch, one learns that the cataloguer of Stosch's gem collection retained its original structure as created by Stosch himself: '*As to the order of the Catalogues, I do not see how I can displace the previous order; everything stays in its old place*'.[106] This helps to understand the qualities of Stosch's sorting system. Winckelmann's catalogue is divided into eight general classes with further sub-classes within them reflecting the subject matter areas concentrating on: I – Egyptian and Persian gems, II – *Mythologie sacrée*, III – *Mythologie historique*, IV *Histoire ancienne* (portraits), V – Festivals, everyday life scenes, vases, etc., VI – ancient

---

96   Justi 1871, p. 24; Potts 2023, p. 91, n. 113.
97   Hansson 2014, p. 26; Dodero 2019, pp. 140–141; Gołyźniak 2022.
98   Justi 1872, p. 344. Apparently Stosch gave or sold to Lorenz Natter some of his cameos already in the 1730s, see: Boardman, Kagan and Wagner 2017, nos 517–519 and 521–525. Some also went to Thomas Hollis collection, see: Boardman, Kagan and Wagner 2017, no. 528.
99   Justi 1872, p. 345; Hansson 2014, p. 21.
100   Winckelmann 1760, p. II: '*Il renferme presque toute la Mythologie des Egyptiens, des Etrusques, des Grecs & des Romains, leur principaux usages, la représentation de beaucoup de Faits mémorables de l'Antiquité, & les Portraits des plus fameux personnages.*'
101   See a detailed analysis of these two gems in: Zazoff and Zazoff 1983, pp. 85–87.
102   The Walters Art Museum, Baltimore, acc. no.: 42.109. For a discussion, see: Platz-Horster 1993; Boardman *et al.* 2009, no. 429 (with more literature) and especially Chapter 10 in this volume.
103   The Fitzwilliam Museum, Cambridge, inv. no.: CG 165/S 25 (CM). For a discussion, see: Henig, Scarisbrick and Whiting 1994, no. 165, see a discussion in Appendix 1, pl. XXVIII.
104   Henig, Scarisbrick and Whiting 1994, p. XV; Zwierlein-Diehl 2007, p. 276; Lang 2012, no. S029 and see a discussion on these gems in Chapter 10 in this volume.
105   Museum of Fine Arts, Boston, acc. no. 99.109. For a discussion, see: Boardman *et al.* 2009, p. 373.
106   Winckelmann 1952–1957, vol. II, pp. 78–79, no. 292 – letter from Johann Joachim Winckelmann to Heinrich Wilhelm Muzell-Stosch dated Rome 11 August 1759: '*Was die Ordnung des Catalogi betrifft, so sehe ich nicht wohl ein, wie es die vorige Ordnung verrücken kann; es bleibet alles an seinem alten Orte.*' This is further confirmed in another letter from Winckelmann to Muzell-Stosch dated 16 June 1759: '*Die Eintheilung in Classen ist nicht die Beste, und scheinet in der That keine andere als eine Ordnung nach so viel Kasten. Da sie aber einmal gemachet ist, so kann und will ich sie nicht ändern*' (Winckelmann 1952–1957, vol. II, pp. 6–7, no. 279).

ships, VII – animals and VIII – Abraxas and oriental gems (magical) as well as modern ones. As discussed in Chapters 6 and 8, a very similar organisation was applied to Stosch's corpus of gem drawings. Moreover, among the drawings preserved in the Princes Czartoryski Museum in Krakow, one finds a series of gems with the same devices but existing in variants differing only in some details.[107] The original structure of Stosch's extensive because numbering 28 000 of gem impressions and casts *dactyliotheca* is not precisely known, but it is suggested to follow the same standards.[108]

It is clear that Stosch's aim was to create a pictorial database covering the widest range of subjects and illustrations of ancient mythologies, customs, rituals, portraits, institutions, etc. on gems imaginable. It was created in accordance with the same principles of antiquarianism as Cassiano dal Pozzo's *Museo Cartaceo*, that is with a tendency to compile a comprehensive corpus of antiquities (in this case engraved gems), according to well-defined categories based on subject matters.[109] The sequence of subjects applied by Stosch is broadly in accordance with the *Synopsis* or *Ordo antiquatum Romanarum* ('*Hierarchy of Roman antiquities*') published in 1664 by Carlo Dati (1619–1676), the disciple of Galileo, in reference to Cassiano dal Pozzo's 23 volumes of drawings of antiquities, architecture and natural history objects. It basically divided the ancient Roman world into two realms – the divine and human, as noticed by Vaiani, evidently inspired by the title of the lost work of Marcus Terentius Varro (116–27 BC), *Antiquitates rerum humanarum et divinarum* ('*Human and divine antiquities*').[110] Stosch makes some advancements to this scheme, though, by, for example, distinguishing the *Mythologie historique* (Winckelmann 1760 class III) but most importantly, probably also taking into account cultural and to some extent also chronological dimensions of antiquities. Therefore, the first class of Winckelmann's catalogue consists of gems with Egyptian, Egyptianising and Persian subjects, while the last one (VIII) magical and modern gems.

As already remarked (cf. Chapter 8), Stosch's corpus of gem drawings was certainly very useful for his day-to-day evaluations of new pieces as a dealer and connoisseur and consultations of the gems he was sent to look at or considered to buy. On the other hand, it reflects Stosch's ambitions towards systematisation of glyptic art and most likely his antiquarian strategy towards creation of an encyclopaedic iconographical aid according to the thematic reading method and comparative iconography combined with ancient practice of gathering *loci communes*.[111] Stosch evidently introduced new qualities of research focusing on systematisation, classification and interpretation of archaeological artefacts, e.g. engraved gems. Already with his book on ancient signed gems, he started to ask new questions, for example, about the identity of the makers of gems, and he consequently investigated gems to show the various degrees of skill of the ancient engravers reflected in their works.[112] Eventually, he not only researched gems with signatures only but analysed those with various kinds of inscriptions holistically.[113] Moreover, Stosch's methodology differs much from, for example, Francesco Bianchini's because his careful, large-scale visual documentation of intaglios and cameos was designed to reflect variety and complexity of the lives of ancient people, their

---

107 For example, there is a series of 127 drawings (Krakow Nos 705–831) depicting masks in various configurations: single ones, conjoined, making compositions of two or more, comedy, tragedy – all sorts. Another such rich but unified category is built by the drawings representing Heracles and subjects related to him. There are 123 drawings by Odam featuring the hero performing his labours, his heads and busts and illustrating his relationships with Omphale, Iole and other characters etc. (Krakow Nos 1032, 1034–1038, 1040–1044, 1046–1054, 1057–1060, 1064–1065, 1067–1096, 1098–1104, 1106–1113, 1115–1123, 1125, 1127, 1129–1131, 1133–1136, 1138–1141, 1143–1146, 1148–1158, 1160–1163, 1165–1166 and 1168–1177). The subject of Eros/Cupid on gems is also richly illustrated since there are 276 drawings related to the God of Love, almost all depict Roman Republican and Roman Imperial intaglios and cameos (Krakow Nos 1982–1990, 1992–1996, 1998–2024, 2026–2046, 2048–2057, 2059–2077, 2079–2086, 2088–2101, 2103–2140, 2142–2143, 2145, 2147–2183, 2185–2207, 2209–2216, 2218–2219 and 2221–2268).

108 The evidence for that has been discussed in Chapter 5 in this volume.

109 On Cassiano dal Pozzo and his antiquarian approach especially, see: Herklotz 1999, pp. 119 and 261.

110 Herklotz 1999, pp. 240–242 and 266–274; Vaiani 2016, pp. 43–46.

111 A similar approach, although applied on a much broader scale, was practiced by Cassiano dal Pozzo, see: Herklotz 1999, pp. 119 and 262–265.

112 Inquiring on much more complex issues related to antiquities such as their functions, producers, users and so on was one of the milestones in the development of antiquarianism and its later transformation into the early archaeological research, see: Schnapp 1997, p. 180. In contrast to the view of Haskell and Penny (1981, p. 100), it was Stosch who systematically studied and organised engraved gems prior to Winckelmann.

113 This is most clear from his correspondence with William Cavendish, 2nd Duke of Devonshire, as he wrote about amassing as many as possible examples of gems with various inscriptions because he wanted to show and explain to other antiquarian fellows the subtle differences between signatures, names of the owners, names of the figures depicted and counterfeited inscriptions. For that purpose, he collected original gems, their impressions, casts and drawings. It is noteworthy that his forthcoming second volume of *Gemmae antiquae caelatae* was meant to include plates exhibiting forgeries as an appendix to warn collectors and other gem enthusiasts. On this aspect, see, especially, Stosch's letter to William Cavendish, 2nd Duke of Devonshire dated Rome 28 August 1728: Chatsworth, the Devonshire Archives, inv. no.: CS1/188.4.

customs, rituals, aesthetic pleasures, etc.; thus, to have aesthetic and informational qualities rather than to prove specific facts from Antiquity and provide milestones for the development of the ultimate chronology.[114]

It is noteworthy that a similar approach is observed in the case of a considerable collection of gem drawings from the archive of Pier Leone Ghezzi, now preserved in the Biblioteca Apostolica Vaticana.[115] The question of whether Ghezzi directly followed Stosch's organisational system for gems or his case simply reflects the current antiquarian approach cannot be answered yet.[116] As Smentek observes, publication of Linnaeus taxonomy in the 1730s shifted the description of nature and art from its irregularity to regularity.[117] Judging by the contents of Stosch's library, one imagines that he was familiar with all new concepts and ideas circulating within the learned societies during his times, including Linnaeus' approach.[118] It was natural for Stosch to organise his collection of original gems, drawings and impressions according to subject matters, which allowed him to study mythologies, history, customs, rituals and everyday life of ancient civilisations from these objects as much as antiquarians did using the passages of ancient written sources, according to the humanist method. However, his attempts at systematisation may go far beyond the traditional antiquarianism and prove that he indeed sought specific features of the objects he studied which would make it possible for him to differentiate one type from another. It should be recalled that while working on his book on ancient signed gems Stosch wanted to show that the beauty of gem engraving varies with the style of individual carvers and later to explain differences between various kinds of inscriptions appearing on gems (see above). Furthermore, Stosch had a close association with contemporary gem engravers for which he is often accused of producing high-quality fakes to sell on the market as ancient pieces, but it might be that this cooperation was more concerned with discovery and exploration of the techniques of ancient gem engraving and making experiments, whose results depended not only on Stosch's decency alone, to say the least.[119]

Because limited archival sources related to Stosch have survived, it is impossible to know what he precisely thought about the gems from his own collection and the ones documented as drawings in general, and if he worked out their strict chronological system.[120] Little remains known about his methodologies as to dating gems and linking them with specific cultural circles. Stosch was certainly concerned with the question of antiquity and genuineness of the examined objects, as he was regarded the most prolific in this matter amongst all antiquarians dealing with engraved gems in Rome and Florence, and because of that he was often called an 'oracle', which he was proud of.[121] Inspired by the success of his first book, Stosch certainly not only continued his study of newly discovered signed gems for the supplement and subsequent problem of detecting fake gems or ancient ones with added fake signatures, but he may have been working on the development of the idea of individual styles and chronology of gems. This would focus on the cultural differences in the first place according to antiquarian principles reflected in iconography, which could be combined with his observations on differences determined also in materials/gemstones used, forms of the gems, and consequently different techniques and styles practised in gem engraving in ancient Egypt, Near East, Etruria, Greece and Rome. As proven by his handwritten corrections to the captions preserved on the drawings from the Kunstbibliothek in Berlin, he certainly discussed the materials the gems were

---

114 On Bianchini's theory of illustrating history using antiquities, see: Schnapp 1997, pp. 182–188; Dixon 2005; Sölch 2007, pp. 41–76.
115 Biblioteca Apostolica Vaticana, Cod. Ott. lat. 3100–3104 and 3106–3109.
116 Gołyźniak (forthcoming – Ghezzi). On the tradition of graphic collections of antiquities to which Stosch's and Ghezzi's corpuses belonged to, see: Herklotz 1999, pp. 251–260.
117 Smentek 2014, p. 117.
118 On Stosch's library as a reflection of his general views and knowledge, see: Hansson 2021a, pp. 119–120; Hansson 2025c.
119 Stosch is said to have had interactions with many contemporary gem engravers like Lorenz Natter (1705–1763), Carlo Costanzi

(1705–1781), Tommaso Costanzi (1700–1747), Flavio Sirletti (1683–1737), Francesco Maria Gaetano Ghinghi (1689–1762), Giuseppe Torricelli (1662–1719), Lorenzo Masini (1713–?), Felice Bernabé (1720–?), and Antonio Pichler (1697–1779). On the traditional view that their cooperation probably resulted in production of fake gems, see: Justi 1872, p. 336; Reinach 1895, p. 148; Osborne 1912, pp. 181–183; Dalton 1915, p. XLVIII; Eggers 1926, p. 222; Borroni Salvadori 1978a, pp. 583 and 595–96; Heringa 1981, p. 103; Zazoff and Zazoff 1983, pp. 188–189; Cremer 1997, pp. 144–145; Arnold-Rutkiewicz 2005, pp. 52 and 63; Fileti Mazza 2006, p. 56; Breckenridge, 1979, p. 11; Campbell and Nesselrath 2006, p. 36; Tassinari 2010a, pp. 31–32; Tassinari 2019, pp. 230–243, Napolitano 2021, pp. 21–22. Naturally, Stosch knew those artists and used their services but the nature of their contacts and potential collaboration was certainly more complex than it may look at the first glance. It remains unclear whether any gem he commissioned at the listed artists was produced with specific intention to deceive, see: Hansson 2021a, p. 119 and especially Gołyźniak (forthcoming – Stosch and forgeries).
120 Eppihimer 2015, p. 16.
121 Justi 1956, vol. II, pp. 283–284; Hansson 2020, p. 59. See also letters and other archival sources confirming his exceptional expertise in detecting forgeries, cited in note 34 and especially in his letter to William Cavendish, 2nd Duke of Devonshire, dated Rome 28 August 1728 – Chatsworth, the Devonshire Archives, inv. no.: CS1/188.4.

made of and their iconography with draughtsmen documenting them for him. Could he also have discussed the chronology of gems and classified them as 'Persian', 'Etruscan', 'Greek' or 'Roman'?

This issue cannot be thoroughly or deeply investigated and Stosch's own manuscript of his collection of gems (now lost) is a particularly irreparable loss in this regard. However, there might be some hints suggesting his engagement into such a discussion as far as particular gems or their groups are concerned. According to the discussion on the commentaries accompanying the gem drawings now preserved in Krakow in Chapters 6 and 8, it is fairly possible that in some instances they reflect what people from Stosch's close circle, notably Joannon de Saint Laurent, thought about individual objects documented as drawings. Careful reading of Winckelmann's catalogue of Stosch gems, which surely reflects Stosch's own views in the case of many gems, even if Winckelmann suggests otherwise, is also helpful. Analysis of these texts as far as the gems' chronology is concerned, combined with limited information on the gems' chronology secured directly from Stosch, brings interesting results. For example, regarding Egyptian scarabs and gems, it should be noted that in the preface of his book, *Gemmae antiquae caelatae*, Stosch notices that the tradition of gem engraving was born in Egypt.[122] This literally means that he considered Egyptian scarabs as the most ancient products of glyptic art.[123] It is also noteworthy that some gem drawings from Krakow are indicated to present Egyptian scarabs and other *Pierres Egiptiennes*. For example, Krakow No. 1792, featuring, in fact, an Assyrian hematite scarab with a Babylonian-looking bearded worshipper gesturing before a goddess and an inscription is described as '*Scarabée avec une gravure Egiptienne*'.[124] A similar case is Krakow No. 1799, an Egyptian heart scarab, once in Stosch's collection, now in the British Museum in London, decorated with six rows of Hieroglyphic text on the base and described as: '*Scarabée avec des caracters hierogliphiques et une balance qui on se voit que tres rarement dans les monuments egyptienns*' (Figs 11.1–11.2).[125] Some further examples also labelled as Egyptian gems can be pointed out (Figs 11.3–11.4).[126] However, some clearly Hellenistic and Roman (mostly magical) gems are also classified as Egyptian due to their iconography. This is the case of Krakow No. 1785, which presents a lost, probably Hellenistic, cameo engraved with a bust of Harpocrates with a headdress and jewellery to the right, raising his finger to the mouth, described as: '*Buste d'Harpocratte avec le Persea sur la tete. Une plume sur l'epaule: cette plume s'apelloit la plume royale que le Dieu Kneph portoit sur le tete: gravure egiptienne*' (Fig. 11.5).[127] Also, it appears that some Sassanian seals were mistaken as Egyptian, like the drawing Krakow No. 1802 demonstrates, being described as: '*Pierre Egiptienne*' (Fig. 11.6).

Within Stosch's collection of engraved gems and glass pastes, there were dozens of those bearing Egyptian subjects (125 to be more precise) gathered by Winckelmann in Class I.[128] In fact, these were mostly Hellenistic and Roman (magical) gems featuring various Egyptian deities, creatures and symbols, as well as single Phoenician,

---

122 Stosch 1724, p. V.
123 Stosch 1724, p. V.
124 London, the British Museum, inv. no.: 1772.3-15.433/E48508 (once in the Stosch, Giovanni Carafa and Hamilton collections); Gori and Passeri 1750, vol. I, pl. XXIV; Raspe and Tassie 1791, no. 654 (scarab, British Museum); Jenkins and Sloan 1996, no. 93; Gołyźniak 2023a.
125 London, the British Museum, inv. no.: EA7911/BS.7911 (Birch Slip Number)/H431 (Miscellaneous number) (once in the Guido, Duca della Gerardesca (1696–1755), Stosch, Carafa and Hamilton collections); Raspe and Tassie 1791, no. 22 (British Museum); Gołyźniak 2023a.
126 Krakow No. 1801, most likely a small figurine made of lapis lazuli, cut in the round, is labelled as '*Pierre Egiptienne*' (Raspe and Tassie 1791, no. 341 (sulphur, Stosch)); Krakow No. 1797, an unidentified Egyptian scarab, is described as: '*Scarabée mal formé. Vilainne gravure Egyptienne*'.
127 Further examples of similar cases are: Krakow No. 1797 documenting a lapis lazuli magical gem now in the British Museum in London, depicting a lion striding right, carrying a throne with lotus frieze and cavetto cornice; on the throne: the head of a crowned Isis, with winged arms, protecting the bust of Horus, adorned with the double crown; in front of Horus, a scorpion represented diagonally from right to left, and a sphinx with a bearded human head, which is described under the drawing as: '*Isis et Osiris mitrés avec un Sphinx sur un autel, devant lequel passe un Lion: Ouvrage egiptien*' (London, the British Museum, inv. no.: G 430, EA 56430 (18th century, once in the Towneley collection); Raspe and Tassie 1791, no. 299 (sulphur, Stosch); Michel 2001, p. 345, no. 603); Krakow No. 1784 represents a lost cameo once in the Capponi collection engraved with a bust of the goddess Hathor with cow's ears and a wig, within a naos flanked by two papyrus columns, on the cornice of the naos and above it, a sun disk with outstretched wings and uraei, which is described on the drawing as '*Buste d'Isis: gravure Egiptienne*' (Dehn/Dolce Vatican, A.20 (22 × 20 mm, cameo); Raspe and Tassie 1791, no. 257 (Capponi at Rome); Cades Grande, 23.II.P.98; Ubaldelli 2001, pp. 175–179, no. 21 (mentioned); Pirzio Biroli Stefanelli 2007, no. I.17; Boardman et al. 2009, no. 660; Borbein, Kunze and Rügler 2019, no. I.39 (with more literature and commentary)); Krakow No. 1803 presents a sardonyx gem engraved on both sides with Egyptian motifs as a cameo and intaglio in one, simply described as '*Fragment Egiptien*' (Raspe and Tassie 1791, nos 297–298 (sulphur, Stosch); Furtwängler 1896, no. 9793; Borbein, Kunze and Rügler 2019, no. I.50 (with full bibliography)).
128 Winckelmann 1760, class I, nos 1–139, pp. 1–32.

Graeco-Phoenician and Cypriote scarabs bearing Egyptian motifs too, while there were just 14 truly Egyptian scarabs.[129] Even at the times of Winckelmann, let alone Stosch, there was virtually no differentiation between the Egyptian glyptics and the gems featuring Egyptian motifs, as these two concepts were thought to be one in the same.

Another interesting group consists of objects, which, at the times of Stosch and his contemporaries, would have been described as 'Persian' or 'Persepolitan'. According to Eppihimer, Near Eastern cylinder and stamp seals and gems appeared in the European collections for the first time in the seventeenth century and they were rarely recognised for what they truly are, usually labelled as of Persian origin.[130] Prior to ca. 1750, they were mostly misunderstood or completely ignored, but apparently not by Stosch and his circle, including de Saint Laurent and Winckelmann. Stosch probably learnt much from Bernard de Montfaucon's writing on Persepolis in *L'antiquité expliquée et representee en figures* published in 1722, which is confirmed by the fact that his *Atlas* contained a good number of drawings, maps and prints representing Persia and Persepolis.[131] Moreover, his collection of engraved gems included 16 examples of seals that could be labelled as 'Persian'.[132] Furthermore, he had some Near Eastern gems from his own and other collections documented as drawings as well. For example, Krakow No. 1793 presents a Neo-Babylonian chalcedony stamp seal, now in the Vorderasiatisches Museum in Berlin, engraved with an Assyrian priest making a sacrifice on an altar in front of him with a sundisc above, which is described under the drawing as: '*Cette pierre est veritablement persanne et de la plus hautle antiquité. Elle represente un pretre faisant un Sacrifier et se trouvoit dans la collectioné de M: Baron Stosch*' (Figs 11.7–11.8).[133] Krakow No. 1794 represents an Old Babylonian cylinder seal with a presentation scene, perhaps once owned by Stosch, now in the British Museum in London, which is described as: '*Cylindre Persan representant quelque ceremonis missterieux*' (Figs 11.9–11.10).[134] Further examples described as 'Persian' or 'Parthian' can be given.[135]

Eppihimer rightly notices disagreements and differences between Winckelmann, who ultimately catalogued Stosch's gems, and Stosch, claiming one of them to be the way to perceive the 'Near Eastern/Persian/Sassanian' gems in Stosch's collection. Indeed, having no precise knowledge of the catalogue of his own gems Stosch was writing with his brother, it is difficult to assess how much Stosch understood them.[136] But the examples of the drawings with the 'Egyptian' and 'Persian' gems evoked above and the fact that Winckelmann explains himself that he classified all Egyptian and Near Eastern seals together in one class because of their limited number and thus limited representativity,[137] even though first, he planned to give them separate sections,[138] actually suggests that his original idea was opposite to Stosch's classification. Moreover, while corresponding with Muzell-Stosch, Winckelmann made it clear that despite the fact that he thinks that Stosch's original organisation of the collection is not ideal, he accepted it and did not move objects between classes.[139] As a result, one should take Winckelmann's explanation on why he put 'Egyptian' and 'Persian' gems together into one class as an excuse, since in this matter he directly followed Stosch's footsteps. From the gem drawings presented and discussed above, it is clear that in the circle of Stosch (e.g. perhaps by Stosch himself) there was a distinction

---

129 These were classified in the beginning of the group: Winckelmann 1760, class I, nos 1–14, pp. 1–7.
130 Eppihimer 2015, pp. 2–3.
131 On Stosch's appreciation of Montfaucon's work, see: Zazoff and Zazoff 1983, pp. 42–44.
132 Thirteenth of them were published by Winckelmann (Winckelmann 1760, class I, nos 126–139, pp. 28–32) and these were in fact mostly Graeco-Persian gems while three Near Eastern cylinder seals were sold to Giovanni Carafa, Duke of Noia (through an antiquary and dealer in antiquities Francesco Alfani (d.1798)), shortly after Stosch's death, see: Eppihimer 2015, pp. 14–15; Dodero 2019, pp. 140–141; Gołyźniak 2023a.
133 Berlin, Vorderasiatisches Museum, inv. no.: VA 769; Ghezzi 1734, III.A.no. 88 (27 × 15 mm); Borbein, Kunze and Rügler 2019, no. I.127 (with full bibliography).

134 London, the British Museum, inv. no.: 1772,0315,GR.418/89303 (once in Stosch (?) and Hamilton collections); Raspe and Tassie 1791, nos 638–641 (British Museum); Collon 1986, no. 57, pl. VIII; Jenkins and Sloan 1996, p. 202, no. 87; Gołyźniak 2023a.
135 Krakow No. 1795 depicts a grey-blue chalcedony Persian cylinder seal with a crowned figure (king?) in combat with a confronting monster, ancillary motifs and symbols, once perhaps in Stosch collection and now in the British Museum in London, described below the drawing as: '*Un Cylindre qu'on supose de Pierre d'eimant ou de Calcedoine portant une gravure Persanne et emblematique. Le pareil existe a Londre, dans le Museum Britannicum*' (London, the British Museum, inv. no.: 1772,0315,GR.419/89781 (once in the Stosch (?) and Hamilton collections); Raspe and Tassie 1791, no. 649–645 (British Museum); Jenkins and Sloane 1996, p. 202, no. 88; Merrillees 2005, no. 62); Gołyźniak 2023a; Krakow No. 1758, presenting unidentified, most likely lost Sassanian gem is described as: '*Tete d'un Roy Parthe inconnu*'.
136 Eppihimer 2015, pp. 15–16.
137 Winckelmann 1952–1957, vol. II, pp. 6–7, no. 279.
138 Winckelmann 1952–1957, vol. I, pp. 432–434, no. 251.
139 Winckelmann 1952–1957, vol. II, pp. 78–79, no. 292 – letter from Johann Joachim Winckelmann to Heinrich Wilhelm Muzell-Stosch dated Rome 11 August 1759; Winckelmann 1952–1957, vol. II, pp. 6–7, no. 279 – letter from Winckelmann to Muzell-Stosch dated 16 June 1759.

of 'Egyptian' and 'Persian' or even 'Parthian' glyptic products, but surely their limited availability resulted in little understanding of these kinds of gems, which is clear from the commentaries accompanying the drawings. Their iconography was obscure but distinctive enough to separate them from the much more popular Graeco-Roman gems. The claim of Eppihimer must stand that while working on the catalogue of Stosch's gems and his synthesis of ancient art Winckelmann did not inherit any art historical paradigms regarding 'Persian' and 'Egyptian' gems.[140] The documentary gem drawings from his corpus, which we know for a fact Winckelmann studied and used during his work, could not help him much to understand these gems and the arts behind them better.[141]

A bit more can be said about Stosch's approach towards Etruscan gems.[142] No single example of Etruscan glyptics appears in Stosch's book *Gemmae antiquae caelatae*, because he rightly considered all the inscriptions appearing on Etruscan scarabs as referring to the names of the heroes and other figures depicted on them.[143] However, this does not mean that Stosch was uninterested in Etruscan gems. On the contrary, over the many years of collecting, he accumulated a substantial number of them[144] and became the owner of some masterpieces, which, as he states by himself, he bought for *'whatever the price was'*.[145] Stosch certainly purchased some Etruscan gems while he was still in Rome, but his interest in them must have developed a great deal when he transferred himself to Florence, where he was completely taken by the local *Etruscomania*.[146]

Stosch arrived at Florence in 1731 and he was quickly surrounded with great enthusiasts of Etruscan culture, like Anton Francesco Gori who published *Museum Etruscum* in 1737, a study presenting and discussing many examples of Etruscan scarabs.[147] Among the gem drawings discovered in Krakow, there are some whose techniques but most importantly commentaries, suggest them to depict Etruscan gems. For example, Krakow No. 570 appears, at the first glance, to be an unfinished drawing until one recognises the Etruscan scarab from Stosch's own cabinet depicting two naked warriors with swords and shields in a fight, cut in the so-called simple *a globolo* style, which is confirmed by the comment below: '*Combat gravure Etrusque*' (Figs 11.11–11.12).[148] Krakow No. 1365 presents an Etruscan scarab from Stosch's own collection too but featuring Heracles at a fountain examining the apples of Hesperides, his club in the field or a Haruspex performing a ritual with his staff in the field within a hatched border, classified as Etruscan because of its size, style and specific hatched border: '*Un homme occupé a faire des balles d'Argile. Le graveure est sur la base d'un Scarabée: et par son geuze, son attitude et par le Guentis qui entoure le bord, elle est decidement Etrusque*' (Figs 11.13–11.14).[149] There are a few more gems classified as Etruscan, according to the texts appearing beneath their drawings; however, some are also mistaken, like Krakow No. 1156, which depicts an unidentified, most likely Roman intaglio engraved with Mithra catching a bull, a hound in the field, apparently taken as an Etruscan piece because the subject had been associated with Heracles: '*Hercule arretant la Biche aux pieds d'airain. Gravau Etrusq*'.[150]

---

140 Eppihimer 2015, pp. 20–21.
141 Letter from Johann Joachim Winckelmann to Antonio Baldani, dated 26–30 September 1758, suggests that originally, a little number of gem drawings had extensive commentaries: '*Non ho altri amminicoli per schiarirmi e facilitarmi il lavoro che i disegni fatti in grande, ma senza veruna spiegazione.*' (Winckelmann 1961, p. 105, no. 31).
142 For a detailed study, see: Kunze 2016.
143 Hansson 2018, p. 84.
144 According to Furtwängler (1896, pp. 20–27 and 36–37), there were 47 Etruscan scarabs in Stosch's collection, which at the time was a considerable success even though the number may seem insignificant compared to the number of Roman Republican and Roman Imperial gems that Stosch amassed in hundreds of examples.
145 Letter from Philipp von Stosch to Giovanni Bianchi dated 18 December 1756 (quoted in Justi 1871, pp. 30–31. no. XVI).
146 Zazoff and Zazoff 1983, pp. 52–53; Hansson 2018, p. 85; Hansson 2020, p. 60. On the rediscovery of the Etruscans and its consequences for development of archaeological scholarship, see: Momigliano 1950, pp. 304–307; Kunze (ed.) 2009.
147 Gori 1737. On engraved gems in the writings and iconography of Anton Francesco Gori, see: Kagan 2006.
148 Berlin, Antikensammlung, inv. no.: FG 243; Furtwängler 1896, no. 243; Borbein, Kunze and Rügler 2019, no. II.981 (with full bibliography).
149 Berlin, Antikensammlung, inv. no.: FG 369; Furtwängler 1896, no. 369; Borbein, Kunze and Rügler 2019, no. II.1768 (with full bibliography).
150 A few more examples are: Krakow No. 150, even though it is, in fact, a glass gem dated to the last third of the 1st century BC depicting a winged and bearded Jupiter, standing next to Semele lying on the ground and bundles of thunderbolts around in the field, is described as: '*Jupiter et Semelé. Gravure etrusque*' (Berlin, Antikensammlung, inv. no.: FG 6219; Raspe and Tassie 1791, no. 1147 (antique paste, King of Prussia); Cades Grande, 2.I.A.174; Furtwängler 1896, no. 6219; Borbein, Kunze and Rügler 2019, no. II.135 (with full bibliography)); Krakow No. 1089 depicting an unidentified, probably lost, Etruscan scarab with Heracles collecting water from a fountain, described as: '*Hercule puisant de l'eau a une fontaine gravure Etrusque*'; Krakow No. 1092 is another example of the same subject on a carnelian Etruscan scarab once in Stosch's collection, now in the Antikensammlung in Berlin, which is described as follows: '*Hercule nomé Fontinalis: graveure Etrusque: il est aupres d'une fontaine qui sort d'un mythe de Lion, il versse en meme tems du vin d'une outre qu'il portte*

Stosch's two Etruscan masterpiece scarabs, the so-called *Gemma Stosch* as well as the scarab with Tydeus scraping his leg, have already been discussed in Chapter 8. However, let us only remark here that regarding the drawing of the latter gem by Georg Abraham Nagel (Krakow No. 1182), its commentary below sounds as follows: '*Tydée un des Sept Chefs qui vinrent au Siége de Thébes qui étant blessé retire le Javelot de sa Jambe. Son nom est gravé en Etrusque*'. Apparently, the name of the hero was considered to be given in the Etruscan language. If the text was originally written in the circle of Stosch, it may help to understand the evolution of Stosch's beliefs in the origin of the inscriptions on Etruscan scarabs, which were much discussed at the time in the context of search for the earliest stages of the ancient production of gems.[151] In the heated debate over the language of the inscriptions appearing on the famous *Gemma Stosch*, Florentine antiquarians like Anton Francesco Gori and Carlo Antonioli believed it to be Etruscan, but it is known that Stosch opted for Greek first, which is also documented on the flyer of the scarab in question engraved in 1756 by Johan Adam Schweickart ('*Literis Graecis Antiquissimis*') on Stosch's commission. He changed his mind later and considered the letters to be reminiscent of Pelasgian, the mother language of Greek and Etruscan. At the end, Stosch admitted that he did not care much about the language of the inscriptions, but he thought that his masterpiece was one of the oldest gems to have survived from Antiquity.[152] However, it could be that prior to being gifted the *Gemma Stosch*, he believed the inscription on his Tydeus gem to be in the Etruscan language, but later he changed his mind first to the Greek language and ultimately came up with an idea of the Pelasgian one, which would be a compromise. The view on the inscriptions from the *Gemma Stosch* that it was written in the Pelasgian language was later accepted by Winckelmann, who, in addition, believed this exceptional scarab to be the oldest artwork of all.[153]

These few examples alone show that in contrast to the 'Egyptian' and 'Persian' gems, the Etruscan ones were recognisable due to their peculiar forms (scarabs), size, hatched borders and most importantly styles, although not always correctly. This is due to the much better availability of Etruscan gems on the art market in Rome and Florence, and the much more advanced studies of Etruscan art overall compared to the Egyptian and Near Eastern ones. Actually, Etruscan gems found their way to the very centre of attention of collectors and antiquarians due to Stosch himself. Stosch and his collaborators producing gem drawings as well as discussing them were aware not only of these distinctive features of Etruscan gems but also of differences in their qualities. This is why the scarabs cut in the distinctive *a globolo* style are clearly drawn differently than others. The few examples evoked above demonstrate that under Stosch's supervision artists developed considerable skills in documenting engraved gems, applying different techniques to reflect technical and stylistic differences between various kinds of them, which proves Stosch's great merit in training them in careful and faithful documentation of gems as reported in his correspondence. It turns out to be not an empty boast.[154]

Regarding the Graeco-Roman gems which constitute the vast majority of the material depicted on the discovered gem drawings in Krakow, it is noteworthy that none bear a clue in the commentary as to depict it as a Greek or Roman intaglio or cameo. It appears that Stosch and his collaborators treated separately only the distinctive 'Egyptian', 'Persian' and 'Etruscan', in other words, non-classical gems.[155] Those which were considered to be from

---

sur l'Epaule' (Berlin, Antikensammlung, inv. no.: FG 206; Raspe and Tassie 1791, no. 4626 (sulphur, Stosch); Furtwängler 1896, no. 206; Borbein, Kunze and Rügler 2019, no. II.1769 (with full bibliography)).

151 Hansson 2020, p. 58.
152 Letter from Philipp von Stosch to Giovanni Bianchi dated 18 December 1756 (quoted in Justi 1871, pp. 30–31. no. XVI). Note also '*Literis Graecis Antiquissimis*' appearing on the flyer engraved in 1756 by Schweickart for Stosch. On this issue, see especially: Hansson 2020, p. 61.
153 Winckelmann 1760, class III, no. 172, pp. 344–347.
154 Letter from Walton [Stosch] to Lord Carteret, dated 28 February 1722 (NA Kew SP 85/14 fols 9–12); Hansson 2021b, p. 62.
155 One wonders if the early Christian and Medieval gems were also treated in Stosch's circle as a separate category. Since most of Stosch's own gems of this kind were quickly sold after his death and they consequently do not appear in Winckelmann's catalogue, it is not known how significant this group was. As far as gem drawings are concerned, Krakow No. 1757 reproduces a sapphire intaglio depicting a bust of Alaric II, King of Visigoths (484–507) to the front in a military garb. This magnificent and extremely rare example of the Late Antique/early medieval glyptics was probably since 1574 in the collection of Graf Ulrich von Montfort, later in the Ambras collection and since 1784 it has been housed in the Kunsthistorisches Museum in Vienna (Zwierlein-Diehl 1991, no. 1732 – with more literature). The commentary to the drawing is very laconic, though, and concerns the name of the depicted king: '*ALARIC*'. Another example of a glyptic product from more or less the same epoch is Krakow No. 1759. It reproduces a gold ring engraved with a laureate bust of a Lombard aristocrat named Aufret in a military garb and with the right hand put on the heart to the front, dated to the 7th century AD. The image is decorated by milleting on the edges, and it has the inscription: cross AVF RET. It was found in 1726 in the central Italian town of Bagnoregnio in the ruins of the church of St. Peter, destroyed in an earthquake in 1695. It passed to the local bishop Onofrio Pini (1721–1754) and was

the realm of ancient Greece and Rome have commentaries nearly entirely about their iconography and its potential meaning.[156] Projection of individual styles and highlight of some distinctive features is, generally, not observed neither. No separation between Archaic and Classical Greek (Figs 11.15–11.18) and Roman gems (Figs 11.19–11.25) on the drawings was certainly because the first were largely underrepresented in Stosch's collection of originals, as were the Hellenistic intaglios and cameos. Hence, there was little chance for Stosch and his collaborators to notice the differences between them.[157] However, there are some exceptions proving ongoing reflection on the differences between the Greek and Roman art. For example, Krakow No. 1033 depicting a lost Hellenistic intaglio (Fig. 11.26) is described as follows: 'Tete d'Heracle, coeffé d'une pau de Lion. C'est une des plus belles pierres de l'antiquité. L'idée de la beauté et l'execution de l'ouvrage sont egalement parfaits.' Even though there is no precise reference to the Greek or Roman character of the piece, the aesthetic qualities are clearly praised and those were done in favour of Greek pieces. As a result, even more interesting is the recalled passage from *Deiphnosophistai* by Athenaios of Naucratis, given in Greek and Latin: 'Τότε γαρ οι παϊδες εισι καλοι, ως Γλυκερα εφασκεν η εταιρα, οσον εοικασι γυναικι χρονον / Tum enim formosi pueri sunt ... cum sunt feminae similes.'[158] Despite the fact that Athenaios of Naucratis was a Greek rhetorician and grammarian of the 2nd century AD, the selection of a passage which is a reference to the ideal male beauty having some of the female character is typical for the Greek concept of art rather than the Roman one. The same passage from Athenaios is recalled in the commentary to the Hellenistic carnelian in Stosch's collection depicting the bust of Heracles (Krakow No. 1056) by Winckelmann. Considering the fact that he used the drawings as a scholarly aid in his preparation of the catalogue of Stosch's gems, could some of the texts accompanying them have been inspirational for him? Moreover, should one consider a possibility that the Greek art was praised more in the circle of Stosch than the Roman one which could inspire Winckelmann to forge his concepts regarding the development of ancient art and his own evaluations?

It is noteworthy that in the catalogue of Stosch's collection of engraved gems written by Winckelmann there are also very few (compared to the number of all Stosch's gems) examples where chronology, whether Etruscan, Greek or else are concerned, is somehow described or at least indicated. The list of such cases excerpted from the catalogue by Zazoff and Zazoff demonstrates very similar and brief descriptions to the ones appearing under the gem drawings discussed above.[159] Moreover, Winckelmann makes virtually no clear differentiation between Greek and Roman objects but the mass of more than 3000 of gems and glass pastes is organised according to the subject matter, like Stosch's gem drawings. This is due to the fact that as mentioned above, the organisation of Winckelmann's catalogue closely follows the one created by Stosch earlier. In the preface to the catalogue, Winckelmann himself implies that he wanted to add an aesthetic and historical dimension to Stosch's rather antiquarian approach towards gems.[160] Nevertheless, as Justi

---

later purchased from him by Alessandro Gregorio Capponi, who resided in Rome. It is believed that it joined the collection of the Museo Kircheriano in Rome after Capponi's death in 1746. From there, the ring went into the Vatican collections. In 1857, it was presented to the British collector and aesthete Edmund Waterton whose collection of engraved gems and rings was sold to the Victoria & Albert Museum in London (Ubaldelli 2001, no. 64 (with full bibliography); Gannon 2012). According to the commentary to the drawing, this piece depicts: 'UN ROY GOTS'. Among the drawings from Krakow, there are no more examples that could be suggestive of Stosch or his collaborators distinguishing a separate class of early Christian gems and even the two examples evoked here are not explicit enough to support such a claim.

156 This is typical for the period, see: Burke 2003, pp. 291–292.
157 One notices only a few examples of original Greek gems and glass pastes made after Greek gems (13 in total), such as: Winckelmann 1760, class II, nos 184, 477, 479, 543–544, 547, 731 and 958 and class III, nos 35, 37, 177–178 and 191. Hellenistic gems in Stosch's own collection or glass pastes made after such are the following (51 in total): Winckelmann 1760, class I, nos 20, 37–38, class II, nos 21, 48, 97, 128, 230–231, 357, 446, 461, 538, 541, 563, 710, 718, 1104, 1278, 1440–1442, 1462, 1679, 1771, class III, nos 70, 107–112, class IV, nos 21, 25–40, 47 and class VI, nos 123, 191. Zazoff and Zazoff (1983, p. 92) also notice that Greek gems started to appear in the European collections more frequently only in the nineteenth century.
158 Athen. 13,605d.

159 Please compare them with the list created by Zazoff and Zazoff 1983, pp. 85–99.
160 Winckelmann 1760, pp. IX–X. According to a letter from Winckelmann to Giovanni Lodovico Bianconi (1717–1781), dated Florence, 30 September 1758, Winckelmann wanted to comment on these aspects because even though though the collection was going to be sold, the catalogue could be still consulted with the collection of Stosch's gem impressions: '*Io sto qui alloggiato in casa del Sig^re de Stosch con tutto il comodo e in mezzo de' suoi tesori superiori al grado d'un privato. Ho dato mano, all'istanze di questo Sig^re, ad un catalogo degli'Intagli suoi, ma volendo evitare la secchezza d'un Semplice Indice e farvi qualche rifflessione intorno all'Arte, al disegno e all'Antichità, mi sono ingolfato in un mare dove non mi mancherà per lungo tratto acqua da navigare. Le pietre stanno per vendersi come le altre raccolte: ma il Catalogo può essere proseguito sopra gli impronti e i Solfi.*' (Winckelmann 1961, p. 112, no. 34).

rightly pointed out, in fact, Winckelmann's merits in this matter are a disappointment because he usually only suggests that some gems are cut in the fine manner and he rarely delivers more extensive comments on the style, techniques and artistic virtuosity.[161] Actually, this happens only when he writes about exceptional gems like the *Gemma Stosch* or the Tydeus scarab – both masterpieces of Etruscan glyptics, which in the eyes of Winckelmann could compete with the best Greek works.[162]

In conclusion, the gem drawings from Stosch's corpus confirm that his organisation of glyptics was governed by the antiquarian principle of subject matter as a determinative of cultural affiliation and subsequently chronology.[163] Only individual gems have their chronology discussed, which demonstrates first attempts to determine their dates. This is also slightly later practiced by Winckelmann, who was apparently inspired by Stosch. The discovered materials bring to the table plenty of new information about Stosch's strategies towards collecting and studying ancient engraved gems. It demonstrates his encyclopaedic approach, since there was no category of gems and seals that he was uninterested or had a preference for. The encyclopaedic classification that was applied by Stosch for his collections of gems and their reproductions whether impressions or drawings reflects one of the two fundamental approaches to the ancient history and material culture in the European Enlightenment – antiquarianism with elements of proto-archaeology.[164] The main criterion for organisation of the collections was subject matter, but, for example, as far as it can be judged, although Stosch and his collaborators seem to have evoked ancient literary sources while describing gem drawings, they do so only when it is indeed useful rather than to find justification for interpretation of the engraved gem like was the habit among the antiquarians at the time.[165] Furthermore, it is worthy to recall that Stosch's book, *Gemmae antiquae caelatae*, has an explanatory preface and then the gems are commented on individually and they are organised in an alphabetical order, not chronologically. This was probably because at that point Stosch could only say whether the gem was ancient or modern and the aim was also to reflect the original designs as accurately as possible and to show that each engraver had his individual style of engraving.[166] Ultimately, one may say that the individualism of the engravers ruled out the organisation of the book, which was a completely innovative approach. Finally, Stosch seems to be more of a practical man, particularly effective in collecting, managing and studying of gems rather than writing erudite dissertations on them by himself. After all, it is widely supposed that the entries in the *Gemmae antiquae caelatae* book were ghost-written by Francesco Valesio.[167]

Stosch's obsessive need to document everything he could put his own hands on resulted in accumulation of a substantial number of visual reproductions of gems, out of which, at least some originally had commentaries originating from his close circle (his own, his brother Heinrich Sigismund, the draughtsmen working for him and Joannon de Saint Laurent, at least). They testify that various dimensions of gems were discussed, including their chronology. They were later used by Winckelmann while writing the catalogue of Stosch's collection of gems alongside his original inventory list. Apparently, both helped him to publish Stosch's collection of original gems considerably, notably by providing categorisation of gems and structure of the whole collection. Certainly, the much-added value of gem drawings was their very high accuracy and faithfulness with the originals, which allowed Winckelmann to evaluate individual pieces. The much-enlarged images made recognition of the depicted scenes and consequently writing the catalogue easier and faster.[168] As far as chronology, techniques and styles are concerned, the drawings and their commentaries confirm that there was little information to be had directly from Stosch. He would share his knowledge during discussions with visitors of his house and through correspondence with other representatives of the *Republic of Letters*. A good example of that is his

---

161 Justi said that the classification of the gems in Stosch collection as well as explanations of their devices were entirely by Stosch himself and he assumed that Winckelmann based considerable parts of his text on Stosch's original catalogue, see: Justi 1956, vol. II, pp. 307–309. For a discussion on the structure of the catalogue of Stosch's gem collection written by Winckelmann, see: Lang 2017, pp. 206–207.

162 Zazoff and Zazoff 1983, pp. 85–99; Harloe 2013, pp. 80–86.

163 Rügler in Winckelmann 2013, pp. XIII–XIV; Hansson 2014, p. 21.

164 Jenkins 2003, p. 174.

165 Schnapp 2002, p. 55.

166 Stosch 1724, p. v. These ideas are also expressed by Stosch in his letter to Gijsbert Cuper dated 8 August 1716 – Koninklijke Bibliotheek, The Hague, inv. 72H25 (quoted in Heringa 1976, p. 77. n. 41).

167 On this issue, cf. Chapter 9 here and Reinach 1895, p. 156; Engelmann 1908, p. 333, n. 2; Heringa 1976, pp. 82–83; Zazoff and Zazoff 1983, pp. 11–13; Dorati da Empoli 2008, p. 69, n. 68; Ridley 2015, p. 79; Hansson 2014, p. 20.

168 In his letter to Antonio Baldani, dated 26–30 September 1758, Winckelmann appreciates enlarged images of Stosch's gems he found on the drawings from his *Paper Museum*: 'Non ho altri amminicoli per schiarirmi e facilitarmi il lavoro che i disegni fatti in grande, ma senza veruna spiegazione.' (Winckelmann 1961, p. 105, no. 31).

detailed discussion of the famous *Gemma Stosch* in his letter to Giuseppe Biancini.[169]

The corpus of gem drawings, most likely to some extent, compensates for the lost inventory of Stosch's collection of gems, which must have included similar loads of information.[170] Justi said that the classification of the gems in Stosch's collection as well as explanations of their devices were entirely by Stosch himself and he assumed that Winckelmann based considerable parts of his own text on Stosch's original catalogue.[171] This cannot be now completely verified; however, from the rediscovered gem drawings, it is deduced that Stosch and his collaborators clearly distinguished major classes of gems like the 'Egyptian', 'Persian', 'Etruscan' and 'Graeco-Roman' ones, but only occasionally commented on peculiarities of individual pieces. They had much more to offer as far as determination of the gemstones used, provenance, interpretation of iconography was concerned using suitable passages from literary sources, according to the humanist method much in the antiquarian vein of the epoch. All of this helps to better understand and appreciate Winckelmann's contribution to the catalogue of Stosch's collection of gems published in 1760.

The discovered archival and visual resources allow to contextualise Stosch within the circles of antiquarians, collectors and connoisseurs of antiquities and early archaeologists of the second half of the seventeenth and the first half of the eighteenth century. The interactions between Stosch and his wide network of contacts were greatly inspirational, and overall they resulted in regarding collections no longer as just accumulations of remains of the Classical World, but as opportunities to explore and penetrate it. Activities of antiquaries resulted in the elaboration of social behaviours and production of tools for

such exploration.[172] One of them was drawings and book illustrations, as already remarked, habitually criticised for their inaccuracy. Stosch's empirical, direct contact with objects of his studies (engraved gems) combined with his attempts to make their drawings as faithful to the originals as possible, made the drawings platforms transmitting a specific amount of information about the objects, not (only) making them pieces of art *per se*. In such a vein, Stosch followed other antiquarians who progressed with observation of antiquities through careful examination of their visual potential, e.g. what they represented. Whether these were coins, inscriptions or gems did not matter since the most important aspect of study was to inquire about the meaning of the analysed objects, and subsequently explain their use and function and date. This change had occurred already in the second half of the seventeenth century because of application of the philological model, which turned discovered and collected artifacts into instruments of a serious archaeological analysis.[173]

Stosch's collecting and documenting activities are particularly valuable for the research on the development of proto-archaeology because they reflect that the dichotomy between the antiquarian approach largely based on the traditional, philological and literate principles reflected in the order of his collection of gems and his gem drawings, and the new more scientific, archaeological one, including attempts towards systematisation and creation of typologies of his own gems and the documented ones was, in his case, an illusion.[174] Assuming that at least a portion of the commentaries by Czartoryska copy the texts originating from Stosch's circle, it can be said that in this case antiquarian research was closely tied to philological and historical scholarship. This is supported, for example, by Stosch's suggestion in his book, *Gemmae antiquae caelatae*, that an emerald intaglio in a Dutch collection reproduced the famous statue of Apollo Sauroctonos by Praxiteles, known only from its description by Pliny the Elder.[175] The character of this comment is essentially philological and applied to a non-literary object of ancient art – a gem. Therefore, in spite of Momigliano's theory about the antiquarian dichotomy, Stosch, like Cassiano dal Pozzo a century earlier, is an example combining various approaches to ancient art together, including the

---

169　Justi 1871, p. 30, no. XVI – letter from Stosch to Giuseppe Bianchini dated Florence 18 December 1756. It is also clear from some correspondence of Winckelmann that Stosch was an authority on antiquities in general and some of his theories and interpretations of pieces of ancient art were widely circulating through correspondence which did not survive, like his interpretation of the so-called Belvedere Antinous statue as depicting the god Mercury or the Borghese Gladiator, which he took as a Discobolous, or the statue of Papirius and his mother now in the Museo Nazionale Romano in Rome, which Stosch interpreted as Andromache and Astyonax or the famous marble of Cleopatra now in the Vatican Museums, which he considered to be Semele, see: Winckelmann 1952–1957, vol. I, pp. 254–256, no. 164a.

170　On the lost inventory of Stosch's gems, cf. Chapter 8 here and: Rügler in Winckelmann 2013, p. XVII; Hansson 2014, p. 27.

171　Justi 1871, p. 3; Justi 1956, vol. II, pp. 289 and 307–309. This view has since been accepted by scholars almost without much reflection, see: Cristofani 1981, p. 24; Zazoff and Zazoff 1983, p. 78; Tassinari 2010b, p. 93; Anderson 2015, p. 104; Lang 2017, p. 207.

172　Momigliano 1950, pp. 285–287; Schnapp 1997, pp. 179–181.
173　Schnapp 1997, pp. 180–185.
174　Such a dichotomy was observed by Momigliano (1950, pp. 286–287) in his general observation of activities of antiquarians.
175　Stosch 1724, pp. XVIII–XIX; Pliny the Elder, *Historia Naturalis*, XXXIV.69–70.

application of more scientific methods.[176] Together with his draughtsmen, Stosch documented a vast number of gems, partially for his studies and book projects as discussed in previous chapters, but it is clear that this was done without making much of a selection to the material as far as chronology and cultural affiliation were concerned. Moreover, from the lecture of the above-mentioned commentaries, one notices that Stosch and his circle did not repeat the mistake of Bianchini, who often confused images with symbols and symbols with causes. Stosch mastered what Schnapp calls comparative iconography, a necessary branch of archaeology, which was primarily concerned with images and their collecting as well as correct reading and interpretation.[177]

4   Opening a New Era for Glyptic Studies, Archaeology and Ancient Art History

Stosch's broad interest in engraved gems and critical examination of his collecting, documenting and scholarly activities prove him to be the most influential figure in the first half of the eighteenth century, contributing to the outburst of real glyptomania around the 1750s and 1760s. This is observed on several levels, for example, due to his largely influential book as outlined above, his considerable influence as a well-connected dealer and agent, his cooperation with neo-classical gem engravers and his profound impact on the career of Christian Dehn and subsequently production of *dactyliothecae* in general.[178] However, the most profound influence was made through his collection of original gems and accumulated impressions, casts as well as drawings of intaglios, cameos, scarabs and seals. Stosch's collecting and documentary activities represent the first, although in some respects tentative, attempts at a focused, systematic exploration of ancient glyptic art in a modern, scholarly sense.[179]

For a long time, archaeologists consider Winckelmann the founding father of modern archaeology and ancient art history, and the achievements of antiquarians and scholars from the Baroque epoch like Cassiano dal Pozzo, Francesco Bianchini, Paolo Alessandro Maffei, Anton Francesco Gori and Philipp von Stosch were largely ignored.[180] Stosch's various activities paved the way for others, notably Winckelmann, to write on ancient art in a holistic way. His legacy endured long after his death and it provided essential elements for the construction of modern archaeological and art historical science, notably as far as attribution of cultural affiliation and ordering chronology of antiquities (engraved gems in particular) are concerned. Stosch's unprecedented accumulation of engraved gems and their visual documentation delivered mass evidence for different approaches to art by ancient Egyptians, 'Persians', Etruscans, Greeks and Romans. The wide availability of various collections in his *Museo* in Florence as well as his far-reaching correspondence significantly contributed to the spread of knowledge about Antiquity and had inspired others to include engraved gems to their studies.

For example, there was a rapid development of the research on 'Persian' art and the Near Eastern seals resulting in incorporation of 'Persian' gems into the path of development of gem engraving by Pierre-Jean Mariette and Comte de Caylus around the middle of the eighteenth century.[181] Pierre-Jean Mariette's exemplary *Traité des pierres gravées* in two volumes discussed the history of gem engraving and the French royal collection of intaglios and cameos and included a section on the

---

176   Herklotz 1999, pp. 285–286.
177   On comparative iconography and its usefulness for early archaeological research, see: Schnapp 1997, pp. 182–188.
178   Hansson 2021a, p. 119. According to a letter from François Hemsterhuis to Adelheid Amalia von Schmettau, sent from The Hague on 28 September 1783 Stosch's sulphur gem impressions were of exceptional quality and Stosch was credited to contribute greatly to the development of production of *dactyliothecae* in the eighteenth century, see: FINA Wiki Database (ID 8801), https://fina.oeaw.ac.at/wiki/index.php/François_Hemsterhuis_-_Adelheid_Amalia_von_Schmettau_-_1783-9-28 [retrieved on 15 August 2022]; Sluis 2010, pp. 174–176, letter 4/68.
179   Hansson 2014, p. 30. This is especially clear once Stosch's studies are compared to those of his predecessors, on which see: Zazoff and Zazoff 1983, pp. 30–48.
180   For example, Sichtermann 1996. Also, such studies like Glyn 1981 and Haskell and Penny 1981, pp. 101–107 pay insufficient attention to the role of antiquarians in the evolution of archaeological science crediting solely Winckelmann as the author of groundbreaking innovations. More recent work of Décultot (2012) tentatively mentions studies of antiquarians only to draw a contrast between them and Winckelmann. Herklotz (1999 especially pp. 298–306) with his detailed study of the Cassiano dal Pozzo case, proves that antiquarians from the Renaissance to the Baroque epoch had a fundamental impact on the development of modern archaeology. Slightly before him, Schnapp (1997, pp. 179–221 and 260) also notices their profound contribution, although he clearly separates the approach of the Renaissance enthusiasts of Antiquity from later antiquarians of the second half of the seventieth and eighteenth century. See also a more general overview of this problem in: Kaufmann 2001, especially pp. 523–525 – with an extensive list of publications devoted to Winckelmann and his significant contribution to the development of modern archaeology and art history (note 3) as well as a list of publications cultivating the myth of Winckelmann's sole foundation of modern archaeology (note 4).
181   Smentek 2014, pp. 191–243; Eppihimer 2015, pp. 5–13.

'Persian' gems.[182] Caylus, who certainly exchanged letters and apparently also drawings of gems with Stosch, tried to organise the remains of Antiquity into a logical order in a broader sense in his monumental study *Recueil d'antiquités égyptiennes, étrusques, grecques et romaines* and in his case engraved gems played a significant role too.[183] He proposed the new approach towards the 'Persian' and 'Egyptian' gems seen as a cross-development of Persian and Egyptian art during the Persian rule over Egypt.[184] Both Mariette and Caylus in the 1750s attempted to change the emphasis of studying classical societies from literary sources to ancient art and products of craftsmanship.[185] They possessed small collections of engraved gems themselves, and, very much like Stosch, they had a lot of appreciation for them, seeing in the images engraved upon them lost sculptures and paintings of Antiquity, among others.[186]

The phenomenon of Stosch and later also Mariette and Caylus was that they considerably changed the traditional antiquarian approach towards gems, focusing less on iconography and offering more empirical and scientific analyses in contrast, for instance, to Bernard de Montfaucon or Anton Francesco Gori, who, as late as 1767, while publishing *Dactyliotheca Smithiana*, still used the philological method when describing the gems and referring to the passages from Ovid, Vergil and Suetonius.[187] This was also a somewhat different approach than the one later offered by Winckelmann, who concentrated on style as the most important aspect of ancient art.[188] Stosch and his meticulous studies of vast numbers of gems that he evidently attempted to group seem particularly close to the methodologies of Caylus and had an impact on Anton Francesco Gori.[189] His empirical direct contact with objects combined with attempts to make their drawings as faithful to the originals as possible is also similar to what Caylus did a bit later.[190]

Despite some criticism from contemporaries (including Mariette, cf. above), Stosch's particular attention and care on how to represent gems in the most faithful and accurate way in his book, *Gemmae antiquae caelatae*, and gem drawings corpus is undeniable. As discussed in Chapter 8, the standards in which gems were documented by the draughtsmen working for him and the surviving commentaries, which almost certainly originate from his circle, despite still heavy use of ancient literary sources for explanation of specific motifs appearing on gems (accordingly to the philological method popular among the antiquarians of the seventeenth and early eighteenth century) also connected gems with coins, sculpture, wall paintings etc. All of this is a sign of taking the study of intaglios and cameos to a new level. One may still be dissatisfied that Stosch's chronological system relied more on the iconography rather than technique and style. However, much of Stosch's original ideas and 'knowledge' were probably never preserved in written form or have been lost (for example, the inventory of his gems). Thus, it is beyond any power today to get a full picture of his accomplishments for the development of antiquarianism and modern archaeology. In addition, Smentek proposes an interesting viewpoint that Stosch and Picart decided not to elaborate too much on styles and techniques but focused on iconography because this was expected from the market. It was safer to publish erudite commentaries with evocation of ancient literary sources because this would guarantee success in the book's sale.[191] Indeed, one should take into account such possibilities as well given the fact that in the case of numismatics, where dating of coins was much easier than gems, the issue of quality, e.g. technological advancement and artistic style, was rarely discussed too.[192]

In any case, as far as techniques and styles are concerned, Mariette offered more in his *Traité* as his entries and commentaries as well as the text of the first volume were, to a considerable degree, focused on stylistic and technical aspects of intaglios. For example, Mariette

---

182   Mariette 1750; Zazoff and Zazoff 1983, pp. 127–128; Harloe 2013, p. 78; Smentek 2014, pp. 192 and 195–199.
183   On Caylus contributions to antiquarianism, see: Haskell 1993, pp. 180–186.
184   On Caylus views on this matter see: Eppihimer 2015, pp. 6–13. On Caylus and his contribution to the gem studies in general, see: Zazoff and Zazoff 1983, pp. 130–131.
185   Haskell 1993, pp. 180–186; Pomian 2002; Harloe 2013, pp. 78 and 109–110; Smentek 2014, pp. 199–200; Lang 2017, p. 202.
186   Smentek 2014, pp. 200–201. It is noteworthy that Stosch himself also expresses usefulness of gems in this matter in the preface to his book *Gemmae antiquae caelatae* (1724, p. XIX).
187   Haskell and Penny 1981, pp. 43–45. On Caylus' and Mariette's contribution to the development of antiquarianism and proto-archaelogy, see: Haskell 1993, pp. 180–186; Pomian 2002; Lang 2017, p. 202. On Gori and his traditional approach, see: Gori 1767; Kagan 2006, p. 88.
188   Lang 2017, p. 207. On the difference in the approach to ancient art between Caylus and Winckelmann, see: Haskell and Penny 1981, pp. 104–105; Schnapp 2002, pp. 53–54. See also an extensive commentary to Winckelmann's application of style as a category of art historical analysis in Harloe 2013, pp. 108–111 and 121–122.

189   Micheli 1986, pp. 40–41; Kagan 2006, p. 83.
190   Caylus 1752–1767, vol. I, p. 121. On Caylus' similar approach, see: Haskell 1993, pp. 180–186; Schnapp 1997, p. 280; Schnapp 2002, p. 54.
191   Smentek 2014, pp. 204–205.
192   On this issue, see: Haskell 1993, pp. 112–113.

was the first to propose that glyptic art started around 1200 BC in Greece and reached its climax in the Hellenistic period.[193] He also pointed out that regional styles existed and showed differences between Greek and Roman gems. However, it should be recalled that, at the same time, Mariette organised his book according to the subject matter criteria, although he complains that this was against his own intentions.[194] Also, as already remarked, the illustrations in his book were heavily criticised, for instance by Étienne-Maurice Falconet,[195] which brings us to the conclusion that the role of faithful illustrations was instrumental for those aspects of ancient art at the time, and in that respect Stosch was unbeatable.

The fundamental change in the approach to engraved gems and ancient art in general came in only with Winckelmann, and there is no point in denying that.[196] However, as rightly raised by Kaufmann, one should not ignore the accomplishments of his predecessors – the antiquarians, including Stosch.[197] Winckelmann was a direct benefactor of Stosch's legacy, whether in terms of his collections or intellectual spirit. Stosch had great influence on Winckelmann's early career due to his recommendation to Cardinal Alessandro Albani, but as the young German scholar admits he benefited immensely while writing a catalogue of Stosch's gems from the collector's own inventory and various archives, including gem drawings, he amassed.[198] As mentioned above, although Winckelmann thought necessary to improve Stosch's organisation system, ultimately he left it untouched.[199] He also considered his ideas conservative and many times he claimed that because of that he avoided writing what Stosch had already written about specific gems, presenting his own innovative commentaries.[200] From his correspondence, one also learns that he indeed sometimes profoundly disagreed with Stosch about such critical issues as antiquity of some signatures on gems.[201] Stosch's *Paper Museum of Gems* proves that as far as the visual and descriptive aspects of studying of engraved gems are concerned, Stosch made a major advancement in comparison to his predecessors and contemporaries, but as far as the chronology and general reconstruction of the past are concerned, he was probably not particularly original. As a result, Winckelmann's criticism of Stosch is to some extent constructive, but one must keep in mind that it was a habit of the time to criticise previous publications and research to justify one's own, which Stosch did himself while preparing his book on ancient signed gems. Therefore, one supposes Winckelmann's criticism to be partially a justification of his own work on the catalogue of Stosch's gems as well, for which he wanted to be credited as a full author rather than editor.[202]

There is a heated debate on Winckelmann's contribution to the catalogue of Stosch's gems. Justi pointed out that in fact Winckelmann rarely wrote extensive comments on the style, techniques and artistic virtuosity of individual pieces from Stosch's collection.[203] Zazoff and Zazoff are of the same opinion.[204] Décullot and Harloe observe that only in very few cases, like the masterpiece Etruscan scarab depicting a meeting of Five out of Seven

---

193 Smentek 2014, p. 221.
194 Smentek 2014, p. 203.
195 Smentek 2014, pp. 203–204 and 207–210. Consequently, Caylus followed his example distinguishing a separate class of 'Galic antiquities' in his monumental study *Recueil d'antiquités égyptiennes, étrusques, grecques et romaines*, see a commentary to this issue in: Haskell 1993, p. 181; Schnapp 2002, pp. 62–63.
196 For a thorough discussion on Winckelmann's accomplishments, see, for example: Haskell 1993, pp. 218–224; Schnapp 1997, pp. 258–266.
197 Kaufmann 2001.
198 Winckelmann 1952–1957, vol. I, pp. 444–445, no. 262; Winckelmann 1961, p. 105, no. 31. The similarity between Stosch and Winckelmann not only in terms of their scientific accomplishments but also in the ways of life are often noticed, for instance, by Bodart (1976, p. 22) and Donato (2019). It should be also noted that Winckelmann collected engraved gems, although not on the same scale as Stosch, see: Neverov 1981.
199 His complaints in this respect are similar to those of Mariette regarding his book from 1750 – both sound to be overpowered, which, in fact, is probably nothing more than justification of their shortcomings in the matter of chronology of engraved gems or a reflection of high ambitions that could not have been fully realised yet.
200 For example, in a letter from Winckelmann to Hieronymus Dietrich Berendis, dated 5 February 1758, see: Winckelmann 1952–1957, vol. I, p. 330, no. 202; Décullot 2012, p. 169; Lang 2017, pp. 205–206.
201 A god example of that is Winckelmann's letter to Giovanni Lodovico Bianconi (1717–1781), dated Rome 17 April 1757, according to which he informed Cardinal Alessandro Albani that he did not accept Pyrgoteles' signature on the famous cameo with a bust of Phocion to be ancient despite the considerable fame this piece acquired over decades and the fact that Stosch thought otherwise, see: 'L'ultima volta ch'io ebbi l'onore di riverirlo, mi mostrò lui stesso le sue rarità e fra l'altre la famosa testa di Focione, intagliata, secondo l'iscrizione da Pirgotele. Gli eposi i miei dubbj intorno l'antichità della scrittura e non dubito punto di dichiararla per contrafatta non ostante la sua celebrità.' (Winckelmann 1961, p. 50, no. 6).
202 On Winckelmann's criticism of his predecessors in other aspects of history of art and archaeology, see: Kaufmann 2001, pp. 537–538. Even though Haskell and Penny believe that it was Winckelmann who first systematised engraved gems, which is untrue, as our research presented in this book demonstrates, they still call Winckelmann's work on the catalogue of Stosch's gems, indeed, quite rightly, an 'edition' (1981, p. 100).
203 Justi 1956, vol. II, pp. 307–308.
204 Zazoff and Zazoff 1983, pp. 82–83.

against Thebes, Winckelmann develops and fully presents his innovative ideas commenting the styles of gem engravers, while he describes the rest in the traditional antiquarian way – surely, as now can be more firmly said, reflecting what Stosch himself already thought about them.[205] Indeed, one supposes that the German scholar was often inspired by Stosch's earlier inventory because it is mentioned several times by him in the final version of his catalogue: class II, nos 534, 909 and 1768; class III, nos 226 and 247; class IV, nos 22, 26 and 83. However, an important observation is that in the case of the listed entries, it is Winckelmann who comments on style as an indicator of more or less ancient workmanship, not Stosch. Furtwängler believed that Winckelmann was not educated enough on gems, and therefore he could not improve Stosch's opinions. Moreover, according to him, Winckelmann's inferior understanding of glyptics, and thus the reliability of the earlier manuscript of Stosch (now we know this must have included gem drawings as well), is best proved by the fact that he was unable to separate many glass pastes from regular ancient intaglios and ancient glass gems within Stosch's assemblage, which were added to the core of the collection.[206] This view seems to be a bit far-fetched since from the early works of Winckelmann it is clear that he was familiar with the use of the objects of *minor arts* like coins, medals and engraved gems.[207] Moreover, assuming that Stosch's original inventory of his collection of gems consisted mostly of entries of a similar sort as the captions to the rediscovered gem drawings, much closer to the truth seems to be the judgement of Sénéchal, Pomian and Décultot, who think that even though Winckelmann's catalogue structure followed the one already created by Stosch himself, he still added much value to the gems' descriptions and analysis.[208] What is more, from Winckelmann's correspondence it is clear that Stosch was impressed by his innovative views on ancient art in general, which was necessary to deal with his gems. Otherwise, he would not have recommended him to Cardinal Alessandro Albani and designated him his 'spiritual heir' with the main goal of publishing his gems, apparently choosing him over Joannon de Saint Laurent.[209]

Naturally, there were other figures offering more advanced concepts, in fact closer to Winckelmann's own, on the development of ancient art, which probably also made a considerable impact on him.[210] For example, Mariette's vision of Greek art being superior to the Roman one was very much in the vein of Winckelmann's thinking.[211] Still, the work on Stosch's collection of gems, access to his extensive library and archives, including his *Paper Museum of Gems* was a decisive step in Winckelmann's career, paving the way to writing his synthesis of ancient art – *Geschichte der Kunst des Alterthums*. The catalogue of Stosch's gems was a testing ground for many of Winckelmann's theories.[212] It was published in 1760 in Florence, and it was initially not as well received as Winckelmann and Muzell-Stosch had hoped for. Most criticism concerned the lack of illustrations, and thus the usefulness of the book was questioned.[213] This criticism perfectly demonstrates the considerable importance of illustrations for the antiquarian and early archaeological scholarship at the time. Stosch's corpus of gem drawings, like the drawings and prints of antiquities assembled by Cassiano dal Pozzo among others, constitutes a lacking visual database that provides us with a significant tool for understanding the culture and intellectual concerns of a period, during which the foundations of our own scientific methods of research and classification were formed. By all means, Winckelmann's catalogue ought not to be disregarded due to the lack of illustrations. It was the first systematic catalogue of its kind, which was later much appreciated, in fact. This was because Winckelmann combined the traditional knowledge on gems (he applied Stosch's organisation system) with an antiquarian attitude (accurate descriptions) and presented his new reflections

---

205 Décultot 2012, pp. 178–179; Harloe 2013, pp. 80–84.
206 Furtwängler 1896, pp. V–VII; Furtwängler 1900, vol. III, pp. 416–417.
207 Zazoff and Zazoff 1983, pp. 80–81; Harloe 2013, p. 77.
208 Sénéchal 1986, pp. 174–176; Pomian 2000, pp. 36–37; Décultot 2012, pp. 178–184.
209 Zazoff and Zazoff 1983, pp. 63–65. Stosch's appreciation of Winckelmann clearly resonates, for example, in Winckelmann's

letter to Giovanni Lodovico Bianconi, dated Rome 17 April 1757: '*Il Sig^re Barone di Stosch à communicato a s.e. una mia lettera prolississima nella quale avevo io rifiutato una sua scritta a me dove mettea in un certo rango ricevuto da molti le Statue di primo ordine, da questa deriva la buona grazia di s.e. verso di me.*' (Winckelmann 1961, pp. 50–51, no. 6).
210 On this issue, see: Kaufmann 2001, pp. 526–541.
211 Zazoff and Zazoff 1983, pp. 127–128; Smentek 2014, pp. 221–227. This in turn shifted the balance in the approach to elaboration of collections of archaeological artifacts, a good example of which is Pierre-François Hugues d'Hancarville (1719–1805) and his study of Sir William Hamilton (1730–1803) ancient vases and antiquities – d'Hancarville 1766–1767. See also Haskell 1984 for a general discussion on d'Hancarvile and his combination of antiquarian and systematic approach to archaeological artefacts.
212 Hansson 2014, p. 30.
213 Zazoff and Zazoff 1983, pp. 76–77; Arbeid, Bruni and Iozzo 2016, pp. 133–134, no. 42; Lang 2017, p. 208.

on ancient art (technical and stylistic commentaries).[214] The overall positive reception of his catalogue was due to its firm basis in the traditional antiquarian vein practised by Stosch and others earlier, and this was also the case of his other writings.[215] Again, there is no need to deny Winckelmann's originality, but there is a need to properly acknowledge Philipp von Stosch and his accomplishments in collecting, documenting and research on engraved gems, now much better understood and visualised thanks to the discovery of his *Paper Museum of Gems*, as a decisive step in the formation of modern archaeological scholarship.

The classification system of gems created by Stosch and developed by Winckelmann was evidently well-received and proved quite influential for a long time. It became a model for other publications on gems, whether catalogues of original collections or *dactyliothecae*.[216] For example, Giuseppe Bencivenni Pelli (1729–1808), in his diary, stated that the catalogue of Stosch's gems written by Winckelmann became a source of inspiration in his cataloguing gems of the Uffizi Gallery in Florence.[217] Moreover, in 1827, Eduard Gerhard concluded that despite the many publications on gems following Winckelmann's catalogue, in fact, there had been little or no real progress in the glyptic studies since publication of Stosch's collection of gems.[218]

Only in the late nineteenth century did a series of Adolf Furtwängler's publications completely change the face of gem studies. This was in accordance with general shifts occurring in the first half of the nineteenth century, especially in Germany, where a new popular tool was invented – typology.[219] Furtwängler became a master of this new methodology, which he successfully applied to the study of a massive amount of ancient engraved gems. His approach to the study of glyptics was based on several crucial criteria: analysis of the gemstones (their forms, shapes, types, etc.), techniques of engravings and styles as well as archaeological context (if possible) and finally, iconography. Stosch's impact on these developments was still considerable, since his huge collection ended up in the Antikensammlung in Berlin, where it became a base for Furtwängler's studies; first his articles on the subject of gems signed by ancient masters (1888–1889), his catalogue of the gems housed there (1896) and finally his *opus magnum* entitled *Die antiken Gemmen: Geschichte der Steinschneidekunst im klassischen Altertum*. It can be said that Furtwängler was a more complete version of Stosch 150 years later because, very much like him, he started from re-evaluation of ancient signed gems and worked out the publication of a catalogue of the huge Berlin collection for which he was a keeper. Finally, basing his research on a thorough examination of the almost the whole corpus of gems preserved in public and private collections and those documented only as casts, etc., he presented a holistic study of ancient glyptics. One cannot escape the impression that he fully realised what Stosch also hoped for, but naturally at a much higher level of expertise basing his classification of gems on the qualities listed above. Furtwängler directly acknowledged his indebtedness to Stosch, and indeed Stosch should be credited for expansion from the Roman oriented collection (and study) to the one including also Egyptian, Near Eastern, Greek and Etruscan gems, even if their numbers were not considerable either in his own cabinet or among the impressions and casts, he made himself or procured from others, as well as the drawings he commissioned. But, above all, he should be appreciated the most for his unprecedented studies of glyptic art and noticing its great potential in delivering us insights into ancient politics, society, religion and daily life. Even though approached with new methodologies today, still ancient glyptics offers probably the most comprehensive visual record of Antiquity, which is the best illustrated, for example, by the large number of gems appearing in the series of *Lexicon Iconographicum Mythologiae Classicae*[220] and the more than 3000 gem drawings made for Stosch, collected and discussed in this book.

---

214 Décultot 2012, p. 167; Lang 2017, p. 207. For a thorough analysis of Winckelmann's catalogue of Stosch's gems, see: Zazoff and Zazoff 1983, pp. 78–134.
215 Schnapp 1997, p. 262; Kaufmann 2001, p. 541. For a more extensive critical reception of Winckelmann's contribution to the development of archaeology and ancient art history, see: Schnapp 1997, pp. 263–266.
216 Justi 1956, vol. II, pp. 306–307; Zazoff and Zazoff 1983, pp. 76–77 and 79; Herklotz 1999, p. 299; Hansson 2014, p. 29.
217 Florence, Biblioteca nazionale centrale, inv. no.: N.A. 1050, Efemeridi, II, III, 1775, c. 462r–462v, https://fina.oeaw.ac.at/wiki/index.php/Giuseppe_Bencivenni_Pelli_-_1775-5-14 [retrieved on 5 August 2022].
218 Gerhard 1827, p. 289.
219 On this issue, see: Schnapp 1997, pp. 275–324.

220 LIMC I–VIII and LIMC Supplement.

FIGURE 11.1

FIGURE 11.2

FIGURE 11.3

FIGURE 11.4

FIGURE 11.5

FIGURE 11.6

PLATE 98

FIGURE 11.7

FIGURE 11.8

FIGURE 11.9

FIGURE 11.10

FIGURE 11.11

FIGURE 11.12

FIGURE 11.13

FIGURE 11.14

PLATE 100

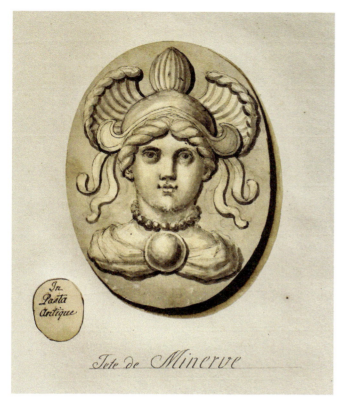

FIGURE 11.15

FIGURE 11.16

FIGURE 11.17

FIGURE 11.18

FIGURE 11.19

FIGURE 11.20

FIGURE 11.21

FIGURE 11.22

PLATE 102

FIGURE 11.23

FIGURE 11.24

FIGURE 11.25

FIGURE 11.26

Bibliography

Unpublished Material

Cortona, Biblioteca del Comune e dell'Accademia Etrusca (BCAE).
Florence, Archivio di Stato (ASF).
Florence, Biblioteca Nazionale Centrale (BNCF).
The Hague, Nationaal Archief (NA The Hague).
Kew, National Archives (NA Kew).
Rome, Biblioteca Hertziana (BH).
Vatican, Biblioteca Apostolica Vaticana (BAV).

Abbreviations

AGDS I.3   E. Brandt, W. Gercke, A. Krug and E. Schmidt 1972. *Antike Gemmen in deutschen Sammlungen Band 1 Staatliche Münzsammlung München. Teil 3. Gemmen und Glaspasten der römischen Kaiserzeit sowie Nachträge.* Munich: Prestel Verlag.

AGDS II   Zwierlein-Diehl E. 1969. *Antiken Gemmen in deutschen Sammlungen 2: Staatliche Museen Preußischer Kulturbesitz, Antikenabteilung Berlin.* Munich: Prestel Verlag.

AGDS IV Hannover   Schlüter, M., Platz-Horster, G. and Zazoff, P. 1975. *Antike Gemmen in deutschen Sammlugen 4, Kestner-Museum Hannover, Museum für Kunst und Gewerbe Hamburg.* Wiesbaden: Franz Steiner Verlag.

Auction Amsler and Ruthardt 1906   *Amsler & Ruthardt Kunstantiquariat Katalog LXXV (1906). Sammlung von Handzeichnungen und Aquarellen aus verschiedenen Hinterlassenschaften: alte Meister des XV. bis XVII. Jahrhunderts, Meister des Goethe-Jahrhunderts, darunter zahlreiche reizvolle Entwürfe in Aquarellfarben für Kupfer und Einbanddecken zu Taschenkalendern und Almanachen von Johann Heinrich Bamberg, Neuere Meister …, Ornamente, Städteansichten; Versteigerung zu Berlin, Donnerstag, den 22. November und folgende Tage.* Berlin.

Auction Fagel 1801   *The catalogue of all that perfect and beautiful assemblage of cabinet pictures, the property of the Greffiers Fagel: selected with infinite taste and judgement, brought from the Hague to England: which will be sold by auction by Peter Coxe, Burrell, and Foster at Mr. Squibb's Great Room, Saville Passge, Conduit Street, on Friday, the 22d of May, 1801, and following day, at one o'clock.* London.

Auction Max Perl 1937   *Graphik-Handbücher, Graphik des 15.–19. Jahrhunderts, Handzeichnungen, Städteansichten, japanische und chinesische Rollbilder und Farbenholzschnitte, Bücher des 15.–20. Jahrhunderts, Exlibris … 8. und 9. Juni 1937 (Katalog Nr. 197).* Berlin.

Auction Muzell-Stosch 1783   *Verzeichniss einer Sammlung hauptsächlich zu den Alterthümern, der Historie, den schönen Künsten u. Wissenschaften gehöriger mehrentheils italienischer, englischer und französischer Bücher: auch Landcharten, Zeichnungen, und Kupferstiche von berühmten Meistern, auch einiger Gemählde, imgl. einer Sammlung Schwefel-Abdrücke von antiken Gemmen &c. welche der verstorbene Herr Heinrich Wilhelm Muzel genamt Stosch Walton hinterlassen und am 22sten April 1783 und folgende Tage Nachnmittags von 2 bis 4 Uhr in der Wohnung des Verstorbenen an der Ecke der Linden-Allee und Kirchgasse, im Bastideschen Hause dem Meistbiethenden in öffentlicher Auction gegen baare Bezahlüngzugeschlagen werden sollen. Das Verzeichniss wird im Wachsmurhischen Hause bey dem Königl. Auctions Commissarius Herrn Böhme, Vormittags von 9 bis 11 Uhr gratis ausgegeben.* Berlin.

Auction Picart 1737   *Catalogue D'une belle Collection de Desseins, Parmi lesquels se trouvent tous les Desseins de Bernard Picart (...), Le tout laissé par la veuve du célèbre Bernard Picart.* Philippe Van Der Land, 25 November 1737 and following days. Amsterdam.

Auction Stosch I   *A catalogue of the genuine and curious collection of prints and drawings, of Baron Stosch of Italy, lately deceas'd; which, by order of the executor, who consign'd them from thence, will be sold by auction, by Mr. Langford, at his house in the Great Piazza, Covent-Garden, on Wednesday the 6th of this instant February 1760, and the three following evenings.* London.

Auction Stosch II   *A catalogue of the Genuine and Choice Collection of Pictures, of that Eminent Collector Baron Stosch of Italy, Lately Deceased; amongst which are the Works of the following Masters, viz. Carlo Dolci, Carlo Marratti, Luca Giordano, Tintoretto, Spagnolo di Bologna, Guercino, Bronzino, Gia. Brandi, Rubens, Brueghell, Jordaens, Zuccarelli [...] which will be sold, by auction by Mr. Langford, being consign'd to Him by the executor, at his house in the Great Piazza, Covent Garden, on Wednesday, the 12th of this Instant March 1760.* London.

Auction Stosch III   *A catalogue of the entire collection of bronzes, of the Palazzo Gaddi, Palazzo Marucelli, and the late eminent antiquary Baron Stosch; consisting of great variety of groupes, statues, busts, priapi, animals, basso and alto relievo's sacrificing vessels, instruments, &c. of Roman, Grecian, Etruscan and Egyptian workmanship; with some few modern bronzes of Mich. Anglo, Giov. di Bologna, Benv. Cellini, Fiamingo, Tacca, Algardi, and other celebrated masters. Which will be sold by auction, by Mr. Langford and Son, at their house in the Great Piaaza, Covent Garden, on Wednesday the 21st of this Instant March 1764, and the two following days.* London.

Auction Stosch IV   *A catalogue of the remainder of the bronzes, of the Palazzo Gaddi, Palazzo Marucelli, and the late eminent antiquary Baron Stosch, which had been mislaid; and which, with several Egyptian and other curious Antiquities; some valuable paintings in crayons and in oil; and a book of drawings in architecture, for publick buildings, by Raphael; will be sold by auction, by Mr. Langford and Son, at their House in the Great Piazza, Covent Garde, on Saturday the 24th of this Instant March 1764.* London.

Cades Grande   Cades, T. The 'Große Edition' preserved in the Deutsches Archaeologisches Institut in Rome.

Dehn/Dolce Vatican   Christian Dehn's Dactyliotheca, the edition preserved in the Biblioteca Apostolica Vaticana (Gbinetto di Medagliere) relevant to Dolce, F.M. 1772. *Descrizione Istorica Del Museo Di Cristiano Denh.* Rome.

Epistolario di Anton Francesco Gori   Online database of the Firenze University Press, Epistolario di Anton Francesco Gori (https://sol.unifi.it/gori/gori).

Lippert[1] I[1]   Lippert, Ph.D. 1755. *Dactyliotheca Universalis signorum exemplis nitidis redditae*, vol. 1, part 1, 1st ed. Leipzig.

Lippert[1] I[2]   Lippert, Ph.D. 1755. *Dactyliotheca Universalis signorum exemplis nitidis redditae*, vol. 1, part 2, 1st ed. Leipzig.

Lippert[1] III[2]   Lippert, Ph.D. 1762. *Dactyliotheca Universalis signorum exemplis nitidis redditae*, vol. III, part 2, 1st ed. Leipzig: Officina Breitkopfia.

Lippert[2] I   Lippert, Ph.D. 1767. *Dactyliotheca Universalis signorum exemplis nitidis redditae*, vol. I, 2nd ed. Leipzig: Officina Breitkopfia.

Lippert[2] II   Lippert, Ph.D. 1767. *Dactyliotheca Universalis signorum exemplis nitidis redditae*, vol. II, 2nd ed. Leipzig: Officina Breitkopfia.

Medina 1742   *Catalogo del prezioso museo di pietre intagliate e cammei appresso le signore de Medina in Livorno.* Livorno: con licenza de' Superiori.

Medina Sale 1761   *A Catalogue of the genuine and capital collection of Antique Gems of Signor De Medina, Late of Leghorn, Merchant, Deceased; Consisting of 125 Intaglias's and 100 Camaeo's, which he had, with great Care and Expence, been many Years collecting; most of which are richly set in Gold, several engraved by Mons.* MARRIETTE *of*

PARIS, and Mr. *NATTER*, and likewise particularly taken Notice of in their Books of Gems. Which (by Order of the Executors) Will be sold by *AUCTION* by Mr. *LANGFORD*, At his House in the Great Piazza, Covent Garden, on Tuesday the 10th of this Instant February 1761, and the Two following Days. London: Langford.

Rkps. 6097 II Izabela z Flemingów Czartoryska. Korespondencja rodzinna. Kopie listów Adama Jerzego Czartoryskiego do matki z l. 1789–1801. Przepisane przez Różę z Potockich Zamoyską w 1888 r. Archive of The Czartoryski Library (manuscript).

Rkps. 6285 II Adam Jerzy Czartoryski. Korespondencja rodzinna. Listy od Ojca Adama Kazimierza, vol. 1. Archive of The Czartoryski Library (manuscript).

Rkps. 6288/1 III Adam Jerzy Czartoryski. Korespondencja rodzinna. Listy do matki Izabeli, vol. 1. Archive of The Czartoryski Library (manuscript).

Rkps. 6070/3 III Izabela z Flemingów Czartoryska. Melanges pour la Maison Gothique, 1808–1820. Archive of The Czartoryski Library (manuscript).

Rkps 12154 Description of the Czartoryski Library in the Puławy Manor, ca. 1830. Archive of The Czartoryski Library (manuscript).

Rkps 12181 Catalogue of the Czartoryski Library in Puławy, vol. 10, ca. 1830. Archive of The Czartoryski Library (manuscript).

Rkps 12214 Catalogue of the Czartoryski Library in Puławy, vol. 43, ca. 1830. Archive of The Czartoryski Library (manuscript).

Rkps 12232 Index of the Czartoryski Library in Puławy, ca. 1830. Archive of The Czartoryski Library (manuscript).

RRC Crawford, M.H. 1974. *Roman Republican Coinage*. Cambridge: Cambridge University Press.

Vettori Vatican Set of gem impressions taken in red wax preserved in the Biblioteca Apostolica Vaticana (Gabinetto di Medagliere).

References

Aa, van der P. 1729. *La galerie agréable du monde, où l'on voit en un grand nombre de cartes très exactes et de belles tailles douces les principaux empires, roïaumes, républiques, provinces, villes, bourgs et forteresses … les îles, côtes rivières, ports de mer … les antiquitez, les abbayes, églises, académies … comme aussi les maisons de campagne, les habillemens et moeurs des peuples … dans les quatre parties de l'univers. Divisée en LXVI tomes, les estampes aiant été dessinées sur les lieux et gravées exactement par les célèbres Luyken, Mulder, Goerée, Baptist, Stopendaal et par d'autres maîtres renomez*. Leiden.

Adams, A.J. 2010. Reproduction and authencity in Bernard Picart's *Impostures Innocentes*, in: L. Hunt, M.C. Jacob and W.W. Mijnhardt (eds), *Bernard Picart and the First Global Vision of Religion*. (Issues & Debates), 75–104. Los Angeles: Getty Research Institution.

Adhémar, J. 1953. *David. Naissance du génie d'un peintre*. Monaco: Raoul Solar.

Agostini, L. 1657. *Le gemme antiche figurate*, vol. I. Rome: appresso dell'autore.

Agostini, L. 1669. *Le gemme antiche figurate*, vol. II. Rome: appresso Michele Hercole.

Agostini, L. 1686. *Le gemme antiche figurate*. Rome: appresso Gio. Battista Bussotti.

Aleksandrowicz, A. 1998. *Izabela Czartoryska: Polskość i europejskość*. Lublin: Wydawnictwo Uniwersytetu Marii Curie-Skłodowskiej.

Alexander, J. 1994. *The Painted Page: Italian Renaissance Book Illumination, 1450–1550*. Munich and New York: Prestel Verlag.

Alteri, G. 1987. Le collezioni di calchi del Medaglieredella Biblioteca Apostolica Vaticana. *Miscellanea Bibliothecae Apostolicae Vaticanae* I: 7–32.

D'Ancona, P. 1914. *La miniatura fiorentina (secoli XI–XVI)*. Florence: Leo S. Olschki.

Anderson, J. 2015. *Reception of Ancient Art: the Cast Collections of the University of Tartu Art Museum in the Historical, Ideological and Academic Context of Europe (1803–1918)*. Tartu: University of Tartu Press.

Anon. 1664. *Nota delli musei, librerie, gallerie e ornamenti di statue e pitture ne' palazzi, nelle case e ne' giardini di Roma*. Rome: appresso Biagio Deuersin e Felice Cesaretti.

Anon. 1725. *New memoirs of literature …*, January 1725, vol. I, London 1725, article XLI: 282–283.

Anon. 1781. *Historischdiplomatisches Magazin für das Vaterland und angrenzende Region*, vol. 1. Nuremberg: Verlag der M.J. Bauerischen Buchhandlung.

Anon. 1791. Leben Herrn Schweikharts, berühmten Kupferstechers in Nürnberg. *Neue Bibliothek der schönen Wissenschaften und der freyen Künste* 42 (2): 250–255.

Arbeid, B., Bruni, S. and Iozzo, M. 2016. *Winckelmann, Firenze e gli Etruschi. Il padre dell'archeologia in Toscana. Catalogo della mostra Firenze, Museo Archeologico Nazionale 26 maggio 2016–30 gennaio 2017*. Florence: Edizioni ETS.

Arnold-Rutkiewicz, B. 2005. O kolekcji odlewów gemm w Zamku Królewskim w Warszawie. *Kronika Zamkowa* 1–2/49–50: 45–65.

Avisseau-Broustet, M. 2002. Madame de Pompadour et la glyptique, in: X. Salmon (ed.), *Madame de Pompadour et les arts*, 252–267. Versailles: Réunion des Musées Nationaux.

Aymonino, A. and Varick Lauder, A. (eds) 2015. *Drawn from the Antique: Artists & the Classical Ideal. An exhibition at Teylers Museum, Haarlem, 11 March–31 May 2015 and at the Sir John Soane's Museum, London, 25 June–26 September 2015*. London: Sir John Soane's Museum.

Babelon, E. 1894. *La gravure en pierres fines*. Paris: Alicide, Picard & Kaan.

Babelon, E. 1897. *Catalogue des camées antiques et modernes de la Bibliothèque Nationale*. Paris: Ernest Leroux éditeur.

Balbaa, N. 1968. Edmé Bouchardon, his work and catalogue raisonné. Unpublished Ph.D. dissertation, University of Oxford.

Baldi, E. 1960. *L'Alba. La prima loggia massonica a Firenze, l'Inquisizione, il processo Crudeli*. Firenze: Tip. B. Coppini & C.

Bandinelli, R. 1996. La formazione della dattilioteca di Antonio Maria Zanetti (1680–1767), in: M. Fano Santi (ed.), *Venezia, l'Archeologia e l'Europa, Atti del Congresso Internazionale (Venezia 27–30 giugno 1994)*, (Rivista di Archeologia, Supplementi 17), 59–65. Rome: G. Bretschneider.

Bandinelli, R. 2002. I due Zanetti ad Anton Francesco Gori. Lettere 170–181, in: A. Bettagno and M. Magrini (eds), *Lettere artistiche del Settecento veneziano vol. 1*, 343–370. Vicenza: Nera Pozzi Editore.

Barocchi, P. and Gallo, D. 1985. *L'Accademia etrusca*. Milan: Electa.

Bartelings, N. 2001. Bernard Picart Tempel der memorie, 1724, in: N. Bartelings, B. de Klerck, E.J. Sluijter and J. Schaeps (eds), *Uit het Leidse Prentenkabinet. Over tekeningen prenten en foto's, bij het afscheid van Anton Boschloo*, 91–94. Leiden: Primavera Press.

Barthélemy, J.-J. 1802 [1801]. *Voyage en Italie de M. l'Abbé Barthélemy*. Paris: F. Buisson.

Bartoli, P.S. and Galeotti, N. 1751–1752. *Museum Odescalcum*. Rome: ex typographia Sancti Ignatii. Excudebat Joannes Generosus Salomoni.

Bartolozzi, F. 1780–1791. *The Marlborough Gems: Gemmarum antiquarum delectus: ex praestantioribus desumptus, quae in dactyliothecis Ducis Marlburiensis conservantur*. London: n.p.

Bartolozzi, F. 1845. *The Marlborough Gems: Gemmarum antiquarum delectus: ex praestantioribus desumptus, quae in dactyliothecis Ducis Marlburiensis conservantur*. London: J. Murray.

Bartsch, von A. 1813. *Le peintre graveur*. Vol. XV. Vienna: J.V. Degen.

Bartsch, von A. 1818. *Le peintre graveur*. Vol. XVI. Vienna: J.V. Degen.

Battista, L. 1993. La collezione di gemme dell'abate Andreini. *Antichità Viva* XXXII: 53–60.

Baudelot de Dairval, Ch.C. 1717. *Lettre sur le prétendu Solon des pierres gravées. Explication d'une medaille d'or de la famille Cornuficia*. Paris: chez Jean-Baptiste Lamesle.

Bean, J. and Griswold, W. 1990. *Eighteenth-Century Italian Drawings in the Metropolitan Museum of Art*. New York: Metropolitan Museum of Art.

Beaurepaire, P.-Y. 2019. *Les Lumières et le Monde. Voyager, explorer, collectionner*. Paris: Belin.

Beger, L. 1696–1701. *Thesaurus Brandenburgicus Selectus, Sive, Gemmarum et Numismatum Graecorum in Cimeliarchio Electoraii Brandenburgico*. 3 vols, Coloniae Marchicae: Ulricus Liebpert.

Berti, L. (ed.) 1979. *Gli Uffizi. Catalogo Generale*. Florence: Centro Di.

Betlej, A. 2021. Kolekcja Czartoryskich w Puławach. Wokół genezy – między tradycją a przyszłością, in: K. Płonka-Bałus and N. Koziara (eds), *Muzeum Książąt Czartoryskich*, 7–11. Kraków: Muzeum Narodowe.

Bettagno, A. 2001. Una vicenda tra collezionisti e conoscitori: Zanetti, Mariette, Denon, Duchesne, in: *Mélanges en hommage à Pierre Rosenberg: peintures et dessins en France et en Italie, XVIIe–XVIIIe siècles*, 82–86. Paris: Editions de la Reunion des musees nationaux.

Bianchini, F. 1697. *La Istoria Universale provata con monumenti e figurate con simboli degli antichi*. Rome: Antonio de Rossi.

Bickendorf, G. 1998. *Die Historisierung der italienischen Kunstbetrachtung im 17. und 18. Jahrhundert*. Berlin: Mann.

Birke, V. and Kertész, J. 1994. *Die italienischen Zeichnungen der Albertina, Band II: Inventar 1201–2400*. Vienna: Böhlau Verlag.

Blanc, J. Winckelmann et l'invention de la Grèce. *Cahiers 'Mondes anciens'* 11/2018, online.

Blunt, A. 1974. Newly identified drawings by Poussin and his followers. *Master Drawings* 12 (3): 239–248 and 295–319.

Blunt, A. 1979. Further newly identified drawings by Poussin and his followers. *Master Drawings* 17 (2): 119–146 and 173–190.

Blunt, A.F. and Schilling, E. 1971. *The German Drawings in the Collection of Her Majesty the Queen at Windsor Castle, and Supplement to the Catalogues of Italian and French Drawings with a History of the Royal Collection of Drawings*. London – New York: Phaidon.

Boardman, J. (ed.) 2002. *The Lewes House Collection of Ancient Gems by John D. Beazley, Student of Christ Church 1920*. (British Archaeological Reports IS 1074). London: Archaeopress.

Boardman, J. and Wagner, C. 2018. *Masterpieces in Miniature. Engraved Gems from Prehistory to the Present*. London: Philipp Wilson Publishers.

Boardman, J., Kagan, J. and Wagner, C. 2017. *Natter's Museum Britannicum. British gem collections and collectors of the mid-eighteenth century*. Oxford: Archaeopress.

Boardman, J., Scarisbrick, D., Wagner, C. and Zwierlein-Diehl, E. 2009. *The Marlborough gems formerly at Blenheim Palace, Oxfordshire*. Oxford: Oxford University Press.

Bodart, D. 1976. Pier Leone Ghezzi disegnatore. *Print Collector* 7 (31): 12–31.

Bogaert, A. 1697. *De Roomsche Monarchy, vertoont in de Muntbeelden der Westersche en Oostersche Keizeren; beginnende van Cesar, en eindigende met Leopoldus, den tegenwoordigen Roomschen Keizer: alle naer ae vermaarde Muntpenningen van haare Zweedsche Majesteit Christina to Rome getekent, en in't koper gesneden*, Utrecht: Francois Halma and Willem van de Water.

Bonfait, O. and Brugerolles, E. 2019. *Poussin, Géricault, Carpeaux ... à l'école de l'Antique* (Carnets d'études 47). Paris: ENSBA.

Borbein, A.H., Kunze, M. and Rügler, A. 2019. *Description des pierres gravées du feu Baron de Stosch. Kommentar*, vols 1–2. Mainz am Rhein: Philipp von Zabern.

Borchia, M. 2019. *Le reti della diplomazia: arte, antiquaria e politica nella corrispondenza di Alessandro Albani*. Provincia autonoma di Trento: Soprintendenza per i beni culturali. Ufficio beni archivistici, librari e Archivio provinciale.

Borioni, A. and Venuti, R. 1736. *Collectanea antiquitatum Romanarum: quas centum tabulis aeneis incisas et a Rodulphino Venuti Academico Etrusco Cortonensi notis illustratas exhibet Antonius Borioni*. Rome: Ex Typographia Rochi Bernabò.

Borroni, F. 1956. *I Due Antonio Maria Zanetti*. Florence: Sansoni.

Borroni Salvadori, F. 1978a. Tra la fine del Granducato e le reggenza: Filippo Stosch a Firenze. *Annali della Scuola Normale Superiore di Pisa. Classe di Lettere e Filosofia* III 8 (2): 565–614.

Borroni Salvadori, F. 1978b. Marcus Tuscher, artista norico fra la Toscana e Roma, in *Miscellanea di studi in memoria di Anna Saitta Revignas*, 85–118. Florence: L.S. Olschki.

Borroni Salvadori, F. 1982. Riprodurre in incisione per far conoscere dipinti e disegni: il Settecento a Firenze. *Nouvelles de la République des Lettres* I: 7–69.

Borroni Salvadori, F. 1983. Personaggi inglesi inseriti nella vita fiorentina del '700: Lady Walpole e il suo ambiente. *Mitteilungen des Kunsthistorischen Institutes zu Florenz* 27 (1): 83–124.

Bortoluzzi, V. 2014. Antonio Maria Zanetti e il ruolo di promotore della cultura artistica del suo tempo; I carteggi con l'elite fiorentina. Ph.D. diss. Universita' Ca'Foscari, Venice.

Bottari, G.G. 1757. *Raccolta di lettere sulla scultura, pittura ed architettura scritte da' più celebri personaggi dei secoli V, VI e VII secoli*. Vols I–VII. Rome: Appresso Niccolò e Marco Pagliarini.

Börner, L. 1997. *Die italienischen Medaillen der Renaissance und des Barock (1450–1750)*, (Berliner Numismatische Forschungen 5). Berlin: Gebr. Mann Verlag.

Bracci, D.A. 1784–1786. *Memorie degli antichi incisori che scolpirono i loro nomi in gemme e cammei con molti monumenti inediti di antichità statue bassorilievi gemme opera di Domenico Augusto Bracci della Società reale antiquaria di Londra*, vols I–II. Florence: Gaetano Cambiagi.

Breckenridge, J.D. 1979. Three Portrait Gems. *Gesta* 18 (1): 7–18.

Broglie, de E. 1891. *Bernard de Montfaucon et les Bernardins*, vol. I. Paris: E. Plon, Nourrit et Cie.

Brummel, L. 1925. *Frans Hemsterhuis. Een philosofenleven*. Haarlem: H.D. Tjeenk Willink.

Brunet, J.-C. 1810. *Manuel du libraire et de l'amateur de livres*, vol. II. Paris: Librarie Brunet.

Brunet, J.-C. 1863. *Manuel du libraire et de l'amateur de livres*, vol. IV. Paris: Librarie de Firmin Didot.

Bruni, S. 1998. Contuccio Contucci et le Museo Kircheriano, in: J. Raspi Serra and F. Polignac (eds), *La fascination de l'Antique 1700–1770. Rome découverte, Rome inventé*, 44–47. Paris: Somogy.

Bruschetti, C. 1984. Francesco Valesio erudito ed archeologo, in: G. Matezke, M.G. Marzi Costagli and L. Tamagno Perna (eds), *Studi di antichità in onore di Guglielmo Maetzke*, vol. 3: 601–607. Rome: Giorgio di Bretschneider.

Bruschetti, di P. 1985–1986. Gemme del Museo dell' Accademia Etrusca di Cortona. *Annali dell'Academia Etrusca di Cortona* 22: 7–70.

Bruschetti, di P., Giullerini, J.G., Reynolds, P. and Swaddling, S. 2014. *Seduzione etrusca. Dai segreti di Holkham Hall alle meraviglie del British Museum*. Milano: Skira.

Buonarroti, F. 1698. *Osservazioni istoriche sopra alcuni medaglioni antichi all'altezza serenissima di Cosimo III Granduca di Toscana*. Rome: Domenico Antonio Ercole in Parione.

Bull, M. 1997. Poussin and the Antique. *Gazette des Beaux-Arts* (March 1997): 115–130.

Burke, P. 2003. Images as evidence in seventeenth-century Europe. *Journal of the History of Ideas* 64 (2): 273–296.

Burnett, A. 2020. *'The Hidden Treasures of This Happy Island'. A History of Numismatics in Britain from the Renaissance to the Enlightenment*, (British Numismatic Society Special Publication 14/Royal Numismatic Society Special Publication 58), vols I–III. London: Spink.

Buttler, K. 2011. Die Sammlung italienischer Figurenzeichnungen von Friedrich Wilhelm vonErdmannsdorff. Zu ihrer Entstehung, Funktion und Provenienz aus den Sammlungen Bartolomeo Cavaceppis und Pier Leone Ghezzis. *Jahrbuch der Berliner Museen* 53: 73–97.

Cacciotti, B. 2001. Gli scavi di antichità del cardinale Alessandro Albani ad Anzio. *Bollettino dei Musei comunali di Roma*, N.S. 15: 25–60.

Callataÿ, F. de 2007. Winckelmann et les monnaies antiques. *Revue des études grecques* 120 (2): 553–601.

Campbell, I. and Nesselrath, A. 2006. The Codex Stosch: surveys of ancient buildings by Giovanni Battista da Sangallo. *Pegasus Berliner Beiträge zum Nachleben der Antike* 8: 9–90.

Camper, P. 1794. *The Works of the late Professor Camper, on the Connexion between the Science of Anatomy and the Arts of Drawing, Painting, Staturary, &c. &c.* (translated from the Dutch by T. Cogan). London: Charles Dilly.

Campinelli, M. 2021. *'Eja Age Dic Satyram'. La Musa Pedestre nel Bosco Parrasio*, (Il Bosco Parrasio 1). Rome: Accademia dell'Arcadia.

Canini, G.A. 1731. *Images des heros et des grands hommes de l'Antiquité*. Amsterdam: chez Bernard Picart.

Carpita, V. 2012. Pier Leone Ghezzi, Anton Francesco Gori e Francesco Vettori: un inedito progetto editoriale sulle lucerne antiche. *Symbolae Antiqvariae* 5: 107–132.

Casini, P. 1972. The Crudeli Affair. Inquisition and Reason of State, in: P. Gay (ed.), *Eighteenth-Century Studies Presented to Arthur M. Wilson*, 131–142. Hannover: University Press of New England.

Caylus, A.C.P. de 1752–1767. *Recueil d'antiquités égyptiennes, étrusques, grecques et romaines*, vols 1–7. Paris: Chez Desaint et Saillant.

Caylus, A.C.P. de and Bouchardon, E. 1737. *Suite de sujets dessinés d'après l'Antique par Edme Bouchardon sculpteur du Roy et gravés à l'eau forte par Mr le C. de C. Terminés au burin par J. P. LeBas graveur du Roy*. Paris: n.p.

Caylus, A.C.P. de 1775. *Recueil de trois cent tetes et sujets de composition graves par Mr. le Comte de Caylus d'apres les pierres gravees antiques du Cabinet du Roi*. Paris: n.p.

Cazort, M. and Percy, A. 2004. *Italian Master Drawings at the Philadelphia Museum of Art*. Philadelphia: Penn State University Press.

Chabouillet, A. 1858. *Catalogue général et raisonné des camées et pierres gravées de la Bibliothèque impériale: suivi de la description des autres monuments exposés dans le Cabinet des médailles et antiques*. Paris: Au Cabinet des médailles.

Champion, J.A.I. 2006. Enlightened Erudition and the Politics of Reading in John Toland's Circle. *The Historical Journal* 49 (1): 111–141.

Chapron, E. 2009. *'Ad utilità pubblica'. Politique des bibliothèques et pratiques du livre à Florence au XVIIIe siècle*, (École Pratique des Hautes Études Sciences Historiques et Philologiques 6). Paris: Droz.

Chennevières de Ph. and de A. Montaiglon (eds) 1859–1860. *Abecedario de P.J. Mariette: et autres notes inédites de cet amateur sur les arts et les artistes*. Paris: J.B. Dumoulin.

Chéron, E.S. 1728. *Pierres antiques gravées tirées des principaux cabinets de la France*. Paris.

Churchill, W.A. 1935. *Watermarks in Paper in Holland, England, France etc. in the XVII and XVIII centuries and their interconnection*. Amsterdam: Hes & De Graff.

Chłędowski, K. 1935. *Z przeszłości naszej i obcej*. Lwów: Ossolineum.

Chwalewnik, E. 1926. *Zbiory polskie: archiwa, bibljoteki, gabinety, galerje, muzea i inne zbiory pamiątek przeszłości w ojczyźnie i na obczyźnie*, vol. 1: A–M. Warszawa: J. Mortkowicz.

Cicognara, L. 1821. *Catalogo ragionato dei libri d'arte e d'antichità*. Pisa: Nicolò Capurro.

Clark, A.M. 1962. Review of Lewis, L. 1961 Connoisseurs and Secret Agents in Eighteenth Century Rome by Lesley Lewis. *The Art Bulletin* 44 (2): 150–151.

Clark, A.M. 1963. Pier Leone Ghezzi's Portraits. *Paragone* 14 (165): 11–21.

Coen, P. 2010. *Il mercato dei quadri a Roma nel Diciottesimo secolo. La domanda, l'offerta e la circolazione delle opere in un grande centro artistico europeo*, vols 1–2. Florence: Leo S. Olschki.

Coen, P. and Fidanza, G.B. (eds) 2011. *Le pietre rivelate: Lo «Studio di molte pietre» di Pier Leone Ghezzi, Manoscritto 322 della Biblioteca Universitaria Alessandrina*. Rome: Istituto Poligrafico e Zecca dello Stato, Libreria dello Stato.

Coggins, C. 1968. Tracings in the Work of Jacques-Louis David. *Gazette des beaux-arts* (November 1968), 6th series, vol. 72: 260–62, 264 and no. 8.

Cohen, H. and de Ricci, S. 1912. *Guide de l'amateur de livres à gravures du XVIIIe siècle*, 6th revised edition. Paris: Librairie Rouquette.

Cojannot-LeBlanc, M. and Prioux, E. 2018. *Rubens. Des camées antiques à la galerie Médicis*. Paris: Le Passage.

Collon, D. 1986. *Catalogue of the Western Asiatic Seals in the British Museum: Cylinder Seals III: Isin-Larsa and Old Babylonian Periods*. London: British Museum Press.

Colonna, C. and Haumesser, L. (eds) 2019. *Dessiner l'Antique. Les recueils de Jean-Baptiste Muret et de Jean-Charles Geslin*. Paris: Bibliothèque nationale de France, Louvre éditions and Institut national d'histoire de l'art.

Connell, D. 2009a. Recently identified at Burton Constable Hall. The collection of William Dugood FRS – jeweller, scientist, freemason and spy. *Journal of the History of Collections* 21 (1): 33–47.

Connell, D. 2009b. William Dugood and the Farnese Numismatic and Glyptic Collections. *Annali dell'Istituto italiano di numismatica* 55: 231–255.

Connor Bulman, L.M. 2008. Richard Topham's collection of drawings, in: C.M. Sicca (ed.), *John Talman. An Early-Eighteenth-Century Connoisseur*, 287–307. New Haven: Yale University Press.

Cornini, G. and C. Lega (eds) 2013. *Preziose antichità. Il Museo Profano al tempo di Pio VI*. Vatican City: Edizioni Musei Vaticani.

Corp, E. 2011. *The Stuarts in Italy 1719–1766. A Royal Court in Permanent Exile*. Cambridge: Cambridge University Press.

Corsi, L. and Crudeli, T. 2003. *Il calamaio del Padre Inquisitore. Istoria della carcerazione del Dottor Tommaso Crudeli di Poppi e della processura formata contro di lui nel tribunale del S: Offizio di Firenze*, ed. R. Rabboni. Udine: Istituto di Studi Storici Tommaso Crudeli/De Bianco Editore.

Craievich, A. 2018. *La vita come opera d'arte: Antonio Maria Zanetti e le sue collezioni*. Exhib. Cat. Venice: Ca'Rezzonico.

Cremer, M. 1997. Eine Unbekannte Arbeit des Gemmenschneiders Lorenz Natter in Köln. *Wallraf-Richartz-Jahrbuch* 58: 143–152.

Cristofani, M. 1983. *La scoperta degli Etruschi. Archeologia e Antiquaria nel '700* (Contributi alla storia degli studi etruschi e italici 2). Rome: Consiglio Nazionale delle Ricerche – Roma.

Crosera, C. 2013. Antonio Maria Zanetti. Le Gemme antiche di Anton-Maria Zanetti di Girolamo illustrate colle annotazioni latine di Anton-Francesco Gori volgarizzate da Girolamo Francesco Zanetti di Alessandro, in: V. Donvito and D. Ton (eds), *Tiepolo Piazzetta Novelli. L'incanto del libro illustrato nel Settecento veneto, catalogo della mostra (Padova, Musei Civici agli Eremitani e Palazzo Zuckermann 24 novembre 2012–7 aprile 2013)*, 400–403. Padua: Antiga Edizioni.

Csapodi, C. and Csapodi-Gárdonyi, K. 1969. *Bibliotheca Corviniana: the library of King Matthias Corvinus of Hungary*. Budapest: Praeger.

Cunyngham, A. 1853. A visit to Rome in the year 1736. *The Gentleman's Magazine* (January–June 1853): 22–26, 159–165, 263–266, 579 and 583.

Czartoryski, A.J. 1904. *Pamiętniki ks. Adama Czartoryskiego i korespondencyja jego z cesarzem Aleksandrem I*. Introduction by Lubomir Gadon, foreword by Karol de Mazade, transl. Karol Scipio. Kraków: Drukarnia "Czasu".

Czepielowa, E. 2006. Pierwotna ekspozycja rysunku i grafiki w Muzeum Książąt Czartoryskich, in: J.A. Chrościcki, T. Grzybkowska and A. Małkiewicz (eds), *Arma virumque cano. Profesorowi Zdzisławowi Żygulskiemu jun. w osiemdziesięciopięciolecie urodzin*, 87–93. Kraków: Muzeum Narodowe.

Czepielowa, E. 2008. Kolekcja rycin i rysunków Muzeum Książąt Czartoryskich. O trudnościach w ustalaniu proweniencji zbiorów, in: E. Frąckowiak and A. Grochala (eds), *Polskie kolekcjonerstwo grafiki. Ludzie i inwestycje*, 167–178. Warszawa: Neriton.

Dacos, N., Grote, A., Giuliano, A., Heikamp, D. and Pannuti, U. 1980. *Il Tesoro di Lorenzo il Magnifico. Le gemme*. Florence: Sansoni Editore.

Dalton, O.M. 1915. *Catalogue of the Engraved Gems of the Post Classical Periods in the Department of British and Mediaeval Antiquities and Ethnography in the British Museum*. London: British Museum Press.

D'Amelio, A.M. 2006. Thomas Patch caricaturista: le due serie de incisioni fiorentine nel Museo di Roma. *Bollettino dei Musei Communali di Roma* 20: 41–76.

Dania, L. (ed.) 2015. *Pier Leone Ghezzi e le caricature dell'album Passionei nella Biblioteca Civica di Fossombrone*. Fermo: Andrea Livi Editore.

Danowska, E. 2006. *Tadeusz Czacki 1765–1813. Na pograniczu epok i ziem*. Kraków: Polska Akademia Umiejętności.

Davis, C.E. 2018. John Toland and Eugène de Savoie. Philosophy, Politics and Patronage in Early Enlightenment Europe. Ph.D. diss., University of St Andrews.

De Brosses, C. 1858. *Le président de Brosses en Italie. Lettres familières écrits en Italie en 1739 et 1740*. Paris: Didier et Cie.

De Brosses, C. 1861 [1768]. *Le président de Brosses en Italie. Lettres familières écrits en Italie en 1739 et 1740*. Paris: Perrin.

Décultot, E. 2012. Eine Geschichte der antiken Kunst im Kleinen. Zu Johann Joachim Winckelmanns «Description des Pierres Gravées du feu Baron de Stosch». *Antike und Abendland* LVIII: 167–188.

De'Rossi, D. 1704. *Raccolta di statue antiche e moderne data in Luce Sotto I gloriosi auspice della santita di N.S: Papa Clemente XI illustrata colle sposizioni a ciascheduna immagine di Pávolo Alessandro Maffei, Patrizio Volterrano e Cav. Dell'Ordine di S. Stefano e della Guardia Pontificia*. Rome: Stamperia alla Pace.

De'Rossi, D. and Maffei, A.P. 1707–1709. *Gemme antiche figurate date in luce da Domenico De' Rossi colle sposizioni di Paolo Alessandro Maffei*, vols I–IV. Rome: Stamperia alla Pace.

Desmas, A.-L., Kopp, E., Scherf, G. and Trey, J. 2017. *Bouchardon: Royal Artist of the Enlightenment*. Los Angeles, CA: Getty Publications.

DeGrazia Bohlin, D. 1979. *Prints and related drawings by the Carracci family*. Washington DC: National Gallery of Arts.

D'Hancarville, P.-F.H. 1766–1767. *Antiquités étrusques, grecques et romaines, tirées du cabinet de M. William Hamilton ...*, vols 1–4. Naples: F. Morelli.

D'Hancarville, P.-F.H. 1778. *MS Catalogue des antiquités recueillies, depuis l'an 1764 jusque vers le milieu de l'année 1776 par Mr. Le Chevalier Guillaume Hamilton, acquises par Acte du Parlement en 1772 et maintenant déposéés dans le Muséum Britannique*. London: The British Museum Trust.

De Wilde, J. 1703. *Gemmae selectae antiquae e museo Jacobi de Wilde: sive L. tabulae diis deabusque gentilium ornatae, per possessorem conjecturis, veterumque poetarum carminibus illustratae*. Amsterdam: sumptibus auctoris.

Devonshire 1730. *Collectio figuraria gemmarum antiquarum ex dactyliotheca Ducis Devoniae*, drawn by A. Gosmond de Vernon and engraved by C. Du Bosc. London.

Dębicki, L.Z. 1887. *Puławy (1762–1830): Monografia z życia towarzyskiego, politycznego i literackiego na podstawie archiwum książąt Czartoryskich w Krakowie*, vol. II. Lwów: Księgarnia Gubrynowicza i Schmidta.

Dębicki, L.Z. 1888. *Puławy (1762–1830): Monografia z życia towarzyskiego, politycznego i literackiego na podstawie archiwum książąt Czartoryskich w Krakowie*, vol. III. Lwów: Księgarnia Gubrynowicza i Schmidta.

Di Fiore, R.G. 2010. La collezione di antichità di Francesco Vettori. Ph.D. diss. Università degli studi di Firenze.

Di Franco, L. and La Paglia, S. 2019. *Un museum ritrovato. La collezione settecentesca di antichità di Giovanni Carafa duca di Noja*, (Le archeologie. Storie, ricerche e metodi 2). Napoli: Naus editorial.

Dimier, L. (ed.) 1928. *Peintres français du XVIIIᵉ siècle. Histoire des vies et catalogue des oeuvres*. Vol. 1. Paris – Brussels: Les Éditions G. van Oest.

Dixon, S.M. 2005. Francesco Bianchini's images and his legacy in the mid-eighteenth century: from capricci to playing cards to proscenium and back, in: V. Kockel and B. Sölch (eds), *Francesco Bianchini (1662–1729) und die europäische gelehrte Welt um 1700*, 83–106. Berlin: Akademie Kunstverlag.

Dmitrieva, E. 2018. *Дактилиотека – Studiensammlung эпохи классицизма (по материалам эрмитажной коллекции слепков с античных гемм)*, i.e. 'A Dactyliotheca – Studiensammlung of the Neoclassical era (on the materials of the Hermitage collection of casts from antique engraved gems)'. Ph.D. dissertation, the State Institute for Art Studies of the Ministry of Culture of the Russian Federation.

Dmitrieva, L. 2022a. The Hermitage set of casts from the collection of engraved gems in the Berlin Antiquarium. *Terra Artis. Art and Design* 2022 (1): 124–134.

Dmitrieva, E. 2022b. On the history of J.-B. Mallia's collection of engraved gems in the Hermitage. *Сообщения Государственно Эрмитажа/Reports of the State Hermitage Museum* 80: 94–103.

Dmitrieva, E. (forthcoming). Russian buyers of antique and modern gems in the Roman art market in the second half of the 18th century, in: *La compra de arte y antigüedades en la Italia del siglo XVIII/Buying Art and Antiquities in Eighteenth Century Italy (Madrid, November–December 2021)*, (Studies in the History of Collection & Art Markets). Leiden: Brill (forthcoming).

Dodero, E. 2019. *Ancient Marbles in Naples in the Eighteenth Century. Findings, Collections, Dispersals*, (Brill Studies in the History of Collecting & Art Markets 7). Leiden-Boston: Brill.

Donato, M.P. 1993a. Un collezionista nella Roma del primo Settecento. Alessandro Gregorio Capponi. *Eutopia* 2 (1): 91–102.

Donato, M.P. 1993b. Corrispondenti di A.G. Capponi tra Roma e la Repubblica delle Lettere. *Eutopia* 2 (2): 39–47.

Donato, M.P. 2004. Il vizio virtuoso. Collezionismo mercato a Roma nella prima metà del Settecento. *Quaderni Storici* 115 (April 2004): 139–160.

Donato, M.P. 2017. L'affirmation d'un amateur aristocrate entre Rome et la République des Lettres. Alessandro Gregorio Capponi et ses collections, in: E. Chapron, E., I. Luciani and G. Le Thiec (eds), *Érudits, collectionneurs et amateur. France méridionale et Italie XVIᵉ et XIXᵉ siècle*, 63–81. Aix-en-Provence: Presses universitaires de Provence.

Dorati da Empoli, M.Ch. 2008. *Pier Leone Ghezzi. Un protagonista del Settecento romano*. Rome: Gangemi editore.

Dorati da Empoli, M.Ch. 2009. Il diario "figurato" di Pier Leone Ghezzi nella Biblioteca Vaticana, in: E. Debenedetti (ed.), *Collezionisti, disegnatori e teorici dal Barocco al Neoclassico Fundstelle*, 151–176. Rome: Bonsignori Editore.

Dorati da Empoli, M.Ch. 2017. *Pier Leone Ghezzi e il contesto artistico della prima metà del Settecento*. Rome: Viella.

Draper, J.D. and Schref, G. 1997. *Augustin Pajou dessinateur en Italie 1752–1756*, (Nouvelles archives de l'Art français XXXIII). Paris: Arts et Metiers.

Duchesne, J. 1826. *Description des objets d'arts qui composent le cabinet de feu M. le Baron V. Denon: estampes et ouvrages à figures*. Paris: imprimerie d'Hippolyte Tilliard.

Duchińska, S. 1891. *Listy ks. Izabeli z hr. Flemingów Czartoryskiej do starszego syna Adama*. Collected by Seweryna Duchińska. Kraków: G. Gebethner i spółka.

Dunkelman, M. 2010. From Microcosm to Macrocosm: Michelangelo and Ancient Gems. *Zeitschrift für Kunstgeschichte* 73 (3): 363–376.

Dury, C. (ed.) 2019. *Le dessin à Port-Royal: Bernard Picart (1673–1733) dessinateur de Paris à Amsterdam*. Gand: Snoeck.

Dziewanowski, M.K. 1998. *Książę wielkich nadziei: biografia księcia Adama Jerzego Czartoryskiego*. Wrocław: Atla 2.

Earle, J. 1628. *Micro-cosmographie or a Piece of the World discovered in Essayes and Characters*. London: William Stansby for Edward Blount.

Ebert, F.A. 1937. *A General bibliographical dictionary*. Oxford: Oxford University Press.

Eckermann, J.P. 1884. *Gespräche mit Goethe, in den letzten Jahren seines Lebens*. Leipzig: Reclam.

Eckhel, J.H. 1788. *Choix des pierres gravées du Cabinet impérial des antiques*. Vienna: De l'imprimerie de J.N. Dekurzbek.

Edgcumbe, R. 2000. *The Art of the Gold Chaser in Eighteenth Century London*. Oxford: Oxford University Press.

Eggers, H. 1926. Philipp von Stosch und die für seinen Atlas beschäftigen Künstler, in: J. Bick (ed.), *Festschrift der Nationalbibliothek in Wien, herausgegeben zur Feier des 200-Jahrigen Bestehens des Gebäudes*, 221–234. Vienna: Oesterr. Staatsdruckerei.

Ehrlich, V.H. 2018. Sculpting heroic action: a new model for Bertoldo di Giovanni's Bellerophon taming Pegasus. *Notes in the History of Art* (Fall 2018): 5–14.

Engelmann, R. 1908. Vier Briefe an Filippo und Rudolfino Venuti. *Archiv für Kultur-Geschichte* 7 (3): 322–338.

Engelmann, R. 1909. Die Manuskripte des Barons Philipp von Stosch. *Centralblatt für Bibliothekswesen* 26: 547–577.

Eppihimer, M. 2015. Caylus, Winckelmann, and the art of 'Persian' gems. *Journal of Art Historiography* 13: 1–27.

Eppihimer, M. 2016. A paradox of eighteenth-century antiquarianism. 'Persian' gems among the Tassie casts. *Journal of the History of Collections* 28 (2): 191–208.

Fabréga-Dubert, M.-L. 2020. *Une histoire en image de la collection Borghèse. Les antiques de Scipion dans les albums Topham*. Paris: Mare et Martin and Louvre éditions.

Falconnet, E. 1771. *Observations sur la statue de Marc-Aurèle*. Amsterdam: Marc-Michel Rey.

Falconet, E.-M. 1781. Observations sur la statue de Marc-Aurèle, in: *Œuvres d'Etienne Falconet, statuaire, contenant plusieurs écrits relatifs aux beaux-arts, dont quelques-uns ont déjà paru, mais fautifs ; d'autres sont nouveaux*, vol. I, 157–348. Lausanne: chez La Société Typographique.

Faliu, O. 1988. Bernard Picart dessinateur et graveur, in: O. Faliu (ed.), *Cérémonies et coutumes religieuses de tous les peuples du monde dessinées par Bernard Picart*, 9–30. Paris: Herscher.

Favaretto, I. 2018. Anton Maria collezionista e cultore di gemme, in: A. Craievich (ed.), *La vita come opera d'arte: Antonio Maria Zanetti e le sue collezioni*, 277–291. Exhib. Cat. Crocetta del Montello and Venezia: Antiga edizioni and MOVE Venezia.

Favaretto, I. 2021. La Dactyliotheca Zanettiana: un'avventura editoriale nella Venezia del Settecento. *Gemmae: an international journal on glyptic studies* 3: 121–137.

Femmel, G. and Heres, G. 1977. *Die Gemmen aus Goethes Sammlung*. Leipzig: E.A. Seeman Buch- und Kunstverlag.

Feola, V. 2014. Prince Eugene and His Library. A Preliminary Analysis. *Rivista Storica Italiana* 126 (3): 742–787.

Ferrara, D. and T. Bergamo Rossi (eds) 2019. *Domus Grimani 1594–2019. The collection of classical sculptures reassembled in its original setting after four centuries*. Venice: Marsilio.

Ficoroni, F. de' 1730. *Le memorie più singolari di Roma, e sue vicinanze notate in una lettera da Francesco de Ficoroni diretta all'illustrissimo signor cav. Bernard inglese aggiuntavi nel fine la spiegazione d'una medaglia d'Omero*. Rome: Giovanni Maria Salvioni.

Ficoroni, F. de' 1744. *Le vestigia e rarità di Roma antica ricercate e spiegate*. Rome: Stamperia di Girolamo Mainardi.

Fielding, W. and Berkvens-Stevelinck, C. 1983. Les Chevaliers de Jubilations, maçonnerie ou libertinage? A propos de quelques publications de Margaret C. Jacob. *Quaerendo* 13 (1): 50–73.

Fileri, E. 2001a. Il cardinale Filippo Antonio Gualtieri (1660–1728), collezionista e scienziato, in: M. Gallo (ed.), *I Cardinali di Santa Romana Chiesa, Collezionisti e mecenati*, II, "Sal terrae, ac lucernae positae super candelabrum", 36–47. Rome: Associazione Culturale Shakespeare and Company.

Fileri, E. 2001b. La "Stanza delle Terracotte" del Museo Cardinale Gualtieri. *Archeologia Classica* 52: 343–384.

Fileri, E. 2022. Piacere, prestigio, erudizione le collezioni di antichità del cardinale Filippo Antonio Gualtiero, in: M.C. Cola (ed.), *Mostrare il sapere. Collezioni scientifiche, studioli e raccolte d'arte a Roma in età moderna*, (Dentro il Palazzo), 69–100. Vatican City: Edizioni Musei Vaticani.

Fileti Mazza, M. 1996. Note su Domenico Augusto Bracci "antiquariolo" a Roma dal 1747 al 1769, in: F. Caglioti, M. Fileti Mazza and U. Parrini (eds), Ad Alessandro Conti (1946–1994) (Quaderno del Seminario di Storia dell'Arte 6), 221–246. Pisa: Scuola Normale Superiore di Pisa.

Fileti Mazza, M. 2006. *Fortuna della glittica nella Toscana mediceo-lorenese e storia del 'Discorso sopra le gemme intagliate' di G. Pelli Bencivenni*. Florence: SPES.

Fleming, J. 1962. *Robert Adam and His Circle in Edinburgh and Rome*. London: John Murray.

Florisoone, M. 1948. *David: Exposition en l'honneur du deuxième centenaire de sa naissance*. Paris: Éditions des Musées nationaux.

Foy-Vaillant, J. 1701. *Historia Ptolemaeorum Aegypti regum, ad fidem numismatum accomodata*. Amsterdam: G. Gallet.

Foy-Vaillant, J. 1703. *Nummi Antiqui Familiarum Romanarum*. Amsterdam: G. Gallet.

Francisci Osti, O. 2000. Key figures in Eighteenth-Century Rome, in E.P. Bowron (ed.), *Art in Rome in the Eighteenth Century*, 77–103. Philadelphia: Merrell Publishers.

Fresco, M.F., Geeraedts, L. and K. Hammacher (eds) 1995. *Frans Hemsterhuis (1721–1790). Quellen, Philosophie und Rezeption = Sources, Philosophy and Reception = Sources, Philosophie et Réception. Symposia in Leiden und Münster zum 200. Todestag des niederländischen Philosophen*. Münster and Hambourg: Lit.

Friedlaender, W. and Blunt, A. 1974. *The Drawings of Nicolas Poussin, catalogue raisonné, vol. V: Drawings after the antique. Miscellaneous drawings addenda*. London: Warburg Institute.

Furtwängler, A. 1888. Studien über die Gemmen mit Künstlerinschriften. *Jahrbuch des Deutschen Archäologischen Instituts* 3 (1888): 105–139, 193–224 and 297–325.

Furtwängler, A. 1889. Studien über die Gemmen mit Künstlerinschriften. *Jahrbuch des Deutschen Archäologischen Instituts* 4 (1889): 46–87.

Furtwängler, A. 1896. *Beschreibung der Geschnittenen Steine im Antiquarium*. Berlin: Spemann Verlag.

Furtwängler, A. 1900. *Die antiken Gemmen. Geschichte der Steinschneidekunst im klassischen Altertum*, vols 1–3. Berlin – Lipsk: Giesecke & Devrient.

Furtwängler, A. 1913. *Kleine Schriften*. Munich: C.H. Beck.

Fusco, L. and Corti, G. 2006. *Lorenzo de'Medici, Collector of Antiquities*. Cambridge: Cambridge University Press.

Fusconi, G. 1994. Da Bartoli a Piranesi: spigolature dai Codici Ottoboniani Latini della Raccolta Ghezzi. *Xenia Antiqua* III: 145–172.

Füßli, J.R. 1810. *Allgemeines Künstlerlexikon oder Kurze Nachricht von dem Leben und den Werken der Mahler, Bildhauer, Baumeister, Kupferstecher, Kunstgießer, Stahlschneider*. Zürich: Orell, Füßli & Compagnie.

Gaehtgens, T. and Lugand, J. 1998. *Joseph-Marie Vien peintre du Roi (1716–1809)*. Paris: Arthena.

Gaetani, P. 1766. *Museum Mazzuchellianum, seu, Numismata virorum doctrina praestantium, quae apud Jo. Mariam comitem Mazzuchellum Brixiæ servantur*. Venice: typis Antonii Zatta.

Galestin, M.C. 1990. De Corazzi collective in het Rijksmuseum van Oudheiden te Leiden. *Tijdschrift voor Mediterrane Archeologie* 6 (2): 23–26.

Gallo, D. (ed.) 1986. *Filippo Buonarroti e la cultura antiquaria sotto gli ultimi Medici*. Florence: Cantini Scolastica.

Gallo, D. 1997. I cataloghi illustrate delle collezioni di antichità nel Settecento, in: M.G. Tavoni and F. Waquet (eds), *Gli spazi del libro nell'Europa del XVIII secolo. Atti del Convegno (Ravenna, 15–16 dicembre 1995)*, 279–294. Bologna: Pàtron.

Gallo, D. 1999. Per una storia degli antiquari romani nel Settecento. *Mélanges de l'École française de Rome. Italie et Méditerranée* 111 (2): 827–845.

Gamba, B. 1836. Bracci, Domenico Augusto, in: Tipaldo de E. (ed.), *Biografia degli Italiani illustri nelle scienze, lettere ed arti del secolo XVIII*. Vol. 3, 172–173. Venice: Tipografia di Alvisopoli.

Gambaro, C. 2008. *Anton Francesco Gori collezionista. Formazione e dispersion della raccolta di antichità*, (Accademia Toscana di Scienze e Lettere 'La Colombara' Studi). Florence: Leo S. Olschki.

Gannon, A. 2012. The double life of Aufret – revealed. *The Antiquaries Journal* 92: 1–13.

Garzelli, A. 1985. *Miniatura fiorentina del Rinascimento, 1440–1525: un primo censimento*. Florence and Scandicci: Giunta regionale toscana and La nuova Italia.

Garzelli, A. 1996. L'Antico' nelle miniature dell'età di Lorenzo, in: *La Toscana al tempo di Lorenzo il Magnifico: Politica, economia, cultura, arte. Convegno di Studi promosso delle Università di Firenze, Pisa e Siena. 5–8 novembre 1992*, vol. I: 163–172. Pisa: Pacini.

Gasparri, C. 1977. Gemme antiche in età neoclassica. Egmagmata, Gazofiliaci, Dactyliothecae. *Prospettiva* 8: 25–35.

Gasparri, C. (ed.) 1994. *Le gemme Farnese*. Naples: Electa.

Gennaioli, R. 2007. *Le gemme dei Medici al Museo degli Argenti*. Florence: Giunti.

Gennaioli, R. 2010. *Pregio e bellezza. Cammei e intaglio dei Medici*. Florence: Sillabe.

Gent, B.E. ca. 1690. A *New Dictionary of the Terms Ancient and Modern of the Canting Crew*. London: Printed for W. Hawes, P. Gilbourne and W. Davis.

Gere, Ch., Rudoe, J., Tait, H. and Wilson, T. 1984. *The Art of the Jeweller, A Catalogue of the Hull Grundy Gift to the British Museum*. London: The British Museum Press.

Gerhard, E. 1827. Zur Gemmenkunde. *Kunst-Blatt des Morgenblattes für gebildete Stände* 73–75: 289–299.

Ghezzi, P.L. 1734. Pier Leone Ghezzi's Dactyliotheca, the edition preserved in the Biblioteca Apostolica Vaticana (Gbinetto di Medagliere) with a relevant manuscript (catalogue) – Ms. Vat. Lat. 14928 dated 1734.

Gialluca, B. 2014. Filippo Buonarroti, in: P. Bruschetti, J.G. Giullerini, P. Reynolds and S. Swaddling (eds), *Seduzione etrusca. Dai segreti di Holkham Hall alle meraviglie del British Museum*, 291–317. Milan: Skira.

Gialluca, B. 2016. Marcus Tuscher, Marcus Meijers, Philipp Stosch e un'erma-ritratto di Marcello Venuti. *Symbolae Antiqvariae* 9: 49–109.

Gianfermo, S. 1986. *Settecento fiorentino, erudite e massone*. Ravenna: Longo Editore.

Ginori Lisci, L. 1985. *The Palazzi of Florence. Their History and Art*. Firenze: Giunti Barbèra.

Giometti, C. 2012. 'Per accompagnare l'antico'. The restoration of ancient sculpture in early eighteenth-century Rome. *Journal of the History of Collections* 24 (2): 219–230.

Giuliano, A. 1973. Un cammeo con Oreste e Ifigenia in Tauride. *Archeologia Classica* 25–26: 303–305 (reprinted with addenda by Lucia Pirzio Biroli Stefanelli, in *Studi di Glittica*, Rome 2009, pp. 163–166).

Giuliano, A. 2009. Catalogo delle gemme che recano l'iscrizione: LAV.R.MED, in: A. Gallottini (ed.), *Studi di glittica*, 83–118. Rome: L'Erma di Bretschneider.

Glyn, D. 1981. A Short History of Archaeology. London: Themes & Hudson.

Goethe, J.W. 1851. *Goethes sämmtliche Werke in dreißig Bänden*. Stuttgart – Tübingen: J.G. Cotta'scher Verlag.

Gołyźniak, P. 2017. *Ancient Engraved Gems in the National Museum in Krakow*. Wiesbaden: Dr. Ludwig Reichert Verlag.

Gołyźniak, P. 2020. *Engraved Gems and Propaganda in the Roman Republic and under Augustus*. Oxford: Archaeopress.

Gołyźniak, P. 2021. From antiquarianism to proto-archaeology: Philipp von Stosch (1691–1757) and the study of engraved gems. *Antiquity* 95 (383): 1–9, e28.

Gołyźniak, P. 2022b. Enjoy life and fear death! – the 'Macabre Gems' of the late Roman Republic and early Roman Empire. *Gemmae: an international journal on glyptic studies* 4: 51–84.

Gołyźniak, P. 2023a. From Stosch through Carafa to Hamilton and the British Museum: Provenance and study of some Egyptian scarabs and Near Eastern cylinder seals in the eighteenth century. *Journal of the History of Collections* 35 (3): 441–454.

Gołyźniak, P. 2023b. Hieronymus Odam, engraved gems, and antiquarianism. *Opuscula* 16: 183–224.

Gołyźniak, P. (forthcoming – Ghezzi). Pier Leone Ghezzi and the antique.

Gołyźniak, P. (forthcoming – Stosch and forgeries). Philipp von Stosch (1691–1757) and forgery (?) of ancient engraved gems.

Gołyźniak, P. and Rambach H.J. (forthcoming). Philipp von Stosch (1691–1757) and his collection of coins and medals.

Gonzalez-Palacios, A. 2014. *Persona e maschera. Collezionisti, antiquari, storici dell'arte*. Milan: Archinto.

Goorle, von A. 1601. *Abrahami Gorlaei Antverpiani Dactyliotheca seu Annulorum sigillarium quorum apud Priscos tam Graecos quam Romanos usus. E Ferro Aere Argento & Auro Promptuarium. Accesserunt variarum Gemmarum quibus antiquitas in Sigillandouti Solita Scalpturae*. Nuremberg.

Goorle, von A. 1609. *Dactyliotheca seu annulorum sigillarium quorum apud Priscos tam Graecos quam Romanos usus e ferro aere argento & auro promptuarium. Accesserunt variarum gemmarvm quibus antiquitas in sigillando uti solita scalptuae*. Nuremberg.

Gori, A.F. 1727. *Monumentum sive columbarium libertorum et servorum Liviae Augustae Et Caesarum: Romae Detectum in Via Appia*. Florence: Regie Celsitudinie.

Gori, A.F. 1731–1732. *Museum Florentinum: exhibens insigniora vetustatis monumenta quae Florentiae sunt*. Vols 1–2. Florence: Ex typographia Michaelis Nestenus et Francisci Moücke.

Gori, A.F. 1731–1737. *Museum Florentinum: exhibens insigniora vetustatis monumenta quae Florentiae sunt*. Vols 1–12. Florence: Ex typographia Michaelis Nestenus et Francisci Moücke.

Gori, A.F. 1737. *Museum etruscum exibens insignia veterum etruscorum monumenta aereis tabulis C.C. nunc primum edita et illustrate*, vols 1–3. Florence: Caietanus Albizinius typographus.

Gori, A.F. 1742. *Difesa dell'alfabeto degli antichi Toscani pubblicato nel 1737 dall'autore del Museo Etrusco disapprovato dall'illustrissimo … Scipione Maffei nel tomo 50 delle sue Osservazioni letterarie date in luce in Verona*. Florence: Anton Maria Albizzini.

Gori, A.F. and Passeri, G.B. 1750. *Thesaurus gemmarum antiquarum astriferarum*. Florence: Ex Officina Typogr. Albiziniana.

Gori, A.F. and Zanetti, A.G.F. 1750. *Le gemme antiche di Anton-Maria Zanetti*. Venice: ex typographio Joan. Baptiste Albritii Hier. f. sumtibus auctoris.

Gori, A.F. 1767. *Dactyliotheca Smithiana*. Venice: Ex typographio J.B. Pasqualii.

Gosmond, A. 1730. *Collectio figuraria gemmarum antiquarum ex dactyliotheca Ducis Devoniae*. London: n.p.

Gould, R. 2014. Antiquarianism as genealogy: Arnaldo Momigliano's method. *History and Theory* 53 (2): 212–233.

Górska, P. 2021. Muzeum Czartoryskich: historia, ludzie, zbiory, in: K. Płonka-Bałus and N. Koziara (eds), *Muzeum Książąt Czartoryskich*, 13–37. Kraków: Muzeum Narodowe.

Griener, P. 2010. *La République de l'œil. L'Expérience de l'art au siècle des Lumières*. Paris: Odile Jacob.

Griggs, T. 2008. The local antiquary in eighteenth-century Rome. *Princeton University Library Chronicle* 69 (2): 280–314.

Griggs, T. 2009. The Local Antiquary in Eighteenth-Century Rome, in A. Stahl (ed.), *The Rebirth of Antiquity*, 66–100. Princeton (NJ): Princeton University Library.

Gronovius, J. 1695. *Dactyliothecae, seu Annulorum sigillarium quorum priscos tam Graecos quam Romanos usus, ex ferro, aere, argento & auro promptuarii*. Leiden: Ex Petrus Vander.

Gross, H. 1990. *Rome in the Age of Enlightenment. The Post-Tridentine Syndrome and the Ancien Regime*. Cambridge: Cambridge University Press.

Grummond, de N.T. 1977. A seventeenth-century book on classical gems. *Archaeology* 30 (1): 14–25.

Guerrieri, M. 2010. Collezionismo e mercato di disegni a Roma nella prima metà del Settecento. Protagonisti, comprimario, compares. Ph.D. dissertation, Università degli studi di Roma III.

Guerrieri Borsoi, M.B. 2004. *Gli Strozzi a Roma. Mecenati e collezionisti nel Sei e Settecento*. Rome: Editore Colombo.

Guerrieri Borsoi, M.B. 2009. Il cavaliere Girolamo Odam: erudizione e disegni di un arcade Romano. *Studiolo* 7: 161–180.

Guerrieri Borsoi, M.B. 2022. Prime considerazioni sul celebre "antiquario" Marco Antonio Sabbatini, in: M.C. Cola (ed.), *Mostrare il sapere. Collezioni scientifiche, studioli e raccolte d'arte a Roma in età moderna*, (Dentro il Palazzo 3), 101–116. Vatican City: Edizioni Musei Vaticani.

Guerrini, L. 1971. *Marmi antichi nei disegni di Pier Leone Ghezzi*. Vatican City: Biblioteca Apostolica Vaticana.

Gurlitt, J. [1798] 1831. Ueber die Gemmenkunde, in: J. Gurlitt (ed.), *Archäologische Schriften, gesammelt und mit Anmerkungen begleitet. Herausgegeben von Cornelius Müller*, 73–156. Altona: bei Joh. Fried. Hammerich.

Hammacher, K. 1971. *Unmittelbarkeit und Kritik bei Hemsterhuis*. Munich: Fink.

Handelsman, M. 1948–1950. *Adam Czartoryski*. Warszawa: Drukarnia Polska.

Hansson, U.R. 2012. On the Study of Engraved Gems: Stosch, Winckelmann, Furtwängler. *Valör: konstvetenskapliga studier* 3-4: 34–48.

Hansson, U.R. 2014. «Ma passion ... ma folie dominante» Stosch, Winckelmann, and the Allure of the Engraved Gems of the Ancients. MDCCC *1800* 4 (Luglio): 13-33.

Hansson, U.R. 2018. Glyptomania: the study, collection, reproduction and re-use of Etruscan engraved gems and jewellery in the eighteenth and nineteenth centuries, in: J. Swaddling (ed.), *An Etruscan Affair: The Impact of Early Etruscan Discoveries on European Culture*, (British Museum Research Publication 211, 81–91). London: British Museum Press.

Hansson, U.R. 2020. "Uno de' più rimarcabili intagli che sinora si è visto". The engraved gems of the ancient Etruscans, from Stosch to Furtwängler and beyond, in K. Mustakallio, M. Silver and S. Örmä (eds), *Mehr Licht, More Light, Più Luce. Studia in honorem Arja Karivieri*, 57–72. Turku: Sigillum.

Hansson, U.R. 2021a. "An Oracle for Collectors": Philipp von Stosch and the Collecting and Dealing in Antiquities in Early Eighteenth-Century Rome and Florence, in: S. Bracken and A. Turpin (eds), *Art Markets, Agents and Collectors: Collecting Strategies in Europe and the USA 1550–1950*, 113–128. New York: Bloomsbury Academic.

Hansson, U.R. 2021b. Philipp von Stosch, in M. Magrini (ed.), *Antonio Maria Zanetti di Girolamo. Il carteggio*, (Lettere artistiche del Settecento Veneziano 6), 59–69. Venezia: Fondazione Cini.

Hansson, U.R. 2022. Philipp von Stosch and his «Museo», in: M.C. Cola (ed.), *Mostrare il sapere: biblioteche, camerini, studioli e raccolte antiche tra Barocco e primo Settecento (Dentro il palazzo)*, 45–68. The Vatican City: Edizioni Musei Vaticani.

Hansson, U.R. 2025a. 'False as His Gems and Canker'd as His Coins'. Notoriety and the Construction of Self in the Case of Baron Philipp von Stosch, in: C. Donato, U.R. Hansson, V. Lagioia and P. Palmieri (eds), *Identità e rappresentazioni nel Settecento*. Rome: Viella.

Hansson, U.R. 2025b. '*Bene qvi vixit latvit bene vixit*': Philipp von Stosch and his portrait medallists. *Médailles* 2022–2023.

Hansson, U.R. 2025c. Bibliotheca Stoschiana. A Key Site for Antiquarianism and the Radical Enlightenment in Italy, in: B. Heinecke and V. Riedl (eds), *Von Joachim I zu Winckelmann. Bibliotheken zwischen Humanismus und Aufklärung*. Beiträge zur Tagung auf Schloss Hundigsburg vom 17. bis 19. Mai 2019, (Schriften zum Bibliotheks- und Büchereiwesen in Sachsen-Anhalt). Halle: Universitäts- und Landesbibliothek Sachsen-Anhalt.

Harloe, K. 2013. *Winckelmann and the Invention of Antiquity: History and Aesthetics in the Age of Altertumswissenschaft*. Oxford: Oxford University Press.

Haskell, F. 1980. *Patrons and painters. A study in the relations between Italian art and society in the age of the baroque*. New Haven and London: Yale University Press.

Haskell, F. 1984. The Baron d'Hancarville. An adventurer and art historian in eighteenth-century Europe, in: E. Chaney and N. Ritchie (eds), *Oxford, China and Italy. Writings in honour of Sir Harold Acton on his eightieth birthday*, 177–191. Florence: Passigli.

Haskell, F. 1988. *The Painful Birth of the Art Book*. New York: Thames & Hudson.

Haskell, F. 1993. *History and Its Images: Art and the Interpretation of the Past*. New Haven: Yale University Press.

Haskell, F. and Penny, N. 1981. *Taste and the Antique*. New Heaven: Yale University Press.

Heawood, E. 1950. *Watermarks Mainly of the 17th and 18th centuries*. Hilversum: The Paper Publications Society.

Heilbron, J.L. 2022. *The Incomparable Monsignor: Francesco Bianchini's World of Science, History, and Court Intrigue*. Oxford: Oxford University Press.

Hemsterhuis, F. 1769. *Lettre sur la sculpture à Monsieur Théod. de Smeth, ancien président des échevins de la ville d'Amsterdam*. Amsterdam: Marc Michel Rey.

Henig, M. 2008. Gems from the collection of Henry, Prince of Wales, and Charles I (Ms.Ashmole 1138), in: J. Boardman and K. Aschengreen Piacenti (eds), *Ancient and Modern Gems and Jewels in the Collection of Her Majesty the Queen*, 269–281. London: Royal Collection Publications.

Henig, M., Scarisbrick, D. and Whiting, M. 1994. *Classical Gems: Ancient and Modern Intaglios and Cameos in the Fitzwilliam Museum, Cambridge*. Cambridge: Cambridge University Press.

Henry, J. 1805. *Allgemeines Verzeichniß des Königlichen Kunst-, Naturhistorischen und Antiken-Museums*. Berlin.

Henry, C. 2002. Les Impostures innocentes de Bernard Picart ou la revanche du "marchand forain", in: M.-C. Heck, F. Lemerle and Y. Pauwels (eds), *Théorie des arts et création artistique dans l'Europe du nord du XVIe au début du XVIIIe siècle*, 313–332. Villeneuve d'Asq: Université Charles-de-Gaulle – Lille 3.

Heres, G. 1987. Johann Carl Schotts Beschreibung des Berliner Antikenkabinetts. *Forschungen und Berichte* 26: 7–28.

Heringa, J. 1976. Die Genese von Gemmae Antiquae Caelatae. *Bulletin Antieke Beschaving* 51: 75–91.

Heringa, J. 1981. Philipp von Stosch als Vermittler bei Kunstankäufen François Fagels. *Nederlands Kunsthistorisch Jaarboek* 32: 55–110.

Heringa, J. 1982. *François Fagel. Portret van een honnête homme*. Den Haag: De Walburg Pers.

Herklotz, I. 1999. *Cassiano Dal Pozzo und die Archäologie des 17. Jahrhunderts*, (Römische Forschungen der Bibliotheca Hertziana 28). Munich: Hirmer Verlag.

Herklotz, I. 2004. Excavations, collectors and scholars in seventeenth-century Rome, in: I. Bignamini (ed.), *Archives and Excavations: Essays on the History of Archaeological Excavations in Rome and Southern Italy from the Renaissance to the Nineteenth Century* (Archaeological Monographs of the

British School at Rome 14), 55–88. Rome: British School at Rome.

Hiesigner, U.W. and Percy, A. (eds) 1980. *A Scholar Collects. Selections from the Anthony Morris Clark Bequest*. Philadelphia: Philadelphia Museum of Art.

Hill, G.F. 1930. *A Corpus of Italian Medals of the Renaissance before Cellini*. London: British Museum Press.

Hill, G.F. and Pollard, G. 1967. *Renaissance Medals from the Samuel H. Kress Collection at the National Gallery of Art*. London: Phaidon.

Hindman, S. 2020. *The Althorp Leopard: The Celebrated Life of a Renaissance Cameo*. Paris – New York – Chicago: Les Enluminures.

Hoefer, J.Ch.F. 1865. *Nouvelle biographie Générale*. Paris: Petit Palais, musée des Beaux-arts de la Ville de Paris.

Homberg, G. 1712. Manière de copier sur le verre coloré les pierres gravées. *Mémoire de l'Académie Royale des Sciences*. (1712): 189–197.

Hunt, L., Jacob, M.C. and Mijnhardt, W.W. 2010a. *The Book that Changed Europe: Picart & Bernard's Religious Ceremonies of the World*. Cambridge: Harvard University Press.

Hunt, L., Jacob, M.C. and Mijnhardt, W.W. (eds) 2010b. *Bernard Picart and the First Global Vision of Religion*. (Issues & Debates). Los Angeles: Getty Research Institution.

Hyży, E. (ed.) 1998. *Muzeum Czartoryskich: Historia i zbiory*. Kraków: Muzeum Narodowe.

Ingamells, J. 1997. *A Dictionary of British and Irish Travellers in Italy 1701–1800*. New Haven and London: Yale University Press.

Israel, J.D. 2002. *Radical Enlightenment. Philosophy and the Making of Modernity, 1650–1750*. Oxford: Oxford University Press.

Jacob, M.C. 1970. An Unpublished Record of a Masonic Lodge in England 1710. *Zeitschrift für Religions- und Geistesgeschichte* 22 (2): 168–171.

Jacob, M.C. 1981. *The Radical Enlightenment. Pantheists, Freemasons and Republicans*. London: George Allen and Unwin.

Jacob, M. 2005. Bernard Picart and the Turn to Modernity. *De Achttiende eeuw* 37 (1): 1–16.

Jaffé, M. 1994. *The Devonshire Collection of Italian Drawings: volume II: Roman and Neapolitan Schools*. London: Phaidon.

Janssen, L. 1866. *Les inscriptions Grecques et Étrusques des pierres gravées du Cabinet de S.M. le roi des Pays-Bas*. The Hague: Martinus Nijhoff.

Jenkins, I. and Sloan, K. 1996. *Vases & Volcanoes: Sir William Hamilton and his Collection*. London: British Museum Press.

Jenkins, I. 2003. Ideas of antiquity: classical and other ancile civilizations in the age of Enlightenment, in: Sloan, K. (ed.), *Enlightenment: Discovering the World in the Eighteenth Century*, 168–177. London: British Museum Press.

Ježková, M. 2015. Unpublished drawings by Hans von Aachen: cameos from the collection of the Granvelle Family. *Studia Rudolphina* 15: 37–47.

Justi, C. 1871. *Antiquarische Briefe des Baron Philipp von Stosch, gesammelt und erläutert von Carl Justi*. Marburg: C.L. Pfeil.

Justi, C. 1872. Philipp von Stosch und seine Zeit. *Zeitschrift für bildende Kunst* 7: 294–308 and 333–346.

Justi, C. 1956. *Winckelmann und seine Zeitgenossen*, vols I–III, 4th ed. Cologne: Phaidon.

Kafker, F.A. and Pinault-Sørensen, M. 1995. Notices sur les collaborateurs du recueil de planches de l'Encyclopédie. *Recherches sur Diderot et sur l'Encyclopédie* 18–19: 200–230.

Kagan, J. 1985. Philipp von Stosch in Porträts auf geschnittenen Steinen aus den Sammlungen der Leningrader Ermitage und der Berliner Museen und einige Fragen der Ikonographie. *Forschungen und Berichte* 25: 9–15.

Kagan, J. 2006. Engraved gems in the writings and the iconography of Antonio Francesco Gori, in: M. Buora (ed.), *Le gemme incise nel Settecento e Ottocento. Continuità della tradizione classica. Atti del Convegno Di Studio, Udine, 26 Settembre 1998 in memoria di Martha McCrory*, (Cataloghi e monografie archeologiche dei Civici Musei di Udine 7), 81–99. Rome: L'erma di Bretschneider.

Kagan, J. 2010. *Gem engraving in Britain from antiquity to the present*, (Studies in Gems and Jewellery 5, British Archaeological Reports IS 40). Oxford: Archaeopress.

Kagan, J, and Neverov, O. 1984. Lorenz Natter's Museum Britannicum. Gem Collecting in Mid-Eighteenth-Century Britain. *Apollo* 217: 114–121.

Kagan, J. and Neverov, O. 2000. *Splendeurs des collections de Catherine II de Russie. Le cabinet de pierres gravées du Duc d'Orléans*. Paris: Centre Culturel du Pantheon.

Kammerer Grothaus, H. 1979. Camere sepolcrali de' liberti e liberte di Livia Augusta ed altri caesari. *Mélanges de l'École française de Rome, Antiquité* 91 (1): 315–342.

Kanzler, P. 1900. *Un congresso di archeologi nell'anno MDCXXVIII: Caricatura di Pier Leone Ghezzi pubblicata in occasione del II Congresso di Archeologia Cristiana*. Rome: Tipografia della Pace di F. Cuggiani.

Kaufmann, T.D. 2001. Antiquarianism, the history of objects, and the history of art before Winckelmann, *Journal of the History of Ideas* 62 (3): 523–541.

Kashcheev, V. 1999. Винкельман и коллекция гемм барона Филиппа фон Штоша (Winckelmann and the gem collection of Baron Philip von Stosch), in *Art collections of museums and traditions of gathering. Materials of the sixth Bogolyubov lectures dedicated to the 175th anniversary of the birth of A. P. Bogolyubov*. Saratov: House Word (in Russian).

Kelly, J.M. 2012. Leters from young painter abroad: James Russel in Rome, 1740–63. *The Volume of the Walpole Society* 74: 61–164.

Kent Hill, D. 1975. From Venuti and Winckelmann to Walters. *Apollo* 162 (August): 100–103.

Keysler, J.G. 1760. *Travels Through Germany, Hungary, Bohemia, Switzerland, Italy and Lorrain*. 4 vols London: J. Scott.

Keyßler, J.G. 1751 [1740]. *Neueste Reisen durch Deutschland, Böhmen, Ungarn, die Schweiz, Italien und Lothringen, worinnen der Zustand und das Merkwürdigste dieser Länder beschreiben* …. Hannover: Nicolai Förster.

Kieven, E. 1991. La collezione dei disegni di architettura di Pier Leone Ghezzi, in E. Debenedetti (ed.), *Collezionismo e ideologia. Mecenati, artisti e teorici dal classico al neoclassico*, (Studi sul Settecento Romano 7): 143–175. Rome: Edizioni Quasar.

Kinauer, R. 1950. *Der Atlas des Freiherrn Philipp von Stosch der Österreichischen Nationalbibliothek: ein Beitrag zu seiner Rekonstruktion und zur Geschichte der Atlanten*. Ph.D. dissertation, Universität Wien.

King, C.W. 1860. *Antique Gems: their origin, uses, and value*. London: Murray.

Klesse, B. 1999. Zum Werk des Nürnberger Glas- und Edelsteinschneiders Johann Christoph Dorsch (1676–1732). *Anzeiger des Germanischen Nationalmuseums*: 141–176.

Klesse, B. 2000. Zum Werk des Nürnberger Edelsteinschneiderin Susanna Maria Preißler, geborene Dorsch (1701–1765). *Anzeiger des Germanischen Nationalmuseums*: 25–66.

Klesse, B. 2001. Die Alexander-Gemme und andere figurenreiche Steinschnitte aus der Nürnberger Werkstatt Dorsch-Preisler. *Anzeiger des Germanischen Nationalmuseums*: 73–92.

Klotz, C.A. 1786. *Über den Nutzen und Gebrauch der alten und geschnittenen Steine und ihrer Abdrücke*. Altenburg: in der Richterischen Buchhandlung.

Knüppel, H.C. 2009. *Daktyliotheken. Konzepte einer historischen Publikationsform*. Ruhpolding – Mainz am Rhein: Verlag Franz Philipp Rutzen.

Kockel, V. and Graepler, D. (eds) 2006. *Daktyliotheken: Götter & Caesaren aus der Schublade: antike Gemmen in Abdrucksammlungen des 18. und 19. Jahrhunderts*. Munich: Biering and Brinkmann.

Kopp, É. 2017. *The Learned Draftsman: Edme Bouchardon*. Los Angeles: Getty Publications.

Korteweg, A.S. and de Heer, E. 1988. *Inventaris van prenten, tekeningen en foto's uit de handschriftencollectie van de Koninklijke Bibliotheek: deel 1: kastnummers 66–72 A*. The Hague: Koninklijke Bibliotheek.

Kowalczyk, B.A. 2022. William Cavendish, II duca di Devonshire; Hugh Howard; Joseph Smith; Arthur Pond; Henry Howard, IV conte di Carlisle; George Spencer, IV duca di Marlborough, in: Magrini, M. (ed.), *Antonio Maria Zanetti di Girolamo, il carteggio*, (Lettere artistiche del Settecento veneziano 6), 97–124. Venice: Fondazione Cini.

Köhler, H.K.E. 1851. Abhandlung über die geschnittenen Steine mit den Namen der Künstler, in: H.K.E. Köhler (ed.), *Gesammelte Schriften. Im Auftrage der Kaiserlichen Akademie der Wissenschaften herausgegeben von Ludolf Stephani*, vol. III. St. Petersburg: Kaiserliche Akademie der Wissenschaften.

Krings, V. (ed.) 2021. *L'Antiquité expliquée et représentée en figures de Bernard de Montfaucon. Histoire d'un livre*. Bordeaux: Ausonius.

Kruse, J. 1989. *Johann Henrich Lips 1758–1817. Ein Zürcher Kupferstecher zwischen Lavater und Goethe*. Coburg: Kunstsammlungen d. Veste Coburg.

Kseniak, M. 1998. *Rezydencja książąt Czartoryskich w Puławach*. Lublin: Idea Media.

Kukiel, M. 1955. *Czartoryski and European Unity 1770–1861*. New Jersey: Greenwood Press.

Kukiel, M. 1993. *Książę Adam*. Warszawa: PAVO.

Kunze, M. (ed.) 1998. *"Außer Rom is fast nichts schönes in der Welt". Römische Antikensammlungen im 18. Jahrhundert*. Mainz am Rhein: Philipp von Zabern.

Kunze, M. (ed.) 2009. *Die Etrusker: Die Entdeckung ihrer Kunst seit Winckelmann. Katalog einer Ausstellung im Winckelmann-Museum vom 19. September bis 29. November 2009*. Ruhpolding-Mainz: Verlag Franz Philipp Rutzen.

Kunze, M. 2016. Winckelmann e le gemme etrusche della Collezione Philipp von Stosch, in: B. Arbeid, S. Bruni and M. Iozzo (eds), *Winckelmann, Firenze e gli Etruschi. Il padre dell'archeologia in Toscana. Catalogo della mostra Firenze, Museo Archeologico Nazionale 26 maggio 2016–30 gennaio 2017*, 157–175. Florence: Edizioni ETS.

La Chausse, M.A.C. de 1690. *Romanum Museum sive Thesaurus eruditae Antiquitatis*. Rome: Ex Typographia Joannis Jacobi Komarek Böemi.

La Chausse, M.A.C. de 1700. *Le gemme antiche figurate di Michel Angelo Causeo dela Chausse*. Rome.

La Chausse, M.A.C. de 1706. *Le Grand Cabinet romain ou recueil d'antiquitez romaines qui consistent en bas reliefs, statues des Dieux et des Hommes, Instruments Sacerdotaux, Lampes, Urnes, Seaux, Brasselets, Clefs, Anneaux et Phioles lacrimales, que l'on trouve à Rome*. Amsterdam: Francois l'Honore & Zacharie Chastelain le Fils.

La Chausse, M.A.C. de 1707. *Michaelis Angeli Causei De La Chausse Parisini Romanum Museum Sive Thesaurus Eruditae Antiquitatis*. Rome: Jo. Franciscus Chracas.

La Gravelle, L. de 1732–1737. *Recueil des pierres gravées antiques*. 2 vols Paris: De l'imprimerie de P.J. Mariette.

Lami, G. 1742. *Memorabilia Italorum*. Florentiae: ex Typographio Societatis ad Insigne Centauri.

Lami, G. 1757. [Philippe de Stosch]. *Novelle Letterarie* 46: 720–723.

La Monica, D. 2002. Progressi verso una "Dactyliotheca Ludovisiana". *Annali della Scuola Normale Superiore di Pisa, Classe di Lettere e Filosofia* Ser. IV 7 (1): 35–84.

La Monica, D. 2014. Battista Franco, Enea Vico e le stampe dei cammei Grimani. *Annali della Scuola Normale Superiore di Pisa*, series 5, vol. 6 (2): 781–810 and 886–903.

Lanciani, R. 1882. Memorie inedite di trovamenti di antichità tratte dai codici Ottoboniani di Pier Leone Ghezzi. *Bulletino della Commissione Archeologica di Roma* 10: 205–254.

Landon, C.P. and Mersan, du T.M. 1818. *Numismatique du voyage du jeune Anacharsis; ou, Médailles des beaux temps de la Grèce, accompagné de descriptions et d'un essai sur la science des médailles, par T.M. Dumersan*. Paris: Au Bureau des Annales du Musée.

Landon, C.P. and Mersan, du T.M. 1823. *Numismatique du voyage du jeune Anacharsis; ou, Médailles des beaux temps de la Grèce, accompagné de descriptions et d'un essai sur la science des médailles, par T.M. Dumersan*. Paris: Au Bureau des Annales du Musée.

Lang, J. 2007. Netzwerke von Gelehrten: Eine Skizze antiquarischer Interaktion im 18. Jh. Am Beispiel des Philipp von Stosch (1691–1757), in J. Broch, M. Rasiller and D. Scholl (eds), *Netzwerke der Moderne: Erkundungen und Strategien*, 203–226. Würzburg: Königshausen and Neumann.

Lang, J. 2012. *Mit Wissen geschmückt? Zur bildlichen Rezeption griechischer Dichter und Denker in der römischen Lebenswelt*, (MAR 39). Wiesbaden: Dr. Ludwig Reichert Verlag.

Lang, J. 2017. Description des pierres gravées du feu Baron Stosch, in: M. Disselkamp and F. Testa (eds), *Winckelmann-Handbuch. Leben-Werk-Wirkung*, 199–210. Stuttgart: J.B. Metzler Verlag.

Lang, J. 2022. "Niemand weiß, was für ein Mensch er war". Philipp von Stosch (1691–1757) und die Leidenschaft des Sammelns im Spiegel von Selbst- und Fremdzeugnissen, in: W. Cortjaens and C.E. Loebens (eds), *Queer Archaeology. Winckelmann and his Passionate Followers. Queer Archaeology, Egyptology and the History of Arts Since 1750*, 269–287. Rahden: VML Verlag Marie Leidorf.

Lang, J. and Cain, H.-U. 2015. *Edle Steine. Lehrreiche Schätze einer Bürgerstadt. Sonderausstellung im Antikenmuseum der Universität Leipzig anlässlich des Stadtjubiläums 1000 Jahre Lepizig Mai–August 2015*. Leipzig: Antikenmuseum der Universität Leipzig.

Lanzi, L. 1809. *Storia pittorica della Italia. Dal risorgiménto delle belle arti fin presso al fine del XVIII secolo*. Third edition. Bassano: Presso Giuseppe Remondini e Figli.

Lapatin, K. 2011. Grylloi, in: N. Adams and Ch. Entwistle (eds), *'Gems of Heaven': Recent Research on Engraved Gemstones in Late Antiquity, AD 200–600*, (British Museum Research Publication 177), 88–98. London: The British Museum Press.

Lapatin, K. 2015. *Luxus: The Sumptuous Arts of Greece and Rome*. Los Angeles, CA: The J. Paul Getty Museum.

Laska, A. 1986. Kolekcjonerzy i grawerzy gemm w Polsce w XVI–XIX wieku. *Opuscula Musealia* 1: 9–31.

Laska, A. 1994. *Kolekcjonerzy gemm antycznych w Polsce od drugiej połowy XVIII wieku do końca XIX wieku*. Ph.D. diss. Jagiellonian University, Kraków.

Latteur, O. 2012. Philipp von Stosch et Bernard Picart, in: M. Lefftz and C. Van Hoorebeek (eds), *L'antiquité de papier. Le livre d'art, témoin exceptionnel de la frénésie de savoir (XVIe–XIXe siècles)*, 32–33. Paris: Namur.

Lauterbach, I. 1991. Pier Leone Ghezzi und Clemens XI. Albani. Die Vorzeichnungen zu Buchillustrationen im Berliner Kupferstichkabinett. *Jahrbuch der Berliner Museen* 33: 149–171.

Lavia, L. 2004. Francesco de' Ficoroni e l'ambiente antiquario romano nella prima metà del Settecento, in: M.G. Mazri, C. Cardone and C. de Benedictis (eds), *Epistolario di Anton Francesco Gori: saggi critici, antologia delle lettere e indici dei mittenti*, 131–146. Florence: Firenze University Press.

Le Blanc, Ch. 1854. *Manuel de l'amateur d'estampes*. Vol. 3. Paris: Emile Bouillon Éditeur.

Le Blond and La Chau 1780–1784. *Description des principales pierres gravées du cabinet de SAS Monseigneur le Duc d'Orléans, premier Prince du Sang*. Paris: Pissot.

Leclerc, J. 1721. *Bibliothèque ancienne et modern*, vol. XVI. The Hague: Les Frères Wetstein.

Leclerc, J. 1724. *Bibliothèque ancienne et modern*, vol. XXII. The Hague: Les Frères Wetstein.

Le Gall, C. 2019. Giovanni Poleni (1683–1761), correspondant padouan de Jean-François Séguier. Entre érudition et expérience, in: E. Chapron and F. Pugnière (eds), *Écriture épistolaire et production des savoirs au XVIIIe siècle. Les réseaux de Jean-François Séguier*, 159–180. Paris: Classiques Garnier.

Leitschuh, F.F. 1886. *Die Familie Preisler und Markus Tuscher. Ein Beitrag zur Geschichte der Kunst im 17. Und 18. Jahrhundert*. Leipzig: Verlag von E.A. Seemann.

Lenzuni, A. (ed.) 1992. *All'ombra del lauro: Documenti librari della cultura in eta laurenziana: Firenze, Biblioteca medicea laurenziana, 4 maggio–30 giugno 1992*. Florence: Silvana editore.

Levine, J. 1898. *Bibliography of eighteenth-century art and illustrated books*. London: Sampson Low, Marston & company limited.

Lewis, L. 1961. *Connoisseurs and Secret Agents in Eighteenth Century Rome*. London: Chatto and Windus.

Lewis, L. 1967. Philipp von Stosch. *Apollo* 85: 320–327.

LIMC I–VIII = *Lexicon Iconographicum Mythologiae Classicae* 1981–1999. Zürich-Munich-Düsseldorf: Artemis & Winkler Verlag.

LIMC Supplement = *Lexicon Iconographicum Mythologiae Classicae. Supplement* 2009. Düsseldorf: Artemis Verlag.

Lippold, G. 1922. *Gemmen und Kameen des Altertums und der Neuzeit*. Stuttgart: Julius Hoffman.

Lo Bianco, A. 1985. *Pier Leone Ghezzi*. Palermo: Ila Palma.

Lo Bianco, A. (ed.) 1999. *Pier Leone Ghezzi. Settecento Alla Moda*. Venice: Marsillio.

Lo Bianco, A. 2010. Pier Leone Ghezzi e l'antico, in: C. Brook and V. Curzi (eds), *Roma e l'antico: realtà e visione nel '700*, 27–32. Milan: Skira.

Loisel Legrand, C. 1999. Pier Leone Ghezzi disegnatore, in: A. Lo Bianco (ed.), *Pier Leone Ghezzi. Settecento alla moda. I Ghezzi dalle Marche all'Europa*, 55–69. Venice: Marsilio.

Longhi, R. 1958. *Arte Lombarda dai Visconti agli Sforza*. 3rd ed. Milan: Silvana editoriale d'arte.

Loon, van G. 1723–1731. *Beschryving der Nederlandsche Historipenningen*, vols I–IV. In's Graavenhaage; Christian van Lom, Pieter Grosse, Rutger Alberts, en Pieter de Hondt.

Lorenzetti, G. 1917. *Un dilettante incisore veneziano del XVIII secolo. Antonio Maria Zanetti di Gerolamo*. Venezia: Regia Deputazione.

Lucchese, E. 2020. Zanetti, Anton Maria, in: *Dizionario Biografico degli Italiani* 100: 507–510.

Lucci, D. 2017. Deism, Freethinking and Toleration in Enlightenment England. *History of European Ideas* 43 (4): 345–358.

Luez, Ph. (ed.) 2019. *Bernard Picart (1673–1733) dessinateur de Paris à Amsterdam. Exposition présentée au musée national de Port-Royal des Champs, Magny les Hameaux (21 mars–23 juin 2019)*. Gand: Snoeck.

Lugt, F. 1921. *Les Marques de Collections de Dessins & d'Estampes*. Amsterdam: Vereenigde Drukkerijen.

Luther, E. 1988. *Johann Friedrich Frauenholz (1758–1822). Kunsthändler un Verleger in Nürnberg*. Nürnberg: Schriftenreihe des Stadtarchivs Nürnberg.

Lyons, C. 2003. Antiquities and art theory in the collections of Vicente Vittoria, in: J. Fejfer, T. Fischer-Hansen, A. Rathje (eds), *The Rediscovery of Antiquity: the Role of the Artist*, (Acta Hyperborea 10), 481–508. Copenhagen: Museum Tusculanum Press, University of Copenhagen.

Maaskant-Kleibrink, M. 1978. *Catalogue of the Engraved Gems in the Royal Coin Cabinet, The Hague*. The Hague: Government Publishing Office, Wiesbaden: Steiner Verlag.

Maaskant-Kleibrink, M. 1997. Engraved Gems and Northern European Humanists, in: C.M. Brown (ed.), *Engraved gems: survivals and revivals*, (Studies in the History of Art (Washington DC) 54, Symposium Papers XXXII), 229–247. Washington-Hannover: National Gallery of Art-University Press of New England.

Macandrew, H. 1978. A group of Batoni drawings at Eton College, and some eighteenth-century Italian copyists of classical sculpture and Catalogue of the drawings by Batoni in the Library of Eton College. *Master Drawings* XVI (2): 131–144 and 144–150.

MacKay Quynn, D. 1941. Philipp von Stosch. Collector, Bibliophile, Spy, Thief (1611[sic]–1757). *Catholic Historical Review* 27 (3): 332–344.

Maggioni, L. 1991. Antonio Maria Zanetti tra Venezia, Parigi e Londra: incontri ed esperienze artistiche, in: E. Debenedetti (ed.), *Collezionismo e ideologia, mecenati, artisti e teorici dal classico al neoclassico*, 91–110. Roma: Multigrafica.

Magrini, M. 2009. Antonio Maria Zanetti il Vecchio, in: L. Borean and S. Mason (eds), *Il collezionismo d'arte a Venezia. Il Settecento*, 317–319. Venice: Marsilio.

Magrini, M. (ed.) 2021. *Antonio Maria Zanetti di Girolamo. Il carteggio*, (Lettere artistiche del Settecento Veneziano 6). Venice: Fondazione Cini.

Maioglio, R. 2011. Un fregio d'armi nei disegni di Pier Leone Ghezzi, in: D. Manacorda, R. Santangeli Valenzani (eds), *Il primo miglio della Via Appia a Roma*, 209–215. Rome: Università degli studi Roma TRE.

Malgouyres, Ph. 2022. *Pierres gravées. Camées, intailles et bagues de la collection Guy Ladrière*. Paris: Mare & Martin.

Mangeart, D.T. 1763. *Introduction a la science des médailles: pour servir a la connoissance des dieux, de la religion, des sciences, des arts et de tout ce qui appartient a l'histoire ancienne, avec les preuves tirées des médailles; Ouvrage propre à servir de supplément à l'Antiquite expliquée par Dom Montfaucon*. Paris: D. Houry.

Manteyer, G. de 1897–1899. Les manuscrits de la reine Christine au Vatican. *Mélanges d'archéologie et d'histoire de l'École française de Rome* 17 (1897): 285–322; 18 (1898): 525–35; 19 (1899): 85–90.

Marchesano, L. 2010. The *Impostures Innocentes*: Bernard Picart's Defense of the Professional Engraver, in: L. Hunt, M.C. Jacob and W.W. Mijnhardt (eds), *Bernard Picart and the First Global Vision of Religion. (Issues & Debates)*, 105–138. Los Angeles: Getty Research Institution.

Mare, de la A.C. 1985. New research on Humanistic Scribes in Florence, in: A. Garzelli and A.C. de la Mare (eds), *Miniatura fiorentina del Rinascimento 1440–1525: un primo censimento*, vol. I, 393–600. Florence: Giunta regionale toscana.

Mariette, P.-J. 1741. *Description sommaire des pierres gravées du cabinet de feu M. Crozat*. Paris: Chez Pierre-Jean Mariette.

Mariette, P.J. 1750. *Traité des pierres gravées*. Paris: l'imprimerie de l'auteur.

Mariette, P.-J. 1851. *Abecedario*. Vol. I. Paris: J.B. Dumoulin.

Mariette, P.-J. 1853–1854. *Abecedario de J. Mariette et autres notes inédites de cet auteur sur les arts et les artistes. Ouvrage publié d'après les manuscrits autographes, conservés au cabinet des estampes de la Bibliothèque impériale, et annoté par MM. Ph. de Chennevières et A. de Montaignon*. Paris: J.-B. Dumoulin.

Mariotti, F. 1892. *La legislazione delle belle arti*. Rome: Unione Cooperativa Editrice.

Martinelli, V. (ed.) 1990. *Giuseppe e Pier Leone Ghezzi*. Rome: Palombi Editori.

Mastiti, F. 1997. Le antichità di Casa Ottoboni. *Storia dell'arte* 90: 201–249.

Mastrocinque, A. 1993. Orpheos Bakchikos. *Zeitschrift für Papyrologie und Epigraphik* 97: 16–24.

Matile, M. 2018. La genesi della raccolta di varie stampe a chiaroscuro, in: A. Craievich (ed.), *La vita come opera d'arte: Antonio Maria Zanetti e le sue collezioni*, 88–107 and 121–169. Exhib. Cat. Venice: Ca'Rezzonico.

Merrillees, P.H. 2005. *Catalogue of the Western Asiatic seals in the British Museum: Pre-Achaemenid and Achaemenid periods*. London: British Museum Press.

Metz, P. and Rave P.O. 1957. Eine Neuerworbene Bildnisbüste des Barons Philipp von Stosch von Edme Bouchardon. *Berliner Museen* 7 (1): 1–26.

Meulen, van der M. 1994. *Corpus Rubenianum Ludwig Burchard: Part XXIII: Copies After the Antique*. London: Harvey Miller Publishers.

Meyer, G. 2022. Moulages de monnaies antiques, ou comment produire des copies (XVIe–XVIIIe siècles), in: F. de Callataÿ (ed.), *Numismatic antiquarianism through correspondence (16th–18th c.). In the Margin of the Project Project Fontes Inediti Numismaticae Antiquae*, 19–46. New York: American Numismatic Society.

Michaelis, A. 1882. *Ancient Marbles in Great Britain*. Cambridge: Cambridge University Press.

Michel, S. 1999–2000. Nürnberg und die Glyptik: Steinschneider, Sammler und die Gemmenkunde im 17. und 18. Jahrhundert. *Nürnberger Blätter zur Archäologie* 16: 65–90.

Michel, S. 2001. *Die Magischen Gemmen im Britischen Museum*. London: British Museum Press.

Micheli, M.E. 1984. Lo scarabeo Stosch. Due disegni e una stampa. *Prospettiva* 37: 51–55.

Micheli, M.E. 1986. "Gemmae Antiquae Caelatae" di Anton Francesco Gori. *Prospettiva* 47: 38–51.

Micheli, M.E. 2000. La glittica al tempo del Bellori, in: E. Borea and G. Gasparri (eds), *L'idea del bello: viaggio per Roma nel Seicento con Giovan Pietro Bellori*, vol. II: 543–561. Rome: De Luca Editori d'Arte.

Middleton, C. 1745. *Antiquitates Middletonianae. Germanae quaedam antiquitates eruditae monumenta quibus romanorum veterum ritus varii tam sacri quam profani, tum graecorum atque aegyptiorum nonnulli illustrantur, Romae olim maxima ex parte collecta*. London: apud R. Manby & H.S. Cox.

Middleton, J.H. 1891. *Descriptive catalogue of the engraved gems in the Fitzwilliam Museum*. Cambridge: Cambridge University Press.

Mikocki, T. 1990. *Najstarsze kolekcje starożytności w Polsce (lata 1750–1830)*. Wrocław-Warszawa-Kraków-Gdańsk-Łódź: Zakład Narodowy im. Ossolińskich.

Miller, M. (ed.) 2005. *Staatliche Museen zu Berlin, Dokumentation der Verluste, Vol. V.1 Antikensammlung, Skulpturen, Vasen, Elfenbein und Knochen, Goldschmuck, Gemmen und Kameen*. Berlin: Antikensammlung Staatliche Museen zu Berlin.

Miller, P.N. 2013. A tentative morphology of European antiquarianism, 1500–2000, in: A. Schnapp (ed.), *World Antiquarianism. Comparative Perspectives*, 67–87. Los Angeles: J. Paul Getty Research Institute.

Miller, P.N. (ed.) 2014. *Momigliano and Antiquarianism. Foundations of the Modern Cultural Sciences*. Toronto: University of Toronto Press.

Miller Gray, J. 1894. *James and William Tassie. A Biographical and Critical Sketch with a Catalogue of Their Portrait Medallions of Modern Personages*. Edinburgh: W.G. Patterson.

Millin, A.L. 1805. Dactyliotheca Stoschiana. *Magasin encyclopédique, ou Journal des sciences, des lettres et des arts* V: 436–443.

Miner, D. 1968–1969. Since de Ricci. Western illuminated manuscripts acquired since 1934. *The Journal of the Walters Art Gallery* 31–32: 40–117.

Minor, H.H. 2001. Rejecting Piranesi. *The Burlington Magazine* 143 (1180): 412–419.

Miranda, S. 2000. *Francesco Bianchini e lo scavo farnesiano del Palatino (1720–1729)*. Firenze: La Nuova Italia Editrice.

Moenkemeyer, H. 1975. *François Hemsterhuis*. Boston (MA): Twayne.

Momigliano, A. 1950. Ancient history and the antiquarian. *Journal of the Warburg and Courtauld Institutes* 13 (3/4): 285–315.

Mongan, A. 1975. Some Drawings by David from his Roman Album I, in: A. Châtelet and N. Reynaud (eds), *Etudes d'art français offertes à Charles Sterling*, 319–326. Paris: Presses Universitaires de France.

Mongan, A. 1996. *David to Corot: French Drawings in the Fogg Art Museum*. Cambridge (MA): Harvard University Press.

Montanari, T. 1997. La dispersione delle collezioni di Cristina di Svezia. Gli Azzelini, gli Ottoboni, gli Odescalchi. *Storia dell'Arte* 90: 250–300.

Montfaucon, B. de 1719–1724. *L'antiquité expliquée et representée en figures*, vols 1–15. Paris: Chez Florentin Delaulne, Hilaire Foucault and Michel Clousier.

Morelli Timpanaro, M.A. 1996. *Per una storia di Andrea Bonduci (Firenze 1715–1766). Lo stampatore, gli amici, le loro esperienze culturali e massoniche*, (Studi di storia moderna e contemporanea 18). Roma: Istituto Storico Italiano per l'Età Moderna e Contemporanea.

Morelli Timpanaro, M.A. 2003. *Tommaso Crudeli, Poppi 1702–1745. Contributo per uno studio sulla inquisizione a Firenze nella prima metà del XVIII secolo*. Florence: Leo S. Olschki.

Möhsen, J.K.W. 1773. *Beschreibung einer Berlinischen Medaillen-Sammlung, die vorzüglich aus Gedächtnis-Münzen berühmter Aerzte bestehet: in welcher verschiedene Abhandlungen, zur Erklärung der alten und neuen Münzwissenschaft, imgleichen zur Geschichte der Arzneigelahrtheit und der Litteratur eingerücket sind*. Berlin – Leipzig: George Jacob Decker, Königl. Hof-Buchdrucker.

Mura Sommella, A. (ed.) 1990. *Il Tesoro di Via Alessandria*. Rome: Silvana editore.

Muzell-Stosch, W. 1781. *Johann Winckelmanns Briefe an Einen Seiner Vertrautesten Freunde in Den Jahren 1756. Bis 1768. Nebst Einem Anhange Von Briefen an Verschiedene Andere*. Berlin and Stettin: Friedrich Nicolai.

Müller, F. 1864. *Die Künstler aller Zeiten und Völker oder Leben und Werke der berühmtesten Baumeister, Bildhauer, Maler ... etc.*, vol. 3. Stuttgart: Verlag von Ebner & Seubert.

Nagler, G.K. 1846. *Neues allgemeines Künstler-Lexicon oder Nachrichten von dem Leben und Werken der Maler, Bildhauer, Baumeister, Kupferstecher, Formschneider, Lithographen, Zeichner, Medailleure, Elfenbeinarbeiter, etc.*, vol. 16. Munich: Fleischmann.

Nagler, G.K. 1849. *Neues allgemeines Künstler-Lexicon oder Nachrichten von dem Leben und Werken der Maler, Bildhauer, Baumeister, Kupferstecher, Formschneider, Lithographen, Zeichner, Medailleure, Elfenbeinarbeiter, etc.*, vol. 19. Munich: Fleischmann.

Nagler, G.K. 1871. *Die Monogrammisten und diejenigen bekannten und unbekannten Künstler aller Schulen, welche sich zur Bezeichnung ihrer Werke eines figürlichen Zeichens, der Initialen des Namens, der Abbreviatur desselben etc. bedient haben*. Munich: Georg Franz'sche Buch- und Kunsthandlung.

Napolitano, M. 2021. Dattilioteca Nissardi: Impronte di gemme nella collezione di Filippo Nissardi. Ph.D. diss. Università degli Studi di Cagliari, Cagliari.

Nardelli, B. 1999. *I cammei del museo archeologico nazionale di Venezia*, (Collezioni e Musei Archeologici del Veneto 43). Rome: Giorgio Bretschneider editore.

Natter, L. 1754. *Traité de la méthode antique de graver en pierres fines comparée avec la méthode moderne et expliqué en diverses planches*. London: De l'imprimerie de J. Haberkorn & Comp.

Natter, L. 1761. *Catalogue des pierres gravées tant en relief qu'en creux de Mylord Comte de Bessborough*. London: J. Haberko.

Nau, E. 1966. *Lorenz Natter 1705–1763. Gemmenschneider und Medailleur*. Biberach an der Riss: Bieberacher Verlagsdruckerei.

Neverov, O. 1971. *Antique Cameos in the Hermitage Collection*. Leningrad: Aurora Publishers.

Neverov, O. 1976. *Antique Intaglios in the Hermitage Collection*. Leningrad: Aurora Publishers.

Neverov, O. 1981. La raccolta di antichità di J.J. Winckelmann: precisazioni sulla sua dispersion. *Prospettiva* XXIV: 53–59.

Neverov, O. 2002. Die Sammlung des Studiolo Grimani, in: L. Altringer, G. Macchi, and G. Romanelli (eds), *Venezia! Kunst aus venezianischen Palästen. Sammlungsgeschichte Venedigs vom 13. Bis 19. Jahrhundert*, 145–148. Bonn: Hatje Cantz Verlag.

Nisard, Ch. (ed.) 1877. *Correspondance inédite du Comte de Caylus avec le P. Paciaudi : théatin (1757–1765) suivi de celle de l'abbé Barthélemy et de Mariette avec le même*. Paris: imprimerie nationale.

Noack, F. von 1907. *Deutsches Leben in Rom, 1700 bis 1900*. Stuttgart: J.G. Cottásche.

Noack, F. von 1928–1929. Stosch, Albani und Winckelmann: urkundliche Ergänzungen zu ihrer Geschichte. *Belvedere* 13 (68): 41–48; 13 (69): 67–71; 13 (70): 87–93; (9): 301–308.

Norden, F.L. 1755. *Voyage d'Egypte et de Nubie*. Copenhagen: The Royal Danish Academy of Sciences and Letters.

Oeschlin, W. 1979. Storia e archeologia prima del Piranesi. Nota su Francesco Bianchini, in: *Piranesi nei loughi di Piranesi*, 107–111. Rome: Multigrafica/Fratelli Palombi.

Olszewski, E.J. 1983. The New World of Pier Leone Ghezzi. *Art Journal* 43 (4): 325–330.

Olszewski, E.J. 2002. The enlightened art patronage of Cardinal Pietro Ottoboni (1667–1740). *Artibus et Historiae* 23 (45): 139–165.

Omont, H. 1891. Le vol d'Aymon à la Bibliothèque du Roi e le baron de Stosch. *Revue des Bibliothèques* 1: 468–469.

Orlandi, P.A. 1733. *L'Abecedario pittorico*. Venice: Giambatista Pasquali.

Orléans 1786. *Catalogue des pierres gravées du cabinet du feu de son altesse sérenissime Monseigneur le Duc d'Orléans, premier Prince du sang dont la vente sera indiquée dans le papiers publics*. Paris: chez Barrois l'aîné.

Orsini, F. 1570. *Imagines et Elogia Virorum Illustrium et Eruditorex Antiquis Lapidibus et Nomismatis Expressa cum Annotationis*. Rome: Antoine Lafréry.

Orsini, F. 1598. *Illustrium imagines: ex antiquis marmoribus, nomismatibus, et gemmis expressae: quae exstant Romae, maior pars apud Fulvium Ursinum/Theodorus Gallaeus delineabat Romae ex archetypis incidebat*. Antwerp: Plantiniana Officina.

Osborne, D. 1912. *Engraved gems, signets, talismans and ornamental intaglios: ancient and modern*. New York: H. Holt.

Ottinger, B. 1997. *La Fable des Dieux. Gravures, dessins & moulages de pierres fines antiques au XVIIIe*. Exhibition and catalogue, Musée d'Art de Senlis, Talmont-Saint-Hilaire: Printéditions.

D'Ottone-Rambach, A., Rambach, H.J. and Zwierlein-Diehl, E. 2020. The Roman past in 7th/13th-century Ḥamā (Syria): A bronze cast with the portrait of Nero in the treasure of al-Malik al-Manṣūr II, in: L. Capezzone (ed.), *Before Archaeology. The meaning of the past in classical and pre-modern Islamic thought*, (Sapienza University – Atlas of the Ancient Near East), 143–176. Rome: Artemide edizioni.

Palma Venetucci, B. 1994. *L'abate Carlo Antonio Pullini. Il manoscritto di un erudito e il collezionismo di antichità in Piemonte nel '700*. Rome: De Luca Editori d'Arte.

Pampalone, A. 2005. Parrocchia di San Lorenzo in Lucina-Rione Colonna, in: E. Debenedetti (ed.), *Artisti e Artigiani a Roma, II dagli Stati delle Anime del 1700, 1725, 1750, 1775*, (Studi sul Settecento Romano 21), 11–139. Rome: Edizioni Quasar.

Pannuti, U. 1994. *Catalogo della collezione glittica Museo Archeologico Nazionale di Napoli*, vol. 2. Rome: Libreria dello Stato.

Panofka, T. 1852. *Gemmen mit Inschriften in den königlichen Museen zu Berlin, Haag, Kopenhagen, London, Paris, Petersburg und Wien*. Berlin: Druckerei der königl. Akademie der Wissenschaften.

Paoli, M.P. 2015. I tanti volti dell'onore. Conflitti del quotidiano e pratiche di pacificazione nella Toscana del Settecento. *Krypton. Identità, potere, rappresentazioni* 3 (5–6): 57–70.

Pächt, O. and Alexander, J. 1966–1973. *Illuminated manuscripts in the Bodleian Library*. Oxford: Clarendon Press.

Pelickmans, P. 1987. *Hemsterhuis sans rapports. Contribution à une lecture distante des Lumières*. Amsterdam: Brill.

Pellicer, L. and Hilarie, M. 2008. *François-Xavier Fabre (1766–1837) de Florence à Montpellier*. Paris: Somogy éditions d'art.

Pennestrì, S. 2021. Dalla Biblioteca al museo. Il Nummophylaceum casanatense e l'eredità di Giovanni Battista Audiffredi. *Notiziario del Portale Numismatico dello Stato* 15: 58–266.

Pforr, H. and Roserot, A. 2016. *Edme Bouchardon*. Gennevilliers: Prisma.

Picart, B. 1734. *Impostures innocents ou, Recueil d'estampes d'apres divers peintres illustres, tels que Rafael, Le Guide, Carlo Maratti, Le Poussin, Rembrandt, &c. Gravées à leur imitation, & selon le gout particulier de chacun d'eux, & accompagnées d'un discours sur les préjugés de certains curieux touchant la gravure, par Bernard Picart, dessinateur et graveur. Avec son eloge historique, et le catalogue de ses ouvrages*. Amsterdam: B. Picart.

Pietrzak, A. 2018. Fameux amateur Baron Philipp von Stosch and the unknown provenance of lost old masters' drawings from the collection of Count Stanisław Kostka Potocki. *Polish Libraries* 6: 115–163.

Piggott, S. 1989. *Ancient Britons and the Antiquarian Imagination*. London: Thames and Hudson.

Piranesi, G.B. 1765. *Parere sull'architettura protopiro e didascalo ovvero il confronto fra le ragioni di verità scientifica con i diritti di varietà fantastica*. Rome: n.p.

Pirzio Biroli Stefanelli, L. 1993. Una raccolta di "zolfi" del Museo Boncompagni per il Medagliere Capitolino. *Bollettino dei Musei Comunali di Roma* 3: 128–136.

Pirzio Biroli Stefanelli, L. 2006. Fortuna delle gemme Farnese nell XVIII e XIX secolo. Calchi, paste vitree e riproduzioni in pietra dura, in: C. Gasparri (ed.), *Le Gemme Farnese, Museo Archeologico Nazionale Napoli*, 101–106. Naples: Electa.

Pirzio Biroli Stefanelli, L. 2007. *La collezione Paoletti. Prima parte. Stampi in vetro per impronte di intagli e cammei*, vol. 1. Rome: Gangemi editore.

Pirzio Biroli Stefanelli, L. 2009. L'incisione in pietra dura a Roma. La grande fioritura del XVIII e XIX secolo, in: A. Gallottini (ed.), *Studi di glittica*: 173–187. Rome: L'Erma di Bretschneider.

Pirzio Biroli Stefanelli, L. 2012. *La collezione Paoletti. Seconda parte. Stampi in vetro per impronte di intagli e cammei*. Rome: Gangemi editore.

Piva, C.M. 2012. Antonio Maria Zanetti e la tradizione della tutela delle opere d'arte a Venezia: dalla critica d'arte all'attività sul campo, in: C.M. Piva (ed.), *Il restauro come atto critico. Venezia e il suo territorio*, 32–43. Venice: Edizioni Ca'Foscari – Digital Publishing.

Plantzos, D. 1999. *Hellenistic Engraved Gems*. Oxford: Clarendon Press.

Platz-Horster, G. 1993. Der "Ölgießer" des Gnaios Granat in der Walters Art Gallery. *The Journal of the Walters Art Gallery* 51: 11–21.

Platz-Horster, G. 2012. *Erhabene Bilder: Die Kameen in der Antikensammlung Berlin*. Wiesbaden: Dr Ludwig Reichert Verlag.

Platz-Horster, G. 2017. Some cameos in Leiden – Roman to neoclassicism, in: B.J.L. van der Bercken and V.C.P. Baan (eds), *Engraved Gems. From Antiquity to the Present*, (Papers on Archaeology of the Leiden Museum of Antiquities 14), 47–64. Leiden: Sidestone Press.

Płonka-Bałus, K. and Koziara, N. (eds) 2021. *Muzeum Książąt Czartoryskich*. Kraków: Muzeum Narodowe.

Pomian, K. 1976. Médailles/coquilles = erudition/philosophie, in: Th. Besterman (ed.), *Studies on Voltaire and the Eighteenth Century. Vol. CLIV: Transactions of the Fourth International Congress on the Enlightenment*, 1677–1703. Oxford: The Voltaire Foundation; reprinted in Pomian, K. 1987. *Collectionneurs, amateurs et curieux. Paris, Venise: XVIe–XVIIIe siècles*, 143–162. Paris: Gallimard; translated in Pomian, K. 1991. *Collectors and curiosities*, 121–138. Cambridge: Polity.

Poulouin, C. 1995. L'Antiquité expliquée et représentée en figures (1719–1724) par Bernard de Montfaucon. *Dix-Huitième Siècle* 27: 43–60.

Pomian, K. 2000. Mariette e Winckelmann. *Revue germanique internationale* 13: 11–38.

Pomian, K. 2002. Caylus et Mariette: une amitié, in: I. Aghion (ed.), *Caylus mécène du roi. Collectionner les antiquitiés au XVIIIe siècle*, 45–52. Paris: Institut national d'histoire de l'art.

Pollard, J.G. 2007. *Renaissance Medals. The Collections of the National Gallery of Art Systematic Catalogue*. Oxford: Oxford University Press.

Prat, L.A. 2011. *Le dessin français au XIXe siècle*. Paris: Somogy Éditions d'Art.

Preaud, M. 1996. Bernard Picart, in: J. Turner (ed.), *The Dictionary of Art*, vol. 24, 712. London: Macmillan.

Preißler, G.M. 1732. *Philippo L Baroni de Stosch antiqvitatis amatori bonarvmqve artivm cvltori statvas hasce antiqvas ab Edmvndo Bovchardon gallo scvlptore egregio Romae delieatas Io. Ivstinvs Preißler noricvs pictor a se in aes incisas favtori svo optime merito*. Nuremberg: Georg Martin Preißler.

Prosperi Valenti Rodinò, S. 1993. I disegni di casa Albani, in: E. Debenedetti (ed.), *Alessandro Albani patrono delle arti. Architettura pittura e collezioni nella Roma del Settecento*, 15–70. Rome: Bonsignori.

Prosperi Valenti Rodinò, S. 2004. Alessandro Gregorio Capponi, un collectionneur de dessins du XVIIIe siècle. *Revue de l'art* 143 (1): 13–26.

Prosperi Valenti Rodinò, S. 2014. Ghezzi e gli altri caricature di Salvator Rosa, Burrini, Mitelli, Maratti e Mola nei volumi di Pier Leone Ghezzi alla Biblioteca Apostolica Vaticana. *Miscellanea Bibliothecae Apostolicae Vaticanae* XX: 657–677.

Quartino, L. 1978. Studi inediti sulla glittica antica. Filippo Buonarroti senatore fiorentino, in: N. Lamboglia (ed.), *Miscellanea di storia italiana e mediterranea*, 289–340. Genoa: Universita di Genova.

Quérard, J.M. 1838. *La France littéraire, ou dictionnaire bibliographique*. Paris: chez Firmin Didot, père et fils, libraires.

Rambach, H.J. 2008. Un livre royal, tant par le sujet que par la provenance. *Bulletin de la Société Française de Numismatique* 63 (6): 132–135.

Rambach, H.J. 2011. Reflections on the gems depicting the contest of Athena and Poseidon, in: N. Adams and Ch. Entwistle (eds), *'Gems of Heaven': Recent Research on Engraved Gemstones in Late Antiquity, AD 200–600*, (British Museum Research Publication 177), 274–285. London: British Museum Press.

Rambach, H.J. 2014. The Gem Collection of Prince Poniatowski. *American Numismatic Society Magazine* 13.2: 34–49.

Rambach, H.J. 2017. A manuscript description in Kraków of the 'Trivulzio Museum' in Milan. *Studies in Ancient Art and Civilization* 21: 261–274.

Rambach, H.J. (forthcoming – Baron von Schellersheim). Friedemann Heinrich Christian Ludwig Schelhaß von Schellersheim (1752–1836) and his collection of engraved gems.

Ranieri, T. 1729. *Delle lodi dell'abate Pier Andrea Andreininobile fiorentino accademico etrusco. Orazione funerale detta nell'Accademia Etrusca di Cortona del dì primo dicembre 1729*. Firenze: appresso Piero Matini.

Raspe, R.E. 1786. *Account of the Present State and Arrangement of Mr. James Tassie's Collection of Pastes and Impressions from Ancient and Modern Gems: with a Few Remarks on the Origin of Engraving on Hard Stones, and the Methods of Taking Impressions of them in Different Substances*. London.

Raspe, R.E. and Tassie, J. 1791. *A descriptive catalogue of a general collection of ancient and modern engraved gems, cameos as well as intaglios, taken from the most celebrated cabinets in Europe and cast in coloured pastes, white enamel, and sulphur, by James Tassie, modeller*. London: Printed for and sold by James Tassie.

Ratouis de Limay, P. 1949. Un chanteur de l'Opéra, graveur et collectionneur, au début du XIXe siècle. Michel Nitot-Dufresne. *Bulletin de la Société de l'Histoire de l'Art français* (1949): 70–78.

Rave, P.O. 1957. Eine Neuerworbene Bildnisbüste des Barons Philipp von Stosch von Edme Bouchardon. *Berliner Museen* 7 (1): 19–26.

Rave, P.O. 1965. *Kunst in Berlin*. Berlin: Staneck Verlag.

Reed, M. 2010. Bernard Picart on China, in: L. Hunt, M. Jacob and W. Mijnhardt (eds), *Bernard Picart and the First Global Vision of Religion*, 215–234. Los Angeles (CA): Getty Research Institute.

Rée, P.J. 1891. Schweickart, Johann Adam, in: *Allgemeine Deutsche Biographie* 33: 329–330.

Reilly, R. 1994. *Wedgwood jasper*. London: Thames & Hudson.

Reinach, S. 1895. *Pierres gravées des collections Marlborough et d'Orléans: des recueils d'Eckhel, Gori, Lévesque de Gravelle, Mariette, Millin, Stosch, réunies et rééditées avec un texte nouveau*. Paris: Firmin-Didot et Cie.

Renouvier, J. and Montaiglon, de A. 1863. *Histoire de l'art pendant la Révolution, 1789–1804*. Paris: Jules Renouard.

Revue 1882. Revue critique d'histoire et de littérature 24 (12 June 1882): 472–473.

Richter, G.M.A. 1956. *Catalogue of Engraved Gems: Greek, Etruscan and Roman (Metropolitan Museum of Art, New York)*. Rome: L'Erma di Bretschneider.

Richter, G.M.A. 1968. *The Engraved Gems of the Greeks, Etruscans and Romans Part I: Engraved Gems of the Greeks and Etruscans*. London: Phaidon Press.

Richter, G.M.A. 1971. *The Engraved Gems of the Greeks, Etruscans and Romans Part II: Engraved Gems of the Romans*. London: Phaidon Press.

Ridley, R.T. 2015. Francesco Valesio's diary and "Archaeology" in Rome in the first half of the Eighteenth Century. *Bullettino della Commissione Archeologica Comunale di Roma* 116: 79–88.

Ridley, T.R. 2017. *The Prince of Antiquarians. Francesco de Ficoroni*. Rome: Edizioni Quasar.

Righetti, R. 1940. *Incisori di gemme e cammei in Roma dal Rinascimento all'Ottocento. Brevi cenni sulle attuali collezioni romane di opere di glittica*. Rome: Palombi.

Righetti, R. 1954–1955. Le opere di glittica dei musei annessi della BibliotecaVaticana. *Atti della Pontificia Accademia di Archeologia. Rendiconti* 28: 279–348.

Righetti, R. 1955. *Opere di glittica dei Musei Sacro e Profano*. The Vatican City: Biblioteca Apostolica Vaticana.

Rizzini, P. 1889. *Illustrazione dei Civici Musei di Brescia*. Brescia: F. Apollonio.

Roettgen, S. 1999. *Anton Raphael Mengs 1728–1779. Band 1: Das malerische und zeichnerische werk*. Munich: Hirmer Verlag.

Roland Michel, M. 1999. Dessiner à Rome au temps de Pajou, in: G. Schref (ed.), *Augustin Pajou et ses contemporains, Actes du colloque du musée du Louvre, 7–8 novembre 1997*, 285–308. Paris: la Documentation française.

Rosenberg, G.D. and Clary, R.M. 2018. *Museums at the Forefront of the History and Philosophy of Geology: History Made, History in the Making*. Colorado: Boulder.

Rosenberg, P. and Prat, L.-A. 2002. *Jacques-Louis David 1748–1825: Catalogue raisonné des dessins*. Milan: Leonardo Arte.

Rosset, T. de 2005. *Polskie kolekcje i zbiory artystyczne we Francji w latach 1795–1919. Między "skarbnicą narodowa" a galerią sztuki*. Toruń: Wydawnictwo Uniwersytetu Mikołaja Kopernika.

Rostriolla, G. 2001. *Il "mondo novo" musicale di Pier Leone Ghezzi*. Milan – Rome: Skira – Accademia nazionale di Santa Cecilia.

Rostirolla, G. 2010. Pier Leone Ghezzi disegnatore di antiche lire: Un excursus tra antiquaria, organologia, musicografia e mito. *Music in Art* 35 (1/2): 157–199.

Rubechini, V. 2016. *Giovanni Domenico Campiglia (1691–1775) 'bravo pittore e perfettissimo disegnatore'*. Ph.D. dissertation. Sapienza Università di Roma.

Rudoe, J. 1996. Eighteenth and nineteenth-century engraved gems in the British Museum; collectors and collections from Sir Hans Sloane to Anne Hull Grundy. *Zeitschrift für Kunstgeschichte* 59 (2): 198–213.

Rudoe, J. 2003. Engraved gems: the lost art of antiquity, in: K. Sloan and A. Burnett (eds), *Enlightenment, Discovering the World in the Eighteenth Century*, 132–138. London: British Museum Press.

Ruysschaert, J. 1964–1965. La lamelle de bronze apollinienne du Médallier Vatican (CIL VI, 3721) et le chevalier Jérôme Odam. *Rendiconti Atti della Pontificia Accademia Romana di Archeologia* 37: 325–336.

Sacconi, A. 1996. I cugini Zanetti e il "Delle Antiche Statue": nascita e diffusione di un'opera, in: M. Fano Santi (ed.), *Venezia, l'archeologia e l'Europa, atti del Congresso internazionale (Venezia 27–30 giugno 1994)*, 163–172. Rome: l'Erma di Bretschneider.

Saint Laurent, J. de 1746. *Description abrégée du fameux cabinet de M. Le Chevalier De Baillou, pour servir a l'Histoire Naturelle des Pierres précieuses, Métaux, Minéraux, et autres fossils*. Lucca: Sauveur et Jean Dominique Marescandoli.

Saint Laurent, J. de 1747. *Description et explication d'un camée de lapis-lazuli, fait en dernier lieu par Mr. Louis Siries, artiste françois, orfèvre du roi de France, et employé dans la Galerie de Florence, ou, Lettres de deux amis sur diverses productions de l'art : avec des notes curieuses & intéressantes : on a joint à la fin du livre la description d'un camée en onyce, travaillé fort singulierement, le tout avec des figures de très-bonne main*. Florence: De l'Imprimerie à l'enseigne d'Apollon.

Saint Laurent, J. de 1751. Sopra le pietre preziose degli antichi e sopra il modo col quale furono lavorate. *Saggi di dissertazioni accademiche: pubblicamente lette nella nobile Accademia Etrusca dell'antichissima città di Cortona* VI: 1–76.

Sapori, G. 2010. *Collezionismo e mercato di disegni a Roma nella prima metà del Settecento: protagonisti, comprimari, compares*. Ph.D. dissertation, Università degli Studi Roma Tre, Rome.

Savattieri, C. 2007. La Galerie de Florence de J.B. Wicar et Antoine Mongez: tradition et originalité à l'époque de la Révolution, in: M.T. Caracciolo and G. Toascano (eds), *Jean-Baptiste Wicar et son temps 1762–1834*, 123–152. Villeneuve d'Ascq: Presses Universitaires du Septentrion.

Sbigoli, F. 1967. *Tommaso Crudeli e i primi framassoni in Firenze. Narrazione storica corredata di documenti inedita*. Bologna: Forni.

Scarfò, G.C. 1739a. *D. Jo. Chrysostomi Scarfo Doctoris Theologi Basiliani in Collectanea Antiquitatum Romanarum ab Antonio Borioni exhibita, & à Rodulphino Venuti Academico Cortonensi explicata Observationes Criticae*. Venice: n.p.

Scarfò, G.C. 1739b. *Lettera nella quale vengono espressi colle figure in rame e dilucidati colle Annotazioni, dal P.D. Giangrisostomo Scarfò, dottor teologico basiliano, vari antichi Monumenti*. Venice: Bonifazio Viezzeri.

Scarisbrick, D. 1979. A.M. Zanetti and Althorp Leopard. *Apollo* 110: 425–427.

Scarisbrick, D. 1981. Henry Walters and the Marlborough Gems. *Journal of the Walters Art Gallery* 39: 49–58.

Scarisbrick, D. 1987. Gem Connoisseurship – The 4th Earl of Carlisle's Correspondence with Francesco de Ficoroni and Antonio Maria Zanetti. *The Burlington Magazine* 129 (1007): 90–104.

Scarisbrick, D. 1990. Piranesi and the 'Dactyliotheca Zanettiana'. *The Burlington Magazine* 132: 413–414.

Scarisbrick, D. 1996. The Arundel Gems Cabinet. *Apollo* 414: 45–48.

Scher, S.K. (ed.) 2019. *The Scher collection of commemorative medals*. New York & London: Guiles.

Schlichtegroll, F. 1792a. *Abbildungen aegyptischer, griechischer und roemischer Gottheiten mit mythologischen und aestetischen Erlaeuterungen. Erste Lieferung*. Nuremberg: J.F. Frauenholz.

Schlichtegroll, F. 1792b. *Choix des principales pierres gravées de la collection qui appartenait autrefois au Baron de Stosch et qui se trouve maintenant dans le cabinet du roi de Prusse : Accompagné de notes et d'explications relatives à la mythologie et aux beaux arts*. Nuremberg: J.F. Frauenholz.

Schlichtegroll, F. 1794. *Abbildungen aegyptischer, griechischer und roemischer Gottheiten mit mythologischen und aestetischen Erlaeuterungen. Zweyte Lieferung*. Nuremberg: J.F. Frauenholz.

Schlichtegroll, F. 1797. *Auswahl vorzüglicher Gemmen aus derjenigen Sammlung die ehmals der Baron Philipp von Stosch besass, die sich jetzt aber in dem Kön. preussischem Cabinette befindet. Mit mythologischen und artistischen Erlaeuterungen begleitet von Friedrich Schlichtegroll.* Erster Band. Nuremberg: J.F. Frauenholz.

Schlichtegroll, F. 1798. *Choix Des Principales Pierres Gravées De La Collection Qui Appartenait Autrefois Au Baron De Stosch Et Qui Se Trouve Maintenant Dans Le Cabinet Du Roi De Prusse Accompagné De notes Et Explications relatives À La Mythologie Et Beaux Arts.* Premier Volume. Nuremberg: J.F. Frauenholz.

Schlichtegroll, F. 1805. *Dactyliotheca Stoschiana Oder Abbildung Aller Geschnittenen Steine Die Ehemals Der Baron Philipp Von Stosch Besass, Die Sich Jetzt Aber In Dem Kön. Preussischen Museum Befinden,* vols I–II. Nurnberg: Friedrich Frauenholz.

Schlosser, J. von 1897. Die ältesten Medaillen und die Antike. *Jahrbuch der Kunsthistorischen Sammlungen des allerhöchsten Kaiserhauses* 15: 64–108.

Schnapp, A. 1997. *The Discovery of the Past.* New York: Harry N. Abrams.

Schnapp, A. 2002. La méthode de Caylus, in: I. Aghion (ed.), *Caylus mécène du roi. Collectionner les antiquitiés au XVIIIe siècle,* 53–63. Paris: Institut national d'histoire de l'art.

Schneider von, R. 1907. Ein Brief Philipp von Stosch an Heraeus. *Jahreshefte des Österreichischen archäologischen Instituts in Wien* 10: 345–348.

Schweickart, J.A. 1775. *Description Des Pierres Gravées Du Feu Baron de Stosch, Par Feu l'Abbé Winckelmann, Dessineés D'Après Les Empreintes Et Graveés En Taille-Douce Par Jean Adam Schweikart.* Nuremberg: Johann Adam Schweickart.

Sectani, Q. 1700. *Satyrae, numero auctae, mendis purgatae et singulae locupletiores. Editio novissima. Accedunt Argumenta ac Indices Rerum, Verborum et Nominum necnon Commentaria ex Notis Anonimi concinnante P. Antoniano,* vols I–II. Amsterdam: apud Elsevirios.

Sena Cheisa, G., Magni, A. and Tassinari, G. 2009. *Gemme dei civici musei d'arte di Verona.* Rome: G. Bretschneider.

Sénéchal, P. 1986. Originale e copia. Lo studio comparato delle statue antiche nel pensiero degli antiquari fino al 1770, in: S. Settis (ed.), *Memoria dell'antico nell'arte italiana 3, Dalla tradizione all'archeologia,* 150–180. Torino: Giulio Einaudi editore.

Sénéchal, P. 2000. Attaché entièrement à l'Antiquité et à mon caprice: die Büste des Barons Philipp von Stosch von Edme Bouchardon, in: U. Fleckner (ed.), *Jenseits de Grenzen. Französische un deutsche Kunst vom Ancien Régime bis zur Gegenwart,* 136–148. Cologne: Dumont.

Sérullaz, A. and Sandt, U. van der (eds) 1981–1982. *David e Roma: dicembre 1981-febbraio 1982.* Rome: De Luca.

Sérullaz, A. 1991. *Dessins de Jacques-Louis David 1748–1825.* Paris: Réunions des musées nationaux.

Sichelstiel, L. 2012. Die Künstlerfamilie Preißler, in: M. Henkel and U. Kubach-Reutter (eds), *1662–1806. Die Frühzeit der Nürnberger Kunstakademie,* 70–81. Nuremberg: Tümmels.

Sichtermann, H. 1996. *Kulturgeschichte der klassischen Archäologie.* Munich: C.H. Beck.

Sieveking, J. and Curtius, L. (eds) 1913. *Kleine Schriften von Adolf Furtwängler,* vol. II. Munich: C.H. Beck.

Simonet-Lenglart, M. 1979. *Louis David, 1748–1825: dessins du premier séjour romain, 1775–1780.* Paris: Galerie de Bayser.

Sinkansas, J. 1993. *Gemology: an annotated bibliography.* Metuchen (NJ): Scarecrow Press.

Skowronek, J. 1986. *Czartoryski Adam Jerzy. Pamiętniki i memoriały polityczne 1776–1809.* Selection and elaboration of the materials – Jerzy Skowronek. Warszawa: Instytut Wydawniczy PAX.

Skowronek, J. 1994. *Adam Jerzy Czartoryski 1770–1861.* Warszawa: Wiedza Powszechna.

Sloan, K. (ed.) 2003. *Enlightenment: Discovering the World in the Eighteenth Century.* London: British Museum Press.

Sluis, van J. 2010. *François Hemsterhuis. Ma toute chère Diotime. Lettres à la princesse de Gallitzin, 1783, Hemsterhusiana,* vol. 4. Berltsum: Van Sluis.

Sluis, van J. 2015. *Lettres de Diotime à François Hemsterhuis tome II: 1782–1784, Hemsterhusiana,* vol. 15. Berltsum: Van Sluis.

Smentek, K. 2014. *Mariette and the Science of the Connoisseur in Eighteenth-Century Europe.* London – New York: Routledge.

Smith, A.H. 1888. *Catalogue of Engraved Gems in the British Museum (Department of Greek and Roman Antiquities).* London: William Clowes and Son.

Smith, J.P. 1995. *James Tassie 1735–1799. Modeller in Glass. A Classical Approach.* London: Mallett.

Sölch, B. 2007. *Francesco Bianchini (1662–1729) und die Anfänge der öffentlichen Museen in Rom.* Berlin: Deutcher Kunstverlag.

Spence, J. 1966. *Observations, Anecdotes, and Characters of Books and Men.* Oxford: W.H. Carpenter.

Spier, J. 1999. Conyer Middleton's gems, in: M. Henig and D. Plantzos (eds), *Classical to Neo-Classical. Essays Dedicated to Gertrud Seidmann,* (British Archaeological Reports IS 793), 205–216. Oxford: Archeopress.

Spier, J. 2007. *Late Antique and Early Christian Gems.* Wiesbaden: Dr. Ludwig Reichert Verlag.

Spier, J. 2014. A cameo from the Medici collection. *Antike Kunst* 57: 67–77.

Spier, J. 2021. Rubens and the Study of Ancient Gems, in: A.T. Woollett, D. Gasparotto and J. Spier (eds), *Rubens. Picturing Antiquity,* 56–69. Malibu: Getty Publications.

Spier, J. and Kagan, J.H. 2000. Sir Charles Frederick and the Forgery of Ancient Coins in Eighteenth-Century Rome. *Journal of the History of Collections* 12: 35–90.

Spon, J. 1685. *Miscellanea eruditae antiquitatis, in quibus marmora, statuae, musiva, toreumata, gemmae, numismata, Grutero, Ursino, Boissardo, Reinesio, aliisque antiquorum monumentorum collectoribus ignota, et hucusque inedita referuntur ac illustrantur: cura & studio Iacobi Sponii, Lugdunensium medicorum collegio, Patavinae recuperatorum, et regiae Nemausensi academiae aggregati.* Leiden: Sumptibus fratrum Huguetan & Soc.

Stahl, A.M. and Waldman, L. 1993–1994. The earliest known medallists: the Sesto Brothers of Venice. *American Journal of Numismatics* NS 5–6: 167–188.

Stante, D. 2006. L'esprit des originaux – Der Geist der Originale. Die Diskussion um die Reproduzierbarkeit von Gemmen durch druckgraphische Medien, in: V. Kockel and D. Graepler (eds), *Daktyliotheken: Götter & Caesaren aus der Schublade: antike Gemmen in Abdrucksammlungen des 18. Und 19. Jahrhunderts*, 110–120. Munich: Biering & Brinkmann.

Stein, P. (ed.) 2022. *Jacques Louis David, radical draftsman*. New York (NY): The Metropolitan Museum of Art.

Story-Maskelyne, M.H. 1870. *The Marlborough Gems. Being a collection of works in cameo and intaglio formed by George, Third Duke of Marlborough*. Printed by the author.

Stosch, P. von 1724. *Gemmae antiquae caelatae, scalptorum nominibus insignitae. Ad ipsas gemmas, aut earum ectypos delineatae & aeri incisae, per Bernardum Picart. Ex praecipuis Europae museis selegit & commentariis illustravit Philippus de Stosch / Pierres antiques gravées, sur les quelles les graveurs ont mis leurs noms. Dessinées et gravées en cuivre sur les originaux ou d'après les empreintes par Bernard Picart. Tirées des principaux cabinets de l'Europe, expliquées par M. Philippe de Stosch*. Amsterdam: Bernard Picart.

Stosch, von P. 1754. Geschichte des Freiherrn Baron Philipp von Stosch, Königlich Großbritannischen Ministers und Königl. Polnischen Raths zu Florenz. *Das neue gelehrte Europa. Fünfter Theil*, 1–54. Wolfenbüttel: J.Ch. Meißner Verlag.

Stosch, von P. 1757. Fortsetzung der Geschichte des Freiherrn Baron Philipp von Stosch zu Florenz. *Das neue gelehrte Europa. Zehntel Theil*, 257–301. Wolfenbüttel: J.Ch. Meißner Verlag.

Stosch, von P. 1758. Neue Zulätze zu Geschichte des Freiherrn von Stosch. *Das neue gelehrte Europa. Dreizehntel Theil*, 242–243. Wolfenbüttel: J.Ch. Meißner Verlag.

Stosch, von P. 1759. *Bibliotheca Stoschiana, sive catalogus selectissimorum librorum*. Florence: n.p.

Strada, J. 1553. *Epitome Thesauri Antiquitatum*. Lyon: Jean de Tournes.

Strong, R. 1986. *Henry Prince of Wales and England's Lost Renaissance*. London: Thames and Hudson.

Sturm, J.W. 1863. Originalaufzeichnungen zur Geschichte der Preisler'schen Künstlerfamilie. *Archiv für die zeichnenden Künste* 9: 373–391.

Szyndler, B. 1997. *Biblioteka króla Stanisława Augusta Poniatowskiego*. Kielce: Antykwariat Naukowy Andrzeja Metzgera.

Tassinari, G. 1994. La riproduzione delle gemme attraverso le incisioni nei secoli XVII e XVIII e alcuni intagli raffiguranti Vulcano o un fabbro. *Xenia Antiqua* III, 1994: 33–72.

Tassinari, G. 2007a. I disegni di gemme di Leopoldo Zuccolo: qualche osservazione, in: M. Buora and A. Marcone (eds), *La ricerca antiquaria nell'Italia nordorientale. Dalla repubblica veneta all'unità*, (Antihcità Alto Adriatiche LXIV), 367–381. Trieste: Edizioni Quasar.

Tassinari, G. 2007b. I disegni di gemme appartenuti a Leopoldo Zuccolo (1760/61–1833). *Aquileia Nostra* LXXVIII: 457–518.

Tassinari, G. 2010a. Antonio Pichler e gli incisori di pietre dure a Napoli ipotesi e suggestioni. *Napoli Nobilissima* LXVII: 23–52.

Tassinari G. 2010b. Lettere dell'incisore di pietre dure Francesco Maria Gaetano Ghinghi (1689–1762) ad Anton Francesco Gori. *LANX* 7: 61–149.

Tassinari, G. 2012. *Giovanni Pichler. Raccolta di impronte di intagli e di cammei del Gabinetto Numismatico e Medagliere delle Raccolte Artistiche del Castello Sforzesco di Milano*, (Dattilioteche 1). Milan: Ennerre.

Tassinari, G. 2018. L'Iliade, un intaglio Marlborough e una gemma al Museo di Como. *Rivista Archeologica dell'antica provincia e diocesi di Como* 200: 28–50.

Tassinari, G. 2019. Winckelmann e la glittica del suo tempo, in: E. Agazzi and F. Slavazzi (eds), *Winckelmann, l'antichità classica e la Lombardia. Atti del Convegno Bergamo/Milano 11–13 aprile 2018*, 223–250. Rome: Artemide.

Tassinari, G. 2022. Collezionisti, committenti e incisori di pietre dure a Venezia nel Settecento, in: A. Gariboldi (ed.), *Collezionisti e collezioni di antichità e di numismatica a Venezia nel Settecento. Atti del convegno del 6–7 dicembre 2019*, 99–211. Trieste: Edizioni Università di Trieste.

Te Rijdt, R.J.A. 1993. Bernard Picart (1673–1733). *Delineavit et Sculpsit. Tijdschrift voor Nederlandse prent-en tekenkunst tot omstreeks 1850* 11: 34–37.

Thomson, D. 2003. The letters of James and William Tassie to Alexander Wilson 1778 to 1826. *The Volume of the Walpole Society* 65: 1–87.

Tondo, L. and Vanni, F.M. 1996. *Le gemme dei medici e dei Lorena nel Museo Archeologico di Firenze*. Florence: Centro Di.

Totaro, G. 1990. Nota su due manoscritti delle *Adnotationes* al *Tractatus Theologico-Politicus* di Spinoza. *Nouvelles de la République des Lettres* 2: 107–115.

Totaro, G. 1993. Da Antonio Magliabechi a Philipp von Stosch. Varia fortuna del *De Tribus Impostoribus* e de *L'Esprit de Spinoza* a Firenze, in: E. Canone (ed.), *Bibliothecae selectae da Crisano a Leopardi*, 377–417. Florence: Leo S. Olschki.

Toutain, Q. 2007. Antonio Maria Zanetti a Paris. L'inspiration retrouvée. *Revue de l'art* 157: 9–22.

Toynbee, P.J. 1903. *The letters of Horace Walpole, fourth earl of Orford. Chronologically arranged and edited with notes and indices by Paget Toynbee. Vol. 1: 1732–1743*. Oxford: n.p.

Trevor-Roper, H. 1985. *Renaissance Essays*. Chicago: University of Chicago Press.

Treu, G. 1874. *De ossium humanorum larvarumque apud antiquos imaginibus*. Berlin: Gustav Schade.

Trigger, B.G. 1996. *A History of Archaeological Thought*. 2nd ed. Cambridge: Cambridge University Press.

Ubaldelli, M.-L. 1998. Le milieu romain des "amateurs d'antiquités". Les collectionneurs de gemmes, in: J. Raspi Serra and F. de Polignac (eds), *La fascination de l'Antique 1700–1770. Rome découverte, Rome inventé*, 40–43. Paris: Somogy éditions d'art.

Ubaldelli, M.-L. 2001. *Corpus Gemmarum: Dactyliotheca Capponiana*. Rome: Istituto poligrafico e Zecca dello Stato.

Ursinus, F. 1606. *Illustrium imagines, ex antiquis marmoribus, nomismatibus et gemmis expressae, quae exstant Romae*. Rome: n.p.

Vaiani, E. 2016. *The Antichita Diverse Album*, (Paper Museum of Cassiano Dal Pozzo. Series A: Antiquities and Architecture V). Turnhout: Brepols.

Valesio, F. 1977–1979. *Il diario di Roma*. Milan: Longanesi.

Valesio, F., Gori, A.F. and Venuti, R. 1750. *Museum Cortonense in quo vetera monumenta complectuntur, quae in Academia Etrusca ceterisque nobilium virorum domibus adservantur, notis illustratum*. Rome: Giovanni Generosis.

Venturelli, P. 2005. *Le collezioni Gonzaga. Cammei, cristalli, pietre dure, preficerine, cassettine, stipeti. Intorno all'elenco dei beni del 1626–1627*. Milan and Mantova: Silvana editore.

Venuti, R. 1740. *Risposta alla critica fatta dal P. D. Giovan-Crisostomo Scarfò ... al libro dell'Illustrissimo Signore Abate Rodolfino Venuti intitolato Collectanea Romanarum Antiquitatum*. Paris: n.p.

Vettori, F. 1732. *Veteris gemmae ad Christianum usum exscalptae brevis explanatio ad academicos Etruscos Cortonenses*. Rome: ex typografia Rochi Bernabò.

Vettori, F. 1739. *Dissertatio glyptographica, sive Gemmae duae vetustissimae emblematibus et graeco artificis nomine insignitae quae exstant Romae in Museo Victorio explicatae, et illustratae. Accedunt nonnulla veteris elegantiae, & eruditionis inedita Monimenta*. Florence: Zempelianis.

Vickers, M. 1983. The Felix Gem in Oxford and Mantegna's Triumphal Programme. *Gazette des Beaux-Arts* CXXV (March 1983): 97–102.

Vieillard-Baron, J.-L. 1975. Hemsterhuis, platonicien (1721–1790). *Dix-huitième siècle* 7: 129–146.

Vincent, A. and Picart B. 1734. *Impostures innocentes ou recueil d'estampes d'après divers peintres illustrés tels que Rafael, le Guide ... et accompagnées d'un discours sur les prejuges de certains curieux touchant la gravure*. Amsterdam: Bernard Picart.

Vinet, E. 1877. *Bibliographie méthodique et raisonnée des Beaux-Arts*, vol. II. Paris: Firmin Didot Frères Fils et Cie.

Vivian, F. 1971. *Il console Smith, mercante e collezionista*. Vicenza: Neri Pozza Editore.

Vollenweider, M.-L. 1966. *Die Steinschneidekunst und ihre Künstler in spätrepublikanischer und augusteischer Zeit*. Baden-Baden: Bruno Grimm.

Vollenweider, M.-L. 1972–1974. *Die Porträtgemmen der römischen Republik*. Mainz am Rhein: Verlag Philipp von Zabern.

Vollenweider, M.-L. and Avisseau-Broustet, M. 1995. *Camées et intailles. Tome 1: Les portraits grecs du Cabinet des médailles. Catalogue raisonné*. Paris: Bibliothèque nationale de France.

Voorn, H. 1960. *De Papiermolens in de Provincie Noord Holland*. Haarlem: Papierwereld.

Wagner, C. 2017. Post-classical cameos, their makers and users, in: B.J.L. van den Bercken and V.C.P. Baan (eds), *Engraved Gems. From Antiquity to the Present*, (Papers on Archaeology of the Leiden Museum of Antiquities 14), 113–122. Leiden: Sidestone Press.

Wagner, C. and Boardman, J. 2009. *Gem Mounts and the Classical Tradition. Supplement to A Collection of Classical and Eastern Intaglios, Rings and Cameos (2003)*. Oxford: Archaeopress.

Wagner, C. and Boardman, J. 2018. *Masterpieces in Miniature: Engraved Gems from Prehistory to the Present*. London: Philip Wilson Publishers.

Wall, E. 2019. Un nouveau dossier : la glyptique dessinée par Muret. https://digitalmuret.hypotheses.org/1090 (retrieved on 7 August 2023).

Walpole, H. 1927–1983. *The Yale Edition of Horace Walpole's Correspondence*. New Haven: Yale University Press.

Walters, H.B. 1926. *Catalogue of Engraved Gems & Cameos, Greek, Etruscan & Roman in the British Museum*. London: British Museum Press.

Wethered, N. 1923. *Mediaeval craftsmanship and the modern amateur*. London: Longmans, Green and Coompany.

Weiner, M.N. 1990. *Mia N. Weiner. Old Master Drawings. Auction Catalogue*. New York.

Whiteley, J.J.L. 1999. Philipp von Stosch, Bernard Picart and the Gemmae Antiquae Caelatae, in: M. Henig and D. Plantzos (eds), *Classicism to Neo-classicism. Essays Dedicated to Gertrud Seidmann*, (British Archaeological Reports IS 793), 183–190. Oxford: Archaeopress.

Wicar, J.-B. 1789–1807. *Tableaux, statues, bas-reliefs et camées de Florence et du Palais Pitti*, vols 1–4. Paris: chez Lacombe.

Wiebel, Ch. 2007. *Aquatinta oder? Die Kunst mit dem Pinsel in Kupfer zu stechen*. Coburg: Deutscher Kunstverlag.

Wierzbicki, P. 2021. O Bibliotece Książąt Czartoryskich, in: K. Płonka-Bałus and N. Koziara (eds), *Muzeum Książąt Czartoryskich*, 237–241. Kraków: Muzeum Narodowe.

Wilton, A. and Bignamini, I. (eds) 1996. *Grand Tour. The Lure of Italy in the Eighteenth Century*. London: Tate Gallery Publishing.

Williams, K.J. 2017. Antiquarianism: A Reinterpretation. *Erudition and the Republic of Letters* 2 (1): 56–96.

Winckelmann, J.J. 1760. *Description des pierres gravées du feu Baron de Stosch*. Florence: André Bonducci.

Winckelmann, J.J. 1952–1957. *Briefe*. In Verbindung mit Hans Diepolder; herausgegeben von Walther Rehm, vol. I: 1742–1759, vol. II: 1759–1763, vol. III: 1764–1768, vol. IV: Dokumente zur Lebensgeschichte. Berlin: De Gruyter.

Winckelmann, J.J. 1961. *Lettere italiane*. Ed. G. Zampa. Milan: Feltrinelli Editore.

Winckelmann, J.J. 2002. *Geschichte der Kunst des Alterthums* (Johann Joachim Winckelmann. Schriften und Nachlass 4.1: Text, A.H. Borbein, T.W. Gaehthgens, J. Irmscher and M. Kunze (eds)). Mainz am Rhein: Philipp von Zabern.

Winckelmann, J.J. 2013. *Description des Pierres gravées du feu Baron de Stosch*. Edited by A. Borbein, M. Kunze and A. Rügler. Mainz am Rhein: Philipp von Zabern.

Witte, A.A. 2018. Pier Leone Ghezzi's albums with drawings between studio practice and noble passtimes, in: Segreto, V. (ed.), *Libri e album di disegni 1550–1800*, 169–174. Rome: De Luca Editori d'Arte.

Wolohojian, S. (ed.) 2003. *A Private Passion: 19th-Century Paintings and Drawings from the Grenville L. Winthrop Collection, Harvard University*. New York (NY): The Metropolitan Museum of Art and Yale University Press.

Wood, L. 1994. *The Lady Lever Art Gallery Catalogue of Commodes*. London: HMSO.

Worlidge, T. 1768. *A Select Collection of Drawings from Curious Antique Gems; most of them in the possession of the Nobility and Gentry of this Kingdom; etched after the manner of Rembrandt by T. Worlidge, Painter*. London: Dryden Leach.

Worsley, R. 1824. *Museum Worsleyanum; or a Collection of Antique Basso-Relievos, Bustos, Statues, and Gems; with Views of Places in the Levant. Taken on the Spot in the Years MDCCLXXXV. VI. and VII*. London: Septimus Prowett.

Wyss, E. 1996. *The Myth of Apollo and Marsyas in the Italian Renaissance*. Newark: University of Delaware Press.

Wyss-Giacosa, P. 2006. *Religionsbilder der frühen Aufklärung. Bernard Picarts Tafeln für die Cérémonies et coutumes religieuses de tous les peuples du monde*. Wabern-Bern: Benteli.

Zadoks-Josephus, J.A.N. 1952. *La Collection Hemsterhuis au Cabinet Royal des Médailles à la Haye*. The Hague: Imprimerie de l'État.

Zamoyski, A. (ed.) 2001. *The Princes Czartoryski Museum. A History of the Collections*. Kraków: The National Museum.

Zanetti, A.M. 1740–1743. *Delle Antiche Statue Greche E Romane, Che Nell'Antisala Della Libreria di San Marco, e in altri luoghi publici di Venezia si trovano*. Venice: n.p.

Zawadzki, W.H. 1993. *A Man of Honour. Adam Czartoryski as a statesman of Russia and Poland, 1770–1831*. Oxford: Oxford University Press.

Zazoff, P. 1968. *Etruskische Skarabäen*. Mainz am Rhein: Philippe von Zabern.

Zazoff, P. 1974. Zur Geschichte der Stosch'schen Steines. *Archäologischer Anzeiger* 1974 (3): 466–484.

Zazoff, P. 1983. *Die antiken Gemmen*. Munich: C.H. Beck.

Zazoff, P. and Zazoff, H. 1983. *Gemmensammler und Gemmenforscher, von einer noblen Passion zur Wissenschaft*. Munich: C.H. Beck.

Zeno, A. 1752. *Lettere di Apostolo Zeno, Cittadino Veneziano Istorico e Poeta Cesareo. Nelle quali si contengono molte notizie attenenti all'Istoria Letteraria de' suoi tempi; e si ragiona di Libri, d'Iscrizioni, di Medaglie, e d'ogni genere d'erudita Antichità*. Venice: Pietro Valvasense.

Zeno, A. 1785. *Lettere di Apostolo Zeno cittadino veneziano istorico e poeta cesareo nelle quali si contengono molte notizie attenenti all'istoria letteraria de' suoi tempi, e si ragiona di libri, d'iscrizioni, di medaglie, e d'ogni genere d'erudita antichità. Seconda edizione in cui le lettere già stampate si emendano, e molte inedite se ne pubblicano*. Jacopo Morelli (ed.), vol. II. Venice: Francesco Sansoni.

Zwierlein-Diehl, E. 1969. Geschichte der Berliner Gemmensammlung. *Archäologischer Anzeiger* 1969 (1): 524–531.

Zwierlein-Diehl, E. 1973. *Die antiken Gemmen des Kunsthistorischen Museums in Wien: Die Gemmen von der minoischen Zeit bis zur frühen römischen Kaiserzeit*, vol. 1. Munich: Prestel Verlag.

Zwierlein-Diehl, E. 1986. *Glaspasten im Martin-von-Wagner-Museum der Universität Würzburg. Band I: Abdrücke von antiken und ausgewählten nachantiken Intagli und Kameen*. Munich: Prestel Verlag.

Zwierlein-Diehl, E. 1989. Thamyras-Gemmen, in: H.-U. Cain, N. Himmelmann, H. Gabelmann and D. Salzmann (eds), *Beiträge zur Ikonographie und Hermeneutik. Festschrift für Nikolaus Himmelmann*, 425–431. Mainz: Philipp von Zabern.

Zwierlein-Diehl, E. 1991. *Die antiken Gemmen des Kunsthistorischen Museums in Wien: Band III. Die Gemmen der späteren römischen Kaiserzeit, Teil 2; Masken Masken-Kombinationen, Phantasie- und Märchentiere, Gemmen mit Inschriften / Christliche Gemmen/Magische Gemmen / Sasanidische Siegel, Rundplastik aus Edelstein und verwandten Materialien/Kameen, Rundplastik, Gegenstände mit figürlichem Relief und Einlegearbeiten aus Glas, Antike Glyptik in Wiederverwendung/Nachantike Glyptik, Nachträge und Ergänzungen zu Band I und II*. Munich: Prestel Verlag.

Zwierlein-Diehl, E. 2005. Gemmen mit Künstlerschriften, in: M.V. Strocka (ed.), *Meisterwerke. Internationales Symposion anläßlich des 150. Geburtstages von Adolf Furtwängler. Freiburg im Breisgau 30. Juni–3. Juli 2003*: 321–343. Munich: Hirmer Verlag.

Zwierlein-Diehl, E. 2007. *Antike Gemmen und ihr Nachleben*. Berlin – New York: De Gruyter.

Zwierlein-Diehl, E. 2013. Gemmen aus der Sammlung Sibylle Mertens-Schaaffhausen. *Kölner Jahrbuch* 46: 209–333.

Zwierlein-Diehl, E. 2023. *Glaspasten im Martin von Wagner Museum der Universität Würzburg. Band II: Abdrücke von neuzeitlichen Kameen und Intaglien mit Nachträgen und ergänzungen zu Band I*. Berlin – Boston: Deutscher Kunstverlag.

Żygulski jr., Z. 2009. *Dzieje zbiorów puławskich. Świątynia Sybilli i Dom Gotycki*. Kraków: Fundacja Książąt Czartoryskich, Muzeum Nawiślańskie w Kazimierzu Dolnym.

Index

Aachen, Hans von (1552–1615)   40
Académie royale de peinture et de sculpture in Paris   76, 259
Accademia di Belle Arti in Florence   81, 84, 87
Accademia di San Luca   68–69, 81
Accademia Etrusca di Cortona   12, 28–29, 150, 156, 164, 288n, 289
Adam, James (1732–1794)   15n
Agostini, Leonardo (1593–1676)   29, 156
Albani, Alessandro, Cardinal (1692–1779)   6, 7n, 9, 12–14, 40, 71, 85–86, 99, 156, 165, 249–250, 289
Albrecht, Konrad Adolf von, Baron (unknown dates)   156–157, 159
Aldenburg Bentinck, Charlotte Sophie, Gräfin von (1715–1806)   219n
Alexander I of Russia (1801–1825)   104, 106
Alexander VIII, Pope (1689–1691)   70, 251–252, 261
Alexeievna, Elizabeth, Empress of Russia (1779–1826)   104
Alfieri, Vittorio, Count (1749–1803)   104, 106–107
Amalienborg Palace Square in Copenhagen   82, 143
Anders, Friedrich (fl. until 1816)   42
Andreini, Pietro Andrea (1650–1729)   6, 29, 70, 137, 139, 143–144, 157, 220, 227
Ansidei, Vincenzo (unknown dates)   30, 85, 157
August II the Strong, Elector of Saxony (1670–1733)   7–8, 157, 159
Aymon, Jean (1661–1734)   8

Baldelli, Onofrio (1667–1728)   30
Bandini, Angelo Maria (1726–1803)   15, 149
Banduri, Anselmo (1671–1743)   5n, 23
Barberini, Urbano III, Prince of Palestrina   157
Barbo, Pietro (1417–1471)   253
Barth, Joseph (1745–1818)   48
Barthélemy, Jean-Jacques (1617–1795)   13, 30, 216, 228
Bartoli, Pietro Santi (1635–1700)   25n, 28n
Bartolozzi, Francesco (1727–1815)   42
Baudelot de Dairval, Charles-César (1648–1722)   3, 5, 23, 133, 220, 282
Bellori, Giovanni Pietro (1613–1696)   29, 40, 157
Benedetti, Tommaso (1797–1863)   48
Bentinck, George von, Baron (1715–1759)   143, 157
Bentivoglio, Cornelio, Cardinal (1668–1732)   11n, 216
Bentley, Sir Richard (1662–1742)   5
Bernabé, Felice (1720-?)   293n
Bertoli, Anton Daniele (1677–1743)   42
Bessborough, Earl – see Ponsonby, William
Beverley collection   157

Bianchi, Sebastiano (1662–1738)   7n, 29
Bianchini, Francesco (1662–1729)   6, 10, 24n, 216n, 218, 281, 293n, 301
Biblioteca Marucelliana   15, 71n, 112, 139, 147–149
Bignon, Jean-Paul (1662–1743)   5, 23
Blacas collection   27n, 72n, 86n, 133n, 138n, 245, 247
Blacas d'Aulps, Pierre-Louis Jean Casimir, Duc de (1771–1839)   107
Blaeu, Joan (1596–1673)   8
Blundell, Henry (1724–1810)   22
Boccardino il Vecchio (1460–1529)   39
Boileau, Jacques (1635–1716)   5n, 47n
Boisselier, Félix (1776–1811)   42
Boissieu, Jean-Jacques de (1736–1810)   42
Bonaccorsi, Ottaviano (unknown dates)   14, 81n, 84, 100, 245
Bonaccorsi, Piero (1501–1547)   40
Boncompagni, Francesco (1592–1641)   26
Boncompagni-Ludovisi collection   25n, 157, 226
Boncompagni-Ludovisi, Gaetano, Duke of Sora, Prince of Piombino (1706–1777)   26
Borioni, Antonio (ca. 1690-aft. 1737)   24–26, 28, 31, 47, 78, 80, 157, 239, 256
Borromini, Francesco (1599–1667)   10
Bouchardon, Edmé (1698–1762)   37, 42, 50, 77, 81, 136n, 142, 149
Bourdaloue collection   157
Bourdeaux, Etienne-Laurent de (active 1736–1793)   110
Bouzonnet-Stella, Antoine (1637–1682)   40
Bracci, Augusto Domenico (1717–1795)   111–112, 244–245, 256, 261
Brandenburg-Schwedt, Frederick William, Prince (1700–1771)   6
Brosses, Charles de (1709–1777)   23
Brühl collection   157
Brühl, Heinrich von, Count (1700–1763)   159
Buonarroti, Filippo (1661–1733)   7, 11, 25, 29, 30n, 43, 137, 148, 157, 283n, 289n
Byres, James (1734–1817)   157

Cades, Tommaso (1772/5–1850)   20
Campiglia, Giovanni Domenico (1691–1768)   43
Camps, François de (1643–1723)   5n
Canini, Giovanni Angelo, a.k.a. Giannangiolo (1609–1666)   40
Capponi, Alessandro Gregorio, Count (1683–1746)   10, 24, 26–28, 30, 44–46, 66, 69, 71, 77–78, 157, 220, 243, 289, 294, 298
Carafa, Giovanni, Duke of Noja (1715–1768)   13, 31, 157, 291, 294, 295n
Carlisle collection   157, 242, 250–252
Carlisle, Earl of – see Howard, Henry; Howard, Charles
Carpegna, Gaspare, Cardinal (1625–1714)   25

Carracci, Annibale (1560–1609)   40
Carstens, Asmus Jakob (1754–1798)   43
Carteret, George, 1st Baron (1667–1695)   8n
Carteret, John, Earl Granville (1690–1763)   8
Casanova, Giovanni Battista (1730–1795)   48n, 111n, 157
Caselli, Giovanni (1698–1752)   43
Castiglioni, Anton Maria (1639–1711)   157
Cavendish, Charles Lord (aft. 1700–1783)   21
Cavendish, William, 2nd Duke of Devonshire (1672–1729)   21, 77n, 78, 133, 160, 162–163, 237, 241, 260, 282, 291–292
Caylus, Anne Claude de Tubières-Grimoard de Pestels de Lévis, Count (1692–1765)   13, 30n, 42–43, 151, 157, 215, 223, 259–260, 281, 302
Cerretani collection   7, 29, 157
Cerretani, Francesco (d. 1763)   7
Chambers/Chalmers, William (fl. 1794–1795)   44
Chamillard, Étienne (1656–1716)   5
Charles VI, Holy Roman Emperor (r. 1711–1740)   7, 157, 222, 239
Chassériau, Théodore (1819–1856)   48
Chausse, Michel-Ange de la (ca. 1660–1724)   24, 27, 29, 137, 140, 157, 159, 254, 281
Cheroffini, Francesca, Countess (née Gherardi, 1709–1778)   157, 250–251
Chesterfield collection   22, 157, 257
Chéron, Élisabeth Sophie (1648–1711)   97, 138, 226n, 282
Christina of Sweden (1626–1689)   25, 28
Cienfuego, Juan Álvaro Villazón, Cardinal (1657–1739)   8
Cipriani, Giovanni Battista (1727–1785)   44
City of Leipzig collection   158
Clement V, Pope (1305–1314)   256
Cocchi, Antonio (1695–1758)   12
Coke, Thomas, 1st Earl of Leicester (1691–1759)   11
Collins, Anthony (1676–1729)   5n
Colman, Francis (1691–1733)   13
Collaur, Cristiano (see Dehn, Christian)   10
Colonna collection   157
Comtesse de Luneville   239
Consalvi, Ercole, Cardinal (1757–1824)   104
Constable, William (1721–1791)   13n, 14n
Contucci, Archangelo Contuccio di (1688–1768)   10, 25
Corazzi, Galeotto Ridolfino (1690–1769)   30, 157
Corsini, Lorenzo, Pope Clement XII (r. 1730–1740)   6, 11
Cosimo III de' Medici (r. 1670–1723)   7
Costanzi, Carlo (1705–1781)   3, 20, 217, 293n
Costanzi, Tommaso (1700–1747)   293n
Cracherode, Clayton Mordaunt (1730–1799)   157
Craon, Marc de Beauvais, Prince of (1676–1754)   13

INDEX

Crispi, Girolamo (1667–1746) 137, 157
Crozat, Pierre (1665–1740) 5, 8, 23, 29–30, 42, 52, 74, 157, 159, 239–240
Crudeli, Tommaso (1702–1745) 12
Czartoryska (née Jabłonowska), Barbara (1760–1834) 107
Czartoryska, Izabela (1746–1835) 103–106, 109, 112–117, 166, 170
Czartoryski, Adam Jerzy (1770–1861) 103–110, 137
Czartoryski, Adam Kazimierz (1734–1823) 103, 105–106, 108

Dacier, André (1651–1722) 5n
Dacier, Anne (1647–1720) 5n
Danish Academy of Painting and Drawing 82
Dati, Carlo (1619–1676) 292
David, Jacques Louis (1748–1825) 48
D'Ayton, Margaret Rolle, Countess Orford, Lady Walpole (1709–1781) 82
Dehn (Denh), Christian (1696–1770) 4, 10–11, 67, 77, 85, 88, 97, 155, 218, 252
Dering, Edward, Sir 6th Baronet (1732–1798) 157, 249
Devonshire, Duke of – see Cavendish, William
Dolce, Federico (d. 1790) 85
Dugood/Dugud/Ducat/Duckett, William (active 1715–1767) 14n, 25n
Duke of Stiualis (?) collection in Rome 138, 158
Duncannon, Viscount – see Ponsonby, William

Edict of Nantes 76
Egizio, Matteo (1674–1740) 6
Elbeuf, Emmanuel Maurice, Duke of (1677–1763) 6, 116n
Esterházy collection 157
Ettore, Salvatore (unknown dates) 44
Eugene, Prince of Savoy (1663–1736) 5, 7, 23, 74, 133, 161, 245

Fabre, François-Xavier (1766–1837) 48, 106
Fagel, François (1659–1746) 5–8, 10, 21, 73, 83n, 99n, 135–137, 220, 222, 224, 226, 254, 284
Fane, Charles, 1st Viscount Fane (1676–1744) 13
Farnese collection 25, 30, 43, 75, 137, 143, 157, 246, 249, 253–254
Farnese, Odoardo, Cardinal (1573–1626) 25
Ferdinand VI, King of Spain (r. 1746–1759) 14, 101n, 170n
Ficoroni, Francesco de' (1664–1747) 6, 22, 24–27, 46, 50, 66–67, 69, 71–72, 78, 137, 157, 160, 215, 243, 252
Finch, Daniel, 7th Earl of Winchilsea and 2nd Earl of Nottingham (1647–1730) 21
Flemming, Jacob Heinrich (1667–1728) 8n, 12n
Fontanini, Giusto (1666–1736) 24n, 26, 216n

Fora, Gherardo del (1445–1497) 39
Fountaine, Sir Andrew (1676–1753) 5, 21
Fragonard, Jean-Honoré (1732–1806) 44
Franceschini, Vincenzo (1680-?) 44
Francis I, Holy Roman Emperor (r. 1745–1765) 14, 101, 164n
Franco, Battista (bef. 1510–1561) 52
Franz de collection 157, 159
Frauenholz, Johann Friedrich (1758–1822) 79, 87, 100n, 110–111, 141, 239, 240n, 255
Frederick II of Prussia (r. 1740–1786) 14–15, 83, 101, 124, 148n, 168, 219, 262, 290
Frederick William of Prussia (r. 1713–1740) 8, 20
French Royal collection 137, 143, 157, 159, 259
Fritsch, Gaspar (1677–1745) 12n
Fritsch, Thomas von, Baron (1700–1775) 157, 159

Gabburri, Niccolò (1676–1742) 147
Galeotti, Niccolò (1692–1758) 157
Gareis, Franz (1775–1803) 48
George III (r. 1760–1820) 31
Germain, John, Sir 1st Baronet (1650–1718) 21, 157
Gesura collection 157
Géricault, Théodore (1791–1824) 48
Ghezzi, Caterina Peroni (ca. 1694–1762) 145
Ghezzi, Giuseppe (1643–1721) 68
Ghezzi, Pier Leone (1674–1755) 6–7, 10–11, 24–27, 30, 44, 66–70, 78, 81, 97, 132–135, 138–139, 144–145, 155, 157, 161, 216, 218, 221, 224, 227, 238, 242–243, 248, 252–253, 293
Ghinghi, Francesco Maria Gaetano (1689–1762) 3, 217n, 293n
Giornale dei Letterati 12, 148, 161
Gleichen-Rußwurm, Karl Heinrich von, Baron (1733–1807) 157, 250
Goeree, Jan (1670–1731) 44
Goorle (or Gorlaeus), Abraham van, of Delft (1549–1608) 241
Gori, Anton Francesco (1691–1757) 7, 12, 29, 38, 45, 47–48, 71, 73, 82, 112, 138, 140, 147–149, 157, 247, 282, 296
Gosmond de Vernon, Augustin (1697–176?) 44
Gravelle, Michel Pierre Philippe l'Evesque de la (1699–1752) 108, 285
Greville, Charles Francis (1749–1809) 219
Gronovius, Jakob (1645–1716) 241
Gualtiero, Filippo Antonio, Cardinal (1660–1728) 10, 24
Guido, Duca della Gherardesca (1696–1755) 157

Hackert, Jacob Philipp (1737–1807) 239
Hamilton, William, Sir (1730–1803) 47, 157, 294n
Harper, Robert (ca. 1700–1772) 157
Hem, Laurens van der (1621–1678) 8

Hemsterhuis, Frans (1721–1790) 44
Hemsterhuis, Tiberius (1685–1766) 4n, 21n, 44, 99n, 102, 112, 219, 229, 301n
Heraeus, Carl Gustav (1671–1725) 7n, 9, 97–98, 139, 154
Herbert, Thomas, 8th Earl of Pembroke (1656–1733) 21
Hollis, Thomas (1720–1774) 30, 157
Homberg, Wilhelm (1652–1715) 5, 23, 97, 218
Howard, Henry, 4th Earl of Carlisle (1693–1758) 22, 28, 47, 71, 74, 84, 143, 228, 243, 253
Howard, Thomas, the 14th Earl of Arundel (1586–1646) 241n
Hutin, Charles François (1715–1776) 157, 159

Imperiali, Giuseppe Renato, Cardinal (1651–1737) 6
Ingres, Jean Auguste Dominique (1780–1867) 48

Jabłonowski, Józef Aleksander (1711–1777) 158
Joubert, Philippe-Laurent de (1729–1792) 106

Kalf, Nicolaas (1677–1734) 222
Kate, Lambert ten (1674–1731) 222
Keyßler, Johann Georg (1693–1743) 10
King of Prussia collection 137
Kostka Potocki, Stanisław (1755–1821) 110, 217

Lami, Giovanni (1697–1770) 12
Le Clerc, Jean (1657–1736) 4n
Leicester, Earl of – see Coke, Thomas
Levier, Charles (d. 1735) 8, 10, 12n
Lippert, Philipp Daniel (1702–1785) 20, 250, 285
Louise, Princess of Stolberg-Gedern (1752–1824) 104, 107
Lucatelli, Giovanni Pietro (fl. 1747–1750) 158

Mabillon, Jean (1632–1707) 29
Maffei, Paolo Alessandro (1653–1716) 26–27, 281, 301
Maffei, Scipione (1675–1755) 6–7, 29, 281
Mallia, Jean-Baptiste (1756/1757–1812) 48
Manchester, Duke of – see Montagu, Robert
Mann, Horace, 1st Baronet (1706–1786) 13–14, 23, 50, 100, 256
Mansfeld, Johann Georg (1772–1817) 48
Mantegna, Andrea (1431–1506) 39
Maratta, Carlo (1625–1713) 6, 68, 70
Marchand, Prosper (1678–1756) 8, 12n, 224n
Marck heer van Leur, Hendrik Adriaan, van de (ca. 1667–1726) 158
Mariette, Pierre-Jean (1694–1774) 7, 23, 37, 42, 50, 74, 133, 161, 163, 220, 240, 254, 285–287, 301–304
Marlborough collection 21, 42, 44, 71, 145, 158, 244, 249, 256–257

Marlborough, Duke of – see Spencer, George
Marmi, Anton Francesco (1665–1736)   7, 26, 75
Marsigli, Luigi Ferdinando (1658–1730)   6, 218
Masini, Lorenzo (1713-?)   3, 215, 257, 293n
Massimo collection   25, 158
Mazzei, Filippo (1730–1816)   104
Mead, Richard (1673–1754)   29
Medici collection   29, 137, 143–145, 158, 253
Medici, Gian Gastone de' (r. 1723–1737)   7, 11, 29, 139, 144
Medici, Leopoldo de' (1617–1675)   29
Medina, Gabriel de (d. before 1761)   22, 30, 143, 158
Mehus, Lorenzo (1717–1802)   12, 15, 29
Mengs, Anton Raphael (1728–1779)   44
Michelangelo (1475–1564)   40
Middlesex, Earl of – see Sackville, Charles
Middleton, Conyers (1683–1750)   22, 28
Mieris, Willem van (1662–1747)   45
Miniato, Monte di Giovanni di (1448–1532)   39
Molinari, Giovanni Carlo (1715–1763)   71, 86, 158
Montagu, Robert, 3rd Duke of Manchester (ca. 1710–1762)   12n
Montfaucon, Bernard de (1655–1741)   5, 23, 156, 163, 214, 221, 281, 295
Mordaunt, Henry, 2nd Earl of Peterborough (1621–1697)   158
Moreau, Gustave (1826–1898)   48
Morell, Andreas (1646–1703)   20, 223
Morpeth, Viscout – see Howard, Henry
Moszyński, August (1731–1786)   158
Muratori, Antonio (1672–1750)   6
Muret, Jean-Baptiste (1795–1866)   48
Museo Kircheriano in the Collegio Romano   10, 25–27, 158, 298n
Museo Cartaceo of Cassiano dal Pozzo   116, 163, 280, 289–290, 292
Muzell, Heinrich Wilhelm von (1723–1782)   13–14, 25, 31, 83–84, 86, 99–102, 109, 112, 123, 163, 170, 214, 290n, 291, 295, 304

Nahl the Younger, Johann August (1752–1825)   45
Natter, Lorenz (1705–1763)   3, 4n, 22, 44–45, 47, 72, 82, 145, 151, 158, 215, 242, 250, 253, 257
Néaulme, Jean II (1694–1780)   110
Netscher, Theodorus (1661–1728)   45, 73
Nitot (dit Dufresne), Michel (1759–1828)   49
Notti Coritane   21, 150, 161
Nottingham, Earl of – see Finch, Daniel
Novelli, Pietro Antonio (1729–1804)   45
Nucherini, Pietro (unknown dates)   45

Odam, Girolamo (1681–1741)   6–7, 24, 45, 67–68, 70–73, 97, 132–140, 154, 158, 160, 220, 224, 238, 282

Odescalchi, Livio (1658–1713)   25, 28, 158
Orléans, Philippe II, Duke of (1674–1723)   5, 8, 23, 29, 47, 74, 158, 218, 239
Orsini (Ursinus), Fulvio (1529–1600)   25, 244–245, 280n
Otto, Ernst Peter (1724–1799)   110
Ottoboni, Pietro, Cardinal (1667–1740)   22, 24–25, 28, 70, 158, 252–253, 261

Paciaudi, Paolo Maria (1710–1785)   160
Painting Academy in Nuremberg   79, 81
Pajou, Augustin (1730–1809)   45
Palatine, Anne Elisabeth, Madame (1652–1722)   5, 23
Palazzi, Francesco (?-1745)   22, 24, 28, 31, 158
Palmieri, Pietro Giovanni (unknown dates)   46
Paoletti, Bartolomeo (1757–1834)   20, 218
Paoletti, Pietro (1785–1844/5)   20, 218
Pasquali, Giovanni Battista (1702–1784)   31
Pasqualigo, Domenico (1698–1766)   30n
Pasqualini, Lelio (1549–1611)   26
Passionei, Silvio Card. (1682–1761)   15
Patarol, Lorenzo (1674–1724)   30n
Patin, Charles (1633–1693)   282
Paul I of Russia (1796–1801)   104
Pedrusi, Paolo (1644–1720)   25n
Peiresc, Nicolas-Claude Fabri de (1580–1637)   41n
Pembroke, Earl of – see Herbert, Thomas
Picart, Bernard (1673–1733)   8, 37, 47, 70, 73, 75–76, 98, 110, 134–137, 213–214, 220–226, 236, 283
Piccini, Gaetano (active 1702–1740)   26, 46, 66, 72, 218
Piccolomini, Mario (1651–1728)   24, 218
Pichler, Antonio (1697–1779)   46n, 293n
Pinelli, Bartolomeo (1781–1835)   49
Pini, Onofrio (1721–1754)   158, 297n
Piombino, Prince of – see Boncompagni-Ludovisi, Gaetano
Piranesi, Giovanni Battista (1720–1778)   46
Pius VII, Pope (1800–1823)   105
Polignac, Melchior de, Cardinal (1661–1742)   10–11, 68, 72, 81, 221
Poniatowski, Stanislas, Prince (1754–1833)   49, 220n, 251n
Ponsonby, William, 2nd Earl of Bessborough (1704–1793)   22, 23n, 157, 216, 256–257
Pope, Alexander (1688–1744)   215
Potocka, Pelagia (1909–1994)   108–109
Poussin, Nicolas (1594–1665)   40
Pozzo, Carlo Antonio dal (1606–1689)   163n, 280
Pozzo, Cassiano dal (1588–1657)   8, 40, 66n, 116, 156, 163, 280, 289–290, 292
Praun, Paul von (1548–1616)   111, 143
Preißler, Georg Martin (1700–1754)   80–81
Preißler, Johann Justin (1698–1771)   10–11, 47, 67, 76–80, 82, 88, 140–143, 153–154, 162, 219, 239–243

Recanati, Giovanni Battista (1687–1734)   30n
Riccardi collection   29, 158, 226
Rigacci, Giuseppe (b. 1710)   12n, 82
Ristori, Antonio (1707–1785)   12n
Rossi, Ferdinando Maria de, Cardinal (1696–1775)   158
Rost, Carl (1742–1798)   110
Rousset de Missy, Jean (1686–1762)   8
Rubens, Peter Paul (1577–1640)   39–41
Rushout, George John, 3rd Baron Northwick (1811–1887)   225
Rushout, John, 2nd Lord Northwick (1770–1859)   225
Rzewuski, Franciszek (1730–1800)   104, 106–107

Sabbatini, Marcantonio (1637–1724)   6, 24, 26, 27n, 28, 74, 158–159, 239
Sackville, Charles, Earl of Middlesex (1711–1769)   12n
Saint-Aubin, Augustin de (1736–1807)   47
Saint-Aubin, Gabriel de (1724–1780)   47
Saint Laurent, Joannon de (1714–1783)   126, 164–166, 168–170, 294–295, 299, 304
Salvini, Anton Maria (1653–1729)   7, 29, 148
Sandrart, Joachim von (1606–1688)   41
Sangallo, Giovanni Battista da (1496–1548)   10, 14
Santarelli, Emilio (1801–1889)   107
Santarelli, Giovanni-Antonio (1758–1826)   104–105, 107
Schinkel, Karl Friedrich (1781–1841)   49
Schlichtegroll, Johann Friedrich (1765–1822)   45, 79, 87, 111, 124, 141, 156, 240
Schmettau, Adelheid Amalie von, Princess Gallitzin (1748–1806)   99n, 102, 112
Schmettau, Wolfgang Freiherr von (1648–1711)   5, 45n
Schott, Johann Carl (1672–1717)   20, 21n
Schönborn, Lothar-Franz von (1655–1729)   158, 229n
Schulenburg, Johann Matthias von, Reichsgraf (1661–1747)   6
Sellari, Reginaldo (unknown dates)   158, 228
Sévin, François (1682–1741)   5n, 158
Sirleti, Flavio (1683–1737)   3, 4n, 20, 30, 68
Sloane, Sir Hans (1660–1753)   5, 22, 28
Smith, Joseph (1674–1770)   31, 48
Società Colombaria   12, 161, 164, 288
Società del Museo Fiorentino   161
Spada, Virgilio (1596–1662)   25n
Spanheim, Ezechiel von (1629–1710)   20
Spence, Joseph (1699–1768)   216
Spencer, George, 4th Duke of Marlborough (1739–1817)   21n, 22, 74, 244, 249, 257
Spencer, John, 1st Earl Spencer (1734–1783)   74, 245n
Spencer-Churchill, Edward (1853–1911)   225
Spinola, Giorgio, Cardinal, apostolic nuncio in Vienna (1667–1739)   7n

Spon, Jacob (1647–1685)   282
Sterbini, Bernardo (active 1718–1751)   22, 28
Stosch, Heinrich Siegismund (1699–1747)   10*n*, 67, 153, 155, 219, 254
Stosch, Ludwig (1688–1717)   4*n*
Stosch, Luise Hedwig (1692–1748)   4*n*
Stosch, Philipp Siegismund (1656–1724)   4
Stosch's *Atlas*   8, 10, 14, 70, 77, 81, 86–87, 142, 155, 236, 244, 261, 289–290, 295
Stosch's collection of medals   82–84
Stosch's *dactyliotheca*   99
Strimesius, Johann Samuel (1648–1730)   4
Strodtmann, Johann Christoph (1717–1756)   4*n*, 100
Strozzi, Leone, Count (1657–1722)   6, 24, 27, 70, 86, 138, 158, 218
Stuart, James Francis Edward (1688–1766)   8
Susterli, Giuseppe (dates unknown)   10*n*
Suvorov, Alexander (1729/1730–1800)   104

Tassie, James (1735–1799)   4, 14, 100*n*, 110, 218, 257
Thoms, Friedrich de Graf (1669–1746)   28, 70–71, 158, 160, 225, 245–247, 251
Tiepolo, Giovanni Domenico (1650–1730)   30, 75, 158
Tischbein, Johann Henrich Wilhelm (1751–1829)   47
Toelken, Ernst Heinrich (1785–1864)   124, 143
Toland, John (1670–1722)   5
Torre di Rezzonico, Carlo della (1693–1769)   86, 158
Torricelli, Giuseppe (1662–1719)   293*n*
Townley, Charles (1737–1805)   42, 44
Tuscher, Markus (1705–1751)   3, 10–11, 47, 67, 70, 81–84, 98, 124, 142–143, 150, 153–154, 221, 237, 254, 256–257

Vaini, Anton Maria (1660–1737)   3*n*, 28, 69, 138–139, 158, 161, 222
Valesio, Francesco (1670–1742)   9, 11*n*, 24, 26, 28, 30, 69, 82, 221, 228, 299
Valletta, Francesco Saverio (1680–1760)   6
Van der Aa, Pieter Boudewijnsz (1659–1733)   12*n*, 44*n*
Vechnerinn, Luyse/Luise (dates unknown)   4
Venuti, Filippo (1706–1768)   30, 84, 245
Venuti, Marcello (1700–1755)   30
Venuti, Ridolfino (1705–1763)   28, 30, 66*n*, 78, 84, 141, 158, 245
Vettori, Francesco (1693–1770)   10, 25, 70, 72, 140, 158, 248–249, 291
Viczay of Hédervár, Mihály, Count (Hungary) (unknown dates)   158
Vien, Joseph-Marie (1716–1809)   50
Vigna, Pietro della (1190–1249)   7*n*
Vitelleschi-Verospi collection   138, 158
Vitzthum von Eckstädt, Friedrich (1675–1726)   159
Vleughels, Nicolas (1668–1737)   24

Wackerbarth-Salmour, Joseph Anton Gabaleon, Count (1685–1761)   7, 159, 250
Wales, George Frederick William, Prince of (1738–1820)   14, 15*n*, 101*n*, 170*n*
Walpole, Horace (1717–1797)   11*n*, 13, 21*n*, 22–23, 50, 215, 216*n*, 252, 256
Wandelaar, Jan (1690–1759)   47
Warburton, Augusta (1854–1941)   225
Wassenaer-Opdam, Johan Hendrik, Graf van (1683–1745)   45, 71, 159
Watermarks – drawings from Krakow   112–113

Watermarks – drawings from Berlin   125–126
Wenzel, Joseph, Prince of Liechtenstein (1696–1772)   30, 74, 159
Werden, Jacob van (fl. 1643–1669)   41
Whiston, William (1667–1752)   5
Wicar, Jean-Baptiste (1762–1834)   47
Wilde, Jacob de (1645–1721)   21
William IV, Prince of Orange (1711–1751)   158
Winchilsea, Earl of – see Finch, Daniel
Winckelmann, Johann Joachim (1717–1768)   4, 13–14, 31, 71, 82, 85–86, 98–99, 111–112, 115–116, 123, 149, 155–156, 163–170, 239, 242, 250, 253, 258, 290–292, 294–305
Winckler, Jacob Benedict (1699–1779)   159, 237–238

Zanetti, Anton Maria di Girolamo (1689–1767)   27, 30, 48, 73–76, 135, 159, 218, 243–245, 251, 282, 288
Zanetti the Younger, Anton Maria (1706–1778)   48
Zelada, Francesco Saverio de, Cardinal (1717–1801)   25
Zeno, Apostolo (1668–1750)   6, 75, 159, 222, 256
Zuccolo, Leopoldo (1760/1761–1833)   50
Zuccolo, Santo (unknown dates)   50